Adolescence

Development, Diversity, and Context

Series Editor
Richard M. Lerner
Tufts University

A GARLAND SERIES

Series Contents

1. Theoretical Foundations and Biological Bases of Development in Adolescence
2. Cognitive and Moral Development and Academic Achievement in Adolescence
3. The Development of Personality, Self, and Ego in Adolescence
4. Adolescents and Their Families
5. Risks and Problem Behaviors in Adolescence
6. Social Interactions in Adolescence and Promoting Positive Social Contributions of Youth

The Editors of this series are grateful to the several colleagues who facilitated our work on this series. Foremost, we are grateful to the authors of the selections reprinted in this volume. Their scholarship has shaped the study of adolescent development and we appreciate greatly their allowing us to include their work in this book.

We are especially grateful to Sofia T. Romero, Editor at the Boston College Center for Child, Family, and Community Partnerships, and to Imma De Stefanis, Graduate Research Assistant at the Center, for all their many contributions. Ms. Romero provided us with sage and professional editorial advice. Her wisdom, judgment, and skills enhanced the quality of our work and made it much more productive. Sr. De Stefanis collaborated extensively with us in the selection and organization of the scholarship included in the series. Her knowledge of and enthusiasm for the study of adolescence was an invaluable asset in our work.

We appreciate as well the excellent work of Carole Puccino, Editor at Garland Publishing. Her productivity and organizational skill enabled the volume to be produced with efficiency and quality. Finally, we thank Leo Balk, Vice President of Garland, for his enthusiasm for this project and for his support, encouragement, and guidance.

Theoretical Foundations and Biological Bases of Development in Adolescence

Edited, with an introduction by

Richard M. Lerner
Tufts University

Jacqueline V. Lerner
Boston College

GARLAND PUBLISHING, INC.
A MEMBER OF THE TAYLOR & FRANCIS GROUP
New York & London
1999

Library of Congress Cataloging-in-Publication Data

Theoretical foundations and biological bases of development in
   adolescence / edited, with an introduction by Richard M. Lerner and
   Jacqueline V. Lerner.
       p.   cm. — (Adolescence : development, diversity, and context
   ; 1)
       Includes bibliographical references.
       ISBN 0-8153-3290-4 (alk. paper)
       1. Adolescent psychology. I. Lerner, Richard M.   II. Lerner,
   Jacqueline V. III. Series: Adolescence (New York, N.Y.) ; 1.
   BF724.T48 1999
       155.5—dc21   99-33732
                                                    CIP

Printed on acid-free, 250-year-life paper
Manufactured in the United States of America

Contents

ix   Introduction
      Adolescence: Theoretical and Empirical Issues in the
      Understanding of Development, Diversity, and Context
          Richard M. Lerner and Jacqueline V. Lerner

HISTORICAL AND THEORETICAL FOUNDATIONS

1   Presidential Address: Creating Adolescents:
      The Role of Context and Process in Developmental Trajectories
          Anne C. Petersen

19   The Philosophical and Historical Roots
      of Theories of Adolescence
          Rolf E. Muuss

37   Theoretical Propositions of Life-Span Developmental
      Psychology: On the Dynamics Between Growth and Decline
          Paul B. Baltes

53   Theories of Adolescent Development
          Rachna Talwar and Jacqueline V. Lerner

61   Stress Absorbing Systems in Black Families
          Harriette P. McAdoo

71   The Life Course as Developmental Theory
          Glen H. Elder Jr.

84   The Stormy Decade: Fact or Fiction?
          Albert Bandura

93   Adolescent Turmoil: Fact or Fiction?
          Michael Rutter, et al.

115   Adolescence as a Developmental Disturbance
          Anna Freud

121   New Maps of Development: New Visions of Maturity
          Carol Gilligan

135 Implications of an Interactional Paradigm for Research
on Human Development
David Magnusson

159 Generational Difference and the Developmental Stake
Vern L. Bengston and Joseph A. Kuypers

172 Children and Adolescents as Producers
of Their Own Development
Richard M. Lerner

201 Relative Plasticity, Integration, Temporality, and Diversity in
Human Development: A Developmental Contextual Perspective
About Theory, Process, and Method
Richard M. Lerner

BIOLOGICAL BASES

207 Menarche, Secular Trend in Age of
James M. Tanner

212 Hormones, Emotional Dispositions, and Aggressive Attributes
in Young Adolescents
Elizabeth J. Susman, et al.

233 Biological Maturation and Social Development:
A Longitudinal Study of Some Adjustment Processes
from Mid-Adolescence to Adulthood
David Magnusson, Håkan Stattin, and Vernon L. Allen

251 The Study of Maturational Timing Effects in Adolescence
J. Brooks-Gunn, Anne C. Petersen, and Dorothy Eichorn

265 The Effects of Delayed Menarche in Different Contexts:
Dance and Nondance Students
J. Brooks-Gunn and Michelle P. Warren

281 Menarcheal Status and Parent-Child Relations
in Families of Seventh-Grade Girls
John P. Hill, et al.

297 Impact of Puberty on Family Relations:
Effects of Pubertal Status and Pubertal Timing
Laurence Steinberg

308 Dialectics, Developmental Contextualism,
and the Further Enhancement of Theory
About Puberty and Psychosocial Development
Richard M. Lerner

331 Objective and Subjective Attractiveness
and Early Adolescent Adjustment
Jasna Jovanovic, Richard M. Lerner, and Jacqueline V. Lerner

337 Acknowledgments

Introduction

Adolescence:
Theoretical and Empirical Issues
in the Understanding of
Development, Diversity, and Context

*Richard M. Lerner, **Jacqueline V. Lerner*

Adolescence has been described as a phase of life beginning in biology and ending in society (Petersen, 1988). This characterization of adolescence underscores the idea that, whereas pubertal changes may be the most visible and universal features of this period, the social and cultural context within which youth develop in large measure textures this phase of life. Accordingly, adolescence may be defined as the period within the life span when most of a person's biological, cognitive, psychological, and social characteristics are changing in an interrelated manner; they change from what is typically considered childlike to what is considered adult-like (Lerner and Spanier, 1980).

For the adolescent, this period is a dramatic challenge requiring adjustment to changes in the self, in the family, and in the peer group. In contemporary Western society, adolescents experience institutional changes as well. Among young adolescents, there is a change in school setting, typically involving a transition from elementary school to either junior high school or middle school; and in late adolescence, there is a transition from high school to the worlds of work, university, or childrearing.

The hopes, challenges, fears, and successes of adolescence have been romanticized or dramatized in novels, short stories, and news articles. It is commonplace to survey a newsstand and to find a magazine article describing the "stormy years" of adolescence, the new crazes or fads of youth, or the "explosion" of problems with teenagers (e.g. involving crime or sexuality). Until the past 25-30 years, when medical, biological, and social scientists began to study intensively the adolescent period, there was relatively little sound scientific information available to verify or refute the literary characterizations of adolescence. Today, however, such information does exist, and it is clear that although adolescence presents many challenges, the evidence is not consistent with the frequently reported belief that adolescence is a protracted period of storm and stress for most individuals (Feldman and Elliott, 1990; Lerner, 1995; Lerner and Galambos, 1998; Offer, 1969; Petersen, 1988).

The purpose of the six volumes in *Adolescence: Development, Diversity, and Context* is to present the range of scholarship that provides the best information currently available about the actual features of the adolescent period. The contributions to the literature found in these volumes attest to the fact that adolescence is a dynamic, developmental period, one marked by diverse sorts of changes for different youth, changes brought about because — for all features of adolescence — development involves changing *relations* among biological, psychological, and social/ecological processes. Diversity in adolescent development occurs as a consequence of dynamic (reciprocal, systemic) relations between youth and their contexts: Contemporary scholarship emphasizes that a developmental systems orientation is most useful in the study of development, diversity, and context in adolescence (Lerner and Castellino, 1998).

Key Features of Adolescent Development

In many ways, the study of adolescence has provided a model for scholarship about the rest of the life span. Today, human development theory and research is marked by the use of dynamic, developmental systems models of person-context relations (e.g., Ford and Lerner, 1992; Sameroff, 1983; Thelen and Smith, 1998); by the use of multivariate longitudinal and multilevel (and often multidisciplinary) research aimed at understanding the nature of development-in-context (e.g., Bronfenbrenner and Morris, 1998; Magnusson and Stattin, 1998); and by an integration of basic and applied scholarship, that is, by a concern with applying developmental science to promote policies and programs enhancing the life chances of youth (e.g., Fisher and Lerner, 1994).

In our view, scholarship about adolescence has championed these themes. This field of scholarship continues to provide the best examples in the human development literature about: the reciprocal relations between biology and context in human behavior and development; the role of temporality — including, quite centrally, historical variation — in promoting both commonalities and differences in human functioning; and thus the need for a contextual- and cohort-comparative perspective to understand both nomothetic patterns of behavior and development and individual differences (diversity) in trajectories of change.

Over the past 30 years, the results of research on adolescence have come to exemplify for biomedical, behavioral, and social scientists the importance of individual differences, diversity, and contextual sensitivity — and thus of gender, racial, ethnic, and cultural variations — for understanding the nature of human life and development (Lerner and Galambos, 1998; Petersen, 1988). Research on adolescence has served as an exemplar of the importance of the collaborative contributions of scholars from multiple disciplines. Today, neither a biologically reductionistic, nor a psychogenic, nor a sociogenic viewpoint characterizes the study of adolescence. Rather, models and methods that seek to understand the synthesis, or fusion, of influences from multiple levels of organization are at the "cutting-edge" of the field. Accordingly, the literature about adolescence allows several generalizations about this period of life and provides ideas about how best to intervene when adolescents are experiencing difficulties. We review these themes below.

Multiple Levels of Context Are Influential During Adolescence

The study of adolescence focuses on the relations between the developing individual and his or her multilevel, changing context (e.g., Lerner and Galambos, 1998; Petersen, 1988). An increasing conceptual and empirical stress has been placed on both the ecology of adolescent development and on the dynamic interactions between this ecology and both intraindividual change processes and interindividual differences in (the diversity of) such processes.

Current scholarship reflects and advances — theoretically and empirically — the view that dynamic (i.e., bidirectional or, perhaps better, "fused"; Tobach and Greenberg, 1984) adolescent-context relations constitute the basic process of human behavior and development. Numerous empirical studies demonstrate this focus on (a) the relation between, and thus the integration of, individual and contextual levels of organization (ranging from biology through history); and (b) interindividual differences in adolescent behavior, and diversity of developmental trajectories, which derive from variation in temporal patterns of individual-context relations (cf. Elder, Modell, and Parke, 1993).

The context or ecology of human development (Bronfenbrenner, 1979; Lerner, 1995) is composed of multiple, integrated levels of organization, including the biological, individual-psychological, social-interpersonal, institutional, cultural, and historical. There are ubiquitous individual differences in adolescent development involving connections among biological, cognitive, psychological, and sociocultural factors. No single influence acts either alone or as the "prime mover" of change (Brooks-Gunn and Petersen, 1983; Lerner, 1995).

For example, adolescence is a period of rapid physical transitions in such characteristics as height, weight, and body proportions. Hormonal changes are part of this development. Nevertheless, hormones are not primarily responsible for the psychological or social developments of this period (Petersen, 1988). In fact, the quality and timing of hormonal or other biological changes influence and are influenced by psychological, social, cultural, and historical contexts (Elder, 1998; Magnusson and Stattin, 1998; Tanner, 1991). Caspi et al. (1993), for example, found that the biological changes of early pubertal maturation were linked to delinquency in adolescent girls, but only among girls who attended mixed-sex schools. Early maturation among girls in single-sex schools was not linked with higher delinquency (see too Magnusson and Stattin, 1998).

Research on cognitive development suggests that there are integrated, multilevel changes in thinking that occur during adolescence (Graber and Petersen, 1991). For instance, there are no global and pervasive effects of puberty on cognitive development, but pubertal changes interact with contextual and experiential factors (e.g. the transition to junior high school) to influence academic achievement (Simmons and Blyth, 1987). Although a universalistic storm-and-stress perspective about adolescence might lead to the assumption that there are general cognitive disruptions across adolescence because of the presumed ubiquitous upheavals of this period, the evidence does not support this assumption. Rather, cognitive abilities are enhanced in early adolescence as individuals become faster and more efficient at processing information

— at least in settings in which they feel comfortable in performing cognitive tasks (Ceci and Bronfenbrenner, 1985).

Changing Relations Between Adolescents and Their Contexts Produce Development in Adolescence

The period of adolescence is one of continual change and transition between individuals and their contexts (Lerner, 1995). Indeed, adolescence represents a natural ontogenetic "laboratory" for the study of dynamic person-context relations. These changing relations constitute the basic process of development in adolescence; they underlie both positive and negative outcomes that occur (Lerner, 1995).

Accordingly, when the multiple biological, psychological, cognitive, and social changes of adolescence occur simultaneously (e.g., when menarche occurs at the same time as a school transition), there is a greater risk of problems occurring in a youth's development (Simmons and Blyth, 1987). In adolescence, poor decisions (e.g. involving school, sex, drugs) have more negative consequences than in childhood (Dryfoos, 1990), and the adolescent is more responsible for those decisions and their consequences than in childhood (Petersen, 1988).

Nevertheless, most developmental trajectories across this period involve positive adjustment on the part of the adolescent. Furthermore, for most youth there is a continuation of warm and accepting relations with parents (Guerney and Arthur, 1984). The most optimal adjustment occurs among adolescents who are encouraged by their parents to engage in age-appropriate autonomy while maintaining strong ties to their family (Galambos and Ehrenberg, 1997).

Accordingly, adolescence is an opportune time in which to intervene into family processes when necessary. For instance, whereas minor parent-child conflicts (for example, regarding chores and privileges) are normative in adolescence, major conflicts are less frequent; thus, when major conflicts occur often in a family, parents should be concerned (Galambos and Almeida, 1992). The continued salience of the family in the adolescent period makes such conflicts an appropriate intervention target.

Individual Differences — Diversity — Characterize Adolescence

There are multiple pathways through adolescence (Offer, 1969). Interindividual (between-person) differences and intra-individual (within-person) changes in development are the "rule" in this period of life. Normal adolescent development involves such variability. Temperamental characteristics involving mood and activity level are good examples (Lerner and Lerner, 1983). There are differences among adolescents in such characteristics, which may influence adolescent behaviors such as substance use and delinquency (Henry et al., 1996). There is also diversity between and within all ethnic, racial, or cultural minority groups. Therefore, generalizations that confound class, race, and/or ethnicity are not useful (Lerner, 1995).

Accordingly, to enhance both basic knowledge and the quality of the research base used for applications aimed at enhancing youth development, future scholarship in adolescence must continue to elucidate the course of development of diverse adolescents. All policies and programs — all interventions — must be tailored to the specific target population and, in particular, to a group's developmental and environmental circumstances (Lerner, 1995). Moreover, because adolescents are so different from one another, one cannot expect any single policy or intervention to reach all of a given target population or to influence everyone in the same way.

In sum, the themes of developmental diversity, adolescent-context relations, and the links among theory, research, and application (to youth policies and programs) are key intellectual themes in contemporary scholarship about adolescence. As such, these themes frame both the present volume and the succeeding volumes in this series.

The Plan of This Volume

There are two main sections of this volume. The initial section presents key articles in the adolescent literature pertinent to the historical and theoretical bases of this field of scholarship. These articles convey the evolution of the study of the adolescent period and of its emergence as an area of inquiry marked by the dynamic, systems orientation to the conceptualization of youth development that we described above.

The articles describe the philosophical foundations of the scientific study of adolescence and discuss the several theoretical viewpoints that have been used to frame research and application. Views of adolescence that stressed universalistic features of the period, instead of diverse patterns of development, are presented. By representing the breadth of the ideas that have been used to conceptualize and study the adolescent period, the articles in this portion of the volume provide an understanding of how and why the field of adolescence has become focused on the themes of diversity, individual-context relations, and application.

The developmental systems orientation to the study of adolescence that emerges across the articles found in the first portion of the volume provide a theoretical grounding for the papers that comprise the second portion of the book. These articles pertain to the biological bases of adolescent physical and behavioral characteristics and development. In early theoretical accounts of the adolescent period biology was seen as the "prime mover" of changes during this period (e.g., A. Freud, 1969) and, as such, the study of adolescence was often virtually equated with the study of biology (McCandless, 1970).

However, consistent with the individual-context relational view of development found within a developmental systems perspective, a key point made in these papers is that biology per se is not linked *directly* to development in adolescence. Rather, the features of the context within which biological changes are expressed, such as those associated with early versus late pubertal maturation, shape the import of biology for youth development. For instance, the very emergence of puberty is influenced by such variables as the quality of nutrition and health services present in a given setting at a particular time in history (Tanner, 1991). Similarly, whether pubertal change is linked to behavioral problems is related to the nature of the peer and family contexts of adolescents (Magnusson and Stattin, 1998).

In short, the articles in this volume document the emergence of a dynamic, individual differences approach to adolescence, one that links theory and application in all areas of empirical inquiry within this field of scholarship. Not only is this theoretical frame useful for understanding the literature on biological bases of adolescent development but, in addition, it is similarly applicable to the substantive topics that are the foci of the other volumes in this series.

The Succeeding Volumes

Volume 2 of this series discusses several related areas of empirical inquiry that, like the study of biological bases, has been expanded through the application of a development systems perspective: cognitive and moral development, academic achievement, and school effects on youth development. As is the case in Volume 1, scholarship framed by both non-systems and developmental systems-related ideas are included in Volume 2. Nevertheless, the importance of the context of adolescent development is ubiquitous across all the substantive foci reviewed in Volume 2.

Research framed by contrasting theoretical perspectives is present as well in Volume 3. This volume focuses on personality development and on the concepts of "self" and "ego" that are central in the understanding of adolescent individuality. The articles in this volume underscore the point that person-context relations are a central focus in contemporary scholarship about adolescent personality development. Neither individual nor contextual variables alone suffice in accounting for such development.

Given the salience of the context for all facets of individual development during this period, Volume 4 is devoted to a context that continues to be of central importance to the person during this period of life, that is, the family. The volume includes articles that describe the importance of the family context and of processes of social interaction in it. In addition, the volume describes variations in family structure and function, and discusses the impact of economic stress on families and the problems associated with teenagers becoming parents.

Volume 5 expands on the treatment of problems that arise in adolescent development. The articles in the volume discuss the behavioral and social risks that adolescents encounter. In addition, the papers describe both the internalizing problems that emerge during this period (e.g., depression) as well as some of the major externalizing problems prototypic of contemporary adolescents (e.g., problems relating to sexual behavior, substance use and abuse, delinquency, and school dropout).

Volume 6 emphasizes the ways in which adolescent-context relations can be structured to promote positive development, to not only prevent problems from emerging during this time of life but, in addition, to provide resources for healthy adolescent development. Accordingly, the roles of peers, parents, love, and work in adolescent development are discussed. In addition, the papers describe the ways in which youth programs and policies may be structured and implemented in order to assure problem prevention and to foster the promotion of positive development during this dynamic and challenging period of life.

Conclusions

Across the articles reprinted in the six volumes of this series a key theoretical point linked to a developmental systems perspective emerges: If we are to have an adequate and sufficient science of adolescent development, we must integratively study individual and contextual levels of organization in a relational and temporal manner (Lerner and Castellino, 1998; Lerner and Galambos, 1998). Anything less will not constitute adequate science. And if we are to serve America's youth through this science, if we are to help develop successful policies and programs through our scholarly efforts, then we must accept nothing less than the integrative temporal and relational model of the adolescent that is embodied in the developmental systems perspective forwarded in contemporary research in adolescent development.

Through such research, the field of adolescence has an opportunity to serve both scholarship and the communities, families, and youth of our world. By integrating policies and programs sensitive to the diversity of our communities and our youth, by combining the assets of our scholarly and research traditions with the strengths of our young people (Scales and Leffert, 1999), we can improve on the often-cited idea of Kurt Lewin (1943), that there is nothing as practical as a good theory. We can, through the application of our science to serve our world's youth, actualize the idea that there is nothing of greater value to society than a science devoted to using its scholarship to improve the life chances of all young people.

*Richard M. Lerner holds the Bergstrom Chair in Applied Developmental Science at Tufts University. A developmental psychologist, Lerner received a Ph.D. in 1971 from the City University of New York. He has been a fellow at the Center for Advanced Study in the Behavioral Sciences and is a fellow of the American Association for the Advancement of Science, the American Psychological Association, the American Psychological Society, and the American Association of Applied and Preventive Psychology. Prior to joining Tufts University, he was on the faculty and held administrative posts at Michigan State University, Pennsylvania State University, and Boston College, where he was the Anita L. Brennan Professor of Education and the director of the Center for Child, Family, and Community Partnerships. During the 1994–95 academic year Lerner held the Tyner Eminent Scholar Chair in the Human Sciences at Florida State University. Lerner is the author or editor of 40 books and more than 275 scholarly articles and chapters, including his 1995 book, *America's Youth in Crisis: Challenges and Options for Programs and Policies*. He edited Volume 1, on "Theoretical models of human development," for the fifth edition of the *Handbook of Child Psychology*. He is known for his theory of, and research about, relations between life-span human development and contextual or ecological change. He is the founding editor of the *Journal of Research on Adolescence* and of the new journal, *Applied Developmental Science*.

**Jacqueline V. Lerner is Professor of Education in the Applied Developmental Psychology Program in the School of Education at Boston College. A developmental psychologist, Lerner received her Ph.D. in 1980 from the Pennsylvania State University. She has been a Visiting Scholar at the Center for Research on Women and the Boystown Center for Youth Development at Stanford University. Prior to joining Boston College, she was on the faculty and held administrative posts at Michigan State University and the Pennsylvania State University. She is currently an Associate Editor of *Child Development*. Lerner is the author or editor of seven books or monographs and more than 75 scholarly articles and chapters. She is known for her research on temperament and social development in children, early adolescent transitions, and maternal employment and daycare.

References

Bronfenbrenner, U. (1979). *The ecology of human development: Experiments by nature and design.* Cambridge, MA: Harvard University Press.

Bronfenbrenner, U., and Morris, P.A. (1998). "The ecology of developmental processes." In R.M. Lerner (Ed.), *Theoretical models of human development.* Vol. 1, *Handbook of Child Psychology* (5th ed., pp. 993–1027). Editor in chief: W. Damon. New York: Wiley.

Brooks-Gunn, J., and Petersen, A.C. (1983). *Girls at puberty: Biological and psychosocial perspectives.* New York: Plenum.

Caspi, A., Lynam, D., Moffitt, T.E., and Silva, P.A. (1993). "Unraveling girls' delinquency: Biological, dispositional, and contextual contributions to adolescent misbehavior." *Developmental Psychology, 29,* 19–30.

Ceci, S.J., and Bronfenbrenner, U. (1995). "'Don't forget to take the cupcakes out of the oven:' Prospective memory, strategic time monitoring, and context." *Child Development, 56,* 152–164.

Dryfoos, J.G. (1990). *Adolescents at risk: Prevalence and prevention.* New York: Oxford University Press.

Elder, G.H., Jr. (1998). "The life course and human development." In R.M. Lerner (Ed.), *Theoretical models of human development* (5th ed., Vol. 1, pp. 939–991). New York: Wiley.

Elder, G.H., Jr., Modell, J., and Parke, R.D. (Eds.). (1993). *Children in time and place: Developmental and historical insights.* New York: Cambridge University Press.

Feldman, S.S., and Elliot, G.E. (1990). *At the threshold: The developing adolescent.* Cambridge, MA: Harvard University Press.

Fisher, C.B., and Lerner, R.M. (Eds.). (1994). *Applied developmental psychology.* New York: McGraw-Hill.

Ford, D.L., and Lerner, R.M. (1992). *Developmental systems theory: An integrative approach.* Newbury Park, CA: Sage.

Freud, A. (1969). "Adolescence as a developmental disturbance." In G. Caplan and S. Lebovier (Eds.), *Adolescence* (pp. 5–10). New York: Basic Books.

Galambos, N.L., and Almeida, D.M. (1992). "Does parent-adolescent conflict increase in early adolescence?" *Journal of Marriage and the Family, 54,* 737–747.

Galambos, N.L., and Ehrenberg, M.F. (1997). The family as health risk and opportunity: A focus on divorce and working families. In J. Schulenberg, J.L. Maggs, and K. Hurrelmann (Eds.), *Health risks and developmental transitions during adolescence* (pp. 139–160). Cambridge: Cambridge University Press.

Graber, J.A., and Petersen, A.C. (1991). Cognitive changes at adolescence: Biological perspectives. In K.R. Gibson and A.C. Petersen (Eds.), *Brain maturation and cognitive development: Comparative and cross-cultural perspectives* (pp. 253–279). New York: Aldine de Gruyter.

Guerney, L., and Arthur, J. (1984). Adolescent social relationships. In R.M. Lerner and N.L. Galambos (Eds.), *Experiencing adolescence: A sourcebook for parents, teachers, and teens* (pp. 87–118). New York: Garland.

Henry, B., Caspi, A., Moffitt, T.E., and Silva, P.A. (1996). "Temperamental and familial predictors of violent and nonviolent criminal convictions: Age 3 to age 18." *Developmental Psychology, 32,* 614–623.

Lerner, R.M. (1995). *America's youth in crisis: Challenges and options for programs and policies.* Thousand Oaks, CA: Sage.

Lerner, R.M., and Castellino, D. (1998). Contemporary developmental theory and adolescence: Developmental systems and applied developmental science. Paper prepared for the Invitational Conference: *Health Future of Youth II: Pathways to Adolescent Health.* Sponsored by the Maternal and Child Health Bureau, U.S. Department of Health and Human Services. Annapolis, Maryland, September 14–16, 1998.

Lerner, R.M., and Galambos, N.L. (1998). Adolescent development: Challenges and opportunities for research, programs, and policies. In J.T. Spence (Ed.), *Annual Review of Psychology* (Vol. 49, pp. 413–446). Palo Alto, CA: Annual Reviews.

Lerner, R.M., and Lerner, J.V. (1983). Temperament-intelligence reciprocities in early childhood: A contextual model. In M. Lewis (Ed.), *Origins of intelligence: Infancy and early childhood* (pp. 399–421). New York: Plenum Press.

Lerner, R.M., and Spanier, G.B. (1980). A dynamic interactional view of child and family development. In R.M. Lerner and G.B. Spanier (Eds.), *Child influences on marital and family interaction: A life-span perspective* (pp. 1–20). New York: Academic Press.

Lewin, K. (1943). "Psychology and the process of group living." *Journal of Social Psychology, 17,* 113–131.

Magnusson, D., and Stattin, H. (1998). Person-context interaction theories. In R.M. Lerner (Ed.),

Theoretical models of human development. Vol. 1, *Handbook of Child Psychology* (5th ed., pp. 685–759). Editor in chief: W. Damon. New York: Wiley.

McCandless, R.R. (1970). *Adolescents.* Hinsdale, IL: Dryden.

Offer, D. (1969). *The psychological world of the teen-ager.* New York: Basic Books.

Petersen, A.C. (1988). Adolescent development. In M.R. Rosenzweig (Ed.), *Annual review of psychology* (Vol. 39, pp. 583–607). Palo Alto, CA: Annual Reviews, Inc.

Sameroff, A.J. (1983). Developmental systems: Contexts and evolution. In W. Kessen (Ed.), *Handbook of child psychology:* Vol. 1, *History, theory, and methods* (pp. 237–294). New York: Wiley.

Scales, P.C., and Leffert, N. (1999). *Developmental assets: A synthesis of the scientific research on adolescent development.* Minneapolis: Search Institute.

Simmons, R.G., and Blyth, D.A. (1987). *Moving into adolescence: The impact of pubertal change and school context.* Hawthorne, NJ: Aldine.

Tanner, J. (1991). Menarche, secular trend in age of. In R.M. Lerner, A.C. Petersen, and J. Brooks-Gunn (Eds.), *Encyclopedia of adolescence* (Vol. 1, pp. 637–641). New York: Garland.

Thelen, E., and Smith, L.B. (1998). Dynamic systems theories. In R.M. Lerner (Ed.), *Theoretical models of human development.* Vol. 1, *Handbook of child psychology* (5th ed., pp. 563–633), Editor in chief: W. Damon. New York: Wiley.

Tobach, E., and Greenberg, G. (1984). The significance of T.C. Schneirla's contribution to the concept of levels of integration. In G. Greenberg and E. Tobach (Eds.), *Behavioral evolution and integrative levels* (pp. 1–7). Hillsdale, NJ: Erlbaum.

JOURNAL OF RESEARCH ON ADOLESCENCE, 3(1), 1–18
Copyright © 1993, Lawrence Erlbaum Associates, Inc.

Presidential Address: Creating Adolescents: The Role of Context and Process in Developmental Trajectories

Anne C. Petersen
University of Minnesota

Research on adolescence has grown dramatically, both quantitatively and qualitatively, over the past 20 years. This research has contributed to debunking several myths about adolescence, including (a) that it is inevitably a period of storm and stress, (b) that difficulties are caused by hormones, and (c) that there is an inevitable and negative generation gap between adolescents and their parents. Several exciting and important emerging issues hold great promise on future knowledge. These include (a) developmental processes, (b) context effects, and (c) interventions. Research on adolescence is important for public policy. At least some part of our efforts should be oriented toward policy issues.

There has been an explosion of research in adolescence over the past 20 years, especially in the last decade (e.g., Dornbusch, Petersen, & Hetherington, 1991; Feldman & Elliott, 1990). For example, in collaboration with Brooks-Gunn and Compas, I recently reviewed the research on depression in adolescence (Petersen et al., in press). We planned this review under the impression that we were familiar with much of the research on this topic. The PsycLIT review conducted by one of Compas's students in the spring of 1991 generated more than 2,000 entries since 1987 using the key words *adolescent depression*. Most of these entries were previously unknown to the three of us. This dramatic example of how rapidly this particular aspect of research on adolescence

---

Requests for reprints should be sent to Anne C. Petersen, 321 Johnston Hall, University of Minnesota, 101 Pleasant Street S.E., Minneapolis, MN 55455-0421.

1

has flourished is surely replicated in most other subfields of adolescence. Compared with two decades ago there are now many more researchers generating significantly more data to enhance knowledge on the second decade of life.

ACCOMPLISHMENTS OF THE PAST DECADE

It is remarkable how far researchers have come in their understanding of adolescence. There has been a dramatic increase in research knowledge, at least on some subgroups of adolescents in the U.S. and Europe. In particular, many myths have been debunked by recent research on adolescence, three of which are discussed here: (a) storm and stress, (b) hormonal influences, and (c) the generation gap in adolescent–parent relationships.

Storm and Stress

Researchers no longer believe that storm and stress are inevitable consequences of adolescence (cf. Petersen, 1988). Many studies have contributed to debunking this myth (e.g., Offer & Offer, 1975; Rutter, 1980). The stereotype of adolescence as a tumultuous period of life still appears in the popular media, but, as a result of recent research, adolescence is now considered much more differentiated, with better understanding of manifestations inherent to the life period versus those attributable to situations or contexts of adolescence. In addition, it is clear that there is more than one healthy way to traverse the adolescent decade (e.g., Block, 1971; Hauser, Borman, Powers, Jacobson, & Noam, 1990).

The belief that psychological turmoil is normal in adolescence had an unfortunate consequence in that it was often assumed that young people with psychological problems would grow out of them. The evidence is now clear that psychological difficulties in adolescence usually persist and should be treated; they seldom disappear spontaneously (Rutter, Graham, Chadwick, & Yule, 1976; Weiner & DelGaudio, 1976).

Hormone Influences

Another myth that has been debunked is that difficulties during adolescence are caused by developmental changes in pubertal hormones (Kestenberg, 1968). My own longitudinal study began 14 years ago with this as the primary hypothesis. We have since learned that increasing pubertal hormones play an important role in a broad set of somatic and physiological changes during this time (e.g., Gupta, Attanasio, & Raaf, 1975). In addition, pubertal hormones influence some aspects of behaviors such as sex and aggression (e.g., Olweus, 1979; Susman et al., 1987; Udry, Billy, Morris, Groff, & Raj, 1985; Udry, Talbert, & Morris, 1986). Even so, Udry (1992) commented that there are mainly single, unreplicated findings that fit no clear hypothesis or pattern. In addition, I think the wrong questions are being asked.

The hypothesis that a universal change such as puberty would influence a nonuniversal outcome such as psychosocial problems now seems illogical. It may be found that mature individual differences in hormonal processes are related to psychological or behavioral problems; such evidence already exists for some symptoms (e.g., Backstrom et al., 1983; Dennerstein, Spencer-Gardner, Brown, Smith, & Burrows, 1984). However, this is not necessarily an issue of puberty or adolescence.

An exciting area likely to be illuminating is that of situation-based effects on the pubertal process. For example, situations that affect physiological processes have been described by Worthman (1992). She found fascinating effects of gender differences on the rate and timing of pubertal development, reducing or even reversing the pattern found in the U.S. in which girls develop 1½–2 years before boys. Another example with behavioral and physiological effects is the hypothesis that prepubertal sexual abuse stimulates earlier pubertal development and altered behavior patterns, a hypothesis supported by preliminary results (Trickett & Putnam, in press). A third example is the provocative hypothesis proposed by Belsky, Steinberg, and Draper (1991) that family conflict causes earlier puberty. An SRA symposium conducted in 1992 presented tests of this hypothesis, with some confirmatory and some nonconfirmatory results (e.g., Steinberg, 1992). These examples propose social influences on the timing of the pubertal process, not on hormonal levels per se. Most important, they are the reverse of the usual direction of effects described in the literature.

Adolescent–Parent Relationships

A final example of a debunked myth, from among many additional examples that I could cite is that adolescence is the period when young people separate from their parents, with overt conflict being the extreme most typically portrayed in the popular media. Research demonstrates that the nature of relationships with parents changes during adolescence beginning with puberty but that this altered relationship typically becomes a more mature interdependent one (Collins, 1990; Steinberg, 1990), rather than one characterized by the dependency typical of childhood.

Other Advances

All of what I have termed *myths* have some element of truth to them. Recent research has identified the limits of their generality or reframed the issues to reflect more complexity than provided by simple cause–effect models.

Recent research has also provided elaborate descriptions of adolescent development in a number of areas. It is known, for example, that in most aspects of individual development during adolescence, there are positive changes in the direction of increasing competence (e.g., Crockett & Petersen, in press). For example, puberty involves biological changes that bring adult size and shape and mature reproductive potential (Marshall & Tanner, 1969, 1970). In addition, young people develop the capacity to think abstractly during adolescence (Keating, 1990; Petersen, 1983). Psychological development also involves enhancement, as is seen in increasing levels of self-esteem over the adolescent decade (Damon & Hart, 1982; Savin-Williams & Demo, 1983). Social development also moves in the direction of increasing capacity to develop and maintain relationships (Crockett, Losoff, & Petersen, 1984; Hartup, 1983; Youniss & Smollar, 1985). Therefore, normal adolescent development is a positive process bringing adult maturity and competence, in contrast to the existing negative stereotypes.

Research on adolescent development is not conclusive because of limitations in the samples typically studied (e.g., Feldman & Elliott, 1990). As many have noted, recent research at least includes both boys and girls, unlike earlier research that focused only on boys. However, it typically includes only White middle-class populations. More research is needed on other populations of adolescents (e.g., Spencer & Dornbusch, 1990).

EMERGING ISSUES

In addition to the varied accomplishments in adolescent research, there are several emerging issues that I would like to highlight. These focus on developmental processes, context effects, and interventions.

Developmental Processes

Developmental processes, or the processes of change over the life course, involve more complex relationships than singular cause–effect models. Most theorists of adolescence posit that development is complex, requiring complex models. Transactional approaches such as that of Sameroff (1982) appear to best fit the current understanding of adolescent development.

Developmental transitions provide a major approach to understanding developmental processes. Developmental transitions are periods in the life course that involve significant changes in biological or social spheres and as such provide a window on development through which one can view the complex interactive processes of development (Petersen, Kennedy, & Sullivan, 1991). Early adolescence has been identified as one such period, involving change in every aspect of individual development and every important social context (Hill, 1983; Petersen, 1987).

What has been learned about development by studying the early adolescent transition is that although the period provides the opportunity for increased growth, negative outcomes are typical responses to added changes or challenges. For example, Simmons and Blyth (1987) found linear relationships between more changes and worse psychosocial outcomes. Similarly, it has been found that changes in early adolescence predict the emergence of depression by middle adolescence (Petersen, Sarigiani, & Kennedy, 1991). The changes that predicted the emergence of depression included the number of changes in the family, such as parental divorce or death, and whether the transition from elementary to secondary school was synchronous with pubertal change. An interesting aspect of these findings is that boys and girls showed similar outcomes when the nature of changes was controlled. Gender differences in depression resulted in middle adolescence because more girls than boys experienced family changes and simultaneous or earlier pubertal change relative to the school transition.

Research by Stattin and Magnusson (1990) has demonstrated that the effects of changes during a developmental transition can be long-lasting. They found that early developing girls were more likely to have lower educational and occupational attainment in adulthood. This process appears to be mediated by social relationships, in that when early developing girls "hang out" with older adolescents, they are consequently introduced into earlier sexual experiences and other problem behaviors. I speculate that the process through which this effect works is that early developing girls are still immature socially and psychologically and therefore are particularly vulnerable to older boys or even young men who are attracted to them. As a consequence of their psychosocial and cognitive immaturity, they are manipulated into early involvement in these problem behaviors because they do not recognize the dramatic effect such behaviors are likely to have on their lives.

Another aspect of these developmental effects and trajectories, exemplified in the work of Caspi and Moffitt (1991) and others (e.g., Block, 1971), demonstrates that some of the differences emerging after a developmental transition, or any period of stress and adversity, can be identified prior to the transition and are accentuated by it. For example, Caspi, Lynam, Moffitt, and Silva (1993) found that young people who engaged in delinquency were different prior to early adolescence. The early adolescent transition amplified preexisting changes. Researchers need to know for which behaviors this accentuation occurs. Likely candidates are behaviors in which rates increase during adolescence. If accentuation occurs, behavior rates or levels increase in or just after early adolescence.

Elliott (in press) has thoughtfully analyzed developmental changes in problem behaviors during adolescence. Figure 1 is particularly interesting for what it suggests about different processes for different

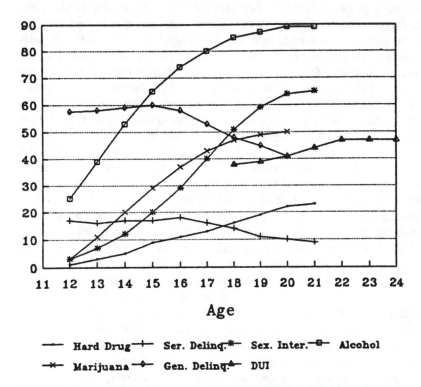

FIGURE 1   Age-specific prevalence rates for selected lifestyle behaviors (3-year running averages). From "Health Enhancing and Health Compromising Lifestyles" (p. 132), by D. S. Elliott, in *Promoting the Health of Adolescents: New Directions for the Twenty-First Century* edited by S. G. Millstein, A. C. Petersen, and E. O. Nightingale, in press, New York: Oxford University Press. Copyright 1993 by Oxford University Press. Used by permission.

behaviors. The timing of onset and peak rate of the behavior in the population were two variables that Elliott considered. Note from the figure that whereas most behaviors increased over adolescence, delinquency actually decreased. Two behaviors that become normative (i.e., engaged in by at least half the population) in adolescence are alcohol consumption, which reaches 50% by age 15, and sexual intercourse, which reaches 50% by age 17. Because these are behaviors expected of adults in most Western societies, one should not be surprised that they are actively pursued by adolescents. It is the case, however, that the age at which these behaviors begin has been declining over recent decades in the U.S., but early engagement in these behaviors is predictive of longer lasting negative outcomes.

The primary focus of the Elliott (in press) chapter was lifestyle development. He concluded from his prior research (e.g., Elliott, Huizinga, & Menard, 1989) that a major difference between lower and middle-income youth is that lower income youth are more likely to adopt a problem behavior lifestyle, whereas middle-income youth experiment with some of the more serious behaviors but then move on to a healthier lifestyle. Elliott speculated that the adoption of a problem-behavior lifestyle is likely to be linked to the lack of positive alternatives. Thus, the opportunities available, and whether they are risky or protective, shape the nature of the developmental trajectory.

Context Effects

As these findings illustrate, the context or situation can influence the developmental course. My colleagues and I examined the Stattin and Magnusson (1990) hypothesis for negative effects of early maturation in girls in our sample of upper-middle-class youth. Although we found long-term effects of pubertal timing on outcomes such as depression (Petersen, Kennedy, & Sullivan, 1991; Petersen, Sarigiani, & Kennedy, 1991), Dubas (1992) did not find effects on educational and occupational attainment in young adulthood like those found in the Swedish study (Stattin & Magnusson, 1990). We hypothesized that higher income status provides a protective or buffering influence that decreases the likelihood that early maturing girls will be vulnerable to the manipulation of boys or young men who influence early developing, lower income girls.

Several years ago I gave a talk in the Federal Republic of Germany to a group of college students at the University of Giessen at the invitation of Rainer Silbereisen. In discussing societal images and media portrayals of adolescence, I used as an example a song then popular by Madonna: "Papa Don't Preach." I intended the introduction of the song, which the students knew, to permit a discussion of adolescent childbearing, but I quickly realized that the German students were not understanding my point. I then learned that adolescent childbearing is not a problem in the Federal Republic of Germany. At that point I, like many others in the U.S., tended to link adolescent pregnancy and childbearing with the developmental period of adolescence. There are many hypotheses about adolescent pregnancy, such as those based on pubertal timing or on cognitive development, that link it to adolescent development (e.g., Petersen & Crockett, 1992). The fact that adolescent pregnancy occurs at much lower rates in other countries emphasizes the nature of context effects on adolescent development (Jones et al., 1985). Many factors seem to influence this particular cross-national difference in teenage pregnancy rates, including sex education and the provision or availability of contraception (Petersen, 1991). Rates of sexual activity in the Federal Republic of Germany and the U.S. are nearly identical (Department of International Economic and Social Affairs, 1988).

Another example of context effects may be seen in the transition to adulthood (e.g., Petersen, Hurrelmann, & Leffert, in press). In the U.S., there is only one pathway to adult work roles: college. The half of youth who do not go on to college have been labeled *forgotten* by a recent William T. Grant Foundation Commission report (1988). Employers regard noncollege youth as unreliable and do not offer them meaningful work opportunities until the early to mid-20s. The problem behaviors seen among these youths have been attributed to adolescent development rather than to the situation in which they find themselves. Such an attribution to the developmental period removes the need to do anything but wait for youth to grow out of adolescence.

Evidence that this is an inappropriate inference may be drawn from my experience in Germany. Although fewer young people go on to the University in Germany compared with the United States (about 25% vs. 50%, respectively), about 85% of all 18-year-olds are in some kind of educational system, including apprenticeships (Bertram, in press). These youth are regarded as a valuable national resource, an attitude that facilitates the development of adult work skills.

Cross-national comparisons provide a significant opportunity for making policy-relevant inferences about adolescent development. The goal of the Academia Europaea Study Group on Youth and Social Change is to chart historical trends in adolescent problem behaviors across countries in Europe to make inferences or develop hypotheses about the societal causes of these behaviors. This is a challenging goal, especially given variations in the nature and quality of data, but any inferences will be important. Cross-national similarities and differences can elucidate what is attributable to adolescent development and what is attributable to context.

Researchers in the U.S. should engage in a similar effort because there are some overwhelming areas of morbidity and mortality seen among U.S. youth that are not typical of other developed countries. The two I have mentioned already are certainly major ones: (a) adolescent pregnancy and childbearing and (b) the transition to adult work roles. Other examples that stand out are mortality caused by motor vehicle accidents and their link to alcohol consumption, and guns. The rates of death in these two areas grossly exceed those in any other developed country (Petersen, 1991). In addition, I think one could argue that these policies foster the demise of U.S. youth.

Because many of these policies are made at the state level, it would be useful to link state-by-state variations in adolescent outcomes to state policies. Apart from presentations of state-by-state variations in child outcomes (e.g., Center for the Study of Social Policy, 1991), I do not know of any existing research efforts of this kind. Another more common approach is the comparison of samples identified by demographic features such as ethnic group or social class. Existing examples of this approach include the recent comparisons of parenting style and adolescent outcomes by ethnic group and other features (Steinberg, Mounts, Lamborn, & Dornbusch, 1991). More research of this kind is needed.

In pursuing this line of research, my colleagues and I have been comparing developmental trajectories and influences in two communities: one suburban and resource rich in both capital and human resources and the other rural and resource poor in both respects (e.g., Bingham, Meyer, & Crockett, 1991; Stemmler, Bingham, Crockett, & Petersen, 1991). Figure 2 shows a developmental change in emotional tone, a measure of positive affect, in the two communities by gender. As one can see, the resource-rich community was higher in emotional tone and boys were higher than girls in both communities. Comparing only 8th- and 12th-grade data, boys showed parallel trends in the two communities, with lower levels in the resource-poor community, but girls showed converging patterns (Petersen, Sarigiani, & Kennedy, 1991). To differentiate social class from other community differences, we looked at the subsample whose parents were college educated. This control for parental education decreased but did not eliminate the significant community effect, suggesting that there is a community effect beyond that of the family. We are examining other behaviors as well in our community comparisons (Crockett, Stemmler, Bingham, & Petersen, 1991).

Gender differences in developmental processes provide another way of looking at context–individual interactions. There may be different gender-related processes by context, as suggested by patterns of positive affect development for girls in two communities, as well as by the

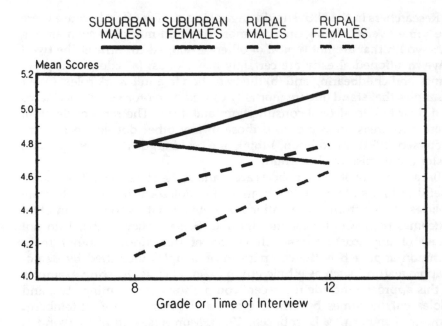

SUBURBAN SUBURBAN   RURAL   RURAL
MALES   FEMALES   MALES   FEMALES

FIGURE 2   The development of emotional tone by gender and community.

different relative timing of puberty between the genders found by Worthman (1992). Gender remains a powerful variable in the U.S. and most other societies.

Another important focus of recent work has been on neighborhoods. This research has moved beyond families, but has incorporated family variables, to characteristics of the neighborhood. Recent examples include the work of Brooks-Gunn, Duncan, Klebanov, and Sealand (1992), Burton and Allison (1992), and others (e.g., Aber, Allan, Mitchell, & Seidman, 1992; Connell, Clifford, & Crichlow, 1992). A committee of the Social Science Research Council seems to have stimulated much of the advance in this area. Burton and Allison (1992) and Spencer (1992), for example, used "drive-by" ratings to assess the physical features of a neighborhood (e.g., the nature of buildings as well as their condition) and the human resources (e.g., social service agencies and the nature of street activity) with ratings obtained at different times of day and night, day of week, and season. Brooks-Gunn et al. (1992) based their assessment of neighborhoods on census tract data. This level of analysis permits examination of the processes between macrolevel variables such as social class and the individual.

This is an exciting area that should permit examination of some of the questions posed by Elliott (in press), described earlier. What are the processes by which adolescents are drawn into problem behaviors? Burton and Allison's (1992) research combined neighborhood assessment with intensive ethnographic research and should yield important findings about the underlying processes. Silbereisen and colleagues (Silbereisen, Schoenpflug, & Albrecht, 1990; Walper & Silbereisen, in press), using survey methods, have also been engaged in identifying the factors assessed cross-nationally that influence different developmental trajectories in self-esteem and problem behaviors. It is highly important that researchers discover what sets a developmental course and what maintains or offsets it.

Interventions

Another approach to studying the processes of developmental change is through systematic interventions. A well-designed intervention can serve two purposes: (a) It can provide information about the underlying processes and (b) it can provide information about the effectiveness of the intervention. Bandura (1982, 1988) has provided many of the best hypotheses and approaches in this area.

I have become particularly interested in preventive interventions. I was drawn into this area several years ago by my students, who noted that we were learning what went wrong in adolescence and that we ought to be trying to change these predicted negative outcomes. We began to design a preventive intervention to decrease the likelihood of depression during early adolescence (Petersen, 1988). Our intervention provides knowledge about early adolescent development and teaches skills to cope with the many changes that take place during this period (Meyer et al., 1992)

There are now many promising models for preventive interventions, with accumulating data on effectiveness. Researchers have not yet discovered the "gold standard," but they are gaining valuable information about what works. It does appear that interventions providing basic skills in problem solving and managing interpersonal relationships are essential (Hamburg, 1990; Price, Cioci, Penner, & Trautlein, 1990). In addition, prevention of specific problems requires some specific focus.

Many lines of evidence suggest that preventive interventions for adolescent problems should be targeted no later than early adolescence. Elliott's data on rates of alcohol consumption and sexual involvement, for example, suggest that these behaviors are normative at ages 15 and 17 years, respectively (Elliott, in press). Interventions to delay onset need to take place much earlier. Interventions to provide lifetime prevention, rather than delay, are likely to require repeated exposure and reinforcement.

There are debates about how early to provide interventions. Ideally, the necessary skills for healthy development would be taught continually by teachers and parents in developmentally appropriate ways, throughout middle childhood and early adolescence (e.g., Schorr, Both, & Copple, 1991). Given that this does not always happen, researchers need to identify the best times for various kinds of interventions.

Most preventive interventions have been focused at the individual level, but it is important to recognize that an individual focus alone may be inappropriate when there are powerful contextual effects (e.g., Dryfoos, 1990). As described earlier, neighborhood effects have been increasingly recognized and must be addressed. For example, results of an individual-focused intervention attempting to decrease illicit behavior will be minimized in a neighborhood in which the incentives for criminal behavior are high and the protective influences of alternative routes to adult status or income are limited. Similarly, some school environments have such an overwhelming negative influence on young people that an intervention to enhance individual achievement or social skills may be unsuccessful in that context.

As anyone who has consulted with programs learns quickly, those working on the "front lines" with adolescents are eager for the results of this research. Many have doubts about the effectiveness of conventional programs and want to know what to do—today. The weight of the negative indicators on youth outcomes in terms of problem behaviors, together with the evidence from developmental research demonstrating increasing capacity in adolescence, suggest that researchers must do better than they have in providing useful information to youth-service providers. Significant potential is being wasted in U.S. youth. Researchers identify ways to capitalize on the strengths of adolescents so that they can become happy, healthy adults making productive contributions to society.

Somehow, intervention research, like applied research more generally, has come to be viewed as less rigorous and less valuable scientifically. From everything I have learned, the opposite is true. It is much more difficult to conduct rigorous intervention research. Furthermore, this avenue of research can yield information about basic developmental processes. Therefore, this challenging scientific work should be attracting the best scientists.

SUMMARY

Adolescence has received much more attention recently by the popular media and by various national and international groups. A great deal of information supports the urgency of the needs of adolescents.

Researchers have the responsibility to provide information to inform various inquiries. Many have shared my experience of frustration at not having answers to perfectly reasonable questions raised by colleagues working in program or policy areas. I have come to believe strongly that researchers need to understand the kind of information needed by others and that they have a responsibility to study these issues. I am not arguing that all research must be applied, but at least some of the research needs to provide information that people want and need.

The stakes are raised by evidence that many problems are becoming increasingly worse for adolescents. Only in the area of illicit drug use and cigarette smoking are the indicators moving in an improved direction, and even so, these problems are still evident in overwhelming proportions (e.g., Johnston, O'Malley, & Bachman, 1987). In the U.S., other indices of mortality and morbidity, such as suicide and criminal behavior, are moving in the direction of increased rates (Dryfoos, 1990; Elliott et al., 1989). These trends may also be true cross-nationally (Rutter, 1992). It is imperative that researchers begin to understand these processes so that they can provide some guidance as to their solution and reversal. Researchers do not presently have this knowledge. I challenge everyone during the next decade to contribute knowledge that will enhance the lives of adolescents in the U.S. and abroad.

ACKNOWLEDGMENTS

This article was presented as the Presidential Address at the Fourth Biennial Meeting of the Society for Research on Adolescence, March 1992, in Washington, DC.

Research described in this article was supported by Grant MH38142 from the National Institute of Mental Health and Grant 91090702 from the William T. Grant Foundation.

I am grateful to all of the colleagues and organizations that have provided a forum for discussion and learning, particularly the Carnegie Corporation of New York, the William T. Grant Foundation, and the recent Office of Technical Assessment Panel on Adolescent Health. In Europe, the Johann Jacobs Foundation and the study group on Youth and Social Change of the Academia Europaea have provided similar forums for comparing ideas extending cross-nationally. I also thank the many colleagues, in both the U.S. and Europe, who have influenced my thinking, especially my many research collaborators, both faculty and current, as well as former students. I gratefully acknowledge the research assistance of Nancy Leffert, PhD, in the preparation of this article for publication.

REFERENCES

Aber, L., Allan, L., Mitchell, C., & Seidman, E. (1992, March). Neighborhood social isolation and adolescent academic achievement: Gender and race specific patterns and processes. In L. Aber (Chair), *The effects of urban neighborhoods on adolescent development and school achievement: Gender and race/ethnic differences*. Symposium conducted at the biennial meeting of the Society for Research on Adolescence, Washington, DC.

Backstrom, T., Sanders, D., Leask, R., Davidson, D., Warner, P., & Bancroft, J. (1983). Mood, sexuality, hormones, and the menstrual cycle: 2. Hormone levels and their relationship to the premenstrual syndrome. *Psychosomatic Medicine, 45*, 503–507.

Bandura, A. (1982). Self-efficacy mechanism in human agency. *Psychology in the Schools, 1*, 224–231.

Bandura, A. (1988). Self-regulation of motivation and action through goal systems. In V. Hamilton, G. H. Bower, & N. H. Frijda (Eds.), *Cognitive perspectives on emotion and motivation* (pp. 37–61). Dordrecht, The Netherlands: Kluwer Academic Publishers.

Belsky, J., Steinberg, L., & Draper, P. (1991). Childhood experience, interpersonal development and reproductive strategy: An evolutionary theory of socialization. *Child Development, 62*, 647–670.

Bertram, H. (in press). Youth: Work and unemployment. In A. C. Petersen & J. Mortimer (Eds.), *Youth, unemployment, and society*. New York: Cambridge University Press.

Bingham, C. R., Meyer, A., & Crockett, L. J. (1991, February). *Rural and suburban differences in adolescent adjustment and expectations for adulthood*. Poster presented at the forum for the initiation of Policy, Research, and Intervention for Development in Early Adolescence, Pennsylvania State University, University Park.

Block, J. (1971). *Lives through time*. Berkeley, CA: Bancroft Books.

Brooks-Gunn, J., Duncan, G. J., Klebanov, P. K., & Sealand, N. (1992). *Do neighborhoods influence child and adolescent behavior?* Manuscript submitted for publication.

Burton, L., & Allison, K. (1992, March). *Family process and developmental outcomes for African American adolescents*. Paper presented at a conference on adolescent social development and change in the Americas, Panamerican Health Organization, Society for Adolescent Medicine, and the Society for Research on Adolescence, Washington, DC.

Caspi, A., Lynam, D., Moffitt, T. E., & Silva, P. A. (1993). Unraveling girls' delinquency: Biological, dispositional, and contextual contributions to adolescent misbehavior. *Developmental Psychology, 29*, 19–30.

Caspi, A., & Moffitt, T. E. (1991). Individual differences are accentuated during periods of social changes: The sample case of girls at puberty. *Journal of Personality and Social Psychology, 61*, 157–168.

Center for the Study of Social Policy. (1991). *Kids count data book: State profiles of child well-being*. Greenwich, CT: Annie E. Casey Foundation.

Collins, W. A. (1990). Parent–child relationships in the transition to adolescence: Continuity and change in interaction, affect, and cognition. In R. Montemayor, G. R. Adams, & T. P. Gullotta (Eds.), *From childhood to adolescence: A transitional period?* (pp. 85–106). Newbury Park, CA: Sage.

Connell, J. P., Clifford, E., & Crichlow, W. (1992, March). Gender and ethnic variation in contextual influences on adolescent school performance. In L. Aber (chair), *The effects of urban neighborhoods on adolescent development and school achievement: Gender and race/ethnic differences*. Symposium conducted at the biennial meeting of the Society for Research on Adolescence, Washington, DC.

Crockett, L., Losoff, M., & Petersen, A. C. (1984). Perceptions of the peer group and friendship in early adolescence. *Journal of Early Adolescence, 4*, 155–181.

Crockett, L. J., & Petersen, A. C. (in press). Adolescent development: Health risks and opportunities for adolescent health promotion. In S. G. Millstein, A. C. Petersen, & E. O. Nightingale (Eds.), *Promoting the health of adolescents: New directions for the twenty-first century.* New York: Oxford University Press.

Crockett, L. J., Stemmler, M., Bingham, R., & Petersen, A. C. (1991, July). *Subcultural variation in the development of adolescent problem behaviors.* Poster presented at the biennial meeting of the International Society for the Study of Behavioral Development, Minneapolis, MN.

Damon, W., & Hart, D. (1982). The development of self understanding from infancy through adolescence. *Child Development, 53,* 841–864.

Dennerstein, L., Spencer-Gardner, C., Brown, J. B., Smith, M. A., & Burrows, G. D. (1984). Premenstrual tension-hormonal profiles. *Journal of Psychosomatic Obstetrics and Gynecology, 3,* 37–51.

Department of International and Economic and Social Affairs. (1988). *Adolescent reproductive behavior: Evidence from developed countries* (Population Studies No. 109). New York: United Nations.

Dornbusch, S. M., Petersen, A. C., & Hetherington, E. M. (1991). Projecting the future of research on adolescence. *Journal of Research on Adolescence, 1,* 7–17.

Dryfoos, J. G. (1990). *Adolescents at risk.* New York: Oxford University Press.

Dubas, J. S. (1992, March). The long term effects of pubertal timing on achievement, work, and family roles. Poster presented at the biennial meeting of the Society for Research on Adolescence, Washington, DC.

Elliott, D. S. (in press). Health enhancing and health compromising lifestyles. In S. G. Millstein, A. C. Petersen, & E. O. Nightingale (Eds.), *Promoting the health of adolescents: New directions for the twenty-first century.* New York: Oxford University Press.

Elliott, D. S., Huizinga, D., & Menard, S. (1989). *Multiple problem youth: Delinquency, substance use and mental health problems.* New York: Springer-Verlag.

Feldman, S. S., & Elliott, G. R. (Eds.). (1990). *At the threshold: The developing adolescent.* Cambridge, MA: Harvard University Press.

Gupta, D., Attanasio, A., & Raaf, S. (1975). Plasma estrogen and androgen concentrations in children during adolescence. *Journal of Clinical Endocrinology and Metabolism, 40,* 636–643.

Hamburg, B. A. (1990). *Life skills training: Preventative interventions for young adolescents.* Report of the Life Skills Training Working Group, Carnegie Council on Adolescent Development, Washington DC.

Hartup, W. W. (1983). Peer relations. In P. H. Mussen (Ed.), *Handbook of child psychology* (Vol. 4, 103–196). New York: Wiley.

Hauser, S. T., Borman, E. H., Powers, S. I., Jacobson, A. M., & Noam, G. G. (199). Paths of adolescent ego development: Links with family life and individual adjustment. *Psychiatric Clinics of North America, 13,* 489–510.

Hill, J. (1983). Early adolescence: A framework. *Journal of Early Adolescence, 3,* 1–21.

Johnston, L. D., O'Malley, P. M., & Bachman, J. G. (1987). *National trends in drug use and related factors among American high school students and young adults, 1975–86* (CDHHS Publication No. ADM87-1535). Rockville, MD: National Institute on Drug Abuse.

Jones, E. F., Forrest, J. D., Goldman, N., Henshaw, S. K., Lincoln, R., Rosoff, J. I., Westoff, C. F., & Wulf, D. (1985). Teenage pregnancy in developed countries: Determinants and policy implications. *Family Planning Perspectives, 17,* 53–63.

Keating, D. P. (1990). Adolescent thinking. In S. S. Feldman & G. R. Elliott (Eds.), *At the threshold: The developing adolescent* (pp. 54–89). Cambridge, MA: Harvard University Press.

Kestenberg, J. S. (1968). Phases of adolescence with suggestions for a correlation of psychic and hormonal organizations: Part 3. Puberty growth, differentiation, and consolidation. *Journal of the American Academy of Child Psychiatry, 7,* 108–151.

Marshall, W. A., & Tanner, J. M. (1969). Variations in pattern of pubertal changes in girls. *Archives of Diseases in Childhood, 44,* 291–303.

Marshall, W. A., & Tanner, J. M. (1970). Variations in the pattern of pubertal changes in boys. *Archives of Diseases in Childhood, 45,* 13–23.

Meyer, A., Miller, S., Grund, E., Herman, M., Rice, K., Sullivan, P., & Kennedy, R. (1992). *Penn State Adolescent Study Intervention Program manual.* University Park, PA: Penn State Adolescent Study.

Offer, D., & Offer, J. B. (1975). *From teenage to young manhood: A psychological study.* New York: Basic Books.

Olweus, D. (1979). Stability and aggressive reaction patterns in males: A review. *Psychological Bulletin, 86,* 852–875.

Petersen, A. C. (1983). Pubertal change and cognition. In J. Brooks-Gunn & A. C. Petersen (Eds.), *Girls at puberty: Biological and psychosocial perspectives* (pp. 179–198). New York: Plenum.

Petersen, A. C. (1987). The nature of biological-psychological interactions: The sample case of early adolescence. In R. M. Lerner & T. T. Foch (Eds.), *Biological-psychosocial interactions in early adolescence.* (pp. 173–188). Hillsdale, NJ: Lawrence Erlbaum Associates, Inc.

Petersen, A. C. (1988). Adolescent development. *Annual Review of Psychology, 39,* 583–607.

Petersen, A. C. (1988). *Coping with early adolescent challenge: Gender related mental health outcomes.* Report to William T. Grant Foundation (Grant #89–1272–89). University Park, PA: Author.

Petersen, A. C. (1991, April). *American adolescence: How it affects girls.* Paper presented at the 1991 Gisela Konopka Lecture, University of Minnesota, Minneapolis.

Petersen, A. C., Compas, B., Brooks-Gunn, J., Stemmler, M., Ey, S., & Grant, K. (in press). Depression in adolescence. *American Psychologist.*

Petersen, A. C., & Crockett, L. J. (1992). Adolescent sexuality, pregnancy, and child rearing: Developmental perspectives. In M. K. Rosenheim & M. F. Testa (Eds.), *Early parenthood and coming of age in the 1990s* (pp. 34–45). New Brunswick, NJ: Rutgers University Press.

Petersen, A. C., Hurrelmann, K., & Leffert, N. (in press). Adolescence and schooling in Germany and the United States: A comparison of societal socialization to adulthood. *Teachers College Record.*

Petersen, A. C., Kennedy, R., & Sullivan, P. (1991). Coping with adolescence. In M. E. Colten & S. Gore (Eds.), *Adolescent stress: Causes and consequences,* (pp. 93–110). New York: Aldine de Gruyter.

Petersen, A. C., Sarigiani, P. A., & Kennedy, R. E. (1991). Adolescent depression: Why more girls? *Journal of Youth and Adolescence, 20,* 247–271.

Price, R. H., Cioci, M., Penner, W., & Trautlein, B. (1990). *School and community support programs that enhance adolescent health and education.* Report prepared for the Carnegie Council on Adolescent Development, Washington, DC.

Rutter, M. (1980). *Changing youth in a changing society: Patterns of adolescent development and disorder.* Cambridge, MA: Harvard University Press.

Rutter, M., Graham, P., Chadwick, O., & Yule, W. (1976). Adolescent turmoil: Fact or fiction? *Journal of Child Psychology and Psychiatry, 17,* 35–56.

Rutter, M. (1992, March). *Adolescence as a transition period: Continuities and discontinuities in conduct disorder.* Gallagher Lecture Paper presented at the joint meetings of the Society for Research on Adolescence and the Society for Adolescent Medicine, Washington, DC.

Sameroff, A. J. (1982). Development and the dialectic: The need for a systems approach. In W. A. Collins (Ed.), *The Minnesota Symposium on Child Psychology* (Vol. 15, pp. 83–103). Hillsdale, NJ: Lawrence Erlbaum Associates, Inc.

Savin-Williams, R., & Demo, D. (1983). Situational and transituational determinants of adolescent self-feelings. *Journal of Personality and Social Psychology, 44,* 824–833.

Schorr, L. B., Both, B., & Copple, C. (Eds.). (1991). *Effective services for children: Report of a workshop.* Washington, DC: National Academy Press.

Silbereisen, R. K., Schoenpflug, U., & Albrecht, H. T. (1990). Smoking and drinking in mid-teens: Prospective analyses in German and Polish adolescents. In K. Hurrelmann & F. Lösel (Eds.), *Health hazards in adolescence* (pp. 167–190). New York: Aldine de Gruyter.

Simmons, R. G., & Blyth, D. A. (1987). *Moving into adolescence: The impact of pubertal change and school context.* New York: Aldine de Gruyter.

Spencer, M. B. (1992, May). *The violence of poverty and the abuse of power: Implications for scholarship and stewardship.* Paper presented at the Gisela Konopka Lectureship, University of Minnesota, Minneapolis.

Spencer, M. B., & Dornbusch, S. (1990). Challenges in studying minority youth. In S. S. Feldman & G. R. Elliott (Eds.), *At the threshold: The developing adolescent* (pp. 123–146). Cambridge, MA: Harvard University Press.

Stattin, H., & Magnusson, D. (1990). Pubertal maturation in female development. *Paths through life* (Vol. 2). Hillsdale, NJ: Lawrence Erlbaum Associates, Inc.

Steinberg, L. (1990). Autonomy, conflict, and harmony in the family relationship. In S. S. Feldman & G. R. Elliott (Eds.), *At the threshold: The developing adolescent* (pp. 255–276). Cambridge, MA: Harvard University Press.

Steinberg, L. (1992, March). Discussant's comments. In R. K. Silbereisen, *Psychosocial antecedents of the timing of puberty.* Symposium conducted at the biennial meeting of the Society for Research on Adolescence, Washington, DC.

Steinberg, L., Mounts, N. S., Lamborn, S. D., & Dornbusch, S. M. (1991). Authoritative parenting and adolescent adjustment across varied ecological niches. *Journal of Research on Adolescence, 1,* 19–36.

Stemmler, M., Bingham, R., Crockett, L. J., & Petersen, A. C. (1991, July). *Normative expectations in different developmental contexts.* Poster presented at the biennial meeting of the International Society for the Study of Behavioral Development, Minneapolis, MN.

Susman, E. J., Inoff-Germain, G., Nottelmann, E. D., Loriaux, D. L., Cutler, G. B., & Chrousos, G. P. (1987). Hormones, emotional dispositions, and aggressive attributes in young adolescents. *Child Development, 58,* 1114–1134.

Trickett, P. K., & Putnam, F. W. (in press). The impact of child sexual abuse on females: Toward a developmental, psychobiological integration. *Psychological Science.*

Udry, J. R. (1992, March). Discussants comments. In B. Hamburg (Chair), *Puberty and biological factors: New research directions.* Symposium conducted at the biennial meetings of the Society for Research on Adolescence, Washington, DC.

Udry, J. R., Billy, J. O. G., Morris, N. M., Groff, T. R., & Raj, M. H. (1985). Serum androgenic hormones motivate sexual behavior in boys. *Fertility and Sterility, 43,* 90–94.

Udry, J. R., Talbert, L. M., & Morris, N. M. (1986). Biosocial foundations for adolescent female sexuality. *Demography, 23,* 217–230.

Walper, S., & Silbereisen, R. K. (in press). Economic hardship in Polish and German families: Some consequences for adolescents. In R. K. Silbereisen & E. Todt (Eds.), *Adolescence in contest: The interplay of family, school, peers, and work adjustment.* New York: Springer.

Weiner, I. B., & DelGaudio, A. (1976). Psychopathology in adolescence. *Archives of General Psychiatry, 33,* 187–193.

William T. Grant Foundation. (1988). *The forgotten half: Non-college youth in America.* Washington DC: William T. Grant Commission on Work, Family, and Citizenship.

Worthman, C. M. (1992, March). Minimally invasive measures of pubertal development. In B. Hamburg (Chair), *Puberty and biological factors: New research directions.* Symposium conducted at the biennial meeting of the Society for Research on Adolescence, Washington, DC.

Youniss, J., & Smollar, J. (1985). *Adolescent relations with mothers, fathers, and friends.* Chicago: University of Chicago Press.

Received September 30, 1992
Accepted September 30, 1992

THE PHILOSOPHICAL AND HISTORICAL ROOTS OF THEORIES OF ADOLESCENCE

Long before psychology became a science, there existed philosophical, theological, and educational theories that contributed to an understanding of human nature and development. As a result of his famous two-volume work *Adolescence* (1916), G. Stanley Hall is considered the father of a scientific "psychology of adolescence." Prior to Hall, it was frequently the philosopher-educator who was especially concerned with the nature of human development and with its implications for teaching and learning. This was the case with Plato, Aristotle, Comenius, Rousseau, Herbart, Froebel, and Pestalozzi.

One difficulty in identifying prescientific theories of adolescent development is that prior to Hall, adolescence was not considered a separate stage of human development. The word "adolescence" first appeared in the fifteenth century, indicating that historically adolescence was subordinated to theoretical considerations about the nature of human development. Contemporary theories of adolescence have their historical roots in more general philosophical ideas about the nature of man and the process of development. Some important ideas about human development come from philosophers who are concerned with the question: What is the nature of man? For example, what Locke and Darwin had to say about the nature of man is so profound that it is reflected in the writings of Rousseau, Hall, and Freud, respectively, and thus provides a philosophical foundation for a theory of development.

EARLY GREEK CONCERN WITH HUMAN NATURE

A historical approach to a theory of adolescence must begin with the early Greek ideas about human development. Their influence remained prevalent throughout the Middle Ages and is still noticeable today. The philosophical idea of dualism, for instance, is essentially Greek. Plato (427–347 B.C.) made a clear distinction between two aspects of human nature: soul and body. He expounded that body and soul are different strata and that although there is some interaction between them, the soul is an entity in itself, capable of leaving the body without losing its identity. The soul can perceive more clearly and reach higher realities when freed from the body; *soma sema* ("the body is the grave of the soul"), he declared. Actually, Plato expressed disdain for the body, favoring the soul which reaches out toward the intangible realm of ideas. The body and sensuality are the fetters that hinder the soul in reaching those higher realities. Body is matter and has all the defects of matter. The idea of dualism between mind and body reappeared later in Christian theology and became of primary importance in the philosophical thinking of the seventeenth century, especially with Descartes, Leibnitz, and Spinoza.

Of greater interest from a developmental point of view is the idea of the layer structure of the soul, which Plato developed in his dialogue, *Phaedo.* According to Plato, the soul has three distinguishable parts, layers, or levels. Thus, probably for the first time in the history of psychology, a threefold division of soul, or mind, is advanced. The lowest layer of the soul is described as man's desires and appetitites. Today we might describe this level in terms of drives, instincts, and needs, and its resemblance to Freud's concept of "id" can hardly be denied. According to Plato, this part of the soul is located in the lower part of the body and is primarily concerned with the satisfaction of the physical needs. ". . . [I]t fills us full of love, and lusts, and fears, and fancies of all kinds, and endless foolery, and . . . takes away the power of thinking at all" (Plato, 1921: 450). The second layer of the soul, the spirit, includes courage, conviction, temperance, endurance, and hardihood; aggressiveness and fierceness also originate here. Man has both the first and the second layer in common with the animal world. These two layers belong to the body and die with it. The third layer is divine, supernatural, and immortal; it constitutes the essence of the universe. This is the real soul, which Plato described as reason and which has only its temporary seat in the body. Plato's theory concerning the layer structure of the soul is reflected in several central European personality theories, which are developed on the assumption of a layerlike stratification of personality. They perceive development as a process by which the lower layers mature earlier and are superseded by higher layers as the child grows older. Plato had already postulated such a developmental theory. Reason is latent during the first stage when perception is most important. Among contemporary theorists, Piaget maintains that percepts develop into concepts which facilitate thinking. The second stage of development is characterized by conviction and understanding and brings the second layer of the soul, spirit, into the foreground of psychological development. The third stage, which we might identify with adolescence, but which, according to Plato, is not reached by all people, relates to the development of the third part of the soul, reason and intelligence.

Interspersed in most of Plato's diaologues—but particularly in *Laws* and *The Republic*—are descriptive accounts of children and youth as well as advice concerning the control of their behavior. While this material does not constitute a theory of development as we understand it today, it does give insight into Plato's conception of the nature of development.

During the first three years of life the infant should be free from fear and pain and sorrow. This point of view would be endorsed by many psychologists today. Interestingly enough, in the dialogue, *Laws,* Cleinias suggests that in addition to freeing the infant from pain we ought to provide pleasure. This is in agreement with Plato's basic goal, which is the possession of happiness. However, the Athenian Stranger objects that this would spoil the child, since during the early years "more than at any other time the character is engrained by habit" (Plato, 1953: 359). Plato postulated that some ideas are innate, present in the mind before experiences. Character is formed at an early age because the experiences and impressions leave a lasting influence. However, Plato did admit that "the characters of young men are subject to many changes in the course of their lives." The argument about the consistency of personality versus its modifiability has continued, and proponents of both of Plato's statements, stability of traits versus the power of situational influences, can still be heard today.

From ages 3 to 6 the child needs sports and social contact with age-mates in order to get rid of his self-will. Plato would punish but not disgrace the child. Social development is taken into consideration at this age, and children ought to come together in a kind of kindergarten arrangement under the supervision of a nurse. However, children should find for themselves the "natural modes of amusement" appropriate to their age.

Plato suggested a division of the sexes at age 6. "Let boys live with boys and girls . . . with girls." The boy now has to learn horsemanship, the uses of bow and arrow, the spear, and the sling. Boys will not be allowed to drink wine until they are 18 because of their easy excitability, "fire must not be poured upon fire." A related adolescent desire is argument for amusement's sake. In their enthusiasm they will leave no stone unturned, and in their delight over the first taste of wisdom they will annoy everyone with their arguments. Plato believed that the character is formed through habit at a very early age.

Plato developed his educational philosophy in *The Republic.* He perceived education as the development of the soul under the influence of the environment, "and this has two divisions, gymnastic for the body, and music for the soul." Reasoning in the young child is undeveloped, but since the young child is impressionable, Plato suggested establishing "a censorship of the writers of fiction," since "anything that he receives into his mind is likely to become indelible and unalterable: and therefore . . . the talks which the young first hear should be models of virtuous thoughts" (Plato, 1921: 642). Rational and critical thought develop mainly during adolescence. The training that began with music and gymnastics during childhood was continued through adolescence with mathematical and scientific studies. The latter brought out critical thought and dissatisfaction with direct sense knowledge; during this training students would develop methods of finding the truth and of distinguishing truth from opinion. In *Laws* Plato spoke of education as "that training which is given by suitable habits to the first instincts of virtue in children;—when pleasure, and friendship, and pain, and hatred are rightly implanted in souls not yet capable of understanding the nature of them, and who find them, after they have attained reason, to be in harmony with her" (Plato, 1953: 218). The meaning of education in this view is to provide experiences for children prior to the development of reason that are nevertheless in agreement with reason when it does develop during adolescence. Plato already recognized the importance of individual differences. He recognized that children are born with different abilities and should be guided into those kinds of activities that are in line with their aptitudes.

Plato postulated that the attainment of knowledge might be explained by his doctrine of innate ideas. Though undeveloped, vague, and nebulous, innate ideas are nevertheless present at birth. Learning is a process of remembering these ideas, which once—probably before the soul entered the body—were clear. Sensations help in reawakening these partially lost ideas. The mind-body dualism is of relevance here, since the body contributes sensation while the mind contains the ideas. Through this distinction, Plato's theory of innate ideas opens the discussion about the influence of heredity and environment.

Aristotle (384–322 B.C.), although a pupil of Plato's, challenged many of his master's ideas. Aristotle denied the separation of body and soul and returned to the older Greek idea of the unity of the physical and mental worlds. Body and soul, according to him, are related in structure and function. The relationship between body and soul is the same as that between matter and form; body is matter and soul is form. Soul-life, for which Aristotle used the word "entelechy," is the principle by which the body lives. Aristotle accepted Plato's idea concerning the levels of the soul-life; however, he viewed soul structure from a biological, almost evolutionary, point of view, in that he drew analogies between biological life forms and human nature. The lowest soul-life form is that of the plant, the life functions of which are supply of nourishment and reproduction. The next higher form of soul-life is also found in animals, its additional functions being sensation, perception, and locomotion. The third soul-life function is distinctly human and sets men apart from the animal world. It includes the ability to think and reason. Consequently, there are three layers of soul-life— the food-supplying, or plant, soul; the perceiving, or animal, soul; and the thinking, or human, soul. Aristotle further divided the thinking, or human, soul into two different parts: the practical soul by which we "deliberate about those things which depend upon us and our purpose to do or not to do" (Aristotle, 1925: 1196), and the theoretical soul, which deals with higher and abstract knowledge such as distinguishing between what is true and what is false. Aristotle saw the ability to think and the use of logic and rational powers as the purpose of development and the essence of mankind.

Aristotle advanced a theory of development concerning the layer structure of the soul that appears to have some resemblance to Darwin's more scientific biological theory of evolution, even though it does not include the idea of evolution of one species from another. Furthermore, Aristotle made an impassable division between the different levels of soul-life. Plato, in describing the stages of development, held that the first (plant) soul level developed before the second (animal) soul level and this, in turn, was a prerequisite for the rational (human) soul level. Aristotle followed this idea of the level structure of the soul and applied it to the development of the child.

> As the body is prior in order of generation to the soul, so the irrational is prior to the rational. The proof is that anger and wishing and desire are implanted in children from their very birth, but reason and understanding are developed as they grow older. Wherefore, the care of the body ought to precede that of the soul, and the training of the appetitive part should follow; none the less our care of it must be for the sake of the reason, and our care of the body for the sake of the soul [Aristotle, 1941c: 1300–1301].

Aristotle divided the developmental period into three distinguishable stages of 7 years each. The first 7 years he named infancy; the period from 7 to the beginning of puberty, boyhood; and from puberty to 21, young manhood. This division of the period of development into three stages was generally accepted during the Middle Ages and recurs in some contemporary theories of development.

Infants and animals are alike in that both are under the control of their appetites and emotions. "Children and brutes pursue pleasures" (Aristotle, 1941a: 1053). Aristotle emphasized that moral character is the result of choice, "for by choosing what is good or bad we are men of a certain character. . . ." Even though young children are able to act voluntarily, they do not have choice, "for both children and the lower animals share in voluntary action, but not in choice, and acts done on the spur of the moment we describe as voluntary, but not as chosen" (Aristotle, 1941a: 967–968). This seems to imply that children first go through an animal-like stage of development; what distinguishes them from animals is that children have the potential for higher development than animals, "though psychologically speaking a child hardly differs for the time being from an animal" (Aristotle, 1941b: 635). It is the characteristic of adolescence to develop the ability to choose. Only if youths voluntarily and deliberately choose will they develop the right kind of habits and thus, in the long run, build the right kind of character. By making choices adolescents actively participate in their own character formation. Voluntary and deliberate choice thus becomes an important aspect in Aristotle's theory of development, since it is necessary for the attainment of maturity. Among contemporary writers, M. Mead and E. Friedenberg claim that prolonged education and dependency have reduced choices to the extent that they interfere with the attainment of maturity.

Although Aristotle did not offer us a systematically stated theory of development, however, in *Rhetorica* he provided us with a detailed description of the "youthful type of character," part of which resembles descriptive statements that could have been written by G. Stanley Hall. "Young men have strong passions, and tend to gratify them indiscriminately. Of the bodily desires, it is the sexual by which they are most swayed and in which they show absence of self-control" (Aristotle, 1941d: 1403). Sexuality in adolescence is a contemporary concern and has become an educational and a public-policy issue. Aristotle, in his description of adolescents, commented on their instability: "They are changeable and fickle in their desires, which are violent while they last, but quickly over: their impulses are keen but not deep-rooted" (Aristotle, 1941d: 1403). Among modern writers, Lewin deals with the instability of the psychological field of the adolescent, who stands in a psychological no man's land. This makes many sociopsychological situations unclear, indefinite, and ambiguous, and the resulting behavior is "changeable and fickle." "For owing to their love and honour they cannot bear being slighted, and are indignant if they imagine themselves being unfairly treated" (Aristotle, 1941d: 1403–1404). Adolescent complaints about being "unfairly treated" in home, school, and society in general are so common today that they need no further elaboration. The list of quotes from *Rhetorica* in which Aristotle described the characteristics of adolescence could be continued, and other analogies to contemporary theories would not be too difficult to find. Aristotle discussed, among other issues, adolescents' desire for success, their optimism, trust, concern with the future rather than the past, their courage, conformity, idealism, friendship, aggressiveness, and gullibility, all of which remain contemporary issues in adolescent psychology and some have been researched extensively.

The education of the adolescent in the fourth century B.C. was based on the study of mathematics and included astronomy, geometry, and the theory of music; these subjects taught abstraction but did not require the life experiences and the wisdom considered necessary in order to become a philosopher or a physicist.

Under the early impact of Christian theology, Aristotelian thought seemed to get lost; however, it was later combined with Christian ideas by Saint Thomas Aquinas. The Aristotelian-Thomistic philosophy became dominant in the twelfth and thirteenth centuries, and its influence was felt during the Middle Ages—particularly in the form of Scholasticism. Aristotle is also considered influential in laying the foundation for a more scientific approach to science and psychology.

MEDIEVAL CHRISTIAN VIEW OF HUMAN DEVELOPMENT

The theological view of human nature and development cannot as readily be identified in terms of one man, a specific historical period, or even a particular denomination. We find the idea of original sin expressed by Tertullian in the second century when he spoke of the depravity of human nature. It was emphasized by John Calvin in the sixteenth century and is prevalent in Catholic Scholasticism, Protestant Calvinism, and American Puritanism.

The theological view of human nature as found in the medieval, early Reformation period encompassed several relevant ideas:

1. Mankind's unique position in the universe, being created in the image of God.
2. Mankind's evil due to Adam's original sin.
3. Mankind's dual nature: a spiritual, immortal soul and a material, mortal body. Salvation and life after death places the immortal soul on a higher level of importance.
4. Knowledge as revealed to mankind from without. It comes from God and is revealed to us through the Bible.
5. The homunculus idea of instantaneous creation. The last point is not so much biblical as medieval.

Most of these ideas can be found in biblical sources, but they were also influenced by Greek philosophy, especially Plato's mind-body dualism. We will see later that theories that followed in the seventeenth, eighteenth, and nineteenth centuries, especially those advanced by Locke, Rousseau, and Darwin, can partly be understood as antitheses to these earlier theological ideas.

The idea that God created mankind in his own image and thus gave it a unique position in the universe is expressed in Genesis 1:27-28: "And God created man to his own image: to the image of God he created him: male and female he created them." Furthermore, he gives them the power to rule over all living creatures. Prior to Darwin man was seen as being divinely created and basically different from the animal world.

The second important idea concerning the nature of humanity is the theological doctrine of human depravity. The human being is seen as having innate tendencies toward ungodliness and sinfulness, as fundamentally bad, with the badness becoming stronger during the developmental years if it is not counteracted by stern discipline. The idea of original sin as based on Genesis 3:6-7 relates the sinfulness of each individual to Adam's first sin. And "as sin came into the world through one man and death through sin, and so death spread to all men because all men sinned. . . . Yet death reigned from Adam to Moses, even over those whose sins were not like the transgression of Adam . . ." (Romans 5:12-14).

This pessimistic view of human nature, prevalent in Catholic theology before the Reformation, received a new impetus with Calvin's theology and thus set the intellectual climate for Puritanism. The educational objective in this theory was to bring forth the innate ideas that are God-given—knowledge of his laws and commands. Such a stern disciplinary approach to education was prevalent under the influence of Catholic Scholasticism and Calvinism in Europe and Puritanism in New England. There was little room for individual differences, since the quality of the mind was the same for all individuals, and the child who failed to learn was seen as willfully resisting the efforts of the teacher. The role of the teacher was defined by the teacher's authority and a belief that learning could be facilitated by physical punishment. The role of the child was defined by obedience. Calvin in particular expressed a strong faith in the value of education.

The theological view that mankind is the result of instantaneous creation results in preformationist thinking (Ausubel, 1958). During the Dark Ages, it was believed that the child came into the world as a miniature adult. The difference between a child and an adult was considered to be only a quantitative one, not a qualitative one. If one were to accept this point of view, then it follows that there should be no difference in the physiological functions of the child and the adult. Therefore, girls wore long dresses and corsets of adult style, only smaller in size, as is obvious from many medieval paintings. The qualitative difference in body build, body function, and mental abilities was disregarded. Growth was understood to be only a quantitative increase of all physical and mental aspects of human nature, not a qualitative one. This is a regression of thought when contrasted with the logical theories of Plato and Aristotle. The theory of preformationism held that children had the same interests as adults and therefore should be treated correspondingly, which meant that adult requirements were put upon them and were enforced by stern discipline. According to this view, the child did not "develop" but was preformed. Figure 1.1 illustrates the homunculus concept; it represents a view of the preformed "little man" in the sperm as conceived by seventeenth-century scientists.

> It was seriously believed that a miniature but fully-formed little man (i.e., an homunculus) was embodied in the sperm, and when implanted in the uterus simply grew in bulk, without any differentiation of tissues or organs, until full-term fetal size was attained at the end of nine months [Ausubel, 1958: 23-24].

This idea of homunculism was soon to be challenged by the beginning of modern science and advancements in the field of medicine. It was learned that young children have qualitative and quantitative characteristics of their own and are not miniature adults. One might speculate that the reason for the limited concern of pre-Hallian writers with the basic physiological changes that take place during pubescence—many of these changes are obvious to the keen observer, and their detection does not require medical knowledge or technology—is due to the theoretical position that the child is a miniature adult. In the philosophical realm it was Rousseau who stated that "nature would have children be children before being man. If we wish to prevent this order, we shall produce precocious fruits which will have neither maturity nor flavor, and will speedily deteriorate; we shall have young doctors and old children" (Rousseau, 1911: 54). Thus a new conception of human nature contributed to a more scientific concept of growth and development.

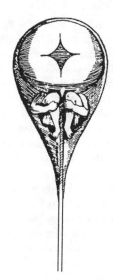

FIGURE 1.1 Drawing of a small man (an homunculus) in a human spermatozoon (adapted from Hartsoeker, 1694).

JOHN AMOS COMENIUS' DEVELOPMENT-CENTERED THEORY OF EDUCATION

The Renaissance may be seen as a revolt against authoritarianism in church, school, and society. The Aristotelian logic, the presupposition of universal ideas, and Scholasticism in general were challenged by Erasmus and Vives. Vives felt that one had "to begin with the individual facts of experience and out of them to come to ideas by the natural logic of the mind" (Boyd, 1965: 179). Learning was no longer seen as a deductive process, but as an inductive process beginning with experiences, and he suggested that an understanding of the learning process came from psychology. Learning, it was believed, was determined by the mind of the learner, and, therefore, education became concerned with individuality in pupils.

Comenius (1592–1670) accepted these ideas of the Renaissance, combined them with Aristotle's classification of development, and advanced a theory of education that was based on psychological assumptions. In his *Great Didactic,* first published in 1657, Comenius suggested a school organization based on a theory of development. Rather than dividing the developmental period into three stages of 7 years, as Aristotle did, Comenius proposed four developmental stages of 6 years each and a different school for each of these four stages.

The suggested school organization was based on assumptions concerning the nature of human development and a specific theory of learning, that of faculty psychology. Interestingly enough, present-day school organization in parts of the United States closely resembles this pattern. Comenius argued that the temporal sequence of the curriculum content should be borrowed from nature; in other words, it should be suitable to the psychological development of the child. "Let our maxim be to follow the lead of nature in all things, to observe how the faculties develope one after the other, and to base our method on this principle of succession" (Comenius, 1923: 257).

In the first 6 years of life children learn at home in the mother-school at their mother's knees. They should exercise the external senses and learn to discriminate among the various objects around them. The nature of the development of the faculty of sense perception is such that it precedes all other faculties, and, consequently, sensory experiences and sensory knowledge should be provided first. The significance of early sensorimotor experiences as the basis for learning and development is emphasized in Piaget's theory.

The child from 6 to 12 attends the vernacular-school and receives a general well-rounded elementary education, which is provided for all children, rich or poor, boy or girl. Included in the curriculum are the correct use of the vernacular language, social habits, and religious training. The program at this level would emphasize training of the "internal senses, the imagination and memory in combination with their cognate organs." Comenius accepted the faculty psychology point of view in respect to memory. "The memory should be exercised in early youth, since practise developes it, and we should therefore take care to practise it as much as possible. Now, in youth, the labour is not felt, and thus the memory developes without any trouble and becomes very retentive" (Comenius, 1923: 152).

For the next 6 years, from ages 12 to 18, which include the adolescent period as we understand it today, education was to be provided in the Latin school. The psychological purpose of the school at this age was to train the faculty of reasoning. The student learned to "understand and pass judgment on the information collected by the senses." Included were judgments about relationships of the things perceived, imagined, and remembered. Understanding here implies utilization of the principle of causality. The curriculum of the school was divided into 6 years, which results in the following six classes: Grammar, Natural Philosophy, Mathematics, Ethics, Dialectics, and Rhetoric.

The following 6 years, from ages 18 to 24, consist of university education and travel, and during this period the faculty of the will is trained. Considering our present conception of will, this appears to be a strange notion and becomes more meaningful only if we consider that the concept of will, as used by Comenius, includes the idea of choice, self-determination and self-direction of one's life. Corresponding ideas can be found in the theories of Erikson and Piaget.

Comenius strongly advocated that the instructional procedure fit the level of comprehension of the child in contrast to the Scholastic education, which he opposed. For Comenius, development is not uniform, continuous, and gradual—as the homunculus theory of development implies—but each stage of development has its own characteristics, "teachable moments" as Havighurst and many developmental stage theorists would say. Development was seen as a process in which the intellectual functions gain progressively more control over the other aspects of the soul.

> To attempt to cultivate the will before the intellect (or the intellect before the imagination, or the imagination before the faculty of sense perception) is mere waste of time. But this is what those do who teach boys logic, poetry, rhetoric, and ethics before they are thoroughly acquainted with the objects that surround them. It would be equally sensible to teach boys of two years old to dance, though they can scarcely walk [Comenius, 1923: 257].

27

The right time for the education of each of the faculties must be chosen correctly, and the sequence must be "borrowed from nature." In Comenius' continuous focus on what children can do, know, and are interested in at each stage of development, one can find the historical roots of a child-centered theory of education.

JOHN LOCKE'S EMPIRICISM

The idea of homunculism with its emphasis on preformationism and Plato's theory of innate ideas—a basic Scholastic principle—was most seriously challenged and opposed by John Locke (1632–1704). Locke was influenced by Thomas Hobbes' (1588–1679) idea that the human being, both body and mind, is part of the natural order; he further expanded Hobbes' theoretical position, known today as empiricism, that all of our knowledge is derived from sensation. Hobbes stated in *Leviathan* that "there is no conception in man's mind, which has not at first, totally, or by parts, been begotten upon the organs of sense" (Hobbes, 1651: 7). Locke further developed the theory that there are no innate ideas. Ideas that can be found in consciousness are either obtained through our senses directly or are derived from those ideas that have been obtained through sensations previously. The child's mind at the time of birth is, according to an analogy used by Locke, a *tabula rasa,* a blank tablet, as the following quote implies:

> Let us then suppose the mind to be, as we say, white paper, void of all characters, without any ideas;—How comes it to be furnished? . . . To this, I answer, in one word, from EXPERIENCE. In that all our knowledge is founded, and from that it ultimately derives itself. Our observation, employed either about external, sensible objects, or about the internal operations of our minds, perceived, and reflected on, by ourselves, is that which supplies our understandings with all the materials of thinking. These two are the fountains of knowledge, from whence all the ideas we have, or can naturally have, do spring [Locke, 1753: 76].

This assumption has had far-reaching influence on social theory and has with amplification become the cornerstone of democracy. Since the mind of each person at birth is a *tabula rasa,* all ideas and knowledge come from experience. Since present differences and inequalities found in people are due to environment and experiences, all are completely equal at birth. Thus the principle of democracy is in part derived from a philosophical-psychological theory concerning the child's mind at birth. Locke discussed his views concerning democracy in *Treatise of Civil Government* (1768). He blamed environmental conditions, such as poor education and poor social environment, for the human misery in the world and gave hope to those who lived under unfavorable conditions. Thus emerged a theory that is an expression of faith in the perfectibility of the human race.

Locke found rather enthusiastic followers in Helvetius and Condillac in France. They carried his empiricism to its extreme, since for them even the powers of faculties of the mind were the result of sensation. Furthermore, since poor living conditions existed for the French lower and middle classes prior to the Revolution, many people in France were especially susceptible to such ideas. Thus, the words *liberté, egalité, fraternité* became the powerful symbols of a new concept of human nature. A new hope emerged, that by changing the environment, human nature could be changed.

Locke's proposition that there are no innate ideas and that the mind is a *tabula rasa* contrasts sharply with several theories of development already discussed. The more outstanding examples are as follows:

1. The doctrine of human depravity and original sin appeared to be in contradiction to Locke's new concept of the human mind. If our mind is formed by experience only, then it follows that whether a child becomes "good" or "bad" is due to environmental experiences. Locke's psychology stresses nurture rather than nature.

2. The medieval class system of Europe was based on what are considered today hereditary assumptions. The nobility was noble by birth, regardless of personal merits and qualities. This notion was challenged by the empiricst assumption that "all men are born equal." If everyone is alike and begins life at the same point, then everyone should have the same rights and opportunities to obtain better social positions. King and subject, rich and poor, all begin life at the same point. Therefore, support for social mobility is found in this theory. Locke's early form of environmentalism, even though it is not directly related to behaviorism, social learning theory, and cultural relativism, may be viewed as a historical forerunner to these schools of thought.

3. The doctrine of innate ideas was interpreted during the medieval period to imply that the child is a miniature adult and grows only quantitatively. Locke's *tabula rasa* concept implied that the child at birth is qualitatively and quantitatively different from the adult. If ideas are not innate, then the newborn child is radically different from the adult in respect to intellectual properties. Locke pointed out that the child's personality is different from that of the adult and thus laid the foundation for a new theory of child development; he also urged the scientific study of human nature. Development occurred in a gradual process from mental passivity in the early years of childhood to increased mental activity in adolescence. The rational faculty emerges toward the end of this developmental process and therefore was seen as characteristic of the period of adolescence.

Locke, even though he advanced many important ideas about human nature, foreshadowed rather than developed a specific theory of human development.

JEAN-JACQUES ROUSSEAU'S ROMANTIC NATURALISM

Rousseau (1712–1778) was partly influenced by Locke's ideas, but he developed his own theoretical positions concerning human nature. For Locke reason was the most important aspect of human nature. Rousseau considered human nature as primarily feeling. While Locke was concerned with constitutional government, Rousseau made a strong plea for individualism and individual freedom and directed his critical attack against society and social institutions. Although he, too, was concerned with the social well-being of all, he distinguished between the "will of all" (majority will, determined by vote) and the "general will" (that which is really best for every member of society). Rousseau was not truly democratic, for he was afraid that rule by majority vote could be as bad as any monarchy. Ideally, the majority will and the general will would coincide. This, however, would only be possible if men were educated and wise.

Rousseau brought about a revolutionary change in thought concerning the nature of human development, with its corresponding educational implications, the main ideas of which he expressed in *Émile* (1780). The traditional approach toward childhood education had been to see the child from the adult point of view. Rousseau claimed that such an approach is not only false, it may even be harmful. He started with the needs and interests of the child and saw development as a natural preplanned process, as the following ideas reveal. If one were to free the child from the restrictions, unnatural limitations, and rigid discipline of the adult world, nature would assure a harmonious and healthy development. The child was innately good, but the restrictions of adult society and poor education tended to corrupt the child. To prevent this, he advocated a natural development in a sound and healthy environment, which for him was one that posed few restrictions on the child, especially in the first 12 years. Rousseau was one of the strongest proponents of individualism in education, basing his proposition on a deep faith in the natural goodness of man.

Rousseau advocated a revision of the treatment children received at home and in school as well as changes in the methods of instruction; if development were left to the laws of nature, the outcome would be most desirable. Each of Rousseau's four stages of development had specific psychological characteristics. Consideration of these characteristics resulted in definite educational objectives, the attainment of which helped children grow toward maturity. The educational methods, the content to be taught, and the objectives at each age level were to be determined by the characteristics of the child at that developmental level. Learning was most effective if the child had freedom and could learn and grow according to his own impulses, needs, and abilities.

Rousseau most strongly opposed the homunculus idea and asserted that it was the plan of nature that children play, live, and behave like children before they become adults. "Childhood has its own way of seeing, thinking, and feeling, and nothing is more foolish than to try to substitute ours for them" (Rousseau, 1911: 54). Rousseau advised teachers and parents, "You ought to be wholly absorbed in the child—observing him, watching him without respite, and without seeming to do so, having a presentiment of his feelings in advance" (Rousseau, 1911: 169). Even though Rousseau himself had only limited and not always successful educational experiences—his five children lived in a foundling asylum—his theory had a tremendous impact on educational practice in the latter part of the eighteenth and most of the nineteenth centuries. Rousseau's ideas are obvious in the works of Pestalozzi, Froebel, and Spencer in Europe, and are reflected in the approach of Horace Mann and John Dewey in the United States.

Rousseau, like Aristotle, saw the development of the chid occurring in certain stages; however, he identified four stages rather than three and believed that teaching and training should be in harmony with the developmental nature of each of these stages. According to Rousseau, these various stages are qualitative transformations in the developmental process, and each can be distinguished by its special characteristics and functions. He spoke of a metamorphosis that takes place when the child changes from one stage to another. Thus, Rousseau introduced a saltatory theory of human development according to which the nature of development is seen as change that is more sudden at certain age levels than at others. He, like G. Stanley Hall, spoke of puberty as a new birth. New functions may emerge rather suddenly and become dominant in the psychological organization. This saltatory aspect of Rousseau's theory can be better understood in the light of his own temperamental saltatory experiences.

The first stage, that of infancy, includes the first 4 to 5 years of life. The child is dominated by the feeling of pleasure and pain. This period is called the animal stage, because the child is like an animal in regard to its physical needs and undifferentiated feelings. This idea had been expressed earlier in the writings of Aristotle and later by Freud. Education, such as training motor coordination, sense perception, and feelings, is primarily physical. He advocated that the method of nature be followed in everything and proposed the following rule: "Observe nature, and follow the route which she traces for you. She is ever exciting children to activity; she hardens the constitution by trials of every sort; she teaches them at an early hour what suffering and pain are."

The second stage, which Rousseau characterized as the savage stage, includes the years from 5 to 12. Dominant during this stage is the faculty of sense. Sensory experiences are provided by play, sport, and games, and the curriculum is centered on the training of the senses. During this stage, self-consciousness and memory develop, and human life in the proper sense begins here. The child still lacks reasoning ability and is not yet sufficiently aware of moral considerations. Education during this stage should be free from external, social, and moral control. Formal training in reading and writing are seen as harmful and therefore postponed until the beginning of the third developmental stage. In the first 12 years, education

. . . ought to be purely negative. It consists not at all in teaching virtues or truth, but in shielding the heart from vice, and the mind from error. If you could do nothing and allow nothing to be done, if you could bring your pupil sound and robust to the age of twelve years without his being able to distinguish his right hand from his left, from your very first lesson the eyes of his understanding would be open to reason [Rousseau, 1911: 59].

Rousseau's method of "negative education," which assumes that there is an innate developmental plan that cannot be improved upon by environmental factors, finds its corresponding modern expression in maturational theories. The defenders of the maturational concept of development frequently advocate, as did Rousseau, a permissive and unrestricted atmosphere for childrearing, and let the child be guided by his/her own inclinations, based on an assumption of "the wisdom of the body."

The third stage, the years from 12 to 15, is characterized by an awakening of the rational functions, including reason and self-consciousness. Youth at this age possess an enormous amount of physical energy and strength. The excess of energy leads to curiosity, which the school curriculum should utilize by encouraging exploratory behavior and the desire to discover what is true about the world. The only book that should be read is *Robinson Crusoe*. Rousseau saw in Crusoe the great model and ideal for the preadolescent, since his style of life was characterized by exploration of the world and a primitive curiosity, which corresponds to the needs and interests of this developmental stage. The curriculum should be geared to the study of nature, astronomy, science, art, and crafts. Rousseau, in agreement with contemporary educational theory, emphasizes the learning process rather than the product. "He is not to learn science, he is to find out for himself." This is the age of reason; curiosity and personal utility are the main motives for behavior; social conscience and emotionality are still undeveloped. It is interesting to observe that, in opposition to other developmental theories, the rational aspect of personality develops prior to the emotional. Rousseau placed great value on emotional development. His theory was a reaction to the historically earlier philosophy of rationalism, with which he differed.

The fourth period, adolescence proper, from the age of 15 to 20, finally culminates in the maturation of the emotional functions and brings about a change from selfishness to social consideration and self-esteem. The adolescent is no longer dominated by self-interest but develops a strong interest in other people and a need for genuine affection. This stage is characterized by the emergence of the sex drive (late by comparison to knowledge about youth today) which Rousseau considered a second birth. "We have two births, so to speak—one for existing and the other for living; one for the species and the other for the sex" (Rousseau, 1911: 193). Now conscience is acquired, and morals and virtues become possible. This is the period of preparation for marriage, which ideally coincides with the attainment of maturity.

Maturity could be considered as a fifth stage in the process, but it is less clearly defined. The faculty that becomes dominant during this period is will. Comenius also placed the development of the will at the time of late adolescence. The will is the faculty of the soul by which we make decisions and choose between alternatives.

These stages of development, according to Rousseau, correspond to certain stages in the development of the human race. Thus, it was assumed by this recapitulation theory that the human race had gone through the stages of animal-like living, the stage of savagery, the stage of reason, and, finally, through a stage of social and emotional maturity. He used the historical development of the race in order to explain the development of the individual child. This hypothesis was further developed by educators such as Froebel and Ziller, as well as by G. Stanley Hall and the Child Study Movement of America.

Critics feel that Rousseau overemphasized the individual nature and the emotional aspect of development and underemphasized the importance of education, society, and culture in the growth process and especially in the formation of the personality. He saw the influence of society and culture as negative forces in personality development; he wanted to remove their detrimental influences to make possible the free, unrestricted, natural unfolding of what is good in the child.

CHARLES DARWIN'S THEORY OF BIOLOGICAL EVOLUTION

A new trend of thought concerning the nature of development emerged with the publication of Darwin's *Origin of Species* (1859). Darwin's (1809–1882) idea of evolution—growth and development from the simpler to the more complex forms of organic life—has been one of the most revolutionary and influential ideas in man's thinking about himself and the nature of his development. Every living organisms from the simplest structure to the most complex, man himself, is brought together under the order of natural explanation. The psychological implications resulting from this biological concept of development were accepted, elaborated, and applied to adolescence by G. Stanley Hall, and also by Freud, thus leading to a science of adolescent development.

Since Darwin's theory is well known and does not propose a psychological or educational theory of development, only its basic principles will be stated. Darwin collected substantial, though not complete, evidence for a theory that claimed that the evolution of biological life is continuous, from a single-cell organism through numerous higher developmental stages to the complexity of human mind and body. This evolutionary theory assumed variability and adjustability in all organisms as well as the overproduction in the number of offspring of each species. Darwin showed that the overproduction of offspring threatened a species' capacity to survive. The result is a "struggle for existence." In this struggle of the selection of some and elimination of others, a "natural selection process" takes place by which the increase in population is checked. The stronger, healthier, faster, more immune, more intelligent, and physically better-adjusted organisms survive and reproduce, while the weak, sick, and less adaptable species perish. In time this leads to the "survival of the fittest." The qualitites that account for the survival of the fittest are inherited by the offspring. Since the conditions for survival frequently differ in various kinds of environments, changes in the organisms occur. Thus in the selection process, variations, new kinds, new races, and eventually new organisms come into existence. This process began with the simple one-cell organism, and from the lower forms of organic life more and more complex forms have developed. The last link in this biological evolution is the human being. Since climatic, geological, and general life conditions change, the evolutionary process is a perpetual one.

This theory of evolution stands in complete contrast to the theological doctrine of the divine creation of humankind. Through Darwin's theory mankind was placed in the order of nature. Most theological and many philosophical positions previous to Darwin's—for example, that of Aristotle—had postulated an essential dichotomy between man and nature. This absolute distinction between human nature and the nature of the organic world was seriously challenged by Darwin. Humans lost their special position and were now seen as part of the organic world, albeit a more advanced and more intelligent species.

G. STANLEY HALL'S BIOGENETIC PSYCHOLOGY OF ADOLESCENCE

G. Stanley Hall (1844–1924) was the first psychologist to advance a psychology of adolescence in its own right and to use scientific methods in his study of adolescence. It can be said that he bridged the philosophical, speculative approach of the past and the scientific, empirical approach of the present.

Hall expanded Darwin's concept of biological "evolution" into a psychological theory of recapitulation. This theory postulated that the experiential history of *homo sapiens* had become part of the genetic structure of each individual. The law of recapitulation asserted that each individual, during his or her development, passes through stages that correspond to those that occurred during the history of mankind. That is, as the child's development progresses he or she relives the development of the human race from early animal-like primitivism, through a period of savagery, to the more recent civilized ways of life that characterize maturity.

Hall assumed that development is brought about by physiological changes. He further assumed that these physiological factors are genetically determined, that internal maturational forces predominantly control and direct development, growth, and behavior. There was little room in this theory for the influence of environmental forces. It follows that development and its behavioral concomitants occur in an inevitable and unchangeable pattern that is universal, regardless of the social and cultural environment. Cultural anthropologists and sociologists have challenged this point and asserted that Hall's position was extreme and untenable. They further refuted the claim that the behavioral predispositions of physiological drives, as expressed in the recapitulation theory, are highly specific. Hall held that socially unacceptable types of behavior—those characteristic of earlier historical phases—must be tolerated by parents and educators, since they are necessary stages in social development. He, like Rousseau before him, and Gesell subsequently, advocated childrearing practices of leniency and permissiveness. However, he reassured parents and educators that unacceptable behavior would disappear in the following developmental stage without any corrective educational or disciplinary efforts.

A corollary of Hall's theory of recapitulation is his concept of stages of human development; the characteristics of a certain age in the development of the individual correspond to some primitive historical stage in the development of the human race. Hall did not divide human development into three stages, as advocated by Aristotle and many present-day "stage" psychologists. He followed a four-division pattern similar to that proposed by Comenius and Rousseau. Hall's developmental stages are infancy, childhood, youth, and adolescence.

The period of infancy includes the first 4 years of life. While children are still crawling, they are recapitulating the animal stage of the human race when the species was still using four legs. During this period, sensory development is dominant; the child acquires those sensorimotor skills that are necessary for self-preservation.

The period of chidlhood—the years from 4 to 8—recapitulates the cultural epoch when hunting and fishing were the main activities of man. This is the time when the child plays hide-and-seek, cowboys and Indians, uses toy weapons, slings, and bow and arrows. The building of caves, shacks, tree houses, and hiding places parallels the cave-dwelling culture of early history.

Youth—from 8 to 12—includes the period that today is referred to as "preadolescence." During this stage the child recapitulates the "humdrum life of savagery" of several thousand years ago. This is the period when the child has a favorable predisposition to practice and discipline, when routine training and drill are most appropriate.

> Never again will there be such susceptibility to drill and discipline, such plasticity to habituation, or such ready adjustment to new conditions. It is the age of external and mechanical training. Reading, writing, drawing, manual training, musical technic, foreign tongues and their pronunciation, the manipulation of numbers and of geometrical elements, and many kinds of skill have now their golden hour, and if it passes unimproved, all these can never be acquired later without a heavy handicap of disadvantage and loss [Hall, 1916: xii].

Adolescence is the period from puberty until full adult status has been attained. According to Hall, it ends comparatively late, between the twenty-second and twenty-fifth years. Hall described adolescence as a period of *Sturm und Drang,* "storm and stress." In German literature, the period of *Sturm und Drang* includes, among others, the works of Schiller and the early writings of Goethe. It is a literary movement full of idealism, commitment to a goal, revolution against the old, expression of personal feelings, passion, and suffering. Hall saw an analogy between the objectives of this group of writers at the turn of the eighteenth century and the characteristics of adolescence. In terms of recapitulation theory, adolescence corresponds to a time when the human race was in a turbulent, transitional stage. Hall described adolescence as a new birth, "for the higher and more completely human traits are now born" (Hall, 1916: xiii).

The characteristics of adolescent *Sturm und Drang* are pictured in detail by Hall in the chapter, "Feelings and Psychic Evolution" (Hall, 1916). He perceived the emotional life of the adolescent as an oscillation between contradictory tendencies. Energy, exaltation, and supernatural activity are followed by indifference, lethargy, and loathing. Exuberant gaiety, laughter, and euphoria make place for dysphoria, depressive gloom, and melancholy. Egoism, vanity, and conceit are just as characteristic of this period of life as are abasement, humiliation, and bashfulness. One can observe both the remnants of an uninhibited childish selfishness and an increasing idealistic altruism. Goodness and virtue are never so pure, but never again does temptation so forcefully preoccupy thought. Adolescents want solitude and seclusion, while finding themselves entangled in crushes and friendships. Never again does the peer group have such a strong influence. At one time the adolescent may exhibit exquisite sensitivity and tenderness; at another time, callousness and cruelty. Apathy and inertia vacillate with an enthusiastic curiosity, an urge to discover and explore. There is a yearning for idols and authority that does not exclude a revolutionary radicalism directed against any kind of authority. Hall (1916) implies these antithetical impulses of Promethean enthusiasm and deep sentimental *Weltschmerz* (sorrow and sadness about the state of the world) in his use of the concept of *Sturm und Drang,* which for him is so characteristic of the adolescent.

In late adolescence the individual recapitulates the stage of the beginning of modern civilization. This stage corresponds to the end of the developmental process: the adolescent reaches maturity. Hall's genetic psychology did not see the human being as the final product of the developmental process; it allowed for indefinite development.

Developmental Psychology
1987, Vol. 23, No. 5, 611–626

Theoretical Propositions of Life-Span Developmental Psychology: On the Dynamics Between Growth and Decline

Paul B. Baltes
Max Planck Institute for Human Development and Education
Berlin, Federal Republic of Germany

Life-span developmental psychology involves the study of constancy and change in behavior throughout the life course. One aspect of life-span research has been the advancement of a more general, metatheoretical view on the nature of development. The family of theoretical perspectives associated with this metatheoretical view of life-span developmental psychology includes the recognition of multidirectionality in ontogenetic change, consideration of both age-connected and disconnected developmental factors, a focus on the dynamic and continuous interplay between growth (gain) and decline (loss), emphasis on historical embeddedness and other structural contextual factors, and the study of the range of plasticity in development. Application of the family of perspectives associated with life-span developmental psychology is illustrated for the domain of intellectual development. Two recently emerging perspectives of the family of beliefs are given particular attention. The first proposition is methodological and suggests that plasticity can best be studied with a research strategy called testing-the-limits. The second proposition is theoretical and proffers that any developmental change includes the joint occurrence of gain (growth) and loss (decline) in adaptive capacity. To assess the pattern of positive (gains) and negative (losses) consequences resulting from development, it is necessary to know the criterion demands posed by the individual and the environment during the lifelong process of adaptation.

The study of life-span development is not a homogeneous field. It comes in two major interrelated modes. The first mode is the extension of developmental studies across the life course without a major effort at the construction of metatheory that emanates from life-span work. The second mode includes the endeavor to explore whether life-span research has specific implications for the general nature of developmental theory. The second approach represents the topic of this article.

Specifically, the purpose of this article is twofold. First, after a brief introduction to the field of life-span developmental psychology, some "prototypical" features of the life-span approach in developmental psychology are presented. Second, these features are illustrated by work in one domain: intellectual development. Although the focus of this paper is on life-span developmental psychology and its theoretical thrust, it is important to recognize at the outset that similar perspectives on developmental theory have been advanced in other quarters of developmental scholarship as well (Hetherington & Baltes, in press; Scarr, 1986). There is, however, a major difference in the "gestalt" in which the features of the theoretical perspective of life-span psychology are organized.

This article is based on invited addresses to Division 7 of the American Psychological Association (Toronto, Canada, August 1984) and to the International Society for the Study of Behavioral Development (Tours, France, July 1985).

Helpful suggestions by Michael Chapman and many valuable discussions with members of the Social Science Research Council Committee on Life-Course Perspectives in Human Development are acknowledged.

Correspondence concerning this article should be addressed to Paul B. Baltes, Max Planck Institute for Human Development and Education, Lentzeallee 94, D-1000 Berlin 33, Federal Republic of Germany.

Several, if not most, of the arguments presented here are consistent with earlier publications by the author and others on the field of life-span developmental psychology (Baltes, 1983; Baltes & Reese, 1984; Featherman, 1983; Honzik, 1984; Lerner, 1984; Sherrod & Brim, 1986). This article includes two added emphases. First, it represents an effort to illustrate the implications of the theoretical perspectives associated with life-span work for research in cognitive development. Second, two of the more recent perspectives derived from life-span work are given special attention. The first is that *any* process of development entails an inherent dynamic between gains and losses. According to this belief, no process of development consists only of growth or progression. The second proposition states that the range of plasticity can best be studied with a research strategy called *testing-the-limits*.

What is Life-Span Development?

Life-span developmental psychology involves the study of constancy and change in behavior throughout the life course (ontogenesis), from conception to death.[1] The goal is to obtain knowledge about general principles of life-long development, about interindividual differences and similarities in development, as well as about the degree and conditions of individual plasticity or modifiability of development (Baltes, Reese, & Nesselroade, 1977; Lerner, 1984; Thomae, 1979).

---

[1] In this article, the terms *life span* and *life course* are used interchangeably. Since the origin of the West Virginia Conference Series (Goulet & Baltes, 1970), psychologists tend to prefer *life span* (see, however, Bühler, 1933), whereas sociologists lean toward the use of the term *life course*.

It is usually assumed that child development, rather than life-span development, was the subject matter of the initial scholarly pursuits into psychological ontogenesis. Several historical reviews suggest that this generalization is inaccurate (Baltes, 1983; Groffmann, 1970; Reinert, 1979). The major historical precursors of scholarship on the nature of psychological development—by Tetens in 1777, Carus in 1808, Quetelet in 1835—were essentially life-span and not child-centered in approach. Despite these early origins of life-span thinking, however, life-span development has begun to be studied empirically only during the last two decades by researchers following the lead of early twentieth century psychologists such as Charlotte Bühler (1933), Erik H. Erikson (1959), G. Stanley Hall (1922), H. L. Hollingworth (1927), and Carl G. Jung (1933).

Three events seem particularly relevant to the more recent burgeoning of interest in life-span conceptions: (a) population demographic changes toward a higher percentage of elderly members; (b) the concurrent emergence of gerontology as a field of specialization, with its search for the life-long precursors of aging (Birren & Schaie, 1985); and (c) the "aging" of the subjects and researchers of the several classical longitudinal studies on child development begun in the 1920s and 1930s (Migdal, Abeles, & Sherrod, 1981; Verdonik & Sherrod, 1984). These events and others have pushed developmental scholarship toward recognizing the entire life span as a scientifically and socially important focus.

Added justification for a life-span view of ontogenesis and important scholarly contributions originate in other disciplines as well. One such impetus for life-span work comes from sociology and anthropology (Bertaux & Kohli, 1984; Brim & Wheeler, 1966; Clausen, 1986; Dannefer, 1984; Elder, 1985; Featherman, 1983; Featherman & Lerner, 1985; Kertzer & Keith, 1983; Neugarten & Datan, 1973; Riley, 1985; Riley, Johnson, & Foner, 1972). Especially within sociology, the study of the life course and of the interage and intergenerational fabric of society is enjoying a level of attention comparable with that of the life-span approach in psychology.

Another societal or social raison d'être for the existence of life-span interest is the status of the life course in longstanding images that societies and their members hold about the life span (Philibert, 1968; Sears, 1986). In the humanities, for example, life-span considerations have been shown to be part of everyday views of the structure and function of the human condition for many centuries. The Jewish Talmud, Greek and Roman philosophy (e.g., the writings of Solon and Cicero), literary works such as those of Shakespeare, Goethe, or Schopenhauer, all contain fairly precise images and beliefs about the nature of life-long change and its embeddedness in the age-graded structure of the society. Particularly vivid examples of such social images of the life span come from the arts. During the last centuries, many works of art were produced, reproduced, and modified in most European countries, each using stages, steps, or ladders as a framework for depicting the human life course (Joerißen & Will, 1983; Sears, 1986).

These observations on literature, art history, and social images of the life course suggest that the field of life-span development is by no means an invention of developmental psychologists. Rather, its recent emergence in psychology reflects the perhaps belated effort on the part of psychologists to attend to an aspect of the human condition that is part and parcel of our everyday cultural knowledge systems about living organisms. Such social images suggest that the life course is something akin to a natural, social category of knowledge about ontogenesis and the human condition.

Is Life-Span Development a Theory or a Field of Specialization?

What about the theoretical spectrum represented by life-span developmental psychology? Is it a single theory, a collection of subtheories, or just a theoretical orientation? Initial interest often converges on the immediate search for one overarching and unifying theory such as Erikson's (1959). The current research scene suggests that in the immediate future life-span developmental psychology will not be identified with a single theory. It is above all a subject matter divided into varying scholarly specializations. The most general orientation toward this subject matter is simply to view behavioral development as a lifelong process.

Such a lack of theoretical specificity may come as a surprise and be seen as a sign that the life-span perspective is doomed. In fact, the quest for a single, good theory (and the resulting frustration when none is offered) is an occasional challenge laid at the doorsteps of life-span scholars (Kaplan, 1983; Scholnick, 1985; Sears, 1980). Note, however, that the same lack of theoretical specificity applies to other fields of developmental specialization. Infant development, child development, gerontology, are also not theories in themselves, nor should one expect that there would be a single theory in any of these fields. In fact, as long as scholars look for *the* theory of life-span development they are likely to be disappointed.

A Family of Perspectives Characterizes the Life-Span Approach

Much of life-span research proceeds within the theoretical scenarios of child developmental or aging work. In addition, however, efforts have been made by a fair number of life-span scholars to examine the question of whether life-span research suggests a particular metatheoretical world view (Reese & Overton, 1970) on the nature of development. The theoretical posture proffered by this endeavor is the focus of the remainder of this article.

For many researchers, the life-span orientation entails several prototypical beliefs that, in their weighting and coordination, form a *family of perspectives* that together specify a coherent metatheoretical view on the nature of development. The significance of these beliefs lies not in the individual items but in the pattern. Indeed, none of the individual propositions taken separately is new, which is perhaps one reason why some commentators have argued that life-span work has little new to offer (Kaplan, 1983). Their significance consists instead in the whole complex of perspectives considered as a metatheoretical world view and applied with some degree of radicalism to the study of development.

What is this family of perspectives, which in their coordinated application characterizes the life-span approach? Perhaps no single set of beliefs would qualify in any definite sense. However, the beliefs summarized in Table 1 are likely to be shared by many life-span scholars. They can be identified pri-

Table 1

Summary of Family of Theoretical Propositions Characteristic of Life-Span Developmental Psychology

Concepts	Propositions
Life-span development	Ontogenetic development is a life-long process. No age period holds supremacy in regulating the nature of development. During development, and at all stages of the life span, both continuous (cumulative) and discontinuous (innovative) processes are at work.
Multidirectionality	Considerable diversity or pluralism is found in the directionality of changes that constitute ontogenesis, even within the same domain. The direction of change varies by categories of behavior. In addition, during the same developmental periods, some systems of behavior show increases, whereas others evince decreases in level of functioning.
Development as gain/loss	The process of development is not a simple movement toward higher efficacy, such as incremental growth. Rather, throughout life, development always consists of the joint occurrence of gain (growth) and loss (decline).
Plasticity	Much intraindividual plasticity (within-person modifiability) is found in psychological development. Depending on the life conditions and experiences by a given individual, his or her developmental course can take many forms. The key developmental agenda is the search for the range of plasticity and its constraints.
Historical embeddedness	Ontogenetic development can also vary substantially in accordance with historical–cultural conditions. How ontogenetic (age-related) development proceeds is markedly influenced by the kind of sociocultural conditions existing in a given historical period, and by how these evolve over time.
Contextualism as paradigm	Any particular course of individual development can be understood as the outcome of the interactions (dialectics) among three systems of developmental influences: age-graded, history-graded, and nonnormative. The operation of these systems can be characterized in terms of the metatheoretical principles associated with contextualism.
Field of development as multidisciplinary	Psychological development needs to be seen in the interdisciplinary context provided by other disciplines (e.g., anthropology, biology, sociology) concerned with human development. The openness of the life-span perspective to interdisciplinary posture implies that a "purist" psychological view offers but a partial representation of behavioral development from conception to death.

marily from the writings in psychology on this topic (Baltes & Reese, 1984; Baltes, Reese, & Lipsitt, 1980; Lerner, 1984; Sherrod & Brim, 1986), but they are also consistent with sociological work on the life course (Elder, 1985; Featherman, 1983; Riley, 1985).

The family of beliefs will be illustrated below, primarily using the study of intellectual development as the forum for exposition. Because, historically, the period of adulthood was the primary arena of relevant research, that age period receives most coverage. It will also be shown, however, that the metatheoretical posture may shed new light on intellectual development in younger age groups as well.

Empirical Illustration: Research on Intellectual Development

The area of intellectual functioning is perhaps the best studied domain of life-span developmental psychology. The discussion and elaboration of the empirical and conceptual bases of the family of perspectives presented here is selective. The intent is not to be comprehensive but to offer examples of areas of research. (Different research findings and agendas—see, for instance, Keating & MacLean, in press; Perlmutter, in press; Sternberg, in press, for other similar efforts—could have been used were it not for the particular preferences of the author.) More detailed information on the topic of life-span intelligence is contained in several recent publications (Baltes, Dittmann-

Kohli, & Dixon, 1984; Berg & Sternberg, 1985; Denney, 1984; Dixon & Baltes, 1986; Labouvie-Vief, 1985; Perlmutter, in press; Rybash, Hoyer, & Roodin, 1986; Salthouse, 1985).

Intellectual Development Is a Life-Long Process Involving Multidirectionality

The first two of the family of perspectives (see Table 1) state that behavior-change processes falling under the general rubric of development can occur at any point in the life course, from conception to death. Moreover, such developmental changes can display distinct trajectories as far as their directionality is concerned.

Life-long development. The notion of life-long development implies two aspects. First, there is the general idea that development extends over the entire life span. Second, there is the added possibility that life-long development may involve processes of change that do not originate at birth but lie in later periods of the life span. Considered as a whole, life-long development is a system of diverse change patterns that differ, for example, in terms of timing (onset, duration, termination), direction, and order.

One way to give substance to the notion of life-long development is to think of the kinds of demands and opportunities that individuals face as they move through life. Havighurst's (1948/ 1972; Oerter, 1986) formulation of the concept of developmental tasks is a useful aid for grasping the notion of a life-long system of demands and opportunities. Developmental tasks involve a series of problems, challenges, or life-adjustment situations that come from biological development, social expectations, and personal action. These problems "change through life and give direction, force, and substance to . . . development." (Havighurst, 1973, p. 11).

Thus, the different developmental curves constitutive of lifelong development can be interpreted to reflect different developmental tasks. Some of these developmental tasks—like Havighurst's conception—are strongly correlated with age. However, as will be shown later, such developmental tasks are also constituted from certain historical and nonnormative systems of influence.

Multidimensionality and multidirectionality. The terms *multidimensionality* and *multidirectionality* are among the key concepts used by life-span researchers to describe facets of plurality in the course of development and to promote a concept of development that is not bound by a single criterion of growth in terms of a general increase in size or functional efficacy.

Research on psychometric intelligence illustrates the usefulness of multidimensional and multidirectional conceptions of development. The psychometric theory of fluid-crystallized intelligence proposed by Cattell (1971) and Horn (1970, 1982) serves as an example (Figure 1). First, according to this theory, intelligence consists of several subcomponents. Fluid and crystallized intelligence are the two most important clusters of abilities in the theory. The postulate of a system of abilities is an example of multidimensionality. Second, these multiple-ability components are expected to differ in the direction of their development. Fluid intelligence shows a turning point in adulthood (toward decline), whereas crystallized intelligence exhibits the continuation of an incremental function. This is an example of the multidirectionality of development.

Meanwhile, the Cattell-Horn theoretical approach to lifespan intellectual development has been supplemented with other conceptions, each also suggesting the possibility of multidimensional and multidirectional change. Berg and Sternberg (1985), for example, have examined the implications of Sternberg's triarchic theory of intelligence for the nature of life-long development. They emphasized that the age trajectories for the three postulated components of Sternberg's theory of intelligence (componential, contextual, experiential) are likely to vary in directionality.

Current work on life-span intelligence (Baltes et al., 1984; Dixon & Baltes, 1986) has also expanded on the Cattell-Horn model by linking it to ongoing work in cognitive psychology. Two domains of cognitive functioning are distinguished in a dual-process scheme: the "fluid" mechanics and the "crystallized" pragmatics of intelligence. The *mechanics of intelligence* refers to the basic architecture of information processing and problem solving. It deals with the basic cognitive operations and cognitive structures associated with such tasks as perceiving relations and classification. The second domain of the dual-process scheme, the *pragmatics of intelligence,* concerns the context- and knowledge-related application of the mechanics of intelligence. The intent is to subsume under the pragmatics of intelligence (a) fairly general systems of factual and procedural knowledge, such as crystallized intelligence; (b) specialized systems of factual and procedural knowledge, such as occupational expertise; and (c) knowledge about factors of perfor-

mance, that is, about skills relevant for the activation of intelligence in specific contexts requiring intelligent action. The explicit focus on the pragmatics of intelligence demands (like Sternberg's concern with contextual and experiential components) a forceful consideration of the changing structure and function of knowledge systems across the life span (see also Featherman, 1983; Keating & MacLean, in press; Labouvie-Vief, 1985; Rybash et al., 1986).

New forms of intelligence in adulthood and old age? What about the question of later-life, "innovative" emergence of new forms of intelligence? It is one thing to argue in principle that new developmental acquisitions can emerge at later points in life with relatively little connection to earlier processes and quite another to demonstrate empirically the existence of such innovative, developmentally late phenomena. A classic example used by life-span researchers to illustrate the developmentally late emergence of a cognitive system is the process of reminiscence and life review (Butler, 1963). The process of reviewing and reconstructing one's life has been argued to be primarily a late-life phenomenon. The phenomenon of autobiographical memory is another example (Strube, 1985).

For the sample case of intelligence, it is an open question whether adulthood and old age bring with them new forms of directionality and intellectual functioning, or whether continuation and quantitative (but not qualitative) variation of past functioning is the gist of the process. On the one hand, there are Flavell's (1970) and Piaget's (1972) cognitive-structuralist accounts, which favor an interpretation of horizontal *décalage* rather than one of further structural evolution or transformation. These authors regard the basic cognitive operations as fixed by early adulthood. What changes afterwards is the content domains to which cognitive structures are applied.

On the other hand, there are very active research programs engaged in the search for qualitatively or structurally new forms of adult intelligence (Commons, Richards, & Armon, 1984). The work on dialectical and postformal operations by Basseches (1984), Labouvie-Vief (1982, 1985), Kramer (1983), Pascual-Leone (1983), and other related writings (e.g., Keating & MacLean, in press) are notable examples of this effort. This line of scholarship has been much stimulated (or even launched) by Riegel's work on dialectical psychology and his outline of a possible fifth stage of cognitive development (Riegel, 1973, 1976).

Other work on adult intellectual development proceeds from a neofunctionalist perspective (Beilin, 1983; Dixon & Baltes, 1986) and is informed by work in cognitive psychology. Models of expertise (Glaser, 1984) and knowledge systems (Brown, 1982) guide this approach in which the question of structural stages is of lesser significance. Aside from an interest in the aging of the "content-free" mechanics of intelligence (Kliegl & Baltes, in press), the dominant focus is on changes in systems of factual and procedural knowledge associated with the "crystallized" pragmatics of intelligence. The crystallized form of intelligence was highlighted already as an ability cluster exhibiting stability or even positive changes into late adulthood. The concept of crystallized intelligence, however, needs further expansion to cover additional domains of knowledge and to permit consideration of forms of knowledge more typical of the second half of life.

Expertise, a concept currently in vogue in cognitive and developmental psychology (Ericsson, 1985; Glaser, 1984; Hoyer,

Multidimensionality
Multidirectionality

Different Forms of Intelligence

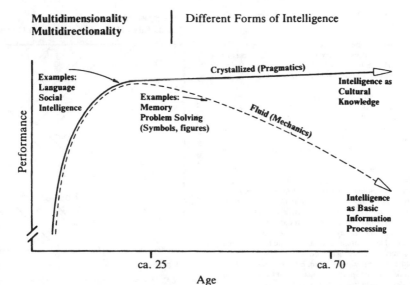

Figure 1. One of the best known psychometric structural theories of intelligence is that of Raymond B. Cattell and John L. Horn. (The two main clusters of that theory, fluid and crystallized intelligence, are postulated to display different life-span developmental trajectories.)

1985; Weinert, Schneider, & Knopf, in press), can be used to illustrate this avenue of research. This concept denotes skills and knowledge that are highly developed and practiced. The sciences, chess, or job-related activities (e.g., typing) are often used as substantive domains in which performance in relation to the acquisition and maintenance of expertise is studied. The life course of many individuals most likely offers opportunity for the practice of such forms of expertise. Therefore, one would expect that further growth of intellectual functioning may occur in those domains in which individuals continue to practice and evolve their procedural and factual knowledge (Denney, 1984; Dixon & Baltes, 1986; Hoyer, 1985; Rybash et al., 1986). In other words, expertise in select facets of the pragmatics of intelligence can be maintained, transformed, or even newly acquired in the second half of life if the conditions are such that selective optimization in the associated knowledge system can occur.

Two areas of knowledge have been identified as key candidates for domains in which the pragmatics of intelligence may exhibit positive changes during the second half of life: practical intelligence (Sternberg & Wagner, 1986) and knowledge about the pragmatics of life, such as is evident in research on social intelligence and wisdom (Clayton & Birren, 1980; Dittmann-Kohli & Baltes, in press; Holliday & Chandler, 1986; Meacham, 1982). Wisdom, in particular, has been identified as a prototypical or exemplar task of the pragmatics of intelligence that may exhibit further advances in adulthood or whose origins may lie primarily in adulthood.

In one approach (Dittmann-Kohli & Baltes, in press; Dixon & Baltes, 1986; Smith, Dixon, & Baltes, in press), wisdom is defined as an "expertise in the fundamental pragmatics of life." In order to capture wisdom, subjects of different age groups are asked, for example, to elaborate on everyday problems of life planning and life review. The knowledge system displayed in protocols of life planning and life review is scored against a set of criteria derived from the theory of wisdom. First evidence (Smith et al., in press) suggests, as expected by the theory, that some older adults indeed seem to have available a well-developed system of knowledge about situations involving questions of life planning. For example, when older adults are asked to explore a relatively rare or odd life-planning situation involving other older persons, they demonstrate a knowledge system that is more elaborated than that of younger adults.

The study of wisdom is just beginning. Thus, it is still an open question whether the concept of wisdom can be translated into empirical steps resulting in a well-articulated psychological theory of wisdom. We are somewhat optimistic, inasmuch as cognitive psychologists are increasingly studying tasks and reasoning problems that, like the problems to which wisdom is applied, have a high degree of real-life complexity, and whose problem definition and solution involve uncertainty and relativism in judgment (Dörner, in press; Neisser, 1982). In the present context, the important point is that research on wisdom is an illustration of the type of knowledge systems that developmental, cognitive researchers are beginning to study as their attention is focused on later periods of life.

41

Intellectual Development as a Dynamic Between Growth (Gain) and Decline (Loss)

The next belief (see Table 1) associated with life-span work is the notion that any process of development entails aspects of growth (gain) and decline (loss). This belief is a fairly recent one and its theoretical foundation is not yet fully explored and tested.

The gain/loss argument. The gain/loss view of development emerged primarily for two reasons. The first relates to the task of defining the process of aging in a framework of development. The second reason deals with the fact of multidirectionality described earlier and the ensuing implication of simultaneous, multidirectional change for the characterization of development.

Concerning the issue of the definition of aging versus development: Traditionally in gerontology, there has been a strong push—especially by biologists (Kirkwood, 1985)—to define the essence of aging as decline (i.e., as a unidirectional process of loss in adaptive capacity). Behavioral scientists, because of their findings and expectations of some gains in old age, have had a tendency to reject this unidirectional, decline view of aging. Thus, they wanted to explore whether aging could be considered as part of a framework of development.

How could this integration of aging into the framework of development be achieved in light of the fact that the traditional definition of development was closely linked to growth, whereas that of aging was linked predominantly to decline? The suggestion of life-span researchers was to redefine or expand the concept of development beyond the biological conception of growth or progression. Specifically, the proposal was to expand the concept of development to include not only phenomena of growth (gain), but other directions of change as well (Baltes, 1983). As a result, development was defined as *any* change in the adaptive capacity of an organism, whether positive or negative. In developmental psychology, this proposal was consistent with other trends. Social learning theory, for example, had suggested a similar expansion of the directional nature of ontogenesis (Bandura, 1982).

The second and related reason for the emergence of the theme of gain–loss relations in development is a further elaboration of the notions of multidimensionality and multidirectionality of life-span intelligence. The separate concern for multiple-ability systems associated with multidirectionality was taken one step further to the examination of the relation and perhaps even the dynamic interplay *between* the various subsystems. The question guiding this investigation is whether the occurrence of multidirectional change, concurrently in separate components of the system (e.g., fluid vs. crystallized intelligence), requires a new conception of development itself. One possible avenue is to view development as a gain–loss relation (see also Baltes & Kliegl, 1986; Labouvie-Vief, 1980, 1982; Perlmutter, in press). According to this view, development at all points of the life course is a joint expression of features of growth (gain) and decline (loss). It is assumed that any developmental progression displays at the same time new adaptive capacity as well as the loss of previously existing capacity. No developmental change during the life course is pure gain.

The view of development as a gain/loss phenomenon, of course, does not imply that throughout life gain and loss exist

Life-span Development: Gain/Loss Ratios in Adaptive Capacity

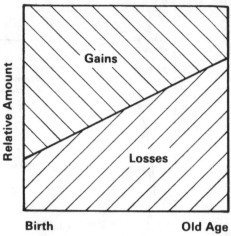

Figure 2. One theoretical expectation concerning the average course of gain/loss ratios is a proportional shift across the life span.

in equal strength. Systematic age-related changes in the gain/loss proportion are likely to be present. A possible life-span scenario of the dynamic between gains and losses is illustrated in Figure 2. Summarizing evidence across a wide spectrum of functions, the proposition contained in Figure 2 is that the sum total of possible gains and losses in adaptive capacity shifts proportionally with increasing age. As a whole, life-span development proceeds within the constraints created by this dynamic.

The concern with an ongoing, developmental dynamic of positive (gains) and negative (losses) change has spurred new research in life-span work. One example is the attempt to specify a general process of adaptation that would represent the lifelong nature of development as a gain/loss relation. Some of this work (M. Baltes, 1987; Baltes et al., 1984; Dixon & Baltes, 1986) has outlined a theoretical framework that is aimed at making explicit the dynamic relation between gain and loss in development. In Table 2, what is described for the case of cognitive aging is perhaps a prototypical change mechanism of "successful aging"—*selective optimization with compensation*.

The process of selective optimization with compensation has three features, each indicative of a gain/loss relation: (a) continual evolution of specialized forms of adaptation as a general feature of life-span development; (b) adaptation to the conditions of biological and social aging with its increasing limitation of plasticity; and (c) individual selective and compensatory efforts dealing with evolving deficits for the purpose of life mastery and effective aging.

Although the process of selective optimization and associated investments in terms of time, space, and behavior budgeting is assumed to be general and prototypical, its specific manifesta-

Table 2

Selective Optimization With Compensation: A Process
Prototypical of Adaptive Life-Span Development
of Cognitive Functioning

- A general feature of life-span development is an age-related increase
  in specialization (selection) of motivational and cognitive resources
  and skills.

- There are two main features of the aging of cognitive functions:
  (a) The reserve capacity for peak or maximum performances in
      fluid functioning (mechanics of intelligence) is reduced.
  (b) Some procedural and declarative knowledge systems (pragmatics
      of intelligence) can continue to evolve and function at peak
      levels.

- When, and if, limits (thresholds) of capacity are exceeded during the
  course of aging for a given individual, the following developmental
  consequences result:
  (a) Increased selection (channeling) and further reduction of the
      number of high-efficacy domains;
  (b) Development of compensatory and/or substitute mechanisms.

Note. This model is adapted from Baltes and Baltes (1980).

tion will vary depending on the individual life history. The emergence of compensatory and substitutive cognitive skills will also vary. For example, B. F. Skinner (1983) described in a personal account how and under which conditions he evolved compensatory or substitutive skills in the face of reduced effectiveness in select aspects of intellectual functioning.

Research by Salthouse (1984) on typing skills in old age is one persuasive example of how specialization and compensation interact in older adults to produce a high level of selective efficacy. Older expert typists—although showing less efficient reaction times than young expert typists when confronted with the typing of individual characters—nevertheless display good efficacy. They cope with their loss in reaction time when typing individual letters by developing more extensive forward-processing of letter and word sequences. As a result, older typists use a different combination of component skills than younger typists to produce a comparable level of overall performance.

Relevance of the gain/loss argument for other developmental questions. For historians interested in the study of social change and the idea of progress (Nisbet, 1980), the gain/loss argument is a truism. Few theorists would maintain that all of social change is progress.

What about ontogenesis? The notion that any ontogenetic change entails a dynamic interplay between gain and loss can be found also in biological conceptions such as Waddington's (1975) work on ontogenesis as differentiation and specialization (canalization). Beginning on the cellular level (Cotman, 1985; Lerner, 1984), differentiation clearly implies the loss of alternate courses of cell differentiation. Sociologists, too, have argued that the life course entails a process of specialization in the sense of commitment to and practice in selected domains of life (Featherman, 1983). Such a process of life-course specialization is assumed to imply a loss of alternative options.

Does the consideration of gains and losses as intrinsic to any developmental process have relevance for cognitive development in younger age groups? The fact that progress is not the only feature of age-related cognitive development has been known for quite some time. Weir's (1964) research with chil-

dren on the developmental progression from maximization to optimization strategies in solving nonperfect probability tasks is a concrete example. This work shows that higher-level cognitive functioning (associated with the so-called optimization strategy) can have its costs when the task in question has no perfect solution. Specifically, when a cognitive task is logically unsolvable, because it has no perfect solution, young children can outperform older children and adults. This is so because older children and adults assume the existence of a logically perfect solution and, therefore, engage in a problem-solving behavior that is criterion-inadequate.

One additional example is Ross's (1981) research on the development of judgmental heuristics. Developmentally later or more "mature" heuristics can be less efficient, depending on the problem to be solved. Another case is second-language learning. Although there is disagreement about the sources of this gain/loss phenomenon, the fact seems accepted: The more and more efficient acquisition of a first language is associated with increasing difficulty in learning a second language (Davies, Criper, & Howatt, 1984; Kellerman & Smith, 1986).

The gain/loss idea is also contained in the work of Piaget, even though Piagetian theory is likely seen by most as the hallmark of a conception of development that features unidirectional growth. In the study of the age-development of visual illusions, for example, Piaget (1969) described illusions that increase with age and others that decrease with age. When visual illusions increase with age, Piaget ascribed this loss in visual accuracy to advancement in cognitive stage. A related example in Piaget's work (see Chapman, in press) is what he called the "repression" effect associated with a dynamic between perceptual and cognitive operations. With children of 7 to 8 years of age, Piaget found that their "veridical" perceptual knowledge was repressed by the (in this case, nonveridical) advancement in conceptual schemata. In effect, cognition "repressed" perception. A by-product of cognitive advancement, then, was a loss in veridical judgment involving perception.

It seems worthwhile to explore with greater force the idea that any process of cognitive development entails positive and negative aspects of change in adaptive capacity. In the long run, the treatment of this question is likely to be tied to the topic of adaptive fitness. In other words, as is true for evolutionary theories (as exemplified in the work of Gould and Lewontin [Lerner, 1984]), ontogenesis may not fundamentally be a process of general gain in the sense of a total increase in adaptive efficacy. As specific forms of mind and behavior are "selected" during ontogenesis for activation and growth, some adaptive capacities may actually become reduced. Whether the reduction is manifest would depend (as is true for evolutionary change) on the criterion demands posed by the individual and the environment in subsequent phases of life, or by the experimenter for that matter.

Plasticity of Development

Another belief (Table 1) held by many life-span scholars is that there is much plasticity in the course of life-span development. Plasticity refers to within-person variability and designates the potential that individuals have for different forms of behavior or development (Gollin, 1981; Lerner, 1984). Would the same individual develop differently if conditions were

43

different? The question of plasticity is, of course, one that has excited developmental psychologists for a long time (e.g., Mc-Graw's [1985] work in the 1930s on motor development in identical twins). It is of equal interest to current work in developmental biology (e.g., Cotman, 1985) and developmental sociology (Dannefer & Perlmutter, 1986; Featherman & Lerner, 1985).

Cognitive training research with the elderly. Whether it proves to be true, the conclusion that the plasticity of cognitive age differences found in the second half of life is larger than what is known from childhood research has impressed life-span researchers. The salience of the topic of plasticity for researchers in life-span development and the general approach used to study it can be illustrated easily in work on intellectual development during adulthood and old age. Initially, in life-span research the idea of plasticity was promulgated in connection with the question of whether intellectual aging is a simple process of gradual decline (Baltes & Schaie, 1976; Horn & Donaldson, 1976). One of the attractive ways to explore this question was to conduct intervention research.

Since the early 1970s, various research programs have been underway to examine the extent to which the observed aging losses in that cluster of psychometric intelligence evincing most definite decline—fluid intelligence—could be simulated for by performance variation (plasticity) within individuals. For example, elderly people were given practice in solving the type of intelligence problems used to measure fluid intelligence (Baltes & Kliegl, 1986; Willis, 1985). The key research hypothesis was that older persons, on the average, have relatively little test experience and everyday practice in fluid intelligence, but that they possess the reserve—the latent competence—to raise their level of performance on fluid intelligence tasks to that of younger adults.

The cognitive training research conducted with older adults offered strong evidence of sizeable plasticity. After a fairly brief program of cognitive practice, many older adults (age range, 60–80 years) exhibited levels of performance comparable with those observed in many "untreated" younger adults. Such findings have been replicated consistently and in other domains of cognitive functioning (e.g., Denney, 1984; Labouvie-Vief, 1985; Willis, 1985). Meanwhile, the evidence has been extended from cross-sectional to longitudinal age comparisons (Schaie & Willis, 1986).

These studies illustrate the emergence of the strong belief of life-span researchers in sizeable plasticity. Knowledge about plasticity of intelligence was judged to be as important as knowledge about the average course of age development. In order to achieve a comprehensive understanding of a given developmental process, such as intellectual development, one must forcefully advance the study of conditions that produce differences in development and highlight the potential for alternate courses of development. The resulting interpretive posture is that whatever one observes concerning the aging of intelligence is but one of many possible outcomes (Brandtstädter, 1984; Lerner, 1984). Knowing the range and limits of intraindividual functioning, therefore, is a cornerstone of the life-span perspective.

From plasticity to limits of plasticity. Current work on plasticity of life-span intellectual development has added new perspectives beyond those associated with cognitive training re-

search. The focus has changed from demonstration of plasticity toward using research on plasticity as a strategy by which limits and boundaries of development can be identified (Kliegl & Baltes, 1987). This strategy is similar to child research on the "zone" of proximal development in childhood (Brown, 1982; Ferrara, Brown, & Campione, 1986).

The resulting focus in the life-span study of plasticity is not on the normal range of intellectual functioning, but on limits of performance. The research strategy chosen to examine different aspects of plasticity and its boundary conditions is known as *testing-the-limits* (M. Baltes & Kindermann, 1985; Guthke, 1982; Wiedl, 1984). Testing-the-limits involves the systematic application of (a) variations in modes of assessment, (b) methods of intervention aimed at identifying latent reserve capacity, and (c) strategies of identification of the mechanisms involved in growth and decline.

In our research efforts (Baltes et al., 1984; Kliegl & Baltes, 1987) intended to determine age-correlated changes in limits of intellectual functioning, three aspects of plasticity are distinguished: (a) baseline performance, (b) baseline reserve capacity, and (c) developmental reserve capacity. *Baseline performance* indicates a person's initial level of performance on a given task, that is, what a person can do in a specified task without intervention or special treatment. *Baseline reserve capacity* denotes the upper range of an individual's performance potential, when, at a given point in time, all available resources are called on to optimize an individual's performance. It is measured by tests of "maximum" performance. When conditions have been added that strengthen an individual's baseline reserve capacity through intervention (or development), we speak of an individual's *developmental reserve capacity.*

Distinguishing between these three aspects of plasticity permits the study not only of plasticity but also of constraints (Keil, 1981) and of what behavior geneticists have called the *norm of reaction* (see Lerner, 1984). Concepts such as constraint and norm of reaction are intended to index those limits—biological and sociocultural—that restrict the formation of a given behavior and its open development. In the long run, assessment of maximum reserve capacity aspires to identify biological boundaries of the plasticity of development. Note, however, that the range and level of maximum reserve capacity is inherently unknowable (see also Keating & MacLean, in press); it can only be approximated. The possibility always exists that new conditions or agents may be found that produce new levels and forms of intellectual performance on a given task.

The general expectation of testing-the-limits research is to predict developmental differences to be most pronounced, perhaps even approaching the condition of irreversibility (Wohlwill, 1973), near maximum levels of performance. Conversely, age changes are easily masked or modified as long as they are studied within the "normal" range of functioning. Figure 3 illustrates how a testing-the-limits strategy is used to obtain information about the range and limits of plasticity during adulthood.

The data presented in Figure 3 are based on subjects of different adult age groups who participated in extensive longitudinal intervention studies. In these studies, high levels of cognitive functioning in the use of a mnemonic skill are engineered in the laboratory. Specifically, subjects participated in 30 sessions of training of expert memory for digits and nouns using the Method

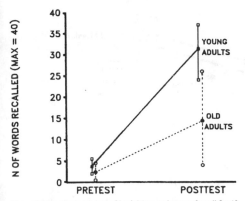

Figure 3. Expertise in Method of Loci: Mean and range of recall for 40 words in two subject groups of young and old adults (for data on digit span, see Kliegl, Smith, & Baltes, 1986).

of Loci (Kliegl, Smith, & Baltes, 1986; Smith, Kliegl, & Baltes, 1987). The results demonstrate, as expected, the dual nature of results from application of testing-the-limits methodology. On the one hand, sizeable plasticity continues to be evident into old age. The reserve capacity is substantial in all age groups, so that subjects of all ages can learn to remember exceedingly long strings of numerical digits and nouns. On the other hand, pronounced age differences in limits also exist. When subjects are tested under more and more difficult conditions, such as with increased speed of presentation, age differences are magnified. In the present example, the magnification of age differences is of such a degree that, at "limits," IQ-comparable young and older subjects barely overlap in their performance.

With such research on the limits of development, the concern for plasticity has taken a new turn. The task is no longer to focus on the demonstration of plasticity as a sole feature of development. Rather, the search is simultaneously for potential (reserve capacity) and constraints. Testing-the-limits research has a broad range of ramifications. It is not only relevant for the study of intellectual development and aging; its possible usefulness also extends to many other fields of study. Consider the study of behavioral and developmental genetics. A possible view is that the role of genetics in regulating interindividual differences can be best examined when the investigation is focused on limits of performance. Another example is the identification of developmental dysfunctions. Like the stress tests used in biology and medicine (M. Baltes & Kindermann, 1985; Coper, Jänicke, & Schulze, 1986; Fries & Crapo, 1981), psychological tests conducted under conditions of high difficulty or following testing-the-limits-like interventions are likely to be more sensitive to the detection of dysfunctions (such as depression, senile dementia of the Alzheimer type, or reading difficulty) than testing under conditions of the normal range of demand and expertise.

Development Is Codetermined by Multiple Systems of Influence

The fifth and sixth belief systems (historical embeddedness, contextualism) associated with life-span research have ex-

panded the spectrum of influences that are considered determinants of behavioral development. A new taxonomy of influence systems has evolved that entails factors beyond the ones considered in past work on psychological ontogeny.

Ontogenesis and evolution. The perspective of historical embeddedness deals with the relation between individual development (ontogenesis) and evolutionary development (Baltes, 1983; Brent, 1978; Dannefer, 1984; Featherman & Lerner, 1985; Nesselroade & von Eye, 1985; Riegel, 1976). The processes of individual development are governed both by principles of ontogenesis and by factors associated with the concurrent process of biocultural change. Together, ontogenesis and biocultural change constitute the two major systems generating development. As individuals develop, society changes as well.

The role of a changing society in codetermining individual development initially came to the forefront in life-span research on cohort differences (Baltes, 1968; Riley et al., 1972; Schaie, 1965); later, its significance was amplified because of theoretical issues such as dialectics and contextualism (Lerner, 1984; Lerner & Kauffman, 1985; Riegel, 1976). In research on cohort effects, the age-development of several birth cohorts is studied in a comparative manner. The basic designs are known as cross-sectional and longitudinal sequences. An excellent up-to-date review of design and analysis of cross-sectional and longitudinal sequences is presented by Labouvie and Nesselroade (1985).

Life-span research with sequential methods has been conducted with many age groups, cohorts, and measurement systems (see Baltes, Cornelius, & Nesselroade, 1979, and Nesselroade & von Eye, 1985, for review). The empirical story began in the periods of adulthood and old age and subsequently extended into earlier segments of the life span. In adulthood and old age, Schaie (1979, 1983) could show that much of the variance contained in cross-sectional studies of age differences in adult intelligence is associated with historical cohort factors rather than age factors.

In adolescence, Nesselroade and Baltes (1974) obtained data that showed that the level and direction of change in adolescent personality development was as much influenced by the historical context (in this case surrounding the Vietnam War) as by age-associated factors. Elder's (1974; Elder & Liker, 1982) work on the life-span development of children and adolescents stemming from the period of the Great Depression offered clear evidence of the impact of historical factors associated with childhood on adult personality.

With respect to infancy, Porges (1976) argued that much of the controversy about conditionability of neonates may be due to historical changes in prenatal and postnatal care. Since then, the possible impact of cohort variation has been explored in a variety of other areas related to infant and child development, including the structure and function of family systems such as the changing characteristics of fatherhood (Parke & Tinsley, 1984).

In the present context, Schaie's 28-year cohort-sequential study on adult intelligence is particularly relevant. In Schaie's (1979, 1983) data, the historical embedding of intellectual development is paramount. Intelligence does not only change with age. It also changes with history or cohort time. Consider, for instance, 50- or 60-year-olds. Cohort differences between these two age levels can be as large as longitudinal aging changes within the same subjects (Schaie, 1983). In Figure 4, such co-

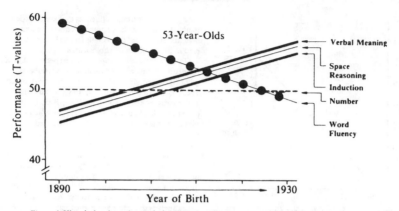

Figure 4. Historical, cohort changes in intellectual performance concern level of functioning as well as directionality. (The simplified trends represent the average performance of 53-year-olds from different birth cohorts on five measures of primary mental abilities, as estimated by Schaie [1979] on the basis of time-lag comparisons.)

hort-related changes in same-age individuals are illustrated for a larger range of birth cohorts based on Schaie's (1983) work. For one age group—53-year-olds—levels of performance are estimated and plotted in a simplified manner separately for the five primary mental abilities studied (number, reasoning, space, verbal meaning, and word fluency). Three of the five abilities show positive historical change; one is cohort-invariant; the fifth evinces negative directionality with historical time. Changes in intelligence, then, are multidirectional not only with chronological age but also with historical time.

Cohort effects of the magnitude reported in studies of adult intelligence are novel in psychological research. Therefore, it is not surprising that classical psychological theory has little to offer when it comes to interpreting the substantive meaning and origin of such cohort effects (see, however, Dannefer, 1984; Featherman & Lerner, 1985; Riley, 1985). The fields of cultural anthropology, historical sociology, and historical medicine may prove to be more relevant.

Three clusters of influences appear to be primarily involved as origins of cohort effects in life-span development of intelligence: education, health, and work. Successive generations, for example, exhibit, on the average, more formal education and other kinds of education-related experiences, such as those associated with the introduction of television or computers. The work life of recent generations may also entail, on the average, a stronger and differential focus on cognitively oriented labor. Furthermore, historical changes have occurred in health care, including, for example, the better treatment of hypertension, a factor implicated in lowered intellectual functioning among the elderly. Together, these examples indicate that many facets of the texture of everyday life exhibit sociocultural change possibly related to the level and rate of intellectual functioning. At present, however, the factors responsible for the cohort changes observed in intellectual aging have not yet been specified.

In summary then, results from cohort-sequential research on intelligence during adulthood and old age suggest much variability in the level and course of intellectual aging. Part of the nature of the reported findings is that they cannot be generalized to other cultural settings and historical epochs. But this feature of research on the aging of intelligence is at the very core of the argument: Depending on the prevailing cultural conditions, the level and course of intellectual aging can vary markedly. Any single cohort-specific observation does not tell the final story on the nature of intellectual aging.

Are cohort differences and biocultural change always relevant for the study of psychological development? Most likely they are not. Cohort differences are more likely to be a concern for those aspects of development that are not stabilized in the process of genetic and cultural evolution. Thus, it is not surprising that in developed countries, because of the high degree of biocultural stabilization in early life, cohort variation in cognitive development during childhood is relatively small and primarily involves differences in rate (Kendler, 1979; Reese, 1974).

Because cohort differences can have rather different empirical and theoretical significance, Baltes, Cornelius, and Nesselroade (1979) have distinguished among several ways in which cohort variation can be treated in developmental psychology (e.g., as error, historical disturbance, quantitative variation in frequency and rate, or as a theoretical/dialectical process). On the basis of this theoretical analysis of cohort effects, it is recommended that researchers examine carefully which logical status they are prepared to assign to cohort effects. Such a decision will influence the way cohort-sequential research is designed and ensuing data are analyzed.

Other contextual factors and contextualism. In life-span work, the argument for the historical embeddedness of human development was joined by another facet of embeddedness involving additional classes of contextual influences. Historically, the emerging focus on life events (Bandura, 1982; Brim & Ryff, 1980; Dohrenwend & Dohrenwend, 1974; Filipp, 1981;

Hultsch & Plemons, 1979) was the initial forum for dialogue about such additional contextual factors and their role in human development. It was proposed that the course of adult development is not only dependent on age-correlated factors of socialization. Rather, "significant" live events—with rather distinct patterns of individual occurrence and sequencing—were identified as important regulators of the nature of change during adulthood.

An additional reaction to the evidence on cohort effects and the role of other contextual factors was metatheoretical. Following the lead of Riegel (1973, 1976) and the concurrent emergence of interest in Marxist and Hegelian thought (Datan & Reese, 1977), life-span psychologists began to proffer a metatheoretical view of development that was inherently dialectical and contextual (Dixon, 1986; Featherman & Lerner, 1985; Labouvie-Vief & Chandler, 1978; Lerner & Kauffman, 1985). In its radical form (Gergen, 1980), the metatheoretical argument was that ontogeny, in principle, is not universal. Rather, the nature of psychological ontogeny is always newly created for any given birth cohort or cultural setting.

Meanwhile, this radical view has given way to more moderate but also more refined positions (Dannefer, 1984; Featherman & Lerner, 1985; Lerner & Kauffman, 1985). Note, however, that the metatheoretical argument associated with contextualism in life-span developmental psychology is not necessarily synonymous—on a theoretical level—with the general advancement of an ecological approach evident in other developmental scholarship. Bronfenbrenner (1977) surely emphasized context. His conceptualization of context, however, does not explicitly follow the metatheoretical principles of contextualism. The metatheoretical guidelines of contextualism, for instance, suggest a general conception of development, which Lerner and Kauffman (1985) have called dynamic and probabilistic interactionism. That a focus on the same notion (such as the role of context) does not imply an identical metatheoretical treatment is illustrated in the exchange between Kendler (1986) and Lerner and Kauffman (1986).

A taxonomy of influences. The preceding discussion of interindividual variability and cohort effects and other contextual factors points toward a search for a new conception of developmental influences. The strategy chosen by life-span researchers is to argue that pluralism and complexity in the descriptive form of development is paralleled by a certain pluralism and complexity in the causal scheme of developmental factors and mechanisms.

For the heuristic purpose of organizing the multitude and complexity of developmental influences, a trifactor model has been proposed (Baltes et al., 1979; Baltes et al., 1980). In this model, three categories of influences, which developing individuals need to deal with (i.e., process, react to, act on) as their lives progress, are identified: *age-graded* influences, *history-graded* influences, and *nonnormative* influences. These three influences operate throughout the life course, their effects accumulate with time, and, as a dynamic package, they are responsible for how lives develop.

Age-graded influences are identical to what most child psychologists and gerontologists have considered the major source of influence on development. They are defined as those biological and environmental determinants that (a) have a fairly strong relation with chronological age and are therefore fairly predict-

able in their temporal sequence (onset, duration), and (b) are, for the most part, similar in their direction among individuals. Biological maturation and age-graded socialization events are examples of age-graded influences.

History-graded influences also involve both biological and environmental determinants. These influences, however, are associated with historical time (Elder, 1985; McCluskey & Reese, 1984; Neugarten & Datan, 1973; Riley et al., 1972) and define the larger evolutionary, biocultural context in which individuals develop. Two types of history-graded influences are likely to exist: those that evince long-term change functions (e.g., toward modernity), and others that are more time or period-specific (e.g., war).

Nonnormative influences also include both biological and environmental determinants (Bandura, 1982; Callahan & McCluskey, 1983; Filipp, 1981). Their major characteristic is that their occurrence, patterning, and sequencing are not applicable to many individuals, nor are they clearly tied to a dimension of developmental time, whether ontogenetic or historical. Nonnormative influences do not follow a general and predictable course.

The trifactor model is easily misunderstood in two respects. First, it may be seen as static. The intent, rather, is to emphasize temporal dynamics (the systems themselves are not historically invariant) and the notion that codeveloping individuals (such as grandparents, parents, and children; Tinsley & Parke, 1984) participate in different segments of the streams of influences. Second, the model may suggest that its focus is more on "normative," average regularities in development than interindividual differentiation. It is important to note, therefore, that systematic interindividual differences exist within each of the categories. In an exchange with Dannefer (1984), for example, Baltes and Nesselroade (1984) emphasized that macrostructural processes of stratification (related to sex, social class, ethnicity, etc.) are associated with clear-cut patterns of individual differences within the stream of age-graded, history-graded, and nonnormative influences.

Some of the influences identified in life-span models, particularly the age-graded ones, result in interindividual similarity in the direction of development. They are the basic components of those classic ontogenetic theories that have been associated with physical maturation and age-graded socialization, such as Piaget's theory of cognitive development, or Freud's theory of psychosexual development. The second category of influences, those that are history-graded, compounds the variability of human development through the impact of historical changes on the course of life-span development. The third category of influences, the nonnormative, renders the individuality or idiosyncrasy of behavioral development most apparent.

In summary then, life-span researchers focus on complex and pluralist explanations of behavioral development. From the recognition of the historical embeddedness of development and the finding of sizeable individual variability in the nature of aging, they have joined other developmental researchers in the recognition of contextual factors and the unique combination of influences that shape a given life course. Some life-span researchers (e.g., Dixon, 1986; Lerner & Kauffman, 1985) have gone beyond the identification of the important role of contextual factors and pushed forcefully in the direction of elevating at least a version of the paradigm of contextualism as the primary metatheoretical avenue for understanding the nature of human development.

Child Intellectual Development in Life-Span Perspective

Concern for the family of perspectives advanced by life-span researchers (as expressed, for instance, in the following concepts: multidimensionality, multidirectionality, gain/loss dynamic, plasticity, and contextualism) has not been as strong on the part of cognitive-developmental researchers concerned with earlier segments of the life span. Aside from the possibility that this evaluation is wrong (Scarr, 1986), there may be a good reason. The data suggest that, in the early phases of the life span, cognitive change toward an increasingly "mature" organism occurs with much regularity. In contrast to the overall regularity surrounding the earlier portion of the life span (McCall, 1979), adulthood and old age are characterized by more openness, variability, and plasticity.

One possible interpretation of this difference between findings on childhood and adulthood locates the origins for this difference in the macro-context surrounding human development. In adulthood and old age, biological and cultural stabilization is less apparent. The biocultural dynamics shaping adulthood and old age are of fairly recent origin and fluctuate in a manner that permits a fair degree of change and active control by the developing individual (Dixon & Baltes, 1986). Conversely, in childhood, biological and societal conditions have converged to form a relatively more solid fabric of influences that generates regularity.

This possible life-span difference in the relative degree of stability of developmental influences has led Baltes et al. (1980) to consider the existence of a general profile of the varying, relative importance of the three types of influences (age-graded, history-graded, nonnormative) through the life course. The argument advanced suggested that, on the average, age-graded influences may be the most pronounced in childhood. This is perhaps the reason why developmental psychologists interested in infancy and childhood have focused in their research and theory foremost on developmental conceptions that entail age-graded changes, factors, and mechanisms. History-graded and nonnormative factors, on the other hand, may gain in prominence as individuals move beyond childhood.

On Multidisciplinary Conceptions of Development

The multitude of influences forming a framework for the origins and directionality of life-span development and its variations also makes explicit why life-span researchers believe so strongly that any single-discipline account of behavioral development is incomplete. The sources of and the mechanisms associated with age-graded, history-graded, and nonnormative influences do not lie within the scientific province of a single discipline such as psychology. History-graded influences, for example, are difficult to approach with psychological concepts and methodology.

An in-depth articulation of the conceptual nature of multidisciplinary connections in the study of life-span development is beyond the scope of this article (see Featherman, 1983). A minimum understanding of other disciplines is mandatory for a number of reasons. First, a multidisciplinary perspective helps

one to appreciate the incompleteness of any discipline's theory of behavioral development. Psychologists, for example, study vocational interests and career development; sociologists and economists, however, are ready to point out that these phenomena are influenced by social stratification and the conditions of the labor market. Similarly, psychologists investigate parent-child relationships, but family sociologists point to the important role of historical changes in defining family structure and functioning, including aspects of household structure and fertility patterns.

Second, interdisciplinary work is more than the mere recognition of the incompleteness of one's own discipline and the strength of other disciplines. The quest is also for interdisciplinary efforts in the sense of integration of knowledge, as opposed to the separatist differentiation of disciplinary knowledge bases. The life-span perspective offers a unique opportunity as a forum for transdisciplinary integrative efforts. Elder's (1974; Elder & Liker, 1982) work on the relation between conditions of history (e.g., economic depression) and personality development is an example, as is Featherman and Lerner's (1985) recent effort to link sociological with psychological perspectives in arriving at a new conception of development.

Retrospect and Prospect

Life-span developmental psychology is presented not as a theory, but as a theoretical perspective. As a perspective, the life-span view coordinates a number of substantive, theoretical, and methodological principles about the nature of behavioral development. Although none of these principles is new, the variation in the strength of the beliefs and the kind of emphasis and coordination contributes uniqueness and novelty.

Essays on historical and theoretical developments in developmental psychology are bound to be somewhat egocentric, topic-centric, and data-centric, to name but a few of the possible centrisms. The field of developmental psychology is more complex and rich than is expressed in this article, where the life-span approach was occasionally juxtaposed with putative theoretical emphases in other fields of developmental specialization. In this respect, the present article surely is an oversimplification.

Having taken the avenue of summarizing what is innovative and possibly useful about the metatheoretical beliefs of life-span developmental psychology, the following observations are offered, both as self-protective disclaimer and as an effort toward achieving better communication between life-span scholars and other developmentalists. Not unlike the gain/loss argument advanced as characteristic of any process of development, the family of beliefs presented here as prototypical of life-span developmental psychology has its dangers and costs. First, there is the question of scientific imperialism. In this sense, life-span scholars are occasionally regarded as holding the opinion that nothing but a life-span view is acceptable (Kaplan, 1983; Sears, 1980). To conclude that the theoretical propositions on the nature of development advanced here have been invented by life-span scholars or to proffer life-span developmental psychology as the royal road of developmental psychology or as the superior approach would be inappropriate. Life-span developmental psychology is but one of the many specializations in developmental scholarship.

Second, there is the issue of theoretical overload. The contributions to metatheory and metamethodology offered by life-span developmental researchers are important. What meta-theoretical discourse can achieve, however, is limited. For example, enlarging and opening up the concept of development has its costs, especially if one or the other of the family of perspectives is taken to its extreme (Baltes, 1983; Lerner, 1984; Montada, 1979). As for plasticity, for a few years the emerging position on intellectual aging was one of complete openness, rather than plasticity within a set of constraints. Similarly, the issue of cohort effects was occasionally taken to a posture of full-blown dialectics or historicism, as if there were no regularity to development at all (for a critical evaluation, see Montada, 1979; Scholnik, 1985). Third, life-span researchers disproportionately emphasize adulthood and old age rather than childhood, yet no strong psychology of life-span development can exist without solid research on earlier phases of life.

Such criticisms, putting life-span developmental psychology and life-span developmentalists into jeopardy, are serious. One approach to these dangers is to call for more intellectual modesty and more communication between the different quarters of developmental research (see also Hetherington, Lerner, & Perlmutter, in press). If we achieve such communication without unnecessary irritation, the future of the life-span approach is likely to be productive. Otherwise, life-span developmental psychology will be not only an edifice without a foundation, but also a network of scholars without partners.

References

Baltes, M. M. (1987). Erfolgreiches Altern als Ausdruck von Verhaltens-kompetenz und Umweltqualität [Successful aging as a function of behavioral competence and environmental quality]. In C. Niemitz (Ed.), *Der Mensch im Zusammenspiel von Anlage und Umwelt* (pp. 353–376). Frankfurt, West Germany: Suhrkamp.

Baltes, M. M., & Kindermann, T. (1985). Die Bedeutung der Plastizität für die klinische Beurteilung des Leistungsverhaltens im Alter [The significance of plasticity in the clinical assessment of aging]. In D. Bente, H. Coper, & S. Kanowski (Eds.), *Hirnorganische Psychosyndrome im Alter: Vol. 2. Methoden zur Objektivierung pharmakotherapeutischer Wirkung* (pp. 171–184). Berlin: Springer Verlag.

Baltes, P. B. (1968). Longitudinal and cross-sectional sequences in the study of age and generation effects. *Human Development, 11,* 145–171.

Baltes, P. B. (1983). Life-span developmental psychology: Observations on history and theory revisited. In R. M. Lerner (Ed.), *Developmental psychology: Historical and philosophical perspectives* (pp. 79–111). Hillsdale, NJ: Erlbaum.

Baltes, P. B., & Baltes, M. M. (1980). Plasticity and variability in psychological aging: Methodological and theoretical issues. In G. Gurski (Ed.), *Determining the effects of aging on the central nervous system* (pp. 41–60). Berlin: Schering.

Baltes, P. B., Cornelius, S. W., & Nesselroade, J. R. (1979). Cohort effects in developmental psychology. In J. R. Nesselroade & P. B. Baltes (Eds.), *Longitudinal research in the study of behavior and development* (pp. 61–87). New York: Academic Press.

Baltes, P. B., Dittmann-Kohli, F., & Dixon, R. A. (1984). New perspectives on the development of intelligence in adulthood: Toward a dual-process conception and a model of selective optimization with compensation. In P. B. Baltes & O. G. Brim, Jr. (Eds.), *Life-span development and behavior* (Vol. 6, pp. 33–76). New York: Academic Press.

Baltes, P. B., & Kliegl, R. (1986). On the dynamics between growth and decline in the aging of intelligence and memory. In K. Poeck, H. J. Freund, & H. Gänshirt (Eds.), *Neurology* (pp. 1–17). Heidelberg, West Germany: Springer Verlag.

Baltes, P. B., & Nesselroade, J. R. (1984). Paradigm lost and paradigm regained: Critique of Dannefer's portrayal of life-span developmental psychology. *American Sociological Review, 49,* 841–847.

Baltes, P. B., & Reese, H. W. (1984). The life-span perspective in developmental psychology. In M. H. Bornstein & M. E. Lamb (Eds.), *Developmental psychology: An advanced textbook* (pp. 493–531). Hillsdale, NJ: Erlbaum.

Baltes, P. B., Reese, H. W., & Lipsitt, L. P. (1980). Life-span developmental psychology. *Annual Review of Psychology, 31,* 65–110.

Baltes, P. B., Reese, H. W., & Nesselroade, J. R. (1977). *Life-span developmental psychology: Introduction to research methods.* Monterey, CA: Brooks Cole.

Baltes, P. B., & Schaie, K. W. (1976). On the plasticity of intelligence in adulthood and old age: Where Horn and Donaldson fail. *American Psychologist, 31,* 720–725.

Bandura, A. (1982). The psychology of chance encounters and life paths. *American Psychologist, 37,* 747–755.

Basseches, M. (1984). *Dialectical thinking and adult development.* Norwood, NJ: Ablex.

Beilin, H. (1983). The new functionalism and Piaget's program. In E. K. Scholnick (Ed.), *New trends in conceptual representation.* Hillsdale, NJ: Erlbaum.

Berg, C. A., & Sternberg, R. J. (1985). A triarchic theory of intellectual development during adulthood. *Developmental Review, 5,* 334–370.

Bertaux, D., & Kohli, M. (1984). The life story approach: A continental view. *Annual Review of Sociology, 10,* 215–237.

Birren, J. E., & Schaie, K. W. (1985). *Handbook of the psychology of aging* (2nd ed.). New York: Van Nostrand Reinhold.

Brandtstädter, J. (1984). Personal and social control over development: Some implications of an action perspective in life-span developmental psychology. In P. B. Baltes & O. G. Brim, Jr. (Eds.), *Life-span development and behavior* (Vol. 6, pp. 1–32). New York: Academic Press.

Brent, S. B. (1978). Individual specialization, collective adaptation, and rate of environmental change. *Human Development, 21,* 21–23.

Brim, O. G., Jr., & Ryff, C. D. (1980). On the properties of life events. In P. B. Baltes & O. G. Brim, Jr. (Eds.), *Life-span development and behavior* (Vol. 3, pp. 368–388). New York: Academic Press.

Brim, O. G., Jr., & Wheeler, S. (1966). *Socialization after childhood: Two essays.* New York: Wiley.

Bronfenbrenner, U. (1977). Toward an experimental ecology of human development. *American Psychologist, 32,* 513–532.

Brown, A. L. (1982). Learning and development: The problem of compatibility, access, and induction. *Human Development, 25,* 89–115.

Bühler, C. (1933). *Der menschliche Lebenslauf als psychologisches Problem* [The human life course as a psychological topic]. Leipzig, East Germany: Hirzel.

Butler, R. N. (1963). The life-review: An interpretation of reminiscence in the aged. *Psychiatry, 26,* 65–76.

Callahan, E. C., & McCluskey, K. A. (Eds.). (1983). *Life-span developmental psychology: Nonnormative life events.* New York: Academic Press.

Carus, F. A. (1808). *Psychologie. Zweiter Theil: Specialpsychologie* [Psychology: Vol. 2. Special Psychology]. Leipzig, East Germany: Barth & Kummer.

Cattell, R. B. (1971). *Abilities: Their structure, growth, and action.* Boston: Houghton Mifflin.

Chapman, M. (in press). *Constructive evolution: Origins and development of Piaget's thought.* Cambridge, England: Cambridge University Press.

Clausen, J. A. (1986). *The life course: A sociological perspective.* Englewood Cliffs, NJ: Prentice-Hall.

Clayton, V. P., & Birren, J. E. (1980). The development of wisdom across the life span: A reexamination of an ancient topic. In P. B. Baltes & O. G. Brim, Jr. (Eds.), *Life-span development and behavior* (Vol. 3, pp. 103–135). New York: Academic Press.

Commons, M. L., Richards, F. A., & Armon, C. (Eds.). (1984). *Beyond formal operations: Late adolescent and adult cognitive development.* New York: Praeger.

Coper, H., Jänicke, B., & Schulze, G. (1986). Biopsychological research on adaptivity across the life span of animals. In P. B. Baltes, D. L. Featherman, & R. M. Lerner (Eds.), *Life-span development and behavior* (Vol. 7, pp. 207–232). Hillsdale, NJ: Erlbaum.

Cotman, C. W. (Ed.). (1985). *Synaptic plasticity.* New York: Guilford Press.

Dannefer, D. (1984). Adult development and social theory: A paradigmatic reappraisal. *American Sociological Review, 49,* 100–116.

Dannefer, D., & Perlmutter, M. (1986). Lifelong human development: Toward decomposition of the phenomenon and explication of its dynamics. Unpublished manuscript, University of Michigan, Ann Arbor.

Datan, N., & Reese, H. W. (Eds.). (1977). *Life-span developmental psychology: Dialectical perspectives on experimental research.* New York, Academic Press.

Davies, A., Criper, C., Howatt, A. P. R. (Eds.). (1984). *Interlanguage.* Edinburgh, Scotland: Edinburgh University Press.

Denney, N. W. (1984). A model of cognitive development across the life span. *Developmental Review, 4,* 171–191.

Dittmann-Kohli, F., & Baltes, P. B. (in press). Toward a neofunctionalist conception of adult intellectual development: Wisdom as a proto-typical case of intellectual growth. In C. Alexander & E. Langer (Eds.), *Beyond formal operations: Alternative endpoints to human development.* New York: Oxford University Press.

Dixon, R. A. (1986). Contextualism and life-span developmental psychology. In R. L. Rosnow & M. Gergoudi (Eds.), *Contextualism and understanding in behavioral science* (pp. 125–144). New York: Praeger.

Dixon, R. A., & Baltes, P. B. (1986). Toward life-span research on the functions and pragmatics of intelligence. In R. J. Sternberg & R. K. Wagner (Eds.), *Practical intelligence: Origins of competence in the everyday world* (pp. 203–235). New York: Cambridge University Press.

Dörner, D. (in press). Heuristics and cognition in complex systems. In R. Groner, M. Groner, & W. F. Bischof (Eds.), *Methods of heuristics.* Hillsdale, NJ: Erlbaum.

Dohrenwend, B. S., & Dohrenwend, B. P. (Eds.). (1974). *Stressful life events.* New York: Wiley.

Elder, G. H., Jr. (1974). *Children of the Great Depression.* Chicago: University of Chicago Press.

Elder, G. H., Jr. (Ed.). (1985). *Life course dynamics.* Ithaca, NY: Cornell University Press.

Elder, G. H., Jr., & Liker, J. K. (1982). Hard times in women's lives: Historical influences across forty years. *American Journal of Sociology, 88,* 241–269.

Ericsson, K. A. (1985). Memory skill. *Canadian Journal of Psychology, 39,* 188–231.

Erikson, E. H. (1959). Identity and the life cycle. *Psychological Issues Monograph 1.* New York: International University Press.

Featherman, D. L. (1983). The life-span perspective in social science research. In P. B. Baltes & O. G. Brim, Jr. (Eds.), *Life-span development and behavior* (Vol. 1, pp. 1–59). New York: Academic Press.

Featherman, D. L., & Lerner, R. M. (1985). Ontogenesis and sociogenesis: Problematics for theory and research about development and socialization across the life span. *American Sociological Review, 50,* 659–676.

Ferrara, R. A., Brown, A. L., & Campione, J. C. (1986). Children's learning and transfer of inductive reasoning rules: Studies of proximal development. *Child Development, 57,* 1087–1099.

Filipp, S.-H. (Ed.). (1981). *Kritische Lebensereignisse* [Critical life events]. Munich, West Germany: Urban & Schwarzenberg.

Flavell, J. H. (1970). Cognitive changes in adulthood. In L. R. Goulet & P. B. Baltes (Eds.), *Life-span developmental psychology: Research and theory* (pp. 247–253). New York: Academic Press.

Fries, J. F., & Crapo, L. M. (1981). *Vitality and aging.* San Francisco, CA: Freeman & Co.

Gergen, K. J. (1980). The emerging crisis in life-span developmental theory. In P. B. Baltes & O. G. Brim, Jr. (Eds.), *Life-span development and behavior* (Vol. 3, pp. 32–65). New York: Academic Press.

Glaser, R. (1984). Education and thinking: The role of knowledge. *American Psychologist, 39,* 93–104.

Gollin, E. S. (1981). Development and plasticity. In E. S. Gollin (Ed.), *Developmental plasticity: Behavioral and biological aspects of variations in development* (pp. 231–251). New York: Academic Press.

Goulet, L. R., & Baltes, P. B. (Eds.). (1970). *Life-span developmental psychology: Research and theory.* New York: Academic Press.

Groffmann, K. I. (1970). Life-span developmental psychology in Europe. In L. R. Goulet & P. B. Baltes (Eds.), *Life-span developmental psychology: Research and theory* (pp. 54–68). New York: Academic Press.

Guthke, J. (1982). The learning test concept. An alternative to the traditional static intelligence test. *The German Journal of Psychology, 6,* 306–324.

Hall, G. S. (1922). *Senescence: The last half of life.* New York: Appleton.

Havighurst, R. J. (1972). *Developmental tasks and education* (3rd ed.). New York: McKay. (Original work published 1948)

Havighurst, R. J. (1973). History of developmental psychology: Socialization and personality development through the life span. In P. B. Baltes & K. W. Schaie (Eds.), *Life-span developmental psychology: Personality and socialization* (pp. 3–24). New York: Academic Press.

Hetherington, E. M., & Baltes, P. B. (in press). Child psychology and life-span development. In E. M. Hetherington, R. M. Lerner, & M. Perlmutter (Eds.), *Child development and the life-span perspective.* Hillsdale, NJ: Erlbaum.

Hetherington, E. M., Lerner, R. M., & Perlmutter, M. A. (Eds.). (in press). *Child development and the life-span perspective.* Hillsdale, NJ: Erlbaum.

Holliday, S. G., & Chandler, M. J. (1986). Wisdom: Explorations in adult competence. In J. A. Meacham (Ed.), *Contributions to human development* (Vol. 17). Basel, Switzerland: Karger.

Hollingworth, H. L. (1927). *Mental growth and decline: A survey of developmental psychology.* New York: Appleton.

Honzik, M. P. (1984). Life-span development. *Annual Review of Psychology, 33,* 309–331.

Horn, J. L. (1970). Organization of data on life-span development of human abilities. In L. R. Goulet & P. B. Baltes (Eds.), *Life-span developmental psychology: Research and theory* (pp. 423–466). New York: Academic Press.

Horn, J. L. (1982). The theory of fluid and crystallized intelligence in relation to concepts of cognitive psychology and aging in adulthood. In F. I. M. Craik & S. E. Trehub (Eds.), *Aging and cognitive processes* (pp. 847–870). New York: Plenum Press.

Horn, J. L., & Donaldson, G. (1976). On the myth of intellectual decline in adulthood. *American Psychologist, 31,* 701–719.

Hoyer, W. J. (1985). Aging and the development of expert cognition. In T. M. Schlechter & M. P. Toglia (Eds.), *New directions in cognitive science* (pp. 69–87). Norwood, NJ: Ablex.

Hultsch, D. F., & Plemons, J. K. (1979). Life events and life-span development. In P. B. Baltes & O. G. Brim, Jr. (Eds.), *Life-span development and behavior* (Vol. 2, pp. 1–37). New York: Academic Press.

Joerißen, P., & Will, C. (1983). *Die Lebenstreppe: Bilder der menschlichen Lebensalter* [The steps of life: Art and the human ages]. Cologne, West Germany: Rheinland-Verlag.

Jung, C. G. (1933). *Modern man in search of a soul.* New York: Harcourt, Brace, & World.

Kaplan, B. (1983). A trio of trials. In R. M. Lerner (Ed.), *Developmental psychology: Historical and philosophical perspectives* (pp. 185–228). Hillsdale, NJ: Erlbaum.

Keating, D., & MacLean, D. (in press). Reconstruction in cognitive development: A post-structuralist agenda. In P. B. Baltes, D. L. Featherman, & R. M. Lerner (Eds.), *Life-span development and behavior* (Vol. 8). Hillsdale, NJ: Erlbaum.

Keil, F. C. (1981). Constraints on knowledge and cognitive development. *Psychological Review, 88,* 187–227.

Kellerman, E., & Smith, M. S. (1986). *Crosslinguistic influence in second language acquisition.* Oxford, England: Pergamon Press.

Kendler, T. S. (1979). Cross-sectional research, longitudinal theory, and a discriminative transfer ontogeny. *Human Development, 22,* 235–254.

Kendler, T. S. (1986). World views and the concept of development: A reply to Lerner and Kauffman. *Developmental Review, 6,* 80–95.

Kertzer, D. I., & Keith, J. (Eds.). (1983). *Age and anthropological theory.* Ithaca, NY: Cornell University Press.

Kirkwood, T. B. L. (1985). Comparative and evolutionary aspects of longevity. In C. E. Finch & E. L. Schneider (Eds.), *Handbook of the biology of aging* (pp. 27–44). New York: Van Nostrand Reinhold.

Kliegl, R., & Baltes, P. B. (1987). Theory-guided analysis of development and aging mechanisms through testing-the-limits and research on expertise. In C. Schooler & K. W. Schaie (Eds.), *Cognitive functioning and social structure over the life course* (pp. 95–119). Norwood, NJ: Ablex.

Kliegl, R., Smith, J., & Baltes, P. B. (1986). Testing-the-limits, expertise, and memory in adulthood and old age. In F. Klix & H. Hagendorf (Eds.), *Human memory and cognitive capabilities: Mechanisms and performances* (pp. 395–407). Amsterdam, Netherlands: North Holland.

Kramer, D. A. (1983). Postformal operations? A need for further conceptualization. *Human Development, 26,* 91–105.

Labouvie, E. W., & Nesselroade, J. R. (1985). Age, period, and cohort analysis and the study of individual development and social change. In J. R. Nesselroade & A. von Eye (Eds.), *Developmental and social change: Explanatory analysis* (pp. 189–212). New York: Academic Press.

Labouvie-Vief, G. (1980). Beyond formal operations: Uses and limits of pure logic in life-span development. *Human Development, 23,* 141–161.

Labouvie-Vief, G. (1982). Dynamic development and mature autonomy: A theoretical prologue. *Human Development, 25,* 161–191.

Labouvie-Vief, G. (1985). Intelligence and cognition. In J. E. Birren & K. W. Schaie (Eds.), *Handbook of the psychology of aging* (2nd ed., pp. 500–530). New York: Van Nostrand Reinhold.

Labouvie-Vief, G., & Chandler, M. (1978). Cognitive development and life-span developmental theory: Idealistic versus contextual perspectives. In P. B. Baltes (Ed.), *Life-span development and behavior* (Vol. 1, pp. 181–210). New York: Academic Press.

Lerner, R. M. (1984). *On the nature of human plasticity.* New York: Cambridge University Press.

Lerner, R. M., & Kauffman, M. B. (1985). The concept of development in contextualism. *Developmental Review, 5,* 309–333.

Lerner, R. M., & Kauffman, M. B. (1986). On the metatheoretical relativism of analyses of metatheoretical analyses: A critique of Kendler's comments. *Developmental Review, 6,* 96–106.

McCall, R. B. (1979). The development of intellectual functioning in infancy and the prediction of later IQ. In J. Osofsky (Ed.), *Handbook of infant development* (pp. 707–741). New York: Wiley.

McCluskey, K. A., & Reese, H. W. (Eds.). (1984). *Life-span developmental psychology: Historical and generational effects.* New York: Academic Press.

McGraw, M. (1985). Professional and personal blunder in child development research. In J. Osofsky (Ed.), *Newsletter of the Society for Research in Child Development.* Special Supplement to Winter Newsletter.

Meacham, J. A. (1982). Wisdom and the context of knowledge: Knowing that one doesn't know. In D. Kuhn & J. A. Meacham (Eds.), *On the development of developmental psychology* (pp. 111–134). Basel, Switzerland: Karger.

Migdal, S., Abeles, R., & Sherrod, L. (1981). *An inventory of longitudinal studies of middle and old age.* New York: Social Science Research Council.

Montada, L. (1979). Entwicklungspsychologie auf der Suche nach einer Identität [Developmental psychology in search of an identity]. In L. Montada (Ed.), *Brennpunkte der Entwicklungspsychologie* [Current foci in developmental psychology] (pp. 31–44). Stuttgart, West Germany: Kohlhammer.

Neisser, U. (Ed.). (1982). *Memory observed: Remembering in natural contexts.* San Francisco, CA: Freeman.

Nesselroade, J. R., & Baltes, P. B. (1974). Adolescent personality development and historical change: 1970–72. *Monographs of the Society for Research in Child Development, 39*(1, Serial No. 154).

Nesselroade, J. R., & von Eye, A. (Eds.). (1985). *Developmental and social change: Explanatory analysis.* New York: Academic Press.

Neugarten, B. L., & Datan, N. (1973). Sociological perspectives on the life cycle. In P. B. Baltes & K. W. Schaie (Eds.), *Life-span developmental psychology: Personality and socialization* (pp. 53–69). New York: Academic Press.

Nisbet, R. (1980). *History of the idea of progress.* New York: Basic Books.

Oerter, R. (1986). Developmental task through the life span: A new approach to an old concept. In P. B. Baltes, D. L. Featherman, & R. M. Lerner (Eds.), *Life-span development and behavior* (Vol. 7, pp. 233–269). Hillsdale, NJ: Erlbaum.

Parke, R. D., & Tinsley, B. R. (1984). Fatherhood: Historical and contemporary perspectives. In K. A. McClusky & H. W. Reese (Eds.), *Life-span developmental psychology: Historical and generational effects.* New York: Academic Press.

Pascual-Leone, J. (1983). Growing into human maturity: Toward a metasubjective theory of adulthood stages. In P. B. Baltes & O. G. Brim, Jr. (Eds.), *Life-span development and behavior* (Vol. 5, pp. 118–156). New York: Academic Press.

Perlmutter, M. (in press). Cognitive development in life-span perspective: From description of differences to explanation of changes. In E. M. Hetherington, R. M. Lerner, & M. Perlmutter (Eds.), *Child development in life-span perspective.* Hillsdale, NJ: Erlbaum.

Philibert, M. (1968). *L'échelle des ages* [The ladder of ages]. Paris: Seuil.

Piaget, J. (1969). *The mechanisms of perception.* London: Routledge & Kegan Paul.

Piaget, J. (1972). Intellectual evolution from adolescence to adulthood. *Human Development, 15,* 1–12.

Porges, S. W. (1976). Cohort effects and apparent secular trends in infant research. In K. F. Riegel & J. A. Meacham (Eds.), *The developing individual in a changing world* (Vol. 2, pp. 687–695). Chicago: Aldine.

Quetelet, A. (1835). *Sur l'homme et le développement de ses facultés* [On man and the development of his faculties]. Paris: Bachelier.

Reese, H. W. (1974). Cohort, age, and imagery in children's paired-associate learning. *Child Development, 45,* 1176–1178.

Reese, H. W., & Overton, W. F. (1970). Models of development and theories of development. In L. R. Goulet & P. B. Baltes (Eds.), *Life-span developmental psychology: Research and theory* (pp. 115–145). New York: Academic Press.

Reinert, G. (1979). Prolegomena to a history of life-span developmental psychology. In P. B. Baltes & O. G. Brim, Jr. (Eds.), *Life-span development and behavior* (Vol. 2, pp. 205–254). New York: Academic Press.

Riegel, K. F. (1973). Dialectical operations: The final period of cognitive development. *Human Development, 16,* 346–370.

Riegel, K. F. (1976). The dialectics of human development. *American Psychologist, 31,* 689–700.

Riley, M. W. (1985). Age strata in social systems. In R. H. Binstock & E. Shanas (Eds.), *Handbook of aging and the social sciences* (Vol. 3, pp. 369–411). New York: Van Nostrand Reinhold.

Riley, M. W., Johnson, M., & Foner, A. (Eds.). (1972). *Aging and society: Vol. 3. A sociology of age stratification.* New York: Russell Sage.

Ross, L. (1981). The "intuitive scientist" formulation and its development implications. In L. Ross & J. Flavell (Eds.), *Social cognitive development* (pp. 1–42). New York: Cambridge University Press.

Rybash, J. M., Hoyer, W., & Roodin, P. A. (1986). *Adult cognition and aging: Developmental changes in processing, knowing, and thinking.* New York: Pergamon Press.

Salthouse, T. A. (1984). Effects of age and skill in typing. *Journal of Experimental Psychology: General, 113,* 345–371.

Salthouse, T. A. (1985). *A theory of cognitive aging.* Amsterdam, Netherlands: North Holland.

Scarr, S. (1986). How plastic are we? *Contemporary Psychology, 31,* 565–567.

Schaie, K. W. (1965). A general model for the study of developmental problems. *Psychological Bulletin, 64,* 92–107.

Schaie, K. W. (1979). The primary mental abilities in adulthood: An exploration in the development of psychometric intelligence. In P. B. Baltes & O. G. Brim, Jr. (Eds.), *Life-span development and behavior* (Vol. 3, pp. 67–115). New York: Academic Press.

Schaie, K. W. (Ed.). (1983). *Longitudinal studies of adult psychological development.* New York: Guilford Press.

Schaie, K. W., & Willis, S. L. (1986). Can adult intellectual decline be reversed? *Developmental Psychology, 22,* 223–232.

Scholnick, E. K. (1985). Unlimited development. *Contemporary Psychology, 30,* 314–316.

Sears, R. R. (1980). A new school of life span? *Contemporary Psychology, 25,* 303–304.

Sears, E. (1986). *Ages of man: Medieval interpretations of the life cycle.* Princeton, NJ: Princeton University Press.

Sherrod, L. R., & Brim, O. G., Jr. (1986). Retrospective and prospective views of life-course research on human development. In A. B. Sorensen, F. E. Weinert, & L. R. Sherrod (Eds.), *Human development and the life course: Multidisciplinary perspectives.* Hillsdale, NJ: Erlbaum.

Skinner, B. F. (1983). Intellectual self-management in old age. *American Psychologist, 38,* 239–244.

Smith, J., Dixon, R. A., & Baltes, P. B. (in press). Expertise in life planning: A new approach to investigating aspects of wisdom. In M. L. Commons, J. D. Sinnott, F. A. Richards, & C. Armon (Eds.), *Beyond formal operations II.* New York: Praeger.

Smith, J., Kliegl, R., & Baltes, P. B. (1987). *Testing-the-limits and the study of age differences in cognitive plasticity: The sample case of expert memory.* Manuscript submitted for publication.

Sternberg, R. J. (in press). Lessons from the life span: What theorists of intellectual development among children can learn from their counterparts studying adults. In E. M. Hetherington, R. M. Lerner, & M. Perlmutter (Eds.), *Child development in life-span perspective.* Hillsdale, NJ: Erlbaum.

Sternberg, R. J., & Wagner, R. K. (Eds.). (1986). *Practical intelligence: Nature and origins of competence in the everyday world.* New York: Cambridge University Press.

Strube, G. (1985). *Knowing what's going to happen in life: 2. Biographical knowledge in developmental perspective.* Unpublished manuscript, Max Planck Institute for Psychological Research, Munich, West Germany.

Tetens, J. N. (1777). *Philosophische Versuche über die menschliche Natur und ihre Entwicklung* [Philosophical essays on human nature and its development]. Leipzig, East Germany: Weidmanns Erben und Reich.

Thomae, H. (1979). The concept of development and life-span developmental psychology. In P. B. Baltes & O. G. Brim, Jr. (Eds.), *Life-span development and behavior* (Vol. 2, pp. 282–312). New York: Academic Press.

Tinsley, B. R., & Parke, R. D. (1984). Grandparents as support and socialization agents. In M. Lewis (Ed.), *Beyond the dyad.* New York: Plenum.

Verdonik, F., & Sherrod, L. (1984). *An inventory of longitudinal research on childhood and adolescence.* New York: Social Science Research Council.

Waddington, C. H. (1975). *The evolution of an evolutionist.* Edinburgh, Scotland: Edinburgh University Press.

Weinert, F. E., Schneider, W., & Knopf, M. (in press). Individual differences in memory development across the life span. In P. B. Baltes, D. L. Featherman, & R. M. Lerner (Eds.), *Life-span development and behavior* (Vol. 9). Hillsdale, NJ: Erlbaum.

Weir, M. W. (1964). Developmental changes in problem-solving strategies. *Psychological Review, 71,* 473–490.

Wiedl, K. H. (1984). Lerntests: Nur Forschungsmittel und Forschungsgegenstand? [Tests of learning: Only a strategy and topic of research?]. *Zeitschrift für Entwicklungspsychologie und Pädagogische Psychologie, 16,* 245–281.

Willis, S. L. (1985). Towards an educational psychology of the adult learner. In J. E. Birren & K. W. Schaie (Eds.), *Handbook of the psychology of aging* (pp. 818–847). New York: Van Nostrand Reinhold.

Wohlwill, J. F. (1973). *The study of behavioral development.* New York: Academic Press.

Received July 22, 1986
Revision received March 16, 1987
Accepted March 23, 1987 ∎

Theories of Adolescent Development

Rachna Talwar
Jacqueline V. Lerner
The Pennsylvania State University

Numerous theories of development have been advanced to account for development during adolescence. These theories can be placed into three major explanatory categories: nature theories, nurture theories, and interaction theories (Lerner & Spanier, 1980). The nature theories of adolescent development were the first historically, and stress that biology, or the person's *nature*, is the source of adolescent development, and that experience and environment have little impact on the quality of behavior or on the sequence of change in behaviors occurring across adolescence. Nurture theories, on the other hand, stress that experience, learning, and environment are the major sources of variables influencing behavior and behavior change. Some of the nurture theorists emphasize the functional link between stimulus and response and eschew cognitive and mental factors in behavior change. Other theorists stress that attention, observation, and modeling of behaviors leads to the acquisition of new responses.

The third group, "interaction" theories of adolescent development, stress the interplay of both nature (biology) and nurture (environment) in shaping development. According to Lerner and Spanier (1980), interaction theories of adolescent development can be categorized as "weak," "moderate," and "strong." Weak interaction theories emphasize that either nature or nurture is more important. The moderate interaction theory gives equal conceptual weight to both nature and nurture, but views them as being independent of each other. The strong interaction theory sees nature and nurture as always embedded with each other, as dynamically interacting (Lerner, 1978). Examples of the above types of theories are presented below.

Nature Theories of Adolescent Development

Nature theories place primary stress on purportedly evolutionarily shaped, hereditary mechanisms in explaining individual behavior and development. As a consequence, such theories explain ontogenetic change on the basis of the presumed relevance of phylogenetic history and biogenetic mechanisms for the individual's life span. Although several instances of such theories exist (e.g., see Lerner, 1986, for reviews), one has been central across the history of the study of adolescence.

G. Stanley Hall's recapitulation theory (Hall, 1904), was the first scientific theory to define adolescence as a specific period in ontogeny after childhood. Hall asserted that human beings relive or pass through stages in their course of ontogenetic development that correspond to the major evolutionary stages involved in the history of mankind. That is, individuals repeat the development of the human race from its early primitive existence to its more recent, civilized state. Since, in this view, evolutionary-shaped biological (e.g., maturational) factors control and direct development, growth, and behavior, this theory paid little attention to the influence of environmental factors on the quality or sequential emergence of behavior.

Adolescence was a period of transition between childhood and adulthood. This ontogenetic period corresponded to a time when—in evolution—the human race was in a turbulent and transitional stage between its beastlike past and its current, civilized state. Thus, adolescence, in recapitulating this stage, involved stormy and stressful transition too, here a change involving being dominated by instinctual drives associated with physical growth while adapting to socializing demands made by significant others (Hall, 1904).

Nurture Theories of Adolescent Development

Generally, nurture theories suggest that there is a functional relationship that exists between stimulus and response (e.g., see Bijou & Baer, 1961). However, there is a great diversity in nurture theories, and no consensus exists about what is the nurture view of behavior (Lerner, 1986; Lerner & Spanier, 1980). This situation is complicated further because no general nurture theory has been specifically developed to deal with the phenomena of human development (White, 1970). However, some nurture theories are useful in understanding adolescent development.

DAVIS'S THEORY OF SOCIALIZED ANXIETY ■ Davis (1944) has proposed a theory of socialized anxiety. He argues that individuals learn to anticipate punishment for behaviors that are disapproved. This anticipation of punishment, termed socialized anxiety, is experienced as an unpleasant state by the individual. Because of this unpleasant state, a person's behavior will be aimed at reducing or avoiding it, that is, behavior will be aimed at diminishing or eliminating this anxiety. Adolescence, according to Davis, is a period where there is less certainty about what behaviors are punished and what behaviors are rewarded. As such, there is no certain way of diminishing socialized anxiety. Accordingly, storm and stress may be involved during adolescence.

However, according to Davis, socialized anxiety during adolescence is important because it serves as a motivating and, through its reduction, as a reinforcing agent in the process of socialization. Nevertheless, too much or too little socialized anxiety during adolescence hinders the attainment of mature behavior.

McCANDLESS'S DRIVE THEORY ■ A "drive theory" of adolescent behavior and development was proposed by McCandless (1970). This

theory was predicated on the view that all human behavior is based on drives (e.g., hunger or sex) and that the direction behavior takes is a consequence of a particular drive. Over time, the individual learns that certain behaviors reduce drive-states; while some of these behaviors are rewarded, others are punished by society (McCandless, 1970). Social learning involves, then, acquiring those drive-reducing behaviors that will likely attain rewards and eliminating or avoiding those drive-reducing behaviors likely to result in punishment.

The relevance of this theory to adolescence is that, during adolescence, a new drive, the sex drive, emerges. Because of this emergence, adolescents have to learn socially acceptable ways of reducing this drive. As males and females are differentially rewarded for male or female sex-appropriate behavior, adolescents will adopt specific roles appropriate for their sex (McCandless, 1970).

COGNITIVE SOCIAL LEARNING THEORIES OF ADOLESCENT DEVELOPMENT ■ As there is no one nurture view of human development, there is no one cognitive social learning theory of adolescent development. One cognitive social learning theory proposed by Albert Bandura (1977) used nurture-based learning principles to explain the role of the social environment in controlling human behavior. According to Bandura, human development is a lifelong process of socialization in which modeling and reinforcement of behavior shape biological drives. Through modeling, adolescents observe and imitate the behavior of others, and through reinforcement, adolescents learn that behaviors that are rewarded are approved while behaviors that are punished are disapproved.

Interaction Theories of Adolescent Development

Interaction theories stress the contributions of both nature and nurture in shaping development. Theories of this type differ, however, in whether this interaction is conceived of as weak, moderate, or strong. Weak interaction theories stress that one source, typically nature, is the prime mover of development and that the second source only acts to hamper or facilitate the action of the first. Moderate interaction theories see both nature and nurture as equal sources of change. However, each source is unaffected by the other over the course of their interaction. Strong interaction theories emphasize the dynamic, systemic, transactional, or dialectic relation between nature and nurture. Examples of each type exist in relation to the study of adolescent development.

SIGMUND FREUD'S PSYCHOSEXUAL STATE THEORY ■ According to the psychoanalytic theory of Sigmund Freud (1949), adolescent and adult development are determined in the first five years of life. Therefore, little emphasis is placed on pubescence and adolescence. Thus, in order to understand adolescent development one has to understand the libidinal fixations and conflicts that occurred in the first three psychosexual stages, namely the oral stage, the anal stage, and the phallic stage.

According to Freudian theory, during the time of pubertal development the libido, or psychic energy, resurfaces after being dormant, and it is localized in the genital area. This stage is termed the genital stage and is marked by the emergence of sexuality that may take an adult form (depending on prior fixations in earlier psy-

55

chosexual stages). Thus, if the adolescent has been successful in his/her previous psychosexual development, there emerges the potential for adult reproductive sexuality, a sexuality directed towards heterosexual relationships and development.

Since the stages of psychosexual development occur in a predetermined and universal sequence, nature, or biological, factors predominate in the sequence of development. However, Freud contends that nature or experiential factors serve as inhibitors or facilitators of this nature-based sequence (that is, nurture is the source of fixations of nature-based changes). Thus, Freud's theory is a "weak" interaction theory.

ANNA FREUD'S THEORY OF ADOLESCENT DEFENSE MECHANISMS ■ Sigmund Freud's

theory placed relatively little emphasis on adolescence. Despite his neglect concerning this period of life, it has been a major concern of Freud's daughter, Anna. Anna Freud (1969) believed that adolescence is a period marked by turbulence because of new, internal demands on the adolescent arising from his/her sexual maturation and the intensified sexual drive associated with it. An increased sexual drive brings with it an increase in most impulse activity, a change leading to the enhancement of aggressiveness, inquisitiveness, and egocentricity in adolescence. Along with this set of changes comes a reactivation of the psychosexual conflicts of childhood, an occurrence leading to ambivalent behavior in adolescents; that is, adolescents tend to alternate between emotional extremes, such as excessive independence and clinging dependence.

In her discussion of adolescence Anna Freud (1969) emphasizes that the relationship between the id, the ego, and the superego undergoes qualitative change. The process of physiological growth and sexual maturation leads to a disequilibrium between the id and the ego, resulting in increased conflict during this period. In turn, the superego, which is developed through the assimilation of the moral values of the people with whom the adolescent identifies, comes into conflict with the ego that is yielding to the id impulses.

Since the conflicts of this period arouse much anxiety in the adolescent, the adolescent tries to cope through the development of new defense mechanisms as well as through the continuation of the use of prior defense mechanisms. As with the defense mechanisms used in earlier periods, new defense mechanisms are unconscious, but they are also influenced by learning. Since the adolescent learns that certain ways of acting out sexual impulses are not condoned by society (e.g., incest is forbidden), some defense against these manifestations of sexual impulses is established. One defensive strategy typically drawn from use in prior periods of life is sublimation, where sexual impulses are transformed into more socially acceptable endeavors such as intellectual and artistic activity. Displacement is another major defense, one wherein the adolescent displaces his/her impulses to other things or persons. Identification with others besides parents, including teachers and peers, may also occur.

Anna Freud held that not only does the adolescent try the above defenses, but he or she also forms new types of defense mechanisms, such as intellectualism and asceticism. In intellectualism the adolescent uses his/her newly developed abstract thinking and intellectual reasoning to justify his or her behavior. This helps in creating an emotional distance between ideas and impulses. In asceticism the adolescent unconsciously denies that he or she has any sexual desires. This is an effort to impose control on their sexual needs.

In sum, Anna Freud sees adolescence as a necessarily and universally developmentally turbulent period, a period having these features because of the emergence of the sexual drive during puberty. Her view is consistent with that of Sigmund Freud, who sees nurture as only an inhibitor or facilitator of nature. Both of their theories are therefore weak-interaction ones.

ERIK ERIKSON'S THEORY OF IDENTITY DEVELOPMENT ■

Erikson's (1959, 1968) theory is an expansion and modification of the Freudian theory of psychosexual development and can be characterized also as a "weak" interaction theory. This theory shifts the emphasis of development from an exclusively psychosexual, as in classical Freudian theory, to a psychosocial emphasis.

In his theory, Erikson describes eight stages of psychosocial development. In each stage the person has to develop a capacity (an ego function) to meet societal demands. Thus, each stage involves an "ego crisis," the resolution of which depends on whether the person meets the demands of the society and develops appropriate ego capabilities.

The core concept in Erikson's theory in regard to adolescence is the acquisition of ego-identity, and the identity crisis is the most prominent and essential characteristic of adolescence (Erikson, 1950). During adolescence the person has to adopt behaviors (that is, a *role*) that involves the perpetuation of society and, as such, the establishment of a sense of identity. Thus, the adolescent experiences a crisis between identity formation at one end and identity diffusion (or role confusion) at the other.

PIAGET'S THEORY OF MODERATE NATURE-NURTURE INTERACTION ■

A moderate interaction between nature and nurture involves the view that heredity and environment, acting independently of each other, are both equally important in development. Jean Piaget's theory of cognitive development falls into this moderate interaction category.

Piaget forwarded a stage theory of development, wherein the posited stages are universal and invariant. These stages are brought about by the organism acting on the environment and the environment acting on the organism. Although Piaget accepts the role of organism and environment in development, a close examination of this theory has led to the belief that experience or environment is not as fully considered as are maturational factors (Brainerd, 1978). Perhaps, for this reason, some consider Piaget's theory as a weak interaction theory.

Piaget (1950, 1970) believed that cognitive development, that is, the processes involved in the acquisition of knowledge, involve a progressive development through four stages. The fourth stage involves the attainment of formal operations, or abstract thought, during adolescence. Formal operations are most representative of adolescents in Western society. With the attainment of such abstract thinking abilities, the person can now deal with hypothetical situations, and can make deductions in order to find solutions to problems, both real and counterfactual. The emergence of this capacity constitutes a turning point in the development of the structure of adolescent thought. Indeed, because the individual centers so much on this newly acquired thinking ability, egocentrism in adolescents is believed, by some scientists, to emerge. That is, the adolescent believes that others are as preoccupied with the object of his or her thought (for example, his or her own physical appearance) as he or she is. The failure to distinguish between his or her thoughts and those of others

57

leads to the construction of an imaginary audience (Elkind, 1967). Along with this emergence of an imaginary audience, the adolescent also constructs a personal fable, that is, a belief that he or she is a unique or special person.

In sum, with the attainment of formal operations, Piaget (1950, 1970, 1972) believes that the last stage of cognitive development is achieved. However, research indicates that not all people achieve formal operational ability. Moreover, some researchers believe that cognitive changes proceed beyond adolescence and involve a fifth stage of cognitive development (Arlin, 1975; Labouvie-Vief, 1980).

STRONG INTERACTION THEORIES

■ Strong interaction theories see nature and nurture as dynamically or reciprocally interactive with each other, with each acting as a product and producer of the other (Lerner & Spanier, 1980). Adolescent development involves a combined influence of the inner-biological, individual-psychological, outer-physical, and sociocultural-historical levels of analyses (Riegel, 1975). The basis of adolescent development involves the interdependence among all levels, and is not the product of a single level (Lerner & Spanier, 1980; Petersen & Taylor, 1980).

Lerner and Spanier (1980) have elaborated this idea within the framework of a "dynamic interactional" model of adolescent development. From the point of view of this model, the potential for change is continual. The phenomena associated with puberty, for example, are not merely biological events. Rather, such changes are linked to changes in the social context of the adolescent. At a molar level these changes involve nutritional and medical care that can affect the timing and quality of pubertal change. In turn, the resulting changes in pubertal development can fur-

ther impact on society and culture as it evolves across history. For instance, some possible implications for society of females experiencing puberty earlier in life—when they are less cognitively and emotionally developed—are increased incidences of illegitimate births and more teenagers dropping out of school. The implications for adolescents are also problematic because reaching puberty and reproductive maturity at an early age can result in an increase in stress for the adolescent. At a more molecular level pubertal changes can influence how others in the social context react to the adolescent and these different reactions may feed back to the youth and alter his or her ensuing psychosocial development (Lerner & Lerner, 1989).

Conclusions

Nature, nurture, and interaction theories of adolescent development represent quite contrasting orientations to understanding the phenomena involved in this period of development. Yet all theories put forward concepts that bear on the core conceptual issues of adolescent development, that is, of the role of biology and context in the lives of young people. Accordingly, the empirical ideas and concomitant research done by researchers associated with each respective approach are inevitably valuable in shedding light on these issues. Thus, these different theoretical approaches to conceptualizing adolescent development are vital for providing ideas and data needed to understand the complexities of this period of life.

References

Arlin, P. K. (1975). Cognitive development in adulthood: A fifth stage? *Developmental Psychology, 11*, 602-606.

Bandura, A. (1965). A stormy decade: Fact or fiction? *Psychology in the School, 1*, 224-231.

Bandura, A. (1977). *Social learning theory*. Englewood Cliffs, NJ: Prentice-Hall.

Bandura, A., & Walters, R. H. (1959). *Adolescent aggression*. New York: Ronald Press.

Bijou, S. W., & Baer, D. M. (1961). *Child development: A systematic and empirical theory* (Vol. 1). New York: Appleton-Century-Crofts.

Brainerd, C. J. (1978). The stage question in cognitive-developmental theory. *Behavioral and Brain Sciences*, *2*, 173–182.

Davis, A. (1944). Socialization and the adolescent personality. *Forty-third year book of the National Society for the Study of Education* (Vol. 43). Chicago: University of Chicago Press.

Elkind, D. (1967). Egocentricism in adolescence. *Child Development*, *38*, 1025–1034.

Erikson, E. H. (1950). *Childhood and society*. New York: W. W. Norton.

Erikson, E. H. (1959). Identity and the life-cycle. *Psychological Issues*, *1*, 18–164.

Erikson, E. H. (1968). *Identity, youth, and crisis*. New York: Norton.

Freud, A. (1969). Adolescence as a developmental disturbance. In G. Caplan & S. Lebovice (Eds.), *Adolescence* (pp. 5–10). New York: Basic Books.

Freud, S. (1949). *Outline of psychoanalysis*. New York: Norton.

Hall, G. S. (1904). *Adolescence*. New York: Appleton.

Labouvie-Vief, G. (1980). Beyond formal operations: Uses and limits of pure logic in life-span development. *Human Development*, *23*, 141–161.

Lerner, R. M. (1978). Nature, nurture, and dynamic interactionism. *Human Development*, *21*, 1–20.

Lerner, R. M. (1986). *Concepts and theories of human development* (2nd ed.). New York: Random House.

Lerner, R. M., & Lerner, J. V. (1989). Organismic and social-contextual bases of development: The sample case of early adolescence.

In W. Damon (Ed.), *Child development today and tomorrow* (pp. 69–85). San Francisco: Jossey-Bass.

Lerner, R. M., & Spanier, G. B. (1980). *Adolescent development: A life-span perspective*. New York: McGraw-Hill.

McCandless, B. R. (1970). *Adolescents*. Hinsdale, IL: Dryden Press.

Petersen, A. C., & Taylor, T. (1980). The biological approach to adolescence: Biological change and psychological adaptation. In Adelson (Ed.), *Handbook of adolescent psychology* (pp. 117–155). New York: Wiley.

Piaget, J. (1950). *The psychology of intelligence*. London: Routledge & Kegan Paul.

Piaget, J. (1970). Piaget's theory. In P. H. Mussen (Ed.), *Carmichael's manual of child psychology* (Vol. 1, pp. 703–732). New York: Wiley.

Piaget, J. (1972). Intellectual evolution from adolescence to adulthood. *Human Development*, *15*, 1–12.

Riegel, K. F. (1975). Toward a dialectical theory of development. *Human Development*, *18*, 50–64.

Sampson, E. E. (1977). Psychology and the American ideal. *Journal of Personality and Social Psychology*, *35*, 767–782.

White, S. H. (1970). The learning theory tradition and child psychology. In P. H. Mussen (Ed.), *Carmichael's manual of child psychology* (pp. 657–702). New York: Wiley.

See Also

Critical Periods; Developmental Contextualism and Adolescent Development; Developmental Tasks; Life-Span View of Human Development and Adolescent Development; Multivariate, Replicated, Single-Subject, Repeated Measures Design: Studying Change in the Adolescent; Psychoanalytic Theory.

Jacqueline V. Lerner's work on this paper was supported in part by a grant to Richard M. Lerner and Jacqueline V. Lerner from the William T. Grant Foundation, and by NIMH grant MH39957.

Stress Absorbing Systems in Black Families*

HARRIETTE P. McADOO**

Upwardly mobile black families were examined in an attempt to ascertain the possible relationships between stress, economic mobility and kin network support within their social/interactional systems. Despite high ratings on stress and high frequencies of major life change events most families studied exhibited high levels of satisfaction with family life situations. Families upwardly mobile over three generations and in the highest social status classification had the lowest stress scores. Kin support systems greatly facilitated stress management.

One of the traditional and continuing stress absorbing systems for black and other minority families has been the wide supportive network of their families. These reciprocal exchange systems have enabled blacks to cope with and sometimes transcend severe environmental stress. The boundaries have included nuclear and extended forms and have often incorporated nonrelatives as "fictive kin." This study was conducted in order to explore the presence of stress in one group of blacks, that is those who were upwardly mobile and who achieved solid middle-class status. One secondary purpose of this research effort was to determine if certain cultural patterns were maintained as sources of support in the management of stress after economic mobility had occurred. This particular group was selected for study in order to examine whether and how black families not adversely affected by precarious economics, were able to escape

*The research for this report was supported by the Office of Child Development, Department of Health, Education and Welfare, Grant 90-C-631(1)

**Harriette P. McAdoo is Professor, School of Social Work, Howard University, Washington, D.C. 20059.

Key Concepts: Black families, stress. stress absorbing systems, kin networks.

(Family Relations, 1982. 31, 479-488.)

the pressure of discrimination as they moved into suburbia and stable urban areas.

The most oppressive sources of stress for blacks continue to be the presence of racism, discrimination, and economic isolation. These, coupled with the lack of majority appreciation of culture and the denigration of their ethnic group, may not be as overt as in the past, but are covertly present and do not appear to be decreasing. The economic and historical stress has resulted in some differential patterns in lifestyles that have produced lower incomes for blacks at all social levels, regardless of education and occupation, surpluses of marriage aged females and a resultant higher proportion of one parent homes. The impact of low income on family structure is shown by the fact that in black families with less than $4,000, only 20% of children live with both parents vs. 37% for similar white families. But for black families earning $15,000 or more, 86% of children live with both parents, a pattern similar to non-black families in the same level (U.S. Bureau of the Census, 1979). These figures indicate that black families under economic restrictions have to endure greater stresses that in turn impact upon the family to a seemingly harsher extent. Public support policies have contributed to the patterns found at lower income levels.

The orientation of the present research effort was that these families, through blending of African and American cultures over generations, had been able to develop lifestyles and family patterns that were similar to but different, in many subtle ways, from other families. While the similarities may outweigh the differences, those differences have formed the core of cultural content. This cultural content, or ethnicity, has now been recognized in many diverse ethnic religious and nationality groups as the soul satisfying component of contemporary family life (Mindel & Habenstein, 1977; Levin & Giordano, Note 1). The cultural patterns that have been found in most black families of all income levels have been documented as: strong reliance on the family (Billingsley, 1968; Hill, 1971; McAdoo, 1978; Stack, 1975); a strong sense of movement and religiosity (Nobles, 1978); an active involvement of both parents in children rearing and decision making (Mack, 1974; Staples, 1971); and the continual defense against discrimination.

Sample Selection

Black families of school aged children with middle income parents were selected to evaluate the level of stress and means of resolving stress. One-half were urban and one-half were suburban; they resided in the middle Atlantic area. The suburban families were randomly selected from a nearly complete list of families that were generated from the black churches, social and professional groups, and public and private schools. Once their education and income were known, similar census tracts were selected in a city located 15 miles away.

Procedure

Interviewing

In each family, the father was interviewed for two hours by a black male interviewer. The mother was then interviewed separately for two-and-a-half hours by a black female interviewer. Parents were then each asked to fill in personal data sheets, at their leisure, for 45 minutes, that provided background demographic information and three separate scales.

In one parent homes, the head of household present in the home was asked to fill out a background data sheet on the other parent. While there were some missing data on the nonresident or deceased parent, background data on both sides of all of the families were obtained. While data were gathered from or about both parents in the home, the family as a whole was the unit of analysis.

Instruments

The instrument used contained sections on: (a) basic background information; (b) schedule of recent life experiences; (c) satisfaction with life; and, (d) preference for the utilization of family support systems. The Holmes and Rahe (1967) scale of critical events was used to measure stress. The instrument measures changes that have been both fortunate and unfortunate. Too great a degree of change, even of a desirous nature, can cause stress. The instrument attempts to measure the amount of change that a given event requires of an individual or family. No cultural based items were included in the scale. The subjects were asked to complete an instrument that measures the amount of change that they have experienced within the past two years. Different events have been weighted on hundreds of actual populations across the country on a scale giving a higher score for major changes (divorce, 73; death of a child, 63), and lower scores for less traumatic events (vacation, 13). Based on clinical follow-up, Holmes and Rahe (1967) had grouped the scores into three categories: Mild stress (150-199), moderate stress (200-299), and major stress (300+). Those in higher stress groups had a greater chance of becoming physically or mentally ill within a six month period of time.

The Standard Happiness Scale used widely in nationwide surveys offers a measure of the global degree of satisfaction with the environment. The decision to use this scale to measure global constructs was based on the work of several authors (Bradburn & Caplovitz, 1965; Gurin, Veroff, & Feld, 1960; Hill, 1971; Harrison Note 2). It has been used repeatedly to measure very global attitudes such as marital happiness and life satisfaction in general. The physical satisfaction part of the scale dealt with how the families decided to live in the urban or suburban sites and the specific reasons for their last move. We also asked them to compare this setting with where they had lived before. It allowed us to compare our families with black and non-black families in nationwide samples. Families were then asked in general about their level of happiness and their satisfaction with their present family situation.

Sample

Three hundred and five parents were included, 174 mothers and 131 fathers, representing 178 family units. The same proportion of one parent (28%) to two parent (72%) families was found in each site. Of the 50 one parent families only four were father headed. Almost all families were nuclear, composed of either one or both parents, (93%), while a few (6%) were extended in form. The average ages were 39 years for fathers and 37 years for mothers.

Of the subjects' 423 children, 51% were boys and 49% were girls, with an average of 2.37 children per family. This was consistent with earlier studies that have shown that black families have fewer children than white families of comparable educational level. When heads of families are college graduates, more blacks than whites have two or fewer children (Glick, 1957). An average of 4.18 people lived in each household. Since 1930, the size of the black household has fluctuated from 3.8 to 4.1 persons (Glick & Mills, Note 3). These families were at the upper limit of that range.

The average income was $19,749 for males and $11,247 for females. The income for males and females in one parent homes was lower than in two parent units. The one parent mothers all worked and earned an average of $8,920, while one parent fathers earned $15,250. As reflected in the U.S. Census data for the total population, the one parent mother was the most economically vulnerable unit when compared to all other units. Although the educational levels of both parents were comparable in two parent homes, the fathers on an average earned wages significantly higher than that of the mothers who worked. Eighty-five percent of these mothers worked outside of the home. Mothers in two parent homes earned $12,133 and fathers earned $19,919, with a combined average income of $33,000.

This was a geographically stable sample, as both mothers and fathers in the sample lived most of their lives generally in the middle Atlantic area (48%) and in the South (23%). The subjects were mostly the children of migrants from the South who had moved to the metropolitan Baltimore-Washington area and they had remained in close proximity to their families. These families had not been as mobile as reported in areas of white middle class families, probably because of more limited occupational opportunities and preferences for proximity to kin.

Socioeconomic status. Although all of the parents had been identified as middle class in the Census tracts, a systematic reassessment of their SES was made. The Hollingshead scale, often used in research, places greater emphasis on the occupation than on the education of the individual. This form was not felt to be satisfactory for black adults, who often are unable to obtain jobs appropriate to their education (Scanzoni & Scanzoni, 1976). Discrimination against blacks has consistently meant that employment status is determined more by race than educational attainment. Concurrently, Heiss (1975) stated that the usual methods of controlling for SES will not result in comparable groups when compared across racial groups. Heiss found that in his nationwide study blacks and whites, equal in the number of years of education, were not equal in earning power. He used a technique of combining education, occupation of main wage earner, and family income to determine status. Therefore, each parent was coded that standard way, and then reverse coded as suggested by Baldwin (Note 4), giving more weight to education. Specifically, the Hollingshead factor loading of occupation (7) and education (4) scores were reversed. The modified SES scoring presented similar patterns to the standard SES scoring (in parentheses), but the modified scoring placed more in the higher status: Class I-51% (43); Class II-39% (47), and Class III-10% (10). This supported the contention that black adults are not able to maintain employment commensurate with their level of education.

When the parents were asked to rate their own status using any criteria that made sense to them, as a group they rated themselves as lower than they actually were when outside criteria were applied. Few (7%) saw themselves as upper class, while most saw themselves as middle class (74%), and some (19%) saw themselves as working class. They also rated their neighbors as similar to themselves. The majority rated their parents as solid working class (68%). One-fourth (26%) had well educated parents; a few had parents whom they had rated as lower (4%) or upper class (2%). The majority of their grandparents were rated as working class (72%). Some were poverty stricken (16%) and only a few were middle class (11%).

Results

Stress Levels

The stress measurement indicated a high and continuing level of stress for the family members. The majority of the families had experienced significant life changes within the past two years. The families in the present study had stressful life changes that were in the moderate range. Their mean score of life change units over two years was 247.93, indicating that the parents had experienced a good deal of stress. Holmes and Rahe (1967) found that 51% of the individuals in their study within this score range were likely to develop a major illness associated with this moderate continuing level of stress. Additionally, these parents appeared to have recently experienced greater stress than expected. In the most recent six month period they experienced a sufficiently high level of stress to obtain a mean score of 103.65. Parents reported that they had experienced a mean of 10.96 such events over two years, and 4.98 of them in just the past six months. This would indicate, assuming accuracy of reporting, an increasingly tense environment for these families. If this high rate of stress continued at this accelerated level over the next year and a half, these families would be near the top of Holmes' major stress category.

One parent families, who had significantly lower income levels, experienced more intense stress than two-parent families ($t(159) = 2.54, p < .01$). Not only were the life changes of a more severe nature, they also occurred with greater frequency ($t(159) = 3.05, p < .003$). The family units with the fewest financial resources and with fewer adults to care for the children were being bombarded with more stress inducing events. All of the single mothers and fathers were employed.

Socioeconomic Status and Stress

A comparison was made of stress by present SES status. No significant differences in intensity or frequency were found on stress scores of families who were rated as upper class compared to those who were rated middle class. There also were no income differences between families which were rated high or low in stress.

In two parent homes it would appear that the socioeconomic status of the father in the home is closely related to stress. The group with the *lowest* stress had the highest average income, highest, occupational status, and highest education of the father. It also had the *lowest* level of maternal employment (76%) outside of the home. In contrast, the group with the *highest* stress scores had the lowest status in income, occupation, and education. This highly stressed group also had the highest level of maternal employment (89%).

The sample was divided using the median stress score into two groups for analysis: those with high and those with low stress. No income differences were found between these two groups. There were no SES differences between either the mothers or the fathers of the high and low stress group.

Upward Mobility Patterns and Stress

It was anticipated that stress would be greater for families who experienced a change in social status than for those who remained socially stable for several generations, but this was not supported. Those who experienced a mobility change did not report more stress than others who had been middle class for one or more generations. In fact, there was a strong tendency ($F(3,106 = 2.58, p < .057$) for the families who had been middle class for three generations to report higher stress ($M = 318.24$) than those whose families had risen in status from poverty to working to middle class, over three generations ($M = 140.85$). The evidence of high stress of the families who were middle class was shown in their significantly higher stress level for six months ($F(3,106 = 2.65, p < .05$). In just six months these families had experienced great stress ($M = 133.24$) that was almost equivalent to the two year ($M = 150-199$) mild stress range of the Holmes and Rahe scale. The third generation group had experienced intense stress ($M = 133.47$) that was much greater than the other groups (newly mobile $M = 90.46$; mobile in parents' generation $M = 59.27$; mobile in each generation $M = 58.86$). Yet the frequency of stressful events was similar for all groups. They had the same amount of stress but their stressful events were more severe during the previous six months. Because the frequency data were based on fathers, the mothers' family role was excluded. When mother's family of orientation were examined alone by mobility pattern, their stress during the previous six months was also significantly higher for those in third generation middle class families ($M = 140.35$). Stress in the maternal line was very low in those whose parents were upwardly mobile ($M = 56.90$; $F(3.106) = 2.65, p < .05$). On both maternal and paternal mobility lines, those who became middle class in the previous generation had experienced more stress.

Maternal Employment and Stress

The level of the employment of the mothers outside the homes was similar in both the high and low stress groups. Fifty percent of the mothers worked full-time and 10% worked part-time outside of the home.

While there was no difference based on maternal employment and stress levels, some very interesting patterns were found in the maternal grandmother's employment outside of the home and the stress levels that these families are now experiencing. Women who were now in families with low stress had mothers who had provided them with the role model of a working mother. Significantly more of the maternal grandmothers of the low stressed families worked than the maternal grandmothers of families who were now under intense stress ($X^2(6) = 12.35, p < .02$). In addition, more of the grandmothers of the low stressed families were in higher skilled or managerial level jobs than the grandmothers of the highly stressed families.

Another interesting picture obtained was that of the fathers of the women who were now in highly stressed families. While their mothers had comparatively lower status jobs, their fathers had significantly higher status jobs than those of the families under low stress ($X^2(4) = 10.98, p < .03$). It could be that the higher status of the father resulted in higher income, thus allowing the mother more of a choice to work or to stay home. More of them, therefore, may have stayed home and did not provide the image of a working mother to their daughters. These same daughters are now in a situation of having to work to maintain their middle class status. They may not have been able to assimilate the juggling skills or coping strategies which allowed the daughters of employed women to stay ahead of their multiple roles. This assessment is further corroborated by the subjective impressions that each interviewer made after leaving the home. Significantly more of the homes in the high stressed group were described as being "cluttered" by the interviewers ($x^2(3) = 11.23, p, < .01$). This could be a reflection of the extent to which the mother was overwhelmed.

Another finding was the statistically significant difference between high and low stressed mothers in two parent homes in the ages of their children and type of child care used when the mother was employed ($X^2(6) = 10.01, p < .03$). Mothers under greater stress were working and had younger children. Levels of stress were associated with ages of the children. One-third of the low stressed, compared to one-fourth of high stressed, had no need for child care because their children were in school all day. The high stress group had the extra problems of finding and keeping adequate child care, plus the added cost of this care. More highly stressed (20%) than low (11%) used relatives for day care. One-third of each group used paid sitters. More than twice as many low stressed families (18%) compared to high (7%) used day care or nurseries for child care during work. The stressed mothers had more children who needed care and used relatives rather than day care.

Kin assisted more in child care when parents faced significant life changes. The stress of the families may be increased when children are younger, more dependent, and therefore requiring more primary care. The reliance on kin did not appear to be because of financial need, since both groups had similar incomes but rather that the care of children was indicative of the concern of the kin network for a member in need. No difference in child care were found for social occasions.

65

The Holmes and Rahe scale does not include a dimension for stress associated with racism and discrimination that is a continuing component of the ecology of black existence. Undoubtedly, the addition of such a scale would have brought these families well into the major stress range, for many of the parents reported that they felt extra stress because they were black. Based on self reports, they felt that at work insidious and sometimes overt discrimination interfered with their career development. They reported that they continually were forced to act as a buffer between their children and their teachers and community institutions. They related small events that were not perceived as serious in another context, such as being treated harshly by a store clerk, but which led to feelings of rage when they became regular occurrences across many settings.

Because the positive association between stress, illness, and reduced life span has been well documented, the parents were asked to respond to the statement that "on the average, blacks die ten years earlier than non-blacks." The majority (97%) agreed with the statement. They gave several reasons why they felt this differential in life span existed. The major reason (38%) was that the psychological and social pressures of racism in their everyday environment was the greatest contributor to black stress. They also argued that forces beyond their control in their environment were an additional critical factor behind blacks having high levels of stress and shorter life expectancies. A sense of powerlessness on the racial issue as expressed by one parent:

> They cut off expectations. I mean no matter how good you are, you will always be a nigger. Hey, that puts strains on people. I mean you can be smart, have a lot of bread, but you know that you will not be able to give your children or yourself an equal chance and this takes its toll. A lot of really good blacks, that have a lot on the ball, end up on dope, alcohol, or one thing or another. I mean everyone that I know has one of these problems because of this racist society. Let me

tell you, I do not have any hope for the future.

The stress from a sense of powerlessness and frustration has an effect on their parenting. Parents are still being forced to provide conflicting messages to their children in relation to the American dream. They looked upon education as the tool for mobility but did not expect to get the full benefit for their efforts. They, therefore, tended to be more protective of their children and act as a buffer to help the children develop their potential while maintaining feelings of self-worth.

No significant differences on race related stress were found between urban and suburban respondents, but the surburban parents tended to be more concerned with discrimination (25%) than those in the city (17%). Suburban black families were living in a more integrated environment and they interacted to a greater extent with non-blacks. This could expose them to more abrasive attitudes and behavioral cues that could be perceived to be discriminatory. Likewise, the lack of stress and degree of comfort felt within all black settings was one of the reasons given for preferences for all black social interactions.

Parents under greater stress were more involved in integrated or almost all white groups. Lower stress parents were more active in all black activities. These lower stress parents appeared to be attempting to maintain a balance between their aspirations of upward mobility and economic stability, while not electing the option of total assimilation into the dominant culture. No particularly racial ideology appeared dominant. They felt that their culture was ignored for the most part by schools and the media and that it was too important an element to allow to disappear. Many were actively involved with their families and friends in organizations that reinforced their culture. They also indicated that the dominant culture had not given Afro-American ethnicity the valid recognition that other cultural groups had received.

Stress and Kin Help Exchange

The sample families were undergoing significant changes in their lives that, when added to the ever present strain provided by racism, required that a continuing level of internal and external support be provided for them. The strains faced by these families led to their continued involvement in the cultural pattern of the kin help system. It would follow that parents undergoing greater stress would be more involved in the kin help system than those who were under less stress. The families under high stress appeared to be more dependent on the kin network and interacted more frequently with relatives. While high and low stress families lived similar distances from their relatives, the frequency of contact was much higher for those under high stress ($X^2(5)$ = 12.12, p < .03). Of the mothers under high stress, 42% saw relatives about twice a week, while low stressed families tended to see relatives about twice a month. Only 29% of those in the low stress category interacted with relatives twice a week. Fathers under more stress also indicated greater contact with family members. Since the broad family network is called upon more during stress, they, therefore, would have greater involvement with kin during that period. Active participation within their ethnic cultural groups had become an important stress absorbing factor.

The low stress families received less help and the high stress families received help in many more areas ($X^2(2)$ = 7.64, p < .02). Of the low stress families 54% received no help, but only 26% of the high stress received no help from relatives. High stress families (65%) tended to receive more help in more different areas than low stress families (43%). The real difference in help received was in child care for the high stress families in spite of the fact that both groups had the same level of maternal employment.

The reciprocity inherent in kin support did not appear to differ between family stress level groups for help or money given to them. The mothers under high stress (62%) did feel more obligated than low stress mothers (39%) to help other members of the wider family who were not as fortunate as they were ($X^2(2)$ = 10.16 p < .01). Because their interaction was more intense, and because they had received greater assistance in many areas, the obligations to help those in need were great.

Friends were an active part of their support networks. They actively exchanged help with their friends. Both high and low stress groups received the same amount and type of help. When asked to evaluate the contacts that they had with their friends, high stress families (81%) felt their contact was just right while 39% of the low stress families felt their contact was too little with friends ($X^2(2)$ = 6.61, p < .04). Mothers held similar attitudes about obligations, but high stress fathers felt a greater obligation to repay for help given by their friends ($X^2(2)$ = 7.11, p < .02). The greater frequency of contact of high stress may indicate that there was a greater dependency with friends when undergoing changes. The level of stress for these parents was related to the intensity of involvement with kin, giving support to the concept of a cultural pattern of preference of black families for reliance on kin rather than institutions when in need.

Family Supportive Needs

The ecology of the black family predisposes it to continuing stress with little chance of changing; therefore, all of the family's internal cultural supports will continue to be functional and depended upon. Because their kin are in even more vulnerable situations and will not always be able to provide the needed support, external programs will need to be provided. For this reason the parents' utilization of and attitudes toward existing programs were explored, along with the kind of support they would like to have in light of their family's present situation and the stress they have faced in the immediate past.

In light of the high rate of mobility, change, and stressful events these families had experienced in the past few years, they were asked to consider how they had handled problems in the past and what external support they needed from community agencies. The interviewers asked them to think for a minute about the crises they had faced in the past few years and tell how they met them. When crises occurred, the majority of the families went first to their family and discussed it, and then they made a decision (62%). The second most frequent response was to "think about it myself, stay calm, and do what was needed" (23%). Five percent indicated that they would get outside help. Only one family indicated that they were unable to cope and one said they go to nobody outside of the family. Nine percent in-

67

dicated that their family had not met a crisis.

Both surburban and urban families had similar reactions in going to the family first for help. More of the suburban families (30%) worked out their problems by themselves, as compared to the urban ones (18%). More urban (7%) got outside help than suburban (2%). The suburban families, all of whom had lived there only a few years, had faced crises, but 15% of the urban families, who had been established for nine or more years, had not faced a crisis. The family network system had helped most in crises, followed by taking the situation in one's own hands. Fewer urban families had faced crises, and tended to be more willing to seek outside help. Families differed depending on urban and suburban residence. Urban families needed more help in meeting their family's basic needs of health, education, recreation and child care but were comfortable in a predominantly black environment. Suburban families with seemingly more resources available to them were under greater financial strain. They appeared also to be reacting to their minority status by seeking greater involvement within the black social community and were particularly sensitive to the race of the provider of these need related services.

Conclusions

The families in the present study were high achievers who valued education, were under a continuing moderate degree of stress, and were acutely aware of the impact of racism on their lives and on their children. The resultant picture is one in which families with greater resources were facing fewer stressful changes. The higher socioeconomic level plus the greater availability of the mother as a full time homemaker appear to be associated with less stress. It is impossible to say exactly what the causal factor is. Did having fewer resources mean that stressful change could not be prevented? Or did stressful changes result because of the underemployment of the fathers, thus requiring more mothers to work, which then made families less prepared for change when it did come?

In spite of the stress and the frequency of changes in their lives, the sample families exhibited a high level of satisfaction with their family life situations. They were aware of the limits placed on them personally by discrimination and had no expectation that this situation would change in the next few generations, if ever. They felt that they had achieved against great odds and therefore felt satisfaction with their lot, especially in relation to their reference group of the wider black community.

It had been anticipated that the families in the second and third generations of middle class status would have higher present status and lower stress because of the head start they had been provided by the greater resources of their families. Instead it was found that they had the lowest achieved status and the highest level of stress. They also were found to have achieved much less than the earlier two generations of their families. Meanwhile, those who were highest in status and were lowest in stress were from those families who had been upwardly mobile in each of the past three generations. Their grandparents had been born in abject poverty, their parents had moved to stable working class status, and they had moved into middle class status as the direct result of their own effort and achievements.

This unexpected mobility difference appears to be the result of the decisions made by those who were born middle class which resulted in lower levels of education and, therefore, income and status. This required the mothers to work, limiting their choices relevant to employment vs. parenting. The result was role overload. These women also had been raised by women who did not work and they may not have been prepared for their multiple roles.

What then are the implications for mothers in one parent families? In the present study their incomes were lower and they had had no choice about working. They did not have another person with whom to share the child rearing tasks and they experienced greater stress. Those with the greatest needs had the fewest resources. Their supportive needs would likely be greater and would require the family and community programs to absorb more of their stress. In a period of changing priorities and economic instability, they will likely find it more difficult to gather the needed resources from outside of the family.

Consistent with the findings of Stack (1975) and the cultural patterns presented by Hill (1971), the extended families of the sample respondents were a source of emotional and instrumental strength, especially during periods of high stress. The "kin insurance policies" were very active because goods and services flowed in both directions between mobile and non-mobile family members. The serial reciprocal obligations to kin were not felt to be excessive, but were felt more strongly by the more recently upwardly mobile. While the pattern of obligation existed, it was not as severe as in Stack's poverty level families and was, therefore, not a serious drain on the family's resources.

The main finding on family supportive needs was that black families studied preferred not to seek help outside of their wider family because they felt community agencies were unsympathetic to their unique stresses, and because of the tradition of reliance upon family members. External support from existing community agencies appeared to be requested only after no internal solution could be found or internal resources were exhausted. The parents indicated that their ideal family support systems would involve an extensive counseling program for both personal, marital, and financial matters that would augment family support. They needed to augment rather than replace the help exchange, to allow families to absorb their own stress as much as possible.

Agencies should also be sensitive to the variety of differences in preferences for same or opposite race counselors and should provide the necessary alternatives of both black and white staff. Policy makers and program planners will need to be sensitive to demographic differences and allow program sensitivity and flexibility to meet blacks' unique needs.

The stress absorbing systems used to protect the family unit in a hostile setting—kin help exchange, shared parenting, and maternal employment—were all operational for these families. These ethnic cultural patterns were not eliminated when the families became mobile, but contributed to the maintenance of achievements. The extended kin exchange patterns had continued with more help being provided to those in more precarious situations. The families under greater stress had reached out beyond the nuclear family to receive help

from their relatives and friends. These exchanges of help, emotional support, and active involvement within the social and cultural life of their communities had become crucial stress absorbing approaches for the families studied.

REFERENCE NOTES

1. Levine, I., & Giordano, J. "Informal coping system and the family." Paper presented at Consultation on Strengthening American Families through the Use of Informal Support Systems, Wingspread Center, Racine, Wisconsin, April 19, 1978.
2. Harrison, A. "Components of family survival." Paper presented at symposium, The Black Family: Survival Organization, annual meeting of the Association of Black Psychologists, Chicago, August 14, 1976.
3. Glick, P., & Mills, K. Black families: Marriage patterns and living arrangements. Bureau of the Census, U.S. Department of Commerce, 1974. Paper published in proceedings of W.E.B. DuBois' conference on American Blacks, Atlanta, October 3-5, 1974.
4. Baldwin, C. "Comparison of mother-child interaction at different ages and in families of different education levels and ethnic backgrounds." Paper presented at annual meeting of Society for Research in Child Development, Philadelphia, 1973.

REFERENCES

Billingsley, A. Black families in white America. Englewood Cliffs, NJ: Prentice-Hall, 1968.
Bradburn, N., & Caplovitz, D. Reports on happiness: A pilot study of behavior related to mental health. NORC Monograph in Social Research #3 Chicago: Aubine Publishing Co., 1965.
Glick, P. American families. New York: Wiley & Sons, 1957
Gurin, G., Veroff, J., & Feld, S. Americans view their mental health: A nationwide study. New York: Basic, 1960.
Heiss, J. The case of the black family: A social inquiry. New York: Columbia University Press, 1975.
Hill, R. The strength of black families. New York: Emerson Hall, publishers, 1971.
Holmes, T. H., & Rahe, R. H. The social readjustment rating scale. Journal of Psychosomatic Research, 1967, 11, 213-218.
Mack, D. The power relationship in black families and white families. Journal of Personality and Social Psychology, 1974, 30, 409-413.
McAdoo, H. Factors related to stability in upwardly mobile black families. Journal of Marriage and the Family, 1978, 40 (4), 761-776.

Mindel, C., & Habenstein, R. *Ethnic families in America.* New York: Elsevier, 1977.

Nobles, W. Toward an empirical and theoretical framework for defining black families. *Journal of Marriage and the Family,* 1978 40(4), 679-690.

Scanzoni, L., & Scanzoni, J. *Men, women, and change: A sociology of marriage and family.* New York: McGraw-Hill, 1976.

Stack, C. *All our kin: Strategies for survival in a black community.* New York: Harper & Row, 1975.

Staples, R. *The black family: Essays and studies.* Belmont,CA.: Wadsworth, 1971.

U.S. Bureau of the Census. Social and economic status of the black population in the United States: An historical view, 1790-1978. Washington D.C.: U.S. Government Printing Office, 1979.

70

Child Development, February 1998, Volume 69, Number 1, Pages 1-12

The Life Course as Developmental Theory

Glen H. Elder, Jr.

The pioneering longitudinal studies of child development (all launched in the 1920s and 1930s) were extended well beyond childhood. Indeed, they eventually followed their young study members up to the middle years and later life. In doing so, they generated issues that could not be addressed satisfactorily by available theories. These include the recognition that individual lives are influenced by their ever-changing historical context, that the study of human lives calls for new ways of thinking about their pattern and dynamic, and that concepts of human development should apply to processes across the life span. Life course theory has evolved since the 1960s through programmatic efforts to address such issues.

INTRODUCTION

A central premise ties together the studies presented in this article: *the notion that changing lives alter developmental trajectories.* I address the developmental relevance of these social pathways in the life course, beginning with findings based on *Children of the Great Depression* (Elder, 1974) and their theoretical meaning for life course study and developmentalists in general. Next I turn to the challenges we have pursued over recent decades and the responses that have fostered advances in life course theory. I conclude with some developmental implications of successive life transitions, from the early years to later life.

Empirical Origins

During the late 1920s and early 1930s, three pioneering longitudinal studies of children were launched at the University of California, Berkeley: the Oakland Growth Study (birth years 1920–1921), under the direction of the late Harold and Mary Jones; the Berkeley Guidance Study (birth years 1928–1929), directed by the late Jean Macfarlane; and the Berkeley Growth Study (also 1928–1929), managed by the late Nancy Bayley. No one could have imagined at the time what this collective effort would mean for an emerging field of child development. From their Berkeley Institute of Child Welfare (now called Human Development), the investigators saw few other projects engaged in studying children over time. The modest beginning established by these studies represents a key event in the remarkable growth of longitudinal research, centered on human development across the life course.[1]

1. An account of the three longitudinal studies at the Institute of Human Development can be found in volumes edited by Eichorn, Clausen, Haan, Honzik, and Mussen (1981) and by

I first encountered these studies in the early 1960s after arriving at the institute (now called Human Development) to work with John Clausen on a study of careers using data from the Oakland Growth Study. The archival records from year to year broadened my vision of lives and revealed the dramatic instability of families under changing economic conditions, the Great Depression. A good many study members could say that they were once "well off" and then "quite poor." Life histories noted frequent changes of residence and jobs, such as they were. A child in an economically deprived family who seemed "old beyond his time" recovered his youthful spirit when family income improved. Overall, the Depression children who did well in their adult years left many puzzles behind.

Such events focused my attention on ways of thinking about social change, life pathways, and individual development as modes of behavioral continuity and change. These pathways represent the most distinctive area for exploration. In my view, they refer to the social trajectories of education, work, and family that are followed by individuals and groups through society. Life transitions (e.g., entry into first grade, birth of a child) are always part of social trajectories that give them distinctive meaning and form

Jones, Bayley, Macfarlane, and Honzik (1971). One of the most important studies based on the Oakland Growth and Guidance samples following participants into adulthood was produced by Jack Block (with the assistance of Norma Haan), entitled *Lives through Time* (1971). Other major studies include Clausen's *American Lives* (1993) and Elder's *Children of the Great Depression* (1974). The growth of longitudinal studies has been documented in a number of volumes, including Cairns, Elder, and Costello (1996), Elder (1985), Magnusson and Bergman (1990), Nesselroade and Baltes (1979), and Rutter (1988).

(Elder, 1998). The multiple trajectories of individuals and their developmental implications are basic elements of the "life course," as conceptualized in research and theory.

Historical forces shape the social trajectories of family, education, and work, and they in turn influence behavior and particular lines of development. Some individuals are able to select the paths they follow, a phenomenon known as human agency, but these choices are not made in a social vacuum. All life choices are contingent on the opportunities and constraints of social structure and culture. These conditions clearly differed for children who grew up during the Great Depression and World War II. Such thinking prompted the way I studied children of the Great Depression, based on the Berkeley Institute studies. It also influenced how I proceeded to carry out a series of investigations of human life and development in different times and places—World War II and the Korean War, the Chinese Cultural Revolution, rural disadvantage in contemporary America, and inner-city poverty.

The Oakland and Berkeley cohorts were subject to the influence of other historical times, including World War II and the Korean conflict. The Oakland males were old enough to serve in World War II, whereas the younger Berkeley males typically experienced this war in terms of mobilized life on the homefront. They served mainly in the Korean War. Later in this article I draw upon accounts of such experiences, as reported in a series of papers (Elder, 1986, 1987; with Clipp [Elder & Clipp, 1988, 1989; see also Clipp & Elder, 1996]). The talented men and women in Lewis Terman's sample (born between 1903 and the 1920s) also encountered the Great Depression and World War II, but later in life (Holahan & Sears, 1995). Our studies show that this later timetable made a lasting imprint on their lives (Elder, Pavalko, & Hastings, 1991), a point well documented by the impact of World War II.

Another effort to examine the role of the state in social mobilization took us to Shanghai and a life history study of the Cultural Revolution in the lives of men and women just prior to the crisis of Tiananmen Square (Elder, Wu, & Yuan, 1993). In collaboration with the Institute of Sociology (Shanghai University) and the Carolina Population Center, we used retrospective life history methods in a survey of 1,300 adults in Shanghai during the winter and spring of 1987–1988. Especially among urban young people who were sent to peasant communities and mines, the disruptive forces and sanctions of the Cultural Revolution led to the postponement of family formation and to the loss of education and conventional career prospects. Because prospective longitudinal studies are not available on the near or distant past in developing societies, this study proved unusually valuable in showing us the effectiveness of retrospective life history techniques for recovering knowledge about the enduring effects of past events.

In the 1980s, hard times returned to rural America with a collapse of land values reminiscent of the Great Depression's jolt. This event led to collaboration with Rand Conger and colleagues at Iowa State University on a panel study of economic stress in family relationships and children's life experiences (Conger & Elder, 1994; Elder, 1992). A third of the families in this north central region of Iowa were engaged in farming, and a fifth had no exposure to agriculture, either in childhood or in their adult years. Launched in 1989, this study of 451 families drew upon analytic models in studies of "children of the Great Depression" and also extended them in fruitful ways through better documentation of the "linking" or intervening experiences and processes.

As in the Depression research, we viewed the family and its adaptations as a central link between a generalized economic decline and the well-being of children. Indebtedness, income loss, and unstable work increased the felt economic pressure of families. The stronger this reported pressure, the greater the risk of depressed feelings and marital negativity among parents. These processes tended to undermine nurturant parenting and increased the likelihood of emotional distress, academic trouble, and problem behavior among boys and girls. Countering such cumulative adversities are resourceful paths to adulthood, most commonly associated with families that have ties to the land (Elder & Conger, in press). The Iowa Youth and Families Project is currently following these children into their adult years of advanced education, family formation, and work.

At the same time, inner-city poverty became an important issue, as the rate of poverty climbed steadily higher in the neighborhoods of our large northern cities (Jargowsky, 1997; Wilson, 1987). To understand the implications of this change for minority children in particular, I joined a research team that was beginning to focus on families and young adolescents in the central city of Philadelphia. In neighborhoods that range from a poverty rate of 10% to 40%, we investigated pathways of success and trouble among African American and European American youth ($N = 487$, ages 11–14 in 1991—Elder, Eccles, Ardelt, & Lord, 1995; Furstenberg, Cook, Eccles, Elder, & Sameroff, in press). As in the Iowa study, we identified a similar process by which economic hardship adversely influenced Black and White children.

Family resources and strategies proved to be more potent in fostering successful outcomes in youth (in academic achievement, social involvement, emotional health, avoidance of problem behavior) than neighborhood influences. There were greater differences within particular neighborhoods, among families and children, than between them. In high-risk neighborhoods, we asked how parents sought to minimize children's exposure to dangers (e.g., keeping children in the house) and maximize opportunities beyond the household (e.g., involving children in recreational and education programs in the area). This project is part of a research program sponsored by the MacArthur Foundation Research Network on Successful Adolescent Development among Youth in High-Risk Settings.

Children of the Great Depression: Some Theoretical Implications

Longitudinal data at the University of California's Institute of Human Development at Berkeley contributed to these research themes and approaches by encouraging me to think holistically about lives and development over time and across changing contexts. I had to move beyond the early longitudinal projects that were known for child-based studies in single domains, such as problem behavior in the work of Jean Macfarlane (Macfarlane, Allen, & Honzik, 1954) on the Berkeley Guidance sample.

This also applied to the Oakland Growth Study (1930–1931) established by Harold Jones and Herbert Stolz. They were interested in normal growth and development, including physical maturation. Neither developmental nor health effects of the encompassing Depression crisis were on their agenda. Over 30 years later, I was privileged to use the data archive they had constructed and saw the possibility of bringing these larger contextual forces to an understanding of the lives of the Oakland men and women, then in their forties. I asked how the economic depression of the 1930s affected them as children with a background in middle- and working-class families before the economic collapse.

Members of the Oakland Study were born at the beginning of the 1920s, entered childhood during this prosperous decade, and then encountered the economic collapse as adolescents through the hardship experience of parents and relatives. Their historical location placed them at risk of this deprivational event. Some were exposed to severe hardships through the family, whereas others managed to avoid them altogether. These contrasting situations, deprived and nondeprived, established an "experi-

ment in nature" with empirical findings that affirm the principle of (1) *historical time and place:* that *the life course of individuals is embedded in and shaped by the historical times and places they experience over their lifetime.*

The full significance of this principle is clarified by comparing the adolescent experience of the Oakland cohort with that of youth who were born a decade earlier and later. For example, a large number of men and women in Lewis Terman's sample (Holahan & Sears, 1995) of highly able youth were born around 1908–1910. They entered grade school during the First World War, and most experienced the relative prosperity of middle-class life during the 1920s. The Oakland children encountered Depression hardships after a relatively secure phase of early development in the 1920s, and they left home after the worst years of the 1930s for education, work, and family.

This life pattern differed strikingly for children who were born at the end of the 1920s or during the Great Depression. A comparative group, the younger Berkeley Guidance children (born 1928–1929), experienced the vulnerable years of childhood during the worst years of the Great Depression, a period of extraordinary stress and instability (see Figure 1—Elder, 1979, 1981; Elder, Caspi, & Downey, 1986; Elder, Liker, & Cross, 1984). Their adolescence coincided with the "empty households of World War II," when parents worked from sunup to sundown in essential industry. We found that the Berkeley children were more adversely influenced by the economic collapse than were the Oakland adolescents, especially the boys.

Even within their respective cohorts, the Oakland and Berkeley study members experienced differences in the temporal order of life events. Some entered marriage before their twentieth birthday, while others were still unmarried 8 years later. Early marriage tended to produce a cumulation of life disadvantages, from socioeconomic hardship to the loss of education. Early childbearing had similar consequences. Later on in life, children of the study members left home at different times in their parents' lives. Whether relatively early or late, the timing of life transitions has long-term consequences through effects on subsequent transitions. The principle of (2) *timing in lives* states that: *the developmental impact of a succession of life transitions or events is contingent on when they occur in a person's life.*

Historical events and individual experience are connected through the family and the "linked" fates of its members. The misfortune of one member is shared through relationships. For example, Depression hardship tended to increase the explosiveness of

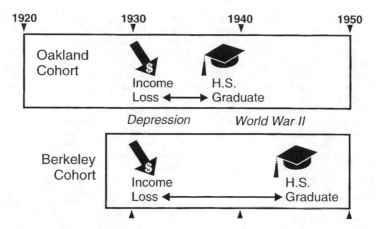

Figure 1   The different historical times of the Oakland and Berkeley cohorts

fathers who were inclined toward irritability. And the more explosive they became under economic stress, the more adversely it affected the quality of marriage and parenting. In these ways, our observations support another principle, that of (3) *linked lives: lives are lived interdependently, and social and historical influences are expressed through this network of shared relationships.*

The Great Depression brings to mind "a world out of control," and yet families often worked out successful adaptations in these circumstances. Parents and children made choices and some engaged in effective adaptations within available options and constraints. I have called this human agency. Under the mounting economic pressures of their households, mothers sought and found jobs amidst scarce options, while their children assumed responsibilities in the home and community. When hard-pressed parents moved their residence to cheaper quarters and sought alternative forms of income, they were involved in the process of "building a new life course." As expressed in this manner, the principle of (4) *human agency* states that *individuals construct their own life course through the choices and actions they take within the opportunities and constraints of history and social circumstances.*

In terms of contemporary knowledge, these early empirical observations already illustrate core principles of life course theory. I use the term "theory" to refer to a framework and orientation (Merton, 1968). Life course theory defines a common field of inquiry by providing a framework that guides research on

matters of problem identification and conceptual development. The key principles are *historical time and place, the timing of lives, linked or interdependent lives,* and *human agency.* Considerations of historical context and social timing enabled us to see how members of the Oakland and Berkeley cohorts were influenced differentially by their life experiences. Moreover, these influences could only be understood through the hardship adaptations of people who were important in their lives—through the agency and dynamic of linked lives.

As one might expect, the principle of historical time is most fully expressed today in the work of historians within the new social history who have played an important role in the development of life course studies. Especially prominent in this group is Tamara Hareven (1978, 1982, 1996), who has pioneered in the historical study of families and lives. In collaboration with her study of Manchester, NH, men, we show that both historical time *and* place (i.e., region) make a difference in life opportunities and adult careers (Elder & Hareven, 1993). Another important contribution is Modell's (1989) study of the emergence of the social institutions of adolescence (such as dating, courtship) across twentieth-century America. A productive collaboration between historians and developmentalists is reported in *Children in Time and Place* (Elder, Modell, & Parke, 1993), and includes an insightful account of ways of studying children in history (see Cahan, Mechling, Sutton-Smith, & White, 1993).

The principle of timing has been associated with

74

the work of Bernice Neugarten on adult development since the 1950s (see Neugarten, 1968; Neugarten & Datan, 1973; and Hagestad & Neugarten, 1985). In the 1960s, sociological studies of age greatly expanded our understanding of the social and individual implications of the temporal pattern of events (see Riley, Johnson, & Foner, 1972). Planned alterations in the timing of life events is one expression of the principle of human agency. People's choices on timing construct their life course (Clausen, 1993). The primacy of human agency in life course thinking has been strengthened by a number of developments, including Bandura's pioneering research on self-efficacy (Bandura, 1997) and greater knowledge of genetic influences on the selection of environments (Dunn & Plomin, 1990; Scarr & McCartney, 1983). But the chance to make certain choices depends on the opportunities and constraints of history.

The principle of linked lives is a key premise of the earliest social account of *pattern* in human lives (see Thomas & Znaniecki, 1918–1920), and it remains a cornerstone of contemporary life course theory, with its notions of role sequence and synchronization. Today the idea of linked lives is central to the ecology of human development (Bronfenbrenner, 1979) and is expressed in models of personal networks (Granovetter, 1973) and in their convoys of friends and family over time (Kahn & Antonucci, 1980). Synchronization in life planning and action refers to the coordination of lives, usually on matters of timing (Hareven, 1991). The concept of family management (Furstenberg, 1993; Sampson, 1992) generally concerns the effectiveness of life synchronization among members, along with other adaptations. A full account of these applications in life course theory and its contribution to an understanding of child development is available in Volume 1 of the new *Handbook of Child Psychology* (Elder, 1998; see also 1995, 1996).

When work began on *Children of the Great Depression* in the mid-1960s, a field of life course studies or relevant theories did not exist. The concept of life course was rarely discussed in the scholarly literature or in graduate seminars. In putting together a study of children in the Great Depression, I drew upon the ideas and research of many people in the social and behavioral sciences who were beginning to work on relevant problems, such as aging (see Elder, 1998). Though neglected at the time, these contexts of developmental relevance are now gaining appropriate visibility through multilevel studies of neighborhood and community effects in children's lives (Furstenberg et al., in press; Sampson, 1997). With advances in statistical models, we are now able to investigate

the interplay of changing behavior and personality with changing social pathways. However, it is still the case that longitudinal studies *seldom* examine the stability and nature of children's social environments over time (Sameroff, 1993, p. 8). As a result, sources of behavioral continuity and change remain poorly understood.

The work ahead is daunting, to be sure, but life course ideas on time, process, and context have continued to spread throughout the social and behavioral sciences. We find examples in both ecological and life-span developmental psychology, in the new social and cultural history of family and children, and in cultural models from anthropology and the sociology of age (see Elder, 1996, 1998; Featherman, 1983). I think of this diffusion in 'terms of research issues that were once posed many years ago by the Berkeley longitudinal studies.

Challenges to Life Course Theory

The Berkeley studies were originally designed for assessments of child development. There was no plan to follow the participants into their twenties and thirties. As they continued into adulthood and even the later years, they acquired greater theoretical significance. I see this significance in the fresh momentum they gave to the study of adult development and its implications for children's lives, along with more awareness of the correlated limitations of child-based models of growth and development.

When the study members reached adulthood, investigators had two ways of thinking about social pathways, and neither placed individuals in history. One involved the notion of careers, usually over a person's worklife. The second is known as the "life cycle"—a sequence of social roles that bear upon stages of parenthood, from the birth of children to their departure from the household and their eventual transition to the role of parent, setting in motion another life cycle.

Neither approach proved satisfactory. The career model dealt with single careers, mainly a person's work life, and thus oversimplified the lives of people who were coping with multiple roles at the same time. The large-scale entry of mothers into the labor force produced circumstances that favored a new concept of multiple, interlocking trajectories that varied in synchronization. Career perspectives also failed to incorporate notions of age-graded expectations in a systematic way and did not orient analyses to the historical context of lives across the generations.

Life cycle theory helped to contextualize people's

lives by emphasizing the social dynamic of "linked lives." These connections extend across the generations and serve to integrate young and old. Social ties to significant others become forms of social control and constraint in channeling individual decisions and actions. Socialization occurs through such networks of social relationships. Though notable, these contributions of life cycle theory did not locate people according to their life stage or historical context.

To address these limitations, studies began to draw upon the insights of a deeper knowledge of age in people's lives. The cultural content of child socialization has much to do with the learning of behaviors that are prescribed and proscribed by age. They constitute "age expectations." These cultural expectations include notions about the timing and order of transitions, such as entry into first grade, and about whether the events are early, on time, or late (Hagestad & Neugarten, 1985). Some events are "out of order" according to conventional expectations, such as births before marriage. Ill-timed or off-timed events (too late or too early) can have adverse effects. In addition, birth year orients analysis to people in specific historical locations, and thus according to particular changes. Consider Americans who were born in the late 1930s. They avoided the generalized pressures of family stress and deprivation, but faced another risk—that of the absence and loss of father during the Second World War.

Children of the Great Depression (Elder, 1974) brought the *life cycle model* together with an *age-based concept of timing* in a framework on the life course. Neither perspective was adequate by itself. In the life cycle approach, the notion of "linked lives" enabled us to understand how Depression hardship influenced children through the family. And it proved helpful in thinking about socialization and the role sequences of adult life. But age distinctions were needed to locate families in history and to mark the transitions of adult life. The meanings of age brought a perspective on "timing" to the study.

A more recent study also shows the insights of a life course model that incorporates ideas of career, life cycle, and age, as expressed in the core principles of timing and linked lives. Among African American families in Los Angeles, Burton (1985; see also Burton & Bengtson, 1985) found that the timing of a young daughter's birth had repercussions well into the grandparent generation. A birth in early adolescence multiplied strains and deprivations, reflecting the violation of deep-seated expectations about "how life should be lived." The young mothers expected their own mothers to help care for their child, but this expectation seldom materialized because they felt "too young" for the grandmother role. As a mother put it, "I can't be a young momma and a grandmomma at the same time."

In this study, the birth of a child defines a life transition, but transitions are frequently a succession of choice points (see Figure 2). In fact, the transition to motherhood in adolescence can be thought of as a *multiphasic process* in which each phase is linked to a choice point. Young girls may choose to engage in premarital sex or not, or to use contraception or not, to seek an abortion or not, and to marry the father or not. Only a handful of options lead to a birth out of wedlock. Not too long ago, unwed motherhood was viewed simply as *one* transition, a concept that obscured appropriate points of preventive intervention along the life course.

What are the consequences of a childbirth that occurs much too early according to expectations? One life course interpretation stresses the *cumulation of disadvantages*—a concatenation of negative events and influences. Birth of a child to an early adolescent may result in the early termination of schooling, with its negative implications for employment. Whether disadvantages cumulate or not depends on the new mother's response to her circumstance. In a Baltimore longitudinal study of African American generations (Furstenberg, Brooks-Gunn, & Morgan, 1987), young mothers who could stay in school through the childcare provided by their mother or who married the father were able to minimize the long-term disadvantage of an ill-timed birth.

As life course theory advanced, it provided a framework for studies that relate social pathways to history and developmental trajectories. In any longitudinal study, the mere step of locating parents in history through their birth year can generate historical insights that would not be achieved otherwise. Consider what we have learned about Lewis Terman's sample of gifted Californians who were born between 1900 and the 1920s (Holahan & Sears, 1995). Selected as the upper 1% of age peers at 19, these "best and brightest" seemed to be invulnerable to the misfortunes of history. However, the twentieth century proved to be no respecter of their high ability (Shanahan, Elder, & Miech, 1997). Men born before 1911 ended up with college degrees and no place to go in the stagnant economy of the 1930s. Their alternative in many cases was to stay in school, piling up degrees. Indeed, they ended up better educated than the younger men, but aspirations had little to do with their achievement.

Life course theory provides a way to study the myriad changes that bear upon children in today's world (see Hernandez, 1993). These include (1) the

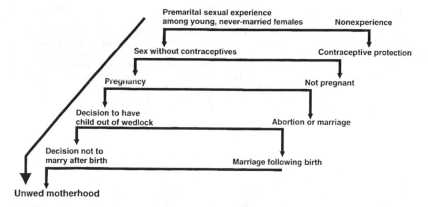

Figure 2   The life course of unwed motherhood

restructuring of the economy through downsizing and other strategies, as expressed through community and family disruption and hardship; (2) the family consequences of expanding levels of economic inequality; (3) the implications of change in the welfare system for children and young families; (4) the concentration of poverty and crime in the inner city; and (5) the redesign of schools and learning through information-age technology. All epochs of social change call for approaches to child development that view children in their changing ecologies. The motivating question focuses on the process by which a particular change is expressed in the way children think, feel, and behave.

More concepts of development are at work today in studies across the life course, and projects are assessing the developmental impact of changing pathways in changing times.[2] The challenge involves the

2. These challenges to life course theory and analysis—thinking about lives, human development, and their relation to changing times—are a large part of the story, but they should be combined with the task of establishing concepts of development that apply across the life course, a major item on the agenda of developmental life-span psychology (Baltes, Lindenberger, & Staudinger, 1998). In "The Life Course and Human Development" (Elder, 1998), I discuss the convergence of these strands in contemporary life course theory. Paul Baltes has been most involved over the years in the development of life-span concepts. In his writings, selection, optimization, and compensation mechanisms aim to minimize the impact of organismic losses and maximize gains. Thus, children may select activities in which they are successful, whether sports or music, and optimize benefits through an investment of time, energy, and relationships. In old age, the musician might restrict the number of pieces and practice more often to compensate for declining physical skill.

analysis of "interlocking trajectories" that connect changing environments with behavioral changes. Consider the following: Using growth curve models, a longitudinal study found that increasing negative life events contributed significantly to the widely documented rise in depressed feelings among girls during early adolescence, especially in the absence of parental warmth (Ge, Lorenz, Conger, Elder, & Simons, 1994). No such effect was observed among boys. In another research example that parallels *Children of the Great Depression* (1974), a nationwide longitudinal study found that mounting economic hardship in families significantly increased the antisocial tendencies and depressed feelings of boys and girls (McLeod & Shanahan, 1996). This type of work provides merely a sampling of the new life course studies.

Transition experiences represent a strategic approach to the possibilities of studying *lives in motion.* Transitions make up life trajectories, and they provide clues to developmental change. The process by which this occurs is captured by the lasting effect of early transitions, my concluding topic.

Transition Experiences in Changing Lives

Early transitions can have enduring consequences by affecting subsequent transitions, even after many years and decades have passed. They do so, in part, through behavioral consequences that set in motion "cumulating advantages and disadvantages." Individual differences are minimized in life transitions when the new circumstances resemble a "total institution" that presses from all angles toward a particular behavior (Caspi & Moffitt, 1993, pp. 265–266). One transition with such impact is military service, a common event for young men in the Oakland and Berkeley studies.

Nine out of 10 males from the Oakland Growth Study served in the military, as did over 70% of the Berkeley Guidance males, most of whom came from economically deprived households in the 1930s (Elder, 1986, 1987). Veterans who entered the service immediately after high school fared better in psychological health and life achievement than nonveterans, regardless of preservice background. This "early entry" occurred before adult careers and thus became a formative influence. In large part, military service accounts for why many "children of the Great Depression" did well in their lives. Three functions of the service offer essential details of this developmental process.

First, military mobilization tends to pull young people from their past, however privileged or deprived, and in doing so creates new beginnings that favor developmental change. This transition, as a Berkeley veteran noted, provided a "passage into manliness."

Second, military service establishes a clear-cut break from the age-graded career, a time-out in which to sort matters and make a new beginning. For another Berkeley veteran, the army "was a place to be for a while, a place for sorting out self."

Third, military service offers a wide range of new experiences for personal growth from group processes, training, and travel. Almost overnight, young men were placed in demanding leadership roles. The G.I. Bill for advanced education was also part of this developmental regime.

Experiences of this kind do not exhaust all features of military service, but they collectively shaped a "developmental turning point" for youth from disadvantaged circumstances. One pathway involved situational changes that made early entrants more ambitious, assertive, and self-directed by mid-life (Elder, 1986). Another pathway led to extensive use of the educational and housing benefits of the G.I. Bill. These trajectories literally changed the kind of parents, husbands, and workers the men became. In this manner, the life change of veterans has special relevance to their children's well-being, a problem explored by Lois Stolz (1954) in the aftermath of World War II.

This research posed important questions regarding the nature of change and continuity in life-span development. Some Guidance Study men experienced dramatic change in their life course, what I describe as a "turning point." The military placed them in a total institution, and the resulting change established a trajectory of greater competence (Clausen, 1995; Rutter, 1996). In other cases, stress symptoms persisted, especially from war combat (Elder & Clipp, 1989). They may have done so through interactions with others that recreated the "trauma" situation or from the progressive cumulation of behavioral consequences (see Caspi, Bem, & Elder, 1989). Explosiveness born of a war experience may elicit responses that legitimize and reinforce such "disruptive" dispositions.

A more complete account of the change mechanisms is presented by a panel study of approximately 1,000 boys from low-income areas of Boston who grew up in the 1920s and 1930s (Sampson & Laub, 1996; see also 1993). More than 70% served in the military. The matched control design of delinquents and controls was originally used for a longitudinal study of delinquency by Sheldon and Eleanor Glueck (Glueck & Glueck, 1968), pioneers in research on juvenile delinquency. Men in both samples generally entered World War II at the age of 18 or 19. Most served at least 2 years and overseas.

As expected, the delinquents were more involved in dishonorable discharges and other forms of official misconduct, but they were also more likely to benefit from the service over their life course, when compared to the controls. And this was especially true for men who entered the service early. These men were young enough to take advantage of such experience through in-service schooling, overseas duty, and the G.I. Bill. In particular, benefits of the G.I. Bill were notably greater for veterans with a delinquent past when they entered the service at a young age. All of these experiences enhanced occupational status, job stability, and economic well-being up to the middle years, independent of childhood differences and socioeconomic origins.

As a whole, these findings provide consistent support for an "early timing hypothesis" on the life course advantages of military service. When military service begins shortly after high school, its training, developmental, and resource advantages are most likely to enhance educational opportunities (e.g., the G.I. Bill) and occupational advancement (e.g., officer training). Later entry, by contrast, is more likely to pull men and women out of adult roles, disrupting their life course. Persistent disadvantages appear among veterans who entered the Second World War at a very late age—in their thirties.

Effects of this kind were observed among California men in Lewis Terman's study of highly able children (Elder, Shanahan, & Clipp, 1994). The older cohort of men hit both the Depression and war years at "an untimely point" in their lives. They tended to follow a path of life-long disadvantage into the later years, when compared to the younger men (Elder & Chan, in press). They suffered more work instability, earned less income over time, experienced a higher rate of divorce, and were at greater risk of an accelerated decline in physical health by their fifties.

"Timeliness," then, represents an important determinant of enduring military influences from the 1940s and its expression in veterans' lives. The service was indeed a bridge to greater opportunity for many, given appropriate timing.

Reflections

In thinking back to the early 1960s at the Berkeley Institute of Human Development, it would be difficult for any of us to appreciate the research challenge of the longitudinal studies. The institute psychologists were students of child development at a time when the study members were entering their middle years. Child-based models of development had little to offer research accounts of the adult years, their pathways, and turning points.

These were the kinds of issues that I recall in exchanges over case histories at the time. The childhood poverty of some adults in the Oakland Growth Study did not square with their high achievements and good health at mid-life. Jean Macfarlane (1963), director of the Berkeley Guidance Study, also noted in the early 1960s that a number of boys in the Guidance Study turned out to be more stable and productive adults than the staff had expected.

Members of the Oakland Growth and Berkeley Guidance studies are "children of the Great Depression," but the central theme of their lives is not the harsh legacy of a deprived family through enduring limitations. It is not the long arm of a Depression childhood. Rather, it is the story of how so many women and men successfully overcame disadvantage in their lives. Some rose above the limitations of their childhood through military service, others through education and a good job, and still others through the nurturing world of family.

These accomplishments amidst adversity were not gained without personal costs, a point that John Clausen (1993) has made so eloquently in *American Lives*. War stresses continue to reverberate through the lives of some combat veterans, though a good many have "learned to manage" (Elder & Clipp, 1988; Hendin & Haas, 1984). Women on the homefront kept families together while working long hours. Other women survived family abuse and have

coped effectively with the stresses of life. Life success can be assessed partly in these terms. Jean Macfarlane (1963, 1971) may have had this in mind some years ago when she spoke about the maturing experience of working through the pain and confusion of life.

But not even great talent and industry can ensure life success over adversity without opportunities. Talented Black youth in our blighted inner cities face this reality every day. Generations of young Chinese also learned this during the Cultural Revolution when important life decisions were made by the work unit, and many thousands were sent down from the city to the rural countryside and mines. Members of this "sent-down generation" were disadvantaged in education, work careers, mate selection, and family formation (Elder, Wu, & Yuan, 1993). Talented women in the Lewis Terman study discovered this lesson when they were barred from career advancement in their chosen fields (Holahan & Sears, 1995, chap. 5). Even some Terman men found their lives going nowhere as they left college for hard times in the Great Depression and later were mobilized into World War II. The constraining realities of social systems are very real.

Life course theory and research alert us to this real world, a world in which lives are lived and where people work out paths of development as best they can. It tells us how lives are socially organized in biological and historical time, and how the resulting social pattern affects the way we think, feel, and act. All of this has something important to say about our field of inquiry. Human development is embedded in the life course and historical time. Consequently, its proper study challenges us to take all life stages into account through the generations, from infancy to the grandparents of old age.

ACKNOWLEDGMENTS

This paper was presented in abbreviated form as a presidential address at the biennial meeting of the Society for Research in Child Development, Washington, DC, April 5, 1997. I wish to express a deep sense of gratitude to many colleagues and students who have been so important in the evolution of my perspective. I am especially pleased that I could share my ideas for the essay with John Clausen before he passed away in February 1996. John brought me to the Institute of Human Development and did much to enhance my accomplishments through this research organization, as did Brewster Smith and Paul Mussen, Jean Macfarlane and Marjorie Honzik, Mary Jones and Dorothy Eichorn, Jeanne and Jack Block, among others. All of us have intellectual homes, and the institute represents one of mine across the years. My professional journey has been blessed by Urie Bronfenbrenner's mentorship. It was he who insisted that I bring my work more fully into the field of developmental science. Lastly, I am indebted to the interdisciplinary vitality of the Carolina Consortium on Human Development (Cairns, Elder, & Costello, 1996). In preparing this essay, I had the benefit of ongoing conversations with Urie Bronfenbrenner. Thanks also to many colleagues and coauthors who have read and commented on drafts of this manuscript. I gratefully acknowledge support by the National Institute of Mental Health (MH 51361, MH 43270, MH 41327, and MH 00567), a contract with the U.S. Army Research Institute, and research support from the MacArthur Foundation Research Network on Successful Adolescent Development Among Youth in High-Risk Settings.

ADDRESS AND AFFILIATION

Corresponding author: Glen H. Elder, Jr., Carolina Population Center, University of North Carolina at Chapel Hill, University Square CB# 8120, 123 West Franklin Street, Chapel Hill, NC 27516-3997; e-mail: glen_elder@unc.edu.

REFERENCES

Baltes, P. M., Lindenberger, U., & Staudinger, U. M. (1998). Life-span theory in developmental psychology. In R. M. Lerner (Ed.), W. Damon (General Ed.), *Handbook of child psychology: Vol. 1. Theoretical models of human development* (5th ed., pp. 1029–1043). New York: Wiley.

Bandura, A. (1997). *Self-efficacy: The exercise of control.* New York: W. H. Freeman.

Block, J., in collaboration with Haan, N. (1971). *Lives through time.* Berkeley, CA: Bancroft.

Bronfenbrenner, U. (1979). *The ecology of human development.* Cambridge, MA: Harvard University Press.

Burton, L. M. (1985). *Early and on-time grandmotherhood in multigenerational black families.* Unpublished doctoral dissertation, University of Southern California.

Burton, L. M., & Bengtson, V. L. (1985). Black grandmothers: Issues of timing and continuity of roles. In V. L. Bengtson & J. F. Robertson (Eds.), *Grandparenthood* (pp. 61–77). Beverly Hills, CA: Sage.

Cahan, E., Mechling, J., Sutton-Smith, B., & White, S. H. (1993). The elusive historical child: Ways of knowing the child of history and psychology. In G. H. Elder, Jr., J. Modell, & R. D. Parke (Eds.), *Children in time and place* (pp. 192–223). New York: Cambridge University Press.

Cairns, R. B., Elder, G. H., Jr., & Costello, E. J. (Eds.). (1996). *Developmental science.* New York: Cambridge University Press.

Caspi, A., Bem, D. J., & Elder, G. H., Jr. (1989). Continuities and consequences of interactional styles across the life course. *Journal of Personality, 57,* 375–406.

Caspi, A., & Moffitt, T. E. (1993). When do individual differences matter? A paradoxical theory of personality coherence. *Psychological Inquiry, 4,* 247–271.

Clausen, J. A. (1993). *American lives: Looking back at the children of the Great Depression.* New York: Free Press.

Clausen, J. A. (1995). Gender, contexts, and turning points in adults' lives. In P. Moen, G. H. Elder, Jr., & K. Lüscher (Eds.), *Examining lives in context: Perspectives on the ecology of human development* (pp. 365–389). Washington, DC: APA Press.

Clipp, E. C., & Elder, G. H., Jr. (1996). The aging veteran of World War II: Psychiatric and life course insights. In P. E. Ruskin & J. A. Talbott (Eds.), *Aging and posttraumatic stress disorder* (pp. 19–51). Washington, DC: American Psychiatric Press, Inc.

Conger, R. D., & Elder, G. H., Jr. (1994). *Families in troubled times: Adapting to change in rural America.* Hawthorne, NY: Aldine DeGruyter.

Dunn, J., & Plomin, R. (1990). *Separate lives: Why siblings are so different.* New York: Basic.

Eichorn, D. H., Clausen, J. A., Haan, N., Honzik, M., & Mussen, P. H. (Eds.). (1981). *Present and past in middle life.* New York: Academic Press.

Elder, G. H., Jr. (1974). *Children of the Great Depression: Social change in life experience.* Chicago: University of Chicago Press.

Elder, G. H., Jr. (1979). Historical change in life patterns and personality. In P. B. Baltes & O. G. Brim, Jr. (Eds.), *Life-span development and behavior* (Vol. 2, pp. 117–159). New York: Academic Press.

Elder, G. H., Jr. (1981). Social history and life experience. In D. H. Eichorn, J. A. Clausen, J. Haan, M. P. Honzik, & P. H. Mussen (Eds.), *Present and past in middle life* (pp. 3–31). New York: Academic Press.

Elder, G. H., Jr. (Ed.). (1985). *Life course dynamics: Trajectories and transitions, 1968–1980.* Ithaca, NY: Cornell University Press.

Elder, G. H., Jr. (1986). Military times and turning points in men's lives. *Developmental Psychology, 22,* 233–245.

Elder, G. H., Jr. (1987). War mobilization and the life course: A cohort of World War II veterans. *Sociological Forum, 2,* 449–472.

Elder, G. H., Jr. (1992, March). *Children of the farm crisis.* Paper presented at the meeting of the Society for Research on Adolescence, Washington, DC.

Elder, G. H., Jr. (1995). The life course paradigm: Social change and individual development. In P. Moen, G. H. Elder, Jr., & K. Lüscher (Eds.), *Examining lives in context: Perspectives on the ecology of human development* (pp. 101–139). Washington, DC: APA Press.

Elder, G. H., Jr. (1996). Human lives in changing societies: Life course and developmental insights. In R. B. Cairns, G. H. Elder, Jr., & E. J. Costello (Eds.), *Developmental science* (pp. 31–62). New York: Cambridge University Press.

Elder, G. H., Jr. (1998). The life course and human development. In R. M. Lerner (Ed.), W. Damon (General Ed.), *Handbook of child psychology: Vol. 1. Theoretical models of human development* (5th ed., pp. 939–991). New York: Wiley.

Elder, G. H., Jr., Caspi, A., & Downey, G. (1986). Problem behavior and family relationships: Life course and intergenerational themes. In A. B. Sørensen, F. E. Weinert, & L. R. Sherrod (Eds.), *Human development and the life course: Multidisciplinary perspectives* (pp. 293–340) Hillsdale, NJ: Erlbaum.

Elder, G. H., Jr., & Chan, C. (in press). War's legacy in men's lives. In P. Moen & D. Dempster-McClain (Eds.), *A nation divided: Diversity, inequality and community in American society.* Ithaca, NY: Cornell University Press.

Elder, G. H., Jr., & Clipp, E. C. (1988). Wartime losses and social bonding: Influences across 40 years in men's lives. *Psychiatry, 51,* 177–198.

Elder, G. H., Jr., & Clipp, E. C. (1989). Combat experience and emotional health: Impairment and resilience in later life. *Journal of Personality, 57,* 311–341.

Elder, G. H., Jr., & Conger, R. D. (in press). *Leaving the land: Rural youth at century's end.* Chicago: University of Chicago Press.

Elder, G. H., Jr., Eccles, J. S., Ardelt, M., & Lord, S. (1995). Inner-city parents under economic pressure: Perspectives on the strategies of parenting. *Journal of Marriage and the Family, 57,* 771–784.

Elder, G. H., Jr., & Hareven, T. K. (1993). Rising above life's disadvantages: From the Great Depression to war. In G. H. Elder, Jr., J. Modell, & R. D. Parke (Eds.), *Children in time and place: Developmental and historical insights* (pp. 47–72). New York: Cambridge University Press.

Elder, G. H., Jr., Liker, J. K., & Cross, C. E. (1984). Parent-child behavior in the Great Depression: Life course and intergenerational influences. In P. B. Baltes & O. G. Brim, Jr. (Eds.), *Life-span development and behavior* (Vol. 6, pp. 109–158). New York: Academic Press.

Elder, G. H., Jr., Modell, J., & Parke, R. D. (Eds.). (1993). *Children in time and place: Developmental and historical insights.* New York: Cambridge University Press.

Elder, Glen H., Jr., Pavalko, E. K., & Hastings, T. J. (1991). Talent, history, and the fulfillment of promise. *Psychiatry, 54,* 215–231.

Elder, G. H., Jr., Shanahan, M. J., & Clipp, E. C. (1994). When war comes to men's lives: Life course patterns in family, work, and health [Special issue]. *Psychology and Aging, 9,* 5–16.

Elder, G. H., Jr., Wu, W., & Yuan, J. (1993). *State-initiated change and the life course in Shanghai, China.* Unpublished project report.

Featherman, D. L. (1983). The life-span perspective in social science research. In P. B. Baltes & O. G. Brim, Jr. (Eds.), *Life-span development and behavior* (Vol. 5, pp. 1–57). New York: Academic.

Furstenberg, F. F., Jr. (1993). How families manage risk and opportunity in dangerous neighborhoods. In W. J. Wilson (Ed.), *Sociology and the public agenda* (pp. 231–258). Newbury Park, CA: Sage.

Furstenberg, F. F., Jr., Brooks-Gunn, J., & Morgan, S. P. (1987). *Adolescent mothers in later life.* New York: Cambridge University Press.

Furstenberg, F. F., Jr., Cook, T., Eccles, J., Elder, G. H., Jr., &

Sameroff, A. (Eds.). (in press). *Managing to make it: Urban families in high-risk neighborhoods.* Chicago: University of Chicago Press.

Ge, X., Lorenz, F. O., Conger, R. D., Elder, G. H., Jr., & Simons, R. L. (1994). Trajectories of stressful life events and depressive symptoms during adolescence. *Developmental Psychology, 30,* 467–483.

Glueck, S., & Glueck, E. (1968). *Delinquents and nondelinquents in perspective.* Cambridge, MA: Harvard University Press.

Granovetter, M. S. (1973). Strength of weak ties. *American Journal of Sociology, 78,* 1360–1380.

Hagestad, G. O., & Neugarten, B. L. (1985). Age and the life course. In R. H. Binstock & E. Shanas (Eds.), *Handbook of aging and the social sciences* (2d ed., pp. 46–61). New York: Van Nostrand Reinhold.

Hareven, T. K. (1978). *Transitions: The family and the life course in historical perspective.* New York: Academic Press.

Hareven, T. K. (1982). *Family time and industrial time.* New York: Cambridge University Press.

Hareven, T. K. (1991). Synchronizing individual time, family time, and historical time. In J. Bender & D. E. Wellbery (Eds.), *Chronotypes: The construction of time* (pp. 167–182). Stanford, CA: Stanford University Press.

Hareven, T. K. (1996). What difference does it make? *Social Science History, 20,* 317–344.

Hendin, H., & Hass, A. P. (1984). *Wounds of war: The psychological aftermath of combat in Vietnam.* New York: Basic.

Hernandez, D. J. (1993). *America's children: Resources from family, government, and the economy.* New York: Russell Sage.

Holahan, C. K., & Sears, R. R. (1995). *The gifted group in later maturity.* Stanford, CA: Stanford University Press.

Jargowsky, P. A. (1997). *Poverty and place: Ghettos, barrios, and the American city.* New York: Russell Sage.

Jones, M. C., Bayley, N., Macfarlane, J. W., & Honzik, M. H. (Eds.). (1971). *The course of human development: Selected papers from the longitudinal studies, Institute of Human Development, the University of California, Berkeley.* Waltham, MA: Xerox College Publishing.

Kahn, R. L., & Antonucci, T. C. (1980). Convoys over the life course: Attachment, roles, and social support. In P. B. Baltes & O. G. Brim, Jr. (Eds.), *Life-span development and behavior* (Vol. 3, pp. 253–286). New York: Academic Press.

Macfarlane, J. W. (1963). From infancy to adulthood. *Childhood Education, 39,* 336–342.

Macfarlane, J. W. (1971). Perspectives on personality consistency and change from the Guidance Study. In M. C. Jones, N. Bayley, J. W. Macfarlane, & M. P. Honzik (Eds.), *The course of human development: Selected papers from the longitudinal studies, Institute of Human Development, the University of California, Berkeley* (pp. 410–415). Waltham, MA: Xerox College Publishing.

Macfarlane, J. W., Allen, L., & Honzik, M. P. (1954). *A developmental study of the behavior problems of normal children between twenty-one months and fourteen years.* Berkeley: University of California Press.

Magnusson, D., & Bergman, L. R. (Eds.). (1990). *Data quality in longitudinal research.* New York: Cambridge University Press.

McLeod, J. D., & Shanahan, M. J. (1996). Trajectories of poverty and children's mental health. *Journal of Health and Social Behavior, 37,* 207–220.

Merton, R. K. (1968). *Social theory and social structure.* New York: Free Press.

Modell, J. (1989). *Into one's own: From youth to adulthood in the United States 1920–1975.* Berkeley: University of California Press.

Nesselroade, J. R., & Baltes, P. B. (Eds.). (1979). *Longitudinal research in the study of behavior and development.* New York: Academic Press.

Neugarten, B. L. (1968). *Middle age and aging: A reader in social psychology.* Chicago: University of Chicago Press.

Neugarten, B. L., & Datan, N. (1973). Sociological perspectives on the life cycle. In P. B. Baltes & K. W. Schaie (Eds.), *Life-span developmental psychology: Personality and socialization* (pp. 53–69). New York: Academic Press.

Riley, M. W., Johnson, M. E., & Foner, A. (Eds.). (1972). *Aging and society: A sociology of age stratification.* New York: Russell Sage.

Rutter, M. (Ed.). (1988). *Studies of psychosocial risk: The power of longitudinal data.* New York: Cambridge University Press.

Rutter, M. (1996). Transitions and turning points in developmental psychopathology: As applied to the age span between childhood and mid-adulthood. *International Journal of Behavioral Development, 19,* 603–626.

Sameroff, A. J. (1993). Models of development and developmental risk. In C. H. Zeanah, Jr. (Ed.), *Handbook of infant mental health* (pp. 3–13). New York: Guilford.

Sampson, R. J. (1992). Family management and child development: Insights from social disorganization theory. In J. McCord (Ed.), *Advances in criminological theory: Vol. 3. Facts, frameworks, and forecasts* (pp. 63–93). New Brunswick, NJ: Transaction Books.

Sampson, R. J. (1997, April). *Child and adolescent development in community context: New findings from a multilevel study of 80 Chicago neighborhoods.* Paper presented at the biennial meeting of the Society for Research in Child Development, Washington, DC.

Sampson, R. J., & Laub, J. H. (1993). *Crime in the making: Pathways and turning points through life.* Cambridge, MA: Harvard University Press.

Sampson, R. J., & Laub, J. H. (1996). Socioeconomic achievement in the life course of disadvantaged men: Military service as a turning point, circa 1940–1965. *American Sociological Review, 61,* 347–367.

Scarr, S., & McCartney, K. (1983). How people make their own environments: A theory of genotype → environment effects. *Child Development, 54,* 424–435.

Shanahan, M. J., Elder, G. H., Jr., & Miech, R. A. (1997). History and agency in men's lives: Pathways to achievement in cohort perspective. *Sociology of Education, 70,* 54–67.

Stolz, L. M. (1954). *Father relations of war-born children.* Stanford, CA: Stanford University Press.

Thomas, W. I., & Znaniecki, F. (1918–1920). *The Polish peasant in Europe and America* (Vols. 1–2). Urbana: University of Illinois Press.

Wilson, W. J. (1987). *The truly disadvantaged: The inner city, the underclass, and public policy.* Chicago: University of Chicago Press.

THE STORMY DECADE: FACT OR FICTION?[1]

ALBERT BANDURA

Stanford University

If you were to walk up to the average man on the street, grab him by the arm and utter the word "adolescence," it is highly probable — assuming he refrains from punching you in the nose — that his associations to this term will include references to storm and stress, tension, rebellion, dependency conflicts, peer-group conformity, black leather jackets, and the like. If you then abandoned your informal street corner experiment, and consulted the professional and popular literature on adolescence, you would become quickly impressed with the prevalence of the belief that adolescence is, indeed, a unique and stormy developmental period (Gallagher & Harris, 1958; Hurlock, 1955; Josselyn, 1948; Mohr & Despres, 1958; Parsons, 1950; Pearson, 1958).

The adolescent presumably is engaged in a struggle to emancipate himself from his parents. He, therefore, resists any dependence upon them for their guidance, approval or company, and rebels against any restrictions and controls that they impose upon his behavior. To facilitate the process of emancipation, he transfers his dependency to the peer group whose values are typically in conflict with those of his parents. Since his behavior is now largely under the control of peer-group members, he begins to adopt idiosyncratic clothing, mannerisms, lingo, and other forms of peer-group fad behavior. Because of the conflicting values and pressures to which the adolescent is exposed, he is ambivalent, frightened, unpredictable, and often irresponsible in his behavior. Moreover, since the adolescent finds himself in a transition stage in which he is neither child, nor adult, he is highly confused even about his own identity.

The foregoing storm and stress picture of adolescence receives little support from detailed information that Dr. Walters and I obtained in a study of middle class families of adolescent boys (Bandura & Walters, 1959). Let us compare the popular version of adolescence with our research findings.

Parental Restrictiveness

At adolescence, parents supposedly become more controlling and prohibitive. We found the very opposite to be true. By the time the boys had reached adolescence, they had internalized the parents' values and standards of behavior to a large degree; consequently, restrictions and external controls had been lightened as the boys became increasingly capable of assuming responsibility for their own behavior, and in directing their own activities. The parents were highly trustful of their boys' judgment and felt that externally imposed limits were, therefore, largely unnecessary. The following interview excerpts provide some typical parental replies to inquiries concerning the restrictions they placed on their boys:

> M. (Mother). I don't have to do anything like that any more.
> I think he's getting so mature now, he's sort of happy medium.
> I don't have to do much with him.

* * * *

---

[1]A revised form of this paper was presented at the televised lecture series, *The World of the Teen-Ager*, sponsored by the University of Minnesota.

I.   (Interviewer). What are some of the restrictions you have for him? How about going out at night?

F.   (Father). We trust the boy. We never question him.

I.   Are there any things you forbid him from doing when he is with his friends?

F.   At his age I would hate to keep telling him that he mustn't do this, or mustn't do that. I have very little trouble with him in that regard. Forbidding I don't think creeps into it because he ought to know at 17, right from wrong.

I.   Are there any friends with whom you have discouraged him from associating?

F.   No, not up to now. They are very lovely boys.

I.   How about using bad language?

F.   Only once, only once have I; of course I'm a little bit hard of hearing in one ear, and sometimes he gets around the wrong side and takes advantage of that.

The boys' accounts were essentially in agreement with those given by the parents. In response to our questions concerning parental demands and controls, the boys pointed out that at this stage in their development parental restraints were no longer necessary. An illustrative quotation, taken from one of the boys' interviews, is given below:

I.   What sort of things does your mother forbid you to do around the house?

B.   Forbid me to do? Gee, I don't think there's ever anything.
The house is mine as much as theirs. . . Oh, can't whistle, can't throw paper up in the air, and can't play the radio and phonograph too loud. Rules of the house; anybody, I mean, it's not just me. . .

I.   Are you expected to stay away from certain places or people?

B.   She knows I do. I'm not expected; I mean, she figures I'm old enough to take care of myself now. They never tell me who to stay away from or where. Well, I mean, they don't expect me to sleep down on Skid Row or something like that. . .

Since the boys adopted their parents' standards of conduct as their own, they did not regard their parents and other authority figures as adversaries, but more as supportive and guiding influences.

Dependence-Independence Conflicts

The view that adolescents are engaged in a struggle to emancipate themselves from their parents also receives little support from our study.

Although the boys' dependency behavior had been fostered and encouraged during their childhood, independence training had begun early and was, therefore, largely accomplished by the time of adolescence. A similar early and gradual decrease in dependency upon adults is reported by Heathers (1955), who compared the dependency behavior of two-year-old and of five-year-old children. He found that, even over this small age range, dependency on adults had declined, whereas dependency on other children had increased.

For most of the boys that we studied, the emancipation from parents had been more or less completed rather than initiated at adolescence. In fact, the development of independence presented more of a conflict for the parents, than it did for the boys. Some of the parents, particularly the fathers, regretted the inevitable loss of the rewards that their sons' company had brought them.

I.   Do you feel that you spend as much time with Raymond as other fathers do with their sons, or more?

F.   I would say about average, but perhaps I should spend more time with him, because as the years go by, I see that he's growing into manhood and I'm losing a lot of him every year. When he was younger, I think I was with him more than I am now. I think, as he gets older, he's had a tendency to get his pleasures from people his own age, this is fine as long as he makes home his headquarters. That's all I want.

Although the boys devoted an increasing amount of time to peer-group activities, they, nevertheless, retained close ties to their parents and readily sought out their help, advice, and support when needed.

Parent Peer-Group Conflicts

The boys' primary reference groups were not selected indiscriminately. Since the adolescents tended to choose friends who shared similar value systems and behavioral norms, membership in the peer-group did not generate familial conflicts. In fact, the peer-group often served to reinforce and to uphold the parental norms and standards of behavior that the boys had adopted. Consequently, the parents were generally pleased with their sons' associates because they served as an important source of control in situations where the parents could not be present.

An essentially similar picture of adolescence, based on an intensive study of middle class families, has been presented by Elkin and Westley (1955; 1956). They summarize their findings as follows:

Family ties are close and the degree of basic family consensus is high. The parents are interested in all the activities of their children, and the adolescents, except for the area of sex, frankly discuss their own behavior and problems with them. In many areas of life, there is joint participation between parents and children. . . In independent discussions by parents and adolescents of the latters' marriage and occupational goals, there was a remarkable level of agreement. The adolescents also acknowledged the right of the parents to guide them, for example, accepting, at least manifestly, the prerogatives of the parents to set rules for the number of dates, hours of return from dates, and types of parties. The parents express relatively little concern about the socialization problems or peer group activities of their children (1955, p.682).

Sources of the Adolescent Mythology

What are the origins of the mythology about adolescence, and why does it persist?

Overinterpretation of Superficial Signs of Nonconformity

The view that adolescence is a period of rebellion is often supported by references to superficial signs of nonconformity, particularly adolescent fad behavior.

It is certainly true that adolescents frequently display idiosyncratic fashions and interest patterns. Such fads, however, are not confined to adolescent age groups. Several years ago, for example, coon skin caps and Davy Crockett apparel were highly fashionable among pre-adolescent boys. When Davy Crockett began to wane a new fad quickly emerged—every youngster and a sizeable proportion of the adult population were gyrating with hoola-hoops. The hoola-hoop also suffered a quick death by replacement.

If pre-adolescent children display less fad behavior than do adolescents, this difference may be primarily due to the fact that young children do not possess the economic resources with which to purchase distinctive apparel, the latest phonograph records, and discriminative ornaments, rather than a reflection of a sudden heightening of peer-group conformity pressures during adolescence. The pre-adolescent does not purchase his own clothing, he has little voice in how his hair shall be cut and, on a 15-cent a week allowance, he is hardly in a position to create new fads, or to deviate too widely from parental tastes and standards.

How about adult fad behavior? A continental gentleman conducts a fashion show in Paris and almost instantly millions of hemlines move upward or downward; the human figure is sacked, trapezed, chemised, or appareled in some other fantastic creation.

At a recent cocktail party the present writer was cornered by an inquiring lady who expressed considerable puzzlement over adolescents' fascination for unusual and bizarre styles. The lady herself was draped with a sack, wearing a preposterous object on her head, and spiked high heel shoes that are more likely to land one in an orthopedic clinic, than to transport one across the room to the olives.

Fashion-feeders determine the styles, the colors, and the amount of clothing that shall be worn. It would be rare, indeed, to find an adult who would ask a sales clerk for articles of clothing in vogue two or three years ago. As long as social groups contain a status hierarchy, and tolerance for upward mobility within the social hierarchy, one can expect imitation of fads and fashions from below which, in turn, forces inventiveness from the elite in order to preserve the status differentiations.

Mass Media Sensationalism

The storm and stress view of adolescence is also continuously reinforced by mass media sensationalism. Since the deviant adolescent excites far more interest than the typical high school student, the adolescent is usually portrayed in literature, television, and in the movies as passing through a neurotic or a semi-delinquent phase of development (Kiell, 1959). These productions, many of which are designed primarily to generate visceral reactions or to sell copy, are generally viewed as profound and sensitive portrayals of the *typical* adolescent turmoil. Holden Caulfield, the central character in *The Catcher in the Rye* (Salinger, 1945), has thus become the prototypic adolescent.

Generalization from Samples of Deviant Adolescents

Professional people in the mental health field are apt to have most contact with delinquent adolescents, and are thus prone to base their accounts of adolescence on observations of atypical samples. By and large, the description of the modal pattern of adolescent behavior fits most closely the behavior of the deviant ten per cent of the adolescent population that appears repeatedly in psychiatric clinics, juvenile probation departments, and in the newspaper headlines.

Our study of the family relationships of adolescents also included a sample of antisocially aggressive boys. In the families of these hyper-aggressive adolescents there was indeed a great deal of storm and stress for many years. The boys' belligerence and rebellion, however, was not a unique product of adolescence. The defiant oppositional pattern of behavior was present all along, but because of their greater size and power the parents were able to suppress and to control, through coercive methods, their sons' belligerence during the early childhood years. By the time of adolescence, however, some of the boys had reached the stage where they were almost completely independent of the parents for the satisfaction of their social and physical needs. Moreover, they had developed physically to the point where they were larger and more powerful than their parents. With the achievement of the power reversal and the decrease of the parents' importance as sources of desired rewards, a number of the boys exhibited a blatant indifference to their parents' wishes about which they could now do little or nothing.

I.   What sort of things does your mother object to your doing when you are out with your friends?

B.   She don't know what I do.

I.   What about staying out late at night?

B.   She says, "Be home at 11 o'clock." I'll come home at one.

I.   How about using the family car?

B.   No. I wrecked mine, and my father wrecked his a month before I wrecked mine, and I can't even get near his. And I got a license and everything. I'm going to hot wire it some night and cut out.

I.   How honest do you feel you can be to your mother about where you've been and what things you have done?

B.   I tell her where I've been, period.

I.   How about what you've done?

B.   No. I won't tell her what I've done. If we're going out in the hills for a beer bust, I'm not going to tell her. I'll tell her I've been to a show or something.

I.   How about your father?

B.   I'll tell him where I've been, period.

The heightened aggression exhibited by these boys during adolescence primarily reflected response predispositions that became more evident following the power reversal in the parent-child relationship, rather than an adolescence-induced stress.

Inappropriate Generalization from Cross-cultural Data

It is interesting to note that many writers cite cross-cultural data as supporting evidence for the discontinuity view of child development in the American society. The reader suddenly finds himself in the Trobriand Islands, or among the Arapesh, rather than in the suburbs of Minneapolis or in the town square of Oskaloosa.

In many cultures the transition from child to adult status is very abrupt. Childhood behavior patterns are strongly reinforced, but as soon as the child reaches pubescence he is subjected to an elaborate initiation ceremony which signifies his abrupt transformation into adult status. Following the ceremonial initiation the young initiate acquires new rights and privileges, new responsibilities and, in some cultures, he is even assigned a new name and a new set of parents who undertake his subsequent social training in the skills and habits required to perform the adult role.

In our culture, on the other hand, except for the discontinuities in the socialization of sexual behavior, there is considerable continuity in social training. As was mentioned earlier, independence and responsibility training, for example, are begun in early childhood and adult-role patterns are achieved through a gradual process of successive approximations. This is equally true in the development of many other forms of social behavior.

It should be mentioned in passing, however, that cross-cultural studies have been valuable in demonstrating that stresses and conflicts are not inevitable concomitants of pubescence, but rather products of cultural conditioning. Indeed, in some societies, adolescence is one of the pleasant periods of social development (Mead, 1930).

Overemphasis of the Biological Determination of Heterosexual Behavior

With the advent of pubescence the adolescent is presumably encumbered by a powerful biologically determined sexual drive that produces a relatively sudden and marked increase in heterosexual behavior. The net result of the clash between strong physiological urges demanding release and even more substantial social prohibitions, is a high degree of conflict, frustration, anxiety and diffuse tension. In contrast to this widely-accepted biological drive theory, evidence from studies of cross-species and cross-cultural sexual behavior reveals that human sexuality is governed primarily by social conditioning, rather than endocrinal stimulation (Ford & Beach, 1951).

The cross-species data demonstrate that hormonal control of sexual behavior decreases with advancing evolutionary status. In lower mammalian species, for example, sexual activities are completely regulated by gonadal hormones; among primates sexual behavior is partially independent of physiological stimulation; while human eroticism is exceedingly variable and essentially independent of hormonal regulation. Humans can be sexually aroused before puberty and long after natural or surgical loss of reproductive glands. Thus, one would induce sexual behavior in a rodent Don Juan by administering androgen, whereas presenting him lascivious pictures of a well-endowed mouse would have no stimulating effects whatsoever. By contrast, one would rely on sexually-valenced social stimuli, rather than on hormonal injections for producing erotic arousal in human males.

The prominent role of social learning factors in determining the timing, incidence and form of sexual activities of humans is also clearly revealed in the wide cross-cultural variability in patterns of sexual behavior. Sex-arousing properties have been conditioned to an extremely broad range of stimuli, but the cues that are sexually stimulating in one culture would, in many instances, prove sexully repulsive to members of another society. A similar diversity exists in the timing of the emergence of sexual interest and in the choice of sexual objects. In cultures that permit and encourage heterosexual behavior at earlier, or at later, periods of a child's development than is true for American youth, no marked changes in sexual behavior occur during adolescence.

It is evident from the foregoing discussion that "sexual tensions" are not an inevitable concomitant of pubescence. Furthermore, any significant increase in heterosexual activities during adolescence is due more to cultural conditioning and expectations than to endocrinal changes.

Stage Theories of Personality Development

Until recently, most of the theoretical conceptualizations of the developmental process have subscribed to some form of stage theory. According to the Freudian viewpoint (1949), for example, behavioral changes are programmed in an oral-anal-phallic sequence; Erickson (1950) characterizes personality development in terms of an eight-stage sequence; Gesell (1943) describes marked predictable cyclical changes in behavior over yearly or even shorter temporal intervals; and Piaget (1948, 1954), delineates numerous different stages for different classes of responses.

Although there appears to be relatively little consensus among these theories concerning the number and the content of stages considered to be crucial, they all share in common the assumption that social behavior can be categorized in terms of a relatively prefixed sequence of stages with varying degrees of continuity or discontinuity between successive developmental periods. Typically, the spontaneous emergence of these elaborate age-specific modes of behavior is attributed to ontogenetic factors. The seven-year-old, for example, is supposed to be withdrawn; the eight-year-old turns into an exuberant, expansive and buoyant child; the fifteen-year-old becomes remote and argumentative; parents are finally rewarded at sweet sixteen (Ilg & Ames, 1955). In truth, all seven-year-olds are not withdrawn, all eight-year-olds are not exuberant, expansive and buoyant, nor are all fifteen year-olds aloof and argumentative. I am also acquainted with sixteen-year-olds who are anything but sweet. The withdrawn five-year-old is likely to remain a relatively withdrawn eight, nine, and sixteen-year-old unless he undergoes social-learning experiences that are effective in fostering more expressive behavior.

Although the traditional stage theories of child development are of questionable validity (Bandura & McDonald, 1963; Bandura & Mischel, 1963; Bandura & Walters, 1963), they have nevertheless been influential in promoting the view that adolescence represents a form of stage behavior that suddenly appears at pubescence, and as suddenly disappears when adulthood is achieved.

Self-fulfilling Prophecy

If a society labels its adolescents as "teen-agers," and expects them to be rebellious, unpredictable, sloppy, and wild in their behavior, and if this picture is repeatedly reinforced by the mass media, such cultural expectations may very well force adolescents into the role of rebel. In this way, a false expectation may serve to instigate and maintain certain role behaviors, in turn, then reinforce the originally false belief.

In discussing our research findings with parents' groups I have often been struck by the fact that most parents, who are experiencing positive and rewarding relationships with their pre-adolescent children are, nevertheless, waiting apprehensively and bracing themselves for the stormy adolescent period. Such vigilence can very easily create a small turbulence at least. When the prophesied storm fails to materialize, many parents begin to entertain doubts about the normality of their youngster's social development.

In closing, I do not wish to leave you with the impression that adolescence is a stress- or problem-free period of development. No age group is free from stress or adjustment problems. Our findings suggest, however, that the behavioral characteristics exhibited by children during the so-called adolescent stage are lawfully related to, and consistent with, pre-adolescent social behavior.

REFERENCES

BANDURA, A., & McDONALD, F. J. The influence of social reinforcement and the behavior of models in shaping children's moral judgements. *J. abnorm. soc. Psychol.*, 1963, *67*, 274-281.

BANDURA, A., & MISCHEL, W. The influence of models in modifying delay-of-gratification patterns. Unpublished manuscript, Stanford Univer., 1963.

BANDURA, A., & WALTERS, R. H. *Adolescent aggression.* New York: Ronald, 1959.

BANDURA, A., & WALTERS, R. H. *Social learning and personality development.* New York: Holt, Rinehart & Winston, 1963.

ELKIN, F., & WESTLEY, W. A. The myth of adolescent culture. *Amer. sociol. Rev.*, 1955, *20*, 680-684.

ERICKSON, E. H. *Childhood and society.* New York: Norton, 1950.

FORD, C. S., & BEACH, F. A. *Patterns of sexual behavior.* New York: Harper, 1951.

FREUD, S. *An outline of psychoanalysis.* New York: Norton, 1949.

GALLAGHER, J. R., & HARRIS, H. I. *Emotional problems of adolescents.* New York: Oxford Univer. Press, 1958.

GESELL, A., & ILG, FRANCES. *Infant and child in the culture of today.* New York: Harper, 1943.

HEATHERS, G. Emotional dependence and independence in nursery school play. *J. genet. Psychol.*, 1955, *87*, 37-57.

HURLOCK, ELIZABETH B. *Adolescent development.* New York: McGraw-Hill, 1955.

ILG, FRANCES L., & AMES, LOUISE B. *Child behavior.* New York: Harper, 1955.

JOSSELYN, IRENE M. *Psychosocial development of children.* New York: Family Service Assoc. of America, 1948.

KIELL, N. *The adolescent through fiction.* New York: International Univer. Press, 1959.

MEAD, MARGARET. Adolescence in primitive and in modern society. In V. F. Calverton, & S. D. SCHMALHAUSEN (Eds.), *The new generation.* New York: Macauley, 1930.

MOHR, G. S., & DESPRES, MARIAN A. *The stormy decade: adolescence.* New York: Random House, 1958.

PARSONS, T. Psycho-analysis and social structure. *Psychoanal. Quart.*, 1950, *19*, 371-384.

PEARSON, G. H. J. *Adolescence and the conflict of generations.* New York: Norton, 1958.

PIAGET, J. *The moral judgement of the child.* Glencoe, Ill.: Free Press, 1948.

PIAGET, J. *The construction of reality in the child.* New York: Basic Books, 1954.

SALINGER, J. D. *The catcher in the rye.* Boston: Little, Brown & Co., 1945.

WESTLEY, W. A., & ELKIN, F. The protective environment and adolescent socialization. *Social Forces*, 1956, *35*, 243-249.

J. Child Psychol. Psychiat., Vol. 17, 1976, pp. 35 to 56. Pergamon Press. Printed in Great Britain.

ADOLESCENT TURMOIL: FACT OR FICTION?*

Michael Rutter, Philip Graham†, O. F. D. Chadwick and W. Yule

Department of Child Psychiatry, Institute of Psychiatry,
De Crespigny Park, Denmark Hill, London SE5 8AF

INTRODUCTION

Although the period of adolescence has provided a constant source of fascination to adults, psychiatric and psychological writings on the topic are characterised more by confident assertion than by the presence of well based knowledge. The flavour of some of the most prevalent views on adolescence is best conveyed by a few quotations. Thus, Blos (1970) asserts (p. 11): "The more-or-less orderly course of development during latency is thrown into disarray with the child's entry into adolescence . . . adolescence cannot take its normal course without regression". Anna Freud (1958) writes: "Adolescence is by its nature an interruption of peaceful growth, and . . the upholding of a steady equilibrium during the adolescent process is in itself abnormal . . . adolescence resembles in appearance a variety of other emotional upsets and structural upheavals. The adolescent manifestations come close to symptom formation of the neurotic, psychotic or dissocial order and merge almost imperceptibly into . . . almost all the mental illnesses". Geleerd (1957) states: "Personally I would feel greater concern for the adolescent who causes no trouble and feels no disturbance". Eissler (1958) thinks of adolescence as predominantly "stormy and unpredictable behaviour marked by mood swings between elation and melancholy".

Psychiatrists and psychologists generally suppose that adolescence is a period of great psychological upheaval and disturbance. Furthermore, psychiatric disorders, which occur during this age period are often thought to be different from those in either childhood or adult life. Thus, Josselyn (1954) maintains that: "A typical adolescent may present a picture today of hysteria while the history indicates that a month ago his behaviour appeared typically impulsive". Eissler (1958) suggests the same variability and unpredictability when he states: ". . . (adolescent) psychopathology switches from one form to another, sometimes in the course of weeks or months, but also from one day to another. . . . The symptoms manifested by such patients may be neurotic at one time and almost psychotic at another. Then, sudden acts of delinquency may occur, only to be followed by a phase of perverted sexual activity".

These suppositions are reflected in psychiatrists' diagnostic habits, at least in the U.S.A. Among adolescents seen at outpatient clinics "transient situational

*Originally delivered by M. Rutter as the Chairman's Address to the Association for Child Psychology and Psychiatry, 13 February, 1974.

†Department of Psychological Medicine, Hospital for Sick Children, Great Ormond Street, London WC1.

Accepted manuscript received 7 November 1974

disorder" constituted much the commonest diagnostic category (Rosen *et al.*, 1965) and even among psychiatric inpatients the diagnosis was made in nearly a quarter of all adolescents (U.S. Department of Health, Education and Welfare, 1966).

Adolescence is the age-period when there is supposed to be an "identity crisis". As they achieve increasing autonomy and independence from their family of origin, youngsters struggle to achieve a sense of their own distinct personality. It is said that adolescents generally become increasingly estranged from their families and that parents complain that they can no longer "get through" to their children. Erikson (1955) has described identity formation as the main characteristic of adolescence. During this period of development the childhood identifications cease to be useful and a new configuration has to develop. The crisis at this point may lead to "role confusion" or "identity diffusion". He writes, ". . . in spite of the similarity of adolescent 'symptoms' and episodes to neurotic and psychotic symptoms and episodes, adolescence is not an affliction, but a *normative crisis*, i.e. a normal phase of increased conflict characterized by a seeming fluctuation in ego strength . . . what under prejudiced scrutiny may appear to be the onset of a neurosis, often is but an aggravated crisis which might prove to be self-liquidating and, in fact, contributive to the process of identity formation".

Social scientists have sometimes gone further in arguing that adolescents form a separate culture which has little in common with the rest of society. Coleman (1961), one of the most influential writers on this topic, states firmly (p. 3) that the adolescent: ". . . is 'cut off' from the rest of society, forced inward toward his own age group, made to carry out his whole social life with others his own age. With his fellows he comes to constitute a small society, one that has most of its important interactions *within* itself, and maintains only a few threads of connection with the outside adult society".

All these aspects of adolescence are "known" as part of our folklore but how far are they true? Is adolescent turmoil a fact or is it merely a picturesque fiction? In considering these questions let us first consider the source of these views. Adelson (1964) has argued that the mystique of adolescence is summarised by two caricatures: the "visionary–victim", a noble idealist betrayed, exploited or neglected by the adult world; and the "victimizer", leather-jacketed, cruel, sinister and amoral. He points out that the latter is based on the delinquents who hit the news headlines and who are prominent in films and novels, and that the former is based on the sensitive, articulate, intense, intelligent, estranged middle-class adolescent on whom the psychoanalytic theory of adolescence is almost exclusively based. Neither can be held to be representative of the ordinary teenager and generalizations based on clinical practice are very likely to be seriously misleading. Adelson suggests that epidemiological studies of the general population are required if you are to talk about the characteristics of the normal adolescent and that data should be preferred to personal opinions. All the quotations given above refer to clinical anecdote and opinion, with one exception—that of Coleman (1961). His statement about the separate culture of adolescence came from a book reporting interviews with a representative sample of over 7000 adolescents. It has the air of a definitive study but, as Jahoda and Warren (1965) have pointed out, much of his argument consists either of bald statements of assumption or appeals for agreement and the empirical

94

base is shaky. The Coleman study is much quoted as showing the existence of a separate youth culture, so it is appropriate to consider the evidence provided. For example, in order to assess the relative importance of parents and friends, the youngsters were asked "which . . . would be hardest for you to take—your parents' disapproval . . . or breaking with your friends?" (p. 5). As Epperson (1964) noted, *breaking* with someone and receiving *disapproval* differ in both emotional importance and likelihood of occurrence. In spite of this manifestly loaded question, over half the adolescents still said that parental disapproval counted for more than breaking with a friend. On the next page, Coleman (1961) states, ". . . those who 'set the standard' are more oriented than their followers to the adolescent culture itself. The consequences of this fact are important, for it means that those students who are highly regarded by others are themselves committed to the adolescent group, thus intensifying whatever inward forces the group already has". This supposedly important fact is based on a difference between 53·8 and 50·2%. Moreover, even in the group supposedly committed to youth culture a *majority* actually found parental disapproval harder to take than breaking with a friend. Later in the book (p. 139) much is made of adolescents' resistance to parental pressures but the figures show that some 70% would not join a school club if their parents disapproved. Further on still (p. 286) Coleman comments on the students' alienation from teachers. The table supporting the text shows that only 12·4% of students thought teachers were "not interested in teenagers".

More examples could be given but these are enough to indicate that in this emotionally loaded topic the actual data require careful examination before the conclusions based on those data are accepted. Needless to say, that also applies to the investigations reported in this paper.

Isle of Wight study

Nevertheless, in order to avoid the pitfalls of selective sampling and of personal opinion, the research findings are presented here in some detail and most emphasis is placed on epidemiological studies of the general population rather than on investigations of clinic patients. A variety of published studies are mentioned but most findings refer to the Isle of Wight study of 14–15-yr-olds. The methodology has been fully described previously (Rutter, Tizard and Whitmore, 1970; Graham and Rutter, 1973), but the main research strategy was as follows. Parents and teachers completed behavioural questionnaires for the total population of 2303 adolescents. From this overall group, two subsamples were chosen for individual study, (1) a random sample of the general population ($N = 200$), and (2) all the children with high, that is "deviant", scores on the questionnaires ($N = 304$)*. The children in both these groups were individually interviewed by psychiatrists (who did not know which subsample the child was in), and the parents and teachers of the youngsters were also interviewed using a standardized approach. On the basis of this detailed information an individual psychiatric diagnosis was made for each child who showed any disorder. As well as information relevant to psychiatric status, many systematic data were obtained about the adolescent's leisure activities and about patterns of

*This includes children selected because of contact with psychiatric services or the Juvenile Court during the previous year.

family life using methods developed by Rutter and Brown (Brown and Rutter, 1966; Rutter and Brown, 1966). The children also received psychological testing which included the short WISC (Wechsler, 1949), the Neale Analysis of Reading Ability (Neale, 1958), and the Vernon arithmetic–mathematics test (Vernon, 1949).

In addition to this cross-sectional survey, the study included a follow-up of all the children in the same age group who had been found to have psychiatric disorder at age 10 yr during the course of a previous epidemiological enquiry (Rutter, Tizard and Whitmore, 1970).

Alienation

So much for methodology. Let us now turn to the questions and to the findings. In doing this it is important to be clear just what are the hypotheses to be considered. First, we will take the concept of alienation, which suggests that during adolescence youngsters become increasingly estranged from their parents. A corollary of this is that the peer group comes to take precedence over the family as an influence on young people's behaviour. Coleman's (1961) study has already been mentioned in this connection and it has been suggested that, his claims notwithstanding, his data suggest that most adolescents are still considerably influenced by their parents. The relevant items seem to be; (1) that just over half the sample of American high school students felt that parental disapproval would be harder to take than breaking with a friend, (2) that most would follow parental suggestions regarding club membership, (3) that only a few felt that teachers were not interested in them and (4) that being accepted and liked by other students was rated as below average importance compared with pleasing parents, learning as much as possible at school, and living up to their religious ideals. In fact, the evidence provides few definitive findings. Also, although the findings suggest that parental influence is still high in adolescence, they say nothing about the quality of relationships or the closeness of ties.

Epperson's findings (1964), based on a much smaller survey of high school students, take the issue a little further in that he directly compared parental disapproval and friend's disapproval; 80% of adolescents said that parental disapproval would make them more unhappy than the disapproval of friends. Furthermore, secondary school students were if anything more concerned about parental approval than were younger children.

Douvan and Adelson (1966) were concerned with similar issues in their questionnaire survey of over three thousand American adolescents, mainly aged 14–16 yr. Most of the questions tapped attitudes and some of the findings were; (a) that of all other people parents were most often admired, (b) helping at home was the major source of self-esteem, (c) just over half said they had some part in rule-making at home, (d) most would be honest and trusting with their parents and (e) a quarter never had arguments with their parents. On the other hand, many had disagreements about clothing, dating, or being allowed to go out. Also four-fifths reported that they would like their parents to be less restrictive. About half stated that they thought friendship could be as close as family relationships. Douvan and Adelson conclude that, although inter-generation conflict exists, its importance has been much exaggerated. Normal adolescents share with their parents a common core of values in spite of sharp disagreements about matters of dress, hair length, pop music and how late they can stay out at night.

The findings from other studies are closely similar. For example, Meissner (1965), in another questionnaire survey of high school youngsters, found that about half thought their parents understood them, the great majority were satisfied and happy at home, and three-quarters generally approved of their parents' discipline. Nevertheless, about half thought their parents old-fashioned and although only a minority resisted parental discipline, the proportion was somewhat higher in late adolescence. Offer (1969) in a study of "modal" adolescents (in effect, the most normal third of the population) reported that most got on well with their parents and shared their values.

The Isle of Wight findings, which provide the only English data, are broadly in keeping with the American results.

TABLE 1. PARENT–CHILD ALIENATION AT 14 yr (GENERAL POPULATION SAMPLE)

	Boys $(n = 98)$	Girls $(n = 94)$
Parental account		
Altercation with parents (any)	17·6%	18·6%
Physical withdrawal of child (any)	12·1%	6·9%
Communication difficulties with child (any)	24·2%	9·3%*

* $\chi^2 = 5\cdot93$; 1 $d.f.$; $p < 0\cdot025$.

Table 1 shows some of the relevant findings from the parental interview. Parents were asked if they had any arguments with their adolescent children concerning when and where they went out, or about other activities. Only one in six parents in the randomly selected control group reported any altercations, although twice as many said they disapproved of their youngsters' clothing or hair styles and often prohibitions in these areas were enforced. The great majority of parents approved of their children's friends, and nearly all had discussed with their children what they might do when they left school.

In order to assess the extent to which the adolescents had become alienated or had withdrawn from their families, parents were first asked if their child tended to withdraw by going off to his room, or staying out of the house, or just not doing things with the rest of the family. This was termed "physical withdrawal" and as shown in Table 1 only a tiny minority of adolescents did so. We next asked if the parents had any difficulties "getting through" to their child and how much the youngster discussed with his parents how he was feeling and what were his plans. In the case of boys almost a quarter of the parents reported some emotional withdrawal or difficulty in communication, but in the great majority of cases this difficulty had always been present. In only 4% of cases had difficulties increased during adolescence. Communication difficulties were much less frequent with girls ($\chi^2 = 5\cdot93$; 1 $d.f.$; $p < 0\cdot025$).

Table 2 shows parent–child relationships as assessed from the interview with the adolescent. About two-thirds reported that they never disagreed with their parents about any of their activities and altercations were present in only a minority.

TABLE 2. PARENT–CHILD ALIENATION AT 14 yr (GENERAL POPULATION SAMPLE)

	Boys (n = 98)	Girls (n = 94)
Child's account		
Disagreements with parents (any)	32·3%	26·7%
Altercations with parents (any)	41·7%	30·2%
Criticism of mother (any)	27·1%	36·8%
Criticism of father (any)	31·6%	31·0%
Rejection of mother (any)	3·1%	2·3%
Rejection of father (any)	5·3%	9·2%
No outings with parents	42·7%	27·3%

Even in the minority who did have arguments, these were usually infrequent. All critical remarks concerning parents made at any time during the interview were noted, and only about a third of the adolescents made any criticisms at all. Frank rejection of parents was rarer still. Youngsters were asked about family outings and only a third or so reported that they never went out with their parents.

The findings of all the epidemiological studies are in general agreement. Alienation from parents is *not* common in 14-yr-olds, although it is probably more frequent by the late teens. Most young teenagers continue to be influenced by their parents and get on quite well with them. Most adolescents are *not* particularly critical of their parents and very few reject them. On the other hand, although still occurring in only half the group or less, petty disagreements about clothes, hair and going out are reasonably common. Some of these disagreements may get quite heated and many adolescents would like their parents to be less strict. Even so, most continue to share their parents' values on other things and respect the need for restrictions and control.

As these unexciting conclusions are so much at variance with some psychiatric opinion, we need to ask why there is this discrepancy. Figure 1 provides at least a partial answer.

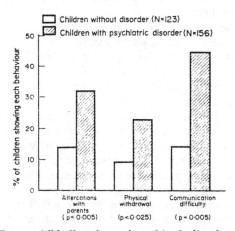

FIG. 1. Parent–child alienation and psychiatric disorder at 14 yr.

This compares altercations, physical withdrawal and communication difficulties in the control group children who showed no psychiatric disorder and the total sample of children with some psychiatric condition. These indications of alienation were two or three times as frequent in the psychiatric group. Thus, opinions based on psychiatric patients are confirmed, in so much as alienation was found to be much more frequent in youngsters with psychiatric problems. Even so, alienation was found in less than half. However, here we have to remember that the Isle of Wight youngsters were not patients and other studies have shown that psychiatric clinic referral is related to stresses in the parent and in parent–child interaction as well as to disorder in the child (Shepherd *et al.*, 1971). In short, alienation is more common in adolescents with psychiatric disorder but also if there is alienation, clinic referral may be more likely other things being equal. In this way, clinic patients may be somewhat unrepresentative of youngsters with psychiatric disorder.

The next question concerns the meaning of the alienation, when it exists. Does it cause psychiatric disorder or is it a result of the child's problems? Before attempting to answer that question let us first consider the prevalence of inner turmoil and of psychiatric disorder in adolescence.

Inner turmoil

The assessment of inner turmoil presents many difficulties and questionnaire surveys are of negligible value in this connection. The Coleman (1961) interviews did not cover this area and the Offer (1969) study is non-contributory in that it excluded all adolescents with difficulties. Masterson (1967) reported that anxiety and depression were as common in ordinary adolescents as in his patient sample, which suggests considerable feelings of distress even in children without psychiatric disorder. That is the only relevant published study. So let us turn straight to the Isle of Wight findings from the psychiatric interview with the adolescent. A sample of results is given on Table 3.

The first four items refer to material reported at interview by the adolescent. Each youngster was asked if he sometimes felt miserable and unhappy to the extent that he was tearful or wanted to get away from it all. Nearly half reported some appreciable misery or depression and this was almost as common in boys as in girls. About a fifth said that they felt that what happened to them was less important than what happened to other people, that they didn't matter very much. Only a small minority admitted to any suicidal thoughts but a quarter said that they sometimes got the feeling that people were looking at them or talking about them or laughing at them.

TABLE 3. FINDINGS FROM PSYCHIATRIC INTERVIEW WITH ADOLESCENT
(GENERAL POPULATION SAMPLE)

	Boys (n = 96)	Girls (n = 88)
Reported misery	41·7%	47·7%
Self-depreciation	19·8%	23·0%
Suicidal ideas	7·3%	7·9%
Ideas of reference	28·1%	30·7%
Observed anxiety	19·8%	28·4%
Observed sadness	12·5%	14·8%

At the end of the interview, the psychiatrist had to note whether the youngster appeared anxious and whether he appeared sad or miserable. Interestingly, the proportion who looked sad was far less than the proportion who reported feelings of misery. Only about one in eight adolescents looked sad or miserable at interview.

The interview data refer to ratings made by psychiatrists on the basis of what the adolescents said to them. Accordingly, it is possible that the high proportion of youngsters said to be miserable and depressed might be due to psychiatrists placing undue weight on phenomena of little depth or meaning to the adolescents themselves. Some check on this is provided by the malaise inventory which is completed by the youngsters without any interpretation by psychiatrists. The findings are shown in Table 4.

TABLE 4. INDIVIDUAL ITEMS ON THE MALAISE INVENTORY (GENERAL POPULATION SAMPLE)

	Boys (n = 96)	Girls (n = 87)	Mothers (n = 170)
Often feels miserable or depressed	20·8%	23·0%	14·3%
Usually has great difficulty in falling asleep or staying asleep	20·8%	17·2%	14·2%
Usually wakes unnecessarily early in the morning	22·9%	24·1%	10·0%

More than a fifth of the boys and girls reported that they felt miserable or depressed, and the same proportion reported great difficulties in sleeping, and waking unnecessarily early in the morning. Although these figures are considerably lower than those from the psychiatric interview, it is striking that they are substantially higher than the equivalent figures for mothers. In short, on the adolescents' own account more of them are depressed or miserable than is the case with their mothers (comparable data for fathers are not available).

There can be no doubt from these findings that many 14–15-yr-olds experience quite marked feelings of affective disturbance which could well be described as "inner turmoil". Although only a small minority appeared clinically depressed, many more reported feelings of misery which were often accompanied by self-depreciation and ideas of reference and occasionally even by suicidal thoughts. Of course, that still leaves half the group who did not experience such inner turmoil. But the findings show that inner experiences of misery and depreciation are very common.

The meaning of these feelings in terms of psychiatric disorder is another question, but before turning to that issue let us consider the prevalence of psychiatric disorder in adolescence.

Prevalence of psychiatric disorder

Apart from the Isle of Wight investigations, the only other studies to examine the prevalence of psychiatric disorder in adolescence are those by Krupinski et al. (1967), Henderson et al. (1971) and by Leslie (1974). Krupinski and his colleagues used medical students to interview all families in an Australian town in order to determine the prevalence of all forms of medical disability. Diagnoses were checked by supervisors and collateral inquiries were made when thought necessary. Some

10 per cent of children, 16 per cent of adolescents and 24 per cent of adults were diagnosed as showing some form of psychiatric disorder. The findings suggested a rate of disorder which increased during adolescence and early adult life, but as, unlike the other surveys, direct psychiatric assessments were not employed comparisons are problematic. Leslie (1974) examined 13–14-yr-old children in Blackburn, basing her diagnosis on interviews with parents and children and on questionnaires from teachers. The prevalence rate found was 21% in boys and 14% in girls. No comparisons with other age groups are possible from her figures. For this purpose, we need to turn to the Isle of Wight findings.

If we are to compare the rate of disorder at 14–15 yr with the rates at other ages, it is necessary to ensure that comparable methods of assessment are used at each age. In this connection we have data on three age-groups on the Isle of Wight— 10-yr-olds, 14–15-yr-olds, and adults (represented by the parents of children in both control groups). The same general strategy was employed in the case of the two groups of children but there were important differences in detail. In the first place, the child interviews were both longer and more thorough at age 14 yr than they had been at 10 yr. In the second place, we had interviews with teachers for the adolescents but only reports from teachers for the 10-yr-olds. Simply on the grounds that our assessments were more searching, we would expect to find more disorder at 14 yr than at 10 yr. With the adults, we had only one source of information— the interview with the mother which had to be used to assess disorder in both parents. In order to equate the methods of assessment as far as possible, only one source of information was used for each age group, in each case the best source available and comparisons were based on the appropriate control groups. The source of information was the parental interview for both groups of youngsters and for adults it was the maternal interview. The results are shown in Table 5.

It is clear that the prevalence of psychiatric disorder is roughly the same at all ages—namely just over 10%. The only group with an appreciably lower rate is that of adult men. In their case the figure may be somewhat of an underestimate because we had to use information from their wives rather than from the men themselves, or it could be truly lower. We have no satisfactory means of testing which is the correct explanation. However, whatever the explanation, the data provide no support for the view that psychiatric disorder is very much commoner during the mid-teens.

TABLE 5. PREVALENCE OF PSYCHIATRIC DISORDER BY AGE
(USING MAIN ACCOUNT)

	Ages		
	10 yr	14 yr	Adult (Parent)
Male	12·7%	13·2%	7·6%
	(n = 55)	(n = 91)	(n = 250)
Female	10·9%	12·5%	11·9%
	(n = 46)	(n = 88)	(n = 270)

In each case n refers to the total sample from the general population who were interviewed in order to determine the proportion with psychiatric disorder.

It could be argued that we should have used the interview with the adolescent himself for this purpose. We did not because the evidence suggested that the parental measure was a better indicator of disorder. Nevertheless, we ought to see how this would affect the results. In the control group, 16·3% of adolescents were diagnosed as having psychiatric disorder on this basis. Therefore, on this measure, psychiatric problems were rather commoner in adolescence than they were in adult life. But caution should be used in drawing conclusions from this comparison as the interviews were different. The same applies to the comparison with 10-yr-olds.

Because of these methodological uncertainties, we need to look to other means of comparison. Let us turn to the teachers' questionnaires. We cannot use the teacher interview because it was undertaken only for the adolescents but the questionnaires were closely comparable at the two ages. At age 10–11 yr some 7% of the population obtain deviant scores (Rutter, Tizard and Whitmore, 1970), and at age 14–15 yr just over 6·5% do so. In short, on information from teachers, the rate of emotional and behavioural problems in adolescence is much the same as that at age 10–11 yr.

Another check is provided by scores on the self-completed health questionnaire which taps emotional and psychosomatic symptoms. This was not used with 10-yr-olds but it was with both adolescents and parents, for whom it has been shown to provide a reasonable indicator of psychiatric disorder. Among the 14–15-yr-old girls 17·2% had scores indicative of possible disorder whereas among the mothers 12·2% had similar scores. The comparable figures for boys and fathers were 10·4% and 3·8%. Accordingly, as judged on the basis of self-completed questionnaires, disorders appear rather more common in adolescence than in adult life.

The findings are largely negative so far, but we have used only separate pieces of information. In the original survey, the final estimate of prevalence was based on a two-stage procedure involving the screening of the total population by means of parents' and teachers' questionnaires and then individual diagnoses based on all available data. On this basis, we obtained a prevalence of 5·7% psychiatric disorder at age 10 yr. At 14–15 yr the figure was 7·7%, just a little higher.

Taking all these comparisons together, it may be concluded that psychiatric disorders occur at a fairly similar rate at age 14–15 yr and at age 10–11 yr, although the prevalence is probably rather higher in adolescence. Comparisons with adulthood are less certain as the findings differ according to which data are used. However, it seems that disorders may be somewhat more frequent in adolescence. It should be noted that psychiatric clinic referral rates are appreciably higher in adult life than in adolescence (Baldwin, 1968), although this difference may reflect referral practices rather than prevalence.

So far so good, but in these last comparisons there has been one missing step and it is that step which throws the whole issue into confusion once more. The missing step is the consideration of how many children with psychiatric disorder are missed by the screening procedures. At 14–15 yr, our data suggest that quite a few children are missed (Graham and Rutter, 1973). Indeed, if a correction is made on the basis of children not picked up on the screening procedures, the rate rises greatly—up to 21%. Unfortunately, the information at age 10 yr is not exactly comparable but the available data indicate that the proportion missed is very much smaller and hence the corrected prevalence is considerably lower (Rutter.

Tizard and Whitmore, 1970). As this one comparison runs counter to all the others we need to look very closely at what it means and search diligently for possible methodological artefacts.

The first point is where do all these extra children who missed the screening procedures come from? On which source of data is the psychiatric diagnosis based? The answer is that the single greatest source is the psychiatric interview with the adolescent himself. In fact no less than 28% are diagnosed *on this basis alone,* without supporting evidence from either the parent or teacher. As this picture is quite different to that in the group selected on the screening procedures, we need to consider whether the interview with the child is a valid and trustworthy indicator of psychiatric disorder.

TABLE 6. VALIDITY OF PSYCHIATRIC INTERVIEW WITH ADOLESCENT

	% with disorder on adolescent interview
Control group (n = 184)	16·3%
Psychiatric group (diagnosed on basis of information from parents/teachers) (n = 158)	48·7% *

* $\chi^2 = 51·78$; 1 $d.f.$; $p < 0·001$.

Table 6 shows the proportion of adolescents diagnosed as having psychiatric disorder (on the basis of the child interview) in two groups. The first group is the random control group where there was a rate of 16·3% and the second is the group of youngsters diagnosed as having psychiatric condition on the information from parents and teachers, where the rate was 48·7%. This provides convincing validation of the interview with the adolescent as a means of detecting disorder so that serious attention must be paid to its findings.

However, the fact remains that many youngsters who appear normal to parents and teachers are diagnosed as showing disorder on the adolescent interview. Thus, in the random control group *not* selected on either the parent or teacher questionnaire nearly one in five are nevertheless diagnosed as showing psychiatric disorder on the adolescent interview. Nearly all these disorders involved some type of emotional disturbance, often depression; and it was clear that the frequently expressed feelings of misery, self-depreciation and the ideas of reference, already noted when considering "inner turmoil", had been used to diagnose psychiatric disorder. Was this correct? No really satisfactory answer can be given to that question on the basis of existing data. Four points may be made, however. First, the data on impairment of functioning were less searching in the adolescent interview than in the parental interview, so that for this reason alone, less reliance can be placed on the diagnosis, if social impairment is required to be present (which it was on our criteria). Second, whether or not it is considered that they indicate psychiatric disorder, the feelings of affective disturbance were real enough. Regardless of what parents and teachers thought or noticed, the adolescents themselves experienced suffering. Thirdly, the proportion of youngsters who looked sad was much smaller than those who reported feeling miserable. This raises the question of whether the reported feelings meant clinical depression or whether they represented inner turmoil which is part of adolescent development rather than an indication of psychiatric disorder. Fourthly, the best test of the psychiatric meaning of these symptoms would be what happened to the youngsters' mental state over the next year or so after the interview. Did the feelings of misery develop into frank depression or some other disorder noticeable to others, *or did the feelings remain purely internal and not observable by other people?* No data on that point are available either from the Isle of Wight study or from other published investigations, but such a study would be most useful and informative.

In the absence of these data any conclusions about the true prevalence of psychiatric disorder in adolescence must remain rather tentative. However, putting the findings together as well as possible, it seems that overt socially handicapping psychiatric disorder is probably somewhat commoner in adolescence than in earlier childhood (and possibly more frequent than in adult life) but the age differences in prevalence are fairly small. But, in addition to these generally recognizable disorders there is a sizable group of adolescents, perhaps 10% of the general population, who suffer from marked internal feelings of misery and self-depreciation. These feelings are obviously important aspects of adolescence but their clinical significance in terms of overt handicapping disorder remains uncertain at present. In view of this uncertainty, from now on when referring to psychiatric disorder in adolescence attention will be confined to the 7·5% who were diagnosed on the basis of the two-stage procedure which involved both *general* population screening *and* individual interviews with parents, teachers and adolescents.

Types of psychiatric disorder in adolescence

It seems, then, that there is probably a slight rise in the rate of psychiatric disorder during early adolescence, but the increase is only moderate. The next issue is whether the disorders occurring in adolescence differ in *type* from those evident at age 10 yr. For the most part the disorders appear closely similar. At both ages there is the same mixture of emotional disorders and conduct disturbances with very few psychotic children. In fact at age 14 yr there were no clear cases of schizophrenia, although there was one boy with a disorder which might reflect the early signs of this condition. The findings emphase the rarity of psychosis in early adolescence.

However, there were two marked differences from the distribution of disorders at age 10 yr. First, depression was much commoner in adolescence. At 10 yr there were only 3 children with a depressive condition whereas at 14 yr there were 9, plus another 26 with an affective disorder involving both anxiety and depression. This difference indicates the beginning of a shift to an adult pattern of disorders, although there is not yet the marked female preponderance of neurotic disorders seen in adults. As shown by Shaffer's study (1974) this rise in affective disorders during adolescence is paralleled by a rise in the incidence of completed suicide. Secondly, at age 14 yr there were 15 cases of school refusal whereas there had been none at age 10 yr. In many cases the school refusal formed part of a more widespread anxiety state or affective disorder, but, in all, the reluctance to go to school constituted one of the main problems. The findings are in keeping with the clinical evidence that school refusal is most prevalent in early childhood and again in adolescence. In the younger children, the main problem is more in keeping with normal developmental patterns and the prognosis is usually very good. In contrast, school refusal in adolescents is more often part of a widespread psychiatric disorder and the prognosis is considerably worse (Rodriguez et al., 1959). In short, although the psychiatric disorders shown at 14 yr are similar in many respects to those evident at age 10 yr, it is clear that the diagnostic pattern is different with respect to affective disorders and in this respect it is beginning to approximate the adult picture.

New disorders and persistent disorders

We now need to turn to the question we started with, whether disorders arising for the first time in adolescence are in some way different from those arising in earlier childhood, and whether adolescent disorders are due in part to the troubles stemming from inner turmoil or alienation from parents. Let us start with the issue of whether the disorders are different. It will be recalled that, as well as the cross-sectional study at 14 yr, we had had a similar study at age 10 yr on the same children. By linking the two studies we were able to sort out the adolescents' disorders into those which were already evident at age 10 yr and those that began at some point between 10 and 14 yr. Table 7 shows how the group divided up.

TABLE 7. AGE OF ONSET IN ADOLESCENT PSYCHIATRIC DISORDERS

	Before 10 yr	After 10 yr	Total
Boys	43 (69·3%)	53 (56·4%)	96
Girls	19	41	60
Total	62	94	156
Sex ratio	2·3 : 1	1·3 : 1	

$\chi^2 = 2·13$; 1 $d.f.$; $N.S.$

There were 48 youngsters who had already shown handicapping psychiatric disorder at age 10 yr. In addition, there were a further 14 who had had deviant scores on the parents' or teachers' questionnaire at the same age, although a handicapping disorder was not diagnosed. These two groups were combined to make a single group of 62 adolescents who were already showing disorder at 10 yr. The remaining 94 children had given no indications of psychiatric problems at 10 yr, so the presumption is that their disorders began some time after that, during early adolescence. (For this comparison, of course, children leaving or coming to the Isle of Wight between 10 and 14 yr have been excluded.)

Thus, just over half the disorders constituted new conditions arising in adolescence and just under half were conditions persisting from earlier childhood. It should be noted that, compared with clinic studies, the proportion of new disorders is unusually high. Both Warren (1965) and Capes et al. (1971) found that among adolescent psychiatric patients the majority of disorders had their origins in early or middle childhood. In the Isle of Wight study there was no difference between those with new and those with persistent disorders in terms of the proportion who were seen by a psychiatrist during the last year (the figures were 15·5 and 17·5%). However, there was some difference in terms of those who had ever received psychiatric care, as would be expected on the basis of the duration of disorder. A third

(33·3%) of the persistent group had seen a psychiatrist compared with less than a fifth (19·0%) of the children with new disorders.

Let us now turn to the question of how the two groups of disorders differed. The first difference which is apparent is that there was a marked preponderance of boys among the persistent cases whereas in the new cases the sex ratio was nearer equal. In short, the disorders arising during adolescence are nearer to the adult pattern than those arising in earlier childhood. Interestingly, however, the diagnostic differences were small and statistically insignificant.

TABLE 8. SEVERITY OF PSYCHIATRIC DISORDER BY AGE OF ONSET

	New disorders	Persistent disorders
Mild	59 (62·8%)	32 (51·6%)
Moderate	29 (30·9%)	21 (33·9%)
Severe	6 (6·4%)	9 (14·5%)
Total	94	62

χ^2 for trends = 3·14; 1 $d.f.$; $N.S.$

Before turning to other differences it is necessary to check whether the two groups differed in terms of the severity of the disorder. This is shown in Table 8. There was a slight tendency for the most severe disorders to be found in the persistent group but the differences fell well short of statistical significance and overall the severity ratings were quite similar in the two groups.

In looking for differences between the groups, it is helpful to have some idea of what features differentiate between the children with psychiatric disorder and those without any psychiatric problems. These variables are summarized in the next two tables. First, there are a variety of cognitive or educational factors. As was the case with the younger children showing psychiatric disorder, there was a slight tendency for the psychiatric group to have a lower I.Q., and a marked tendency for them to have severe reading difficulties. They also had significantly lower arithmetic scores.

Again as with the younger children, psychiatric disorder was associated with various indicators of family pathology, such as break-up of the parent's marriage, the child going into care, marital discord, irritability between the parents, parental irritability towards the child, and mental disorder in the mother.

In addition, there were a number of items, not assessed at age 10 yr, which were associated with psychiatric disorder in adolescents. First, most of the items associated with parent–child alienation were more often found in the psychiatric group. More quarrelled with their parents, more showed physical withdrawal, more showed communication difficulties or emotional withdrawal, more of the parents disapproved of the adolescent's friends and fewer of the adolescents went out with their parents. Second, there was also a mixed group of items referring to the young-sters' leisure activities which were associated with psychiatric disorder. The significant items are just a few out of a large number of non-significant differences on leisure activities, so these few should not receive much emphasis.

These items will be used to look for possible differences between the youngsters with new disorders and those with disorders persisting from earlier childhood. Table

10 shows that there was no I.Q. difference, but the children with persistent disorders had much lower arithmetic scores ($t = 4\cdot30$; 144 $d.f.$; $p < 0\cdot01$).

The difference with respect to reading retardation was even greater, as shown in Table 10 and Figure 2. The children with new disorders had no more reading difficulties than did the general population ($3\cdot3$ vs $4\cdot1\%$). This was in marked

TABLE 9. ITEMS DIFFERENTIATING PSYCHIATRIC GROUP FROM CONTROLS

Low I.Q. Low arithmetic score Reading retardation	Cognitive/educational
Not living with natural parents Child been in care Marital discord Parental irritability Maternal psychiatric disorder	Family pathology
Altercations with parents Physical withdrawal Communication difficulties Parental disapproval of friends Does not go out with parents	Parent–child alienation
Goes to coffee bar Meets friends in public places Has paper round Smokes	Other

TABLE 10. FAMILY AND EDUCATIONAL VARIABLES AND TIME OF ONSET OF DISORDER

	New disorders (at age 14 yr) $n = 94$	Persistent disorders (10–14 yr) $n = 62$	Non-persistent disorders (after age 10 yr) $n = 45$
Not living with both natural parents	18·2%	37·3%**	25·5%
Poor marriage	20·8%	30·2%	18·9%
Child been in care	8·3%	32·8%***	8·7%†
Maternal psychiatric disorder	17·6%	30·2%	21·4%
Reading retardation (age 10 yr)	3·3%	14·3%*	11·1%
Reading retardation (age 14 yr)	2·2%	21·4%***	13·3%††
Mean I.Q.	105·0 ($s.d. = 17\cdot14$)	102·0 ($s.d. = 15\cdot09$)	102·3 ($s.d. = 20\cdot60$)
Mean arithmetic score	31·4 ($s.d. = 11\cdot68$)	23·3 ($s.d. = 10\cdot82$)	27·9 ($s.d. = 13.00$)

Differences between new disorders and persistent disorders
* $p < 0\cdot05$
** $p < 0\cdot025$
*** $p < 0\cdot001$.
Differences between persistent disorders and non-persistent disorders
† $p < 0\cdot001$ ($\chi^2 = 7\cdot28$; 1 $d.f.$).
Differences between new disorders and non-persistent disorders
†† $p = 0\cdot015$ (Fisher's Exact test).

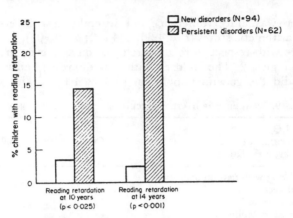

FIG. 2. Reading retardation and time of onset of psychiatric disorder.

contrast to the situation with respect to those with persistent disorders, many of whom (14·3%) were seriously retarded in reading. Interestingly the proportion who showed severe and specific reading retardation was even greater at 14 yr than it had been at age 10 yr. In short, the disorders persisting from earlier childhood were strongly and significantly associated with scholastic problems whereas this was not true at all with the disorders arising *de novo* during adolescence.

Figure 3 and Table 10 show a selection of the family variables associated with psychiatric problems. As is evident, in all cases family difficulties were much more strongly associated with the persistent cases than with the new cases. A third (32·8%) of the children with persistent disorders had been in care compared with only 8·3% of those with new disorders ($\chi^2 = 13\cdot76$; 1 *d.f.*; $p < 0\cdot001$). Almost two-fifths (37·3%) were not living with their two natural parents compared with less than a quarter (18·2%) of those with new conditions ($\chi^2 = 5\cdot77$; 1 *d.f.*; $p < 0\cdot025$). Maternal psychiatric disorder, irritability between parents and paternal irritability with the child were all nearly twice as common in the persistent group, although only the last difference reached statistical significance ($\chi^2 = 7\cdot49$; 1 *d.f.*; $p < 0\cdot01$).

A check was made to see if any of these differences were explicable in terms of diagnostic variation or difference in the severity of disorder. They were not. The differences remained even after the appropriate standardizations had been made.

In summary, as shown in Table 11, whereas persistent disorders at age 14 yr are strongly associated with various indices of family discord, parental difficulty and educational disadvantage (as were disorders at age 10 yr), these associations were much attenuated or non-existent in the case of psychiatric conditions arising for the first time during adolescence. The only association reaching statistical significance was that with marital disharmony.

However, it could be objected that the differences were explicable simply in terms of the different stages in the process of psychiatric disorder. The new disorders were recent whereas the persistent disorders were chronic. It is not possible to determine how far this constitutes an explanation but some check can be provided by a comparison with the 10-yr-old children who had *recovered* before 14 yr, as they,

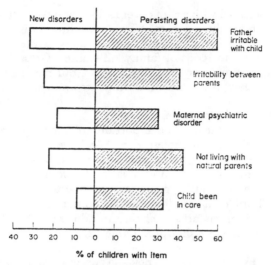

FIG. 3. Family variables and time of onset of disorder.

TABLE 11. FAMILY AND EDUCATIONAL VARIABLES AND DIFFERENCES FROM CONTROL GROUP

	Non-disordered controls (n = 123)	New disorders (n = 94)	Persistent disorders (n = 62)
Not living with both natural parents	14·9%	18·2%	37·3% **
Poor marriage	6·6%	20·8% **	30·2% ***
Child been in care	3·3%	8·3%	32·8%
Maternal psychiatric disorder	9·5%	17·6%	30·2% **
Reading retardation (at age 10 yr)	4·1%	3·3%	14·3% *
Reading retardation (at age 14 yr)	3·3%	2·2%	21·4% ***
Mean I.Q.	108·51 (s.d. = 14·32)	104·98 (s.d. = 17·14)	102·02** (s.d. = 15·09)
Mean arithmetic score	33·9 (s.d. = 11·24)	31·4 (s.d. = 11·68)	23·2*** (s.d. = 10·82)

Differences from controls
  * $p < 0.025$
  ** $p < 0.01$
  *** $p < 0.001$.

too, constituted a group with relatively acute conditions. This comparison is complicated by the fact that the non-persistent disorders from age 10 yr differ somewhat in diagnosis from both the other groups, in being predominantly neurotic conditions. Accordingly, on these grounds alone a lesser association with family and educational variables would be expected. Nevertheless, the findings should be examined.

It is apparent from Table 10 that whereas reading retardation was associated with *both* the non-persistent and persistent disorders from age 10 yr, it was not associated with the disorders arising in adolescence. It may be firmly concluded that this is a difference associated with age of onset rather than with chronicity. However, the reverse is true with family variables. After controlling statistically for diagnostic differences between groups it was evident that the non-persistent group was closely similar to the new group in terms of family difficulties. Gross family pathology is mainly associated with chronic psychiatric disorders, but marital discord at parent–child alienation (see below) is found with both acute and chronic conditions.

Alienation and adolescent psychiatric disorder

We now need to turn to the possible importance of alienation from parents in the genesis of psychiatric disorder in adolescence. We have already seen that all the various measures of alienation are significantly associated with psychiatric problems. Altercations with parents, physical withdrawal and emotional withdrawal were all twice as common in the psychiatric group. But the question is: does alienation lead to disorder or does disorder lead to alienation? In order to answer that question we need to compare the disorders arising *de novo* in adolescence with those persisting from age 10 yr. The findings are shown in Table 12.

TABLE 12. PARENT–CHILD ALIENATION AND TIME OF ONSET OF DISORDER

	New disorders (n = 94)	Persistent disorders (n = 62)
Parental account		
Altercation with parents	28·0%	43·4%
Physical withdrawal	19·3%	29·1%
Emotional withdrawal	43·4%	43·6%
Child's account		
Altercation with parents	35·6%	41·8%
Rejection of mother	2·2%	8·2%
Rejection of father	9·0%	8·6%

No differences are statistically significant.

Alienation was found to be associated with *both* types of disorder, but on the whole it was somewhat more evident in the persistent group even after controlling for differences in the severity of disorder (although the differences fall short of statistical significance). At least in that group, alienation *arising in adolescence* could not have caused psychiatric disorder because the disorder long antedated the adolescent period. Either the association was the other way round, that is the alienation was part of or the *result*, not the cause, of psychiatric problems, or the alienation must have acted as a stress in the pre-adolescent years. Unfortunately the direction of association cannot be conclusively determined in the new group as we had no measure of alienation at age 10 yr. However, two findings militate *against* alienation arising during adolescence being a major causal factor. The first is that most parents said that the alienation began when the child was much younger; only in a very few cases did alienation increase during adolescence. Secondly, the finding that alienation was, if anything, more strong in the persistent disorders argues against alienation being a special causal factor in the new group.

It may be that alienation from parents in earlier childhood predisposes the child to later disorder or it may be that the disorder leads to alienation, or both may be true. Nevertheless, it should not be assumed that the observed association between alienation and psychiatric disorder has the same meaning in the new disorders as it does in those persisting from early or middle childhood.

In the persistent group alienation probably stemmed from the psychiatric disorder in many cases. These children tended to come from disturbed homes in which parents showed psychiatric disorder, or there was severe marital discord, or the family had split up, and often the children had had periods "in care" as a result of the family difficulties. It seems that when marital discord is associated with gross family pathology, psychiatric disorder (if it occurs) is likely to develop in the children well before adolescence. In these cases alienation is probably just part of the general family disturbance.

The new disorders, in contrast, occurred in children from more stable families, although marital discord and alienation were also often present. As far as could be judged from parental reports, the alienation frequently began in earlier childhood *before* the onset of psychiatric disorder. In these cases alienation might well be a causal factor. The findings are in keeping with the hypothesis that deviant relationships and impaired communication patterns (i.e. alienation in the setting of marital discord) in families without severe disturbance may be factors in the development of psychiatric problems which do not become overt until the early or middle teens. On the other hand, our evidence suggests that alienation *arising for the first time* is *not* a common causal factor in either psychiatric group.

Does the same thing apply to "inner turmoil"? The findings are that misery, self-depreciation, suicidal ideas and ideas of reference occur with just the same frequency in the persistent disorders as in the new disorders. In short, if these are taken as reflections of "inner turmoil", "inner turmoil" is *no* more frequent in the children whose disorders have arisen *de novo* during adolescence.

The transience or persistence of adolescent disorders

Before attempting to summarize the findings, there is just one other set of data we have to consider and that refers to the prognosis of adolescent psychiatric conditions. An essential element in the concept of adolescent disorders, as a result of turmoil and alienation, is the supposition that the problems are variable in symptomatology, transient and benign. Is this borne out by the results of follow-up studies? We have no follow-up data on the Isle of Wight youngsters but data are available from several other studies such as those by Annesley (1961), Warren (1965), Masterson (1967) and Capes et al. (1971). As the findings from each are so closely similar they can be discussed together.

First, the question of symptom fluctuation. All the studies have shown that most disorders remain true to type and that symptom fluctuation is not a common feature. There is *no* reason to suppose that symptoms are more variable in adolescence than at any other age.

Secondly, the prognosis for adolescent psychiatric disorders does not appear to be any different (neither better or worse) from that for similar disorders in earlier childhood.

Thirdly, the prognosis varies markedly according to diagnosis. Psychoses have the worst outcome, neurotic conditions the best, with conduct disorders intermediate. This pattern is the same as that found in younger children.

These conclusions apply to the group of adolescent psychiatric disorders as a whole and not just to those whose problems arose *de novo* during adolescence. The evidence is not decisive but, so far as it goes, it suggests that their outlook is no different from the other. Warren (1965) found that the age of onset of the disorder did not influence the prognosis one way or the other. Capes *et al.* (1971) found that the prognosis was better for those whose first five years of life were reasonably trouble-free, but as nearly all of these had emotional disorders a good prognosis would have been expected on the basis of diagnosis alone. Neither Annesley (1961) nor Masterson (1967) presented their findings in a way which allows this comparison.

Generality of findings

The findings from the Isle of Wight study apply to 14–15-yr-old adolescents living in an area of small towns and villages. Whether the same apply to teenagers living in metropolitan or city areas remains uncertain. The level of psychiatric disorder among 10-yr-olds living in inner London is well above that found in Isle of Wight children of the same age (Rutter, 1973) and the same may be true at 14–15 yr. Nevertheless, the limited evidence from other investigations suggests that the *pattern* of findings from the present study may well be fairly general. Doubtless, the extent of parent–child alienation and the frequency of adolescent depression are influenced by socio-cultural factors, but how much so remains to be determined. It is also not known how far the pattern at age 18–19 yr differs from that in mid-adolescence. It is highly likely, however, that the situation will be much influenced by whether the young people are working and financially independent or whether they continue as students and remain dependent on their families.

CONCLUSIONS

The first conclusion is that although parent–child disagreements over items such as dress and hair length are fairly frequent, parent–child alienation is not a common feature at age 14 yr, unless the youngster is already showing psychiatric problems and even then it is present in only about half the group. We have no data concerning alienation during later adolescence but the findings from other studies suggest that it increases somewhat during the late teens but still remains a phenomenon confined to a minority, although possibly a substantial minority. The evidence is meagre and inconclusive but it may be that alienation and rebellion are most evident in those teenagers who, in spite of considerable maturity, remain economically or otherwise dependent on their parents (as would often be the case with respect to those in higher education).

Secondly, parents continue to have a substantial influence on their children right through adolescence. It is certainly true that peer group influences increase markedly during the teen-age period, but except in a minority of youngsters, they do *not* replace parental influences, although they sometimes rival them.

Thirdly, "inner turmoil" as represented by feelings of misery, self-depreciation and ideas of reference are quite common in 14-yr-olds. These feelings cause appreciable personal suffering but often they are unnoticed by adults. It remains uncertain how far these feelings constitute indicators or portents of psychiatric disorder.

Fourthly, psychiatric conditions are probably a little commoner during adolescence than during middle childhood but the difference is not a very great one and most adolescents do *not* show psychiatric disorder. On the other hand, the *pattern* of disorders shows a substantial shift in terms of the increased prevalence of both depression and school refusal.

Fifthly, many adolescent psychiatric problems arise in early childhood so that if prevention is to be attempted it must take place long before the child reaches his teens.

Sixthly, parent–child alienation arising in adolescence is probably not a very common *cause* of psychiatric disorder, in adolescence, although it is commonly *associated* with disorder. Alienation arising in earlier childhood, however, may be aetiologically important.

Seventhly, conditions arising for the first time during adolescence differ in certain important respects from those which persist from earlier childhood. The new conditions are more commonly found in girls, they are *un*associated with educational difficulties, and adverse family factors are less often found than in the early onset conditions.

Lastly, the prognosis for adolescent psychiatric disorders seems to be much more dependent upon diagnosis than upon the age of onset. Although the evidence is limited, there is no indication that disorders arising in adolescence have any different prognosis from those which arise in younger children.

Adolescent turmoil is a fact, not a fiction, but its psychiatric importance has probably been over-estimated in the past. Certainly it would be most *unwise* to assume that adolescents will "grow out" of their problems to a greater extent than do younger children.

SUMMARY

The concept of adolescent turmoil is considered in the context of findings from a total population epidemiological study of Isle of Wight 14–15-yr-olds. It is concluded that parent–child alienation is not a common feature unless the adolescents are already showing psychiatric problems. Inner turmoil, however, as represented by feelings of misery and self-depreciation is quite frequent. Psychiatric conditions are only slightly commoner during adolescence than in middle childhood but the pattern of disorders changes in terms of an increase in depression and school refusal. Many adolescent psychiatric problems arise in early childhood but conditions arising for the first time during adolescence differ in important respect from those with an earlier onset.

Acknowledgements—We are grateful to Professor J. Tizard (co-director of the project with M. R.) and Mr. L. Rigley who were jointly concerned with the organisation and planning of the Isle of Wight studies, and to our many colleagues who participated in the interviewing and testing. The project was supported by grants from the Nuffield Foundation and the Social Science Research Council.

REFERENCES

ADELSON, J. (1964) The mystique of adolescence. *Psychiat.* **27**, 1–5.
ANNESLEY, P. T. (1961) Psychiatric illness in adolescence: presentation and prognosis. *J. ment. Sci.* **107**, 268–278.

BALDWIN, J. A. (1968) Psychiatric illness from birth to maturity: an epidemiological study. *Acta psychiat. Scand.* **44,** 313–333.

BLOS, P. (1970) *The Young Adolescent: Clinical Studies.* Collier–Macmillan, London.

BROWN, G. W. and RUTTER, M. (1966) The measurement of family activities and relationships: a methodological study. *Human Relations* **19,** 241–263.

CAPES, M., GOULD, E. and TOWNSEND, M. (1971) *Stress in Youth.* Oxford University Press, London.

COLEMAN, J. S. (1961) *The Adolescent Society.* Collier–Macmillan, London.

DOUVAN, E. and ADELSON, J. (1966) *The Adolescent Experience.* Wiley, New York.

EISSLER, K. R. (1958) Notes on problems of technique in the psychoanalytic treatment of adolescents. *Psychoanal. Stud. Child* **13,** 223–254.

EPPERSON, D. C. (1964) A re-assessment of indices of parental influence in "The Adolescent Society". *Am. Sociol. Rev.* **29,** 93–96.

ERIKSON, E. H. (1955) The problem of ego identity. *J. Am. Psychoanal. Assoc.* **4,** 56–121.

FREUD, A. (1952) Adolescence. *Psychoanal. Stud. Child* **13,** 255–278.

GELEERD, E. R. (1961) Some aspects of ego vicissitudes in adolescence. *J. Am. Psychoanal. Ass.* **9,** 394–405.

GRAHAM, P. and RUTTER, M. (1973) Psychiatric disorder in the young adolescent: a follow-up study. *Proc. R. Soc. Med.* **66,** 1226–1229.

HENDERSON, A. S., KRUPINSKI, J. and STOLLER, A. (1971) Epidemiological aspects of adolescent psychiatry. In *Modern Perspectives in Adolescent Psychiatry* (Edited by HOWELLS, J. G.). Oliver & Boyd, Edinburgh, pp. 183–208.

JAHODA, M. and WARREN, N. (1965) The myths of youth. *Sociol. Education* **38,** 138–149.

JOSSELYN, I. M. (1954) The ego in adolescence. *Am. J. Orthopsychiat.* **24,** 223–237.

KRUPINSKI, J., BAIKIE, A. G., STOLLER, A., GRAVES, J., O'DAY, D. M. and POLKE, P. (1967) Community mental health survey of Heyfield, Victoria. *Med. J. Aust.* **1,** 1204–1211.

LESLIE, S. A. (1974) Psychiatric disorders in the young adolescents of an industrial town. *Br. J. Psychiat.* **125,** 113–124.

MASTERSON, J. F. (1967) *The Psychiatric Dilemma of Adolescence.* Churchill, London.

MEISSNER, W. W. (1965) Parental interaction of the adolescent boy. *J. genet. Psychol.* **107,** 225–233.

NEALE, M. D. (1958) *Neale Analysis of Reading Ability Manual.* Macmillan, London.

OFFER, D. (1969) *The Psychological World of the Teenager.* Basic Books, London.

RODRIGUEZ, A., RODRIGUEZ, M. and EISENBERG, L. (1959) The outcome of school phobia in a follow-up study based on 41 cases. *Am. J. Psychiat.* **116,** 540–544.

ROSEN, B. M., BAHN, A. K., SHELLOW, R. and BOWER, E. M. (1965) Adolescent patients served in outpatient psychiatric clinics. *Am. J. publ. Health* **55,** 1563–1577.

RUTTER, M. (1973) Why are London children so disturbed? *Proc. R. Soc. Med.* **66,** 1221–1225.

RUTTER, M. and BROWN, G. W. (1966) The reliability and validity of measures of family life and relationships in families containing a psychiatric patient. *Social Psychiat.* **1,** 38–53.

RUTTER, M., TIZARD, J. and WHITMORE, K. (Editors) (1970) *Education, Health and Behaviour.* Longmans, London.

SHAFFER, D. (1974) Suicide in childhood and early adolescence. *J. Child Psychol. Psychiat.* **15,** 275–292.

SHEPHERD, M., OPPENHEIM, B. and MITCHELL, S. (1971) *Childhood Behaviour and Mental Health.* University of London Press, London.

U.S. DEPARTMENT OF HEALTH, EDUCATION AND WELFARE (1966) *Patients in Mental Hospitals.* Public Service Publication No. 1818. Chevy Chase, M.D.

VERNON, P. E. (1949) *Graded Arithmetic–Mathematic Test.* University of London Press, London.

WARREN, W. (1965) A study of psychiatric in-patients and the outcome six or more years later—II. The follow-up study. *J. Child Psychol. Psychiat.* **6,** 141–160.

WECHSLER, D. (1949) *Wechsler Intelligence Scale for Children.* Psychological Corporation, New York.

Adolescence as
a Developmental Disturbance

Anna Freud

THE PSYCHOANALYTIC VIEW
OF MENTAL HEALTH AND ILLNESS

Our psychoanalytic investigations of individuals have convinced us that the line of demarcation between mental health and illness cannot be drawn as sharply as had been thought before. Especially so far as the neuroses are concerned, neurotic nuclei are found in the minds of normal people as regularly as large areas of normal functioning are part of the makeup of every neurotic. Also, people cross and recross the border between mental health and illness many times during their lives.

There is the further point that the concept of health as it is derived from the physical field cannot be taken over to the mental side without alteration. Physically, we are healthy so long as the various organs of the body function normally and, via their specific action, contribute to an over-all state of well-being. Mentally, more than this is needed. It is not enough if each part of the mind, as such, is intact, since the various parts of our personality pursue different aims and since these aims are only too often at cross purposes with each other. Thus, we may be healthy so far as our instinctual drives are concerned; or our sense of reality plus adaptation to the environment may be well up to the mark; or our ideals may be considered admirable by other people. Nevertheless, these single items do not yet add up to the result of mental health. To achieve this, all the agencies in our mind—drives, reasonable ego, and ideals—have to coincide sensibly and, while adapting to the external world, resolve the conflicts inherent in the total situation. To say it in other words: mental health depends on workable compromises and on the resulting balance of forces between the different internal agencies and different external and internal demands.

THE CONCEPT OF DEVELOPMENTAL DISTURBANCES

It is implied in the view above that this balance and these compromises are precarious and easily upset by any alteration in the internal or external circumstances. It is obvious also that such changes are as inevitable as they are continuous and that they occur especially frequently on the basis of development. Every step forward in growth and maturation brings with it not only new gains but also new problems. To the psychoanalyst this means that change in any part of mental life upsets the balance as it had been established earlier and that new compromises have to be devised. Such change may affect the instinctual drives, as happens in adolescence; or it may occur in the ego, that is, in the agency whose function it is to manage and control the drives; or what undergoes change may be the individual's demands on himself, his aims and ideals or his love objects in the external world or other influences in his environment. Changes may be quantitative or qualitative. Whatever they are, they affect the internal equilibrium.

Developmental disturbances of this type are frequent occurrences, for example, in the area of sleep and food intake in early childhood. Infants may be perfect sleepers in the first half-year of life, that is, drop off to sleep whenever they are tired and when no stimuli from inside or outside their bodies are strong enough to disrupt their peace. This will alter with normal further growth when the child's clinging to the people and happenings in his environment make it difficult for him to withdraw into himself and when falling asleep thereby is turned into a conflictful process. Likewise, the disturbing food fads of childhood are no more than the impact on eating of various infantile fantasies, of dirt, of impregnation through the mouth, of poisoning, of killing. These fantasies are tied to specific developmental phases and are transitory accordingly, as are the feeding disorders based on them. In fact, in clinical practice with children, the concept of transitory developmental disturbances has become indispensable to us as a diagnostic category.

It is worth noting here that developmental change not only causes upset but can also effect what is called spontaneous cures. A case in point here is the temper tantrums that serve young children as affective-motor outlets at a time when no other discharge is available to them. This is altered by the mere fact of speech development that opens up new pathways and by which the earlier turbulent and chaotic behavioral manifestation is rendered redundant.

THE ADOLESCENT REACTIONS AS PROTOTYPES OF DEVELOPMENTAL DISTURBANCES

Let us return to the problems of adolescence that, in my view, are the prototypes of such developmental upsets.

Although in the childhood disorders of this nature we are confronted usually with alterations in one or the other area of the child's personality, in adolescence we deal with changes along the whole line. There are, as a basis on the physical side, the changes in size, strength, and appearance. There are the endocrinological changes that aim at a complete revolution in sexual life. There are changes in the aggressive expressions, advances in intellectual performance, reorientations as to object attachments and to social relations. In short, the upheavals in character and personality are often so sweeping that the picture of the former child becomes wholly submerged in the newly emerging image of the adolescent.

A. Alterations in the Drives

So far as the sexual drive in adolescence is concerned, I have found it useful to differentiate between quantitative and qualitative changes. What we see first, in the period of preadolescence, is an indiscriminate increase in drive activity that affects all the facets which have characterized infantile sexuality, that is, the pregenital, sexual-aggressive responses of the first five years of life. At this juncture, the preadolescent individual becomes, as a first step, hungrier, greedier, more cruel, more dirty, more inquisitive, more boastful, more egocentric, more inconsiderate than he has been before. This exacerbation of the pregenital elements is followed then, shortly after, by a change in the quality of the drive, namely the changeover from pregenital to genital sexual impulses. This new element involves the adolescent in dangers which did not exist before and with which he is not accustomed to deal. Since, at this stage, he lives and functions still as a member of his family unit, he runs the risk of allowing the new genital urges to connect with his old love objects, that is, with his parents, brothers, or sisters.

B. Alterations in the Ego Organization

It is these temptations of giving way, first to sexual-aggressive pregenital behavior and, next, to incestuous fantasies or even actions that cause all those ego changes which impress the observer as the adolescent's personal upheaval and also as his unpredictability. Serious attempts are made by the preadolescent to keep the quantitative drive increase under control as drive activity has been controlled in earlier periods. This is done by means of major efforts on the side of the defenses. It means bringing into play more repressions, more reaction formations, more identifications and projections, sometimes also more determined attempts at intellectualizations and sublimations. It means also that the entire defensive system of the ego is overstrained and breaks down repeatedly and that therefore the frantic warding off of impulses alternates with unrestrained upsurges of drive activity. When we approach a young adolescent at this stage, we never know which of these two aspects we are going to meet: his overstrict, highly defended personality or his openly aggressive, openly sexual, uninhibited primitive self.

C. Alterations in Object Relations

What serves the preadolescent as some protection against the quantitative pressure of the drives proves wholly inadequate against the qualitative change to a primacy of the genital urges, that is, adult sexuality proper. Nothing helps here except a complete discarding of the people who were the important love objects of the child, that is, the parents. This battle against the parents is fought out in a variety of ways: by openly displayed indifference toward them—by denying that they are important—by disparagement of them since it is easier to do without them if they are denounced as stupid, useless, ineffective; by open insolence and revolt against their persons and the beliefs and conventions for which they stand. That these reactions alternate also with returns to helplessness and dependence on the part of the young persons does not make it any easier for the parents. Obviously, the task imposed on them is a double one: to be thick-skinned, self-effacing, and reserved, but also to change over at a moment's notice to being as sympathetic, concerned, alert, and helpful as in former times.

The closer the tie between child and parent has been before, the more bitter and violent will be the struggle for independence from them in adolescence.

D. Alterations in Ideals and Social Relations

The adolescent's change in social relationships follows as the direct consequence of his stepping out of his family. He is not only left without his earlier object ties. Together with the attachment to his parents, he has thrown out also the ideals that he shared with them formerly, and he needs to find substitutes for both.

There is a parting of the ways here which, I believe, produces two different types of adolescent culture. Some adolescents put into the empty place of the parents a self-chosen leader who himself is a member of the parent generation. This person may be a university teacher, a poet, a philosopher, a politician. Whoever he may be, he is considered infallible, Godlike, and is followed gladly and blindly. At present, though, this solution is comparatively rare. More frequent is the second course where the peer group as such or a member of it is exalted to the role of leadership and becomes the unquestioned arbiter in all matters of moral and aesthetic value.

The hallmark of the new ideals as well as of the new emotionally important people is always the same: that they should be as different as possible from the former ones. In the remote past, when I myself was adolescent, there had come into being in central Europe the so-called Youth Movement, a first attempt at an independent adolescent culture. This was directed against the bourgeois complacency and capitalistic outlook of the parent generation of the period, and the ideals upheld by it were those of socialism, intellectual freedom, aestheticism, and so on. Poetry, art, and classical music were what parents did not believe in, although adolescents did. We know how far the tide has turned in the last two generations. At present, adolescents are hard put to set up new ideals—constructive or disastrous—which can serve to mark the dividing line between their own and their parents' lives.

CONCLUDING REMARKS

To the abbreviated summary of the main theme given above, I add a few concluding remarks that concern more general issues.

First, it has struck me always as unfortunate that the period of adolescent upheaval and inner rearrangement of forces coincides with such major demands on the individual as those for academic achievements in school and college, for a choice of career, for increased social and financial responsibility in general. Many failures, often with tragic consequences in these respects, are due not to the individual's incapacity as such but merely to the fact that such demands are made on him at a time of life when all his energies are engaged otherwise, namely, in trying to solve the major problems created for him by normal sexual growth and development.

Second, I feel that the obvious preponderance of sexual problems in adolescence is in danger of obscuring the concomitant role of aggression that, possibly, might be of great significance. It is worth noting that countries which are engaged in a struggle for existence, such as, for example, Israel, do not report the same difficulties with their adolescents as we do in the Western world. The main difference in their situation is that the aggression of the young people is not lived out within the family or community but directed against the enemy forces that threaten the state and therefore usefully employed in socially approved warlike activities. Since this is a factor outside the sphere of sexual growth, this should extend our thinking into new directions.

Third and last, it seems to me an error not to consider the details of the adolescent revolt in the light of side issues, disturbing as they may be. If we wish to maintain the developmental point of view, it is of less significance how the adolescent behaves at home, in school, at the university, or in the community at large. What is of major importance is to know which type of adolescent upheaval is more apt than others to lead to a satisfactory form of adult life.

Amer. J. Orthopsychiat. 52(2), April 1982

THEORY AND REVIEW

NEW MAPS OF DEVELOPMENT:
New Visions of Maturity

Carol Gilligan

Graduate School of Education, Harvard University, Cambridge, Mass.

Two modes of moral reasoning are distinguished in boys' and girls' discussions of moral dilemmas: one oriented to justice and rights, one to care and response. These different modes are associated with different forms of self-definition and reflect different images of relationships. The contrasting images of hierarchy and web derive from childhood experiences of inequality and interdependence which give rise to the ideals of justice and of care. The representation of these two lines of development and their interplay yields a new mapping of human growth.

That development is the aim of a liberal education seems clear until we begin to ask what is a liberal education and what constitutes development. The current spirit of reappraisal in the field of education stems in part from the fact that some old promises have failed and new practices must be found if the vision of education for freedom and for democracy is to be realized or sustained. But this current reappraisal in the field of education finds its parallel in the field of developmental psychology where a similar reassessment is taking place, a reassessment that began in the early 1970s when developmental psychologists began to question the adulthood that formerly they had taken for granted and when the exclusion of women from the research samples from which developmental theories were generated began to be noticed as a serious omission and one that pointed to the exclusion of other groups as well. Thus, if the

Presented, in earlier versions, to the National Academy of Education, October 1981, and to the Conference on Adolescent Development and Secondary Schooling, Wisconsin Center for Education Research, November 1981. Research was supported by grant RO3-MH31571 from the National Institute of Mental Health and grant G790131 from the National Institute of Education. Portions of this paper are contained in a full-length work, In a Different Voice: Psychological Theory and Women's Development, *by Carol Gilligan, forthcoming from Harvard University Press in May 1982.*

199

changing population of students, particularly the larger number of adults and especially of adult women entering postsecondary education, has raised a series of questions about the aims of education and the nature of educational practice, the study of adulthood and of women has generated a new set of questions for theorists of human development.

To ask whether current developmental theories can be applied to understanding or assessing the lives of people who differ from those upon whose experience these theories were based is only to introduce a problem of far greater magnitude, the adequacy of current theories themselves. The answer to the initial question is in one sense clear, given that these theories are used repeatedly in assessing the development of different groups. But the question asked in such assessment is how much like the original group is the different group being assessed. For example, if the criteria for development are derived from studies of males and these criteria are then used to measure the development of females, the question being asked is how much like men do women develop. The assumption underlying this approach is that there is a universal standard of development and a single scale of measurement along which differences found can be aligned as higher and lower, better and worse. Yet, the initial exclusion of women displays the fallacy of this assumption and indicates a recognition of difference, pointing to the problem I wish to address. While I will use the experience of women to demonstrate how the group left out in the construction of theory calls attention to what is missing in its account, my interest lies not only in

women and the perspective they add to the narrative of growth but also in the problem that differences post for a liberal educational philosophy that strives toward an ideal of equality and for a developmental psychology that posits a universal and invariant sequence of growth. In joining the subjects of morality and women, I focus specifically on the questions of value inherent in education and in developmental psychology, and indicate how the lives of women call into question current maps of development and inform a new vision of human growth.

The repeated marking of women's experience as, in Freud's terms, "a dark continent for psychology"[5] raises a question as to what has shadowed the understanding of women's lives. Since women in fact do not live on a continent apart from men but instead repeatedly engage with them in the activities of everyday life, the mystery deepens and the suggestion emerges that theory may be blinding observation. While the disparity between women's experience and the representation of human development, noted throughout the psychological literature, has generally been seen to signify a problem in women's development, the failure of women to fit existing models of human growth may point to a problem in the representation, a limitation in the conception of the human condition, an omission of certain truths about life. The nature of these truths and their implications for understanding development and thinking about education are the subjects of this paper.

CONSTRUCTION OF RELATIONSHIPS AND THE CONCEPT OF MORALITY

Evidence of sex differences in the findings of psychological research comes mainly from studies that reveal the way in which men and women construct the relation between self and others. While the differences observed in women's experience and understanding of relationships have posed a problem of interpretation that recurs throughout the literature on psychoanalysis and personality psychology, this problem emerges with particular clarity in the field of moral judgment research. Since moral judgments pertain to conflicts in the relation of self to others, a difference in the construction of that relationship would lead to a difference in the conception of the moral domain. This difference would be manifest in the way in which moral problems are seen, in the questions asked which then serve to guide the judgment and resolution of moral dilemmas. While the failure to perceive this difference has led psychologists to apply constructs derived from research on men to the interpretation of women's experience and thought, the recognition of this difference points to the limitation of this approach. If women's moral judgments reflect a different understanding of social relationships, then they may point to a line of social development whose presence in both sexes is currently obscured.

THEORIES OF MORAL DEVELOPMENT

This discussion of moral development takes place against the background of a field where, beginning with Freud's theory that tied superego formation to castration anxiety, extending through Piaget's study of boys' conceptions of the rules of their games, and culminating in Kohlberg's derivation of six stages of moral development from research on adolescent males, the line of develop-

ment has been shaped by the pattern of male experience and thought. The continual reliance on male experience to build the model of moral growth has been coupled with a continuity in the conception of morality itself. Freud's observation that "the first requisite of civilization is justice, the assurance that a rule once made will not be broken in favour of an individual,"[4] extends through Piaget's conception of morality as consisting in respect for rules[16] and into Kohlberg's claim that justice is the most adequate of moral ideals.[12] The imagery that runs through this equation of morality with justice depicts a world comprised of separate individuals whose claims fundamentally conflict but who find in morality a mode of regulating conflict by agreement that allows the development of life lived in common.

The notion that moral development witnesses the replacement of the rule of brute force with the rule of law, bringing isolated and endangered individuals into a tempered connection with one another, then leads to the observation that women, less aggressive and thus less preoccupied with rules, are as a result less morally developed. The recurrent observations of sex differences that mark the literature on moral development are striking not only in their concurrence but in their reiterative elaboration of a single theme. Whether expressed in the general statement that women show less sense of justice than men[5] or in the particular notation that girls, in contrast to boys, think it better to give back fewer blows than one has received,[16] the direction of these differences is always the same, pointing in women to a greater sense of connection, a concern with relationships more than with rules. But this observation then yields to the paradoxical conclusion that women's preoccupation with relationships constitutes an impediment to the progress of their moral development.

THE MORAL JUDGMENTS OF TWO ELEVEN-YEAR-OLDS

To illustrate how a difference in the understanding of relationships leads to a difference in the conceptions of morality and of self, I begin with the moral judgments of two 11-year-old children, a boy and a girl who see in the same dilemma two very different moral problems. Demonstrating how brightly current theory illuminates the line and the logic of the boy's thought while casting scant light on that of the girl, I will show how the girl's judgments reflect a fundamentally different approach. I have chosen for the purposes of this discussion a girl whose moral judgments elude current categories of developmental assessment, in order to highlight the problem of interpretation rather than to exemplify sex differences per se. My aim is to show how, by adding a new line of interpretation, it becomes possible to see development where previously development was not discerned and to consider differences in the understanding of relationships without lining up these differences on a scale from better to worse.

The two children—Amy and Jake— were in the same sixth grade class at school and participated in a study[8] designed to explore different conceptions of morality and self. The sample selected for study was chosen to focus the variables of gender and age while maximizing developmental potential by holding constant, at a high level, the factors of intelligence, education, and social class that have been associated with moral development, at least as measured by existing scales. The children in question were both bright and articulate and, at least in their 11-year-old aspirations, resisted easy categories of sex-role stereotyping since Amy aspired to become a scientist while Jake preferred English to math. Yet their moral judgments seemed initially to confirm previous findings of differences between the sexes, suggesting that the edge girls have on moral development during the early school years gives way at puberty with the ascendance of formal logical thought in boys.

The dilemma these children were asked to resolve was one in the series devised by Kohlberg to measure moral development in adolescence by presenting a conflict between moral norms and exploring the logic of its resolution. In this particular dilemma, a man named Heinz considers whether or not to steal a drug, which he cannot afford to buy, in order to save the life of his wife. In the standard format of Kohlberg's interviewing procedure, the description of the dilemma itself—Heinz's predicament, the wife's disease, the druggist's refusal to lower his price—is followed by the question, should Heinz steal the drug? Then the reasons for and against stealing are explored through a series of further questions, conceived as probes and designed to reveal the underlying structure of moral thought.

Jake

Jake, at 11, is clear from the outset that Heinz should steal the drug. Constructing the dilemma as Kohlberg did as a conflict between the values of property and life, he discerns the logical priority of life and uses that logic to justify his choice:

For one thing, a human life is worth more than money, and if the druggist only makes $1000, he is still going to live, but if Heinz doesn't steal the drug, his wife is going to die. [*Why is life worth more than money?*] Because the druggist can get a thousand dollars later from rich people with cancer, but Heinz can't get his wife again. [*Why not?*] Because people are all different, and so you couldn't get Heinz's wife again.

Asked if Heinz should steal the drug if he does not love his wife, Jake replies that he should, saying that not only is there "a difference between hating and killing," but also, if Heinz were caught, "the judge would probably think it was the right thing to do." Asked about the fact that, in stealing, Heinz would be breaking the law, he says that "the laws have mistakes and you can't go writing up a law for everything that you can imagine."

Thus, while taking the law into account and recognizing its function in maintaining social order (the judge, he says, "should give Heinz the lightest possible sentence"), he also sees the law as man-made and therefore subject to error and change. Yet his judgment that Heinz should steal the drug, like his view of the law as having mistakes, rests on the assumption of agreement, a societal consensus around moral values that allows one to know and expect others will recognize "the right thing to do."

Fascinated by the power of logic, this 11-year-old boy locates truth in math which, he says, is "the only thing that is totally logical." Considering the moral dilemma to be "sort of like a math problem with humans," he sets it up as an equation and proceeds to work out the solution. Since his solution is rationally derived, he assumes that anyone following reason would arrive at the same conclusion and thus that a judge would

also consider stealing to be the right thing for Heinz to do. Yet he is also aware of the limits of logic; asked whether there is a right answer to moral problems, he says that "there can only be right and wrong in judgment," since the parameters of action are variable and complex. Illustrating how actions undertaken with the best of intentions can eventuate in the most disastrous of consequences, he says

. . . like if you give an old lady your seat on the trolley, if you are in a trolley crash and that seat goes through the window, it might be that reason that the old lady dies.

Theories of developmental psychology illuminate well the position of this child, standing at the jucture of childhood and adolescence, at what Piaget described as the pinnacle of childhood intelligence, and beginning through thought to discover a wider universe of possibility. The moment of preadolescence is caught by the conjunction of formal operational thought with a description of self still anchored in the factual parameters of his childhood world, his age, his town, his father's occupation, the substance of his likes, dislikes, and beliefs. Yet as his self-description radiates the self-confidence of a child who has arrived, in Erikson's terms, at a favorable balance of industry over inferiority—competent, sure of himself, and knowing well the rules of the game—so his emergent capacity for formal thought, his ability to think about thinking and to reason things out in a logical way, frees him from dependence on authority and allows him to find solutions to problems by himself.

This emergent autonomy then charts the trajectory that Kohlberg's six stages of moral development trace, a three-level progression from an egocentric understanding of fairness based on individual need (stages one and two), to a conception of fairness anchored in the shared conventions of societal agreement (stages three and four), and finally to a principled understanding of fairness that rests on the free-standing logic of equality and reciprocity (stages five and six). While Jake's judgments at 11 are scored as conventional on Kohlberg's scale, a mixture of stages three and four, his ability to bring deductive logic to bear on the solution of moral dilemmas, to differentiate morality from law, and to see how laws can be considered to have mistakes, points toward the principled conception of justice that Kohlberg equates with moral maturity.

Amy

In contrast, Amy's response to the dilemma conveys a very different impression, an image of development stunted by a failure of logic, an inability to think for herself. Asked if Heinz should steal the drug, she replies in a way that seems evasive and unsure:

Well, I don't think so. I think there might be other ways besides stealing it, like if he could borrow the money or make a loan or something, but he really shouldn't steal the drug, but his wife shouldn't die either.

Asked why he should not steal the drug, she considers neither property nor law but rather the effect that theft could have on the relationship between Heinz and his wife. If he stole the drug, she explains,

. . . he might save his wife then, but if he did, he might have to go to jail, and then his wife might get sicker again, and he couldn't get more of the drug, and it might not be good. So, they should really just talk it out and find some other way to make the money.

Seeing in the dilemma not a math problem with humans but a narrative of relationships that extends over time, she envisions the wife's continuing need for her husband and the husband's continuing concern for his wife and seeks to respond to the druggist's need in a way that would sustain rather than sever connection. As she ties the wife's survival to the preservation of relationships, so she considers the value of her life in a context of relationships, saying that it would be wrong to let her die because, "if she died, it hurts a lot of people and it hurts her." Since her moral judgment is grounded in the belief that "if somebody has something that would keep somebody alive, then it's not right not to give it to them," she considers the problem in the dilemma to arise not from the druggist's assertion of rights but from his failure of response.

While the interviewer proceeds with the series of questions that follow Kohlberg's construction of the dilemma, Amy's answers remain essentially unchanged, the various probes serving neither to elucidate nor to modify her initial response. Whether or not Heinz loves his wife, he still shouldn't steal or let her die; if it were a stranger dying instead, she says that "if the stranger didn't have anybody near or anyone she knew," then Heinz should try to save her life but he shouldn't steal the drug. But as the interviewer conveys through the repetition of questions that the answers she has given are not heard or not right, Amy's confidence begins to diminish and her replies become more constrained and unsure. Asked again why Heinz should not steal the drug, she simply repeats, "Because it's not right." Asked again to explain why, she states again that theft would not be a good solution, adding lamely, that, "if he took it, he might not know how to give it to his wife, and so his wife might still die." Failing to see the dilemma as a self-contained problem in moral logic, she does not discern the internal structure of its resolution; as she constructs the problem differently herself, Kohlberg's conception completely evades her.

Instead, seeing a world comprised of relationships rather than of people standing alone, a world that coheres through human connection rather than through systems of rules, she finds the puzzle in the dilemma to lie in the failure of the druggist to respond to the wife. Saying that "it is not right for someone to die when their life could be saved," she assumes that if the druggist were to see the consequences of his refusal to lower his price, he would realize that "he should just give it to the wife and then have the husband pay back the money later." Thus she considers the solution to the dilemma to lie in making the wife's condition more salient to the druggist or, that failing, in appealing to others who are in a position to help.

Just as Jake is confident the judge would agree that stealing is the right thing for Heinz to do, so Amy is confident that, "if Heinz and the druggist had talked it out long enough, they could reach something besides stealing." As he considers the law to "have mistakes," so she sees this drama as a mistake, believing that "the world should just share things more and then people wouldn't have to steal." Both children thus recognize the need for agreement but see it as mediated in different ways: he impersonally through systems of logic and law, she personally through communication in relationship. As he relies on the conventions of logic to de-duce the solution to this dilemma, assuming these conventions to be shared, so she relies on a process of communication, assuming connection and believing that her voice will be heard. Yet while his assumptions about agreement are confirmed by the convergence in logic between his answers and the questions posed, her assumptions are belied by the failure in communication, the interviewer's inability to understand her response.

MEASURING MORAL DEVELOPMENT: ASSESSING DIVERSE PERCEPTIONS

While the frustration of the interview with Amy is apparent in the repetition of questions and its ultimate circularity, the problem of interpretation arises when it comes to assessing her development. Considered in the light of Kohlberg's conception of the stages and sequence of moral development, her moral judgments are a full stage lower in moral maturity than those of the boy. Scored as a mixture of stages two and three, they seem to reveal a feeling of powerlessness in the world, an inability to think systematically about the concepts of morality or law, a reluctance to challenge authority or to examine the logic of received moral truths, a failure even to conceive of acting directly to save a life or to consider that such action, if taken, could possibly have an effect. As her reliance on relationships seems to reveal a continuing dependence and vulnerability, so her belief in communication as the mode through which to resolve moral dilemmas appears naive and cognitively immature.

Yet her description of herself conveys a markedly different impression. Once again, the hallmarks of the preadolescent child depict a child secure in her sense of herself, confident in the substance of her beliefs, and sure of her ability to do something of value in the world. Describing herself at 11 as "growing and changing," Amy says that she "sees some things differently now, just because I know myself really well now, and I know a lot more about the world." Yet the world she knows is a different world from that refracted by Kohlberg's construction of Heinz's dilemma. Her world is a world of relationships and psychological truths, where an awareness of the connection between people gives rise to a recognition of responsibility for one another, a perception of the need for response. Seen in this light, her view of morality as arising from the recognition of relationship, her belief in communication as the mode of conflict resolution, and her conviction that the solution to the dilemma will follow from its compelling representation seem far from naive or cognitively immature; rather, her judgments contain the insights central to an ethic of care, just as Jake's judgments reflect the logic of the justice approach. Her incipient awareness of the "method of truth," central to nonviolent conflict resolution, and her belief in the restorative activity of care, lead her to see the actors in the dilemma arrayed not as opponents in a contest of rights but as members of a network of relationships on whose continuation they all depend. Consequently her solution to the dilemma lies in activating the network by communication, securing the inclusion of the wife by strengthening rather than severing connection.

But the different logic of Amy's response calls attention to a problem in the interpretation of the interview itself. Conceived as an interrogation, it appears as a dialogue that takes on moral dimensions of its own, pertaining to the interviewer's uses of power and to the manifestations of respect. With this shift in the conception of the interview, it immediately becomes clear that the interviewer's problem in hearing Amy's response stems from the fact that Amy is answering a different question from the one the interviewer thought had been posed. Amy is considering not *whether* Heinz should act in this situation (*Should* Heinz steal the drug?) but rather *how* Heinz should act in response to his awareness of his wife's need (Should Heinz *steal* the drug?). The interviewer takes the mode of action for granted, presuming it to be a matter of fact. Amy assumes the necessity for action and considers what form it should take. In the interviewer's failure to imagine a response not dreamt of in Kohlberg's moral philosophy lies the failure to hear Amy's question and to see the logic in her response, to discern that what from one perspective appears to be an evasion of the dilemma signifies in other terms a recognition of the problem and a search for a more adequate solution.

Thus in Kohlberg's dilemma these two children see two very different moral problems—Jake a conflict between life and property that can be resolved by logical deduction, Amy a fracture of human relationship that must be mended with its own thread. Asking different questions that arise from different conceptions of the moral domain, they arrive at answers that fundamentally diverge, and the arrangement of these answers as successive stages on a scale of increasing moral maturity calibrated by the logic of the boy's response misses the different truth revealed in the judgment of the girl. To the question, "What does he see that she does not?", Kohlberg's theory provides a ready response, manifest in the scoring of his judgments a full stage higher than hers in moral maturity; to the question, "What does she see that he does not?", Kohlberg's theory has nothing to say. Since most of her responses fall through the sieve of Kohlberg's scoring system, her responses appear from his perspective to lie outside the moral domain.

Yet just as Jake reveals a sophisticated understanding of the logic of justification, so Amy is equally sophisticated in her understanding of the nature of choice. Saying that "if both the roads went in totally separate ways, if you pick one, you'll never know what would happen if you went the other way," she explains that "that's the chance you have to take, and like I said, it's just really a guess." To illustrate her point "in a simple way," she describes how, in choosing to spend the summer at camp, she

. . . will never know what would have happened if I had stayed here, and if something goes wrong at camp, I'll never know if I stayed here if it would have been better. There's really no way around it because there's no way you can do both at once, so you've got to decide, but you'll never know.

In this way, these two 11-year-old children, both highly intelligent, though perceptive about life in different ways, display different modes of moral understanding, different ways of thinking about conflict and choice. Jake, in resolving the dilemma, follows the construction that Kohlberg has posed. Relying on theft to avoid confrontation and turning to the law to mediate the dispute, he transposes a hierarchy of power into a hierarchy of values by recasting a conflict between people into a

conflict of claims. Thus abstracting the moral problem from the interpersonal situation, he finds in the logic of fairness an objective means of deciding who will win the dispute. But this hierarchical ordering, with its imagery of winning and losing and the potential for violence which it contains, gives way in Amy's construction of the dilemma to a network of connection, a network sustained by a process of communication. With this shift, the moral problem changes from one of unfair domination, the imposition of property over life, to one of unnecessary exclusion, the failure of the druggist to respond to the wife.

This shift in the formulation of the moral problem and the concomitant change in the imagery of relationships are illustrated as well by the responses of two eight-year-olds who participated in the same study[8] and were asked to describe a situation in which they weren't sure of the right thing to do:

Jeffrey (age 8): When I really want to go to my friends and my mother is cleaning the cellar, I think about my friends, and then I think about my mother, and then I think about the right thing to do. [*But how do you know it's the right thing to do?*] Because some things go before other things.

Karen (age 8): I have a lot of friends, and I can't always play with all of them, so everybody's going to have to take a turn, because they're all my friends. But like if someone's all alone, I'll play with them. [*What kind of things do you think about when you are trying to make that decision?*] Um, someone all alone, loneliness.

While Jeffrey sets up a hierarchical ordering in thinking about the conflict between desire and duty, Karen describes a network of relationships that includes all of her friends. Both children deal with the issues of exclusion and priority created by choice, but while

Jeffrey thinks about what goes first, Karen focuses on who is left out.

MORAL JUDGMENT
AND SELF-DESCRIPTIONS

In illustrating a difference in children's thinking about moral conflict and choice, I have described two views that are complementary rather than sequential or opposed. In doing so, I go against the bias of developmental theory toward ordering differences in a hierarchical mode. This correspondence between the order of developmental theory and that manifest in the boys' responses contrasts with the disparity between the structure of theory and that manifest in the thought of the girls. Yet, in neither comparison does one child's thought appear as precursor of the other's position. Thus, questions arise about the relation between these perspectives; what is the significance of these differences, and how do these two modes of thinking connect? To pursue these questions, I return to the eleven-year-olds and consider the way they describe themselves.

[*How would you describe yourself to yourself?*]

Jake: Perfect. That's my conceited side. What do you want—any way that I choose to describe myself?

Amy: You mean my character? [*What do you think?*] Well, I don't know. I'd describe myself as, well, what do you mean?

[*If you had to describe the person you are in a way that you yourself would know it was you, what would you say?*]

Jake: I'd start off with eleven years old. Jake [last name]. I'd have to add that I live in [town] because that is a big part of me, and also that my father is a doctor because I think that does change me a little bit, and that I don't believe in crime, except for when your name is Heinz . . . that I think school is boring because I think that kind of changes your

character a little bit. I don't sort of know how to describe myself, because I don't know how to read my personality. [*If you had to describe the way you actually would describe yourself, what would you say?*] I like corny jokes. I don't really like to get down to work, but I can do all the stuff in school. Every single problem that I have seen in school I have been able to do, except for ones that take knowledge, and after I do the reading, I have been able to do them, but sometimes I don't want to waste my time on easy homework. And also I'm crazy about sports. I think, unlike a lot of people, that the world still has hope. . . . Most people that I know I like, and I have the good life, pretty much as good as any I have seen, and I am tall for my age.

Amy: Well, I'd say that I was someone who likes school and studying, and that's what I want to do with my life. I want to be some kind of a scientist or something, and I want to do things, and I want to help people. And I think that's what kind of person I am, or what kind of person I try to be. And that's probably how I'd describe myself. And I want to do something to help other people. [*Why is that?*] Well, because I think that this world has a lot of problems, and I think that everybody should try to help somebody else in some way, and the way I'm choosing is through science.

In the voice of the 11-year-old boy, a familiar form of self-definition appears, resonating to the schoolbook inscription of the young Stephen Daedalus ("himself, his name and where he was")[10] and echoing the descriptions that appear in *Our Town*,[18] laying out across the coordinates of time and space a hierarchical order in which to define one's place. Describing himself as distinct by locating his particular position in the world, Jake sets himself apart from that world by his abilities, his beliefs, and his height. Although Amy also enumerates her likes, her wants, and her beliefs, she locates herself in relation to the world, describing herself through actions that bring her into connection with others, elaborating ties through her ability to provide help. To Jake's ideal of perfection against which he measures the worth of himself,

Amy counterposes an ideal of care against which she measures the worth of her activity. While she places herself in relation to the world and chooses to help others through science, he places the world in relation to himself as it defines his character, his position, and the quality of life.

CONCLUSIONS

As the voices of these children illuminate two modes of self-description and two modes of moral judgment, so they illustrate how readily we hear the voice that speaks of justice and of separation and the difficulty we encounter in listening to the voice that speaks of care and connection. Listening through developmental theories and through the structures of our educational and social system, we are attuned to a hierarchical ordering that represents development as a progress of separation, a chronicle of individual success. In contrast, the understanding of development as a progress of human relationships, a narrative of expanding connection, is an unimagined representation. The image of network or web thus seems more readily to connote entrapment rather than an alternative and nonhierarchical vision of human connection.

This central limitation in the representation of development is most clearly apparent in recent portrayals of adult life, where the insistent focus on self and on work provides scanty representation of an adulthood spent in the activities of relationship and care. The tendency to chart the unfamiliar waters of adult development with the familiar markers of adolescent separation and growth leads to an equation of development with separation; it results in a failure to represent the reality of connection both in love and in work. Levinson,[15] patterning the stages of adult development on the seasons of a man's life, defined the developmental process explicitly as one of individuation, yet reported his distress at the absence of friendships in men's lives. Vaillant,[17] deriving his account of adaptation to life from the lives of the men who took part in the Grant study, noted that the question these men found most difficult to answer was, "Can you describe your wife?" In this light, the observation that women's embeddedness in lives of relationship, their orientation to interdependence, their subordination of achievement to care, and their conflicts over competitive success leave them personally at risk in mid-life, though generally construed as a problem in women's development, seems more a commentary on our society and on the representation of development itself.

In suggesting that the consideration of women's lives and of adulthood calls attention to the need for an expansion in the mapping of human development, I have pointed to a distinction between two modes of self-definition and two modes of moral judgment and indicated how these modes reflect different ways of imagining relationships. That these modes are tied to different experiences may explain their empirical association with gender, though that association is by no means absolute. That they reflect different forms of thought—one relying on a formal logic whose development Piaget has described, the other on a narrative and contextual mode of thought whose development remains to be traced—indicates the implication of this distinction for psychological assessment and education.

The experiences of inequality and of

interdependence are embedded in the cycle of life, universal because inherent in the relationship of parent and child. These experiences of inequality and interdependence give rise to the ethics of justice and care, the ideals of human relationship—the vision that self and other will be treated as of equal worth, that despite differences in power, things will be fair; the vision that everyone will be responded to and included, that no one will be left alone or hurt. The adolescent, capable of envisioning the ideal, reflects on the childhood experiences of powerlessness and vulnerability and conceives a utopian world laid out along the coordinates of justice and care. This ability to conceive the hypothetical and to construct contrary-to-fact hypotheses has led the adolescent to be proclaimed a "philosopher,"[11] a "metaphysician par excellence."[9] But the representation of the adolescent's moral philosophy in the literature of developmental psychology has been limited to the portrayal of changes in the conception of justice that supports the adolescent's claim to equality and the separation of other and self. My own work[7] has expanded this description by identifying two different moral languages, the language of rights that protects separation and the language of responsibilities that sustains connection. In dialogue, these languages not only create the ongoing tension of moral discourse, but also reveal how the dynamics of separation and attachment in the process of identity formation relate to the themes of justice and care in moral growth. This expanded representation of identity and moral development allows a more complex rendering of differences, and points to the need

to understand and foster the development of both modes.

The old promise of a liberal education, of an education that frees individuals from blinding constraints and engenders a questioning of assumptions formerly taken for granted remains a compelling vision. But among the prevailing assumptions that need to be questioned are the assumptions about human development. The lives of women, in pointing to an uncharted path of human growth and one that leads to a less violent mode of life, are particularly compelling at this time in history and thus deserve particular attention. The failure to attend to the voices of women and the difficulty in hearing what they say when they speak has compromised women's development and education, leading them to doubt the veracity of their perceptions and to question the truth of their experience. This problem becomes acute for women in adolescence, when thought becomes reflective and the problem of interpretation thus enters the stream of development itself. But the failure to represent women's experience also contributes to the presentation of competitive relationships and hierarchical modes of social organization as the natural ordering of life. For this reason, the consideration of women's lives brings to the conception of development a much needed corrective, stressing the importance of narrative modes of thought and pointing to the contextual nature of psychological truths and the reality of interdependence in human life.

The process of selection that has shadowed this vision can be seen in Kohlberg's reading of Martin Luther King's letter from the Birmingham jail,[11] since Kohlberg extracted King's justification for breaking the law in the name of justice but omitted the way in which King's vision of justice was embedded in a vision of human connection. Replying to the clergy who criticized his action, King not only offered a justification of his action but also defended the necessity for action, anchoring that necessity in the realization of interdependence:

I am in Birmingham because injustice is here. I cannot sit idly by in Atlanta and not be concerned about what happens in Birmingham. Injustice anywhere is a threat to justice everywhere. We are caught in an inescapable network of mutality, tied in a single garment of destiny. Whatever affects one directly, affects all indirectly.

Thus, like Bonhoeffer,[1] who stated that action comes "not from thought but from a readiness for responsibility," King tied his responsiveness to a caring that arises from an understanding of the connection between people's lives, a connection not forged by systems of rules but by a perception of the fact of relationship, a connection not freely contracted but built into the very fabric of life.

The ideals of a liberal democratic society—of freedom and equality—have been mirrored in the developmental vision of autonomy, the image of the educated man thinking for himself, the image of the ideal moral agent acting alone on the basis of his principles, blinding himself with a Rawlsian "veil of ignorance," playing a solitary Kohlbergian game of "moral musical chairs." Yet the developmental psychologists who dared, with Erikson,[3] to "ask what is an adult," immediately began to see the limitations of this vision. Erikson himself has come increasingly to talk about the activity of caretaking and to identify caring as the virtue and strength of maturity.[2] When integrated into a developmental understanding, this insight should spur the search for the antecedents of this strength in childhood and in adolescence. Kohlberg,[13] turning to consider adulthood, tied adult development to the experiences of "sustained responsibility for the welfare of others" and of the irreversible consequences of choice. The resonance of these themes of maturity to the voice of the 11-year-old girl calls into question current assumptions about the sequence of development and suggests a different path of growth.

The story of moral development, as it is presently told, traces the history of human development through shifts in the hierarchy of power relationships, implying that the dissolution of this hierarchy into an order of equality represents the ideal vision of things. But the conception of relationships in terms of hierarchies implies separation as the moral ideal—for everyone to stand alone, independent, self-sufficient, connected to others by the abstractions of logical thought. There is, then, a need to represent in the mapping of development a nonhierarchical image of human connection, and to embody in the vision of maturity the reality of interdependence. This alternate vision of the web of connection is the recognition of relationship that prevents aggression and gives rise to the understanding that generates response.

REFERENCES

1. BONHOEFFER, D. 1953. Letters and Papers from Prison. Macmillan, New York.
2. ERIKSON, E. 1976. Reflections on Dr. Borg's life cycle. Daedalus 105:1–29.

3. ERIKSON, E. 1970. Reflections on the dissent of contemporary youth. Daedalus 99:154–176.

4. FREUD, S. 1929. Civilization and its discontents. *In* Standard Edition of the Complete Psychological Works of Sigmund Freud, Vol. XXI, J. Strachey, ed. Hogarth Press, London. (1961)

5. FREUD, S. 1926. The question of lay analysis. *In* Standard Edition of the Complete Psychological Works of Sigmund Freud, Vol. XX, J. Strachey, ed. Hogarth Press, London. (1961)

6. FREUD, S. 1925. Some physical consequences of the anatomical distinction between the sexes. *In* Standard Edition of the Complete Psychological Works of Sigmund Freud, Vol. XIX, J. Strachey, ed. Hogarth Press, London. (1961)

7. GILLIGAN, C. 1982. In a Different Voice: Psychological Theory and Women's Development. Harvard University Press, Cambridge, Mass.

8. GILLIGAN, C., LANGDALE, S. AND LYONS, N. 1982. The Contribution of Women's Thought to Developmental Theory: The Elimination of Sex-Bias in Moral Development Theory and Research. Final report to the National Institute of Education, Washington, D.C.

9. INHELDER, B. AND PIAGET, J. 1958. The Growth of Logical Thinking from Childhood to Adolescence. Basic Books, New York.

10. JOYCE, J. 1916. A Portrait of the Artist as a Young Man. Viking Press, New York. (1956, p. 15)

11. KING, M., JR. 1964. Why We Can't Wait. Harper and Row, New York.

12. KOHLBERG, L. 1981. The Philosophy of Moral Development. Harper and Row, San Francisco.

13. KOHLBERG, L. 1973. Continuities and discontinuities in childhood and adult moral development revisited. *In* Life-Span Developmental Psychology: Personality and Socialization, P. Baltes and K. Schaie, eds. Academic Press, New York.

14. KOHLBERG, L. AND GILLIGAN, C. 1971. The adolescent as a philosopher: the discovery of the self in a post-conventional world. Daedalus 100:1051–1086.

15. LEVINSON, D. 1978. The Seasons of a Man's Life. Knopf, New York.

16. PIAGET, J. 1932. The Moral Judgment of the Child. Free Press, New York. (1965)

17. VAILLANT, G. 1977. Adaptation to Life. Little, Brown, Boston.

18. WILDER, T. 1938. Our Town. Coward-McCann, New York.

For reprints: Carol Gilligan, Ph.D., Harvard University Graduate School of Education, Larsen Hall, Appian Way, Cambridge, Mass. 02138

International Journal of Behavioral Development 8 (1985) 115–137
North-Holland

IMPLICATIONS OF AN INTERACTIONAL PARADIGM FOR RESEARCH ON HUMAN DEVELOPMENT *

David MAGNUSSON

University of Stockholm, Sweden

This paper consists of three main parts. First, a brief review of an interactional perspective for research on individual functioning is given. The need for integrated models, taking into consideration both psychological and biological factors on the person side in studying the person-environment interaction is emphasized. Second, empirical studies from a longitudinal program are presented. These studies are used as a basis for a discussion of methodological problems connected with interindividual differences in biological maturation. Thirdly, major implications for further development research in an interactional perspective are suggested, including (a) a need for well planned longitudinal research, (b) careful systematic observation and description of psychological phenomena, (c) integration of psychological and biological variables, (d) more interest devoted to the person as an integrated totality than to variables per se, (e) more interest devoted to lawfulness of processes in human functioning than to prediction of behavior, and (f) systematic analyses of environments and situations. Finally, it is argued that an interactional perspective can serve as a general frame of reference for planning, carrying through and interpreting empirical research, in order to overcome the fragmentation that now impedes real progress.

Introduction

The aim of this paper is to discuss research on human development from an interactional perspective. As a perspective rather than a theory or a model in a restricted sense, an interactional approach to psychological research cannot be sufficiently described in all its facets within the limited space available here. Therefore, as a background to my main points, I can only briefly summarize what I regard as the main aspects of an interactional perspective on human functioning. (For more extensive reviews the reader is referred to Endler (1981); Endler and Magnusson (1976); Magnusson (1976, 1980); Magnusson and Allen (1983); Öhman and Magnusson (1985).)

* This is a revised version of an invited address to the Seventh Biennial Meeting of ISSBD, Munich, 1983.

Author's address: D. Magnusson, Dept. of Psychology, University of Stockholm, S-106 91 Stockholm, Sweden.

An interactional perspective

According to an interactional perspective on human functioning psychological events are determined by two types of interaction processes: (a) the continuously ongoing, bidirectional process of interaction between the individual and his/her environment, and (b) the continuously ongoing reciprocal interaction among subsystems of factors within the individual. The first of these two processes has been emphasized in the past by researchers using very different approaches to psychological research, while the second belongs to what might be called modern interactionism.

Person-environment interaction

In a contemporary perspective behavior always takes place in situations; it does not exist except in relation to certain situational conditions, and cannot be understood and explained in isolation from them. Thus, the situation and all its elements as well as the total environment in which a situation is embedded must necessarily play a decisive role in any effective model of individual functioning. Knowledge of and models for the functional interrelations of the network of individual and situation-bound factors operating in the person-situation interaction process are prerequisites for understanding and explaining individual functioning in its situational context. In order to understand the functioning of an individual in his/her environment, we need (a) knowledge about the effective characteristics of the person, (b) knowledge about the effective operating situational/environmental variables and their interrelations, and (c) a theory linking these two networks of factors together in the framework of dynamic interaction (see Magnusson 1981a).

The current functioning of an individual has its background in his/her past course of *development*; contemporary readiness to respond to current situations have been formed in sequences of continuous interaction with the situations in which he/she has appeared. It is in actual situations with their specific characteristics that we meet the world, form our conceptions of it, and develop our specific kinds of strategies for dealing with it. Situations provide, at various levels of specification, the information that we handle, and they offer us the necessary feedback for building valid conceptions of the outer world as a basis for predictions about what will happen and what will be the outcome of our own behaviors, i.e., for our predictive and behavioral control of the world. In the continuous interaction with the various characteristics of the environment, each individual develops a total integrated system of mental structures and contents that constrain and shape his future behavior. On the basis of, and within the limits of inherited dispositions, affective tones become attached to specific contents and actions, and coping strategies are developed for dealing with various kinds of environments and situations in a continuous process of learning and maturation.

When the process underlying current behavior is described in terms of person-situation interaction and when individual development is discussed in such terms, the problem is not how the person and the situation, as two separate parts of equal importance, interact; it is rather how individuals by their perceptions, thoughts, and feelings, function in relation to the environment. The individual is the active, intentional subject in the interaction process; he both chooses and contributes to changes in his environment. The primary function of the environment is to offer information to the individual, which enables him or her to deal adequately with the external world. Therefore, the crucial role in the person-environment process is played by the properties and functioning of the individual's perceptual cognitive system, characterized by organized contents, goals, and strategies with their attached emotional tones (Forgas 1981; Magnusson and Allen 1983).

Interaction among individual subsystems

The character of the person-environment interaction process in which an individual is involved, depends upon and influences the continuous ongoing, reciprocal interaction among psychological and biological factors in the individual. The individual's partly specific interpretation of the information which is offered by his/her environment not only steers his/her behavior; it also evokes physiological systems which may act back to influence psychological events. Some of the bodily systems, which characterize a person, are reactive to specific situational challenges, and involve the secretion of substances (e.g., adrenaline and nonadrenaline) which have powerful and widespread physiological effects, and also influence both thoughts and behavior. Since these physiological processes also affect the immune system, various desease processes can be more effectively analyzed in terms of person-situation interaction processes as has been done by Carlsson and Jern (1982), and Weiner (1977) for psychosomatic reactions, by Depue (1979) for depression, and by Zubin and Spring (1977) for schizophrenia (see Öhman and Magnusson (1985).

Comments

As emphasized many times during the lively debate on the person-environment issue, interactionistic formulations are not new: In various forms they have been expressed for a long time by researchers with very different approaches to psychological problems (Magnusson 1981a). During the seventies, an interactional perspective and its consequences have been debated vigorously and intensely among researchers interested in contemporaneous aspects of human functioning. However, interactionistic formulations have been accepted more naturally and used as a frame of reference for actual research by researchers investi-gating human functioning in a developmental perspective. This is reflected in developmental models for various aspects of human functioning – cognition, intelligence, motivation, competence, etc. (see e.g., McV. Hunt 1961, 1965, 1966; Lerner 1978; Piaget 1964; Sameroff 1975; Vygotsky 1929, 1963) and in discussions of methodological implications of what is basically an interactionistic view (see e.g., Lerner, Skinner and Sorell 1980).

Expressed in general terms, interactionistic formulations may, to a casual observer, seem too obvious, even trivial. Taken seriously, however, they have important and far-reaching consequences for methodology and strategy in empirical research on human functioning, in both a contemporaneous and a developmental perspective. Now that interactionistic formulations have been widely accepted as a general approach to research on human functioning, one of the important tasks for developmentalists is to analyze these consequences carefully, so as to be able to plan and perform more effective developmental research.

Some of these implications of an interactional perspective for empirical research on human development will be briefly summarized in this paper. As a background I will first present an empirical study from a longitudinal research project, which I have led at the Department of Psychology at the University of Stockholm during the last twenty years and discuss the implications of interindividual differences in growth curves.

A longitudinal project and its background

The general aim of the project is to investigate how person factors and environmental factors – independently and jointly in interaction – operate and influence the course of development from childhood to adulthood, with particular emphasis on social adjustment in adulthood. Within this general frame, subsidiary projects are directed towards the study of aspects of the developmental background of alcoholism, criminality and mental illness. In the planning and implementation of the project, an interactionist view has had explicit and important consequences right from the start. One element in the background of the planning, namely what might be called a person approach in contrast to a variable orientation should be particularly emphasized. (The distinction can only be touched upon here. The reader is referred to more extensive discussions in Bergman and Magnusson (in press); Magnusson and Bergman (1985); and Magnusson and Allen (1983).)

A person orientation

Much developmental research can be characterized as variable oriented; i.e., a variable or variables are the main conceptual and analytical unit. It is the nature of the relationship among variables – simultaneously and across age – that is the main object of interest in this approach; the person, per se, is important as the means of providing measures for the variables. Variables take on meaning mainly as quantitative dimensions when they are observed across individuals. The orientation to psychological research towards variables in general has been strongly fostered by the development and application of appropriate and effective methods for variable analysis and hypothesis testing, ANOVA, regression analytical methods etc.

In summary, an interactional perspective recognizes that human functioning has a complex causal background. Even simple psychological phenomena can be influenced and caused by a multitude of factors which are in continuous interaction with each other, at various levels. An important aspect is that causal factors in the processes underlying individual functioning change with age. This change is partly as a result of the individual's own developmental history. Causal psychological and biological factors in the individual, and physical, social and cultural factors in the environment interact with developmental levels. The

139

effects of this process of interaction on individuals differ depending on the age and the course of the individual's earlier development (see Emmerich 1964, 1968; Flavell 1971; Kagan 1971; McCall 1977; Moss and Susman 1980; Wohlwill 1980). This view leads to an approach in which the individual, rather than the variable, is the conceptual unit for analysis of developmental processes.

A person vs variable approach to developmental research is not just a theoretical issue. For our planning of the longitudinal project, the person-orientation had direct consequences in two main aspects. *The first* consequence was a need to cover a broad spectrum of person factors that may be of importance for development, including biological factors. *The second* consequence for the planning of the project was concerned with the strategy for selection of appropriate types of data at each age level.

In variable-oriented research, a main interest is in measuring 'the same' function reflected in data for different ages. (The question of what constitutes 'the same' is the well-known problem of equivalence of functional measures, a problem that itself has important conceptual and methodological implications – Baltes, Reese and Lipsitt 1980; Loevinger 1966.) A favorable situation for a researcher is then one where he can use the same type of data from the same type of instrument across ages.

In our person-oriented approach, the central consideration with respect to the appropriateness of data has been to cover the factors that have been judged to be important at each developmental stage according to relevant theories and empirical research. Thus, data have been maximized for those factors, irrespective of whether or not they were covered by data at other age levels.

Longitudinal data

Data collection began in 1965. The main sample consisted of a complete cohort of children attending school in a mid-Swedish town, rather more than 1000 boys and girls in total, who were ten years of age at the time. Studies within the project have shown that this group can be regarded as fairly representative of pupils in the compulsory school system in Sweden (Bergman 1973).

The boys and the girls in the main sample were followed up each year throughout their years at school. In the past two years a further comprehensive follow-up has been performed, at the age of 26 to 29, including the administration of an inventory, a test session, an interview, a medical examination, and the collection of data from official records.

With reference to the general considerations that I summarized earlier, the data collections covered a broad spectrum of psychological and biological factors on the person side, and physical and social factors on the environmental side (Dunér 1978; Magnusson 1981b, 1985; Magnusson and Dunér 1981; Magnusson, Stattin and Dunér 1983). Thus for person factors, measures for mediating psychological varibles, social relations, conduct etc., have been supplemented with data for various biological functions of central interest, with emphasis on hormonal functioning. Such biological data have been collected at the age of 12 and 13 and at the age of 27. On the environmental side, the main focus has been on the family situation, for example, parents' education and income, family norms and family activities.

At this stage of the longitudinal research project, data are available on biological and psychological aspects of individual functioning and on relevant environmental variables for a fairly large representative sample of males and females from the age of 10 to the age of 28.

Biological age as an important development factor

In one subproject we were interested in the relation between individual differences in physical maturation among girls and their later adjustment (Magnusson and Stattin 1982). The general assumption was that very early physical maturation may imply greater vulnerability to social pressures and thus lead to problems in social adjustment during the transition from childhood to adulthood (see Frisk, Tenhunen, Widholm and Hortling 1966; McFarlane, Allen and Honzik 1954).

It was assumed that the social stimuli to which girls are exposed will vary with biological maturation. The transition period, of which the menarche is one manifestation, involves changes in the actual environment confronting a girl. A maturing girl seeks new situations, with other roles, other rules, other expectancies and the environment reacts to her differently. Self-perceptions also change, as do the perceptions, interpretations, and evaluations of what is happening in the external world. Thus, the transitional period generally sees changes in the frequency and character of contacts with the opposite sex, along with changes in other habits, leisure activities, relations with peers and parents, etc. In summary, a girl's interaction with her physical and social environment will change (sometimes drastically) during the transitional period both with respect to form and to content.

In one part of this study we investigated the relation between the age of menarche for girls and their alcohol consumption when they were 14:5. We found a significant and very strong relation. Thus, early maturing girls used significantly more alcohol than late maturing girls at the age of 14:5.

This result is open to two interpretations. A first hypothesis would be that the early establishment of a high alcohol consumption among early-maturing girls will lead to a persistent higher alcohol consumption (see fig. 1(a)). Support for this hypothesis would be a negative correlation between the age at menarche and alcohol consumption in adulthood.

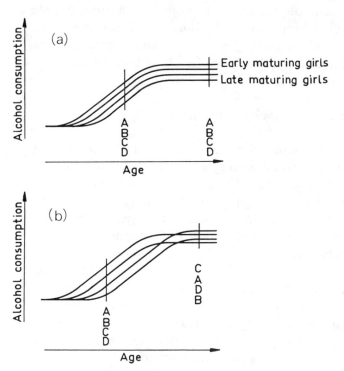

Fig. 1. (a) A model for hypothesis 1.
        (b) A model for hypothesis 2.

The second hypothesis is that heavy drinking among early-maturing girls is simply an expression of these girls starting the normal transition to adult life patterns (which involves exposure to new social stimuli) before their late-maturing peers. Early maturation should not lead to persistent or long-term consequences in terms of alcohol. Individual differences in adult alcohol habits would be determined instead by other person-bound factors than age at menarche and/or by environmental factors unrelated to physical maturity during puberty. A model for this hypothesis is shown in fig. 1(b). If it is valid, the relation between alcohol habits at the age of menarche and in adulthood will attenuate and approach zero.

The differential predictions expressed in the two hypotheses were investigated by collecting data for alcohol consumption on two occasions – at the age of 15 : 10, i.e., one year and five months after the first round of alcohol data, and at the age of 26 – and relating them to age at menarche. For alcohol data at 15 : 10, the relation to age at menarche had decreased to a level of very low significance ($p < 0.20$), while at the age of 26 there was no systematic relation. Late- and early-maturing girls reported almost the same amount and frequency of alcohol at the age of 26. These results support hypothesis 2 for development of alcohol habits.

The results from this and other studies in the project on social adjustment and social relations during puberty among girls – particularly those connected with norms, values and social relationships – show very clearly that these aspects are bound up with interindividual differences in physical maturity. For some behaviors, the interindividual differences in social adjustment are temporary and will disappear after a time, as in the case just described. For other factors, interindividual differences on entering the adult world may lead to more permanent differences in adjustment in adulthood (Magnusson, Stattin and Allen 1985).

The results of this study prompt the following conclusions:
(1) In all matrices of data for variables that relate systematically to physical maturity, a portion of the variance will be determined by interindividual differences in the onset of the physical transitional period. Thus, the coefficients reflecting relationships between these other variables (for example, between aggression and parental relations or between drug abuse and peer relations) will be partly determined by

interindividual differences in physical maturity. This applies, of course, whether or not the matrices include data for physical maturity.

(2) The strength of the correlation between physical maturity (as reflected in age at menarche) and behavioral variables will vary with the chronological age at which these other variables are measured. This implies that the extent to which interindividual differences in physical maturity influence the coefficients for relationships between secondary factors in cross-sectional studies will depend in part upon the chronological age represented in data.

These conclusions imply that considering biological age when studying individual differences in social adjustment during puberty might be as important as considering mental age when investigating factors associated with intelligence.

From a theoretical standpoint the character of the interplay between individuals and environments in the maturation process illustrates an important aspect of an interactional view: It is not the biological maturation per se that leads to increased alcohol consumption. *This effect in an individual is mediated by an environment that changes as a consequence of changes in the individual.* The validity of that conclusion is empirically demonstrated by data from the project presented by Magnusson et al. (1985).

Individual differences in growth curves

The empirical example from the study of physical maturation raises the general issue of interindividual differences in growth curves and the implications for developmental research. Though many researchers have presented and discussed models for growth curves (see Baltes et al. 1980; Jessor and Jessor 1977; Loevinger 1966; Schaie 1972), the methodological consequences in empirical developmental research of the existence of such interindividual differences have not received the attention they deserve. The problem is here illustrated with a few examples chosen from biological factors, for which the growth curves can be confirmed empirically.

The first example is the growth curve for the thymus gland. This curve is characteristic for the lymphoid system, including lymph nodes and intestinal lymphoid masses (Tanner 1978). The typical growth

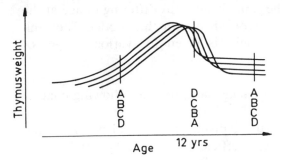

Fig. 2. Fictitious growth curves for the weight of the thymus gland for four individuals A–D.

curve for the weight of the thymus gland is shown in fig. 2 for four hypothetical individuals, A–D, who differ with respect to biological age. (The weight of the thymus reaches a peak at around 12 years of age and then declines rather rapidly, to about half that weight at the age of 20.)

For various chronological ages, the figure shows the rank orders of the individuals with respect to weight of the thymus.

My second example is the growth curve for body height. Summarizing a large number of studies, Garn concluded that 'early maturing girls tend to be taller earlier in life but ultimately shorter, consistent with an earlier cessation of growth' (1980: 134). This model implies that the final level of the person factor is inversely related to chronological age at the onset of the growth spurt. Fig. 3 shows the growth curves for four

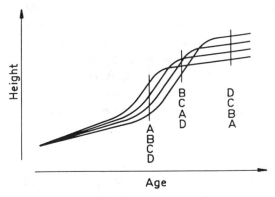

Fig. 3. Fictitious growth curves for body height for four individuals A–D.

hypothetical girls, starting at the same height but differing in age at the onset of the growth spurt, in concordance with this model. The rank order of girls with respect to height is given for various stages of chronological age.

These illustrations can serve as a background for the following conclusions:

(1) Though all individuals pass through the transitional period in the same lawful and predictable way, coefficients for correlations between rank orders obtained for the same function at various age levels can theoretically take any value between $+1$ and -1.

(2) The size of a coefficient for the correlation between rank orders taken at various age levels depends not only on the interval between the data collections and/or age at the first data collection. It also depends upon the stage in the transitional period at which the data are collected. Coefficients covering the time before and after a transitional period may be higher than coefficients covering a shorter period, when data collections occur during the transitional period.

The growth curves that I have just shown represent biological growth. However, as emphasized, for instance, by Loevinger (1966) in her discussion of four models for individual growth curves, there are many examples of interesting psychological functions that display the same general growth curves. In so far as this applies, the conclusions drawn for the biological growth curves can be extended to psychological functions.

Schaie presented a general model for development, holding that 'a response is a function of the age of the organism, the cohort to which the organism belongs, and the time at which measurement occurs' (1965: 93). As Baltes (1968) has noted, Schaie's model implies that two dimensions are free to vary, and that data can be explained by a two-dimensional plane in the three-dimensional space. What has been demonstrated here indicates that adding a fourth dimension, biological age, to the data space will increase the variance that can be explained in developmental data. It may sometimes be more important to take into account biological factors than, say, chronological age.

These statements have obvious consequences for the use of factor analytic research on development, as well as the interpretation of coefficients of correlation between measures taken at different ages, both as indicators of stability of person characteristics and as indicators of the existence of personality traits.

That low coefficients of correlation cannot generally be interpreted as indicators of low relative stability of a certain person factor and cannot be used unreservedly as arguments against the existence of personality traits, as was done, for example, by Mischel (1968), seems obvious. Since factor analysis is based on matrices of correlation coefficients, the effects that I have briefly demonstrated will occur also in factor analytical research on development. These consequences are complex and need careful analysis. Particularly so when we consider the complicated process of interaction in which most factors are involved within each individual and the fact that these interactions may well differ in relation to maturational stage.

The growth curves that I have just discussed have been drawn in order to highlight possible methodological effects of the existence of interindividual differences in physical maturation. Those familiar with psychometrics have already observed that statistical effects are seldom, if ever, as dramatic as the fictitious curves illustrate. The extent to which these effects occur depends, of course, upon the total interindividual variation for the function in question. But this does not absolve us from taking the effects seriously. They do exist, and we have to analyze carefully, whether and to what extent, in order to ascertain when the traditional linear psychometric models are valid for meaningful estimations of stability and interrelations among person functions.

Implications for further developmental research

With these illustrations as background, I would like to point to what I see as main implications for developmental research. These are summarized in six points which reflect what I believe to be current trends in developmental research.

A plea for longitudinal research

A major implication of an interactional view is that we have to follow the same individuals across time, if we are to understand how individuals as totalities develop in a process of maturation and learning in continuous interaction with their environments. In other words, we have to conduct longitudinal research. The empirical study outlined earlier demonstrates very forcefully the necessity of longitudinal research for effective analysis of important developmental problems.

The problems associated with longitudinal research have been demonstrated and discussed very cogently by, among others, Baltes (1968), Nesselroade (Nesselroade and Baltes 1980), and Schaie (1965). In particular they have emphasized the consequences of the inherent confounding of age, the year in which observations are made and the year of the individual's birth. These consequences are important and have to be analyzed thoroughly in each specific case. But when they have been used as an argument against longitudinal research per se, the consequences have been overgeneralized. Whether and to what extent they are relevant will vary with the types of person factors that are involved and with the type of psychological problem that is being investigated. Given the nature of the developmental process, seen in an interactional perspective, there is no adequate alternative to longitudinal research for the study of many important psychological problems. To quote McCall, 'The longitudinal method is the life blood of developmental psychology: it deserves a more thorough, objective and constructive evaluation by all developmentalists' (1977: 341) (see also, e.g., Wohlwill 1970).

Since longitudinal research has become 'à la mode', there is a tendency to designate even rather short-term observations by this title. The preceding discussion clearly demonstrates that if longitudinal studies are to be effective, (a) they must cover the total critical periods of development for the function(s) under consideration, and (b) observations must be made continuously during the critical stages of development so that important transitions are not missed. This means in many cases that longitudinal studies must continue over a considerable period, to avoid misinterpretation of results.

A need for systematic observation and description of phenomena

Whether, and to what extent, interindividual differences in growth curves of the kind I have just discussed do exist and influence our results, is something that differs between variables and with the age span under consideration. This implies both a need for careful theoretical analysis of the nature of the particular psychological variables under consideration and a need for careful empirical description of the pertinent phenomena as a basis for effective planning of longitudinal studies. Solid theorizing which is a necessity in a developing science has to be founded on systematic observations of the space of phenomena under consideration. There would be less risk of missing the obvious – as we sometimes do – and our research would be more realistic and more effective, if we devoted more time and resources to systematic description, based on careful observation of the phenomena that are our real interest, before we apply the sophisticated methods that we have developed for data collection and data treatment (see e.g., Cronbach 1975; Wohlwill 1970). I think this is valid for psychological research in general. It is certainly valid when planning developmental research in an interactional perspective, directed to the study of individuals as totalities.

The importance of biological factors

If we want to understand and explain – in an interactionistic frame of reference – the process underlying individual development, it is obvious that we have to include biological factors in models for individual development and in planning and carrying through of empirical developmental research. This conclusion is illustrated in the empirical study, which was presented above and it is further strongly supported by results from other studies in the longitudinal project (see e.g., Bergman and Magnusson 1979; Magnusson 1985; Magnusson et al. 1983). In my view, one of the most serious drawbacks in traditional developmental research is its lack of interest in the biological aspects of individual functioning.

A plea for a person approach

As was stressed earlier, a natural consequence of an interactional view of development is a person-oriented approach, an interest in the individual as a totality. Needless to say, this does not imply that variable-directed research is meaningless or unnecessary. Careful studies of single factors, yielding valid results, are important prerequisites for effective studies of individuals as totalities.

Some implications of a person-oriented research on development have already been discussed (pp. 119–120). Another implication involves methodology. In a person approach, the person is conceptualized as an integrated totality, characterized by a pattern of variables. The aim is to understand the functioning of this totality by trying to discover the distinctive configuration of psychological and biological functions that will satisfactorily characterize each person, as a basis for understanding the lawful patterning of developmental change (Loevinger 1965; McCall, Appelbaum and Hagerty 1973; Santostefano 1978; Sroufe and Waters 1977). This view leads to demands for a complement to the linear regression methods and models so frequently used for data treatment in a variable approach. The appropriate methods are those by which individuals can be grouped and studied on the basis of their characteristic configurations of crucial factors, as a basis for generalizations. An important task for further research is the development and application of appropriate methods and models for data treatment in this perspective. In a series of empirical studies in the longitudinal project, such methods have been applied to the study of development of patterns of adjustment problems (Bergman and Magnusson 1983, 1984a, 1984b, 1985). More developmental work is needed on this issue, particularly in order to develop methods for studying individuals involved in the developmental process.

Prediction vs lawfulness

I pointed out earlier that one characteristic feature of variable-directed research is its emphasis on prediction. Of course, prediction is a natural element in the research process. What I want to argue against is the tendency in psychology to make perfect prediction the ultimate goal and high prediction the overriding criterion for the scientific status of psychology.

This is not just a matter of words. The conception of prediction as a goal is closely connected with a mechanistic model of man (Overton and Reese 1973). Associated with this view are the concepts of cause-effect relations, independent–dependent variables, and predictor-criterion relations. When motivated by the goal of prediction, the concern of research is most often one or a few variables at a time, in which cause and effect are studied as a uni-directional relationship between independent and dependent variables. Relations between sets of variables are studied in terms of additive, linear effects. This view is also reflected in the operationalization of psychological concepts, in the choice of variables to study at different age levels, in the treatment of data, in the interpretation of empirical results, etc.

An interactional view emphasizes the dynamic character of development, in which both the individual and the environment change in a multi-determined, spiral process over time. The overriding interest then is in the lawfulness and continuity of this process of person-environment interaction. Given the complex, often nonlinear interplay of subsystems of factors within the individual, and the complicated interplay between the individual as a totality and an environment that is functioning in relation to the individual in a probabilistic, sometimes very uncertain and unpredictable way, it is unrealistic to hope for high prediction of molar, social behavior over any considerable age span (Scarr 1981). To foresee molar social behavior is as difficult for psychologists, as it is for meteorologists to foresee the weather even from day to day.

Actually the nature of meteorological phenomena bears a striking resemblance to the phenomena of psychology. Weather is best described by a process model: Many factors are involved, they operate in a continuous and bidirectional interaction and they interplay in a nonlinear way, etc. Though a great deal is known about the effective factors which are associated with a certain change in the weather and about the way each factor operates in relation to other factors, meteorologists cannot predict change in the weather with any great degree of certainty. However, this has not diminished their status in the scientific community.

Analysis of environments and situations

That human functioning cannot be understood and explained without considering the environmental context in which the individual develops and acts has been emphasized for decades, not just by psychologists, but also by anthropologists, sociologists, and by those who take an ethological approach (see Magnusson 1984). Though most of the discussion about the environment has concentrated on contemporaneous functioning, it is obvious that the points made are equally applicable to analyses and discussions of individual functioning from a developmental perspective (Bloom 1964; Bronfenbrenner 1979; Hautamäki 1982; McGurk 1977; Vygotsky 1929; Wohlwill 1973). This is certainly true when the issue under consideration is human development from the perspective of person-environment interaction.

Given the important role of the environment's characteristics for human development, an obvious task for research is to incorporate and consider environmental factors both in models of human functioning and when planning and performing developmental research. This leads to a need for systematic analysis of the environment. This need has been underlined explicitly and strongly by developmental researchers for a long time. In a historical perspective it is interesting to note that W.I. Thomas (1927, 1928) back in the twenties discussed many of the current problems connected with this issue. In psychology, this perspective is represented by several distinguished researchers, Brunswik (1956), Bloom (1964), and Barker (1968), for example. (See also Wohlwill 1973; McGurk 1977; and Bronfenbrenner 1979.) During the seventies, interest in theorizing and empirical research on the environment grew in two directions: In the field of personality, as an element in the intense debate on the person-situation interaction issue and mainly directed to the study of perceived situations, and in the field of environmental psychology, mainly directed to the study of physical environments. However, it is both interesting and noteworthy that in spite of the long tradition of theoretical formulations, we still lack a comprehensive system of concepts about the environment, a 'scientific language' for dealing with the environment in a systematic way in theoretical and empirical analysis of development in an interactional perspective.

   That analysis of how individuals perceive and interpret the environment is necessary for understanding their reactions to and acting in it in a developmental perspective has been aptly demonstrated empirically (Magnusson 1982). Analyzing environments and situations in an effective and meaningful way is certainly feasible (Magnusson 1981a). As long as order and regularity exist in the physical and social environment (and in the cognitive representations of these environments in the minds of the individuals living in them), it is a scientific challenge to map these regularities and express them in relevant terms. The result of such analyses will help to promote real progress in research on human development as seen in the perspective of person-environment interaction. That systematic analyses of the environment involve many difficult conceptual and methodological problems should not prevent us from setting to work.

A final comment

The goal for psychological research is to understand and explain why individuals think, feel, react, and act as they do in real-life situations. I believe that most will agree, when I say that one of the obstacles on the road is the fragmentation of the total field into subareas, each with its own specific theories, methodologies and research strategies. Empirical research is often planned and results are interpreted in the frame of reference of theories and models that are restricted to more or less specific subareas – such as information processing, decision making, cognition, role theories, goal theory, attitude models, etc. – with little or no relation to theories and models in other subareas.

Fragmentation of the total space of psychological phenomena implies that individual functioning is split into components. In this way we risk losing sight of the complete, functioning individual that is a necessary frame of reference when studying and trying to understand the functioning of parts. One important implication of this is that results from empirical research cannot be interpreted in a common frame of reference. This in turn impedes the kind of accumulation of knowledge that is a prerequisite for real progress and a characteristic of a maturing science (Meehl 1978).

There is a rapidly growing awareness, expressed by many researchers, of the need for overriding perspectives that integrate various aspects of human functioning in order to overcome this fragmentation. In my view, an interactionist perspective may serve as just such a general frame, for the formulation of realistic problems, for planning effective research and for the interpretation of results. If it can serve these functions, it will contribute not only to our understanding of why individuals think, feel, react and act as they do, but also to our possibilities of helping to form environments that are better adapted to individuals' needs and potentialities.

References

Baltes, P.B., 1968. Longitudinal and cross-sectional sequences in the study of age and generation effects. Human Development 11, 145–171.

Baltes, P.B., H.W. Reese and L.P. Lipsitt, 1980. Life-span development psychology. Annual Review of Psychology 31, 65–110.

Barker, R.G., 1968. Ecological psychology. Stanford, CA: Stanford University Press.

Bergman, L.R., 1973. Parent's education and mean change in intelligence. Scandinavian Journal of Psychology 14, 273–281.

Bergman, L.R. and D. Magnusson, 1979. Overachievement and catecholamine excretion in an achievement-demanding situation. Psychosomatic Medicine 41, 181–188.

Bergman, L.R. and D. Magnusson, 1983. The development of patterns of maladjustment. Report from the project Individual Development and Environment. Department of Psychology, University of Stockholm, No. 50.

Bergman, L.R. and D. Magnusson, 1984a. Patterns of maladjustment problems at age 10: an empirical and methodological study. Reports from the Department of Psychology, University of Stockholm, No. 615.

Bergman, L.R. and D. Magnusson, 1984b. Patterns of adjustment problems at age 13: an empirical and methodological study. Reports from the Department of Psychology, University of Stockholm, No. 620.

Bergman, L.R. and D. Magnusson, 1985. A person-oriented approach to the study of the development of adjustment problems. Proceedings from the XXIII International Congress of Psychology, Acapulco, Mexico, September 2–7, 1984. (In press.)

Bloom, B.S., 1964. Stability and change in human characteristics. New York: Wiley.

Bronfenbrenner, U., 1979. Contexts of child rearing. Problems and prospects. American Psychologist 34, 844–850.

Brunswik, E., 1956. Perception and the representative design of psychological environments. Berkeley, CA: University of California Press.

Carlsson, S.G. and S. Jern, 1982. Paradigms in psychosomatic research: a dialectic perspective. Scandinavian Journal of Psychology, Suppl. 1, 151–157.

Cronbach, L.J., 1975. Beyond the two disciplines of scientific psychology. American Psychologist 30, 116–127.

Depue, R.A., 1979. The psychobiology of the depression disorders. Implications for the effect of stress. New York: Academic Press.

Dunér, A., 1978. 'Problems and designs in research on educational and vocational career'. In: A. Dunér (ed.), Research into personal development: educational and vocational choice. Amsterdam: Swets & Zeitlinger.

Emmerich, W., 1964. Continuity and stability in early social development. Child Development 35, 311–332.

Emmerich, W., 1968. Personality development and concepts of structure. Child Development 39, 671–690.

Endler, N.S., 1981. 'Persons, situations, and their interactions'. In: A.J. Rabin (ed.), Further explorations in personality. New York: Wiley.

Endler, N.S. and D. Magnusson, 1976. Toward an interactional psychology of personality. Psychological Bulletin 83, 956–974.

Flavell, H., 1971. Age related properties of cognitive development. Cognitive Psychology 2, 421–453.

Forgas, J.P. (ed.), 1981. Social cognition: perspectives on everyday understanding. European monographs in social psychology. New York: Academic Press.

Frisk, M., T. Tenhunen, O. Widholm and H. Hortling, 1966. Physical problems in adolescents showing advanced or delayed physical maturation. Adolescence 2, 126–140.

Garn, S.M., 1980. 'Continuity and change in maturational timing'. In: O.G. Brim, Jr. and J. Kagan (eds.), Constancy and change in human development. Cambridge, MA: Harvard University Press. pp. 113–162.

Hautamäki, A., 1982. Activity environment, social class and voluntary learning. An interpretation and application of Vygotsky's concept. Publications of the University of Joensu, Series A, No. 22.

Hunt, J.McV., 1961. Intelligence and experience. New York: Ronald Press.

Hunt, J.McV., 1965. 'Intrinsic motivation and its role in psychological development'. In: D. Levine (ed.), Nebraska symposium on motivation. Lincoln, NE: University of Nebraska Press. pp. 189–282.

Hunt, J.McV., 1966. 'The epigenesis of intrinsic motivation and early cognitive learning'. In: R.H. Hober (ed.), Current research in motivation. New York: Holt, Rinehart & Winston. pp. 355–370.

Jessor, R. and S.L. Jessor, 1977. Problem behavior and psychological development. A longitudinal study of youth. New York: Academic Press.

Kagan, J., 1971. Change and continuity in infancy. New York: Wiley.

Lerner, R.M., 1978. Nature, nurture and dynamic interactionism. Human Development 21, 1–20.

Lerner, R.M., E.A. Skinner and G.T. Sorell, 1980. Methodological implications of contextual/dialectic theories of development. Human Development 23, 225–235.

Loevinger, J., 1965. 'Measurement in clinical psychology'. In: B.B. Wolman (ed.), Handbook of clinical psychology. New York: McGraw-Hill. pp. 78–94.

Loevinger, J., 1966. Models and measures of developmental variation. Annals from New York Academy of Sciences 134:2. pp. 585–590.

McCall, R.B., 1977. Challenges to a science of developmental psychology. Child Development 48, 333–344.

McCall, R.B., M.I. Appelbaum and P.S. Hagerty, 1973. Developmental changes in mental performance. Monographs of the society for research in child development, 38, serial no 150, vol. 38, no 3.

McFarlane, J.W., L. Allen and M. Honzik, 1954. A developmental study of the behavior problems of normal children between twenty-one months and fourteen years. Berkeley, CA: University of California Press.

McGurk, H., 1977. Ecological factors in human development. Amsterdam: North-Holland.

Magnusson, D., 1976. The person and the situation in an interactional model of behavior. Scandinavian Journal of Psychology 17, 253–271.

Magnusson, D., 1980. Personality in an interactional paradigm of research. Zeitschrift für Differentielle und Diagnostische Psychologie 1, 17–34.

Magnusson, D., 1981a. 'Wanted: a psychology of situations'. In: D. Magnusson (ed.), Toward a psychology of situations: an interactional perspective. Hillsdale, NJ: Erlbaum.

Magnusson, D., 1981b. 'Some methodology and strategy problems in longitudinal research'. In: F. Schulzinger, S.A. Mednick and J. Knop (eds.), Longitudinal research: methods and uses in behavioral science. Boston, MA: Martinus Nijhoff. pp. 192–215.

Magnusson, D., 1982. 'Situational determinants of stress: an interactional perspective'. In: L. Goldberger and S. Breznitz (eds.), Handbook of stress. New York: The Free Press. pp. 231–253.

Magnusson, D., 1984. 'Persons in situations: some comments on a current issue'. In: H. Bonarius, G. van Heck and N. Smid (eds.), Personality psychology in Europe. Lisse: Swets & Zeitlinger. pp. 129–149.

Magnusson, D., 1985. 'Adult delinquency in the light of conduct and physiology at an early age'. In: D. Magnusson and A. Öhman (eds.), Psychopathology: an interactional perspective. New York: Academic Press. (In press.)

Magnusson, D. and V. Allen, 1983. 'An interactional perspective for human development'. In: D. Magnusson and V. Allen (eds.), Human development: an interactional perspective. New York: Academic Press.

Magnusson, D. and L.R. Bergman, 1985. 'Theoretical perspectives on the study of the development of adjustment problems'. In: L. Pulkkinen and P. Lyytinen (eds.), Human action and personality: essays in honour of Martti Takala. Jyväskylä studies in education, psychology and social research. Jyväskylä: University of Jyväskylä. (In press).

Magnusson, D. and A. Dunér, 1981. 'Individual development and environment: a longitudinal study in Sweden'. In: S.E. Mednick and A.E. Baert (eds.), Prospective longitudinal research. Oxford: University Press.

Magnusson, D. and A. Öhman, 1985. Psychopathology: an interactional perspective. New York: Academic Press. (In press.)

Magnusson, D. and H. Stattin, 1982. Biological age, environment, and behavior in interaction: a methodological problem. Reports from the Department of Psychology, University of Stockholm, no. 587.

Magnusson, D., H. Stattin and V. Allen, 1985. 'Differential maturation among girls and its relation to social adjustment: a longitudinal perspective'. In: D. Featherman and R.M. Lerner (eds.), Life span development, Vol 7. New York: Academic Press. (In press.)

Magnusson, D., H. Stattin and A. Dunér, 1983. 'Aggression and criminality in a longitudinal perspective'. In: S.A. Mednick (ed.), Antecedents of antisocial behavior. Boston, MA: Kluwer-Nijhoff. pp. 277–301.

Meehl, P.E., 1978. Theoretical risks and tabular asterisks: Sir Karl, Sir Ronald, and the slow progress of soft psychology. Journal of Consulting and Clinical Psychology 46, 806–834.

Mischel, W., 1968. Personality and assessment. New York: Wiley.

Moss, H.A. and E.J. Susman, 1980. 'Longitudinal study of personality development'. In: O.G. Brim, Jr. and J. Kagan (eds.), Constancy and change in human development. Cambridge, MA: Harvard University Press.

Nesselroade, J.R. and P.B. Baltes, 1980. 'History and rationale of longitudinal research'. In: J.R. Nesselroade and P.B. Baltes (eds.), Longitudinal methodology in the study of behavior and development. New York: Academic Press.

Öhman, A. and D. Magnusson, 1985. 'An interactional paradigm for research in psychopathology'. In: D. Magnusson and A. Öhman (eds.), Psychopathology: an interactional perspective. New York: Academic Press. (In press.)

Overton, W.F. and H.W. Reese, 1973. 'Models of development: methodological implications'. In: J.R. Nesselroade and H.W. Reese (eds.), Life span development psychology: methodological issues. New York: Academic Press.

Piaget, J., 1964. Development and learning. Journal of Research in Science Teaching 2, 176–186.

Sameroff, A.L., 1975. Transactional models in early social relations. Human Development 18, 65–79.

Santostefano, S.A., 1978. A biodevelopmental approach to clinical child psychology. New York: Wiley.

Scarr, S., 1981. Maturation and development: biological and psychological perspectives. London: William Heinemann Medical Books.

Schaie, K.E., 1965. A general model for the study of developmental problems. Psychological Bulletin 64, 92–107.

Schaie, K.W., 1972. Limitations on the generalizability of growth curves of intelligence. Human Development 15, 141–152.

Sroufe, L.A. and E. Waters, 1977. Attachement as an organizational construct. Child Development 48, 1184–1199.

Tanner, J.M., 1978. Foetus into man: physical growth form conception to maturity. London: Open Books.

Thomas, W.I., 1927. The behavior pattern and the situation. Publications of the American Sociological Society: Papers and Proceedings 22, 1–13.

Thomas, W.I., 1928. The child in America. New York: A.A. Kopt.

Vygotsky, L.S., 1929. The problem of the cultural development of the child. Journal of Genetic Psychology 3, 415–432.

Vygotsky, L.S., 1963. 'Learning and mental development at school age'. In: B. Simon and J. Simon (eds.), Educational psychology in the USSR. London: Routledge & Kegan Paul.

Weiner, H., 1977. Psychobiology and human disease. New York: Elsevier.

Wohlwill, J.F., 1970. The age variable in psychological research. Psychological Review 77, 49–64.

Wohlwill, J.F., 1973. The concept of experience: S or R? Human Development 16, 90–107.

Wohlwill, J.F., 1980. 'Cognitive development in childhood'. In: O.G. Brim, Jr. and J. Kagan (eds.), Constancy and change in human development. Cambridge, MA: Harvard University Press. pp. 359–444.

Zubin, J. and B. Spring, 1977. Vulnerability: a review of schiziphrenic. Journal of Abnormal Psychology 86, 103–126.

GENERATIONAL DIFFERENCE AND THE DEVELOPMENTAL STAKE[1]

Vern L. Bengtson and Joseph A. Kuypers

University of Southern California,
University of California, Berkeley

There is drama in the continuing succession of one generation by another. This drama begins with the differences in behavior and attitudes exhibited by emerging generations; it develops with the reaction of older generations to these innovations; and it reaches a climax with the changes in configuration of culture which result. And then the drama begins anew, with yet another cast of actors.

In today's society, something new seems to have been added to the drama: a sense of urgency, of concern that the magnitude of differences between age groups has outstripped the continuity of plot that holds culture together. One wonders about those differences. What causes significant behavioral contrasts between generations? Why do such differences seem so stridently obvious today? Are they, perhaps, more apparent than real? What accounts for the anxiety surrounding generational differences? What explains the contrasting responses of youth and their elders to the manifestation of such differences; why are they welcomed by youth, and perceived with dismay or indignation by parents?

A growing number of analyses have contributed much to understanding the causes of dissimilarity between generations in behavior (see, for example, Cain, 1967, 1970; Elkind, 1970; Neugarten, 1970; Thomas, 1971; Troll, 1970; Hill, 1970.) However, social scientists have not been as successful in identifying those factors affecting the quality of *interactions* and the element of *threat* in intergenerational interchanges. Perhaps prior analyses have focused too little on the issue of attribution—the *perceptions* generational actors have of each other, and the bases for these perceptions. The purpose of this paper is to examine some critical factors which may determine perceptions across generations, under the central assumption that *cross-generational perceptions are just as determinative of the quality of intergenerational relations as are the actual differences* in philosophy, attitude, and action between cohorts.

Our argument is as follows: the perceptions one generation has of another in interaction are related less to the state of the percei*ved* than to the state of the percei*ver*. We will suggest that the individual's personal history, his position in society, and his state of development substantially color his perceptions and expectations of the other generations. Further, we will argue that cross-generation perceptions of their mutual interaction are often based on two processes: the *fear of loss mythology* ("If I don't watch out, I'm going to lose. . . .") and the *developmental stake mythology* ("If the

---

[1] An earlier version of this paper was presented at the symposium on "The Generation Gap: Real or Contrived?" American Psychological Association 78th Annual Convention, Miami Beach, September 4, 1970. We acknowledge the assistance of Marijo Walsh, Rosemary Sundeen, and Chris Lovejoy. Preparation of this paper was supported by Grant MH HD 18158 from NIMH.

Aging and Human Development, Volume 2, 1971

young reject my values, my life has come to nothing."). We submit that these mythologies contribute substantially to the experience of anxiety in the drama of generations, because they work to increase the gap between what is perceived and what is real in generational differences. We will argue, in conclusion, that differences between age groups need not be tinged with such fear, for the drama of generational evolution contains the potential for adaption to, and mastery of, social ills.

In discussing our own perceptions of the drama of generations, we will draw from two ongoing studies at the University of Southern California and the University of California, Berkeley. The first is a large survey of youth, their parents and grandparents, focusing on attitudinal aspects of differences and continuities between cohorts. The second study is an extension of the long-term longitudinal project begun in Berkeley in 1928, in which the aged parents of the original sample are being interviewed in order to examine continuities through time and between generations in aspects of personality and social functioning. These studies are, of course, still in progress and we will be using our impressions gathered from as yet incomplete data to support the argument.

SOME DATA ON DIFFERENCES IN PERCEPTION ACROSS GENERATIONS

We begin with some data from a study of students and their parents more fully described elsewhere (Bengtson, 1969). These data suggest considerable differences in perception between the youthful and mature generation when both look at their common interaction.[2]

Perceptions of Generational Social Distance

First we will review previously reported findings regarding what may be called "social distancing" between generations. Perceptions of within-family interaction were overwhelmingly favorable; for example, on the summary measure of intergenerational integration, a very high proportion of each generation (78 percent of the students and 87 percent of the parents) reported "close" or "very close" relations. Similar responses were elicited by the questions concerning global evaluation of the quality of communication and understanding between parents and students. Even given this favorable assessment, some differences in perception emerge. Parents consistently overestimated the degrees of closeness, understanding, and communication, compared to their childrens' responses. Perceptions of generational interaction outside the family showed the same pattern. When asked if they thought a "generation gap" existed, over 80 percent of the students said "yes," while only 40 percent of the parents responded affirmatively. Further, when asked if this gap is inevitable, 70 percent of the students said "yes," compared to only 58 percent of the parents (percentages based on those cases responding "yes" to the preceding question).

What these data seem to indicate is, first, that in terms of their own family, both parents and students tend to minimize the scope of the "generation gap." In the second place, however, there is a consistent difference between parents and children, with the

---

[2] This material derives from a survey of college students and their parents at a large private university. The study was later replicated with three other samples drawn from public institutions in the same area. A total of 312 students and 371 of their parents provided data in this study. Publication of this report is pending.

Aging and Human Development, Volume 2, 1971

students consistently emphasizing a greater distance and the parents minimizing the distance. These data, admittedly tapping surface perceptions and broad generalizations concerning intergenerational relations, indicate that youth and parents indeed display a different perception of the nature and evaluation of intergenerational relations, both within and outside the family.

Perceptions of Family Discussion and Disagreement

Respondents were also asked to report the extent of discussion between themselves and their parent (or child) on eleven topics selected on the basis of pilot studies as of greatest import for families of young adults. The topics, ranging from religion and politics to sex and dating, were each rated as to the frequency of discussion and then the amount of disagreement. The results of the comparison between the students' reports with those of the parents is presented in Table 1.

It can be seen from this table that there is a statistically stable difference between the amount of discussion reported by the parents and that reported by the children. For both the mother and the father, the estimate of the parent is higher than that of the child. In terms of disagreement perceived in these eleven issues, the obverse pattern emerges. Students report considerably higher disagreement than do the parents.

Why should such differences in the definition of mutual interaction exist? Part of the answer must be found in the *expectations* brought to the interaction by the two generations.

Perceptions of the Nature of Generational Difference

We asked about the specific nature of generational differences as experienced by the Ss. One would expect youth and parents to be concerned with different aspects of the relationship and thus to attend to different factors as being problematic.

A content analysis was carried out on the open-ended responses to several questions: In what ways is there a generation gap in our society, in your opinion? What is it that you

TABLE 1
Differences in Amount of Discussion and Disagreement on Eleven Topics as
Reported by Parents and Children[1]
(n = 312 students, 371 parents)

	Students' Perception		Parents' Perception			
	$\overline{X}$	s.d.	$\overline{X}$	s.d.	t	p
DISCUSSION:						
with father	27.07	6.40	30.37	6.17	5.42	.001
with mother	29.36	6.60	33.69	4.71	7.72	.001
DISAGREEMENT:						
with father	19.89	5.47	17.72	4.16	4.37	.001
with mother	19.56	5.21	17.32	3.15	5.20	.001

[1] Scores are summed means on reported discussion or disagreement on 11 issues, such as values, politics, religion, sex, money, dating, friends, etc. Scores on each item range from 1 (never discuss, never disagree) to 4 (discuss very often, very often disagree).

Aging and Human Development, Volume 2, 1971

disagree most about with your parents (child)? In what ways would you like to see the relationship with your parents (child) changed?

These questions ask for the content of the respondent's perceptions of the generations and, therefore, his own personal concerns as he looks at the drama of generational differences. The issues that parents identify as sources of friction between themselves and their children may be considered as evidence not so much of the student's behavior, but of the dominant concern that the parents have.

With regard to the first question, that of the personal definition of the "gap," it is clear (Table 2) that both parents and students agree on three major areas as basic issues dividing the generations: issues of value and morality; issues of interpersonal interaction, such as tolerance, understanding, and closeness; and the age-status issues having to do with responsibility and freedom. However, there is a difference between the generations regarding the emphasis placed on the different categories. Students maintained that issues of values and morality are the essential definers of the "gap" (35 percent), while parents saw the greatest cause in the area of breakdowns in interaction between the generations (29 percent). Over twice as many parents as students maintained that "there is no gap" or that "the gap is a myth" (4 to 9 percent).

This basic difference in theme becomes even more apparent in the respondents' attempts to define the gap as it most applies to their own families (Table 3). Parents responded in two major areas: grooming, housekeeping, empathy (22 percent), and lack of tolerance, understanding, and closeness (19 percent). Again, the students identified as

TABLE 2
In what ways is there a generation gap? In your own words, define the "gap."

	Student		Parent		Both (total)	
	%	n	%	n	%	n
1. Personal habits and traits (grooming, empathy, stubbornness, underachieving)	4.0	10	4.8	16	4.5	26
2. General personal orientations (use of time, leisure, hypocrisy)	2.8	7	1.8	6	2.2	13
3. Values and morality (life goals, philosophy of life, sex, religion)	34.8	88	19.7	64	26.2	152
4. Age status and generational issues (maturity, responsibility, freedom, independence, age, diff. life exper.)	19.8	50	25.9	85	23.3	135
5. Politics and social relations (social consciousness, patriotism, law and order, race relations, politics)	2.8	7	.6	2	1.6	9
6. Interpersonal interaction (tolerance, understanding, closeness, family rules, choice of friends)	25.0	63	29.0	95	27.2	158
7. Economic Issues	0	0	.3	1	.2	1
8. No gap: gap is a myth	4.0	10	8.6	28	6.6	38
9. Other and non-categorizable	7.1	18	9.5	31	8.4	49
SUB-TOTAL		253		278		581
10. No response	18.9	59	11.6	43	14.9	102
TOTAL	100.0	312	100.0	371	100.0	683

Aging and Human Development, Volume 2, 1971

TABLE 3
What is it you disagree about most with your parents (child)?

	Student		Parent		Both (total)	
	%	n	%	n	%	n
1. Personal habits and traits (grooming, empathy, stubbornness, underachieving)	6.8	21	21.6	72	14.7	93
2. General personal orientations (use of time, leisure, hypocrisy)	6.6	20	9.0	30	7.9	50
3. Values and morality (life goals, philosophy of life, sex, religion)	21.6	65	9.3	31	15.2	96
4. Age status and generational issues (maturity, responsibility, freedom, independence, age, diff. life exper.)	7.2	22	5.1	17	6.2	39
5. Politics and social relations (social consciousness, patriotism, law and order, race relations, politics)	13.4	40	8.1	27	10.6	67
6. Interpersonal interaction (tolerance, understanding, closeness, family rules, choice of friends)	22.9	69	18.6	62	20.8	131
7. Economic Issues	9.0	27	8.7	29	8.9	56
8. No, nothing much	6.7	20	15.6	52	11.4	72
9. Other and non-categorizable	5.0	15	3.6	12	4.3	27
SUB-TOTAL		299		332		531
10. No response	4.3	13	10.5	39	7.6	52
TOTAL	100.1	312	100.0	371	99.9	683

a primary source of disagreement issues relating to values and philosophy of life (22 percent). Problems of interpersonal relations (23 percent) ranked high for the students, as for the parents; but the issues of politics and social relations, while cited as important areas of disagreement by the students (13 percent) were not defined as one of the top three areas of discord by the parents (8 percent). Sixteen percent of the parents said that there is no disagreement whatsoever, compared with 7 percent of the children.

The pattern of responses by the two generations to these and other questions seems consistent. Both parents and students identify disagreement in the dimensions of interpersonal interaction (lack of respect, tolerance, family rules, etc.). From this point the generations diverge. Students point to issues of values, morality, politics, and life goals as major points of friction between generations; while parents attend to the personal habits and traits. Parents tend to minimize the philosophical, abstract, ideological component of differences; while the students maximize these differences. Parents attend to issues of personal habits and traits and the age-status differences and personal maturity.

It is as if the parents were saying, "Yes, there are differences between the generations, but these are not intrinsic; they are simply due to difference in life status and maturity." The students, by contrast, are saying, "The contrasts we see are in values and basic orientations to life. There are differences; and they are important."

These data suggest (a) that there is a consistent pattern of solidarity and warmth between the generations, and (b) that there are also differences in the interpretation each has of their interaction. There must be, therefore, some *expectational processes related to*

Aging and Human Development, Volume 2, 1971

the other generation that color perception. What are these processes? One has to do with *one's own experiences as members of an age group rooted in time,* time measured in both historical and personal terms. Another has to do with *one's own need for the other generation:* It may be termed the "developmental stake."

OBJECTIVE ROOTS OF GENERATIONAL DIFFERENCE: HISTORY, POWER, MATURITY

To understand the differences, both real and perceived, between age groups it is necessary to recognize the historical, social, and personal factors that influence the experiencing of each generation. In some ways a discussion of such factors may seem premature, because of the frequently overlooked fact that the nature, extent, and consequences of differences between generations are still very much open to a variety of interpretations (see Feuer, 1969; Adelson, 1970; Bengtson, 1970; Kalish, 1970; Mead, 1970). In this paper, we have chosen not to focus on the degree to which actual differences in philosophy, action, or moral judgment exist (or do not exist), for we have commented on these elsewhere (Bengtson, 1969, 1970; Birren and Bengtson, 1969; Kobrin and Bengtson, 1970; Kuypers, 1970). Rather, we intend to emphasize the critical factors that determine perceptions across generational lines, under the assumption that one foundation for intergenerational action is its perceptual base. There are four factors which are readily observable (hence "objective") that account for such differences. We will mention these briefly before considering two additional "subjective" factors.

The first factor concerns the different *historical settings* in which different generations find themselves. As much as we are a product of our *zeitgeist,* displacement in historical time will contribute to differences in value, attitude, life style (see, among others Mannheim, 1952; Berger, 1960).

A second factor concerns the point of contact an individual has relative to the historical evolution of *social institutions.* Social systems change; their component parts evolve with the passage of time. It is easy to see that young men of twenty years of age in 1900, in 1940, and in 1970, equated in every other way, would face quite a different spectre of military life, because of the transformations of that institution within our society.

A third factor involves *age-status differentials* and social system positions. Persons at different points along the life cycle typically exhibit differential penetration into, and identification with, the social institutions of their culture. This relates to the succession to higher and higher status with the passage of personal time, and to the differential commitment persons have in maintaining social institutions and personal investments. The picture is abundantly clear in terms of the middle generation having its major involvements and identities defined by the running, governing, educating, parenting, guiding roles in society. The power differential that this social system identification creates becomes a major source of clash between generations (see Feuer, 1969; Musgrove, 1970).

Fourth, there is the critically important factor of differential life tasks and psychological concerns patterned by *psychological development.* While it is clear that society changes over time, that behaviors and orientations of youth and middle age are partly conditioned by the historical context impinging on them, it is also clear that the individual experiences and adapts differently along his life line because of developmental

Aging and Human Development, Volume 2, 1971

changes. If one could, for the moment, hold constant personal history and vary only stage of psychological development, different concerns and interests would be evidenced. The dominant concerns, characteristic needs, or cognitive mechanisms of forty-year-olds are different than those of twenty-year-olds (see Birren, 1969). A recent dissertation by Weimer (1970) demonstrated age-related shifts in dominant psychological concerns from psychophysiological data. The variation in "developmental tasks" (Havighurst, 1953), "ego-developmental crises" (Erikson, 1950, 1959), "decelerated socialization" (Davis, 1940), or "increased inferiority" of personality (Neugarten, 1968), between one stage of life and another, leads inevitably to significant differences in interaction and perspectives between cohorts. Or in the words of one of our respondents, a 43-year-old mother:

> The younger generation cannot feel or think as an older person who has had a myriad of experiences, responsibilities, joys, disappointments, and sadness to color his thinking, perspectives, values, and reactions. Likewise, it is difficult to remember how we felt and thought when we were younger—the plain joy of living, the things we considered important, etc.

Many scholars have commented that differences in value, philosophy, and ego involvements are likely over time. Erikson and Neugarten for example, have noted that the *intimacy* concerns of a young adult have quite a different impact on the person than do the *generative* concerns of the middle-aged man or woman. These concerns, for the young person, are likely to lead to a primary interest in the development and establishment of personally meaningful relationships with peers, the development and establishment of personal philosophies and value systems on which to base action. The middle-aged person, by contrast, is likely to be critically concerned with the maintenance of already developed commitments and value systems and with the development of what might be called *personal heirs*. The concern is not with personal relationships with peers, but with the development and growth of social and personal heirs to extend one's personal history into the future.

These psychological concerns have quite different implications regarding the saliency one generation has relative to another. Youth, for example, is likely to experience the parenting generation, in part, as relatively expendable objects. Their role of parenting and socializing is past, from the youth's point of view. Attempts of the parenting generation to guide and direct, to control or instruct, may be experienced with mild toleration or more dramatic irritation. The parenting generation, on the other hand, is likely to invest a good deal of energy in the progress and development of youth. Great concern and personal meaning is attached to their behavior. In short, they are high saliency objects.

Thus the condition is set in which middle generation adults need to orient, socialize and direct youth, a direction which, itself, is antithetical to the personal concerns of youth. And so we now have the elements which create a *differential of intentionality* between generations. While youth presses for minimization of external controls, the press of the middle generation is just the opposite, to guarantee generational continuity through influence on the youth.

It is interesting to note that Erikson views the grandparenting generation as concerned with personal issues of meaningfulness of life, of personal integrity, and with life review. In this view, other persons of younger generations may be relatively low saliency objects, regardless of age. This is similar to an element in Charlotte Buhler's theory of phases in life goals (see Buhler, 1967). Buhler emphasizes that the fourth phase of the life cycle (45 to 65) involves self-assessment regarding attained or failed goals; while the fifth (after 65) centers around the tendency to establish inner order.

Up to this point we have adhered relatively faithfully to reasoning introduced by scholars of the stature of Erikson, Havighurst, Buhler, and Neugarten. By now a departure is required to examine the foundations for middle and young generational developmental concerns, the relation of these concerns to perception, and their essential mythological character.

SUBJECTIVE ROOTS OF GENERATIONAL PERCEPTION: THE "DEVELOPMENTAL STAKE" AND THE FEAR OF LOSS MYTH

David Elkind (1970) has called attention to the contractual agreements entered into by parents and children. He emphasizes that the terms of the contract must change with the increasing maturity of the child, as the nature of the investment each bases in the other shifts. Bettleheim (1965) has noted that some parents may view as their child's main task in life the justification of a parent; the child is to provide the parent with what was lacking in his (the parent's) own life. Some children may view their goal in life as that of surpassing the parent—socially, economically, or intellectually. These examples focus on our central concern in explaining differences in cross-generational perception: the nature of *interactional expectations* as each generation views the other.

What is it in an individual's condition that determines how he sees another? When one has an investment in the fortunes of another, the expectation is often summarized by saying, "I've got a stake in him." What is the nature of the stakes the generations have in each other, and the roots of these stakes?

For the middle generation, evidence points to the high saliency of issues centering around the meaning, the justification, and, as Haan (1970) has pointed out, the validation of their life and the commitments they have made to it. This is especially true in times of rapid social change when previously assumed cultural values are called into question. At a time when the middle generation may be confronting the realization of their personal mortality, the glimmering realization of the finitude of their own personal history, questions about the essential worth, meaning, and even judgment of their life come to the foreground. Neugarten has suggested that a shift in time perspective occurs in middle age when time left to live becomes the life-cycle yardstick.

We maintain that many in the middle years seek resolution to these issues in the development of the young generation. An experienced continuity with the next generation—which is one's personal extension into the future—becomes the experiential answer to the questions, "What is my life all about? Where will it lead to? Does it make any sense?"

An interesting example of this concern is found in the long history behind inheritance litigation. Recently Back and Baade (1967) presented a social-psychological analysis of "the social meaning of death and the law." They argued that the use of the law and its inheritance restrictions are designed to be safeguards against man's tendency, especially in the wealthy and powerful, to extend his control and influence well past his death. To quote from Back and Baade (p. 316),

... the urge to control the conduct of future generations through conditional or limited testamentary dispositions in favor of natural persons and of charities is deepseated, especially in Great Britain and in the United States.

Aging and Human Development, Volume 2, 1971

The developmental stake which the middle generation has in the young, therefore, creates a view of the young as social heirs, that is, as (a) extension of the self and (b) continuous with the older generation's personal-social order. This developmental concern colors the perception the elders have of the emerging generation. It explains why the middle generation would *minimize the essentiality* of differences perceived between the generations. In the face of behavior which, in reality, reflects both difference and continuity, the middle generation is constrained to believe and perhaps to fabricate the continuity.

The developmental stake of the young is quite different. They have high investment in establishing their personal life styles, in forming their attitudes toward major issues and institutions. As based in their developmental concerns, they are more concerned with the *establishment,* as opposed to the *validation,* of values and strategies. Such issues imply freedom to experience and develop.

In other words, youth is at a point of attempting to establish its existence and its style, to throw off the *stake* of the parenting generation. An oppositional stake is created, a stake which colors youth's view of the middle generation. The young are pressed to see discontinuity across generations, and they tend to *maximize the essentiality* of differences. For them, those of the middle generation are low saliency objects. Thus, they react with the anticipation of differences and with the tendency to view the differences as essential.

Cross-Generational Differences and the "Fear of Loss"

We now have before us the array of influences which explain the "fear of loss" mythology; the backdrop for interpreting the intergenerational drama. For the middle generation, the feared loss is, indeed, quite dramatic. If not one's existence, certainly one's validation is at stake. The completion of our earlier statement is "If I don't watch out, I'm going to lose my identity, reason for being, and value." Difference is indicative of loss. Loss is feared, hence the demand to counteract the feared loss.

There exists in the middle generation a ready vocabulary of motive to explain away the youth revolt. Phrases such as the following are used so often these days—and often by those in highest offices—as adults attempt to explain the violence of youthful confrontation: "only a passing phase . . . a radical minority . . . outside agitators . . . only a bystander . . . a communist plot to undermine . . . breakdown of discipline . . . a function of college administrative spinelessness . . . simply youthful experimentation . . . certainly not true in my family." The message of such euphemisms may be the following: "My stake in the oncoming generation is so great, that there cannot be any basic disruption between us. To so disrupt will seriously question the validity of my own beliefs."

The same fear of loss exists in the younger generation. The fear here is related to powerlessness, to the perceived meaninglessness of the social order into which one is moving, and to the blurring of distinctiveness between oneself and the parenting generation. There exists a ready vocabulary of motive to explain the essentiality of revolt: "You can't trust *any*one over 30 . . . non-negotiable demands . . . so up-tight . . . irrelevant . . . off the pigs." The message here is: "My stake in the future is being cataclysmically endangered by the controls put on by the middle-aged Establishment. My stake in the freedom the older generation wants to deny me is so great that there cannot be any continuity between us. To see continuity is to seriously question the validity of my own beliefs about the nature of man, environment, wealth, and interpersonal affairs."

The Relation of Perception to Control

While identifying the mythological bases for intergenerational perceptions (mythological in the sense that their validation is nonexistent), it is at once apparent that they serve as very real bases for action, especially action in the form of control and influence. As noted earlier, the developmental stake implies differential control of the generations: the middle is more likely to control the destinies of the young, being in command of information, monies, and other resources, and being concerned with generational continuity. The young are predisposed to seek dissociation between themselves and the generation of those in command. The difficulty comes in the extent to which the young experience the forces on them as controlling, and whether these controls violate philosophical roots of life, such as freedom, openness, justice. The middle-aged see youth resenting the legitimate demands for order and continuity while youth experiences arbitrary expression of control and authority.

For the young generation, therefore, the "fear of loss" involves loss of freedom—the freedom to choose and establish personal controls. As with the middle generation, the anticipated fear of loss across the generations is quite dramatic for the young. The stakes are high on both sides of the generational theater.

CONCLUSION

In this paper we have explored the influences, real or mythological, of those factors that lead to differential perceptions across generations. Our analysis has centered on the assumption that perceptions are one foundation for action between generations. We explored the historical, social, and personal causes of differential perception across generations. We concluded by suggesting the existence of a basic contrast in expectations concerning generational interaction, rooted in the developmental stakes each generation has in each other and the mythological bases for these perceptions.

To recapitulate, our argument has been this. For the middle generation, the backdrop for perceiving generational relations concerns the establishment and maintenance of *continuity* over time. Experienced *conflict* arises from their anticipation that youthful emergence, unless guided and controlled, will create disruptive discontinuity. For the young generation, the perception backdrop rests on their focus on individuation, change, and *emergence*. Experienced conflict arises from their anticipation that middle generation influence will delimit their development. For both, perceptions across generations are characterized by *fear*: fear of losing the ability to emerge, on the one hand, and to establish continuity, on the other.

The question naturally arises, after having argued for the sources of fear in the generational drama, of how to reduce the defensive, protective, and what seems to be the self-defeating conflict between generations. While not pretending to approach an inclusive answer to this critical question, we do nurture the hope that *awareness* of the arbitrariness of the essential fear across generations will help. To realize that the perspectives, urgencies and criticisms of youth, for example, do not intrinsically forecast social dissolution but rather offer energy and commitment for constructive change will,

Aging and Human Development, Volume 2, 1971

itself, be helpful. To realize that the power and influence of the middle generation does not automatically predict generational control but, rather, offers the mechanism for rapid social change, itself will be helpful. While the middle generation may be essentially concerned with *continuity* and validation the emergence of youth is not intrinsically oppositional. Nor is the young person's struggle for emergence intrinsically antithetical to a quest for continuity.

Ultimately, all members of the generational drama must acknowledge that there is a moral error in behavior that seeks to control and externally determine the form of another's life, no matter what the reason. *To seek validation for the self through control of another is an error,* for individuals and for generations. Rather, we must evaluate the worth of our social order and its institutions by the experiential meaning they have for people. The meaningful answer to the question of meaning rests not in the continuation through time of currently operative policies and structures, but in the effect they have on the condition of man. A shift is required in which we look not across generations, fearing what is to be lost and preparing to defend against that loss, but in which we seek what can be gained from the constructive utilization of the perspectives of youth and the executing abilities of the middle generation.

REFERENCES

Adelson, J. What generation gap? *New York Times Magazine,* 1970 (Jan. 18), 10-13.

Back, K., & Baade, J. The social meaning of death and the law. In J. McKinney & F. De Vyver (Eds.), *Aging and social policy.* New York: Appleton-Century-Crofts, 1966.

Bengtson, V. L. The "generation gap": Differences by generation and by sex in the perception of parent-child relations. Paper presented at Pacific Sociological Association meetings, 1969.

Bengtson, V. L. The "generation gap": A review and typology of social-psychological perspectives. *Youth and society,* 1970, *2* (1).

Berger, B. How long is a generation? *British Journal of Sociology,* 1960, *II,* 10-23.

Bettleheim, B. The problem of generations. In E. Erikson (Ed.), *Youth: Change and challenge.* New York: Basic Books, 1963.

Birren, J. E., & Bengtson, V. L. The problem of generations: Emotions vs. reality. Paper presented at hearings before the Senate Subcommittee on Aging, held at the Center for the Study of Democratic Institutions, Santa Barbara, Calif., October 17, 1968. Condensation in *The Center Magazine,* 1969, *2* (2), 84-87.

Birren, J. E. Age and decision strategies. In A. T. Welford & J. E. Birren (Eds.), *Decision making and age.* Basel, Switzerland: Karger, 1969.

Buhler, C. Human life as a whole as a central subject in humanistic psychology. In J. Bugehtal (Ed.), *Challenges of humanistic psychology.* New York: McGraw-Hill, 1967.

Cain, L. D. Age status and generational phenomena: The new old people in contemporary America. *Gerontologist,* 1967, *7* (2), 83-92.

Cain, L. D. The 1916-1925 cohort: Their contribution to the "generation gap." Paper presented at the American Sociological Association meetings, September 2, 1970.

Davis, K. The sociology of parent-youth conflict. *American Sociological Review,* 1940, *5* (4), 523-534.

Elkind, D. P. The youth revolt and parental exploitation. *Mental Hygiene,* 1970. *54* (4), 490-497.

Erikson, E. H. *Childhood and society.* New York: W. W. Norton, 1950.

Erikson, E. Identity and the life cycle. *Psychological Issues,* 1959, 1 (1).

Feuer, L. *The conflict of generations: The character and significance of student movements.* New York: Basic Books, 1969.

Haan, N. The generation gap as moral redefinition in families. Paper presented at the American Psychological Association meetings, 1970.

Hill, R. The three-generation technique as a method for measuring social change. In R. Hill & E. Konig (Eds.), *Families east and west.* Paris: Mouton, 1970.

Kalish, R. The young and the old as generation gap allies. *Gerontologist,* 1969, *9* (2), 83-90.

Kobrin, S. & Bengtson, V. L. Generational contrasts in the attribution of legitimacy. Paper presented at the American Sociological Association meetings, 1970.

Kuypers, J. Generational continuities and contrasts in personality: Effects on family interaction. Paper presented at Gerontological Society meetings, Toronto, October 24, 1970.

Aging and Human Development, Volume 2, 1971

Mannheim, K. The problem of generations. In K. Mannheim, *Essays in the sociology of knowledge.* London: Routledge, Kegan, Paul, 1952.

Mead, M. *Conflict and commitment: A study of the generation gap.* New York: Basic Books, 1970.

Musgrove, F. The problem of youth and the structure of society in England. *Youth and Society,* 1969, *1* (1), 39-58.

Neugarten, Bernice L. The young and the old in modern societies. *American Behavioral Scientist* 1970, *12*, 43-57.

Thomas, L. E. Family correlates of student political activism. *Developmental Psychology,* 1971, *4* (1), 58-73.

Troll, L. The generation gap: conceptual models. *Aging and Human Development,* 1970, *1*, 199-218.

Weimer, A. S. Shifts in psychological concerns from adolescence to later maturity. Unpublished doctoral dissertation, University of Southern California, 1970.

DEVELOPMENTAL REVIEW 2, 342–370 (1982)

Children and Adolescents as Producers of Their Own Development

RICHARD M. LERNER

Center for Advanced Study in the Behavioral Sciences

Interest in the historically changing contexts of human life has been associated with the elaboration of a life-span view of human development. This view holds that all levels of the context, including the biological, psychological, and sociocultural, change in reciprocal relation to one another. As a consequence of being embedded in a context which they both influence and are influenced by, children and adolescents may promote their own development. One way this occurs is that as a consequence of their characteristics of physical and behavioral individuality people promote differential reactions in their socializing others (e.g., parents, teachers, or peers); these reactions feed back affecting further development. My colleagues and I have conducted research that describes such child and adolescent contributions to development. We have focused on characteristics of physical individuality, such as body type and physical attractiveness, and on characteristics of behavioral individuality, such as behavioral style or temperament. Findings from these studies are conceptualized in terms of a person–context "goodness-of-fit" model. Adaptive development is associated with congruence, or fit, between a person's attributes of individuality and the demands of his or her setting. Implications of this research for illustrating the use of the life-span perspective, and for theory in and practice of intervention, are discussed.

What My Grandmother Always Knew

I completed my doctoral dissertation at the City University of New York *in absentia*. On the evening before my oral defense I flew in from Michigan, where I was teaching, to New York City. I stayed with my mother and grandmother, who shared an apartment in Brooklyn. Both seemed especially quiet that evening, as if reluctant to disturb what they may have sensed was a delicate homeostasis. When I left for Manhattan the next morning all either said to me was "Good luck".

After a successful defense I returned to Brooklyn feeling quite elated

This paper was written while I was a Fellow at the Center for Advanced Study in the Behavioral Sciences. I am grateful for financial support provided by National Institute of Mental Health Grant 5-T32-MH14581-05 and by The John D. and Catherine T. MacArthur Foundation, and for the assistance of the Center staff. I am also grateful to Paul B. Baltes, Jay Belsky, Orville G. Brim, Jr., Nancy A. Busch-Rossnagel, Robyn M. Dawes, Martin E. Ford, Ruth T. Gross, David F. Hultsch, David Krathwohl, Lewis P. Lipsitt, Jacqueline V. Lerner, Margaret Snow, Mark Snyder, Alexander Thomas, and to two anonymous reviewers for helpful comments on a previous version of this paper. Reprint requests should be sent to Richard M. Lerner, College of Human Development, The Pennsylvania State University, University Park, PA 16802.

0273-2297/82/040342-29$02.00/0

and upon arriving I found my mother's reaction to my success to be more grandiose than mine. My mother and grandmother each had her own phone, with extensions often adjacent to each other in the same room. My mother sat facing the entrance of the apartment with a receiver at each ear. As I entered and answered the all-purpose Yiddish question, "*Nu?*" with "Yes, I passed," my mother sprang into action. The relatives who were holding on each line were given their instructions about how to proceed with a chain call that, to hear my mother explain it, would reach family members of five generations on both sides of the Atlantic.

As my mother continued to dial and talk on two phones simultaneously, my grandmother walked over to where I was standing, incredulous in the apartment entranceway. With a Yiddish accent that remains strong despite her over sixty years in this country she asked, "So tell me Sonny, what did you write your book about?"

While my grandmother is a very bright woman, she has no formal education, especially in the technology (and jargon) of psychology. I immediately recognized that I would have to communicate the main findings of my work without recourse to the vocabulary of my profession. My dissertation dealt with topics that today fall under the headings of "child influences" and "reciprocal socialization," topics that bear directly on key themes in this article. My work assessed whether children and adolescents who differed in their physical characteristics (i.e., their body types) elicited different, stereotyped reactions from their peers and, if so, whether these children and adolescents had body and self-concepts consistent with the appraisals of their peers. This explanation was not, however, the one I related to my grandmother. Rather, my jargon-free account went something like: "Well, Grandma, I found out that children don't like fat kids as much as they do average build kids, and that fat kids don't like themselves very much either."

My grandmother let go of my arm. She took a step back and her eyes narrowed. "Tell me boychick" (I knew something was wrong: she had switched pronouns on me), "how long did it take you to find this out?"

"Well, Grandma, it took me about a year and a half to complete the whole thing."

Her open hand flew up and *klopped* the side of my head. "Stupid," she said, "if you would have asked me I would have told you in two minutes!"

Reformulating My Reply: A Transition in the Study of Human Development

Perhaps I should have given my grandmother more credit for being able to follow a bit more convoluted of an argument. What might I have said?

First, I might have indicated that in a sense it is the job of social science to deal with the obvious. This occurs in two ways. As argued for by Prewitt (1980, pp. xxiii–xxiv), first:

> the greatest discoveries of social science quickly become conventional wisdom . . . social science has the power to label, and therefore the power to reveal empirical constants and patterns of association which would otherwise not be "obvious" to us. Many social science terms have since slipped into common usage; they have become part of the conventional wisdom of society. A partial list from various disciplines would include adolescence, socialization, . . . GNP, . . . hyperactivity, . . . the rising revolution of expectations.

However, second:

> If social science discovers the obvious, and thereby renders it accessible, it also disproves the obvious. It evaluates the truth of conventional wisdom, often finding that accepted assumptions are wrong. . . . The social sciences seldom get credit for their counter-intuitive findings, as legion as they are, because people quickly rearrange their belief systems, claiming that they "knew it all along." Even this obvious fact was not so obvious before psychology began to develop theories of dissonance reduction (Prewitt, 1980 p. xxiv).

Second, I might have then explained how this view of the nature of social science bore on my particular research interests. My dissertation work was completed in early 1971. By that time some of the major conceptual and methodological ideas that not only influenced my thinking, but too were to forge what I view as a revised understanding of the nature of human development, had appeared (Baltes, 1968; Brim & Wheeler, 1966; Goulet & Baltes, 1970; Schaie, 1965; Tobach & Schneirla, 1968). As a consequence of these ideas I might have told my grandmother that my work related to a view of human development that differed from perspectives then traditional in human development.

Conventionally, the study of the child was approached from the framework of ideas that saw the major bases of development as lying either within the child or extrinsic to him or her, i.e., from an organismic or a mechanistic perspective, respectively (Reese & Overton, 1970). My view, however, was a "relational" one (Looft, 1973). There are always both intrinsic and extrinsic influences on the person. However, to appreciate the nature of their impact, to understand the developmental changes with which they are associated, one must recognize that both individual and environment may change and that, often, changes in one affect changes in the other. By being in a context that they both influence and are influenced by, children may promote their own development.

Nevertheless, even after indicating how my dissertation data illustrated the use of this perspective, my grandmother may have responded similarly (although perhaps without a slap), that is, that she knew this all along. Indeed, as noted by Baltes (1979a), the idea that people and their worlds are reciprocally interactive is not new.

Thus, what makes this idea and the recent work associated with it important? Brim (1981), in addressing this very question, provides an answer which links work on this idea with a major, current transition in the understanding of human development. He says:

> The idea that organisms act to create environments to elicit responses from themselves is not new. The plan for getting oneself into the right situation to help one become something else, something more than he or she is today, is exemplified by hanging "THINK" signs at strategic points in one's home and work place, and joining some of the thousands of organized groups devoted to helping one become a different person. What is new and powerful about this . . . is that it is the first major work dealing in broad perspective with the idea, and placing the idea firmly in the theory of life-span development.
>
> Behind this idea, to be sure, is the view that the organism is dynamic, powered by curiosity, growth, expansion, and a drive towards mastery over itself and its world. . . . Behind the idea is also the view that organisms are open to change, are much more malleable than heretofore thought, and that the consequences of early experience and biological endowment are transformed by later experience.

In other words, Brim (1981) sees the idea—that as a consequence of reciprocal relations with their context, children may be producers of their development—as having current importance because of its place in a larger network of ideas, often labeled as the life-span view of human development (Baltes, Reese, & Lipsitt, 1980). Therefore, to best understand how children and adolescents contribute to their own development it is useful to discuss the nature of the life-span perspective and the revisions it has fostered in thinking about human development.

FEATURES OF THE LIFE-SPAN VIEW OF HUMAN DEVELOPMENT

Developmental psychology is not the only scientific discipline concerned with the study of human development. Family and life-course sociologists, developmental and evolutionary biologists, comparative psychologists, physicians, and economists are also concerned with human development (e.g., see Riley, 1979). Human development, or more accurately child development, was often studied in the first several decades of this century within university institutes, e.g., at Iowa, Minnesota, and Berkeley, designed to be multidisciplinary; however, this pluralistic perspective began to erode by the 1950s, and was replaced by a unidisciplinary, psychological view of development.[1] Indeed, some reviewers (e.g., Hartup, 1978) have thus noted that relative disciplinary isolation characterized developmental research in the two decades prior to the 1970s. However, the years following this time were marked by renewed

[1] Lipsitt, L. P., personal communication, December 1979; Palermo, D. S., personal communication, August 1980.

calls for interdisciplinary integration (e.g., Baltes, 1979a; Brim & Kagan, 1980; Bronfenbrenner, 1979; Burgess & Huston, 1979; Hill & Mattessich, 1979; Lerner & Spanier, 1978; Petrinovich, 1979; Riley, 1979). The bases for these calls were primarily conceptual.

Attempts to use a unidimensional biological model of growth, based on an idealistic, genetic–maturational (organismic) paradigm, to account for data sets pertinent to the adult and aged years were not completely successful (Baltes et al., 1980; Baltes & Schaie, 1973). Viewed from the perspective of this organismic conception, the adult and aged years were necessarily seen as periods of decline. However, all data sets pertinent to age changes, e.g., in regard to intellectual performance, during these periods were not consistent with such a unidirectional format for change. That is, increasingly greater interindividual differences in intraindividual change were evident in many data sets (Baltes, 1979a; Baltes & Schaie, 1974, 1976; Schaie, Labouvie, & Buech, 1973).

On the basis of such data Brim and Kagan (1980, p. 13) concluded that "growth is more individualistic than was thought, and it is difficult to find general patterns." Variables associated with membership in particular birth cohorts and/or with normative and nonnormative events occurring at particular times of measurement appeared to account for more of the variance in behavior change processes with respect to adult intellectual development than did age-associated influences (Baltes et al., 1980). Data sets pertinent to the child (Baltes, Baltes, & Reinert, 1970) and the adolescent (Nesselroade & Baltes, 1974) that considered these cohort and time effects also confirmed their saliency in developmental change. Conceptualizations useful for understanding the role of these non-age-related variables in development were therefore induced (e.g., Baltes, Cornelius, & Nesselroade, 1977), and a major conceptual change, if not a paradigm shift, has occurred among many of today's social scientists. This new focus has led to the evolution of a new perspective about human development. Brim and Kagan (1980, p. 1) have summarized the status of this alteration in focus by noting that this

> conception of human development . . . differs from most Western contemporary thoughts on the subject. The view that emerges . . . is that humans have a capacity for change across the entire life span. It questions the traditional idea that the experiences of the early years, which have a demonstrated contemporaneous effect, necessarily constrain the characteristics of adolescence and adulthood . . . there are important growth changes across the life span from birth to death, many individuals retain a great capacity for change, and the consequences of the events of early childhood are continually transformed by later experiences, making the course of human development more open than many have believed.

As a consequence of this empirical and conceptual activity, the point of view labeled as "life-span developmental psychology" or as the "life-span view of human development" has become crystallized. As discussed by Havighurst (1973) and by Baltes (1979a), the historical bases of this perspective can be traced to 18th- and 19th-century European publications by Tetens (1777), Carus (1808), and Quetelet (1835) and, in the 20th century to contributions, in both Europe and in the United States, such as those by Sanford (1902), Hall (1922), Hollingworth (1927), Bühler (1933), Pressey, Janney, and Kuhlen (1939), Erikson (1950), and by the faculty of the Committee on Human Development at the University of Chicago (e.g., Havighurst, 1948, 1953, 1956; Neugarten, 1964, 1966, 1969; Neugarten & Guttman, 1958). For example, in the work of Havighurst (1948, 1953) we find a stress on an active organism changing across life (as a consequence of having to confront new "developmental tasks") and an emphasis on the need to use a multidisciplinary perspective to understand organism–context relations across life.

By the late 1960's and throughout the 1970s these historical antecedents began to be synthesized, and the nature of the life-span view became clear, over the course of several conferences (Baltes & Schaie, 1973; Datan & Ginsberg, 1975; Datan & Reese, 1977; Goulet & Baltes, 1970; Nesselroade & Reese, 1973), the initiation of publication of an annual volume devoted to life-span development (Baltes, 1978; Baltes & Brim, 1979, 1980, 1981), and the publication of numerous empirical and theoretical papers (see Baltes et al., 1980). From this perspective, the potential for developmental change is seen to be present across all of life; the human life course is held to be potentially multidirectional and necessarily multidimensional (Baltes, 1979b; Baltes & Nesselroade, 1973). In addition, the sources of the potentially continual changes across life are seen to involve both the inner-biological and outer-ecological levels of the context within which the organism is embedded. Indeed, although an orientation *to* the study of development and not a specific theory *of* development (Baltes, 1979b), it is clear that life-span developmentalists are disposed to a reciprocal model of organism–context relations. As Baltes (1979b, p. 2) has indicated:

> Life-span developmental psychologists emphasize *contextualistic-dialectic* paradigms of development (Datan & Reese, 1977; Lerner, Skinner, & Sorell, 1980; Riegel, 1976) rather than the use of "mechanistic" or "organismic" ones more typical of child development work. There are two primary rationales for this preference. One is, of course, evident also in current child development work. As development unfolds, it becomes more and more apparent that individuals act on the environment and produce novel behavior outcomes, thereby making the active and selective nature of human beings of paramount importance. Furthermore, the recognition of the interplay between age-graded, history-graded, and nonnormative life events suggests a contextualistic and dialectical conception of development. This dialectic is further accentuated by the fact that individual development is the reflection of multiple forces which are not always in synergism, or convergence, nor do they always permit the delineation of a specific set of end states.

In sum, the development of life-span developmental psychology in the 1970s has led to a view of human development which suggested that individual changes across life are both a product and a producer of the multiple levels of context within which the person is embedded.

Three points about the present status of this view are important to note. First, in order to study the complex interrelations among organism and context life-span developmentalists (e.g., Baltes, 1968; Schaie, 1965) promote the use of particular research designs and methodologies (e.g., sequential designs, multivariate statistics, cohort analysis). Second, they seek both methodological and substantive collaboration with scholars from disciplines whose units of analysis have traditionally been other than individual-psychological, or personological, ones. For example, the work of life-course sociologists has been important in advancing life-span developmental psychology (e.g., Brim, 1968; Brim & Kagan, 1980; Brim & Ryff, 1980; Elder, 1974, 1979; Riley, 1978, 1979). Third, however, these methodological and multidisciplinary activities are undertaken primarily for conceptual reasons. If contextual influences were not seen as crucial for understanding individual development, then neither methods for their assessment in relation to the individual, nor information about the character of these levels of analysis, would be necessary.

Accordingly, the life-span view promotes a model of development that can be described as contextual (Lerner, Hultsch, & Dixon, in press; Pepper, 1942). In so doing, it sees individuals as both products and producers of the context which provides a basis of their development. As such, individuals may be seen as producers of their development. Theoretical and empirical reasons suggest that childhood and adolescence exemplify both the use of the life-span perspective and the role of individuals as producers of their own development.

Childhood and Adolescence as Periods Exemplifying the Use of the Life-Span Perspective

Several data sets illustrate how the person both affects and is affected by variables in his or her relatively proximal familial settings (Belsky, 1981; Hill, 1980a, 1980b; Steinberg & Hill, 1978) and peer contexts (Bengtson & Troll, 1978; Lerner, Karson, Meisels, & Knapp, 1975); by variables in the broader ecological context (Bronfenbrenner, 1979; Garbarino & Bronfenbrenner, 1976), for example, educational (Bachman, 1970; Bachman, Green, & Wirtanen, 1971), and political (Gallatin, 1975) institutions; and finally by variables linked to the historical/evolutionary context (Bengtson & Troll, 1978; Brent, 1978; Lerner & Busch-Rossnagel, 1981).

For example, the secular trend regarding the decreasing mean age of menarche has presumably been brought about by historical changes in nutritional levels and medical and health practices (Garn, 1980; Katch-adourian, 1977; Lerner & Spanier, 1980). However, cohorts of early adolescents who are physiologically capable of reproduction at earlier and earlier ages, do not necessarily achieve formal thought or ego identity earlier. Yet, such earlier-maturing youth can have profound affects on the family, the peer group, and educational institutions. For example, by the beginning of the 1980s an average of more than 30,000 females, aged 14 years or less, gave birth out of wedlock (Jaffe & Dryfoos, 1976). If the secular trend continues even for a few decades more, a large proportion of today's young adults' grandchildren or great grandchildren will be involved in an out-of-wedlock pregnancy or birth while still in their "childhood" years.

Another illustration of the potential for reciprocal influence between children and adolescents and their changing social context may be seen by noting that in the United States there is an increasingly greater proportion of children and adolescents who experience several years of their preadult development in single-parent families and/or in families reconstituted through remarriage. At the same time, changing marital and family patterns, along with changing economic conditions, have led to a proportion of children and adolescents greater than ever before living in a household with a working mother (Hoffman, 1979). In addition, more and more children are experiencing caregiving in day-care or other non-home-setting contexts. These changes in the social context may have an impact on parents, on their interactions with their children, and on the individual development of the children and adolescents themselves.

For example, the adolescent daughters of working mothers are more likely to aspire to nontraditional vocational careers than is the case with adolescent daughters of nonworking mothers (Hoffman, 1979). Similarly, the changing career aspirations of women, as well as the economic pressures of inflationary economies, are leading adolescents to delay age of first marriage and, often, to forego having children until both careers, in an initiated marriage, are established (Lerner, Spanier, & Belsky, 1982). In turn then, the issue is not *whether* having greater proportions of older, career-oriented couples will have an impact on educational, financial, and marital institutions but rather *how* such impacts will be manifest.

Still other data indicate that the nature of early development is altered by historical changes in the social context. One of the best examples of the role of historical change is found in the research of Nesselroade and Baltes (1974), regarding the effects of time of measurement on changes in adolescents' personality factor scores, for example, regarding dimensions such as superego strength and independence. Regardless of whether adolescents were 13, 14, 15, or 16 years old in 1970, and despite their initial

(1970) scores on these two variables, by 1972 all adolescents decreased in superego strength and increasd in independence, to a point where the scores of all age groups were comparable.

Another excellent example is provided by the work of Glen Elder. For example, data in his influential book *Children of the Great Depression* (1974), well document the role of the socioeconomic context, as it existed at particular periods in history, on the nature of both immediate, adolescent, and later, adult personal and interpersonal behaviors. For instance, Elder reports that characteristics of this historical era produced alterations in the influence education had on achievement, affected later, adult health for youth from working-class families who suffered deprivation during this period, and enhanced the importance of children in later, adult marriages for youth who suffered hardships during the Depressions.

The cohort effects illustrated by Elder's (1974, 1980) research, and the time of measurement effects identified in the work of Nesselroade and Baltes (1974), suggest that we consider variables in the historical context of young people in our attempts to account for increasing proportions of the variance in behavior change processes. As a consequence of normative and nonnormative historically related variation,[2] the trajectory of development may change in childhood and adolescence. In other words, because of its multidimensional and dynamic interactional character, child and adolescent development is a potentially multidirectional phenomenon, best studied within the context of research designs sensitive to historical change, and most adequately conceptualized and assessed through multivariate means (Baltes, Reese, & Nesselroade, 1977; Lerner & Spanier, 1980; Nesselroade & Baltes, 1979).

In sum, data sets pertinent to childhood and adolescence (e.g., Elder, 1974, 1980; Nesselroade & Baltes, 1974; Schaie, 1979) have led life-span developmental psychologists and life-course sociologists to forego simplistic, unidimensional, univariate, and/or unidisciplinary approaches to development. Instead, in attempts to integrate personological and contextual (e.g., historically changing social and cultural) levels of analysis, multidisciplinary perspectives about development and change have evolved (Baltes, 1979b; Lerner & Busch-Rossnagel, 1981; Lerner, Hutsch, & Dixon, in press).

However, it is important to note that the above examples of the role of historical change and of reciprocal relations in child and adolescent development are largely descriptive. We need then to consider the explana-

---

[2] Normative experiences are those encountered by most people in a cohort and/or alive at a particular historical moment, e.g., most people living in the United States today experience or will experience marriage and the birth of at least one child; nonnormative experiences are atypical events, encountered rarely in the course of history, e.g., birth of quintuplets, experiencing an atomic bomb attack.

tory bases of such relations. Specifically, what may be the precise processes by which such transactions occur? There may be several means by which such influences proceed, means which may be specific to particular levels of analysis. Lerner and Busch-Rossnagel (1981) have discussed many of these. One process by which children and adolescents might produce their own development may involve the extent to which a person's characteristics of physical and/or behavioral individuality provide a match, or a "goodness of fit," with adaptational demands pertinent to the person's characteristics of individuality extant in the social context. After reviewing the theoretical bases of this goodness-of-fit model of person—context transaction, I will discuss two lines of research conducted by my colleagues and me which support this model.

A "GOODNESS-OF-FIT" MODEL OF PERSON—CONTEXT RELATIONS

Conceptions of development which stress behavioral (Bandura, 1978; Bijou, 1976), organismic (Erikson, 1968), or contextual (Schneirla, 1957; Lerner, 1978, 1979; Thomas & Chess, 1981) mechanisms converge in suggesting that children may affect their own development. As a consequence of characteristics of physical (e.g., sex, body type, or facial attractiveness; Berscheid & Walster, 1974) and/or behavioral (e.g., temperamental; Thomas & Chess, 1977) individuality, children promote differential reactions in their socializing others; these reactions may feed back to children, increasing the individuality of their developmental milieu, and providing a basis of their further development. Through the establishment of such "circular functions" in ontogeny (Schneirla, 1957), children and adolescents may be conceived of as producers of their own development (Lerner, 1978, 1979; Lerner & Busch-Rossnagel, 1981). However, this circular-functions idea needs to be extended; that is, in and of itself the notion is mute regarding the specific characteristics of the feedback (e.g., its positive or negative valence) an organism will receive as a consequence of its individuality.

Thomas and Chess (1977, 1980, 1981) and J. Lerner (in press) have extended these "person—social context reciprocal interaction" ideas by proposing a person—context "goodness-of-fit" model for adaptive development. Just as a child brings his or her characteristics of individuality to a particular social setting there are demands placed on the child by virtue of the social and physical components of the setting. These "demands" may take the form of: (1) attitudes, values, or stereotypes, held by others in the context, regarding the child's attributes (either his or her physical or behavioral characteristics); (2) the attributes (usually behavioral) of others in the context with whom the child must coordinate, or fit, his or her attributes (also in this case usually behavioral) for adaptive interactions to exist: or (3) the physical characteristics of a setting (e. g., presence or absence of access ramps for handicapped people, or the noise level in a setting) which require the person to possess certain attributes (again, usually behavioral abilities) for most efficient interaction within the setting to occur. The child's individuality, in differentially meeting these demands, provides a basis for the feedback he or she gets from the socializing environment.

For example, considering the demand "domain" of attitudes, values, or stereotypes, teachers and parents may have relatively individual and distinct desires for behaviors of their students and children, respectively. Teachers may want students who show little distractibility, since they would not want attention diverted from the lesson by the activity of other children in the classroom. Parents, however, might desire their children to be moderately distractible, for example, when they require their child to move from television watching to dinner or bed. Children whose behavioral individuality was either generally distractible or generally not distractible would thus differentially meet the demands of these two contexts. Problems of adaptation to school or to home might thus develop as a consequence of a child's lack of match (or "goodness of fit") in either or both settings.

Similarly, considering the second domain, of behavioral mismatches, problems for efficient interaction might result when a child who was irregular in his or her biological functions (for example, regarding eating, sleep—waking cycles, and toileting behaviors) existed within a family setting composed of highly rhythmic parents and siblings. Finally, a poor fit with the "demands" of the physical setting might exist when a child with a low threshold for reaction to noise and with a high level of distractibility is placed in a noisy physical setting and given the requirement of attending to a task (e.g., as occurs in studying for an exam).

Thomas and Chess (1977, 1980, 1981) and J. Lerner (in press) believe that adaptive psychological and social functioning does not derive directly from either the nature of the child's characteristics of individuality per se or the nature of the demands of the contexts within which the child functions. Rather, if a child's characteristics of individuality match (or "fit") the demands of a particular setting adaptive outcomes in that setting will accrue. Those children whose characteristics match most of the settings within which they exist should receive support or positive feedback from the contexts and should show evidence of the most adaptive behavioral development. In turn, of course, mismatched children, whose characteristics are incongruent with one or most settings, should slow alternative developmental outcomes.

This sequence of events can best be appraised by observations over time. In addition, repeated measures of both child and context characteristics are required in order to describe the child's effects on the contexts, the contexts' behaviors toward the child, the child's further development, and so forth. Moreover, because children exist in more than one context, and because behavior in one context affects behavior in others (Lewis & Feiring, 1978), i.e., situational "transitivity" exists, the child–context goodness of fit in several contexts should be appraised. Finally, because of transitivity effects, measures of adaptation both within and across contexts appear useful. Enhancement of development in one context may facilitate development in another.

To date, there have been no direct tests of the "goodness-of-fit" model that fulfill all these requirements. Previous research bearing on the use of this model provides at best only indirect support because it has suffered from one or more of the following limitations: (1) it has focused on cross-sectional patterns of covariation, and not on repeated observations enabling the description of intraindividual change; (2) it has failed to include assessments of both child characteristics and contextual demands, and thus the "goodness of fit" between a child and his/her context had to be indirectly inferred; (3) it has assessed children in only one context, has thus ignored the "transitivity" (Lewis & Feiring, 1978) of functioning among contexts; and (4) thus it cannot speak to the use of enhancing adaptation in one context for more general adaptive functioning. Finally, (5) in the few data sets relevant to the model that have had a longitudinal component, methodological problems, due to focus on only one cohort and omission of drop-out- and retest-control groups, have existed (Baltes, Cornelius, & Nesselroade, 1977).

Thus, admittedly, while no existing data set has all the methodological features necessary for a complete test of this goodness-of-fit model, two lines of research followed by my colleagues and me provide data consistent with many of these features. While not providing an exhaustive appraisal of the model, the research allows for a good deal of evaluation of its use. These lines of research pertain to the demands domain of attitudes, values, and stereotypes, and the fit between these cognitive orientations of others in the child's context and the child's physical or behavioral attributes. The first line of research pertains to the role of characteristics of physical individuality in children's and adolescents' contributions to their own development; the second line of research pertains to the role of temperamental individuality in such contributions.

It should be noted that these lines of research bear on two distinct ways in which people may contribute to their own development. One type of "person effect" occurs as a consequence of the individual's active (behavioral) shaping or manipulation of his or her context. The person's behavioral attributes evoke reactions in the socializing context. The second line of research I will discuss pertains to another type of person effect, one which occurs in relation to individual attributes *relatively* more static than behavior may be. Examples of such (relatively) static organism attributes are sex, race, and body type. Here a person's contributions to his/her own development occur as a consequence of: the organismic attributes placing the individual in one or another category of person perception (e.g., male or female; black or white; obese or well built); stereotypic expectations being maintained to all members of the social category; and stereotype-consistent feedback being given the person and behavior being then canalized (Lerner, 1976). The first line of research I will discuss pertains to such contributions by an individual.

The Role of Characteristics of Physical Individuality

Over 10 years ago my colleagues and I initiated a line of research pertinent to the circular-functions, goodness-of-fit ideas outlined above. Our idea was to explore the role of children's and adolescents' characteristics of physical individuality in providing a basis of the person's own development.

To provide support for the goodness-of-fit model several links between characteristics of physical individuality and the social context had to be established. First, we had to demonstrate that there existed distinct sets of expectations, demands, or evaluations pertinent to different characteristics of individuality. Second, we had to demonstrate that children and adolescents whose characteristics of physical individuality fulfilled these expectations (met these demands, or received favorable evaluations), were also accorded social feedback consistent with these appraisals. In turn, of course, we also had to establish that children and adolescents whose characteristics did not match with these social appraisals received feedback consistent with their mismatch. Finally, we had to establish that the different children had characteristics of psychosocial development consistent with their alternative types of feedback.

We have been successful in providing support for all three elements of our model. First, we initially operationalized our concern with the role of characteristics of physical individuality by a focus on variations in body type, or somatotype. Using Sheldon's (1940, 1942) terms of endomorph, mesomorph, and ectomorph as descriptions only of body types essentially fat or chubby, muscular or average, and thin and linear, respectively, we conducted a series of studies to discover: (1) whether general (stereotypic) appraisals exist for male children and adolescents possessing one of these body types; (2) whether the age of the target person possessing the body type moderates the attributions toward him; (3) whether age, sex, or body type of the person doing the attribution significantly moderates the nature of the attributions made; and (4) whether membership in a different cultural (or national) context is associated with any moderation in attributions on the part of the person doing the attribution.

In a series of studies (Iwawaki & Lerner, 1974, 1976; Lerner, 1969a, 1969b, 1971; Lerner & Iwawaki, 1975; Lerner & Korn, 1972; Lerner & Pool, 1972; Lerner & Schroeder, 1971a) it was found that highly positive stereotypes exist for children and adolescents possessing a mesomorph body type, that markedly negative stereotypes exist for endomorphic children and adolescents, and that somewhat less unfavorable, but still essentially negative stereotypes exist in regard to those having an ectomorphic body build. Moreover, the nature and strength of these stereotypes do *not* vary substantially as a function of: (1) age of the person possessing the body type (e.g., the same sets of attributions were shown to target person stimuli representing 5-, 15-, and 20-year-old endomorphs, mesomorphs, and ectomorphs); (2) age of the person doing the attribution (e.g., 5- through 20-year-olds have essentially the same stereotypes regarding the three body builds); (3) body type of the person doing the attribution (e.g., chubby children and adolescents have the same negative stereotypes about endomorphs as do average-build or thin children); (4) sex of the person doing the attribution; and (5) cultural (or national) membership of the person doing the attribution (e.g., Mexican and Japanese male and female children and adolescents have body build stereotypes that are essentially identical to those maintained by their American age and sex peers).

Do male and female children who possess different body types receive feedback from their male and female peers which is consistent with these stereotypes? Several data sets we have gathered suggest the answer is "yes." Using sociometric procedures we have found that as early as in the kindergarten year chubby and thin children receive fewer positive peer nominations (e.g., "who would you choose as leader?") and more negative nominations (e.g., "who is left out of games?") than is the case with average-build children; these latter children receive more positive and fewer negative peer nominations than do their chubby or thin classmates (Lerner & Gellert, 1969; Lerner & Schroeder, 1971b). More importantly, it appears that from kindergarten through the sixth grade (i.e., from middle childhood through early adolescence), different personal space is shown toward fat, average, and thin male and female children by their male and female peers. Differences in personal space usage among children and adolescents are indicative of differences in the type or quality of their social relationships, and children use most personal space toward target person stimuli representing chubby male and female age peers, least space toward average-build peer stimuli, and a level of space intermediate between these two extremes toward ectomorphic peer stimuli (Lerner, 1973; Lerner, Karabenick, & Meisels, 1975a; Lerner, Venning, & Knapp, 1975). These differences in personal space use remain stable over the course of 1 year (Lerner, Karabenick, & Meisels, 1975b). In addition, they have been replicated among corresponding groups of Japanese kindergarten through sixth-graders (Iwawaki, Lerner, & Chihara, 1977; Lerner, Iwawaki, & Chihara, 1976).

Finally, do children and adolescents show evidence of psychosocial functioning which is consistent with such stereotype-based feedback? Again, the answer seems to be "yes." Lerner and Korn (1972) found that the body and self-concepts of chubby 5-, 15-, and 20-year-old males were more negative than those shown by average-build age peers. Similarly, we have found that male and female late adolescents, who have bodily characteristics seen by them and others to be less interpersonally attractive or less individually effective, have lower self-esteems than is the case among late adolescent males and females whose body parts are regarded by them and others as more attractive and effective (Lerner & Brackney, 1978; Lerner & Karabenick, 1974; Lerner, Karabenick, & Stuart, 1973; Lerner, Orlos, & Knapp, 1976; Padin, Lerner, & Spiro, 1981). These relations among body attractiveness, body effectiveness, and adolescent self-esteem have been replicated among Japanese ranging in grade level from seventh grade through the senior year of college (Lerner, Iwawaki, Chihara, & Sorell, 1980).

Moreover, these data linking body attractiveness, effectiveness, and self-esteem suggest that our findings relating individual differences in body type to social context appraisal and feedback may be just instances of a more general relation between individual differences in physical attractiveness and the social context. Indeed, Berscheid and Walster (1974) have also suggested such a correspondence and, in addition, have demonstrated that there exists in society a "beauty is the best" stereotype. Their research, as well as that of others (e.g., Dion, 1973; Langlois & Stephan, 1981; Mussen & Jones, 1957; Richardson, 1971), also documents that, consistent with such a physical attractiveness stereotype, children and adolescents receive differential feedback based on their characteristics of physical individuality, and that such feedback is linked to different personal (e.g., self-esteem) and social (e.g., popularity, interpersonal aggression) developments. Our own research also illustrates such relationships.

Lerner and Lerner (1977) studied a group of fourth- and sixth-grade males and females. Each child posed for a standard photographic slide, and from these slides a group of college students rated the fourth- and sixth-graders' facial physical attractiveness. The teachers of the children rated them in regard to their academic ability and school adjustment, and the children's actual grades in that school year, as well as in the two preceding years, were obtained. In addition, the children responded to a standard measure of personal and social adjustment, and the classroom peers of the children provided sociometric ratings of each child's negative and positive relationships. As compared to their physically attractive classmates, the physically unattractive male and female children had fewer positive peer relations, more negative peer relations, were judged by teachers as less able and adjusted, and actually scored lower on the standardized adjustment test. In addition, in both their present classes and in their classes of the two preceding years the physically unattractive male and female children had lower grades than their physically attractive peers.

In sum, this first line of research conducted by my colleagues and me suggests that by "bringing" different physical characteristics to a situation, a child may affect how others react to, and provide feedback to, him or her; this feedback may be linked to different developments in the child. Although our data supportive of this idea are derived essentially from unitemporal patterns of covariation, and pertain to a relatively static or "passive" characteristic of individuality, they do indicate that there are important psychosocial implications of such attributes: children's physical characteristics may provide a source of their own development by either matching or not matching (i.e., fitting) with, in this case, the physicalistic stereotypes of their social context. Moreover, physical characteristics other than body type, such as sex, or race, may serve as even more potent static attribute contributors of the person to his/her own development, and may do so in manners consistent with the goodness-of-fit model. For example, Kagan and Moss (1962) found that personality characteristics showing continuity from birth to maturity were those consistent with traditional sex-role stereotypes. Similarly, Jones and Haney (1981) indicate that race serves as a physicalistic attribute canalizing people along different developmental pathways. In addition, Busch-Rossnagel (1981) reviews data indicating that physical disabilities lead to handicaps as a consequence of disabled persons being poorly fit with the demands of their social context. Thus, there may be several "static" organismic attributes that alone and in interaction serve to channel a person's development in a manner consistent with the present goodness-of-fit model.

Additional evidence for this goodness-of-fit model of person–context relations derives from the second line of research conducted by my colleagues and me, i.e., the study of the impact of more active characteristics of individual differences: that is, our second line of research considers how temperament, or behavioral style, contributes to the person's own development.

The Role of Characteristics of Temperamental, or Behavioral Style, Individuality

Individual differences in temperament have been a major focus of those theorists and researchers concerned with assessing the child's contribution to his or her own development (Thomas & Chess, 1977, 1980). The major support for the goodness-of-fit model comes from the study of temperament. Temperament has been defined as the stylistic component of behavior, i.e., how an organism does whatever it does (Thomas & Chess, 1977; Thomas, Chess, & Birch, 1970). For example, all children engage in eating, sleeping, and toileting behaviors. While attention to the absence or presence of such contents of the behavior repertoire would not easily differentiate among children, focus on whether these behaviors occur with regularity (i.e., rhythmically or predictably), with a lot or a little motor activity, intensity, or vigor, or whether there is a negative, positive, or neutral mood associated with the behaviors, might serve to differentiate among children.

Results from the New York Longitudinal Study (NYLS; Thomas, Chess, Birch, Hertzig, & Korn, 1963; Thomas, Chess, & Birch, 1968; Thomas et al., 1970) have indicated that particular types of individual differences in temperament are differentially associated with adaptive psychosocial functioning in both handicapped and nonhandicapped children. For example, low rhythmicity or biological functions, high activity levels, high distractibility, low response thresholds, and high-intensity reactions represent a cluster of characteristics which have been found to place samples of both handicapped children (e.g., mentally retarded children or children born with multiple physical handicaps as a result of maternal rubella) and nonhandicapped children "at risk" for behavioral and emotional problems (see Thomas & Chess, 1977). Alternatively, similarly handicapped children, and nonhandicapped children, who either have none of these temperamental characteristics and/or have high rhythmicity and moderate activity, threshold, intensity, and distractibility levels, have fewer problem behaviors. Data from samples other then the NYLS, collected by the Thomas group (Korn, Chess, & Fernandez, 1978; Thomas & Chess, 1977) and others (Sameroff, Note 1; Super & Harkness, 1981), confirm the linkages between differential temperamental repertoires and contrasting psychosocial developments, again among children having various categories of handicap and among nonhandicapped children.

Although these data sets have been limited by an omission of direct focus on a person–context bidirectional relation, the data indicate that individual differences in temperament are associated with differences in adaptive functioning; unfortunately, they do not describe the interactions presumed to be involved in these relations. However, since the Thomas group's conceptualization of temperament is one which sees its impact as lying in whether a particular repertoire provides a "goodness of fit" with the individual characteristics of a specific context, Thomas and Chess (1977, 1981) and their associates (e.g., Korn, Note 2) have speculated about how their data are congruent with a goodness-of-fit model.

The NYLS sample is a white, middle-class one. Such social contexts may have fairly generalizable views about desirable behavioral styles for children. If so, then a child with a repertoire that has been labeled as difficult is only "at risk" insofar as his or her arrhythmicity, negative mood, and high-intensity reactions are not congruent with such demands. However, in another context, having alternative appraisals of such attributes, the "at risk" status would change. Korn (Note 2) and Gannon (Note 3) have presented data indicating that in lower-class Puerto Rican settings not only are these "difficult" attributes not undesirable but they may in fact be highly regarded. In turn, they indicate that, as compared to white middle-class samples, there is less association of such attributes with negative psychosocial development. Sameroff (Note 1) provides similar data in regard to social class and race differences in the implications of a "difficult" temperament.

A more direct, albeit a cross-sectional, test of the goodness-of-fit model was conducted by J. Lerner (in press). Using a psychometrically well developed measure of temperament, the Dimensions of Temperament Survey (DOTS; Lerner, Palermo, Spiro, & Nesselroade, 1982), she measured the temperamental repertoires of early adolescent junior high school students. Lerner also appraised the demands placed on the adolescents in two components of their school context, i.e., the demands of the teacher and of the classroom peer group in regard to temperament were assessed. In addition, for each of the two contexts, both *actual* and *perceived* demands were assessed. Finally, several indices of personal and social adaptation were taken (e.g., measures of grade point average, peer relations, and self-esteem). Children who were fit, or matched, in one context tended to be those matched in the other (i.e., transitivity was evident). Moreover, the greater the level of fit the higher were scores of adaptation—both within and across contexts. For example, a child who met peer demands not only had better peer relations but was seen by the teacher as more academically adjusted and capable. Furthermore, matched children had better scores on the measure of general adaptation (self-esteem) than did mismatched children. Finally, consistent with the idea that the adolescent plays an active role in his or her own development, the results also indicated that the match scores for the perceived contextual demands had more import for prediction than did the match scores for the actual contextual demands.

In another test of this model, J. Lerner, Lerner, and Zabski (Note 4) appraised the relation between goodness of fit and the actual and rated academic abilities of fourth-grade children. The children responded to a self-report version of the DOTS, and teachers responded to a DOTS form which appraised their demands/expectations of their students for each of the five temperamental attributes measured by this instrument. Teachers also rated their students' academic ability and adjustment. Finally, objective measures of the students' academic abilities were obtained through

Comprehensive Tests of Basic Skills and Stanford Achievement Test (Reading) scores. Results indicated that most of the children's temperament attributes were related to teacher-rated and/or objectively measured academic attributes, and that for two of the three temperament attributes for which directional predictions were made, clear support for the model was found; that is, for two of the attributes that were predicted to be important in the school context (i.e., for attention span/distractibility and for reactivity—an attribute comprising activity level, threshold, and intensity items—but not for adaptability/approach−withdrawal), children who had goodness-of-fit scores indicative of better matches with their teacher's demands tended to have higher scores on the teacher-rated and objective ability measures than did less well matched children.

Similarly, Palermo (Note 5) assessed the temperaments of fifth-grade children and, as did J. Lerner (in press) and J. Lerner et al. (Note 4), appraised teachers' demands regarding behavioral style in their classrooms. Teacher judgments of academic ability and adjustment, and peer ratings of positive and negative relations with target children, were also assessed. In addition, the mothers' ratings of their children's behavioral problems were assessed, and mothers also provided an indication of their demands for behavioral style in the home. As above, and both within and across the teacher, peer, and parent social contexts, those children who had goodness-of-fit scores indicative of better matches with either teacher or parent demands tended to have more positive scores on all the outcome measures, i.e., they had higher ability and adjustment teacher ratings, more positive and fewer negative peer relations, and fewer mother-identified behavioral problems.

In sum, findings such as these suggest that when there is a mismatch *between* a particular temperament and a particular context problems of adjustment may arise. As such, the issue in temperament research is whether a particular set of person attributes is congruent of incongruent with the demands of a specific context. One should ask what person characteristics in interaction with what environmental characteristics lead to what outcomes. Moreover, given the evidence found for transitivity effects in J. Lerner's (in press) and in Palermo's (Note 5) results, we suggest that one may enhance the psychosocial adjustment of a child in a context through interventions aimed at that child's functioning in another context. This conclusion regarding the implications for intervention of our model will be amplified as a consequence of the other conclusions we may draw about our model and the life-span perspective from which it is derived.

CONCLUSIONS

It is, of course, no accident that this life-span perspective about development arose largely from data sets pertinent to adolescence and later portions of life (cf., Lerner, 1981). Increasingly greater interindividual differences in intraindividual change occur with development during these periods, as the person becomes exposed to an increasingly more differentiated and singular social context (Baltes, 1979a; Baltes et al., 1980). In turn, the person must respond to, and in some way integrate, the unique set of presses imposed on him or her if adaptation will occur (Brent, 1978). In other words, the person must act on the context, to enhance goodness of fit with it, if he/she is to contribute to his/her own adaptive development.

Adolescence is a time when multiple transitions, in the inner-biological, individual-psychological, physical environmental, and sociocultural contexts, occur. Thus, it is a particularly appropriate time to study the relation between a changing person and his or her changing world. Successful adaptation always involves appropriate coordination between our changing selves and our changing contexts. But it is in adolescence, and particularly early adolescence (Hill, 1980a, 1980b), that such adaptational stresses may be most critical, due to their simultaneity and multidimensionality. One may see our research on physical and temperamental characteristics of individuality as just two instances of the numerous dimensions of the adolescent for which presses for fit occur.

Thus, we may summarize the life-span conceptualization of human development as it impacts on our view of child and, especially, adolescent development and our goodness-of-fit model of person–context relations. First, developmental change is a potentially life-span phenomenon. Second, such change involves a contextual view of the person, that is, that the person is reciprocally embedded in his or her world. Third, such change therefore involves adaptations of changing people to their changing world, of individuals' contributions to their own development. Fourth, adolescence, and again, particularly early adolescence, especially involves changes within the person, in the person's social context, and therefore between the person and the context. Thus, fifth, not only is this period a key time within which to focus research in order to substantiate this view of development, but in turn, in order to understand adolescence one must appreciate the multiple changes involved in development at his time of life, and the integrative presses on the person in order for adaptive fit to occur.

Finally, sixth, these ideas have relevance to the theory and practice of intervention. Although it is often not emphasized in discussions of the goodness-of-fit concept, the term describes only the status of the relation between the person and his or her context at a particular point in time. However, a life-span developmental perspective emphasizes process and, as a consequence, a key concern in the application of the goodness-of-fit notion is the identification of the antecedent changes that resulted in a particular fit at a specific time and, in turn, specification of the consequences of this fit for later development. Only with such information can appropriate intervention be instituted. However, as emphasized by Kendall (1981), intervention can only proceed after necessary assessments are made; there are several cognitive and behavioral variables that would have to be assessed before one could intervene to enhance goodness of fit.

One would have to assess whether the child or adolescent could appropriately evaluate: (1) the demands of a particular context; (2) his or her stylistic attributes; and (3) the degree of match that exists between the two. In addition to these cognitive assessments, other cognitive and behavioral skill assessments are necessary. One has to determine whether the child has the ability to select and gain access to those contexts with which there is a high probability of match, and avoid those contexts where poor fit is likely. In addition, in those contexts that cannot easily be selected, for example, family of origin or assigned elementary school class, one has to assess whether the child has the knowledge and skill necessary to either change himself or herself to fit the demands of the setting or, in turn, alter the context to better fit his or her attributes.

Appropriate interventions after such assessments might involve skill training, behavior modification, and/or various cognitive-behavioral changes. The common goal of all procedures would be to enhance the child's ability for self-regulation, and thereby increase the ability to actively enhance his or her own fit. Recalling J. Lerner's (1982) findings that the match between an adolescent's temperament and his or her perception of the demands placed on him or her was a better predictor of adjustment than the match scores between temperament and actual demands, a prime example of such interventions may be derived from the work of Bandura and his colleagues on perceived self-efficacy (e.g., Bandura, 1980a, 1980b).

Children who do not see themselves as efficacious in a particular setting will tend to withdraw from the situation, have a negative mood in or about the situation, and/or be less active in it (Bandura, 1980a, 1980b). For example, Bandura and Schunk (Note 6) report that such a style behavior was characteristic of elementary school students who were not performing well in mathematics classes. By withdrawing from the situation, the children were acting to enhance their own failure, since by not actively or enthusiastically participating they were not exposing themselves to the experiences and practice opportunities necessary for success in mathematics.

Assessing the children's perceptions of their efficacy before intervention revealed that, quite appropriately, they saw themselves as unable to do what was necessary for success in the situation. However, Bandura and Schunk found that by enhancing the child's perceived self-efficacy, greater approach and activity was engendered. The child, now taking greater advantage of the learning experiences available in the context, eventually showed greater competence in mathematics.

In essence, then, the manipulation of self-efficacy is but one of many behavioral or cognitive-behavioral strategies that may be adopted (see Kendall, 1981, for a review of others) in order to enhance children's abilities to create better fits for themselves in their contexts. In other words, rather than being "passive recipients" of the fit immediately afforded them as a consequence of their characteristics of individuality, assessments and interventions associated with a process view of the goodness-of-fit idea are aimed at providing the child with those abilities necessary to actively create a good fit for himself or herself.

In sum, any theory of intervention compatible with a life-span perspective rests on a view of human development which stresses that there exists a potential for change after the early years of life, and that such change can be enhanced by facilitating individuals to actively engage their contexts, to constructively act as producers of their development in order to transform or fit the presses of their contexts. These optimistic beliefs run counter to more pessimistic ones associated with views of human development which stress that constancy (or developmental fixity) is established early in life and/or that the individual is a passive recipient of either genetically or environmentally determining influences. Characterizing such views, Brim and Kagan (1980, p. 21) have noted that:

> The belief that early experiences create lasting characteristics, like the belief in biological and genetic determinism, makes it possible to assume that attempts to improve the course of human development after early childhood are wasted and without consequence. If society believes that it is all over by the third year of life, it can deal harshly with many people in later life because nothing more can be done, and social programs designed to educate, redirect, reverse, or eliminate unwanted human characteristics cannot be justified. Policies of racial, ethnic, and sex discrimination, incarceration rather than rehabilitation of criminals, ignoring urban and rural poverty, and isolation of the elderly have found shelter in the belief in the determinism of the early years of life.

In conclusion, as a consequence of their embeddedness and plasticity children and adolescents may contribute to their own behavior change processes, and they appear to do so in a manner consistent with a goodness-of-fit model of person–context relations. Fruitful research questions can be formulated on the basis of ideas associated with this model. However, as I have emphasized, no current data set has all the methodological features required by this model. As such, the major contemporary contribution of this perspective is to suggest ways that current theoretical questions and extant empirical literatures can be significantly integrated and extended. Such contributions are among the major goals of the continuing work of my colleagues and me on the implications of individuals' contributions to their own development.

REFERENCES

Bachman, J. C. *Youth in transition: The impact of family background and intelligence on tenth-grade boys.* Ann Arbor: Univ. of Michigan Press, 1970. Vol 2.

Bachman, J. G., Green, S., & Wirtanen, I. D. *Youth in transition: Dropping out—problem or symptom?* Ann Arbor: Univ. of Michigan Press, 1971. Vol. 3.

Baltes, P. B. Longitudinal and cross-sectional sequences in the study of age and generation effects. *Human Development,* 1968, 11, 145–171.

Baltes, P. B. (Ed.) *Life-span development and behavior.* New York: Academic Press, 1978. Vol. 1.

Baltes, P. B. Life-span developmental psychology: Some converging observations on history and theory. In P. B. Baltes & O. G. Brim, Jr. (Eds.), *Life-span development and behavior* (Vol. 2). New York: Academic Press, 1979. (a)

Baltes, P. B. On the potential and limits of child development: Life-span developmental perspectives. *Newsletter of the Society for Research in Child Development,* 1979(Summer), 1–4. (b)

Baltes, P. B., Baltes, M. M., & Reinert, G. The relationship between time of measurement and age in cognitive development of children: An application of cross-sectional sequences. *Human Development,* 1970, 13, 258–268.

Baltes, P. B., & Brim, O. G., Jr. (Eds.) *Life-span development and behavior,* New York: Academic Press, 1979. Vol. 2.

Baltes, P. B., & Brim, O. G., Jr. (Eds.) *Life-span development and behavior.* New York: Academic Press, 1980. Vol. 3.

Baltes, P. B., & Brim, O. G., Jr. (Eds.) *Life-span development and behavior.* New York: Academic Press, 1981. Vol. 4.

Baltes, P. B., Cornelius, S. W., & Nesselroade, J. R. Cohort effects in behavioral development: Theoretical and methodological perspectives. In W. A. Collins (Ed.), *Minnesota symposia on child psychology* (Vol. II). New York: T. Y. Crowell, 1977.

Baltes, P. B., & Nesselroade, J. R. The developmental analysis of individual differences on multiple measures. In J. R. Nesselroade & H. W. Reese (Eds.), *Life-span developmental psychology: Methodological issues.* New York: Academic Press, 1973.

Baltes, P. B., Reese, H. W., & Lipsitt, L. P. Life-span developmental psychology. *Annual Review of Psychology,* 1980, 31, 65–110.

Baltes, P. B., Reese, H. W., & Nesselroade, J. R. *Life-span developmental psychology: Introduction to research methods.* Monterey, Calif.: Brooks/Cole, 1977.

Baltes, P. B., & Schaie, K. W. (Eds.) *Life-span developmental psychology: Personality and socialization.* New York: Academic Press, 1973.

Baltes, P. B., & Schaie, K. W. The myth of the twilight years. *Psychology Today,* 1974, 7, 35–40.

Baltes, P. B., & Schaie, K. W. On the plasticity of intelligence in adulthood and old age: Where Horn and Donaldson fail. *American Psychologist,* 1976, 31, 720–725.

Bandura, A. The self system in reciprocal determinism. *American Psychologist,* 1978, 33, 344–358.

Bandura, A. Self-referent thought: A developmental analysis of self-efficacy. In J. H. Flavell & L. D. Ross (Eds.), *Cognitive social development: Frontiers and possible futures.* New York: Cambridge Univ. Press, 1980. (a)

Bandura, A. The self and mechanisms of agency. In J. Suls (Ed.), *Social psychological perspectives on the self.* Hillsdale, N.J.: Erlbaum, 1980. (b)

Belsky, J. Early human experience: A family perspective. *Developmental Psychology,* 1981, 17, 3–23.

Bengtson, V. L., & Troll, L. Youth and their parents: Feedback and intergenerational influence in socialization. In R. M. Lerner & G. B. Spanier (Eds.), *Child influences on marital and family interaction: A life-span perspective.* New York: Academic Press, 1978.

Berscheid, E., & Walster, E. Physical attractiveness. In L. Berkowitz (Ed.), *Advances in experimental social psychology.* New York: Academic Press, 1974.

Bijou, S. J. *Child development: The basic stage of early childhood.* Englewood Cliffs, N.J.: Prentice–Hall, 1976.

Brent, S. B. Individual specialization, collective adaptation and rate of environment change. *Human Development,* 1978, **21,** 21–33.

Brim, O. G., Jr. Adult socialization. In J. A. Clausen (Ed.), *Socialization and society.* Boston: Little, Brown, 1968.

Brim, O. G., Jr. Foreword. In R. M. Lerner & N. A. Busch-Rossnagel (Eds.), *Individuals as producers of their development: A life-span perspective.* New York: Academic Press, 1981.

Brim, O. G., Jr. & Kagan, J. Constancy and change: A view of the issues. In O. G. Brim, Jr. & J. Kagan (Eds.), *Constancy and change in human development.* Cambridge, Mass.: Harvard Univ. Press, 1980.

Brim, O. G., Jr. & Ryff, C. D. On the properties of life events. In P. B. Baltes & O. G. Brim Jr. (Eds.), *Life-span development and behavior* (Vol. 3). New York: Academic Press, 1980.

Brim, O. G., Jr. & Wheeler, S. *Socialization after childhood: Two essays.* New York: Wiley, 1966.

Bronfenbrenner, U. *The ecology of human development.* Cambridge, Mass.: Harvard Univ. Press, 1979.

Bühler, C. *Der menschliche Lebenslauf als psychologisches Problem.* Leipzig: Hirzel, 1933.

Burgess, R. L., & Huston, T. L. (Eds.) *Social exchange in developing relationships.* New York: Academic Press, 1979.

Busch-Rossnagel, N. A. Where is the handicap in disability? The contextual impact of physical disability. In R. M. Lerner & N. A. Busch-Rossnagel (Eds.), *Individuals as producers of their development: A life-span perspective.* New York: Academic Press, 1981.

Carus, F. A. *Psychologie Zweiter Theil: Specialpsychologie.* Leipzig: Barth & Kummer, 1808.

Datan, N., & Ginsberg, L. H. (Eds.) *Life-span developmental psychology: Normative life crises.* New York: Academic Press, 1975.

Datan, N., & Reese, H. W. (Eds.) *Life-span developmental psychology: Dialectical perspectives on experimental psychology.* New York: Academic Press, 1977.

Dion, K. Young children's stereotyping of facial attractiveness. *Developmental Psychology,* 1973, **9,** 183–188.

Elder, G. H., Jr. *Children of the Great Depression.* Chicago: Univ. of Chicago Press, 1974.

Elder, G. H., Jr. Historical change in life patterns and personality. In P. B. Baltes & O. G. Brim, Jr. (Eds.), *Life-span development and behavior* (Vol. 2). New York: Academic Press, 1979.

Elder, G. H., Jr. Adolescence in historical perspective. In J. Adelson (Ed.), *Handbook of adolescent psychology.* New York: Wiley, 1980.

Erikson, E. H. *Childhood and society.* New York: Norton, 1950.

Erikson, E. H. *Identity, youth and crisis.* New York: Norton, 1968.

Gallatin, J. E. *Adolescence and individuality.* New York: Harper & Row, 1975.

Garbarino, J., & Bronfenbrenner, U. The socialization of moral judgment and behavior in cross-cultural perspective. In T. Lickona (Ed.), *Moral development and behavior.* New York: Holt, Rinehart & Winston, 1976.

Garn, S. M. Continuities and change in maturation timing. In O. G. Brim, Jr. & J. Kagan (Eds.), *Constancy and change in human development*. Cambridge, Mass.: Harvard Univ. Press, 1980.

Goulet, L. R.. & Baltes, P. B. (Eds.) *Life-span developmental psychology: Research and theory*. New York: Academic Press, 1970.

Hall, G. S. *Senescence: The last half of life*. New York: Appleton, 1922.

Hartup, W. W. Perspectives on child and family interaction: Past, present, and future. In R. M. Lerner & G. B. Spanier (Eds.), *Child influences on marital and family interaction: A life-span perspective*. New York: Academic Press, 1978.

Havighurst, R. J. *Developmental tasks and education*. New York: David McKay, 1948.

Havighurst, R. J. *Human development and education*. New York: David McKay, 1953.

Havighurst, R. J. Research on developmental task concept. *School Review*, 1956, **64**, 215–223.

Havighurst, R. J. History of developmental psychology: Socialization and personality development through the life span. In P. B. Baltes & K. W. Schaie (Eds.), *Life-span developmental psychology: Personality and socialization*. New York: Academic Press, 1973.

Hill, J. P. The family. In M. Johnson (Ed.), *Toward adolescence: The middle school years. Seventy-ninth Yearbook of the National Society for the Study of Education* (Part I). Chicago: Univ. of Chicago Press, 1980. (a)

Hill, J. P. *Understanding early adolescence: A framework*. Chapel Hill, N.C.: Center for Early Adolescence, 1980. (b)

Hill, R., & Mattessich, P. Family development theory and life-span development. In P. B. Baltes & O. G. Brim, Jr. (Eds.), *Life-span development and behavior* (Vol. 2). New York: Academic Press, 1979.

Hoffman, L. W. Maternal employment: 1979. *American Psychologist*, 1979, **34**, 859–865.

Hollingworth, H. L. *Mental growth and decline: A survey of developmental psychology*. New York: Appleton, 1927.

Iwawaki, S., & Lerner, R. M. Cross-cultural analyses of body-behavior relations. I. A comparison of body build stereotypes of Japanese and American males and females. *Psychologia*, 1974, **17**, 75–81.

Iwawaki, S., & Lerner, R. M. Cross-cultural analysis of body-behavior relations. III. Developmental intra- and inter-cultural factor congruence in the body build steretypes of Japanese and American males and females. *Psychologia*, 1976, **19**, 67–76.

Iwawaki, S., Lerner, R. M., & Chihara, T. Development of personal space schemata among Japanese in late childhood. *Psychologia*, 1977, **20**, 89–97.

Jaffe, F. S., & Dryfoos, J. G. Fertility control services for adolescents: Access and utilization. *Family Planning Perspectives*, 1976, **8**, 167–175.

Jones, R. T., & Haney, J. I. A body-behavior conceptualization of a somatopsychological problem: Race. In R. M. Lerner & N. A. Busch-Rossnagel (Eds.), *Individuals as producers of their development: A life-span perspective*. New York: Academic Press, 1981.

Kagan, J., & Moss, H. A. *Birth to maturity*. New York: Wiley, 1962.

Katchadourian, H. *The biology of adolescence*. San Francisco: Freeman, 1977.

Kendall, P. C. Cognitive-behavioral interventions with children. In B. Lahey & A. E. Kazdin (Eds.), *Advances in child clinical psychology* (Vol. 4). New York: Plenum, 1981.

Korn, S. J., Chess, S., & Fernandez, P. The impact of children's physical handicaps on marital quality and family interaction. In R. M. Lerner & G. B. Spanier (Eds.), *Child influences on marital and family interaction: A life-span perspective*. New York: Academic Press, 1978.

Langlois, J. H., & Stephan, C. W. Beauty and the beast: The role of physical attraction in peer relationships and social behavior. In S. S. Brehm, S. M. Kassin, & S. X. Gibbons (Eds.), *Developmental social psychology: Theory and research.* New York: Oxford Univ. Press, 1981.

Lerner, J. V. The role of temperament in psychosocial adaptation in early adolescents: A test of a "goodness of fit" model. *Journal of Genetic Psychology,* in press.

Lerner, R. M. The development of stereotyped expectancies of body build-behavior relations. *Child Development,* 1969, **40,** 137–141. (a)

Lerner, R. M. Some female stereotypes of male body build-behavior relations. *Perceptual und Motor Skills,* 1969, **28,** 363–366. (b)

Lerner, R. M. "Richness" analyses of body build stereotype development. *Developmental Psychology,* 1971, **7,** 219.

Lerner, R. M. The development of personal space schemata toward body build. *Journal of Psychology,* 1973, **84,** 229–235.

Lerner, R. M. *Concepts and theories of human development.* Reading, Mass.: Addison–Wesley, 1976.

Lerner, R. M. Nature, nurture, and dynamic interactionism. *Human Development,* 1978, **21,** 1–20.

Lerner, R. M. A dynamic interactional concept of individual and social relationship development. In R. L. Burgess & T. L. Huston (Eds.), *Social exchange in developing relationships.* New York: Academic Press, 1979.

Lerner, R. M. Adolescent development: Scientific study in the 1980s. *Youth and Society,* 1981, **12,** 251–275.

Lerner, R. M., & Brackney, B. The importance of inner and outer body parts attitudes in the self concept of late adolescents. *Sex Roles,* 1978, **4,** 225–238.

Lerner, R. M., & Busch-Rossnagel, N. A. Individuals as producers of their development: Conceptual and empirical bases. In R. M. Lerner & N. A. Busch-Rossnagel (Eds.), *Individuals as producers of their development: A life-span perspective.* New York: Academic Press, 1981.

Lerner, R. M., & Gellert, E. Body build identification, preference, and aversion in children. *Developmental Psychology,* 1969, **1,** 456–462.

Lerner, R. M., Hultsch, D. F., & Dixon, R. A. Contextualism and the character of developmental psychology in the 1970s. *Annals of the New York Academy of Sciences,* in press.

Lerner, R. M., & Iwawaki, S. Cross-cultural analyses of body-behavior relations. II. Factor structure of body build sterotypes of Japanese and American adolescents. *Psychologia,* 1975, **18,** 83–91.

Lerner, R. M., Iwawaki, S., & Chihara, T. Development of personal space schemata among Japanese children. *Developmental Psychology,* 1976, **12,** 466–467.

Lerner, R. M., Iwawaki, S., Chihara, T., & Sorell, G. T. Self-concept, self-esteem, and body attitudes among Japanese male and female adolescents. *Child Development,* 1980, **51,** 847–855.

Lerner, R. M., & Karabenick, S. A. Physical attractiveness, body attitudes, and self-concept in late adolescents. *Journal of Youth and Adolescence,* 1974, **3,** 307–316.

Lerner, R. M., Karabenick, S. A., & Meisels, M. Effects of age and sex on the development of personal space schemata towards body build. *Journal of Genetic Psychology,* 1975, **127,** 91–101. (a)

Lerner, R. M., Karabenick, S. A., & Meisels, M. One-year stability of children's personal space schemata towards body build. *Journal of Genetic Psychology,* 1975, **127,** 151–152. (b)

Lerner, R. M., Karabenick, S. A., & Stuart, J. L. Relations among physical attractiveness, body attitudes, and self-concept in male and female college students. *Journal of Psychology,* 1973, **85,** 119–129.

Lerner, R. M., Karson, M., Meisels, M., & Knapp, J. R. Actual and perceived attitudes of late adolescents and their parents: The phenomenon of the generation gaps. *Journal of Genetic Psychology*, 1975, **126**, 195–207.

Lerner, R. M., & Korn, S. J. The development of body build stereotypes in males. *Child Development*, 1972, **43**, 912–920.

Lerner, R. M., & Lerner, J. V. The effects of age, sex, and physical attractiveness on child-peer relations, academic performance, and elementary school adjustment. *Developmental Psychology*, 1977, **13**, 585–590.

Lerner, R. M., Orlos, J. B., & Knapp, J. R. Physical attractiveness, physical effectiveness, and self-concept in late adolescents. *Adolescence*, 1976, **11**, 313–326.

Lerner, R. M., Palermo, M., Spiro, A., III, & Nesselroade, J. R. Assessing the dimensions of temperamental individuality across the life-span: The Dimensions of Temperament Survey (DOTS). *Child Development*, 1982, **53**, 149–159.

Lerner, R. M., & Pool, K. B. Body build stereotypes: A cross-cultural comparison. *Psychological Reports*, 1972, **31**, 527–532.

Lerner, R. M., & Schroeder, C. Kindergarten children's active vocabulary about body build. *Developmental Psychology*, 1971, **5**, 179. (a)

Lerner, R. M., & Schroeder, C. Physique identification, preference, and aversion in kindergarten children. *Developmental Psychology*, 1971, **5**, 538. (b)

Lerner, R. M., Skinner, E. A., & Sorell, G. T. Methodological implications of contextual/dialectic theories of development. *Human Development*, 1980, **23**, 225–235.

Lerner, R. M., & Spanier, G. B. (Eds.) *Child influences on marital and family interaction: A life-span perspective*. New York: Academic Press, 1978.

Lerner, R. M., & Spanier, G. B. *Adolescent development: A life-span perspective*. New York: McGraw–Hill, 1980.

Lerner, R. M., Spanier, G. B., & Belsky, J. The child in the family. In C. B. Kopp & J. Krakow (Eds.), *The child: Development in a social context*. Reading, Mass.: Addison–Wesley, 1982.

Lerner, R. M., Venning, J., & Knapp, J. R. Age and sex effects on personal space schemata towards body build in late childhood. *Developmental Psychology*, 1975, **11**, 855–856.

Lewis, M., & Feiring, C. The child's social world. In R. M. Lerner & G. B. Spanier (Eds.), *Child influences on marital and family interaction: A life-span perspective*. New York: Academic Press, 1978.

Looft, W. R. Socialization and personality throughout the life-span: An examination of contemporary psychological approaches. In P. B. Baltes & K.W. Schaie (Eds.), *Life-span developmental psychology: Personality and socialization*. New York: Academic Press, 1973.

Meisels, M., & Guardo, C. J. Development of personal space schemata. *Child Development*, 1969, **40**, 1167–1178.

Mussen, P. H., & Jones, M. C. Self-conceptions, motivations, and interpersonal attitudes of late- and early-maturing boys. *Child Development*, 1957, **28**, 242–256.

Nesselroade, J. R., & Baltes, P. B. Adolescent personality development and historical change: 1970–1972. *Monographs of the Society for Research in Child Development*, 1974, **39**(1, Serial No. 154).

Nesselroade, J. R., & Baltes, P. B. (Eds.) *Longitudinal research in the study of behavior and development*. New York: Academic Press, 1979.

Nesselroade, J. R., & Reese, H. W. (Eds.) *Life-span developmental psychology: Methodological issues*. New York: Academic Press, 1973.

Neurgarten, B. L. *Personality in middle and late life*. New York: Atherton Press, 1964.

Neugarten, B. L. Adult personality: A developmental view. *Human Development*, 1966, **9**, 61–73.

Neugarten, B. L. Continuities and discontinuities of psychological issues into adult life. *Human Development*, 1969, **12**, 121–130.

Neugarten, B. L., & Guttman, D. L. Age-sex roles and personality in middle age: A thematic apperception study. *Psychological Monographs*, 1958, **72**, (No. 470).

Padin, M. A., Lerner, R. M., & Spiro, A., III. The role of physical education interventions in the stability of body attitudes and self-esteem in late adolescents. *Adolescence*, 1981, **16**, 371–384.

Pepper, S. C. *World hypotheses: A study in evidence*. Berkeley: Univ. of California Press, 1942.

Petrinovich, L. Probabilistic functionalism: A conception of research method. *American Psychologist*, 1979, **34**, 373–390.

Pressey, S. L., Janney, J. E., & Kuhlen, R. G. *Life: A psychological survey*. New York: Harper, 1939.

Prewitt, K. Annual report of the President. In *Social Science Research Council: 1979–80 Annual Report*. New York: Social Science Research Council, 1980.

Quetelet, A. *Sur l'homme et le développement de ses facultés*. Paris: Bachelier, 1835.

Reese, H. W., & Overton, W. F. Models of development and theories of development. In L. R. Goulet & P. B. Baltes (Eds.), *Life-span developmental psychology: Research and theory*. New York: Academic Press, 1970.

Richardson, S. A. Handicap, appearance and stigma. *Social Science and Medicine*, 1971, **5**, 621–628.

Riegel, K. F. The dialectics of human development. *American Psychologist*, 1976, **31**, 689–700.

Riley, M. W. Aging, social change, and the power of ideas. *Daedalus*, 1978, (Fall), 39–52.

Riley, M. W. (Ed.) *Aging from birth to death*. Washington, D.C.: American Associatoin for the Advancement of Science, 1979.

Sanford, E. C. Mental growth and decay. *American Journal of Psychology*, 1902, **13**, 426–449.

Schaie, K. W. A general model for the study of developmental problems. *Psychological Bulletin*, 1965, **64**, 92–107.

Schaie, K. W. The primary abilities in adulthood: An exploration in the development of psychometric intelligence. In P. B. Baltes & O. G. Brim, Jr. (Eds.), *Life-span development and behavior* (Vol. 2). New York: Academic Press, 1979.

Schaie, K. W., Labouvie, G. V., & Buech, B. V. Generational and cohort-specific differences in adult cognitive functioning: A fourteen-year study of independent samples. *Developmental Psychology*, 1973, **9**, 151–166.

Schneirla, T. C. The concept of development in comparative psychology. In D. B. Harris (Ed.), *The concept of development*. Minneapolis: Univ. of Minnesota Press, 1957.

Sheldon, W. H. *The varieties of human physique*. New York: Harper, 1940.

Sheldon, W. H. *The varieties of temperament*. New York: Harper, 1942.

Steinberg, L. D., & Hill, J. P. Patterns of family interaction as a function of age, the onset of puberty, and formal thinking. *Developmental Psychology*, 1978, **14**, 683–684.

Super, C. M., & Harkness, S. Figure, ground, and gestalt: The cultural context of the active individual. In R. M. Lerner & N. A. Busch-Rossnagel (Eds.), *Individuals as producers of their development: A life-span perspective*. New York: Academic Press, 1981.

Tetens, J. N. *Philosophische Versuche über die menschliche Natur und ihre Entwichlung*. Leipzig: Weidmanns Erben und Reich, 1777.

Thomas, A., & Chess, S. *Temperament and development*. New York: Brunner/Mazel, 1977.

Thomas, A., & Chess, S. *The dynamics of psychological development*. New York: Brunner/Mazel, 1980.

Thomas, A., & Chess, S. The role of temperament in the contributions of individuals to their development. In R. M. Lerner & N. A. Busch-Rossnagel (Eds.). *Individuals as producers of their development: A life-span perspective.* New York: Academic Press, 1981.

Thomas, A., Chess, S., & Birch, H. *Temperament and behavior disorders in children.* New York: New York Univ. Press, 1968.

Thomas, A., Chess, S., & Birch, H. G. The origin of personality. *Scientific American,* 1970, **223**, 102–109.

Thomas, A., Chess, S., Birch, H., Hertzig, M., & Korn, S. J. *Behavioral individuality in early childhood.* New York: New York Univ. Press, 1963.

Tobach, E., & Schneirla, T. C. The biopsychology of social behavior of animals. In R. E. Cooke & S. Levin (Eds.), *Biologic basis of pediatric practice.* New York: McGraw–Hill, 1968.

REFERENCE NOTES

1. Sameroff, A. J. *Differences in infant temperament in relation to maternal mental illness and race.* Paper presented at the Louisville Temperament Conference, Louisville, Ky., September 1978.

2. Korn, S. J. *Temperament, vulnerability, and behavior.* Paper presented at the Louisville Temperament Conference, Louisville, Ky., September 1978.

3. Gannon, P. *Behavioral problems and temperament in middle class and Puerto Rican five-year-olds.* Unpublished Master's thesis, Hunter College of the City of New York, 1978.

4. Lerner, J. V., Lerner, R. M., & Zabski, S. *Temperament and elementary school children's actual and rated academic performance: A test of a "goodness of fit" model.* Unpublished manuscript, The Pennsylvania State University, 1981.

5. Palermo, M. *Child temperament and contextual demands: A test of the goodness of fit model.* Unpublished Ph.D. dissertation, The Pennsylvania State University, 1982.

6. Bandura, A., & Schunk, D. H. *Cultivating competence, self-efficacy, and intrinsic interest.* Unpublished manuscript, Stanford University, 1980.

RECEIVED: October 20, 1981; REVISED: January 12, 1982

Developmental Psychology
1996. Vol. 32, No. 4, 781-786

Relative Plasticity, Integration, Temporality, and Diversity in Human Development: A Developmental Contextual Perspective About Theory, Process, and Method

Richard M. Lerner
Boston College

Current research about adolescent development often is associated with ideas stressing that dynamic individual–context relations provide the bases of behavior and developmental change. The power of these ideas is constituted by 4 assumptive components of contemporary developmental theories: systematic change and relative plasticity; relationism and integration; embeddedness and temporality; and generalizability limits, diversity, and individual differences. A program of research adequate to address these ideas must involve longitudinal designs and diversity- and change-sensitive measures, multiple methods to appraise variables at multiple levels, and multiple cohorts to assess temporal change. Such theory-guided research may legitimate the possibility of enacting policies and programs to promote positive developmental trajectories in children and adolescents and thus capitalize on the human potential for plasticity.

Adolescents and their families, communities, and societies develop; they show systematic and successive changes over time (Lerner, 1986). These changes are interdependent. Changes within one level of organization, for example, developmental changes in personality or cognition within the individual, are reciprocally related to developmental changes within other levels, for example, changes in caregiving patterns or spousal relationships within the familial level of organization (e.g., Hetherington, Lerner, & Perlmutter, 1988; Lerner & Spanier, 1978; Lewis & Rosenblum, 1974).

Moreover, the reciprocal changes among levels of organization are both products and producers of the reciprocal changes within levels. For example, over time, parents' "styles" of behavior and of rearing influence children's personality and cognitive functioning and development; in turn, the interactions between personality and cognition constitute an emergent "characteristic" of human individuality that affects parental behaviors and styles and the quality of family life (e.g., Lerner, 1982; Lerner & Busch-Rossnagel, 1981; Lerner, Castellino, Terry, Villarruel, & McKinney, 1995; Lewis, in press).

These interrelations illustrate the integration of changes within and among the multiple levels of organization constituting the ecology of human life (Bronfenbrenner, 1979; Lerner, 1978, 1984, 1991). Human development within this ecology involves organized and successive changes—that is, systematic changes—in the structure and function of interlevel relations over time (Ford & Lerner, 1992). In other words, the human development system involves the integration, or "fusion" (Tobach & Greenberg, 1984), of changing relations among the multiple levels of organization that compose the ecology of human behavior and development. These levels range from biology through culture and history (Bronfenbrenner, 1979; Elder, 1980; Gottlieb, 1992; Riegel, 1975). Indeed, the embeddedness of all levels of the system within history provides a temporal component to human development (Elder, Modell, & Parke, 1993); makes the potential for change a defining feature of human development (Baltes, 1987); and as such assures that relative plasticity (i.e., the potential for systematic change across ontogeny) characterizes development across the human life span (Lerner, 1984).

Given that human development is the outcome of changes in this developmental system, then, for individual ontogeny, the essential process of development involves *relations* between the developing person and his or her changing context (Lerner, 1991). Similarly, for any unit of analysis with the system (e.g., for the family, studied over its life cycle; Lerner & Spanier, 1978; or for the classroom, studied over the course of a school year; J. V. Lerner & Lerner, 1983), the same developmental process exists. That is, development involves changing relations between that unit and variables from the other levels of organization within the human development system. Accordingly, the concept of development is a relational one: Development is a concept denoting systemic changes—that is, organized, successive, multilevel, and integrated changes—across the course of life of an individual (or other unit of analysis).

I believe that a focus on process and, particularly, on the process involved in the changing relations between individuals and their contexts, is at the cutting edge of contemporary developmental theory and, as such, is the predominant conceptual frame for research in the study of human development (Lerner, in press). Certainly, these theoretical and empirical orientations represent the essential approaches of the preponderant majority of the research articles in this special issue. Indeed, the forefront of contemporary developmental theory and research is represented by theories of process: of how structures function and how functions are structured over time (Lerner, in press).

Correspondence concerning this article should be addressed to Richard M. Lerner, Center for Child, Family, and Community Partnerships, School of Education, Campion Hall, Boston College, Chestnut Hill, Massachusetts 02167-3813.

For example, and as reflected by the articles in this special issue, most contemporary research about human development in general, and about adolescent development more specifically, is associated with theoretical ideas stressing that the dynamics of individual–context relations provide the bases of behavior and developmental change (see too Lerner, 1986, in press; Lerner, Petersen, & Brooks-Gunn, 1991). Indeed, even models that try to separate biological or, more particularly, genetic influences on an individual's development from contextual ones are at pains to (retro)fit their approach into a more dynamic systems perspective (e.g., as found in Ford & Lerner, 1992; Gottlieb, 1992; Thelen & Smith, 1994; Wapner, 1993).

For instance, in the concluding paragraph of their article on the association between (a) autonomic conditioning and electrodermal recovery time and (b) criminal behavior, Raine, Venables, and Williams (1996) noted that "it is always possible that social factors not indexed in this study could underlie group differences in psychophysiological variables. It is not inconceivable, for example, that early environmental factors such as stressful life events or child abuse could alter psychophysiological functioning" (p. 629). In turn, Pike, McGuire, Hetherington, Reiss, and Plomin (1996) argued that "The presence of genetic influence on measures of the family environment is consistent with the idea that socialization is bidirectional. That is, when parents interact with their children, this interaction is affected by the child's behavior as well as that of the parent" (p. 591).

Thus, in emphasizing that systematic and successive change (i.e., development) is associated with alterations in the dynamic relations among structures from multiple levels of organization, the scope of contemporary developmental theory and research is not limited by (or, perhaps better, confounded by an inextricable association with) a unidimensional portrayal of the developing person (e.g., the person seen from the vantage point of only cognitions, or emotions, or stimulus–response connections, or genetic imperatives; e.g., see Piaget, 1970; Freud, 1949; Bijou & Baer, 1961; Rowe, 1994, respectively). Rather, the power of the contemporary stress on processes of dynamic person–context relations is the "design criteria" imposed on research, method, and application pertinent to the study of any content area or dimension of the developing person. This power is constituted by four interrelated, and in fact "fused" (Tobach & Greenberg, 1984), assumptive components of contemporary theories of human development (Lerner, in press). Accordingly, it is useful to discuss these components to illuminate the key theoretical and methodological (e.g., research design and measurement) issues pertinent to understanding how biological, psychological, and contextual processes combine to promote behavior and development across the life span and, certainly as well, within periods such as adolescence.

Change and Relative Plasticity

Contemporary theories stress that the focus of developmental understanding must be on systematic *change* (Ford & Lerner, 1992). This focus is required because of the belief that the potential for change exists across the life span (e.g., Baltes, 1987). Although it is also assumed that systemic change is not limitless (e.g., it is constrained by both past developments and by con-

temporary contextual conditions), contemporary theories stress that *relative plasticity* exists across life (Lerner, 1984).

There are important implications of relative plasticity for the application of development science. For instance, the presence of relative plasticity legitimates a proactive search across the life span for characteristics of people and of their contexts that, together, can influence the design of policies and programs promoting positive development (Birkel, Lerner, & Smyer, 1989; Fisher & Lerner, 1994; Lerner & Hood, 1986).

Relationism and the Integration of Levels of Organization

Contemporary theories stress that the bases for change, and for both plasticity and constraints in development, lie in the relations that exist among the multiple levels of organization that make up the substance of human life (Ford & Lerner, 1992; Schneirla, 1957; Tobach, 1981). These levels range from the inner biological level, through the individual and psychological level and the proximal social relational level (e.g., involving dyads, peer groups, and nuclear families) to the sociocultural level (including key macroinstitutions such as educational, public policy, governmental, and economic systems) and the natural and designed physical ecologies of human development (Bronfenbrenner, 1979; Riegel, 1975). These levels are structurally and functionally integrated, thus requiring a systems view of the levels involved in human development (Ford & Lerner, 1992; Sameroff, 1983; Thelen & Smith, 1994).

Developmental contextualism (Lerner, 1986, 1991, 1995) is one instance of such a developmental systems perspective. Developmental contextualism promotes a *relational* unit of analysis as a requisite for developmental analysis (Lerner, 1991): Variables associated with any level of organization exist (are structured) in relation to variables from other levels; the qualitative and quantitative dimensions of the function of any variable are shaped as well by the relations that variable has with variables from other levels. Unilevel units of analysis (or the components of, or elements in, a relation) are not an adequate target of developmental analysis; rather, the relation itself—the interlevel linkage—should be the focus of such analysis (Lerner, 1991; Riegel, 1975).

Relationism and integration have a clear implication for unilevel theories of development: At best, such theories are severely limited and inevitably provide a nonveridical depiction of development, because of their focus on what are essentially main effects embedded in higher order interactions (e.g., see Walsten, 1990); at worst, such theories are neither valid nor useful. Accordingly, neither biogenic theories (e.g., genetic reductionistic conceptions such as behavioral genetics or sociobiology; Freedman, 1979; Rowe, 1994), psychogenic theories (e.g., behavioristic or functional analysis models; Bijou, 1976; Bijou & Baer, 1961), nor sociogenic theories (e.g., "social mold" conceptions of socialization; e.g., Homans, 1961; and see Hartup, 1978, for a review) provide adequate theoretical frames for understanding human development. Simply, neither nature nor nurture theories provide adequate conceptualizations of human development (cf. Hirsch, 1970). For instance, theories that stress critical periods of development (e.g., Bowlby, 1969; Erikson, 1959; Lorenz, 1965), that is, periods of ontogeny constrained by biology (e.g., by genetics or by maturation), are seen from the perspective of theories that stress relationism and integration as conceptually flawed (and empirically counterfactual).

Moreover, many nature–nurture interaction theories also fall short in this regard; theories of this type often treat nature and nurture variables as separable entities and view their connection in manners analogous to the interaction term in an analysis of variance (e.g., Bijou, 1976; Erikson, 1959; Rowe, 1994; cf. Gollin, 1981; Hebb, 1970; Walsten, 1990). The cutting edge of contemporary theory moves beyond the simplistic division of sources of development into nature-related and nurture-related variables or processes; instead the multiple levels of organization that exist within the ecology of human development are seen as part of an inextricably fused developmental system.

Historical Embeddedness and Temporality

The relational units of analysis of concern in contemporary theories are understood as change units (Lerner, 1991). The change component of these units derives from the ideas that all of the above-noted levels of organization involved in human development are embedded in history, that is, they are integrated with historical change (Elder, 1980; Elder et al., 1993). Relationism and integration mean that no level of organization functions as a consequence of its own, isolated activity (Tobach, 1981). Each level functions as a consequence of its fusion (its structural integration) with other levels (Tobach & Greenberg, 1984). History—change over time—is incessant and continuous, and it is a level of organization that is fused with all other levels. This linkage means that change is a necessary and an inevitable feature of variables from all levels of organization (Baltes, 1987; Lerner, 1984); in addition, this linkage means that the structure, as well as the function, of variables changes over time.

Indeed, at the biological level of organization, one prime set of structural changes across history is subsumed under the concept of evolution (Gould, 1977; Lewontin, 1981; Lewontin, Rose, & Kamin, 1984); of course, the concept of evolution can be applied also to functional changes (Darwin, 1872; Gottlieb, 1992). In turn, at more macrolevels of organization many of the historically linked changes in social and cultural institutions or products are evaluated in the context of discussions of the concept of progress (Nisbet, 1980). The continuity of change that constitutes history can lead to both intraindividual (or, more generally, intralevel) continuity or discontinuity in development, depending on the rate, scope, and particular substantive component of the developmental system at which change is measured (Brim & Kagan, 1980; Lerner, 1986, 1988; Lerner & Tubman, 1989). Thus, continuity at one level of analysis may be coupled with discontinuity at another level; quantitative continuity or discontinuity may be coupled with qualitative continuity or discontinuity within and and across levels; and continuity or discontinuity can exist in regard to both the processes involved in (or the "explanations" of) developmental change and in the features, depictions, or outcomes (i.e., the "descriptions") of these processes (Cairns & Hood, 1983; Lerner, 1986).

These patterns of within-person change pertinent to continuity and discontinuity can result in either constancy or variation in the rates at which different individuals develop in regard to a particular substantive domain of development. Thus, any pattern of intraindividual change can be combined with any instance of interindividual differences in within-person change, that is, with any pattern of stability or instability (Lerner, 1986; Lerner & Tubman, 1989). In other words, continuity–discontinuity is a dimension of intraindividual change and is distinct from, and independent of, stability–instability, which involves between-persons change and is, therefore, a group and not an individual concept (Baltes & Nesselroade, 1973; Lerner, 1986).

In summary, because historical change is continuous, temporality is infused in all levels of organization. This infusion may be associated with different patterns of continuity and discontinuity across people. The potential array of such patterns has implications for understanding the importance of human diversity.

The Limits of Generalizability, Diversity, and Individual Differences

The temporality of the changing relations among levels of organization means that changes that are seen within one historical period (or time of measurement) and/or with one set of instances of variables from the multiple levels of the ecology of human development may not be seen at other points in time (Baltes, Reese, & Nesselroade, 1977; Bronfenbrenner, 1979). What is seen in one data set may be only an instance of what does or what could exist. Accordingly, contemporary theories focus on diversity—of people, of relations, of settings, and of times of measurement (Lerner, 1991, 1995).

Individual differences within and across all levels of organization are seen as having core, substantive significance in the understanding of human development (Baltes, 1987; Lerner, 1991, 1995). Diversity is the exemplary illustration of the presence of relative plasticity in human development (Lerner, 1984). Diversity is also the best evidence that exists of the potential for change in the states and conditions of human life (Brim & Kagan, 1980).

Moreover, the individual structural and functional characteristics of a person constitute an important source of his or her development (Lerner, 1982; Lerner & Busch-Rossnagel, 1981). The individuality of each person promotes variation in the fusions he or she has with the levels of organization within which the person is embedded. For instance, the distinct actions or physical features of a person promote differential actions (or reactions) in others toward him or her (Lerner, 1987). These differential actions, which constitute feedback to the person, shape at least in part further change in the person's characteristics of individuality (Schneirla, 1957; Lerner & Lerner, 1989). For example, the changing match, congruence, or goodness of fit between the developmental characteristics of the person and of his or her context provide a basis for consonance or dissonance in the ecological milieu of the person; the dynamic nature of this interaction constitutes a source of variation in positive and negative outcomes of developmental change (J. V. Lerner & Lerner, 1983; Thomas & Chess, 1977).

The major assumptive components of contemporary theories of human development—systematic change and relative plasticity, relationism and integration, embeddedness and temporality, and generalizability limits and diversity—are very much intertwined facets of a common paradigmatic core. And, as also the case with the levels of organization that are integrated to form the substance of developmental change, the assumptive components form the corpus of superordinate developmental systems views of human development (Ford & Lerner, 1992), for example, developmental contextualism. As is the case with the several defining features of the life span developmental perspective, which, accordingly to Baltes (1987), need to be considered as an integrated whole, the assumptive components of contemporary developmental theories need to be appreciated simultaneously. Such appreciation is required to understand the breadth, scope, and implications for research and application of this "family" of conceptual frameworks.

Methodological Implications

The temporality involved in contemporary theories of human development necessitates change-sensitive measures of structure and function *and* change-sensitive (i.e., longitudinal) designs (Baltes et al., 1977; Brim & Kagan, 1980). The key question vis-à-vis temporality in such research is not whether change occurs; rather, the question is whether the changes that do occur make a difference for a given developmental outcome (Lerner, Skinner, & Sorell, 1980).

Moreover, given that the study of these changes will involve appraisal of both quantitative and qualitative features of change, which may occur at multiple levels of organization, there is a need to use both quantitative and qualitative data collection and analysis methods, ones associated with the range of disciplines having specialized expertise at the multiple levels of organization at which either quantitative or qualitative change can occur. In essence, then, the concepts of historical embeddedness and temporality indicate that a program of developmental research adequate to address the relational, integrated, embedded, and temporal changes involved in human life must involve multiple occasions, methods, levels, variables, and cohorts (Baltes, 1987; Lerner, 1986, 1991; Schaie, 1965).

Thus, the theoretically provocative and substantively important empirical patterns of unitemporal covariation between adolescent functioning and contextual characteristics that are represented in several of the articles in this special issue would be critical to enrich by longitudinal extension. Empirical appraisals of cross-time variation and covariation are more veridical with the character of change phenomena. Moreover, such analyses would afford examination of whether changes are consistent with theoretical propositions about developmental processes. In other words, to study any process and, more basically, to study any change phenomenon, cross-temporal (multioccasion) data must be gathered, and it would be both theoretically interesting and important and empirically useful to recast the cross-sectional data sets in this special issue as longitudinal investigations.

Indeed, change-sensitive (i.e., longitudinal) designs must be used in research that is intended to adequately appraise the alterations over time that are associated with individual behavior across the adolescent period (e.g., Lerner et al., 1991). As noted, these designs must involve the use of measures that are developed to be able to detect change; however, it is typically the case that measures of traits are not developed to be sensitive to developmental change (Lerner, 1988, 1991). Furthermore, multivariate measurement models must be used to appraise the several individual and contextual levels integrated within and across the adolescent period.

However, a dynamic systems theory, such as development contextualism, would move the study of adolescent development beyond just the point of promoting multivariate-longitudinal designs involving change-sensitive measures. In addition, developmental contextualism would lead scholars to design research studies that involve the following: (a) dynamic (fused) relations among levels of organization (Ford & Lerner, 1992; Tobach & Greenberg, 1984) involved in the ecology of human development; (b) the appraisal of levels ranging from the inner-biological, and individual-psychological, to the physical ecological, the sociocultural, and the historical; and here, concepts that stress the ways in which levels interrelate, or are fused—such as the goodness-of-fit notion forwarded by J. V. Lerner and Lerner (1983)—may be particularly helpful; (c) the individual differences (the diversity) that derives from variation (e.g., in the timing) of the interactions among levels; and, because researchers may not be expert in the culture and ecology of all the diverse groups of youth they study; and (d) as necessary, a "co-learning" model for the design of research (and intervention) programs (Birkel et al., 1989; Lerner, 1995); this model relies on the contributions of youths themselves to further knowledge about the issues, assets, and risks affecting their lives. Such research thus diminishes problems of "alienation" between researchers and participants (Riegel, 1975) and suggests that any quantitative appraisal of adolescents rests on a qualitative understanding of their life spaces and meaning systems. Because such understanding is shaped at least in part by the participants' input, research and, especially, programs derived from such information are more likely to be valued and "owned" by, and therefore efficacious in influencing the lives of, young people (Lerner, 1995).

Finally, then, developmental contextualism underscores the need for policies and programs that are derived from research to be diversity-sensitive and to take a change-oriented, multilevel, integrated, and hence a developmental systems approach (Ford & Lerner, 1992), to capitalize on the potential for plasticity present in the human development system. The integrated nature of this system means that one can effect change by entering the system at any one of several levels, or at several levels simultaneously, depending on the precise circumstances within which one is working and on the availability of multidisciplinary and multiprofessional resources (Lerner, 1995).

Conclusion

Contemporary theories of development and the research associated with them take an integrative approach to the multiple levels of organization presumed to constitute the nature of human life; that is, "fused" (Tobach & Greenberg, 1984) relations among biological, psychological, and social and physical contextual levels constitute the process of developmental change in human life. Rather than approach variables from these levels of analysis in either a reductionistic or a parallel-processing approach, theories, such as developmental contextualism (Lerner, 1986, 1991, 1995), rest on the idea that variables from these levels of analysis are dynamically interactive—they are reciprocally influential over the course of human ontogeny.

It is such ideas that shape much of the empirical work presented in this special issue, especially those instances that reflect longitudinal, change-sensitive, multilevel integrated, and dynamic approaches to the study of adolescent–context relations. Only through such research will adequate understanding be developed of the bases and import of the multiple pathways that compose the adolescent period.

In turn, not only do theoretical views such as developmental contextualism provide an agenda for a developmental, dynamic, and systems approach to research about adolescent development, but they also allow researchers to envision the possibility of promoting positive developmental trajectories in adolescents (Lerner, 1995). One may actualize this vision if one remains assiduously committed to a developmental systems orientation; if one recognizes the "double-edged sword" nature of plasticity that derives from the functioning of this system; and if one therefore creates through policies and programs a "convoy of social support" (Kahn & Antonucci, 1980) across the life course of adolescents. Such a convoy would be a network encompassing the familial, community, institutional, and cultural components of the ecology that affects a person's behavior and development across his or her life.

References

Baltes, P. B. (1987). Theoretical propositions of life-span developmental psychology: On the dynamics between growth and decline. *Developmental Psychology, 23,* 611–626.

Baltes, P. B., & Nesselroade, J. R. (1973). The developmental analysis of individual differences on multiple measures. In J. R. Nesselroade & H. W. Reese (Eds.), *Life-span developmental psychology: Introduction to research methodological issues* (pp. 219–251). New York: Academic Press.

Baltes, P. B., Reese, H. W., & Nesselroade, J. R. (1977). *Life-span developmental psychology: Introduction to research methods.* Monterey, CA: Brooks/Cole.

Bijou, S. W. (1976). *Child development: The basic stage of early childhood.* Englewood Cliffs, NJ: Prentice Hall.

Bijou, S. W., & Baer, D. M. (Ed.). (1961). *Child development: A systematic and empirical basis.* New York: Appleton-Century-Crofts.

Birkel, R., Lerner, R. M., & Smyer, M. A. (1989). Applied developmental psychology as an implementation of a life-span view of human development. *Journal of Applied Developmental Psychology, 10,* 425–445.

Bowlby, J. (1969). *Attachment and loss: Vol. 1. Attachment.* New York: Basic Books.

Brim, O. G., Jr., & Kagan, J. (Ed.). (1980). *Constancy and change in human development.* Cambridge, MA: Harvard University Press.

Bronfenbrenner, U. (1979). *The ecology of human development.* Cambridge, MA: Harvard University Press.

Cairns, R. B., & Hood, K. E. (1983). Continuity in social development: A comparative perspective on individual difference prediction. In P. B. Baltes & O. G. Brim, Jr. (Eds.), *Life-span development and behavior* (Vol. 5, pp. 301–358). New York: Academic Press.

Darwin, C. (1872). *The expression of emotion in men and animals.* London: J. Murray.

Elder, G. H., Jr. (1980). Adolescence in historical perspective. In J. Adelson (Ed.), *Handbooks of adolescent psychology* (pp. 3–46). New York: Wiley.

Elder, G. H., Jr., Modell, J., & Parke, R. D. (1993). Studying children in a changing world. In G. H. J. Elder, J. Modell, & R. D. Parke (Eds.), *Children in time and place: Developmental and historical insights* (pp. 3–21). New York: Cambridge University Press.

Erikson, E. H. (1959). Identity and the life-cycle. *Psychological Issues, 1,* 18–164.

Fisher, C. B., & Lerner, R. M. (Eds.). (1994). *Applied developmental psychology.* New York: McGraw-Hill.

Ford, D. L., & Lerner, R. M. (1992). *Developmental systems theory: An integrative approach.* Newbury Park, CA: Sage.

Freedman, D. G. (1979). *Human sociobiology: A holistic approach.* New York: Free Press.

Freud, S. (1949). *Outline of psychoanalysis.* New York: Norton.

Gollin, E. S. (1981). Development and plasticity. In E. S. Gollin (Ed.), *Developmental plasticity: Behavioral and biological aspects of variations in development* (pp. 231–251). New York: Academic Press.

Gottlieb, G. (1992). *Individual development and evolution: The genesis of novel behavior.* New York: Oxford University Press.

Gould, S. J. (1977). *Ontogeny and phylogeny.* Cambridge, MA: Belknap Press of Harvard.

Hartup, W. W. (1978). Perspectives on child and family interaction: Past, present, and future. In R. M. Lerner & G. B. Spanier (Eds.), *Child influences on marital and family interaction: A life-span perspective* (pp. 23–45). New York: Academic Press.

Hebb, D. O. (1970). A return to Jensen and his social critics. *American Psychologist, 25,* 568.

Hetherington, E. M., Lerner, R. M., & Perlmutter, M. (Eds.). (1988). *Child development in life-span perspective.* Hillsdale, NJ: Erlbaum.

Hirsch, J. (1970). Behavior-genetic analysis and its biosocial consequences. *Seminars in Psychiatry, 2,* 89–105.

Homans, G. C. (1961). *Social behavior: Its elementary forms.* New York: Harcourt, Brace, & World.

Kahn, R. L., & Antonucci, T. C. (1980). Convoys over the life course: Attachment, roles, and social support. In P. B. Baltes & O. G. Brim, Jr. (Eds.), *Life-span development and behavior* (Vol. 3, pp. 253–286). New York: Academic Press.

Lerner, J. V., & Lerner, R. M. (1983). Temperament and adaptation across life: Theoretical and empirical issues. In P. B. Baltes & O. G. Brim Jr. (Eds.), *Life-span development and behavior* (Vol. 5, pp. 197–230). New York: Academic Press.

Lerner, R. M. (1978). Nature, nurture, and dynamic interactionism. *Human Development, 21,* 1–20.

Lerner, R. M. (1982). Children and adolescents as producers of their own development. *Developmental Review, 2,* 342–370.

Lerner, R. M. (1984). *On the nature of human plasticity.* New York: Cambridge University Press.

Lerner, R. M. (1986). *Concepts and theories of human development* (2nd ed.). New York: Random House.

Lerner, R. M. (1987). The concept of plasticity in development. In J. Gallagher & C. T. Ramey (Eds.), *The malleability of children* (pp. 3–14). Baltimore: Paul H. Brooks.

Lerner, R. M. (1988). Personality development: A life-span perspective. In E. M. Hetherington, R. M. Lerner, & M. Perlmutter (Eds.), *Child development in life-span perspective* (pp. 21–46). Hillsdale, NJ: Erlbaum.

Lerner, R. M. (1991). Changing organism–context relations as the basic process of development: A developmental–contextual perspective. *Developmental Psychology, 27,* 27–32.

Lerner, R. M. (1995). *America's youth in crisis: Challenges and options for programs and policies.* Thousand Oaks, CA: Sage.

Lerner, R. M. (Ed.). (in press). *Theoretical models of human development: Vol. 1. Handbook of child psychology* (5th ed.). New York: Wiley.

Lerner, R. M., & Busch-Rossnagel, N. A. (Eds.). (1981). *Individuals* as producers of their development: A life-span perspective. New York: Academic Press.

Lerner, R. M., Castellino, D. R., Terry, P. A., Villarruel, F. A., & McKinney, M. H. (1995). A developmental contextual perspective on parenting. In M. H. Bornstein (Ed.), Handbook of parenting: Vol. II. Biology and ecology of parenting (pp. 285-309). Hillsdale, NJ: Erlbaum.

Lerner, R. M., & Hood, K. E. (1986). Plasticity in development: Concepts and issues for intervention. Journal of Applied Developmental Psychology, 7, 139-152.

Lerner, R. M., & Lerner, J. V. (1989). Organismic and social contextual bases of development: The sample case of early adolescence. In W. Damon (Ed.), Child development today and tomorrow (pp. 69-85). San Francisco: Jossey-Bass.

Lerner, R. M., Petersen, A. C., & Brooks-Gunn, J. (Eds.). (1991). Encyclopedia of adolescence. New York: Garland.

Lerner, R. M., Skinner, E. A., & Sorell, G. T. (1980). Methodological implications of contextual/dialectic theories of development. Human Development, 23, 225-235.

Lerner, R. M., & Spanier, G. B. (Eds.). (1978). Child influences on marital and family interaction: A life-span perspective. New York: Academic Press.

Lerner, R. M., & Tubman, J. (1989). Conceptual issues in studying continuity and discontinuity in personality development across life. Journal of Personality, 57, 343-373.

Lewis, M. (in press). Unavoidable accidents and chance encounters. New York: Guilford Press.

Lewis, M., & Rosenblum, L. A. (Eds.). (1974). The effect of the infant on its caregivers. New York: Wiley.

Lewontin, R. C. (1981). On constraints and adaptation. Behavioral and Brain Sciences, 4, 244-245.

Lewontin, R. C., Rose, S., & Kamin, L. J. (1984). Not in our genes: Biology, ideology, and human nature. New York: Pantheon.

Lorenz, K. (1965). Evolution and modification of behavior. Chicago: University of Chicago Press.

Nisbet, R. A. (1980). History of the idea of progress. New York: Basic Books.

Piaget, J. (1970). Piaget's theory. In P. H. Mussen (Ed.), Carmichael's manual of child psychology (Vol. 1, pp. 703-732). New York: Wiley.

Pike, A., McGuire, S., Hetherington, E. M., Reiss, D., & Plomin, R.

(1996). Family environment and adolescent depressive symptoms and antisocial behavior: A multivariate genetic analysis. Developmental Psychology, 32, 590-603.

Raine, A., Venables, P. H., & Williams, M. (1996). Better autonomic conditioning and faster electrodermal half-recovery time at age 15 years as possible protective factors against crime at age 29 years. Developmental Psychology, 32, 624-630.

Riegel, K. F. (1975). Toward a dialectical theory of development. Human Development, 18, 50-64.

Rowe, D. C. (1994). The limits of family influence: Genes, experience, and behavior. New York: Guilford Press.

Sameroff, A. J. (1983). Developmental systems: Contexts and evolution. In W. Kessen (Ed.), Handbook of child psychology: Vol. 1. History, theory, and methods (Vol. 1, pp. 237-294). New York: Wiley.

Schaie, K. W. (1965). A general model for the study of developmental problems. Psychological Bulletin, 64, 92-107.

Schneirla, T. C. (1957). The concept of development in comparative psychology. In D. B. Harris (Ed.), The concept of development (pp. 78-108). Minneapolis: University of Minnesota Press.

Thelen, E., & Smith, L. B. (1994). A dynamic systems approach to the development of cognition and action. Cambridge, MA: MIT Press.

Thomas, A., & Chess, S. (1977). Temperament and development. New York: Brunner/Mazel.

Tobach, E. (1981). Evolutionary aspects of the activity of the organism and its development. In R. M. Lerner & N. A. Busch-Rossnagel (Eds.), Individuals as producers of their development: A life-span perspective (pp. 37-68). New York: Academic Press.

Tobach, E., & Greenberg, G. (1984). The significance of T. C. Schneirla's contribution to the concept of levels of integration. In G. Greenberg & E. Tobach (Eds.), Behavioral evolution and integrative levels (pp. 1-7). Hillsdale, NJ: Erlbaum.

Walsten, D. (1990). Insensitivity of the analysis of variance to heredity-environment interaction. Behavioral and Brain Sciences, 13, 109-120.

Wapner, S. (1993). Parental development: A holistic, developmental systems-oriented perspective. In J. Demick, K. Bursik, & R. D. Biase (Eds.), Parental development (pp. 3-37). Hillsdale, NJ: Erlbaum.

Received February 1, 1996
Revision received March 1, 1996
Accepted March 1, 1996 ∎

Menarche, Secular Trend in Age of

James M. Tanner

University of London

During at least the last 150 years the average age of menarche, the first menstrual period, has decreased in the populations of the industrialized or "developed" countries. Modern data on menarche is collected by what is called the "status quo" method. An accurate sampling is made of all girls aged 9 to 16 in a given city, country, or geographical area and each individual is simply asked her date of birth and whether she has yet experienced a menstrual period (usually defined as bleeding for at least three days). The percentage of girls responding in the affirmative for successive six-month age periods is plotted, and yields a sigmoid curve. The age at which 50% of the girls were postmenarcheal is then estimated, using the statistical technique of probits. (Longitudinal studies giving exact date of menarche have shown that the distribution of age at menarche, at least under good environmental conditions, is Gaussian.) This method is so easy to apply that we now have an enormous list of ages of menarche, including practically all populations in the world (Eveleth & Tanner, 1990). The method yields a standard error of the mean and a test also for homogeneity of the populations examined.

But the status quo method has only been in use since the middle 1950s. Before then most studies relied on questioning adult women—often those admitted to hospital for childbirth—as to their recollection of their age when menstruation occurred for the first time. Some studies are available on the accuracy of this recollection. In a Swedish longitudinal study, 339 girls whose dates were accurately known were questioned some four years after the event. Despite the fact that these girls had participated in a prolonged study that paid particular attention to all aspects of development, the correlation between recollected and true age was only 0.81; less than two-thirds recalled the date to within three months of the true one. In a similar study, at the Harvard University School of Public Health, a correlation of 0.78 was found between the true date and the date recollected 19 years later. Thus recollected ages have to be dealt with cautiously.

Using historical data may also produce sampling problems. Young women attending a certain hospital in the 1870s, for example, may be exclusively from the lower class (since most middle-class women in Europe had their labors at home at that time), while all social classes might be represented in the same hospital during the 1920s.

In spite of these cautions, the data gives rather clear-cut results. Table 1, taken from my *A History of the Study of Human Growth*, lists most of the data available for Europe in the 19th century. Working women had a later menarche than middle-class women, by something approaching two years. The figures for Danish women have recently been carefully reassessed by Helm and Helm (*Annals of Human Biology*, 1987, p. 371). In 1840–50 the average age of menarche for working women was as high as 17.2 years. From 1860 on there was a fairly rapid reduction, amounting to about 0.3 years per decade, so that by 1920 age 15.0 was the average figure. By 1950 the value had fallen to about 13.5. Thereafter the change slowed down; the figure for 1983 was 13.0. Figure 1 summarizes some of the main data.

More detail is available for the city of Oslo, Norway. This data shows that the trend has not always been as linear as it appears in Figure 1. Brudevoll (1973), randomly selected the records of 50 women for each year from the archives of the Oslo City Maternity Hospital and plotted the average recollected age of menarche of these patients year by year. Figure 2 shows the data, with a 21-point moving average line put in. There was a sharp drop between girls born about 1860 and those born about 1880, followed by a period of little change. Then a second sharp drop occurred between those born in 1900 and those born in 1940. There has been little change in the last 30 years.

Brudevoll reports the data in terms of date of birth, and this may well paint a truer historical picture than reporting in terms of date of menarche. The secular trend to earliness is a response to amelioration of the conditions of life, particularly increase of food and decrease of infection. Age at menarche, the end-point of the growth process, is influenced by all the conditions in the preceding years of fetal life and childhood. There is some evidence, however, that it is especially the conditions of the early years, around birth to two, which play the major role (as they do in the secular increase in body size also).

North American data is more limited. About 1890 patients in a Boston and a St. Louis practitioners' dispensary had a recollected age of 14.2 years (see Tanner, 1981); college women had a mean of 13.5 years. Wyshak (1983) studied a large number of mostly middle-class Americans all over the U.S.A. in the course of an epidemiological survey and found a secular trend of 3.2 months per decade between women born around 1920 and those born around 1940. The value for those born in 1940 and later was 12.5, but no further decline has occurred—12.5 is still the expected value for middle-class white Americans.

The greatest of all secular trends in menarche occurred in Japan. From 1900 to 1935 the trend was slight, and from 1935 to 1950 the trend actually reversed, with age at menarche increasing. Then, in improving postwar conditions, there was a decline of some 11 months per decade until 1975, when the trend leveled out to practically zero. The secular change in age at peak height velocity was similar (Marshall & Tanner, 1986).

In a population growing up under optimal circumstances from the points of view of nutrition, infection, exercise, and psychological well-being, age at menarche is a genetically determined characteristic (being simply an element of the more general characteristic called growth tempo). In some developed countries something like these conditions have obtained for several decades, and it seems that menarche has

TABLE 1
AVERAGE AGES OF MENARCHE IN UNITED KINGDOM, SCANDINAVIA, GERMANY, AND RUSSIA IN THE NINETEENTH CENTURY

	YEAR OF MENARCHE (APPROX.)	MEAN AGE AT MENARCHE	PLACE	AUTHOR
Working women				
UK	1815	15.2	Manchester	Roberton (1830)
	1835	15.6	Manchester	Whitehead (1847)
	1830	15.1	London	Guy (1845)
	1830	14.9	London mostly	Murphy (1844–45)
	1855	15.0	London	Rigden (1869)
	1910	15.0	Edinburgh	Kennedy (1933)
Scandinavia,	1785	16.6	Göttingen	Osiander (1795)
Germany, and Russia	1835	16.4	Copenhagen	Ravn (1850)
	1850	16.8	Copenhagen	Hannover (1869)
	1850	16.4	Berlin	Krieger (1869)
	1850	16.8	Munich	Hecker (1864)
	1865	16.6	Bavaria	Schlichting (1880)
	1870	15.6	Oslo	Brudevoll et al. (1979)
	1875	15.7	Russia	Grüsdeff (1894)
	1875	16.5	Helsinki	Malmio (1919)
	1890	15.7	Stockholm	Essen-Möller; in Lenner (1944)
	1895	16.2	Berlin	Schaeffer (1908)
	1900	16.2	Schleswig	Heyn (1920)
	1900	16.0	Helsinki	Malmio (1919)
	1900	14.6	Oslo	Brudevoll et al. (1979)
Middle class				
UK	1835	14.3	Manchester	Whitehead (1847)
	1890	14.4	London	Giles (1901a)
Scandinavia, Germany, and Russia	1820	15.0	Norway	Brundtland and Walløe (1976)
	1835	14.4	Copenhagen	Ravn (1850)
	1875	14.4	Russia	Grüsdeff (1894)
	1895	14.4	Berlin	Schaeffer (1908)

Note: The average date of year of menarche has been calculated from the probable mean age of the women studied: it has an error of up to five years.

reached or very nearly reached its lower threshold; the secular trend has stopped. (There are differences between populations in the value of this threshold: it is about 13.0 for North-West European popula-tions, for example, but nearer 12.3 for Mediterranean European populations). Similarly, in socially advanced countries, such as Norway and Sweden, there are no differences in age at menarche between

209

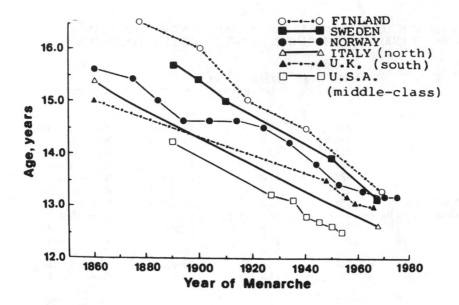

FIGURE 1 Secular changes in age at menarche, 1860–1980 (from Marshall and Tanner, 1986).

children growing up in manual workers' families and those in nonmanual workers' households. But in most other countries, lower-class age of menarche lags behind middle- and upper-class age of menarche.

In the developing countries the trend in age at menarche, which may be zero, is a good guide to whether conditions of life are being ameliorated. Thus economic historians have been interested to interpret data such as those shown in Figure 2, in terms of the history of industrialization. Statistics on age at menarche are one of the most easily obtained indicators of economic well-being.

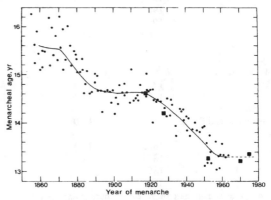

FIGURE 2 Mean menarcheal age for working-class women (up to 1945; thereafter middle-class also) in Oslo from 1860 to 1975. Recollection data; each point represents the average of about 50 maternity clinic patients. The squares represent status-quo probit-fitted data on Oslo schoolgirls. The curve is a 21-term moving average until 1960. Redrawn from Brudevoll, Liestol, and Walloe (1979).

References

Brudevoll. (1973). *Annals of Human Biology.*

Eveleth, P. B., & Tanner, J. M. (1990). *Worldwide variation in human growth.* (2d Ed.) Cambridge: Cambridge University Press.

Marshall, W. A. & Tanner, J. M. (1986). Puberty. In F. Falkner & J. M. Tanner (Eds.), *Human Growth* (2nd ed., Vol. 2, pp. 171–209). New York: Plenum Press.

Tanner, J. M. (1981). *A history of the study of human growth.* Cambridge: Cambridge University Press.

Wyshak. (1983). *Annals of Human Biology.*

See Also

Cognitive Abilities and Physical Maturation; Growth Spurt, Adolescent; History of Research on Adolescence; Maturational Timing, Antecedents of in Girls; Maturational Timing Variations in Adolescent Girls, Consequences of; Menarche and Body Image; Menstrual Cycle; Physical Status and Timing in Early Adolescence, Measurement of; Pubertal Development, Assessment of; Puberty, Body Fat and; Puberty Education; Puberty, Endocrine Changes at; Puberty, Hypothalamic-Pituitary Changes of; Puberty, Precocious, Treatment of; Puberty, Sport and; Spatial Ability and Maturation in Adolescence; Spermarche.

Hormones, Emotional Dispositions, and Aggressive Attributes in Young Adolescents

Elizabeth J. Susman, Gale Inoff-Germain, and Editha D. Nottelmann

National Institute of Mental Health

D. Lynn Loriaux, Gordon B. Cutler, Jr., and George P. Chrousos

National Institute of Child Health and Human Development

SUSMAN, ELIZABETH J.; INOFF-GERMAIN, GALE; NOTTELMANN, EDITHA D.; LORIAUX, D. LYNN; CUTLER, GORDON B., JR.; and CHROUSOS, GEORGE P. *Hormones, Emotional Dispositions, and Aggressive Attributes in Young Adolescents.* CHILD DEVELOPMENT, 1987, 58, 1114–1134. Relations among hormone levels, emotional dispositions, and aggressive attributes were examined in 56 boys and 52 girls, age 9 to 14 years. The adolescents represented all 5 stages of pubertal development. Serum levels of gonadotropins, gonadal steroids, adrenal androgens, and testosterone-estradiol binding globulin were assessed. Levels of these hormones were related to stage of pubertal development and were assumed to represent relatively stable biological characteristics. The emotional dispositions assessed were adolescent self-reported anger, nervousness, sadness, and impulse control. The aggressive attributes assessed were mother-reported acting out and aggressive behavior problems and rebellious and nasty characteristics. Hormone levels were related to emotional dispositions and aggressive attributes for boys but not for girls. For example, higher levels of androstenedione in boys were related to higher levels of acting-out behavior problems. Level of testosterone-estradiol binding globulin was negatively related to sad affect and acting out behavior.

Puberty is a period of physical development accompanied by dramatic increases in the circulating levels of many hormones (Sizonenko, 1978; Williams, 1981). Puberty also is a period of psychological development characterized by increases in aggressive and rebellious behavior in most cultures (Weisfeld & Berger, 1983). How these two sets of changes relate to each other is the focus of the present study.

At a folk-wisdom level, hormonal changes are associated with behavior change in adolescents. The empirical evidence confirming this link is almost nonexistent. It is known that the rapid hormone changes at puberty include increases in androgens, which are presumed to be linked to aggressive behavior. In many species studied, aggression also increases at puberty, most clearly for males (Weisfeld & Berger, 1983).

The link between androgen levels and aggressive behavior in animals has been found consistently for males and sometimes for females (Bouissou, 1983; Eleftheriou & Sprott, 1975; also see Ellis, 1982). Further-more, increases in androgen levels in males are implicated in the increases in aggression at puberty. In elegantly designed studies of aggression in mice, Cairns, MacCombie, and Hood (1983) found that at early sexual maturity, aggression began to rise in male mice. In humans, similar but less consistent androgen-aggression relations have been reported in adult males (Mazur & Lamb, 1980) and in late pubertal male adolescents (Olweus, Mattsson, Schalling, & Low, 1980). Females are less frequently studied than males with regard to hormonal influences on aggression.

The extensive animal literature demonstrating the role of hormones in aggression (e.g., Adams, 1983; Bouissou, 1983; Brain, 1977) and the growing psychoneuroendocrinology literature demonstrating the influence of hormones on the behavior of humans (e.g., Rose & Sachar, 1981; Sachar, 1980) provide the basis for the hypothesis that hormone levels are related to aggression in human adolescents. This study simultaneously examines hormone levels, emotions theoretically related to aggression, and aggression in a sample of male and female young adolescents.

The authors would like to thank Marian Radke-Yarrow for her support for all aspects of this project. Requests for reprints should be sent to Elizabeth J. Susman, Laboratory of Developmental Psychology, NIMH, Building 15K, 9000 Rockville Pike, Bethesda, MD 20892.

Emotions and aggression.—An unanswered question is, What are the mechanisms whereby the effects of hormones become exhibited in aggressive behavior? One approach to answering this question involves emotional states in the hormone-aggressive behavior pathway. The emotions predisposing adolescents to overt aggressive behavior include rage (Berkowitz, 1964; Fonberg, 1979), sadness (Doering, Brodie, Kraemer, Moos, Becker, & Hamburg, 1975), and fear or anxiety (Bouissou, 1983; Ehrenkranz, Bliss, & Sheard, 1974; Frodi, Macaulay, & Thome, 1977; Leshner, 1983). Fear can have activating as well as inhibitory effects on aggression, depending on the circumstances. Emotions that can have inhibitory or antagonistic effects on the expression of aggression also include happiness or elation (Alpert, Cohen, Shaywitz, & Piccirillo, 1981; Fonberg, 1979). Aggression probably is motivated by multiple emotions that may or may not be experienced consciously by the aggressor.

The mechanisms whereby hormones influence emotions and behavior have been conceptualized in terms of the organizing and activating influences of hormones (Hays, 1981; Phoenix, Goy, Gerall, & Young, 1959; Tieger, 1980). Organizational influences stem from prenatal and perinatal hormone exposure, which affects the structure or functioning of the central nervous system such that development and functioning are altered. Activational influences stem from contemporaneous effects of hormones on behavior. Gonadal steroids are involved prenatally and perinatally in the organization of the central nervous system; during and after puberty, they serve primarily an activating function (Rubin, Reinisch, & Haskett, 1981; Young, Goy, & Phoenix, 1964). The organizing and activating influences of hormones may result in differences among groups, such as those found between the sexes as well as differences among individuals.

The organizing influence of hormones, as reflected in the degree of prenatal and perinatal exposure to gonadal steroids, may sensitize individuals in such a way that they differ with respect to their readiness for certain types of emotional responding (Marcus, Maccoby, Jacklin, & Doering, 1985). Individual differences in early hormone exposure were thought to account for sex differences in frequency, intensity, and age patterns of emotional behaviors, such as girls showing more fearfulness than boys and boys showing more anger and frustration reactions than girls. Links between neonatal hormone levels and predominant mood states in early childhood have been reported (Marcus et al., 1985). In most cases, hormones are presumed to be involved in emotions in children but are not examined.

Hormone links to emotions in adults also have been reported. Although not all the evidence has been consistent, findings indicate hormone links to both emotional states (Bardwick, 1976; de Lignieres & Vincens, 1982; Mazur & Lamb, 1980) and traits (Doering et al., 1975; Houser, 1979). Relations between changes in hormone levels and depression and other affective disorders (e.g., see Anisman & LaPierre, 1982; Puig-Antich, 1986) and premenstrual or menopausal symptoms (e.g., see Bardwick, 1976; de Lignieres & Vincens, 1982; Floody, 1983) also have been examined. Additionally, the bidirectional influence of hormone levels affecting behavior and behavior or experience (e.g., defeat) affecting hormone levels is well recognized in psychobiological research (Leshner, 1983). The pathway involving hormonal influences on behavior was the theoretical focus of this study.

In young adolescents, emotional states may undergo major perturbations as a sequelae of the rise in hormone levels at puberty. The activating influences of hormones may be reflected in the emotions of adolescents because neural tissues are target tissues for some puberty-related hormones. Disturbances in emotions also may reflect disequilibrium in biological processes that may stem from the rapidity of change in hormone levels. In our cross-sectional sample of young adolescents, hormone levels had not yet reached adult levels, even for the adolescents in the later stages of puberty. Therefore, the adolescents still may have been experiencing emotional perturbations related to increases in hormone levels.

In this study, four aspects of emotion were examined: anger, nervousness, sadness, and impulsivity. These aspects of emotion are referred to as "emotional dispositions." Rather than describing specific emotional states, they describe traits or dimensions of behavior similar to temperament or the behaviors examined in the Stanford Longitudinal Study (Maccoby, Doering, Jacklin, & Kraemer, 1979; Marcus et al., 1985). Impulsivity is not usually labeled an emotion, but it is considered to reflect characteristics of temperament. Impulsivity also is thought to link hormones and aggression (Olweus et al., 1980; Schlain, 1976).

While hormones may affect both positive and negative emotions, it is negative emotions that are implicated in aggression. If negative emotions are expressed in behavior, they are likely to be expressed as irritability, talking back, or some other similar negative attribute. It is this form of aggression that was investigated in the present study. Irritability and rebellious behaviors are more likely expressions of aggression in normal adolescents than physical attack. As in the case of emotions, the measures of aggression describe traits. They are referred to as "aggressive attributes."

We examined relations among (a) hormones and emotional dispositions, (b) hormones and aggressive attributes, and (c) hormones and emotional dispositions together and aggressive attributes. If the activational influences of hormones at puberty are reflected in emotional dispositions and emotional dispositions are reflected in aggressive attributes, then prediction of aggressive attribute scores should be improved by using both hormones and emotional dispositions, rather than hormones alone.

Sex differences.—Sex differences in the expression of aggression are reported for most species, but the degree and pattern of differences depend on the species and type of aggression being considered (Cummings, Hollenbeck, Iannotti, Radke-Yarrow, & Zahn-Waxler, 1986; Floody, 1983; Frodi et al., 1977). The most marked sex differences are seen in rank-related aggression (Brain, 1977). In most species, males tend to be more aggressive than females (Maccoby & Jacklin, 1974, 1980). Sex differences in socialization practices (Friedman, Richart, & Vande Wiele, 1974) and, as mentioned earlier, the organizing and activating influences of hormones (Gandelman, 1980; Hays, 1981; Tieger, 1980; van de Poll, Smeets, & van der Zwan, 1982) are viewed as important factors in sex differences in the expression of aggression.

State versus trait characteristics.—In addition to short-term variations within individuals, hormone levels also vary across individuals. In adolescents, a major source of the variation in hormone levels across individuals is associated with stage of pubertal development. The hormones examined in this study correlate with stage of pubertal development using Tanner criteria (Marshall & Tanner, 1969, 1970). Therefore, for adolescents progressing through puberty, the hormone levels represent the hormone analogue of psychological traits. In this study, individual differences in hormone levels were examined in

relation to individual differences in typical or average behavior, that is, to psychological traits. The traits were the emotional dispositions and aggressive attributes. For human males, individual differences in testosterone level have related to the traits of aggressiveness, assertiveness, and impulsiveness, especially where provocation and threat were involved (Doering et al., 1975; Ehrenkranz et al., 1974; Houser, 1979; Mattsson, Schalling, Olweus, Low, & Svensson, 1980; Olweus et al., 1980; Persky, Smith, & Basu, 1971; Scaramella & Brown, 1978). Thus, in this study, both the hormone and behavior measures were assumed to assess traits.

Hormone-behavior specificity.—The literature on aggression provides few empirical findings relevant to developing hypotheses about which particular hormones should be related to aggression in healthy human young adolescents under normal conditions. In the Olweus et al. study (1980), testosterone levels related to certain aspects of aggression in adolescent males in the later stages of puberty. Hormone-aggression findings generally are based on studies of experimentally induced changes in hormone level (e.g., Bouissou, 1983), pathological conditions (Hines, 1982; Kelly, 1981; Siris, Siris, Van Kammen, Docherty, Alexander, & Bunney, 1980), unusual or prison samples (e.g., Ehrenkranz et al., 1974; Mattsson et al., 1980), or infrahumans (e.g., Bouissou, 1983; Rose, Bernstein, Gordon, & Lindsley, 1978). Whether these findings can be generalized to normal adolescents of both sexes is an open question.

The groups of hormones examined in this study were: gonadotropins (luteinizing hormone and follicle stimulating hormone), gonadal steroids (testosterone and estradiol), and adrenal androgens (dehydroepiandrosterone, dehydroepiandrosterone sulphate, and androstenedione). Testosterone-estradiol binding globulin also was measured. These hormones were chosen because of their contribution to sexual development (Sizonenko, 1978; Williams, 1981) and because of assumed links between sexual maturation and aggression (Cairns et al., 1983). Along with testosterone, it was hypothesized that higher levels of adrenal androgens would be related to higher levels of aggression. The adrenal glands are a major source of androgens during early puberty for boys and girls and throughout puberty for girls. It also was hypothesized that estrogen would be negatively related to aggression. Estrogen may inhibit aggression, especially in females. Estrogen levels are high during ovulation and pregnancy (Fregly

& Luttge, 1982), periods of the reproductive cycle during which aggression may be antithetical to species survival. Gonadotropins were included as measures to provide preliminary findings on their relation to emotions and aggression (see Lloyd, 1975; Rubin et al., 1981). To summarize, our hypothesis was that hormone levels, particularly androgen levels, would be positively related to negative emotional dispositions and aggressive attributes.

Method

Participants

Ten- to 14-year-old boys ($N = 56$) and 9–14-year-old girls ($N = 52$) and their parents were the participants in the study. The adolescents were assessed three times on both biological and psychological measures at 6-month intervals over 1 year. Information provided by the adolescents and their mothers at the first time of assessment was used in this report. Adolescents at all five stages of pubertal development, based on Tanner criteria (Marshall & Tanner, 1969, 1970), were included in the sample. There were at least seven adolescents of each sex at each stage of pubertal development. The wider age range of girls was necessary in order to include girls in all five stages of pubertal development. The adolescents were from intact families, although the parents were not necessarily the biological parents. The majority of the families were middle to upper middle class (Hollingshead, 1975).

Recruitment of participants was done mainly through notices distributed at churches, health clinics, community centers, and parent-teacher association and scout troop meetings. Families who contacted the project laboratory were sent a written explanation of the study. The project staff then contacted the family to determine if the family wished to participate. If the decision was positive, two appointments were scheduled: (*a*) a 4-hour visit for mother, father, and adolescent at a home-like laboratory, where most of the behavioral data were collected, and (*b*) a 2-hour visit for the adolescent and one parent at an outpatient clinic in a research hospital, where the biological data were collected. Mother and adolescent also made mood ratings at home during the week following the laboratory and clinic visits.

Procedure

Behavioral measures.—The adolescent, mother, and father were given a battery of standardized tests and interviews to assess various aspects of the adolescent's social,

emotional, and cognitive development as well as family relationships. Measures for the present analyses were selected from the larger battery of tests based on the following criteria: (1) The measures had to be relevant to the theoretical perspective of the study. For the emotional dispositions, the following variables were included: (*a*) angry mood (angry-friendly), (*b*) anxious or fearful mood (nervous-calm), (*c*) sad mood (happy-sad and emotional tone), and (*d*) impulse control, which could affect whether or not aggressive tendencies are expressed as aggressive behavior. For the aggressive attributes, variables tapping delinquent (acting out), aggressive, rebellious, and "nasty" behavior were included. (2) The measures needed to be limited in number. The hormone levels, emotional dispositions, and aggressive attributes were analyzed using multiple regression. Therefore, the total number of variables selected was limited to take into account constraints related to number of variables and number of participants.

Angry-friendly, nervous-calm, and happy-sad.—The adolescents were instructed to complete a series of self-ratings at home at the end of every day for 5 consecutive days during the week following the laboratory and clinic visits. These self-ratings included angry-friendly, nervous-calm, and happy-sad. Ratings were made using five-point scales. Scores of 5 represented feeling very friendly to others, feeling very calm, and feeling very sad, respectively. For example, for angry-friendly, 1 = very angry, 2 = angry, 3 = neither angry nor friendly, 4 = friendly, and 5 = very friendly. Scores used in analyses are comprised of means across 5 days of self-ratings.

Stabilities for each of these ratings were assessed by correlating the mean of the scores for the odd days (days 1, 3, and 5) with the mean of the scores for the even days (days 2 and 4). For angry-friendly, nervous-calm, and happy-sad, the respective r's were .55, $p \leq$ .001, .55, $p \leq$ .001, and .33, $p \leq$ .05, for boys and .32, $p \leq$ .05, .26, $p \leq$ .10, and .48, $p \leq$ .001, for girls. Because these self-ratings reflected emotions, it was expected that there would be considerable day-to-day variability. The stability coefficients supported this expectation. In addition to intraindividual variability in emotions, there also was interindividual variability in emotions, which was reflected in the mean scores across 5 days of self ratings. Thus, means for angry-friendly, nervous-calm, and happy-sad were used as indices of emotional dispositions.

215

Emotional tone and impulse control.— Emotional tone and impulse control are subscales from the Offer Self-Image Questionnaire for Adolescents (Offer, Ostrov, & Howard, 1977). Wording of the items was modified for use with younger adolescents. Statements were rated by the adolescent on a six-point scale (1 = describes me very well; 6 = describes me not at all). Cronbach's alphas for the emotional tone and impulse control subscales, based on this sample, were .81 and .65, respectively. Examples of items from the emotional tone subscale are: "Most of the time I am happy" (negative weight) and "I often feel sad." Examples of items from the impulse control subscale are: "I rarely lose my temper (rarely get mad)" (negative weight) and "I get wild if I don't get my way." High scores on emotional tone indicate high levels of sadness. High scores on impulse control indicate problems with impulse control. The Offer Self-Image Questionnaire has been used on more than 120 samples, including younger and older teenagers. It differentiates among groups of normal, delinquent, and psychiatrically disturbed youths (Offer, Ostrov, & Howard, 1984).

Delinquent and aggressive.—The delinquent and aggressive measures are two subscales from the Child Behavior Checklist (CBC) (Achenbach & Edelbrock, 1979). The CBC consists of 113 behavior problems rated on a scale of 0 (not true of my child) to 2 (very true or often true of my child). The items are grouped into nine subscales for boys and eight subscales for girls. Mothers completed the checklist during the evening visit to the laboratory. While these two subscales do not include exactly the same items for boys and girls, they are very similar for both sexes. Examples of items (common to boys and girls) on the delinquent subscale are: disobeys at school, lies and cheats, steals at home, steals outside the home, and poor schoolwork. Examples of items (common to boys and girls) on the aggressive subscale are: argues, demands attention, sulks, stubborn, cruel to others, temper tantrums, and threatens people.

The CBC is a widely used instrument for which reliability and validity data are available (see Achenbach & Edelbrock, 1983). One-week test-retest reliabilities for the delinquent and aggressive subscales have ranged from .94 to .97 and .87 to .95, respectively. These subscales are highly correlated with scales from other instruments assessing similar dimensions. Ninety-eight percent of the items on the scale differentiate clinically

referred from nonreferred but demographically similar children. (While the CBC subscale aggressive was actually labelled "aggressive," the variables delinquent, rebellious, and nasty also were assumed to index aspects of aggression.)

Rebellious.—The mother of each adolescent was instructed to rate her child on 28 items at the end of every day for 5 consecutive days during the week following the laboratory and clinic visits. The items consisted of adjectives (or verbs) that have been used in mood and behavior checklists and rating scales with established reliability and validity (e.g., the Multiple Affect Adjective Check List; Zuckerman & Lubin, 1965). The items were chosen on the basis of hypothesized relevance to emotional states and behaviors of adolescents. Mothers were instructed to rate each item on a seven-point scale (1 = not at all; 7 = very much) in terms of how it described their adolescent's mood or behavior that day. Mean scores across the 5 days of ratings were used in a varimax rotation of a principal components factor analysis. The rebellious attribute is the second of four factors derived from this analysis. High-loading items (with loadings given in parentheses) on the rebellious factor are: rebellious (.88), talks back (.88), sulks (.68), irritable (.64), irresponsible (.52), agreeable (−.52), cries (.51), and assertive (.51). Initial factor analyses were done separately for boys and girls. A four-factor solution identified in these analyses was highly similar for boys and girls. Factor scores used in the regression analyses reported here are based on the combined sample. The factor replicated across two independent samples: The correlation for the factor loadings for boys and girls was $r = .88$. Thus, the rebellious factor was viewed as representing a reliable structure.

Nasty.—Mothers rated their adolescents on 20 items modified from the Adolescent Q-Set (Block, 1971). The ratings were made during the evening visit to the laboratory. Using a seven-point scale (1 = not at all true; 7 = extremely true), each mother rated the degree to which each of the items was descriptive of her adolescent. The nasty attribute measure was the first of two factors derived from a varimax rotation of a principal components analysis. High-loading variables (with factor loadings given in parentheses) on the nasty factor are: tries to see how much he/she can get away with (.75), blames others for things (.71), tries to take advantage of others (.69), is jealous of others (.67), is stubborn (.65), is moody (.63), gets upset when he/she has to wait for things (.62), is obedient and well-behaved (−.58), and gets upset even at unimportant things (.57). Initial factor analyses were done separately for boys and girls. A two-factor solution in these analyses was highly similar for boys and girls. Factor scores used in the regression analyses are based on the combined sample. The factor replicated across two independent samples: The correlation for the factor loadings for boys and girls was $r = .89$. Thus, the nasty factor was viewed as representing a reliable structure.

Biological measures.—The biological measures were obtained during a 2-hour visit at an outpatient clinic. The clinic visit was scheduled within a mean number of 2.3 days from the behavioral measures assessment. The biological measures were obtained by a pediatric nurse practitioner or by an endocrinologist. For this report, pubertal stage was based on genital development for boys and breast development for girls (Marshall & Tanner, 1969, 1970). Interexaminer agreement for pubertal stage for boys and girls was $r = .99$ and 1.00, respectively.

Hormone levels may exhibit many types of variation that are relevant to the interpretation of findings: (1) diurnal variations, (2) minute-to-minute fluctuations because of the pulsatile release of some hormones, (3) variations related to stress responses to the experimental situation, (4) variations with age, (5) variations because of illness or other unusual circumstances such as pregnancy, (6) variations related to the menstrual cycle, and (7) other interindividual variations related to constitutional or genetic characteristics.

To minimize the effects of diurnal variations, blood samples were collected between the hours of 8:00 and 10:00 A.M. To minimize the effects of minute-to-minute fluctuations due to pulsatile release of hormones, three blood samples were drawn at 0, 20, and 40 min. Mean values for the three samples were used in statistical analyses. One sample of testosterone-estradiol binding globulin was obtained at Time 0 only. There were significant differences among the three samples for only one measure—testosterone in boys. Testosterone level decreased across the three samples, but the post hoc tests were not significant. Use of the mean hormone levels based on three samples also minimized the effects of stress on our results. Adolescents may vary in the timing of their physiological stress responses to the phlebotomy procedure. Some adolescents may have heightened physiological responses prior to the venipuncture as a result of anticipatory anxiety.

Others may not respond until they actually experience the venipuncture itself. Therefore, no one sample was viewed, a priori, as more reliable than any other sample.

Hormones also vary with age as a result of timing and rate of maturation. The decision regarding whether or not to control for age in statistical analyses was complicated by the fact that developmental phenomena are of interest in this study. For that reason, statistical analyses were done controlling for age as well as without controlling for age. Variations in hormone levels due to unusual circumstances such as illness or disease were minimized by excluding adolescents with a history of major health problems that could have affected hormone levels (e.g., adolescents with diabetes). The adolescents had no known chronic illnesses or major health problems at the time of study.

Menstrual cycle–related variations in hormone levels in females were not controlled in this study. In the sample of 52 girls, 34 (65%) were premenarcheal and 18 (35%) were menarcheal. The probability of a regular cycle of increases and decreases in hormone levels related to ovulation varies with gynecological age (duration of time since first menses) (Vihko & Apter, 1980). However, menarche does not absolutely differentiate girls who show hormone cycles from those who do not. Menarche merely is the culmination of a long series of endocrine changes that are occurring at least 2 years prior to menarche (Apter & Vihko, 1985). Thus, variations in hormone levels in both the premenarcheal and menarcheal girls may introduce error in the data to an unknown extent.

Finally, no attempts were made to control for interindividual variations related to constitutional or genetic characteristics.

Radioimmunoassays were performed according to the following techniques: luteinizing hormone (Odell, Ross, & Rayford, 1967); follicle stimulating hormone (Cargille & Rayford, 1970); testosterone (Nieschlag & Loriaux, 1972); estradiol (Abraham, Buster, Lucas, Corrales, & Teller, 1972); and dehydroepiandrosterone, dehydroepiandrosterone sulfate, and androstenedione (Cutler, Glenn, Bush, Hodgen, Graham, & Loriaux, 1978). Testosterone-estradiol binding globulin, a glycoprotein produced by the liver that serves in binding and transporting gonadal steroids, was measured by a competitive binding assay (Dunn, Nisula, & Rodbard, 1981). The serum concentrations of this glycoprotein change during puberty in boys (Cunningham, Loughlin, Culliton, & McKenna, 1984). Testosterone-estradiol binding globulin influences the fraction of testosterone that is free (unbound) and active. Findings involving testosterone-estradiol binding globulin indirectly may provide information about the effects of free testosterone. The testosterone to estradiol ratio also was computed and used in the analyses. Interassay and intraassay coefficients of variation and assay detection limits appear elsewhere (Nottelmann et al. 1987b).

Results

Mean Levels and Sex Differences

Behavioral measures.—Means and standard deviations for the behavioral variables for boys and girls appear in the top half of Table 1. Analysis of variance for sex differences was conducted for seven of the nine behavioral variables. There were no significant mean level differences between boys and girls. The two Child Behavior Checklist subscales, delinquent and aggressive behavior problems, are highly similar for boys and

girls, but some of the items are different for the sexes. Therefore, tests for sex differences were not conducted for these two variables.

Hormone levels.—Means and standard deviations for the hormone levels for boys and girls appear in the bottom half of Table 1. The means and standard deviations by pubertal stage appear elsewhere (Nottelmann et al., 1987b). Analysis of variance for sex differences was conducted for the nine hormone measures (see Table 1). Boys were significantly higher than girls for level of testosterone, the testosterone to estradiol ratio, and dehydroepiandrosterone sulphate. Girls were significantly higher than boys for level of luteinizing hormone, follicle stimulating hormone, estradiol, and androstenedione. There were no significant group differences between boys and girls for dehydroepiandrosterone or testosterone-estradiol binding globulin.

Intercorrelations

Behavioral variables.—Intercorrelations among the behavioral measures for boys and girls appear in Table 2. In general, the behav-

TABLE 1

MEANS, STANDARD DEVIATIONS, AND F RATIOS FOR SEX DIFFERENCES FOR BEHAVIORAL MEASURES AND HORMONE LEVELS FOR BOYS AND GIRLS

	BOYS			GIRLS			
	$\bar{X}$	SD	N	$\bar{X}$	SD	N	F
Behavioral measures:							
Angry-friendly.............	3.50	.61	52	3.50	.64	49	.00
Nervous-calm...............	3.51	.68	52	3.29	.67	48	2.84
Happy-sad	2.17	.40	53	2.15	.67	49	.02
Emotional tone	2.22	.68	55	2.22	.73	52	.00
Impulse control.............	2.86	.68	55	2.91	.57	52	.12
Delinquent..................	57.80	4.05	55	58.33	4.73	55	...
Aggressive	58.65	6.17	55	58.50	5.86	52	...
Rebellious	−.11	.86	53	.12	1.13	48	1.31
Nasty	−.04	1.11	56	.05	.88	52	.22
Hormone levels:							
LH (mIU/ml)................	5.66	3.74	54	7.58	5.68	51	4.26*
FSH (mIU/ml)...............	6.97	4.74	54	9.12	4.98	51	5.16*
T (ng/dl)	214.65	204.35	55	19.25	9.24	52	47.43***
E_2 (pg/ml).................	12.79	8.19	48	44.99	49.61	50	19.70***
T/E_2 (ng/l)................	158.10	142.95	48	9.01	8.64	50	54.21***
TeBG (ug/dl)	1.91	1.29	42	1.87	1.16	34	.02
DHEA (ng/dl)	256.01	139.86	54	240.48	162.46	50	.27
DHEAS (ug/dl)	104.57	51.08	55	71.98	41.79	52	12.96***
Δ4-A (ng/dl)	62.27	41.14	52	87.18	54.25	51	6.91**

NOTE.—LH = luteinizing hormone, FSH = follicle stimulating hormone, T = testosterone, E_2 = estradiol, T/E_2 = testosterone to estradiol ratio, TeBG = testosterone-estradiol binding globulin, DHEA = dehydroepiandrosterone, DHEAS = dehydroepiandrosterone sulphate, Δ4-A = androstenedione.

* $p \leqslant .05$.
** $p \leqslant .01$.
*** $p \leqslant .001$.

TABLE 2
INTERCORRELATIONS OF BEHAVIORAL MEASURES FOR BOYS AND GIRLS

	1	2	3	4	5	6	7	8	9
1. Angry-friendly		.59***	-.48***	-.28	-.15	.03	.06	-.09	.19
2. Nervous-calm	.41**		-.20	-.28	-.14	-.06	-.08	-.12	.01
3. Happy-sad	-.39**	-.08		.28	.35**	-.04	.15	.16	.10
4. Emotional tone	-.24	-.07	.14		.57***	-.07	.00	.02	.01
5. Impulse control	-.21	-.17	.10	.60***		.02	.15	.03	.05
6. Delinquent	-.24	-.38**	.04	.20	.30*		.70***	.45***	.49***
7. Aggressive	-.12	-.20	-.13	.07	.27*	.61***		.62***	.72***
8. Rebellious	-.16	.13	.24	.06	.00	-.05	.14		.56***
9. Nasty	-.22	-.21	-.01	.07	.23	.56***	.65***	.27*	

NOTE.—The correlation coefficients below the diagonal are for boys; those above the diagonal are for girls. N's range from 52 to 56 for boys and from 47 to 52 for girls.

* $p \leqslant .05$.
** $p \leqslant .01$.
*** $p \leqslant .001$.

ioral measures showed only minimal to moderate intercorrelations. The strongest relations were among the measures of aggression, although, even there, there was considerable independence of each measure.

Hormone levels.—Intercorrelations of the hormone levels for boys and girls appear in Table 3. There were moderate to high intercorrelations among the hormone levels.

Correlations with Age

Behavioral measures.—Only one of the behavioral measures was significantly correlated with age, emotional tone ($r = .36, p \leq .01$), for males only. High scores on emotional tone denote sad affect.

Hormone levels.—For boys, there were significant positive correlations between age and luteinizing hormone ($r = .46, p \leq .001$), follicle stimulating hormone ($r = .40, p \leq .01$), testosterone ($r = .54, p \leq .001$), the testosterone to estradiol ratio ($r = .56, p \leq .001$), dehydroepiandrosterone ($r = .29, p \leq .05$), and androstenedione ($r = .32, p \leq .05$). There was a significant negative correlation between age and testosterone-estradiol binding globulin ($r = -.40, p \leq .01$). Estradiol and dehydroepiandrosterone sulphate were not significantly correlated with age. For girls, there were significant positive correlations between age and luteinizing hormone ($r = .52, p \leq .001$), follicle stimulating hormone ($r = .40, p \leq .01$), testosterone ($r = .56, p \leq .001$), estradiol ($r = .52, p \leq .001$), dehydroepiandrosterone ($r = .40, p \leq .01$), dehydroepiandrosterone sulphate ($r = .53, p \leq .001$), and androstenedione ($r = .65, p \leq .001$). There was a significant negative correlation between age and the testosterone to estradiol ratio ($r = -.44, p \leq .001$). Testosterone-estradiol binding globulin was not significantly correlated with age.

Regression Analyses

Findings are reported for three separate sets of regression analyses: (*a*) the hormones as predictors of emotional dispositions, (*b*) the hormones as predictors of aggressive attributes, and (*c*) both hormones and emotional dispositions as predictors of aggressive attributes. In the reporting of findings, the terms predictor, dependent variable, and independent variable are used for their statistical meaning and not to imply causality. The zero-order correlations between the hormones and the behavioral variables appear in Table 4.

Both the hormones and the emotional dispositions were entered into the regression equations as sets of independent variables. The hormones were entered as a set into the regression equations because they appear to act in synchrony in bringing about maturation during puberty. The exact mechanisms regulating pituitary, gonadal, and adrenal functioning and, thus, the relative levels of these hormones under various circumstances are currently being examined extensively. What is known is that some combination of these hormones is responsible for normal pubertal maturation. Therefore, the set of hormones was entered into regression equations. There was only a moderate degree of multicollinearity among the hormones.

The emotional dispositions also were entered as a set into the regression equations because they were assumed collectively to reflect important aspects of the emotional development of adolescents. By treating the hormones or the behaviors as sets in terms of how they relate to the dependent variables, the set is effectively reduced to a single variable (Cohen & Cohen, 1975). In each multiple regression analysis, the overall F test for each equation is tested for its statistical significance. The individual variables within the set also are tested for their significance by a standard t test, such that the partial contribution of each individual independent variable is assessed (Cohen & Cohen, 1975). The partial contribution of each individual independent variable to the overall result is reflected in its beta weight. In the analyses reported here, all significant results are reported, but findings involving significant betas should be interpreted with caution if the overall F is not also significant.

Hormones and emotional dispositions.—The hormone values (luteinizing hormone, follicle stimulating hormone, testosterone, estradiol, the testosterone to estradiol ratio, testosterone-estradiol binding globulin, dehydroepiandrosterone, dehydroepiandrosterone sulphate, and androstenedione) were entered into the regression equations as a set of independent variables with adolescent emotional dispositions as the dependent variables (angry-friendly, nervous-calm, happy-sad, emotional tone, and impulse control). For each dependent variable, the betas and overall R, R^2, and F ratio appear in Table 5. The findings shown are for boys only. There were no significant findings for girls.

Emotional tone was the only emotional disposition that was related to chronological age. Therefore, for multiple regression to emotional tone, age was entered into the equation first, so as to control for the relation between age and emotional tone before the

TABLE 3

INTERCORRELATIONS OF HORMONE LEVELS AND PUBERTAL STAGE FOR BOYS AND GIRLS

	LH	FSH	T	E_2	T/E_2	TeBG	DHEA	DHEAS	Δ4-A	Pubertal Stage
LH............		.63***	.47***	.49***	-.32*	-.16	.24	.41**	.57***	.56***
FSH...........	.51***		.47***	.20	-.20	-.23	.22	.26	.39**	.34*
T.............	.61***	.60***		.43**	-.08	.25	.29*	.42**	.62***	.48***
E_2...........	.41**	.43**	.63***		-.51***	.16	.33*	.35**	.76***	.55***
T/E_2.........	.41**	.44**	.68***	.01		-.07	-.21	-.21	-.38**	-.47***
TeBG.........	-.31*	-.30*	-.45**	-.35*	-.34*		-.02	-.23	.03	.02
DHEA........	.26	.39**	.39**	.26	.31*	-.31*		.53***	.60***	.37**
DHEAS.......	.14	.20	.13	.16	-.01	-.25	.59***		.57***	.46***
Δ4-A.........	.27	.42**	.50***	.49***	.41**	-.36*	.56***	.31*		.61***
Pubertal stage[a]	.60***	.53***	.82***	.46***	.69***	-.57***	.38**	.14	.53***	

SOURCE.—Nottelmann et al., 1987b.

NOTE.—LH = luteinizing hormone, FSH = follicle stimulating hormone, T = testosterone, E_2 = estradiol, T/E_2 = testosterone to estradiol ratio, TeBG = testosterone-estradiol binding globulin, DHEA = dehydroepiandrosterone, DHEAS = dehydroepiandrosterone sulphate, Δ4-A = androstenedione. Correlations below the diagonal are for boys; correlations above the diagonal are for girls. N's range from 42 to 55 for boys and 34 to 52 for girls.

[a] Pubertal stage is represented by genital development for boys and breast development for girls.

* $p \le .05$.
** $p \le .01$.
*** $p \le .001$.

TABLE 4
ZERO-ORDER CORRELATIONS OF BEHAVIORAL MEASURES WITH HORMONE LEVELS

BEHAVIORAL MEASURES	HORMONES								
	LH	FSH	T	E_2	T/E_2	TeBG	DHEA	DHEAS	Δ4-A
Boys:									
Angry-friendly..........	−.06	.05	−.05	−.04	−.07	.08	−.20	−.08	−.16
Nervous-calm...........	.25	−.05	.10	.25	−.09	−.17	−.07	−.14	−.01
Happy-sad..............	.17	.12	.13	.32*	−.07	−.15	.35**	.22	.23
Emotional tone.........	.06	.18	−.07	.11	−.13	−.31*	.10	.03	.28*
Impulse control........	−.11	.06	−.13	−.04	−.10	−.26	.19	−.05	.20
Delinquent.............	.01	.17	.10	−.11	.22	−.21	.19	−.02	.41**
Aggressive.............	−.08	−.07	.06	−.12	.15	−.21	.06	−.12	.16
Rebellious.............	.32*	−.15	−.01	.03	−.04	−.24	.28*	.22	−.03
Nasty..................	.01	−.21	.02	−.15	.10	−.06	.02	−.14	.15
Girls:									
Angry-friendly..........	.06	−.18	.08	.17	.09	.24	−.01	.17	.08
Nervous-calm...........	.22	−.04	.18	.08	.14	.20	−.01	.29*	.12
Happy-sad..............	.19	.21	.02	.17	−.22	−.06	.13	−.01	.10
Emotional tone.........	.16	.20	.02	.13	−.09	.15	.10	−.15	.14
Impulse control........	.27*	.29*	−.05	.15	−.26	−.17	.09	.06	.21
Delinquent.............	−.08	−.02	−.15	.00	−.04	.07	−.11	−.17	−.11
Aggressive.............	−.03	−.05	−.21	−.10	.04	−.01	−.26	−.33*	−.22
Rebellious.............	−.13	−.14	−.27	−.09	−.01	−.08	−.20	−.24	−.20
Nasty..................	−.26	−.28*	−.19	−.14	.14	.18	−.12	−.34**	−.27*

NOTE.—LH = luteinizing hormone, FSH = follicle stimulating hormone, T = testosterone, E_2 = estradiol, T/E_2 = testosterone to estradiol ratio, TeBG = testosterone-estradiol binding globulin, DHEA = dehydroepiandrosterone, DHEAS = dehydroepiandrosterone sulfate, Δ4-A = androstenedione. For boys, N's range from 40 to 55; for girls, N's range from 30 to 52.
* $p \leq .05$.
** $p \leq .01$.

TABLE 5

MULTIPLE REGRESSION OF HORMONE LEVELS TO EMOTIONAL DISPOSITIONS FOR BOYS: BETA WEIGHT FOR EACH HORMONE MEASURE, MULTIPLE R, R^2, AND F RATIO

EMOTIONAL DISPOSITIONS	HORMONES										R	R^2	F^a
	AGE	LH	FSH	T	E_2	T/E_2	TeBG	DHEA	DHEAS	Δ4-A			
Angry-friendly..........	...	−.09	.22	.06	−.01	−.03	.03	−.22	.06	−.12	.28	.08	.25
Nervous-calm...........	...	.34	−.23	−.04	.21	−.17	−.20	.04	−.23	−.04	.47	.22	.87
Happy-sad.............	...	.14	−.07	−.27	.37	−.03	−.03	.39	−.03	−.03	.48	.23	.88
Emotional tone.........	.59***	.02	.28	−.15	−.40	−.82**	−.35*	−.04	−.23	.54**	.77	.59	3.74**
Impulse control........	...	−.04	.20	.08	−.53	−.65	−.45*	.35	−.46*	.40	.62	.38	1.87

NOTE.—LH = luteinizing hormone, FSH = follicle stimulating hormone, T = testosterone, E_2 = estradiol, T/E_2 = testosterone to estradiol ratio, TeBG = testosterone-estradiol binding globulin, DHEA = dehydroepiandrosterone, DHEAS = dehydroepiandrosterone sulfate, Δ4-A = androstenedione. Results presented are for boys only. There were no significant findings for girls.

[a] Df's were 9,27 for all measures except emotional tone, for which df was 10,26.

* $p \leq .05$.

** $p \leq .01$.

*** $p \leq .001$.

relation between the set of hormones and emotional tone was assessed. Higher emotional tone, indicating sad affect, was related to older age. The set of hormones was significantly related to emotional tone. Higher emotional tone was related to lower testosterone to estradiol ratios, lower levels of testosterone-estradiol binding globulin, and higher levels of androstenedione. Difficulty with impulse control also was related to lower levels of testosterone-estradiol binding globulin and lower levels of dehydroepiandrosterone sulphate, but the overall F was not significant.

Hormones and aggressive attributes.— The same hormones were entered into the regression equations as a set of independent variables with aggressive attributes as the dependent variables (delinquent, aggressive, rebellious, and nasty behavior). For each independent variable, the betas and overall R, R^2, and F ratio appear in Table 6. These results are for boys only. The set of hormones was significantly related to delinquent and rebellious behavior problems. There were no significant findings for girls. Higher scores on delinquent behavior problems were related to lower levels of estradiol and higher levels of androstenedione. Higher scores on the rebellious attribute were related to higher levels of luteinizing hormone, lower levels of follicle stimulating hormone, and higher levels of dehydroepiandrosterone. Higher scores on the nasty factor also were related to higher levels of androstenedione, but the overall F was not significant.

*Hormones, emotional dispositions, and the aggressive attributes.—*The hormones were entered into the regression equations as a set, followed by the emotional dispositions as a second set of independent variables predicting the aggressive attributes. The hormones were entered into the equation first because they were assumed to be causally prior to the emotional dispositions and aggressive attributes. Emotional dispositions and aggressive behaviors also may affect hormone levels. However, it is unlikely that emotions and aggressive behaviors are totally responsible for the rapid increases in hormones during puberty, and that changes in the emotions and behavior of adolescents during puberty are totally unaffected by these hormone changes. Emotional dispositions were entered into the regression equations second. Therefore, the variance accounted for by emotional dispositions is the increment that is added after controlling for the variance accounted for by the hormones.

For each dependent variable, the betas and overall R, R^2, and F ratio appear in Table 7. The findings shown are for boys only. There were no significant findings for girls. Hormones and emotional dispositions, jointly, were significantly related to delinquent behavior problems in boys. For delinquent behavior problems, three additional single hormones and one emotional disposition became significant when the emotional dispositions were added to the equation. Higher scores on delinquent behavior problems were related to lower testosterone to estradiol ratios, lower levels of testosterone-estradiol binding globulin, lower levels of dehydroepiandrosterone sulphate, and lower levels of calm disposition (higher nervousness), in addition to lower levels of estradiol and higher levels of androstenedione. Further, the multiple R for delinquent behavior problems increased from .66 to .76 as a function of adding the emotional dispositions to the regression equation. The overall F for rebellious attributes became nonsignificant when the additional variables were added. Similarly, the betas for follicle stimulating hormone and dehydroepiandrosterone in predicting rebellious attributes became nonsignificant.

Age, Hormones, Emotional Dispositions, and Aggressive Attributes

As mentioned previously, age was correlated with only one behavioral variable, emotional tone. For the regression analysis predicting to emotional tone, age was entered first into the equation, and the beta for age was significant. Although age was not related to the other behavioral variables, age was related to most hormone levels. Therefore, the relations between hormones and the other behavioral variables were examined when age was controlled for by entering it first into the regression equations. Analyses parallel to those described above were conducted. Including age in the regression equations did not affect the pattern of findings.

*Pubertal stage.—*For boys, pubertal stage was significantly related to luteinizing hormone, follicle stimulating hormone, testosterone, estradiol, the testosterone to estradiol ratio, testosterone-estradiol binding globulin (negative relation), dehydroepiandrosterone, and androstenedione (see Table 3). Pubertal stage did not relate to dehydroepiandrosterone sulphate. For girls, pubertal stage was significantly related to luteinizing hormone, follicle stimulating hormone, testosterone, estradiol, the testosterone to estradiol ratio (negative relation), dehydroepiandrosterone, dehydroepiandrosterone sulphate, and an-

TABLE 6

MULTIPLE REGRESSION OF HORMONE LEVELS TO AGGRESSIVE ATTRIBUTES FOR BOYS: BETA WEIGHT FOR EACH HORMONE MEASURE, MULTIPLE R, R^2, AND F RATIO

AGGRESSIVE ATTRIBUTES	HORMONES									R	R^2	F^a
	LH	FSH	T	E_2	T/E_2	TeBG	DHEA	DHEAS	$\Delta 4\text{-A}$			
Delinquent	-.02	.19	.56	-.95***	-.64	-.25	.03	-.30	.77**	.66	.43	2.28*
Aggressive	-.11	-.11	.60	-.67	-.44	-.31	.09	-.31	.37	.49	.24	.93
Rebellious	.57**	-.44*	-.38	.14	.04	-.25	.46*	-.00	-.23	.67	.45	2.44*
Nasty	.15	-.36	.65	-.73	-.53	-.14	.07	-.30	.51*	.53	.28	1.16

NOTE.—LH = luteinizing hormone, FSH = follicle stimulating hormone, T = testosterone, E_2 = estradiol, T/E_2 = testosterone to estradiol ratio, TeBG = testosterone-estradiol binding globulin, DHEA = dehydroepiandrosterone, DHEAS = dehydroepiandrosterone sulfate, $\Delta 4\text{-A}$ = androstenedione. Results are for boys only. There were no significant findings for girls.

ᵃ Df's were 9,27.

* $p \leq .05$.

** $p \leq .01$.

*** $p \leq .001$.

225

TABLE 7

MULTIPLE REGRESSION OF HORMONE LEVELS AND EMOTIONAL DISPOSITIONS TO AGGRESSIVE ATTRIBUTES FOR BOYS

AGGRESSIVE ATTRIBUTES	HORMONES								
	LH	FSH	T	E_2	T/E_2	TeBG	DHEA	DHEAS	Δ4-A
Delinquent	.15	.16	.52	−.95**	−.85*	−.44*	.06	−.46*	.86**
Aggressive	.04	−.15	.50	−.56	−.54	−.42	.12	−.38	.41
Rebellious	.57*	−.43	−.35	.07	−.03	−.30	.48	−.06	−.21
Nasty	.28	−.41	.60	−.65	−.59	−.21	.05	−.35	.52

	EMOTIONAL DISPOSITIONS							
	Angry-Friendly	Nervous-Calm	Happy-Sad	Emotional Tone	Impulse Control	R	R^2	F^a
Delinquent	−.04	−.43*	−.02	−.19	−.04	.76	.58	2.21*
Aggressive	−.01	−.30	−.16	−.19	.11	.57	.33	.76
Rebellious	−.01	−.06	.06	.04	−.13	.68	.46	1.35
Nasty	−.03	−.31	−.03	−.14	.11	.61	.37	.93

NOTE.—LH = luteinizing hormone, FSH = follicle stimulating hormone, T = testosterone, E_2 = estradiol, T/E_2 = testosterone to estradiol ratio, TeBG = testosterone-estradiol binding globulin, DHEA = dehydroepiandrosterone, DHEAS = dehydroepiandrosterone sulfate, Δ4-A = androstenedione. Results are for boys only. There were no significant findings for girls.

^{a} Df's were 14,22.

* $p \leq .05$.

** $p \leq .01$.

*** $p \leq .001$.

drostenedione. Pubertal stage did not relate to testosterone-estradiol binding globulin.

To determine whether the relations among hormone levels, emotional dispositions, and aggressive attributes were changed by including pubertal stage in the equation, the following regression analyses were conducted: (a) The hormones as a set were entered into the equation first, followed by pubertal stage, in predicting each of the emotional dispositions and aggressive attributes. (b) The hormones as a set were entered into the equation first, followed by pubertal stage, followed by the emotional dispositions as a set, in predicting each of the aggressive attributes. (c) Pubertal stage was entered into the equation first, followed by the emotional dispositions as a set, in predicting each of the aggressive attributes. In all cases, entering pubertal stage into the equations did not change the previous results.

Discussion

Hormone levels were related to both emotional dispositions and aggressive attributes for boys, but not for girls. For the emotional dispositions, the strongest relations were between hormones and sad affect (based on the emotional tone subscale) and anxious affect. For the aggressive attributes, the strongest relations were between hormones and delinquent (acting-out) and rebellious behavior.

Our expectations regarding specific hormone-behavior relations were confirmed in some cases but not in others. The expectation that serum testosterone levels (which include bound and unbound testosterone) would be related to negative emotional dispositions and aggressive attributes was not supported directly. Olweus et al. (1980) reported associations between testosterone and a specific type of aggression, response to provocation and threat and lack of frustration tolerance. Testosterone was not associated with many of the items that also were expected to index aggressive behavior. Our sample of adolescents differed from the Olweus et al. sample. While the Olweus et al. sample was limited to male adolescents in the later stages of puberty, adolescents from each of the five pubertal stages were included in our sample. Thus, the testosterone levels in the Olweus et al. adolescents were likely to be close to reaching adult levels for many of the adolescents, while the testosterone levels in our adolescents had not yet reached adult levels for the majority of adolescents.

Although testosterone levels and aggression were not directly related, there was some evidence linking testosterone and emotional dispositions and aggressive attributes in males. The level of testosterone-estradiol binding globulin, a carrier protein which serves in binding and transporting of gonadal steroids, was negatively related to sad affect. Furthermore, when both hormones and emotional dispositions were used to predict aggressive attributes, testosterone-estradiol binding globulin level was negatively related to delinquent behavior problems. As total testosterone and testosterone-estradiol binding globulin are negatively correlated, these relations between testosterone-estradiol binding globulin in males and the behavioral variables are consistent with our prediction for total testosterone. The pattern of findings for adrenal androgens, androstenedione and, to a lesser degree, dehydroepiandrosterone, in males, was consistent with what was expected for androgens of gonadal origin. Higher levels were related to sad affect and delinquent and rebellious behavior problems. Higher levels of adrenal androgens and higher degrees of negative behavior is a pattern that we have identified in other aspects of our larger study (Nottelmann et al., 1987a). While little is known about the influences of adrenal androgens on behavior, it may be speculated that their effects parallel those of androgens of gonadal origin.

The findings relating specific hormones and emotional dispositions and aggressive attributes should be interpreted with caution. Two factors should be considered. First, the significant beta weights may be affected by the nature of the distribution of each hormone and behavioral variable in the equation. Therefore, the significant betas may reflect random rather than true associations between specific hormones and specific emotional dispositions and aggressive attributes. Thus, a conservative interpretation of our findings is that some linear combination of hormones relates to emotional dispositions and aggressive attributes in boys. Second, a particular relation cannot be interpreted as meaning that that specific hormone is the active metabolic ingredient associated with an emotion or behavior. The hormones that we measured are metabolized into other substances which may, in turn, act on neural tissue. For instance, testosterone may be aromatized into estradiol. Estradiol is generally hypothesized to be the active metabolic substance affecting central nervous system functioning, which in turn may influence the expression of aggression (Clark & Nowell, 1979). Experimental studies or experiments in nature (e.g., with hypogonadal males) are the preferred method for determining the causal role of specific hormones on behavior.

The assumption that emotional states are involved in the hormone-aggressive behavior pathway received only moderate support. The addition of emotional dispositions to the hormones in the regression equations improved the multiple R of the hormones in predicting delinquent behavior problems in boys so as to account for an additional 15% of the variance. In the case of rebellious attributes, the multiple R became nonsignificant when additional variables were added to the equation.

Nervous-calm, an index of anxiety, was the emotional disposition significantly related to delinquent behavior problems in the regression equation in which both hormones and emotions were entered. Higher anxiety was related to more delinquent behavior problems in boys. The role of fear or anxiety in mediating the expression of aggressive behavior has been examined in animals and, to a lesser extent, in humans (Ehrenkranz et al., 1974; Frodi et al., 1977). Determining the specific mechanisms whereby anxiety affects aggression is complicated by the fact that anxiety may have inhibitory as well as activating effects on the expression of aggression. As with the other relations, our cross-sectional findings do not allow us to assign a causal link between anxiety and aggression.

Sad affect also was related to hormone levels. These findings are consistent with research on the psychoneuroendocrinology of emotions in adults. Disturbances in hypothalamic-pituitary-adrenal (Chrousos, Schuermeyer, Oldfield, Doppman, Schulte, Gold, & Loriaux, 1985; Gold & Chrousos, 1985) and hypothalamic-pituitary-gonadal (Rubinow, Roy-Byrne, & Hoban, 1985) axes functioning have been reported in individuals with clinical depression. The findings relating sad affect to specific hormones among boys should be interpreted with caution for the reasons mentioned earlier. However, the question of whether changes in hormone levels are causal factors in the appearance of depressive symptoms in adolescents is an important one. Kandel and Davies (1986) reported that feelings of dysphoria in adolescence predicted similar feelings in adulthood as well as use of habit-forming substances and problems in peer and family relationships. A question for future research is whether the degree of sensitivity to changes in hormones during puberty, when hormone changes are most dramatic, predicts affective disorders or other emotional characteristics later in the lifespan.

Pubertal stage did not relate to the emotional dispositions or the aggressive attributes. Similarly, Olweus and colleagues (1980) failed to find relations between pubertal stage and aggression. Pubertal stage was related to cognitive abilities as well as characteristics of parent-child interactions in previous studies of adolescents (Steinberg, 1981; Steinberg & Hill, 1978). In recent studies, external indices of pubertal status generally have not related to many behaviors during adolescence. When such relations are found, they tend to be small in number and inconsistent across domains of behavior (Susman et al., in press).

The complete absence of relations between hormone level and both emotional dispositions and aggressive attributes for girls was striking. One explanation for this lack of findings involves the error introduced by menstrual cycle–related variations in hormone levels. While only 35% of the girls had reached menarche, these girls were in various phases of the menstrual cycle when they participated in the study. Considerable controversy exists in the literature regarding the validity and reliability of relations between phase of the menstrual cycle and behavioral variability (Rubinow & Roy-Byrne, 1984). If phase of the menstrual cycle influences emotions and aggression, then our findings might have been influenced to an unknown extent by the variations in behavior related to phase of the menstrual cycle. Hormone-level variability even in the girls who were premenarcheal also may have affected our findings to an unknown extent. For example, level of follicle stimulating hormone shows an increase in girls as young as 7 (see Apter & Vihko, 1985, for a comprehensive longitudinal study of hormone level variations in 7–17-year-old girls).

The possibility that error is introduced by menstrual cycle–related variations in hormone levels did not negate the value of measuring hormone levels in girls. Correlations between hormone levels and pubertal stage were similar in boys and girls in this study. Furthermore, in other aspects of our larger study, hormone levels were related to behavioral measures in our sample of girls. For example, girls who were earlier maturers based on hormone levels were found to be higher on sad affect and to spend less time with peers than did later maturers (Susman et al., 1985). However, relations between hormones and behaviors were much stronger and more consistent for boys than for girls for the behaviors that we have examined. The less consistent pattern of findings for girls is also consistent with previous studies by other investigators. Marcus and colleagues (1985) found many of the correlations between neonatal sex steroid levels and behavior in early childhood for girls to be lower and nonsignificant or opposite in sign from the correlations for boys.

Our aggressive attributes failed to discriminate between males and females in level of aggression. There were no differences between males and females on rebellious and nasty attributes, the two attributes for which we could test for sex differences. Males generally are reported to be more aggressive than females (Maccoby & Jacklin, 1980), although sex differences in aggression tend to be greater in younger rather than in older children (Hyde, 1984). Females can be highly aggressive under certain circumstances, for example, those involving defense of one's young (Rose, Bernstein, Gordon, & Catlin, 1974) or those in which aggression is positively sanctioned. For many species, hormonal abnormalities or treatments also can increase aggressive behavior in females (Floody, 1983). In addition to there being no mean level difference between boys and girls on the behavioral measures, the behavioral measures were not related to hormone levels in females. Thus, we are unable to discern whether the measures were inadequate to assess aggression in females or whether aggression in females is unaffected by changes in hormone levels at puberty. It may be that levels of aggressive behavior and dominance shown by females are influenced more by social interactions and relationships than by hormonal changes (Floody, 1983; Marcus et al., 1985). Thus, males and females could show comparable overall levels of aggression but have different correlates of aggression.

In conclusion, relations between hormones and some emotional dispositions and aggressive attributes were found for boys but not for girls. This pattern of findings indicates that puberty-related hormone changes may not be as important in the development of aggression in adolescents as previously speculated. These findings, including the lack of findings for girls, need to be replicated, and future studies need to be extended to include other age groups. The influences of culture, family, and peers as moderators of hormone-aggression links also remain to be explored. Nevertheless, hormones responsible for phys-

ical and sexual development during puberty were related to emotions and the expression of aggression in early adolescent boys. These findings suggest the need for consideration of hormonal processes in future studies of the behavioral development of adolescents.

References

Abraham, G. E., Buster, J. E., Lucas, L. A., Corrales, P. C., & Teller, R. C. (1972). Chromatographic separation of steroid hormones for use in radioimmunoassay. *Analytical Letters*, **5**, 509–517.

Achenbach, T. M., & Edelbrock, C. S. (1979). The Child Behavior Profile: 2. Boys aged 12–16 and girls aged 6–11 and 12–16. *Journal of Consulting and Clinical Psychology*, **47**, 223–233.

Achenbach, T. M., & Edelbrock, C. (1983). *Manual for the Child Behavior Checklist and Revised Child Behavior Profile.* Burlington: Department of Psychiatry, University of Vermont.

Adams, D. B. (1983). Hormone-brain interactions and their influence on agonistic behavior. In B. B. Svare (Ed.), *Hormones and aggressive behavior* (pp. 223–245). New York: Plenum.

Alpert, J. E., Cohen, D. J., Shaywitz, B. A., & Piccirillo, M. (1981). Neurochemical and behavioral organization: Disorders of attention, activity, and aggression. In D. O. Lewis (Ed.), *Vulnerabilities to delinquency* (pp. 109–171). New York: Spectrum.

Anisman, H., & LaPierre, Y. D. (1982). Neurochemical aspects of stress and depression: Formulations and caveats. In R. W. Neufeld (Ed.), *Psychological stress and psychopathology* (pp. 179–217). New York: McGraw-Hill.

Apter, D., & Vihko, R. (1985). Hormonal patterns of the first menstrual cycles. In S. Venturoli, C. Flamigni, & J. R. Givens (Eds.), *Adolescence in females* (pp. 215–238). Chicago: Year Book Medical Publishers.

Bardwick, J. M. (1976). Psychological correlates of the menstrual cycle and oral contraceptive medication. In E. J. Sachar (Ed.), *Hormones, behavior, and psychopathology* (pp. 95–103). New York: Raven.

Berkowitz, L. (1964). Aggressive cues in aggressive behavior and hostility catharsis. *Psychological Review*, **71**, 104–122.

Block, J. (1971). *Lives through time.* Berkeley, CA: Bancroft.

Bouissou, M. F. (1983). Androgens, aggressive behavior and social relationships in higher mammals. *Hormone Research*, **18**, 43–61.

Brain, P. F. (Ed.). (1977). *Hormones and aggression: Vol. 1. Annual research review.* Montreal: Eden.

Cairns, R. B., MacCombie, D. J., & Hood, K. E. (1983). A developmental-genetic analysis of aggressive behavior in mice: I. Behavioral outcomes. *Journal of Comparative Psychology,* 97, 69–89.

Cargille, C. M., & Rayford, P. L. (1970). Characterization of antisera for follicle-stimulating hormone radioimmunoassay. *Journal of Laboratory and Clinical Medicine,* 75, 1030–1040.

Chrousos, G. P., Schuermeyer, T., Oldfield, E., Doppman, J., Schulte, H. M., Gold, P. W., & Loriaux, D. L. (1985). Clinical applications of corticotropin releasing factor. *Annals of Internal Medicine,* 102, 344–358.

Clark, C. R., & Nowell, N. W. (1979). The effect of the antiestrogen CI-628 on androgen-induced aggressive behavior in castrated male mice. *Hormones and Behavior,* 12, 205–210.

Cohen, J., & Cohen, P. (1975). *Applied multiple regression/correlation analysis for the behavioral sciences.* Hillsdale, NJ: Erlbaum.

Cummings, E. M., Hollenbeck, B., Iannotti, R. J., Radke-Yarrow, M., & Zahn-Waxler, C. (1986). Early organization of altruism and aggression: Developmental patterns and individual differences. In C. Zahn-Waxler, E. M. Cummings, & R. J. Iannotti (Eds.), *Altruism and aggression: Social and biological origins* (pp. 165–188). New York: Cambridge University Press.

Cunningham, S. K., Loughlin, T., Culliton, M., & McKenna, T. J. (1984). Plasma sex hormone–binding globulin levels decrease during the second decade of life irrespective of pubertal status. *Journal of Clinical Endocrinology and Metabolism,* 58, 915–918.

Cutler, G. B., Jr., Glenn, M., Bush, M., Hodgen, G., Graham, C. E., & Loriaux, D. L. (1978). Adrenarche: A survey of rodents, domestic animals and primates. *Endocrinology,* 103, 2112–2118.

de Lignieres, B., & Vincens, M. (1982). Differential effects of exogenous oestradiol and progesterone on mood in post-menopausal women: Individual dose/effect relationship. *Maturitas,* 4, 67–72.

Doering, C. H., Brodie, K. H., Kraemer, H. C., Moos, R. H., Becker, H. B., & Hamburg, D. A. (1975). Negative affect and plasma testosterone: A longitudinal human study. *Psychosomatic Medicine,* 37, 484–491.

Dunn, J. F., Nisula, B. C., & Rodbard, D. (1981). Transport of steroid hormones: Binding of 21 endogenous steroids to both testosterone-binding globulin and corticosteroid-binding globulin in human plasma. *Journal of Clinical Endocrinology and Metabolism,* 53, 58–67.

Ehrenkranz, J., Bliss, E., & Sheard, M. H. (1974). Plasma testosterone: Correlation with aggressive behavior and social dominance in man. *Psychosomatic Medicine,* 36, 469–475.

Eleftheriou, B. E., & Sprott, R. L. (1975). *Hormonal correlates of behavior: Vol. 1. A lifespan view.* New York: Plenum.

Ellis, L. (1982). Developmental androgen fluctuations and the five dimensions of the mammalian sex (with emphasis upon the behavioral dimension and the human species). *Endocrinology and Sociobiology,* 3, 171–197.

Floody, O. R. (1983). Hormones and aggression in female mammals. In B. B. Svare (Ed.), *Hormones and aggressive behavior* (pp. 39–89). New York: Plenum.

Fonberg, E. (1979). Physiological mechanisms of emotional and instrumental aggression. In S. Feshbach & A. Fraczek (Eds.), *Aggression and behavior change: Biological and social processes* (pp. 6–53). New York: Praeger.

Fregly, M. J., & Luttge, W. G. (1982). *Human endocrinology: An interactive text.* New York: Elsevier Biomedical.

Friedman, R. C., Richart, R. M., & Vande Wiele, R. L. (Eds.). (1974). *Sex differences in behavior.* New York: Wiley.

Frodi, A., Macaulay, J., & Thome, P. R. (1977). Are women always less aggressive than men? A review of the experimental literature. *Psychological Bulletin,* 84, 634–660.

Gandelman, R. (1980). Gonadal hormones and the induction of intraspecific fighting in mice. *Neuroscience & Biobehavioral Reviews,* 4, 133–140.

Gold, P. W., & Chrousos, G. P. (1985). Clinical studies with corticotropin releasing factor: Implications for the diagnosis and pathophysiology of depression, Cushing's disease and adrenal insufficiency. *Psychoneuroendocrinology,* 10, 401–419.

Hays, S. (1981). The psychoendocrinology of puberty and adolescent aggression. In D. A. Hamburg & M. B. Trudeau (Eds.), *Biobehavioral aspects of aggression* (pp. 107–119). New York: Liss.

Hines, M. (1982). Prenatal gonadal hormones and sex differences in human behavior. *Psychological Bulletin,* 92, 56–80.

Hollingshead, A. B. (1975). *Four-factor index of social status.* New Haven, CT: Yale University.

Houser, B. B. (1979). An investigation of the correlation between hormonal levels in males and mood, behavior, and physical discomfort. *Hormones and Behavior,* 12, 185–197.

Hyde, J. S. (1984). How large are gender differences in aggression? A developmental meta-analysis. *Developmental Psychology,* 20, 722–736.

Kandel, D., & Davies, M. (1986). Adult sequelae of adolescent depressive symptoms. *Archives of General Psychiatry,* 43, 255–262.

Kelly, D. D. (1981). Sexual differentiation of the nervous system. In E. R. Kandel & T. H.

Schwartz (Eds.), *Principles of neural science* (pp. 533–546). North Holland: Elsevier.

Leshner, A. I. (1983). Pituitary-adrenocortical effects on intermale agonistic behavior. In B. B. Svare (Ed.), *Hormones and aggressive behavior* (pp. 27–38). New York: Plenum.

Lloyd, J. A. (1975). Social behavior and hormones. In B. E. Eleftheriou & R. L. Sprott (Eds.), *Hormonal correlates of behavior: Vol. 1. A life-span view* (pp. 185–197). New York: Plenum.

Maccoby, E. E., Doering, C. H., Jacklin, C. N., & Kraemer. H. (1979). Concentrations of sex hormones in umbilical-cord blood: Their relation to sex and birth order of infants. *Child Development, 50,* 632–642.

Maccoby, E. E., & Jacklin, C. N. (1974). *The psychology of sex differences.* Stanford, CA: Stanford University Press.

Maccoby, E. E., & Jacklin, C. N. (1980). Sex differences in aggression: A rejoinder and reprise. *Child Development, 51,* 964–980.

Marcus, J., Maccoby, E. E., Jacklin, C. N., & Doering, C. H. (1985). Individual differences in mood in early childhood: Their relation to gender and neonatal sex steroids. *Developmental Psychobiology, 18,* 327–340.

Marshall, W. A., & Tanner, J. M. (1969). Variations in the pattern of pubertal changes in girls. *Archives of Disease in Childhood, 44,* 291–303.

Marshall, W. A., & Tanner, J. M. (1970). Variations in the pattern of pubertal changes in boys. *Archives of Disease in Childhood, 45,* 13–23.

Mattsson, A., Schalling, D., Olweus, D., Low, H., & Svensson, J. (1980). Plasma testosterone, aggressive behavior, and personality dimensions in young male delinquents. *Journal of the American Academy of Child Psychiatry, 19,* 476–490.

Mazur, A., & Lamb, T. A. (1980). Testosterone, status and mood in human males. *Hormones and Behavior, 14,* 236–246.

Nieschlag, E., & Loriaux, D. L. (1972). Radioimmunoassay for plasma testosterone. *Zeitschrift fuer Klinische Chemie und Klinische Biochemie, 10,* 164–168.

Nottelmann, E. D., Susman, E. J., Blue, J. H., Inoff-Germain, G., Dorn, L. D., Loriaux, D. L., Cutler, G. B., Jr., & Chrousos, G. P. (1987a). Gonadal and adrenal hormone correlates of adjustment in early adolescence. In R. M. Lerner & T. T. Foch (Eds.), *Biological-psychosocial interactions in early adolescence: A life-span perspective.* Hillsdale, NJ: Erlbaum.

Nottelmann, E. D., Susman, E. J., Dorn, L. D., Inoff-Germain, G., Loriaux, D. L., Cutler, G. B., Jr., & Chrousos, G. P. (1987b). Developmental processes in early adolescence: Relations among chronologic age, pubertal stage, height, weight, and serum levels of gonadotropins, sex steroids, and adrenal androgens. *Journal of Adolescent Health Care, 8,* 35–48.

Odell, W. D., Ross, G. T., & Rayford, P. L. (1967). Radioimmunoassay for luteinizing hormone in human plasma or serum: Physiological studies. *Journal of Clinical Investigation, 46,* 248–255.

Offer, D., Ostrov, E., & Howard, K. I. (1977). *The Offer Self-Image Questionnaire for Adolescents: A manual.* Chicago: Michael Reese Hospital.

Offer, D., Ostrov, E., & Howard, K. I. (1984). The self-image of normal adolescents. *New Directions for Mental Health Services, 22,* 5–17.

Olweus, D., Mattsson, A., Schalling, D., & Low, H. (1980). Testosterone, aggression, physical, and personality dimensions in normal adolescent males. *Psychosomatic Medicine, 42,* 253–269.

Persky, H., Smith, K. D., & Basu, G. K. (1971). Relation of psychologic measures of aggression and hostility to testosterone production in man. *Psychosomatic Medicine, 33,* 265–277.

Phoenix, C. H., Goy, R. W., Gerall, A. A., & Young, W. C. (1959). Organizing actions of prenatally administered testosterone propionate on the tissues mediating mating behavior in the female guinea pig. *Endocrinology, 65,* 369–382.

Puig-Antich, J. (1986). Psychological markers: Effects of age and puberty. In M. Rutter, C. E. Izard, & P. B. Read (Eds.), *Depression in young people: Developmental and clinical perspectives* (pp. 341–381). New York: Guilford.

Rose, R., & Sachar, E. (1981). Psychoendocrinology. In R. H. Williams (Ed.), *Textbook of endocrinology* (pp. 646–669). Philadelphia: Saunders.

Rose, R., Bernstein, I. S., Gordon, T. P., & Catlin, S. F. (1974). Androgens and aggression: A review and recent findings in perspective. In R. L. Holloway (Ed.), *Primate aggression, territoriality, and xenophobia: A comparative perspective.* New York: Academic Press.

Rose, R. M., Bernstein, I. S., Gordon, T. P., & Lindsley, J. G. (1978). Changes in testosterone and behavior during adolescence in the male Rhesus monkey. *Psychosomatic Medicine, 40,* 60–70.

Rubin, R. T., Reinisch, J. M., & Haskett, R. F. (1981). Postnatal gonadal steroid effects on human behavior. *Science, 211,* 1318–1324.

Rubinow, D. R., & Roy-Byrne, P. (1984). Premenstrual syndromes: Overview from a methodologic perspective. *American Journal of Psychiatry, 141,* 163–172.

Rubinow, D. R., Roy-Byrne, P., & Hoban, M. C. (1985). Menstrually related mood disorders: Methodological and conceptual issues. In M. Y. Dalwood, J. L. McGuire, & L. M. Demers (Eds.), *Premenstrual syndrome and dysmenorrhea* (pp. 27–40). Baltimore: Urban & Schwartzenberg.

Sachar, E. J. (Ed.). (1980). Advances in psycho-neuroendocrinology. *Psychiatric Clinics of North America*, 3, 203–368.

Scaramella, T. J., & Brown, W. A. (1978). Serum testosterone and aggressiveness in hockey players. *Psychosomatic Medicine*, 40, 262–265.

Schlain, E. A. (1976). A factor analytic study of three aspects of aggression: Assertiveness, hostility, and self-control. *Dissertation Abstracts International*, 37(2-B), 961–962.

Siris, S. G., Siris, E. S., Van Kammen, D. P., Docherty, J. P., Alexander, P. E., & Bunney, W. E., Jr. (1980). Effects of dopamine blockade on gonadotropins and testosterone in men. *American Journal of Psychiatry*, 137, 211–214.

Sizonenko, P. C. (1978). Endocrinology in preadolescents and adolescents: I. Hormonal changes during normal puberty. *American Journal of Diseases of Childhood*, 132, 704–712.

Steinberg, L. D. (1981). Transformations in family relations at puberty. *Developmental Psychology*, 17, 833–840.

Steinberg, L. W., & Hill, J. P. (1978). Patterns of family interaction as a function of age, the onset of puberty, and formal thinking. *Developmental Psychology*, 14, 683–684.

Susman, E. J., Nottelmann, E. D., Inoff, G. E., Dorn, L. D., Cutler, G. B., Jr., Loriaux, D. L., & Chrousos, G. P. (1985). The relation of relative hormonal levels and physical development and social-emotional behavior in young adoles-

cents. *Journal of Youth and Adolescence*, 14, 245–264.

Susman, E. J., Nottelmann, E. D., Inoff-Germain, G., Dorn, L. D., & Chrousos, G. P. (in press). Hormonal influences on aspects of psychological development during adolescence. *Journal of Adolescent Health Care*.

Tieger, T. (1980). On the biological basis of sex differences in aggression. *Child Development*, 51, 943–963.

Van de Poll, N. E., Smeets, J., Van Oyen, H. G., & van der Zwan, S. M. (1982). Behavioral consequences of agonistic experience in rats: Sex differences and the effects of testosterone. *Journal of Comparative and Physiological Psychology*, 96, 893–903.

Vihko, R., & Apter, D. (1980). The role of androgens in adolescent cycles. *Journal of Steroid Biochemistry*, 12, 369–373.

Weisfeld, G. E., & Berger, J. M. (1983). Some features of human adolescence viewed in evolutionary perspective. *Human Development*, 26, 121–133.

Williams, R. H. (Ed.). (1981). *Textbook of Endocrinology*. Philadelphia: Saunders.

Young, W. C., Goy, R. W., & Phoenix, C. H. (1964). Hormones and sexual behavior. *Science*, 143, 212–218.

Zuckerman, M., & Lubin B. (1965). *Multiple Affect Adjective Check List, Today Form*. San Diego: Educational and Industrial Testing Service.

232

Journal of Youth and Adolescence, Vol. 14, No. 4, 1985

Biological Maturation and Social Development: A Longitudinal Study of Some Adjustment Processes from Mid-Adolescence to Adulthood

David Magnusson,[1] Håkan Stattin,[2] and Vernon L. Allen[3]

The role of biological maturity in behaviors in adolescence which most often are considered as negative by adults was investigated for a normal group of girls. In mid-adolescence early matured girls were found to play truant, smoke hashish, get drunk, pilfer, ignore parents' prohibitions, considerably more often than did late maturing girls. These differences between biological age groups were mediated by the association with older peer groups and they leveled out in late adolescence. Data on alcohol consumption and crime at adult age showed little association with biological maturation. A hypothesis was tested suggesting that early biological maturation may have negative long-term consequences within the education domain. In accord with this assumption, a considerably smaller percentage of girls among the early maturers had a theoretical education above the obligatory nine-year compulsory schooling than among the late maturing girls. The association between biological maturation and adult education was significant also after controlling for standard predictors of education, such as the girls' intelligence and the social status of the home. The requirement of conducting longitudinal studies when investigating issues connected with maturation was strongly emphasized.

The research presented here was supported by funds to D. Magnusson from the Swedish Terecentenary Foundation and the Swedish Council for Planning and Coordination of Research.
[1]Department of Psychology, University of Stockholm. Received Ph.D. from the University of Stockholm. Current research interest is development.
[2]Department of Psychology, University of Stockholm. Received Ph.D. from University of Stockholm. Current research interest is development.
[3]Department of Psychology, University of Wisconsin – Madison. Received Ph.D. from University of California at Berkeley. Current research interest is Social psychology.

0047-2891/85/0800-0267$04.50/0 © 1985 Plenum Publishing Corporation

INTRODUCTION

Researchers have become increasingly aware of the complex interplay of biological, psychological, and social factors during adolescence (cf. Magnusson and Allen, 1983; Petersen and Taylor, 1980). In their review of the psychological impact of menarche, Greif and Ullman (1982) concluded with a plea for network analyses as the appropriate way to describe this complex interactive system. The present study, which reports on the relation between biological maturity and norm-breaking behavior, represents such an interactive approach. Consideration is given to the role of social factors in mediating the influence of biological maturity on norm violations, and an attempt is made to determine the conditions under which we can expect the relation to occur. The study also investigates how factors in one sector of the total organization of the individual have short- and long-term repercussions on other sectors.

The empirical portion of the study has three purposes: (1) The first purpose is to present data concerning the influence of biological maturity on teenage behaviors that often are assumed to indicate a risk of further negative social adjustment. Norm violations in mid-adolescence will be investigated for girls at varying levels of biological maturity. (2) Second, in order to elucidate factors that mediate the influence of biological maturation on norm-breaking behaviors, peer relations will be introduced as a moderating factor. (3) To provide illustrations of the short-term changes that occur during adolescence as well as the long-term consequences of differential maturation, data on alcohol use will be analyzed for two occasions in the adolescent period and for a later occasion in adulthood. The search for alternative pathways to adult adjustment will introduce the educational career of the girls as a probable outcome domain.

METHOD

Subjects

The subjects in the present study belong to a group of 1025 individuals who have been followed by repeated data collection from their early school years up into adulthood (Magnusson, *et al.,* 1975).[4] They consist of com-

---

[4]A more extensive presentation and discussion of the research are given in Magnusson *et al.* (in press).

plete school-grade cohort — all pupils who in 1965 (at the age of 10) attended grade 3 of the compulsory school in a mid-Swedish town of about 100,000 inhabitants. All types of schooling within the ordinary school system that year are represented. Less than 1% of the children in the town did not attend the ordinary school system because of severe problems (e.g., severely retarded children or psychotic children). These latter children are not included in the present research. Thus, a very wide range of social and psychological upbringing conditions are included. Studies within the project have shown the group of children to be representative of pupils in the compulsory school system in Sweden (see Bergman, 1973; Magnusson *et al.,* 1975).

The present research group consists of the girls for whom complete menarcheal data were obtained when they were about 15 years of age (in grade 8) in 1970. A total of 588 girls were registered in the school, and data on menarche was obtained for the 509 girls present at school on the days the data were collected. Most of the 509 girls in grade 8 were born in 1955; however, 1.9% were early school starters (born in 1954), and 8.4% were late school starters or pupils who had not moved in the ordinary manner up to the next class. The present investigation is based only on girls in grade 8 who were born in 1955 (466 girls) in order to control for chronological age.[5]

Data

Age at Menarche. Age at menarche was measured by an item in a questionnaire administered in April 1970, when the average age of the girls was 14:10 yrs.[6] The median age of the self-reported menarche was 12.86 years, which corresponds closely to national figures for this age cohort (Lindgren, 1976).

The girls were grouped into four menarcheal groups: (1) menarche before the age of 11, (2) menarche between the ages of 11 and 12, (3) menarche between the ages of 12 and 13, and (4) menarche after the age of 13.

Norm Violations. Data on norm violations were collected at the average age of 14:5 years. At that time the girls answered a norm instrument asking about different situations (see Magnusson, 1981). Several concrete norm-breaking situations were listed. They covered descriptions of violations of norms at home — (1) ignore parents' prohibitions, (2) stay out late without permission; at school — (3) cheat on an exam, (4) play truant; and during leisure time — (5) smoke hashish, (6) get drunk, (7) loiter in town every evening, and

---

[5]An empirical calculation indicated that there were no differences in chronological age among girls grouped according to age at menarche.
[6]References to chronological age use colons to denote average year and month, so that 14:10 years indicates 14 years, 10 months.

(8) pilfer from a shop. Subjects' answers about their actual breaches of norms of this type were analyzed for how many times they had violated rules of the type that the situations describe up to time when the instrument was administered. Answers were given on 5-point Likert scales with the alternatives (1) never, (2) once, (3) 2–3 times, (4) 4–10 times, and (5) more than 10 times (see Magnusson *et al.*, 1975, pp. 100–103).

Peer Evaluations. For each of the listed situations, subjects were asked to state their peers' evaluations of norm breaking. It was stated in the instrument that "By 'peers' we mean those whose opinion you care most about, whether they are in your class, in a gang, or your best friend." After the description of a situation, the specific instruction was "Here you should say what you think your peers think about cheating (etc.). My peers think it is . . . ." The answers were given on 7-point scales with the alternatives (1) "very silly," (2) "silly," (3) "rather silly," (4) "not really OK," (5) "rather OK," (6) "OK," and (7) "quite OK."

Expected Peer Sanctions. Subjects also stated the expected sanctions from their peers if they violated norms of the type the situation described. For expected peer sanctions, the following question was asked: "How do you think your peers would react if they found out that you had cheated (etc.)?" Answers were given on 5-point scales with the alternatives (1) "they would certainly disapprove," (2) "they would probably disapprove," (3) "I am not sure how they would react," (4) "They would probably not care," and (5) "They would certainly not care."

Alcohol Use. Data on alcohol use were obtained for the number of times the subject had been drunk. The question was asked at age 14:5 years in the norm inventory described above and again in a pupil's questionnaire given at age 15:10 years. In connection with a follow-up assessment at adult age, when the girls were 25:10 years old on the average, data on alcohol consumption was collected by a mailed questionnaire covering educational-vocational career, family life, working conditions, social networks, and leisure time activities (Andersson *et al.*, 1982). Two questions concerned alcohol habits— how often the subjects drank alcohol, and how much they consumed on occasions when they drank the most.

Adult Educational Level. Data for attained level of education at an average age of 25:10 years were obtained by a questionnaire. Data were coded into four categories: (1) compulsory school education; (2) higher secondary school education, practical; (3) higher secondary school education, theoretical; and (4) academic and college education.

RESULTS

Biological Maturation and Norm Breaking During Adolescence

In dealing with the issue of social maladaptation in adolescence, the conventional procedure in empirical research has been to view norm breaking at a particular point as an individual difference variable and relate it to other information about the individuals under study. Causes of norm breaking have then been sought in ecological factors, upbringing conditions, social networks, school adjustment, person-bound factors, and so on (see Brooks-Gunn and Petersen, 1983; Jessor and Jessor, 1977). However, when comparing subjects of the same chronological age with each other and relating these individual differences to concurrent and later data, we cannot be certain that at the occasion in question we are measuring the same psychological processes across individuals. Research on physical growth has made clear that the assumption of homogeneous development does not always hold true; hence, chronological age cannot be used as the only meaningful reference scale for development (Goldstein, 1979; Magnusson, 1985; Peskin, 1967).

The starting point for the empirical research presented here was a study (Magnusson and Stattin, 1982) testing the hypothesis that some social behaviors that typically start in adolescence are related to biological maturation, meaning that physical growth is paralleled by accompanying changes in social life, so that early biological maturation corresponds to an earlier display of these social behaviors. This hypothesis implies that obtained individual differences in adjustment among girls at a particular age in the adolescent period partly represent biological time-lag effects.

The relation between biological maturation (measured by age of menarche) and norm violations at the age of 14:5 years is presented in Tables I and II. Table I presents means of norm breaches for girls subdivided into four menarcheal groups, together with statistical tests of differences among the four groups of girls. Table II shows the percentage of girls in each of the four groups who reported frequent norm breaking (four times or more) for each situation.

Table I shows a clear-cut association between age of biological maturation and frequency of norm breaking, and indicates that variations in norm violations at the time of testing are highly related to the girls' physical maturation. As can be seen in Table II, a considerably higher percentage of early than of late maturing girls reported frequent violations of norms. It is also

Table I. Means on Norm breaking for Four Menarcheal Groups of Girls

Norm breaking	Age at menarche (years)				F	p
	-11 ($n = 48$)	11-12 ($n = 98$)	12-13 ($n = 178$)	13- ($n = 112$)	($df = 3, 432$)	
Home						
Ignore parents' prohibitions	2.40	1.93	1.89	1.89	4.84	<0.01
Stay out late without per-						
mission	2.67	2.08	1.96	1.74	9.96	<0.001
School						
Cheat on an exam	2.19	2.05	2.09	2.00	0.48	ns
Play truant	2.77	2.08	1.74	1.74	12.40	<0.001
Leisure time						
Smoke hashish	1.13	1.04	1.01	1.01	6.65	<0.001
Get drunk	2.65	2.14	1.75	1.54	11.43	<0.001
Loiter in town every evening	2.23	2.05	2.01	1.75	2.69	<0.05
Pilfer from a shop	2.02	1.64	1.59	1.50	3.64	<0.05
Total	2.23	1.88	1.76	1.63	10.57	<0.001

Table II. Percentage of Girls in Different Menarche Groups Reporting Frequent Norm Breaking at Age 14:5 Years

	Age at menarche (years)			
	−11 (*n* = 48)	11–12 (*n* = 98)	12–13 (*n* = 178)	13– (*n* = 112)
Home				
Ignore parents' prohibitions	16.7	7.1	2.8	3.6
Stay out late without permission	27.1	12.2	5.6	4.5
School				
Cheat on an exam	17.0	5.1	5.1	7.3
Play truant	39.6	14.3	5.6	7.1
Leisure time				
Smoke hashish	12.0	4.1	1.1	0.9
Get drunk	35.4	20.0	7.9	6.3
Loiter in town every evening	20.8	9.1	8.5	3.6
Pilfer from a shop	14.6	5.2	4.5	1.8

obvious that the relationship is not linear: The earliest developing group of girls differed markedly in mean and frequency of norm breaches from the groups of later developing girls.

Older Friends as Social Mediators

An empirically documented relation between individual variations in age at menarche and frequency of norm violations in adolescence leads us to examine the nature of the factors that contribute to the connection, since a direct causal link is unlikely to exist between bodily or hormonal changes and social behaviors. Rather, the effect is most likely to be mediated by an environment that changes as a consequence of changes in the individual. This proposition requires some form of mediation of the effects of physical maturity.

An early maturing girl will probably be considered older than she actually is. The expectations and demands placed upon her will be different from those placed on her late maturing peers. One can expect the early maturing girl to associate more with chronologically older persons, signifying new and more advanced habits and leisure-time activities. In her association with older peers, the girls may encounter the more tolerant attitudes towards norm breaking that characterize older groups of teenagers. Through association with them, she will more often confront situations that may lead to rule breaking and also encounter more positive attitudes towards norm violations.

For the group of girls in the present study, Magnusson *et al.* (in press) showed that the early maturing girls sought and were sought by others who were congruent with their early biological stage of maturity. Seventy-four percent of the earliest maturing girls reported having older companions, while only 39% of the latest maturing girls said they had older friends at age 14:5 years. Results also showed that the earliest and the latest developed girls tended to prefer other girls in terms of how they matched their own level of biological maturity. Third, the early maturing girls were found to be considerably more advanced in their contacts with the opposite sex. Eighty-three percent of the early maturing girls had been or were going steady with a boy, in comparison with 52% of the late maturing group of girls. Moreover, more than four times (45%) as many girls among the earliest maturing than among the latest maturing girls (77%) had had sexual intercourse with boys at age 14:5 years. Both relationships yielded high levels of significance ($p < 0.001$).

The finding that early maturing girls were more oriented towards older age groups of peers (and towards same-age girls more congruent with their early maturity) suggests the hypothesis that the relationship between early maturation and high norm breaking is mediated by the association with more mature, older peers. If this is the case, the impact of such an association should be stronger for very early maturing girls than for later maturing girls.

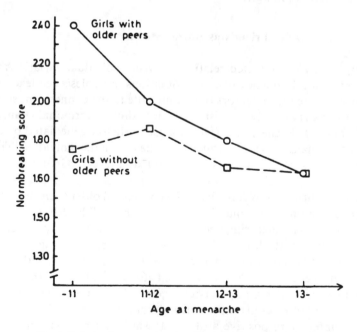

Fig. 1. Relation between norm breaking and menarcheal age for girls with and without older friends.

240

In Figure 1, the relation between norm breaking and menarcheal age is shown for girls with and for girls without older friends. The statistical analysis revealed a significant mean difference between the two groups ($p < 0.01$). For girls who reported having no older friends at age 14:5 yrs, there was no significant difference in norm breaking among the menarcheal groups $F(3, 176) = 1.31$, n.s. However, a clear and significant difference in norm violations among the menarcheal groups was found for girls who reported having older friends ($F(3, 183) = 9.14$, $p < 0.001$). In accord with the hypothesis, the difference in means between girls with and girls without older friends is mainly explained by the difference between very early maturing girls with and very early maturing girls without older friends ($p = 0.059$), which illuminates the results reported in Tables I and II, showing that the group of very early maturing girls differed from the other groups in both frequency and intensity of norm breaking. For the other menarcheal groups, the difference was in the expected direction—having older friends was associated with more norm breaking—but the differences were small and insignificant. For the latest maturing group of girls, the means for norm breaking were actually the same for girls with and girls without older friends.

Friends as Norm Transmitters. The role that friends play as norm transmitters—how the girls perceive their friends' evaluations of norm breaking and the sanctions they expect from friends after their own norm violations—comes into focus against the background of friends' roles as social mediators of maturational influences on behavior. For the girls' judgments of their peers' evaluations of norm breaking, there were no differences between the four menarcheal groups of girls, $F(3, 395) = 1.11$, n.s., suggesting that girls generally are confronted by similar evaluative systems among their peers. On the other hand, the results on expected peer sanctions show the pattern found for the relations between biological maturity and norm violation frequency. Biologically early maturing girls expected weaker sanctions after breaches of norms than did late maturing girls, $F(3, 370) = 3.18$, $p < 0.01$. When chronological age of friends was introduced as a moderator variable, the relation between biological maturity and expected peer sanctions appeared only for girls with older peers (girls with older friends: $F(3, 138) = 4.65$, $p < 0.004$. Girls without older friends; $F(3, 176) = 0.17$, n.s. The results are depicted in Figure 2.)

Longitudinal Implications of Differential Maturation

The results covering mid-adolescence indicate that early maturing girls form a group at higher risk of later social maladaptation. The higher norm violation frequency among early maturing girls might possibly be associated with a lasting pattern of deviance. On the other hand, we may argue that

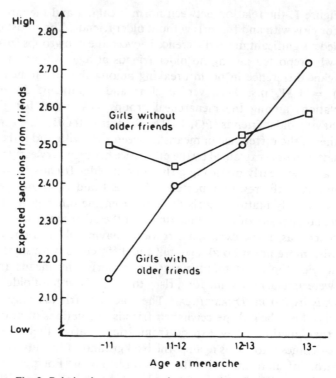

Fig. 2. Relation between expected peer sanctions for norm breaking and menarcheal age for girls with and without older friends.

differences in norm breaking among the menarcheal groups at age 14:5 years are of a temporary nature, merely indicating that some girls enter the normal process of transition in norms earlier than others. Thus, girls pass through a time of liberation from parents and a time of change in norms, roles, and reference groups; but early maturing girls pass through this phase at an earlier time than do their late maturing peers. In this latter case, we would expect the late maturing girls to catch up with the early developing girls at a later time.

To elucidate this problem for one type of behavior, data on use of alcohol have been analyzed from two age points in adolescence, separated by 17 months. Table III presents data on alcohol use at the age of 14:5 years; the same type of data collected at 15:10 years are shown in Table IV.

These tables contain interesting information regarding trends over time for the total group of girls and also regarding intergroup comparisons. As expected, more girls had been drunk at the later test occasion. At age 14:5 years about 40% of girls reported having been drunk. At age 15:10 years the figure was 70%.

Table III. Percentage of Girls in Four Menarcheal Groups with Varying Frequency of Drunkenness up to Age 14:5 years[a]

	Frequency of drunkenness						
	Never	Once	2–3 times	4–10 times	>10 times	N	%
Age at menarche (years)							
−11	37.5	12.5	14.6	18.8	16.7	48	11.0
11–12	51.0	13.3	15.3	11.2	9.2	98	22.5
12–13	62.1	13.0	16.9	3.4	4.5	177	40.7
13–	71.4	10.7	11.6	4.5	1.8	122	25.7
N	258	54	65	31	27	435	
%	59.3	12.4	14.9	7.1	6.2		

[a] $\chi^2(12, N = 435) = 39.88$, $p < 0.001$.

The net increase for the categories of excessive drinking was about the same for early and late maturing girls from the age of 14:5 years to 15:10 years. For example, in the earliest maturing group, the percentage who had been drunk more than 10 times increased from 16.7% to 40% over the 17-month period. For the latest maturing group girls, the increase was from 1.8% to 23%.

Despite the equality in net increase of excessive drinking, a tendency can be discerned for the late maturing girls to catch up with the earlier ones with respect to drinking *per se*. The proportion of girls moving from never having been drunk to having been drunk at least once is considerably higher for the late maturing girls (from 28.6% to 64.7%) than for the late maturing girls (from 62.5% to 75%). Thus, in terms of moderate drinking, the spurt for the late maturing girls came during this 17-month period.

Table IV. Percentage of Girls in Four Menarcheal Groups with Varying Frequency of Drunkenness up to Age 15:10 years[a]

	Frequency of drunkenness						
	Never	Once	2–3 times	4–10 times	>10 times		
Age at menarche (years)							
−11	25.0	7.5	5.0	22.5	40.0	40	9.3
11–12	25.7	5.9	18.8	20.8	28.7	101	23.5
12–13	29.4	10.0	19.4	18.8	22.4	170	39.5
13–	35.3	9.2	20.2	11.8	23.5	119	27.7
N	128	37	78	76	111	430	
%	29.8	8.6	18.1	17.7	25.8		

[a] $\chi^2(12, N = 430) = 15.71$, $p < 0.02$.

A complementary two-way ANOVA was computed with test occasion as a trial factor and menarcheal age as a grouping factor. The dependent variable (drunkenness) was dichotomized, with subjects who had not been drunk scoring 0 and subjects being drunk at least once coded 1. There was a significant main effect of menarcheal age ($F = 3.44$, $p < 0.05$) and of test occasion ($F = 104.97$, $p < 0.001$). In addition there was a significant interaction between test occasions and menarcheal age ($F = 2.59$, $p \leq 0.05$), reflecting the catching up in drunkenness over time by the late maturing girls.

Table V shows the self-reported data at adult age (25:10 years) for frequency of alcohol consumption as related to age of menarche. No significant relation remains at adult age when frequency of alcohol consumption is used as the dependent measure. (This is the case also for amount of alcohol consumed; see Magnusson, et al., in press). The most frequent drinkers come from the group of very late maturing girls as often as from the group of very early maturing girls. The results agree with the data presented at age 15:10 years, which indicated that differences among the menarcheal groups of girls for alcohol use occur for a limited period during adolescence, but do not persist into adulthood.

A broader analysis of the issue of the persistence of norm breaking behavior has been performed by Magnusson et al. (in press). They compared early and late maturing girls with respect to registered crime up to age 26. There was a slight tendency for the early maturing girls to be overrepresented among the girls with criminal records. However, overall the results failed to provide strong evidence for the argument that menarcheal age is connected with crime in adulthood.

Alternative Pathways to Adult Social Adjustment

Are there alternative pathways that adjustment problems in mid-adolescence might take in the long run? Two observations from the data,

Table V. Alcohol Comsumption at Age 25:10 years for Girls in Four Menarcheal Groups[a]

	Frequency of alcohol consumption				
	Never	Sometimes	At least weekly	N	%
Age at menarche (years)					
–11	5.7	82.9	11.4	35	9.9
11–12	7.1	79.8	13.1	84	23.8
12–13	9.0	75.2	15.9	145	41.1
13–	11.2	77.5	11.2	89	25.2
N	31	274	48	353	
%	8.8	77.6	13.6		

[a]$\chi^2(6, N = 353) = 2.58$, ns.

Table VI. Level of Education at Adult Age for Girls in Four Menarcheal Groups[a]

Age at menarche (years)	Academic or college education	Higher secondary school, theoretical	Higher secondary school, practical	Compulsory school education	N
-11	1 (2.3)	11 (25.6)	13 (30.2)	18 (41.9)	43 (10.4)
11-12	13 (13.0)	39 (39.0)	20 (20.0)	28 (28.0)	100 (24.2)
12-13	21 (12.7)	86 (51.8)	25 (15.1)	34 (20.5)	166 (40.1)
13-	16 (15.2)	47 (44.8)	19 (18.1)	23 (21.9)	105 (25.4)
Total	51 (12.3)	183 (44.2)	77 (18.6)	103 (24.9)	414

[a] $\chi^2(9, N = 414) = 21.83$, $p < 0.009$. Percentages are given in parentheses.

when the subjects were in compulsory school, suggest that long-term effects may occur in the educational-vocational domain. First, as shown in Tables I and II, early maturing girls violated school regulations more often than did late maturing girls. Second, greater school maladjustment among early maturing girls was found in an earlier study within the longitudinal project (Andersson, *et al.,* 1980). When a group of early maturing girls were compared with a normative control group of the same chronological age on various aspects of school adjustment at ages 13 and 15, early maturing girls at both ages were found to show more negative attitudes towards school and schoolwork, and they were rated more unfavorably by their teachers. Similar findings (Davies, 1977; Frisk, *et al.,* 1966; Simmons, *et al.,* 1979, 1983) suggest that long-term consequences may be found in the further education of the girls. Therefore, the educational status in adult life was compared among the menarcheal groups of girls (see Table VI).

As can be seen in Table VI, there were marked differences among the four menarcheal groups of girls in level of education at adult age. The difference among the groups of girls was significant at a high level ($p < 0.01$). Most striking is that a minority of the most early developing girls (27.9%) had some form of theoretical education above the obligatory nine-year compulsory schooling, while a majority of the latest developing girls (60.0%) had such an education. Only 2.3% of the earliest maturing girls entered college or university in comparison to 12% to 15% of the rest of the girls. Elsewhere (Magnusson *et al.,* in press) control analyses have been performed investigating the unique contribution of menarcheal age to the variation in adult education status over and above other standard predictors of educational achievement — the educational status of the parents and the girls' intelligence. With the latter measures obtained at the age of 10, a stepwise multiple regression yielded a multiple correlation of 0.49 ($p < 0.001$). A partial correlation coefficient of 0.15 ($p < 0.01$) between menarcheal age and adult education (controlling for intelligence and educational status of the home) indicated that most of the variance that menarcheal age had with adult education was unique. (The original condition was 0.17.)

DISCUSSION

Three issues have been empirically studied: (1) the role of biological maturation in norm-breaking behavior among girls during puberty; (2) peer relations as social mediators and modifiers in the socialization process; and (3) the short- and long-term consequences for behavior of early biological maturation. At the time of the test occasion in mid-adolescence (at the age of 14:5 years), early maturing girls were found to have violated various types of norms considerably more frequently than their late maturing peers. The hypothesis we advanced suggested that biological maturity is related to social adjustment processes via the characteristics of one's circle of peers. In accord with the hypothesis, differences in norm violations among girls with different levels of maturity occurred for girls who had formed close contacts with older and more mature peers; the impact of having older friends was concentrated in the group of very early maturing girls. Illuminating the role of friends as norms transmitters, the girls' conception of their peers' sanctions after own norm violation was found to have the same pattern found for the relation between biological maturity and norm violation frequency.

The third problem investigated was the important question of the longitudinal implications of the impact of menarche. In the short-term perspective, results on one behavior — alcohol use — showed that the strong relation found at age 14:5 years between biological maturity and frequency of drunkenness was considerably weaker by the age of 15:10 years. At adult age no systematic relation with alcohol consumption existed for age of menarche. The same lack of a strong relation to the age of menarche was demonstrated for registered criminal offences up to age 26 by Magnusson, *et al.* (in press).

The absence of systematic long-term consequences in these respects suggests that the higher frequency of norm breaking among early developing girls is not a risk factor for later social maladaptation, but mirrors the approximation of an adult status by these girls earlier than by the late maturing girls. Further support for this acquisition of adult social role model, rather than the deviant model, has been reported by Magnusson *et al.* (in press). They found early maturing girls to consider themselves considerably more mature at age 14:5 years, more romantic, and more looking forward to giving birth to and bringing up their own children. Similarly, Simmons *et al.* (1983) showed that early developers were allowed greater independence from their parents than the late developers, and that early maturing girls took greater responsibility for household activities by babysitting more than did their late developing counterparts.

Investigating the alternative pathways of adjustment problems in adolescence revealed a systematic relationship with the age of menarche for the educational careers of the girls. This finding can be interpreted as a function of the greater influence of the peer culture (especially older peers) on the early developing girls in the adolescent years. Devoting more time to steady contacts with boys and to more intimate relations (sexual relations), viewing themselves as more mature and wanting to bring up their own children, the early developing girls are more likely to engage in activities such as family life than to aspire to higher education, compared to the late maturing girls.

Similar conclusions were arrived at by Simmons *et al.* (1979, 1983). An alternative but related interpretation is that the older peer group with which the early maturing girls associate in mid-adolescence holds lower educational aspirations than do the peers of the late maturing girls.

The results in the present study have some basic implications for developmental research. The study demonstrates, in a very decisive way, the necessity of following the same individuals over a considerable time (i.e., longitudinal research) in order to understand the process involved in individual development. Given the nature of the developmental process, there is no adequate alternative to longitudinal research for the study of many important problems (cf. McCall, 1977; Wohlwill, 1970). A natural consequence of an interactionist perspective on development is also the interest in the individual as a totality, simultaneously incorporating a psycho-bio-social view of individual functioning. One consequence of this view is a need to cover a broad spectrum of psychological, biological, and social aspects of the individual in order to investigate effectively the central issues in individual development. The analysis in the present research of the relationship between age at menarche and adult education is a good example. The long-term consequences of early biological maturation among girls, thus, can be successively investigated only by studying a wide range of personal factors for a representative group followed from an early age to adulthood.

REFERENCES

Andersson, T., Dunér, A., and Magnusson, D. (1980). *Social anpassning hos tidigt utvecklade flickor* (Social adjustment among early maturing girls). Report from the Individual Development and Environment Project, Department of Psychology, University of Stockholm, No. 35 (Not available in English.)

Andersson, T., Magnusson, D., and Dunér, A. (1982). *Basdata -81: Livssituation i tidig vuxenalder* (Base data -81: The life situation at early adulthood). Report from the Individual Development and Environment Project, Department of Psychology, University of Stockholm, No. 49. (Not available in English.)

Bergman, L. R. (1973). Parents' education and mean change in intelligence. *Scand. J. Psychol.* 14: 273-281.

Brooks-Gunn, J., and Petersen, A. C. (eds.) (1983). *Girls at Puberty: Biological and Psychosocial Perspectives,* Plenum, New York.

Davies, B. L. (1977). Attitudes towards school among early and late-maturing adolescent girls. *J. Genet. Psychol.* 131: 261-266.

Frisk, M., Tenhunen, T., Widholm, O., and Hortling, H. (1966). Physical problems in adolescents showing advanced or delayed physical maturation. *Adolescence* 1: 126-140.

Goldstein, H. (1979). *The Design and Analysis of Longitudinal Studies,* Academic Press, New York.

Greif, E. B., and Ulman, K. J. (1982). The psychological impact of menarche on early adolescent females: A review. *Child Dev.* 53: 1413-1430.

Jessor, R., and Jessor, S. L. (1977). *Problem Behavior and Psychosocial Development: A Longitudinal Study of Youth,* Academic Press, New York.

Lindgren, G. (1976). Height, weight, and menarche in Swedish urban school children in relation to socio-economic and regional factors. *Ann. Hum. Biol.* 3: 501-528.

Magnusson, D. (1981). Some methodology and strategy problems in longitudinal research. In Schulzinger, F., Medncik, S. A., and Knop, J. (eds.), *Longitudinal Research: Methods and Uses in Behavioral Science,* Nijhoff, Boston, pp. 192-215.

Magnusson, D. (1985). Implications of an interactional paradigm of research on human development. *Int. J. Behav. Dev.* 8: 115-137.

Magnusson, D., and Allen, V. L. (1983). *Human Development: An Interactional Perspective,* Academic Press, New York.

Magnusson, D., Dunér, A., and Zetterblom, G. (1975). *Adjustment: A Longitudinal Study,* Almqvist & Wiksell, Stockholm.

Magnusson, D., and Stattin, H. (1982). Biological age, environment, and behavior in interaction: A methodological problem. Reports from the Department of Psychology, University of Stockholm, No. 587.

Magnusson, D., Stattin, H., and Allen, V. L. (In press). Differential maturation among girls and its relation to social adjustment: A longitudinal perspective. In Featherman, D. L., and Lerner, R. M. (eds.), *Life Span Development,* Vol. 7, Academic Press, New York.

McCall, R. B. (1977). Challenges to a science of developmental psychology. *Child Dev.* 48: 333-344.

Peskin, H. (1967). Puberal onset and ego functioning. *J. Abnorm. Psychol.* 75: 1-15.

Petersen, A., and Taylor, B. (1980). The biological approach to adolescence: Biological change and psychological adaptation. In Adelson, J. (ed.), *Handbook of Adolescent Psychology,* Wiley, New York, pp. 117-155.

Simmons, R. G., Blyth, D. A., Van Cleave, E. F., and Bush, D. M. (1979). Entry into early adolescence: The impact of school structure, puberty, and early dating on self-esteem. *Am. Sociol. Rev.* 44: 948-967.

Simmons, R. G., Blyth, D. A., and McKinney, K. L. (1983). The social and psychological effects of puberty on white females. In J. Brook-Gunn, J., and Petersen, A. C. (eds), *Girls at puberty: Biological and Psychological Perspectives,* Plenum, New York, pp. 229-272.

Wohlwill, J. F. (1970). The age variable in psychological research. *Psychol. Rev.* 77: 49-64.

Journal of Youth and Adolescence, Vol. 14, No. 3, 1985

The Study of Maturational Timing Effects in Adolescence

J. Brooks-Gunn,[1] Anne C. Petersen,[2] and Dorothy Eichorn[3]

INTRODUCTION

The facts that not all children go through pubertal development at the same time and that children are aware of their actual stage of development vis-à-vis their peers have intrigued psychologists for the past 40 years. The Berkeley, Oakland, and Fels growth studies have explored the effects of early and late maturation upon individuals' social adaptation in adolescence and beyond. Early maturers seemed to have an advantage relative to late maturers in many aspects of social-emotional functioning. In the Oakland Growth Study, for example, early maturing boys were seen as more relaxed and attractive to adults and more attractive and popular with their peers than were the late maturers (Jones and Bayley, 1950; Jones, 1965). In late adolescence, early maturing boys were more likely to be leaders and to display more adult behavior than were late maturers (Clausen, 1975; Mussen and Jones, 1957). Finally, differences in social functioning were still seen when the subjects reached adulthood (Clausen, 1975). In contrast, the Berkeley Guidance Study found that early maturation had detrimental as well as positive behavioral correlates. Peskin (1967) found that early maturing males were more somber, temporarily more anxious, and more submissive around the time of puberty, but this was not the case for the late maturers.

[1] Senior Research Scientist, Educational Testing Service and Adjunct Associate Professor of Pediatrics, University of Pennsylvania. Ph.D. from the University of Pennsylvania. Research Interests: Girls' psychological adaptation to pubertal change, biosocial aspects of female reproductive events, development in at risk children and adolescents.
[2] Professor of Human Development and Head, Department of Individual and Family Studies, The Pennsylvania State University. Ph.D. from University of Chicago. Research Interests: Adolescent development, self-identity, sex-role development.
[3] Associate Director, Institute of Human Development, University of California at Berkeley. Ph.D. from Northwestern University. Research Interests: Biological Behavioral Relationships, Cognitive Development, and Life-Span research.

149

The growth studies produced more divergent findings for girls than for boys with regard to timing of maturation. Early maturation does not seem to be as much of a social advantage for girls as for boys. For example, Jones and Mussen (1958) report that the early maturing girls in the Oakland Growth Study were not likely to be popular or to be in leadership positions, although this relationship was later found to be mediated by social class. In the Berkeley Guidance Study, early maturing girls displayed significantly more diminished sociability and unrest in adolescence than late maturing girls. These negative effects disappeared by the time the girls reached adulthood (Peskin, 1973). And an early study conducted by Faust (1960) found that being average for one's age was more desirable in grade 6 while being advanced was more prestigious in grades 7 and 8.

For a variety of reasons, investigators are currently interested in the role of the timing of maturation during puberty with respect to several aspects of development. One set of hypotheses involves the direct and indirect effects of pubertal hormones on cognition and selected behavioral domains, such as moodiness. Another line of theorizing concerns itself with the social effects of physical maturity. A third distinct, though related, perspective examines the role of being "on" or "off" time with regard to pubertal events. Indeed, social-emotional functioning as it relates to timing of maturation is being recast in light of life-span approaches to on-time and off-time life events (Lerner, next issue; Brooks-Gunn and Petersen, 1983).

Although some recent research has been directed toward each of these perspectives, the results to date are rather contradictory and confusing. First, not all studies have found timing effects, and the effects that have been found are not always consistent, particularly not across samples, gender, or social class groups within samples. Second, all three theoretical perspectives have some support and appear to operate interactively, though not for all population subgroups. Therefore, the theories as well as the results on maturational timing effects would benefit from a reexamination.

The necessity for a "new" look at maturational timing effects became clear at a 1983 Social Science Research Council meeting on Life-Span Development and Early Adolescence. Discussions kept returning to the issue of maturational timing effects, especially after results from three different research groups were presented. It was as though the issues raised by the old growth studies had come back to haunt the field, given the somewhat disparate findings across the current studies.

Our response was to search for explanations of the contradictions in terms of measures, samples, and the new conceptualizations of puberty that have emerged in the 1980s. To that end, a Society for Research in Child Development Study Group was convened, in order to bring together all the psychologists, sociologists, endocrinologists, and pediatricians who were currently examining maturational timing effects. This interdisciplinary group met to report findings, discuss discrepancies, and develop conceptual frameworks for interpreting differences. The end result is the publication of two special issues of the *Journal of Youth and Adolescence.*[4] We are pleased that the *Journal* is sponsoring these issues, as they represent an integration or, at the very least, an up-to-date interpretation of maturational timing effects.

LIFE-SPAN DEVELOPMENT AND MATURATIONAL TIMING RESEARCH

Several themes are highlighted. Perhaps the most salient is the life-span perspective being brought to maturational timing research today. This perspective appears in various guises. First, life-span developmentalists have proposed that age-graded, history-graded, and nonnormative influences may affect the course of development (Baltes, 1968; Baltes and Reese, 1984). By age-graded is meant all normative age-related factors. Petersen (1986) has suggested that at least four age-graded factors are relevant to the study of early adolescence; these are chronological age, biological age, cognitive age, and grade in school. The first reflects amount of life experience, the second maturation (in the case of adolescence, pubertal age), the third intelligence or cognition, and the fourth the amount one has learned academically and socially. Thus, maturation is only one normative factor for which timing effects may be studied. In several of the papers in these special issues of the *Journal of Youth and Adolescence,* the relative effects of different age-related factors are examined within a timing framework. For example, Petersen and Crockett's work (this issue) suggests that when maturational timing and grade are examined, grade-in-school effects are much larger than timing effects. Since the adolescents' social world is organized by grade in school rather than by pubertal development, the primacy of the former should not surprise us. On the other hand, this does not mean that maturation has no influence on behavior, but suggests the need to embed pubertal timing effects within a larger framework.

Another approach to the study of grade and maturational timing not unrelated to the life-span perspective has been taken by Blyth *et al.* (this issue), who have studied the interaction of grade, school transitions, and pubertal timing. They have found that early maturing sixth-grade girls find the transition to middle school more difficult than on-time or late maturing sixth-grade girls or than early maturing sixth-graders not moving to middle

[4]Space limitations made it necessary to devote this issue and the next issue to these papers.

school. This fine-grained individual difference approach suggests that maturational timing may be especially potent at a specific juncture for a subgroup of children defined by their maturational timing — in this case, sixth-graders leaving elementary school.

The life-span perspective also has made a major contribution to our understanding of timing effects by the introduction of the notion of on-time and off-time events. Neugarten (1979) has discussed how the life cycle is perceived in terms of a set of norms about what events should occur as well as when they should occur. The "social clock," which is internalized by individuals, identifies life phases and expected life transitions. Events which are off-time, occurring earlier or later than anticipated, may result in a crisis for the individual (Neugarten, 1969; Neugarten and Hagested, 1976). Critical to this notion is the importance of the individual's perception of timeliness, as well as actual timelines. That is, an event may be perceived to be on time or off time depending on a variety of factors, such as one's referent group, the cohort in which one finds herself, the importance to the individual of being in phase, and an individual's perception of the range of on time.

ASYNCHRONIES AMONG NORMATIVE EVENTS

Related to the notion of being on-time and off-time is the concept of asynchrony. Asynchronies (e.g., Eichorn, 1975) exist between biological status (pubertal age), chronological age, grade-in-school, cognitive functioning, and social maturity. Such asynchronies make it difficult to characterize an individual on any unitary timing dimension. A seventh-grade girl may be on time for biological growth but off time socially and cognitively, vis-à-vis her peers. Or she may be on time socially but off time biologically and cognitively. To circumvent this problem, researchers have adopted several techniques: They may hold some dimensions constant (e.g., only study seventh-graders or those with formal operational thought), focus on two dimensions simultaneously (e.g., compare premenarcheal and postmenarcheal seventh-graders), statistically control for some dimensions through covariate analysis, or examine the relative effects of several dimensions upon an outcome using the general linear model (e.g., in regression analysis or analysis of variance).

The concept of asynchrony also is useful for examining individual variation in pubertal events. Interindividual and intraindividual variability in the attainment of various morphological characteristics is large. Thus, asynchronies may occur with regard to timing of different pubertal status measures. For example, one may be on time with regard to breast but not pubic hair development. Typically, only one pubertal measure is examined, or a scale is comprised of many measures, so that asynchronies are masked. Thus, it is not known whether the classification of individuals as early, on time, or late using different pubertal measures would result in different timing effects, or whether certain pubertal status measures are more salient than others. One study suggests that the onset of breast development, but not pubic hair development, is related to psychosocial functioning in fifth- and sixth-graders (Brooks-Gunn and Warren, 1985). However, little research has examined the effects of pubertal events other than menarche or the relative effects of various events such as menarche, breast development, and pubic hair growth.

Besides variability at any given time, individuals differ in their rates of maturation. Maturation involves a set of processes, not one event. These processes do not occur in an exact time-graded fashion. Thus, some girls may progress through breast development in a few years, and some may take much longer. That rate of development differs means that classification of individuals as on-time and off-time is a static snapshot which may not predict perfectly the classification of individuals at another time. Thus, the classification of girls' timing as a function of breast development in sixth grade may predict timing for the group as a whole in eighth grade, but will not be an accurate reflection of the timing for each individual in eighth grade. Another difficulty is that within individuals, the rate may be different for various pubertal events.

One final asynchrony needs to be mentioned. An individual may perceive herself to be off-time even when by physical indicators, she is not. Tobin-Richards *et al.* (1983) have found that for some aspects of psychosocial functioning, perceived timing may be more important than actual timing.

MEASURING PUBERTAL STATUS

As will be seen in this special issue and the next one, some findings across laboratories and samples are still disparate. The most prominent reasons for the disparities involve measurement issues. One issue in the measurement of maturational timing has been alluded to: Most of the changes are continuous, not discrete. The sexual maturation stages themselves, as outlined by Tanner and his colleagues, are an attempt to superimpose categories upon a continuum. Thus, the label "stages" is a slight misnomer, as qualitative changes in breast, pubic hair, or penile growth do not really occur. A few events, such as menarche and ejaculation, are discrete and more easily used as pubertal event markers. Other pubertal changes, such as the adolescent growth spurt, cannot be used to categorize an individual at any single point during the spurt, but remain important indicators of the entire process and its timing (Brooks-Gunn and Petersen, 1984).

A major measurement problem is the distinction between pubertal status and pubertal timing. The former refers to an absolute, the actual pubertal state at any given point in time. The latter is a relative concept, referring to an individual's status vis-à-vis a referent group or a set of norms.

With regard to pubertal status, many different measures have been used. In the earlier growth studies, bone age as determined by wrist X-ray was typically used. Because of concerns about radiation, the difficulty of collecting data outside the medical setting, and the lack of consensus on convergent validity of bone age with other measures, no current studies employ this measure. Several other approaches are favored at the present. The most popular measures seem to be menarche for girls and peak height velocity for both boys and girls, but other methods are available. Other approaches are illustrated in these special issues. The Stanford group (Duncan *et al.*, this issue), using the National Health Examination Survey data, had pediatricians rate maturation in terms of the Tanner stages (average of breast and pubic hair for girls and pubic hair and penile growth for boys). Petersen and Crockett (this issue) classified subjects as early, average, and late maturers based on age at peak height velocity. In the following paper, Brooks-Gunn and Warren (this issue) have used schematic representations and written descriptions of the five Tanner stages. Mothers or daughters check off the stage that best represents current status. A similar approach has been used successfully by Duke and colleagues (1980). High reliability has been obtained using both of these procedures (Duke *et al.*, 1980; Morris and Udry, 1980).

Even when studies use the same pubertal status measure, definitions of maturational timing may differ. Consider menarche. Blyth *et al.* (this issue) have used grade-in-school as the criterion by which to classify girls, given their interest in school transitions. This had the effect of trichotomizing their sample. Several other research groups have used the grade-in-school cirterion (Greif and Ulman, 1982; Ruble and Brooks-Gunn, 1982). Age of menarche rather than grade at menarche is probably more often used for timing classifications, as is illustrated by our contributors – Rierdan and Koff (this issue), Brooks-Gunn and Warren (next issue), Hill *et al.* (next issue), Hauser *et al.* (next issue), and Meyer-Bahlburg *et al.* (next issue). However, all of these groups have used different age cut-offs for classifying subjects' timing at maturation. Meyer-Bahlburg *et al.* (next issue) studied a clinical sample of girls with precocious puberty, so that their menarcheal age definition was very strict. Rierdan and Koff (this issue) and Brooks-Gunn and Warren (next issue) chose age 14 as a definition of late maturation. Hauser *et al.* (next issue), relying on retrospective data, identified late maturers as those beginning after age 13. Thus, the percentage of adolescents classified as on time and off time varies across studies. Furthermore, relative to some uniform norms, there is across-study variation in the maturational and chronological ages of subjects classified in the same timing group. One might expect more differences to be found in studies identifying more extreme groups of off-time maturers if a deviance hypothesis is operating. That is, the adolescents who are very early or very late (i.e., 2 standard deviations away from the mean), by virtue of the large disparity between themselves and others in maturational status, may find themselves in a very different set of circumstances than adolescents who are less off-time. However, this hypothesis has not been tested.

Differences also exist in whether classification decisions are normative or criterion based. Most studies are criterion based and sample specific. However, national norms may be used to classify students, as was done in the National Health Examination Survey analysis (Duncan *et al.*, this issue). Standard deviations based on national norms also may be used.

Even if only one system is used, different samples, having different distributions, may exhibit various percentages of off-time and on-time subjects. For example, Brooks-Gunn and Warren (next issue) studied dancers and nonathletes, and the former had twice as many late maturers as did the comparison sample. Based on national norms, however, even the nonathletes were somewhat overrepresented in the late maturing group, in part because of the restricted, high social class of the families. Thus, samples will differ in percentage of off-time subjects, even if similar criteria are applied. In addition, being off time in a group where proportionately more adolescents are off time may have a different meaning than in settings where it is more rare. We would like to propose a strategy for overcoming these measurement impediments to comparability. Investigators could reanalyze their data using their colleagues' timing criteria, in order to see whether different criteria alter the findings. To date, this has not been done, although several of the investigators represented in this volume are discussing such a possibility.

Another problem inherent in studying maturational timing is the fact that a complete design almost never is used. By this, we mean that at any one grade level or age, a complete range of pubertal growth will not be seen, or that the number of individuals at the extremes will be quite small. Even in the relatively large samples of Petersen and Crockett (this issue) and Blyth *et al.* (this issue), the ranges are restricted. Thus, while some sixth-graders are physically mature, only a handful will be found in any one study (with the exception of large national health surveys). Several strategies have been employed to overcome this problem.

First, at any one grade level, analyses may be done on the pubertal stage levels more typical of that grade, rather than on the complete range. For example, if we are interested in studying fifth-grade girls, those in sexual maturation stages 1, 2, and 3 would be compared. For seventh-graders, girls in sexual maturation stages 2, 3, and 4 might be compared. In addition, stages may be combined for specific purposes. For example, sexual maturation stages 4 and 5 may not differ much with regard to psychological meaning and are difficult for girls to distinguish on self-report scales; therefore, these two stages may be combined in some studies. With these analyses, it is important to keep the restricted sampling in mind when making inferences.

Second, timing schemes typically do not distinguish between more and less extreme off-time maturers. Instead, extreme groups are examined clinically or selected because they are known to have a large number of off-time individuals. The clinical approach was used by Meyer-Bahlburg and colleagues (next issue) in their study of precocious puberty; the selected group approach was used by Brooks-Gunn and Warren in their study of dancers (next issue). With this design for pubertal timing studies, it is important to control for any age or grade effects.

Third, individuals may be selected on the basis of their sexual maturation rather than their age; in this scenario age or grade vary, and no attempt to obtain a representative age sample is made. Susman and colleagues (this issue) used such an approach in their study of hormone-behavior links; subjects were selected for their sexual maturation stage, and age differences were handled statistically.

Finally, several age groups may be tested and, if no age differences appear, combined in order to obtain a wider range of pubertal development. If the typically strong association between pubertal status and age still exists, covariate analyses may be appropriate.

COMPARING SAMPLES

Besides measurement issues, studies differ as to sample selection. Most of the samples discussed in this special issue are community or school based, making generalizations difficult. The National Health Examination Survey (results reported by Duncan et al., this issue) sampled teenagers in the United States in the late 1960s and is the only nationally representative sample we know of that has assessed pubertal status. Blyth et al. (this issue) randomly chose schools within the Milwaukee School District. Two other community-based studies have been conducted, one in Sweden (Magnusson et al., in press, next issue) and one in Finland (Ojajarvi, 1982). Petersen's study (Petersen and Crockett, this issue) includes a randomly selected group of young adolescents in two Chicago suburban school districts. Brooks-Gunn and Warren's sample (next issue), although very selective, is representative of girls attending private schools in a large northeastern city, where private school attendance is commonplace in middle to upper middle class families. The other studies in these two special issues were not school or community based, drawing students from a variety of sources (Susman *et al.*, this issue; Hill *et al.*, next issue; Hauser *et al.*, next issue).

Across these studies, great variations exist in important demographic factors such as social class, parental educational attainment, maternal employment status, family structure, and religion. Variations in such social context factors are known to influence children's and adolescents' development. However, how these factors might act to mediate or moderate effects of maturational timing has not been studied. One exception to the general neglect of demographic differences is the analysis of the National Health Examination Survey data by the Stanford group (Duncan *et al.*, this issue); in their sample, maturational timing effects are mediated by social class for boys and for specific behavioral domains (i.e., achievement but not problem or socially deviant behavior). Most of the other samples represented in these special issues are primarily White and middle to upper middle class. The concentration on a particular segment of the population may make sense when investigating a new topic. Indeed, this strategy has characterized developmental psychology in general. Only after the general parameters of an area have been established do investigators begin to study context effects. At the same time, such a strategy leaves us with little to say about timing effects for Blacks, Hispanics, or lower middle class groups.

Even with sample limitations, several research groups have begun to explore contextual factors related to timing effects. In this issue, Blyth *et al.* examine different school compositions and timing of school transitions; Petersen and Crockett study two different communities; Brooks-Gunn and Waren focus on school gender composition and athletic activity; and the Stanford group (Duncan *et al.*) focuses on social class differences. In the next issue, Hauser and colleagues study samples of healthy and diabetic adolescents.

MEASURING BEHAVIOR

Investigative groups also differ as to the behavioral domains upon which they have focused. A large range of psychosocial domains is included in these two special issues — familial relationships, parent-adolescent interaction, peer relationships, heterosocial behavior, sexuality, psychopathology, school adjustment, self-esteem, body image, eating problems, and deviant behavior. The mix of constructs varies across research groups, as do the measures relevant to any particular domain. The diversity is laudable in that it provides a way of identifying the domains in which timing effects are found. For example, pubertal timing effects seem to be quite prevalent for social deviancy and body image. Given such results, it may be most profitable to examine these behavioral domains in more detail in order to understand why and how pubertal timing affects them. At the same time, it is important to note the domains for which relationships with pubertal timing are not found across studies.

Another approach has been taken in the study of family relationships. Microanalytic analyses of interaction sequences within the family are providing evidence of pubertal timing and status effects. In the next issue, the research groups of Hill *et al.* and Hauser *et al.* provide excellent examples of the new research assessing familial interactions as a function of maturational timing (see also Papini and Datan, 1983; Steinberg, 1981; Steinberg and Hill, 1978). Other social interactions (e.g., among peers) may be similarly affected (Brooks-Gunn *et al.,* 1986).

CONCEPTUAL MODELS

As a final important note, it is very heartening that so many research groups are deriving conceptual models and then testing them with their data. Several of the hypotheses concerning pubertal timing effects follow. The deviance hypothesis suggests that early and late maturers differ from on-time maturers because of their status being socially deviant compared to their peer group. Early maturing girls and late maturing boys would be at risk for adjustment problems because they constitute the two most deviant groups in terms of maturation. Another hypothesis is the stage termination hypothesis. Early maturation is believed to interrupt the developmental tasks of middle childhood. Girls, especially those maturing early, would be most affected by timing if this hypothesis is correct. The Petersen and Crockett findings in this issue support both, at least to some degree, for girls.

Another model involves the notion of goodness of fit for a particular context (Lerner, next issue). Adolescents may be at risk for adjustment problems when the requirements of a particular social context and their physical and behavioral characteristics are mismatched. On-time dancers are a case in point. While, with regard to the general peer group, they are on-time and should not exhibit any particular problems, they do not have the characteristics deemed ideal by the dance world. That they do look quite different psychologically from late maturers is probably a consequence of having higher weights and less control over eating then the profession demands (Brooks-Gunn and Warren, next issue). Lerner (next issue), in his integrative essay, also provides illuminating examples of goodness of fit models relevant to the study of maturational timing.

Another set of hypotheses is proposed by Blyth *et al.* (this issue) to account for the effects of pubertal development in different school context. All three are related to the salience of potential reference standards or groups for body image. The authors find strong support for a cultural ideal-of-thinness hypothesis as influencing body image and, to a lesser extent, a school transitions hypothesis.

A final explanatory model may be derived from the work of Susman and colleagues (this issue). They have found evidence for direct effects of timing of hormonal change upon select aspects of behavior. Hormonal changes, not being directly observed by the adolescent, may be more purely biological in function than secondary sexual changes, which also carry much social meaning. Indeed, if hormonal effects are found independent of pubertal status effects, the influence of biology may be directly inferred.

In brief, these approaches allow for the refinement of possible explanatory models, as well as a comparison of alternate hypotheses. Of interest is the fact that most models are interactive, in that both biological and social factors are taken into account. Indeed, the value of these two special issues lies in their focus on the biosocial interface; their inclusion of research from pediatrics, endocrinology, developmental psychology, and clinical psychology; their inclusion of work that is programmatic in nature; and their attempt to reconcile alternate approaches to the study of maturational timing effects.

ACKNOWLEDGMENTS

This paper is the culmination of a SRCD Study Group meeting held at Educational Testing Service in October 1983. We wish to thank the Foundation for Child Development and the W. T. Grant Foundation for their support, the conference attendees for their willingness to work together on the development of new conceptual frameworks, and Orville Brim for his commitment to the study of early adolescence from a life-span perspective. Rosemary Deibler, Debra Friedman, and Lorraine Luciano are thanked for their help in manuscript preparation, and R. Gunn and A. Eichorn for listening and sometimes participating in our discussions about these special issues. Last and most important, the enthusiastic commitment of Daniel Offer to the publication of these papers is greatly appreciated.

REFERENCES

Baltes, P. B. (1968). Longitudinal and cross-sectional sequences in the study of age and generation effects. *Hum. Dev.* 11: 145-171.

Baltes, P. B., and Reese, H. W. (1984). The life-span perspective in developmental psychology. In Lamb, M. E., and Bornstein, M. H. (eds.), *Developmental Psychology: An Advanced Textbook,* Erlbaum, Hillsdale, N.J..

Brooks-Gunn, J., and Petersen, A. C. (eds.). (1983). *Girls at Puberty: Biological and Psychosocial Perspectives,* Plenum, New York.

Brooks-Gunn, J., and Petersen, A. C. (1984). Problems in studying and defining pubertal events. *J. Youth Adoles.* 13: 315-327.

Brooks-Gunn, J., and Warren, M. P. (1985). Physical and social maturity in early adolescents: The salience of different pubertal events. Submitted for publication.

Brooks-Gunn, J., Samelson, M., and Warren, M. P. (1986). Changes in girls' friendship patterns: Effects of age and pubertal status. *J. Early Adoles.* 6(1).

Clausen, J. A. (1975). The social meaning of differential physical and sexual maturation. In Dragastin, S. E., and Elder, G. H., Jr. (eds.), *Adolescence in the Life Cycle: Psychological Change and the Social Context,* Halsted, New York.

Duke, P. M., Litt, I. F., and Gross, R. T. (1980). Adolescents' self-assessment of sexual maturation. *Pediatrics* 66(6): 918-920.

Eichorn, D. E. (1975). Asynchronizations in adolescent development. In S. Dragastin, S. E., and Elder, G. H., Jr. (eds.), *Adolescence in the Life Cycle: Psychological change and the Social Context,* Halsted, New York.

Faust, M. S. (1960). Developmental maturity as a determinant in prestige of adolescent girls. *Child Dev.* 31: 173-186.

Greif, E. B., and Ulman, K. J. (1982). The psychological impact of menarche on early adolescent females: A review of the literature. *Child Dev.* 53: 1413-1430.

Jones, M. C. (1965). Psychological correlates of somatic development. *Child Dev.* 36: 899-911.

Jones, M. C., and Bayley, N. (1950). Physical maturing among boys as related to behavior. *J. Educ. Psychol.* 41: 129-148.

Jones, M. C., and Mussen, P. H. (1958). Self-conceptions, motivations, and interpersonal attitudes of early- and late-maturing girls. *Child Dev.* 29: 491-501.

Magnusson, D., Stattin, H., and Allen, V. L. (in press). Differential maturation among girls and its relation to social adjustment in a longitudinal perspective. In Featherman, D. L., and Lerner, R. M. (eds.), *Life-Span Development,* Vol. 7, Academic Press, New York.

Morris, N. M., and Udry, J. R. (1980). Validation of a self-administered instrument to assess stage of adolescent development. *J. Youth Adoles.* 9: 271-280.

Mussen, P. H., and Jones, M. C. (1957). Self-conceptions, motivations, and interpersonal attitudes of late- and early-maturing boys. *Child Dev.* 28: 243-256.

Neugarten, B. L. (1969). Continuities and discontinuities of psychological issues into adult life. *Hum. Dev.* 12: 121-130.

Neugarten, B. L. (1979). Time, age and life cycle. *Am. J. Psychiat.* 136: 887-894.

Neugarten, B. L., and Hagestad, G. O. (1976). Age and the life course. In Binstock, R. H., and Shanas, E. (eds.), *Handbook of Aging and the Social Sciences,* Van Nostrand Reinhold, New York.

Ojajarvi, P. (1982). *The Adolescent Finnish Child. A Longitudinal Study of Anthropometry, Physical Development and Physiological Changes During Puberty.* Helsinki. (In Finnish, English summary.)

Papini, D., and Datan, N. (1983). Transitions into adolescence: An interactionists perspective. Paper presented at the biennial meeting of the Society for Research in Child Development, Detroit, April.

Peskin, H. (1967). Pubertal onset and ego functioning. *J. Abnorm. Psychol.* 72: 1-15.

Peskin, H. (1973). Influence of the developmental schedule of puberty on learning and ego functioning. *J. Youth Adoles.* 2: 273-290.

Petersen, A. C. (1986). The nature of biological-psychosocial interactions: The sample case of early adolescence. in Lerner, R. M., and Foch, T. (eds.), *Biological-Psychosocial Interactions in Early Adolescents: A Life-Span Perspective,* Erlbaum, Hillsdale, N.J.

Ruble, D. N., and Brooks-Gunn, J. (1982). The experience of menarche. *Child Dev., 53:* 1557-1566.

Steinberg, L. D. (1981). Transformations in family relations at puberty. *Dev. Psychol.* 17: 833-840.

Steinberg, L. D., and Hill, J. P. (1978). Patterns of family interaction as a function of age, the onset of puberty, and formal thinking. *Dev. Psychol.* 14: 683-684.

Tobin-Richards, M., Boxer, A., and Petersen, A. C. (1983). Early adolescents' perceptions of their physical development. In Brooks-Gunn, J., and Petersen, A. C. (eds.), *Girls at Puberty: Biological and Psychosocial Perspectives,* Plenum, New York, pp. 127-154.

Journal of Youth and Adolescence, Vol. 14, No. 4, 1985

The Effects of Delayed Menarche in Different Contexts: Dance and Nondance Students

J. Brooks-Gunn[1,3] and Michelle P. Warren[2]

The premise that effects of maturational timing are mediated by social context is explored by comparing adolescent girls in dance and nondance schools. Because the dance student must maintain a relatively low body weight, being a late maturer (who is often leaner than an on-time maturer) is expected to be more advantageous to the dancer than to the student not required to meet a weight standard. Girls aged 14 to 18 were seen; 276 attended private schools and 69 attended national ballet company schools. All Ss were weighed and measured and asked questions about their secondary sexual development, weight-related concerns, eating concerns, adult sex-role expectancies, body image, emotional functioning, and family relationships. Menarcheal age was used to classify girls as early (before 11.5 years of age), on time (between 11.5 and 14 years), and late maturers (after 14 years). More dance than nondance school students were late maturers (55% versus 29%). The dance students weighed less and were leaner, had higher eating scores, and had lower family relationship and impulse control scores than the comparison sample. Across groups, late maturing students weighed less, were leaner, and had lower diet and higher oral control scores than on-time maturers, with the differences more pronounced in the dance than nondance students. In addition, the on-time dancers had higher psychopathology, perfection, and bulimia scores and lower body image scores than the late maturing dancers.

This paper was prepared with the support of grants from the W. T. Grant Foundation and the National Institutes of Health.
[1]Senir Research Scientist, Educational Testing Service and Adjunct Associate Professor of Pediatrics, University of Pennsylvania. Ph.D. from the University of Pennsylvania. Research Interests: Girls' psychological adaptation to pubertal change, biosocial aspects of female reproductive events, development in at-risk children and adolescents.
[2]Associate Professor of Clinical Obstetrics and Gynecology and Clinical Medicine, Columbia University College of Physicians and Surgeons; Co-Director of Gynecologic Endocrinology, St. Luke's–Roosevelt Hospital Center.
[3]Correspondence should be sent to Jeanne Brooks-Gunn, Educational Testing Service, Princeton, New Jersey 08541.

285

The findings are discussed in terms of a goodness of fit between the require-
ments of a social context and a person's physical and behavioral charac-
teristics.

INTRODUCTION

Effects of the timing of maturation may be mediated by social context, cultural beliefs, and individual beliefs about the importance of behaviors associated with maturation. Most timing research has explored relationships between attributes of the person, the features of a context, and the reasons why such features may be salient to an individual (Lerner, in press). The important work of Simmons, Blyth, and colleagues in the Milwaukee study has elucidated the influence of school context upon the effects of maturational timing. Examining the relative advantages and disadvantages of being an early, an on-time, or a late maturer — with menarche as the marker of maturation — Simmons *et al.* (1983) found that the effects of maturational timing differed as a function of school context and transition. For example, the early maturing sixth-grader in a K-6 school was at an advantage compared to her counterpart in a K-8 school setting. Another example of research focusing upon the moderation of maturational timing effects as a function of context is the Swedish study conducted by Magnusson and colleagues. In one analysis, early maturing girls with older friends were more likely to exhibit deviant behavior for their age group than were early maturers without older friends and also had more older friends than later maturing girls (Magnusson *et al.,* in press).

In both studies, only specific behaviors were influenced by contextual factors; timing of maturation by context interactions were found for dating behavior and body image in the Milwaukee study and dating, sexuality, drug use, and deliquency in the Swedish study. Thus, given the demands of a context, only outcomes salient to that context may be affected. Likewise, only certain characteristics may predispose an individual to be at a relative advantage or disadvantage as a function of maturational timing. Individual characteristics and contexts other than school composition and peer group have not been systematically examined with regard to maturational timing. In addition, the relationship of the demands of a context and individual characteristics which may predispose a girl to adapt to that context has not been explicated. The present study explores how maturational timing relates to adaptation within different social contexts. Girls in dance company schools were compared with girls in nondance schools. Not only are great time demands placed on the adolescent girl who dances in a professional company school but she also is expected to maintain a relatively low body weight (Vincent, 1981). Nondancers, while influenced by the general cultural ideal for thinness in our society, may be less concerned about weight, given that less specific and immediate demands are placed upon them for low weight and fewer penalties may occur for not being thin (Vincent, 1981; Garner *et al.,* 1980). In brief, it is expected that dance students will have responded to the demands of the dance world, exhibiting control over eating and concern with weight as well as being relatively thin, compared to students not engaged in dance.

Timing of maturation is expected to affect girls in the two contexts differently. Being a late maturer may be advantageous for dancers, even though it has not been shown to be so for nondancers (Simmons *et al.,* 1983; Petersen and Crockett, 1985; Faust, 1960; Peskin, 1967). Since dancers are more likely to be late maturers than girls not participating in dance (Frisch *et al.,* 1980; 1981; Malina *et al.,* 1979; Warren, 1980), being late may be normative in the dance world. In addition, being late may be a positive attribute: Late maturing dancers may be more likely to enter national companies after adolescence than are on-time maturers. In our recent study of adult classical ballet dancers in national companies, 70% reached menarche at age 14 or later (Hamilton *et al.,* in press). It is expected that on-time and late dancers will differ more than on-time and late nondancers and that the late maturing dancers as compared to the on-time dancers will exhibit the individual attributes deemed desirable for dancers—low weight, concern about weight, and control over eating.[4] In keeping with previous findings of girls attending nondance schools, it is expected that being an early maturer will be somewhat disadvantageous, compared with being an on-time or late maturer (Simmons *et al.,* 1983; Magnusson *et al.,* in press).

METHOD

Subjects

Three hundred and forty-five girls ranging in age from 14 to 18 were seen. The mean age of the sample was 15.60 (SD = 1.22). The majority (276) attended one of four private schools in a large city where public school attendance is the exception rather than the rule for middle class families. The other 76 girls attended one of three national ballet company schools in the same city. All four required initial and yearly auditions as well as biweekly attendance in dance class. The majority (86%) took at least four classes weekly.

---

[4]These comments only apply to thin as compared to normal weight adolescents; being overweight is clearly disadvantageious (Attie & Brooks-Gunn, in press).

All girls were White. Forty-seven percent were first born, 28% were second born, and 25% were later born. Socioeconomic status was high: Virtually all (96%) of the girls' families were in the highest two of Hollingshead and Redlich's (1958) five social classes (based on paternal education and occupation). Seventy-four percent of the girls' mothers had completed college, and 69% of the mothers were working outside the home.

The two samples did not differ with respect to age, birth order, socioeconomic status, maternal education, or maternal work status. However, 75% of the dance students attended private schools, while all of the comparison sample did so.

Procedure

In the private school sample, letters were written to all the parents of students in the upper school. Sixty-five percent of the parents returned the consent form by mail (an additional 6% of the parents returned consent forms on the day of testing; because of scheduling arrangements in the schools, their daughters were not able to be tested). Thus, the response rate was 71%, which is high for adolescent studies deemed sensitive by parents (i.e., studies examining emotional functioning, eating problems, pubertal development, family relationships; Brooks-Gunn and Ruble, 1982).

Girls filled out a questionnaire in the classroom with a research assistant present. Subjects were weighted (wearing their school clothes) and measured in private by our nurse-practitioner after completing the questionnaire. Research staff were available for the remainder of the day to answer any questions about the study in general.

In the ballet schools, a similar procedure was followed. The parental consent rate was comparable (68%). Questionnaires were completed after dance class, and girls were weighed and measured in private. All subjects were paid for their participation.

Measures

Physical Parameters. Height and weight were obtained by the nurse-practitioner, who took the average of two consecutive readings. Girls reported their age at menarche; menarcheal age reports are quite accurate (Bean *et al.,* 1979). A measure of leanness was calculated using a weight over height ratio (Keys *et al.,* 1972). Breast and public hair development were assessed by mothers, who rated their daughters' physical development using schematic drawings and descriptions of the Tanner (1969) stages. Eight five percent of the mothers completed the Tanner rating form. Maternal ratings correlate highly with physician ratings (Brooks-Gunn *et al.,* 1986).

Self-Image. Subjects filled out the Petersen *et al.* (1984) Self-Image Questionnaire for Young Adolescents (SIQYA), an adaptation of the Offer Self-Image Scale (Offer *et al.,* 1977, 1981). Girls were asked to rate how well 78 items described them on a 6-point scale ("not at all true of me" to "very true of me"). Nine scales were identified via factor analyses; high internal consistency has been reported (alpha coefficients more than 0.80; Petersen, *et al.,* 1984). The subscales have been labeled Impulse Control ("I become violent if I don't get may way"), Emotional Tone ("My feelings are easily hurt"), Body Image ("Most of the time I am happy with the way I look"), Social Relationships ("I think that other people just do not like me"), Family Relationships ("I can count on my parents most of the time"), Mastery and Coping ("When I decide to do something, I do it"), Educational Goals ("A job well done gives me pleasure"), Psychopathology ("When I am with people, I am afraid that someone will make fun of me"), and Adjustment ("I am a leader in school").

Eating Behavior. A short version of the EAT-26, an eating problems scale developed by Garner and Garfinkel (1979), was used. Nine items are rated on the same 6-point scale used for the SIQYA. The subscales are Dieting ("I am on a diet much of the time"), Bulimia ("I have the impulse to throw up after meals"), and Oral Control ("I feel that others pressure me to eat").

Adult classical ballet dancers have been shown to have high scores on these three scales. In addition, the revised EAT-26 was significantly related to self-reported anorexia nervosa, low body fat, and low weight; these data provide partial validation for use of the shorter form of the EAT-26 (Hamilton *et al.,* in press, [a,b]

Weight-Related Concerns. Weight-related concerns, as distinguished from eating-related concerns, were assessed by a series of questions including (1) whether *S* is heavier, thinner, or about the same as other girls her age (5-point scale); (2) whether *S* believes she is heavy, thin, or about right (5-point scale); (3) whether *S*'s mother thinks she is thin, heavy, or about right (5-point scale); and (4) *S*'s desired height and weight.

Adult Sex-Role Expectations. Girls rated the importance to them of marriage, children, and careers on a 4-point scale ("not at all" to "a lot").

Attractiveness and Perfection. The importance of being pretty was rated on a 4-point scale ("not at all" to "a lot"). A subscale from the Eating Disorders Inventory (EDI; Garner *et al.,* 1983) was also used. The EDI taps psychological and behavioral traits believed to be related to eating disorders. The Perfection subscale was included, as it examines the importance of doing things well, an imputed characteristic of dancers (Vincent, 1981).

RESULTS

Menarcheal Age

The mean menarcheal age for the dance sample was 13.29 (SD = 1.27) and the 12.76 (SD = 1.12) for the comparison sample; this difference was significant ($t(304)$ = 2.78, p < 0.01).

Timing of Menarche

Girls were classified as early, on-time, or late maturers based on menarcheal age. Based on a mean menarcheal age of 12.6 to 12.8 for American White adolescents (Zacharias *et al.,* 1976; Damon *et al.,* 1969), girls who were ± 1.2 years from the mean were classified as off time; those who reached menarche before 11.5 years were classified as early, and after 14 years as late. In the nondance school sample, 11% of the girls were early, 59% were on time, and 29% were late. In contrast, 6% of the dance students were early, 38% on time, and 57% late ($\chi^2(2)$ = 18.06, p < 0.001). Since so few dancers were early, only on-time and late maturers were compared across social context. A series of 2 (on-time versus late menarche) × 2 (dance by nondance school student) ANOVAS were performed. Individual comparisons among the on-time and late dancers and on-time and late nondance students were performed if significant interaction effects were found. Since all girls were age 14 or older, premenarcheal girls also would be classified as late. In the late maturing group, 84% of the nondance students and 50% of the dance students were postmenarcheal.

A separate analysis was conducted for the nondance school students in order to compare the early maturers to the on-time and late maturers. A series of one-way (early, on-time, and late) ANOVAS were performed. When significant effects were found, planned comparisons were conducted (early versus on-time and early versus late maturers).

Social Context by Maturational Status

Anthropomorphic Measures. The dance students weighted 16 pounds less than the nondance students, as seen in Table I. In addition, the late maturers in both groups weighed 8 pounds less than the early maturers. The weight differences between maturational groups were more pronounced for the dance than the nondance school students (9 versus 5 pounds). The dance students were about three-quarters of an inch shorter than the nondance school students (p < 0.10). No maturational effects for height were seen in either group.

270

Table I. Mean Scores for Dancer and Comparison Students by Timing of Menarche

	Maturational status			
	Total	On time	Late	F test
Anthropomorphic measures				
Weight (pounds)				
Comparison	125.35	127.04	122.01	G: 34.46[f]
Dance	108.80	114.30	104.82	T: 7.95[f]
				G × T: ns
Height (inches)				
Comparison	65.09	65.11	65.06	G: 3.47[d]
Dance	64.27	64.46	64.13	T: ns
				G × T: ns
Secondary sexual characteristics				
Tanner – breast[a]				
Comparison	4.20	4.34	3.95	G: ns
Dance	3.90	4.50	3.50	T: 19.65[f]
				G × T: 4.09[f]
Tanner – pubic hair[a]				
Comparison	4.42	4.54	4.19	G: 2.66[d]
Dance	4.07	4.56	3.78	T: 13.65[f]
				G × T: ns
Eating-related concerns				
Diet[b]				
Comparison	3.16	3.31	2.85	G: 10.29[f]
Dance	3.64	4.24	3.24	T: 12.38[f]
				G × T: ns
Bulimia[b]				
Comparison	2.44	2.47	2.40	G: 9.42[e]
Dance	2.92	3.29	2.67	T: ns
				G × T: 2.82[d]
Oral control[b]				
Comparison	2.11	1.99	2.35	G: 30.54[f]
Dance	3.03	2.69	3.25	T: 10.82[f]
				G × T: ns
Self-image scales				
Impulse control[b]				
Comparison	4.41	4.40	4.43	G: 3.67[d]
Dance	4.22	4.03	4.36	T: ns
				G × T: ns
Body image[b]				
Comparison	3.94	4.01	3.79	G: ns
Dance	4.07	3.68	4.34	T: ns
				G × T: 9.19[e]
Education[b]				
Comparison	5.11	5.17	4.99	G: 5.98[e]
Dance	5.25	5.19	5.29	T: 4.46[e]
				G × T: 3.95[e]
Psychopathology[a]				
Comparison	2.87	2.80	2.99	G: ns
Dance	3.06	3.21	2.96	T: ns
				G × T: 2.71[d]
Family relationship[b]				
Comparison	5.00	4.99	5.00	G: 3.84[e]
Dance	4.78	4.48	4.99	T: ns
				G × T: 3.90[f]

Table I. Continued

	Maturational status			
	Total	On time	Late	*F* test
Emotional tone[b]				
Comparison	4.66	4.66	4.66	G: ns
Dance	4.52	4.40	4.61	T: ns
				G × T: ns
Weight related concerns				
Relative weight[a]				
Comparison	2.77	2.64	3.01	G: 32.96[f]
Dance	3.69	3.23	4.00	T: 15.32[f]
				G × T: ns
Self-perceptions[a]				
Comparison	2.20	2.14	2.34	G: ns
Dance	2.37	2.00	2.62	T: 11.59[f]
				G × T: 4.16[e]
Desired weight loss				
Comparison	12.05	13.12	9.95	G: ns
Dance	10.32	12.45	8.73	T: 5.62[e]
				G × T: ns
Weight want				
Comparison	112.85	113.57	111.40	G: 67.34[f]
Dance	98.36	101.85	95.97	T: 4.60[e]
				G × T: ns
Attractiveness and perfection				
Perfection[b]				
Comparison	2.92	3.40	2.76	G: 19.20[e]
Dance	3.57	3.78	3.42	T: 3.81[e]
				G × T: ns
Importance of being pretty[c]				
Comparison	3.38	3.36	3.42	G: 3.72[e]
Dance	3.54	3.81	3.36	T: ns
				G × T: 8.00[f]
Adult sex-role expectancies				
Marriage[c]				
Comparison	3.43	3.37	3.56	G: 55.22[f]
Dance	2.62	2.54	2.67	T: 3.11[e]
Children[c]				
Comparison	3.31	3.25	3.42	G: 25.17[f]
Dance	2.65	2.62	2.67	T: ns
				G × T: ns

G = group (dance versus comparison).
T = timing of maturation (on-time versus Rate).
G × T = group by timing interaction.
[a]5-point scale.
[b]6-point scale.
[c]4-point scale.
[d]$p < 0.10$.
[e]$p < 0.05$.
[f]$p < 0.01$.

Given the weight differences, it is not surprising that the dancers were leaner than the nondancers and that the later maturers in both groups were leaner than the on-time maturers. These maturational effects were more pronounced in the dancer than the comparison sample.

Secondary Sexual Characteristics. The dancers were less advanced with regard to breast and pubic hair development than were the nondancers. Breast and pubic hair development were less advanced in the late than the on-time maturers, as would be expected, given the relationship of menarcheal status and Tanner staging.

Self-Image. Social context effects were found for five of the nine SI-QYA scales. Dance students had lower family relationships, lower impulse control, and higher education scores than did the comparison students. Context by maturational timing interactions were found for, education, psychopathology, body image, and family relationships. These interactions indicated that maturational effects were found for the dance, but not the nondance, school students. The on-time dancers exhibited higher psychopathology and lower body image, family relationships and education, control scores than did the late maturing dancers (see Table I). The on-time dancers' family relationship and body image scores were lower than those of the other three groups.

Eating Concerns. As seen in Table I, dancers had higher diet, bulimia, and oral control scores than did the nondancers. On-time maturers in both groups had higher diet and bulimia scores and lower oral control scores than did late maturers. A significant interaction was found for the Bulimia subscale, indicating that the maturational effect was only seen in the dancers; the on-time dancers had higher bulimia scores than any other group. In addition, the maturation effects for diet and oral control were more pronounced in the dance than the comparison group.

Weight-Related Concerns. Compared to other girls their age, dance students and late maturers rated themselves as being thinner than comparison students and on-time maturers. With regard to self-perceptions, dancers did not see themselves as lighter than the comparison students saw themselves, even though the former were significantly thinner. Late maturers rated themselves as lighter than did on-time maturers. A significant interaction indicated that the timing effect was only found for the dancers.

In terms of the amount each girl would like to weigh, the dancers wished to weigh 14 pounds less than the nondancers; and across groups, the late maturers wished to weigh less than the on-time maturers. The maturational differences were more pronounced in the dance than the comparison sample.

Adult Sex-Role Expectations. Marriage and children were rated as less important by the dance than the nondance students. Careers were equally important to the two groups. No maturation effects were found.

Attractiveness and Perfection. Dance students exhibited higher perfection scores than did comparison students, as did the on-time maturers as compared to late maturers. These trends were more pronounced for the dancers than nondancers, although the interaction did not reach significance. The dancers rated being pretty as more important than the comparison students. A significant interaction indicated that the on-time dancers rated being pretty as more important than the other three groups.

Early Versus On-Time or Late Menarche. Early maturers were compared to on-time and late maturers in the comparison but not the dancer sample, given the small number of Ss in the latter. The early maturers weighed more than the on-time or late maturers and were not as lean, as Table II

Table II. Mean Scores for the Private School Students by Timing of Menarche

	Maturational status			
	Early (N = 31)	On time (N = 164)	Late (N = 81)	F test
Anthropomorphic measures				
Weight (pounds)	132.99	127.04	122.01	3.94^f
Height (inches)	64.70	65.11	65.06	ns
Leanness (weight/height)	2.05	1.94	1.87	5.70^e
Eating-related concerns[a]				
Diet	3.34	3.31	2.85	3.10^e
Bulimia	2.57	2.47	2.40	ns
Oral control	2.11	1.99	2.35	ns
Self-image scales[a]				
Impulse Control	4.16	4.40	4.43	ns
Body Image	3.67	4.01	3.79	3.08^e
Education	5.12	5.17	4.99	ns
Psychopathology	3.12	2.80	2.99	2.22^d
Family Relationships	4.95	4.99	5.00	ns
Emotional Tone	4.32	4.66	4.66	2.49^d
Weight-related concerns				
Relative weight[b]	2.52	2.64	3.01	4.56^f
Self-perceptions[b]	1.90	2.14	2.34	4.45^f
Desired weight loss	13.69	9.04	6.40	8.46^f
Weight want	115.16	113.57	111.40	ns
Attractiveness and perfection				
Perfection[a]	3.36	3.40	2.76	3.00^e
Importance of being pretty[c]	3.48	3.36	3.42	ns

[a]6-point scale.
[b]5-point scale.
[c]4-point scale.
[d]$p < 0.10$.
[e]$p < 0.05$.
[f]$p < 0.01$.

shows. However, they were the same height as the other two groups. Their secondary sexual development was the same as that of the on-time maturers.

Differences were found between the maturational timing groups on three of the nine SIQYA scales. Early maturers had lower emotioal tone, lower body image, and higher psychopathology scores than the on-time maturers and lower emotional tone scores than the late maturers. Quadratic trends were found for body image and psychopathology, with the on-time maturers having the most positive body images and the lowest psychopathology scores ($F(2, 268) = 4.42, p < 0.05$ and $F(2, 259) = 6.11, p < 0.05$, respectively).

Dieting scores were higher for the early and on-time than the late maturers. No group differences in bulimia or oral control were found.

Differences were found with respect to weight-related concerns. Early and on-time maturers reported that they were heavier than late maturers, compared to other girls their age; self-perceptions of weight exhibited similar trends. The early maturers wished to lose more weight than the on-time or late maturers. However, all three groups wished to weight the same. No differences were found for adult sex-role expectancies or importance of being pretty. Early and on-time maturers had higher perfection scores than late maturers.

DISCUSSION

These results illustrate a goodness of fit between the requirements of a social context and a person's physical and behavioral characteristics. With respect to dancers, the damands are clear: Maintain a low body weight in order to conform to professional standards and devote a great deal of time to practice. Given these environmental constraints, it is not surprising that differences between dance and nondance school students were, for the most part, related to these two demands. Dancers did weigh less and were leaner than nondancers. Dancers' eating behavior also reflected weight requirements, as they had higher dieting, bulimia, and oral control scores than did the nondancers. Dancers were more concerned about weight, in that they wished to weigh less and did not perceive themselves to be thin, even while recognizing that they were thinner than most other girls their age: Their already low weight did not result in satisfaction with their weight. Thus, their weight concerns do not seem to be due to a perceptual distortion, as in the case of anorexia nervosa (Garner and Garfinkel, 1979), since dancers were able to rate themselves accurately as thinner than other girls their age. Instead, the different self-standards of dancers seem to account for the sample differences.

Another demand placed on dancers is for a high degree of control and precision(Vincent, 1981), which may be reflected in the high perfection scores of this group. Finally, the time requirements of dance may make dancers likely to have less time to devote to other pursuits. That family relationships are rated as less harmonious in the dance than the comparison students may be indicative of single-minded pursuit and possibly self-absorption.

With regard to maturation, dancers are more likely to be late maturers than are nondancers, as these results and others have demonstrated (Frisch *et al.*, 1980, 1981; Malina *et al.*, 1979; Warren, 1980). Of interest is the relative effect of environment and genetic influences on the menarcheal delays seen in dancers. Genetics are believed to play a role in that late maturing girls have physical characteristics preferred by dance masters, specifically leanness and angularity. Consequently, girls without these characteristics probably would not be selected for the company schools. However, since girls are choosen for national ballet companies around ages 9 to 10, dance masters may have difficulty differentiating between on-time and late maturers. Early maturers may be selected out at this point (either by themselves or in auditions), as they will have breast buds and may also have more body fat than on-time or late maturing 9- or 10-year-olds. In fact, only 6% of the girls in the dance company schools were early maturers.

If selection of late maturers occurs at the point of selection into dance company schools, one might expect that dancers' mothers would be more likely to have had delayed menarche than nondancers' mothers, given that mother-daughter menarcheal correlations range from 0.26 to 0.40 (Damon *et al.*, 1969; Zacharius *et al.*, 1976). However, in a recent study, no differences between the menarcheal ages of dance and comparison students' mothers were found. In addition, the best predictor of daughter's menarcheal age in the dance sample was leanness, not maternal menarcheal age. Thus, the dancer's predisposition to be a late maturer seems to be environmentally rather than genetically mediated, at least to some degree (Brooks-Gunn and Warren, 1985).

Our findings reflect this possible environmental selection. Dancers with delayed menarche are different physically: They weigh much less than on-time dancers, a condition that is adaptive within the dance context. In addition, late maturers seem to have greater control over eating, which may in part account for their lower weight. These differences may affect the late maturers' behavior and self-expectancies. While the on-time maturers are thin by almost any standards, they are average weight for dancers. That the on-time dancers may be at a relative disadvantage, at least in terms of their weight, is reflected in their negative body images, their ratings of themselves as heavy (even though they are at or below their ideal weight), and their desire to lose weight. With regard to behaviors related to weight, they have higher dieting and bulimia scores, suggesting that food is highly salient. However, they have lower oral control scores then later maturers, suggesting that they may be less successful in restraining themselves. They may be exhibiting the cycle of binging and restraining described by others in nonathletic samples (Polivy *et al.*, 1983). Psychologically, they are less emotionally healthy, which may be a consequence of not meeting the expectations of their profession and of realizing that they are less likely to enter a national company after high school graduation than are their late maturing counterparts. This premise is predicated on the fact that on-time dancers rate dance to be as important to them as do late maturing dancers.

In contrast to the dancers, fewer maturational timing effects were found in the comparison sample and those that were found were of a lesser magnitude. While timing of maturation has been hypothesized to result in different self-expectancies and treatment by others, these differences may be relatively short-lived, may only occur at specific age points, may only occur during rapid physical and/or social changes, and/or may be more salient for early maturers. The age-graded nature of many adolescent experiences may override any maturational timing effects. Or effects of maturation may spread rapidly through an age group. Thus, while early maturers may begin to date earlier than later maturers, as soon as a subgroup exhibits a behavior deemed desirable by the entire group, others will follow suit, regardless of their maturational status. In this scenario, one would expect maturational timing effects to appear at the time that maturation begins, to be relatively short-lived, and to be expressed only in a few behaviors (dating, menarcheal attitudes, adult sex-role expectations). Thus, the early maturers would be more likely to be different from later maturers than would on-time from late maturers. In fact, the results tend to support this. Early maturers, especially in studies that define a more extreme and restricted early group (i.e., 20% versus 33% of the sample) are more likely to be at a disadvantage than later maturers. For example, the early maturer, because of her figure, may be pressured to act more socially mature by her parents and in her dating relationships by peers then the on-time or late maturer (Simmons *et al.*, 1983). In our sample, early maturers weighted more, had poorer body images, and had higher psychopathology and perfectionism scores than later maturers, suggesting that early maturation does have some disadvantages. However, these differences related to weight also characterized the on-time versus the late maturers. Interestingly, a curvilinear trend was found for body image: The on-time maturers had the most positive body images, suggesting that being in phase may be more important than weight in the determination of body image for nondancers as others have suggested (Tobin-Richards *et al.*, 1983). Interestingly, the same trend was found for psychopathology.

Maturational timing similarities are seen between the two samples with respect to weight. Like the dancers, the late maturing nondance students weigh less and report higher oral control scores than the on-time maturers. Unlike the dancers, this state of affairs does not result in nondancers' poorer body images, more weight concerns, higher bulimia scores, or more psychopathology. Weight is only one facet of the self, not the central evaluative feature for most adolescent girls. In contrast, weight may become a major focus of the dance student, since success is in part predicated upon it. Thus, being a late maturer is much more of an advantage to the dancer than the nondancer. And being a late maturer may be a salient feature of a dancer's self-identity, given the importance of weight and leanness to her and their relationship to maturation. In any case. the goodness of fit between late maturation and the environmental demands of the dance world is clear. Girls who, because of predisposing characteristics (i.e., genetic constitution) and/or behavioral characteristics (i.e., lack of control over food intake, binge-restraint cycles), develop late may be more satisfied with their bodies and more emotionally healthy girls who develop on time. The late maturers have adapted, by accident or design, to the requirements of their particular environment.

Of interest is whether the early maturing girl in a nondance school setting is analogous to the on-time maturing girl in the dance world. They are similar in being at a relative disadvantage in terms of specific aspects of self-image such as body image, psychopathology, and weight. Such findings suggest that being "in phase," hypothesized to explain maturational timing effects, may not be the only determining feature of such effects. Late maturing girls also are out of phase, but seem to be at less of a disadvantage than early maturing girls — perhaps because only early maturing girls are deviant with regard to males and females in the peer group. Characteristics of being early (i.e., weighing more) and the context in which the early maturer finds herself (i.e., pressures to date, to act more socially mature, to have older friends) may be salient features of timing. Alternatively, deviance may be more salient when one is the first, rather than the last, to exhibit a characteristic.

The dancer clearly illustrates why the notion of being in phase may not be sufficient to explain timing effects and why more specific models for explaining timing effects are proposed in this special issue and the preceding one. It is difficult to classify the dancers as in or out of phase, as equal numbers are on time and late. Instead, contextual demands make the on-time dancers' physical characteristics disadvantageous. Similarly, early maturing girls' characteristics may lead to different treatment by others and possibly different self-expectancies. These differences lead the early maturing adolescent to develop in a slightly different context than her later maturing peers. Thus, the effects of maturational timing in the dance world provide a model with which to examine more generally the process by which maturational differences may alter self-expectancies and the context in which a girl develops.

ACKNOWLEDGMENTS

We wish to thank Marian Samelson, Linda Ferington, Linda Hamilton, and Debra Friedman for their assistance in data collection, and the ballet and private schools for their enthusiastic participation in the study. Data analyses was conducted by James Rosso and manuscript preparation by Rosemary Deibler; their assistance is also appreciated.

REFERENCES

Attie, I., & Brooks-Gunn, J. (in press). Causes and consequences of weight-related concerns in women. In R. C. Barnett, G. K. Baruch, and L. Biener (Eds.), *Women and stress*. Wellesley, MA: Wellesley College Center for Research on Women.

Bean, J. A., Leeper, J. D., Wallace, R. B., Sherman, B. M., and Jagger, H. (1979). Variations in the reporting of menstrual histories. *Am. J. Epidemiol.* 109: 181-185.

Brooks-Gunn, J., and Ruble, D. N. (1982). The development of menstrual-related beliefs and behaviors during early adolescence. *Child Dev.* 53: 1567-1577.

Brooks-Gunn, J., Warren, M. P., Rosso, J., & Gargiulo, J. (1985). Validity of self-report measures of girls' pubertal status. Submitted for publication.

Damon, A., Damon, S. T., Reed, R. B., & Valadian, I. (1969). Age at menarche of mothers and daughters, with a note on accuracy of recall. *Hum. Biol.* 41: 161-175.

Faust, M. S. (1960). Developmental maturity as a determinant in prestige of adolescent girls. *Child Dev.* 31: 173-184.

Frisch, R. E., Wyshak, G., and Vincent, L. (1980). Delayed menarche and amenorrhea in ballet dancers. *New Engl. J. Med.* 303: 17-18.

Frisch, R. E., *et al.* 1981). *J. Am. Med. Assoc.* 246, 1559.

Frisch, R. E., Gotz-Welbergen, A. V., McArthur, J. W., Albright, T., Witschi, J., Bullen, B., Birnholz, J., Reed, R. B., & Hermann, H. (1981). Delayed menarche and amenorrhea of college athletes in relation to age of onset of training. *J. Am. Med. Assoc.*, 246: 1559-1590.

Garner, D. M., and Garfinkel, P. E. (1979). The Eating Attitudes Test: An index of the symptoms of anorexia nervosa. *Psychol. Med.* 9: 273-279.

Garner, D. M., Garfinkel, P. E., Schwartz, D., and Thompson, M. (1980). Cultural expectations of thinness in women. *Psychol. Rep.* 47: 483-491.

Garner, D. M., Olmstead, M., and Polivy, J. (1983). Development and validation of a multidimensional eating disorder inventory for anorexia nervosa and bulimia. *Int. J. Eating Disord.* 2(2). 15-34.

Hamilton, L. H., Brooks-Gunn, J., and Warren, M. P. (in press a). Sociocultural influences on eating disorders in female professional dancers. *Int. J. Eat. Disord.*

Hamilton, L. H., Brooks-Gunn, J., & Warren, M. P. (in press b). Nutritional intake of female dancers: A reflection of eating problems. *Int. J. Eat. Disord.*

Hollingshead, A. B., and Redlich, F. C. (1958). *Social Class and Mental Illness: A Community Study,* Wiley, New York.

Keys, A., Fidanza, F., Karvonen, M. J., Kimura, N., and Taylor, H. L. (1972). Indices of relative weight and obesity. *J. Chron. Dis.* 25: 329-343.

Lerner, R. M. (in press). A life-span perspective for early adolescence. In Lerner, R. M. and Foch, T. T. (eds.), *Biological-Psychosocial Interactions in Early Adolescence: A Life-Span Perspective,* Erlbaum, Hillsdale, N.J.

Magnusson, D., Stattin, H., and Allen, V. L. (in press). Differential maturation among girls and its relation to social adjustment in a longitudinal perspective. In Featherman, D. L., and Lerner, R. M. (eds.), *Life-Span Development,* Vol. 7, Academic Press, New York.

Malina, R., Bouchard, C., Shoup, R., Demirijian, A., and Lariviere, G. (1979). Age at menarche, family size, and birth order in athletes at the Montreal Olympic Games. *Med. Sci. Sports* 11: 354-358.

Offer, D., Ostrov, E., and Howard, K. I. (1977). *The Offer Self-Image Questionnaire for Adolescents: A Manual,* Michael Reese Hospital, Chicago.

Offer, D., Ostrov, E., and Howard, K. I. (1981). *The Adolescent: A Psychological Self-Portrait,* Basic Books, New York.

Peskin, H. (1967). Pubertal onset and ego functioning. *J. Abnorm. Psychol.* 72: 1-15.

Petersen, A. C., and Crockett, L. (1985). Gender, pubertal timing, and grade effects on adolescent adjustment. *J. Youth Adoles.* 14: 00-00.

Petersen, A. C., Schulenberg, J. E., Abramowitz, R. H., Offer, D., and Jarcho, H. D. (1984). A Self-Image Questionnaire for Young Adolescents (SIQYA): Reliability and validity studies. *J. Youth Adoles.* 13: 93-111.

Polivy, J., Herman, C. P., Olmsted, P., and Jazwinski, C. (1983). Restraint and binge eating. In Hawkins, R. C. II, Fremouw, W., and Clement, P. (eds.), *Binge-Eating: Theory, Research and Treatment,* Springer, New York.

Simmons, R., Blyth, D., and McKinney, K. (1983). Thoe social and psychological effects of puberty on White females. In Brooks-Gunn, J., and Petersen, A. C. (eds.), *Girls at Puberty: Biological and Psychosocial Perspectives,* Plenum, New York.

Tanner, J. M. (1969). Growth and endocrinology of the adolescent. In Gardner, L.I. (ed.), *Endocrine and Genetic Diseases of Childhood,* Saunders, Philadelphia.

Tobin-Richards, M., Boxer, A. M., and Petersen, A. C. (1983). The psychological significance of pubertal change: Sex differences in perceptions of self during early adolescence. In Brooks-Gunn, J., and Petersen, A. C. (eds.), *Girls at Puberty: Biological and Psychosocial Perspectives,* Plenum, New York, pp. 127-154.

Vincent, L. M. (1981). *Competing with the Sylph: Dancers and the Pursuit of the Ideal Body,* Andrews & McMeel, Kansas City, Kans.

Warren, M. P. (1980). The effects of exercise on pubertal progression and reproductive function in girls. *J. Clin. Endocrinol. Metab.* 51(5): 1150-1157.

Zacharias, L., Rand, W. M., and Wurtman, R. J. (1976). *Obstet. Gynecol. Surv., 31,* 325.

Journal of Youth and Adolescence, Vol. 14, No. 4, 1985

Menarcheal Status and Parent-Child Relations in Families of Seventh-Grade Girls[1]

John P. Hill,[1,6] Grayson N. Holmbeck,[2] Lynn Marlow,[3] Thomas M. Green,[4] and Mary Ellen Lynch[5]

The associations between menarcheal status and several child-rearing and outcome variables were examined for mother-daughter and father-daughter dyads. All variables were assessed with questionnaires as an extension of earlier observational studies. Analyses were conducted via multiple regression analyses wherein menarcheal status was treated as a continuous variable and was entered into the regression equation as a set of power polynomial terms. The results indicated that most of the significant relations occurred for the mother-daughter dyad, and most of these relations were curvilinear. When menarche occurs at or around the modal time, changes in parent-child relations may be best thought of as temporary perturbations, but when menarche occurs early the effects may persist.

The research reported here was funded by Father Flanagan's Boys Home, Inc., and by a grant to the senior author from the John D. and Catherine T. MacArthur Foundation, "Family Relations in Early Adolescence."
[1]Professor of Psychology, Virginia Commonwealth University. Received his Ph.D. in clinical psychology from Harvard University.
[2]Graduate student in clinical psychology at Virginia Commonwealth University. Received his M.S. from Virginia Commonwealth University.
[3]Graduate student in counseling psychology at Virginia Commonwealth University. Received her M.S. in counseling psychology from Virginia Commonwealth University.
[4]School Psychologist, Area School Association, Denison, Iowa. Received his M.S. from the University of Nebraska.
[5]Research Associate, Eating Disorders Program, University of Nebraska Medical Center. She received her Ph.D. in developmental psychology from the Department of Human Development and Family Studies, Cornell University.
[6]Correspondence should be sent to John P. Hill, Department of Psychology, Virginia Commonwealth University, 810 West Franklin St., Richmond, Virginia 23284.

301

INTRODUCTION

Individual and familial adaptation to biological change at adolescence has been the subject of influential theoretical speculation (Blos, 1962, 1979; Deutsch, 1944; Erikson, 1968; Freud, 1958; Hall, 1904), but very little empirical study (Greif and Ulman, 1982; Hill, 1980; Petersen and Taylor, 1980). The biological event of interest in the present instance, menarche, has been the subject of more intense investigation in the past decade, yet no studies have examined the impact of menarche upon family relations (see Greif and Ulman, 1982, for a review.) Although negative effects of menarche are associated with earlier timing of menarche, how families may mediate such effects (other than through earlier and better preparation) remains uninvestigated (Brooks-Gunn and Ruble, 1983; Greif and Ulman, 1982). The lack of research on family effects, together with an interest in extending earlier work on effects of pubertal change on family relations in males (Steinberg, 1981; Steinberg and Hill, 1978), provided the motivation for the present study.

In the Steinberg and Hill (1978) cross-sectional study (confirmed by longitudinal follow-up; Steinberg, 1981), changes in parent-child interaction were linked to pubertal development in adolescent boys. Analyses of family interactions during a discussion of hypothetical situations showed that change occurred in the mother-son interaction during the early period of pubertal growth. Both mothers and sons interrupted each other more and explained themselves less during this period; these differences increased as the sons progressed from the onset of puberty to apex pubertal status. Although mothers' interruptions increased, the sons yielding to them decreased. During the later part of the pubertal period, the mothers' interruptions of the sons decreased and maternal deference to sons increased. Influence within the family also shifts during the pubertal cycle, with the mother losing influence and the son gaining it as he matures. The hierarchy shifted from one in which both parents have more influence than the son at the onset of puberty to a father > son > mother structure in later puberty. The longitudinal study also showed that, in general, father dominance and sons' submissiveness increased over the latter part of the pubertal cycle.

Three phenomena are important here: (a) a period of temporarily increased conflict, especially between mothers and sons (when both are interrupting each other more and explaining themselves less), (b) an increasing display of assertiveness and decision influencing by the son with respect to the mother, and (c) increases in paternal dominance and the son's submissiveness to the father. The present study extends these earlier efforts. Can we find similar impacts of biological change on family relations when we examine (a) girls instead of boys, (b) self- and parental reports of menarcheal status rather than observers' reports of pubertal status, and (c) questionnaire reports of family processes and outcomes instead of observational data for a structured laboratory task?

Anticipated Effects for Girls

Over the pubertal cycle, boys appear to become more assertive and influential in family interaction. Alexander (1973) has proposed that such an outcome is common to all adolescents. From this perspective, relations between parents and girls as well as boys should become more equalitarian during the adolescent era. However, we do not believe that parallel results are likely to emerge for two reasons, one empirical and one theoretical. The empirical reason is suggestive only. Employing a structured family interaction task (of the sort employed by Steinberg), Hetherington *et al.* (1971) compared the family interactions of normal adolescents and their families with those of three types of delinquent families. The results for boys and girls differed dramatically. The normal adolescent boys systematically differed from their delinquent counterparts in being more assertive, and the normal adolescent girls were less assertive than the delinquent controls. This difference, which matches traditional sex-typing expectations, led us to believe that conflict around menarche for girls might not be accompanied by the gains in assertiveness and influence that occur for boys. Early adolescence may well be accompanied by an intensification of traditional gender-related role expectations, so that family (and peer) practices foster more assertiveness in boys and more deference in girls than is commonly found in childhood (see Hill and Lynch, 1983, for an examination of this view).

Menarche Versus Pubertal Status

Most of the events of biological change in adolescence occur gradually (Tanner, 1962); the sense of dramatic biological change may be less common than is believed. Menarche, on the other hand, is a singular event. It occurs rather late in the pubertal cycle and it signals reproductive maturity with a definitive quality not associated with any event in the maturation of boys. Studies of menarche and regular menstruation suggest that the timing of these events may be critical to the individual's adaptation, and early menarche may be especially problematical. In part, the association between earlier timing of menarche and poorer adjustment may be a function of lack of preparation for menarche among early maturing girls; lack of preparation in itself is related to poor adjustment (Brooks-Gunn and Ruble, 1983; Greif and Ulman, 1982). At the same time early maturing girls have no advantage among peers in the early grades — as they will later on (Faust, 1960) and appearing "different" so early may be stressful.

In the family, early maturing, in general, and the reproductive maturity that menarche presages, in particular, may lead to parental fears of dating pressure, sexual pressure, and pregnancy. In turn, such fears may evoke the parental "chaperonage" and "vigilance" noted in the literature as characteristic of parents of early adolescent girls (Block, 1978; Newson and Newson, 1968). Early maturing girls may be treated more restrictively, giving rise to more conflict than might be occasioned in families where girls are "on time." Modal girls and their families have more institutionalized social support and social control for dealing with the same issues. Our use of a time since menarche scale and of seventh-graders as subjects permits examination of these issues.

Questionnaire Versus Observational Methods

In designing a program of research with the earlier Steinberg and Hill (1978) and Steinberg (1981) work as a major departure point, we decided to include both questionnaire and observational measures in attempting to reproduce and extend the earlier results. Here we report the results from the questionnaire analysis.

Child-Rearing and Outcome Variables

In view of the absence of empirical studies, one of our strategies was to embed our questions about impacts on families of biological change in the context of the indirectly related work available. Indirect findings suggest that authoritarian rearing during adolescence may produce social and instrumental incompetence and problematic behavior at rates or levels greater than during childhood (Baumrind, 1968; Devereux, 1970; Hill, 1980). Authoritarian rearing may have more negative effects when children are pubertal than before, owing to a failure of authoritarian parents to be responsive to intraindividual change. Overprotective (highly controlling and highly loving) parents may also promote more negative outcomes during adolescence than during childhood (Schaefer and Bayley, 1963).

Authoritarian, authoritative (or democratic), protective, and permissive (or laissez-faire) rearing have been defined in many ways, ranging from single items dealing with who makes decisions in the family (e.g., Kandel and Lesser, 1972) to a location on a "circumplex" of parent behavior (Schaefer, 1955) to more complex congeries of behavioral dimensions (Baumrind, 1968). Here, we are concerned with the Schaefer work. The circumplex of parenting behavior reflects the two dimensions of rearing that consistently emerge and account for the most variance in factor analyses of parental behavior: love-hostility and autonomy-control.

Our interest here is twofold. We wish to identify (a) whether there are differences in parental warmth-hostility and autonomy-control between pre- and postmenarcheal daughters; and (b) whether some psychosocial outcomes (child involvement in family activities, parental influence, oppositionalism, and disagreements over rules) typically associated with these rearing dimensions are greater or lesser for families with postmenarcheal than premenarcheal girls. If menarche brings with it greater equalitarianism, we ought to see fewer postmenarcheal than premenarcheal families where control is stressed. If menarche means intensification of gender-related role expectations and practices, we ought to see more postmenarcheal than premenarcheal families where control is stressed. And if classical storm-and-stress views of the adolescent era are correct, we ought also to see greater manifestations of hostility in the families with post- than in the families with premenarcheal daughters.[7]

METHOD

Subjects

Subjects were 100 seventh-grade girls and their families, recruited through the cooperation of several school districts in a large midwestern city. School principals were asked to provide lists of seventh-graders who were the oldest children in their families and who were living with both parents.

About 50% of the families contacted agreed to participate in the study, and (because of the successful operation of the questionnaire delivery system, described below) all who agreed to participate eventually completed questionnaires. On the Socio-Economic Index (SEI; Duncan, 1977), scores based upon paternal occupation ranged from 8 to 87; 24 subjects fell below an SEI of 40, 16 fell between 40 and 60, 40 fell between 60 and 70, and 20 fell above 70. A comparison of the SEI scores of subjects in the sample with those of

[7]At the most complex level of analysis, we had intended to ask whether menarcheal status moderates the effects of the two rearing dimensions (love-hostility and autonomy-control) on our four outcomes (involvement in family activities, parental influence, oppositionalism, and disagreements over rules). Owing to the curvilinear relations between (a) menarcheal status *and* acceptance and family rules and standards; (b) menarcheal status and our outcome variables; and (c) acceptance and rules and standards *and* the outcome variables — present but not detailed here — an analysis that would permit the examination of menarcheal status as a variable moderating effects of rearing upon the outcomes of interest could not be implemented.

a random sample who refused to participate showed no differences. Twenty-seven of the girls' fathers had some education beyond college, 16 fathers had finished college, 33 had had some college, and 19 had finished high school. Only 5 fathers had not finished high school.

Procedure

All family members were tested in their own homes during a two-to-three-hour period. A research assistant delivered the questionnaire materials at the appointed time and remained with the family while the questionnaires were completed. This permitted the assistants to monitor the independent completion of the questionnaires. Assistants had several hours of training which focused on providing them with standard definitions for terms they might be asked about in the questionnaire, the handling of requests on parents' parts to see their child's questionnaires (a situation that did not arise), and their learning to do global ratings of pubertal status.

Menarcheal Status Measure

Seventh-grade girls and their parents were asked to indicate whether menstruation had not yet begun or had begun within the past 6, within the past 12, or longer than 12 months ago. Around 80% agreement in placing the time of menarche was characteristic of each pair of respondents: mother-father, mother-daughter, and father-daughter. (Correlations between pairs ranged from 0.87 to 0.91.) For the father-daughter dyads, 61 girls were reported as being premenarcheal by their fathers, 13 were reported as experiencing the onset of menarche within the past 6 months, 19 reportedly experienced the onset within the past 12 months, and 7 were reported as experiencing the onset more than 12 months ago. The same frequencies for the mother-daughter dyads were 62, 11, 17, and, 10, respectively. In the analyses to follow, the report of menarcheal status employed is that of the parent whose child-rearing practice or whose report of some psychosocial outcome is being examined.

Rearing Variables: Acceptance and Family Rules and Standards

To assess our subjects' placement on dimensions of love-hostility and autonomy-control, Spence and Helmreich's (1978) Parental Attitudes Questionnaire was incorporated into our child questionnaire. In a second-order factor analysis on 11 first-order parenting scales, three factors emerged for girls and were labeled Mother and Family Acceptance, Father Acceptance, and Family Rules and Standards (Spence and Helmreich, 1978). Low scores on the acceptance factors were indicative of mother and father rejection. Thus, we felt comfortable in using the second-order acceptance factors to assess our subjects' placement on the love-hostility dimension (acceptance-nonacceptance might be a more accurate label). Examination of the Family Rules and Standards items indicated that low scores on this factor were indicative of parental indifference, permissiveness, and lack of control versus high control and parental strictness for high scorers, similar to the Schaefer (1985) autonomy-control rearing dimension.

Before obtaining scores for the second-order factors, items were maintained only on the first-order factors on which they had the highest loading. In the same way, the resulting first-order factors were maintained only on the second-order factors on which they had the highest loading. The factor label for Mother and Family Acceptance was changed to Mother Acceptance because only 4 of its 20 items referred to parents in general; the remainder referred to mothers. The Family Rules and Standards factor was not broken up into mother and father subfactors, given the small number of items (5 mother items, 4 father items, and 3 items that refer to parents in general). Cronbach alphas for Mother Acceptance and Father Acceptance were 0.85 and 0.86, respectively. The alpha for Family Rules and Standards was 0.56.

Outcome Variables

Involvement in Family Activities. This variable was measured with items developed by Blyth *et al.* (1978), Kandel and Lesser (1972), and Garbarino (1978). These 8 items, based on parental report, were tested for internal consistency and the resulting Cronbach alphas were 0.59 for mothers and 0.61 for fathers. Sample items include "In the past few weeks, how often has _____ worked on a project around the house or yard with the family?" "In the past few weeks, how often did _____ eat the evening meal with the family?"

Parental Influence. These items were developed by Kandel and Lesser (1972) and Spence and Helmreich (1978). These 7 items were included in the child questionnaire. Cronbach alphas were 0.83 for the child's report of mother's influence and 0.75 for father's influence. Sample items include "How much do you depend upon your mother for advice and guidance?" "When you have problems, whose ideas and opinions do you respect more, your father's or your best friend's?" "Are your opinions about most things similar to the opinions of your parents, or are they different?"

Oppositionalism. Two items were written by our staff and one was borrowed from Kohn (1977) to assemble the 3 item scales of mother's and father's reports of child oppositionalism. Cronbach alphas were 0.53 for mother's report and 0.47 for father's report. A high score on oppositionalism indicates agreement with such items as "I sometimes think that _____ does the opposite of what I say."

Disagreement over Rules. These 15 items were included in the parent questionnaire. Cronbach alphas were 0.69 for the mother's report and 0.73 for the father's report. Items referred to disagreements that had occurred over rules involving dating, personal habits, and family obligations.

RESULTS

Intercorrelations Among the Rearing and Outcome Variables

Intercorrelations among all rearing and outcome variables are given in Table I. Given that in most cases a small amount of variance in one variable is explained by other variables, independence within most variable pairs is considered to be established. Most correlations are moderate to low. The reasonably high alpha coefficients assure us that, in general, statisfactory internal consistency has been achieved for the variables. Some exceptions to independence were noted. There are high correlations between child report of parental influence and child report of acceptance for both mothers and fathers. Both variables were retained, however, and analyses were designed to take the interrelations between these variables into account. Also included in Table I (on the diagonal) are the correlations between the mother and father variables. Inspection of these correlations reveals that relations between the child-reported variables are stronger than those between the parent-reported variables.

Multiple regression analyses were performed to assess the relations between menarcheal status and the child-rearing and outcome variables. Analyses were completed separately for each of the two parent-child dyads (father-daughter and mother-daughter).

To test the effects of menarcheal status on the dependent variables, menarcheal status was treated as a continuous variable and was entered into a multiple regression equation as a set of power polynomial terms. Such a procedure, when applied to a single variable, can test the linearity and nonlinearity of the relation of this independent variable with a dependent variable. The terms are entered in a hierarchical fashion beginning with the linear term (v) and continuing with the terms that test for a quadratic trend (v^2), a cubic trend (v^3), and other nonlinear trends. By first partialing out the linear term, the squared semi-partial correlation of v^2 with the criterion is the increment in the cumulative R^2 that is due to the addition of the quadratic varia-

Table I. Intercorrelations of the Family Variables[a]

	Parental acceptance	Family rules	Involvement in activities	Parental influence	Child opposi-tionalism	Rule dis-agreement
Parental acceptance	*0.61*	0.13	0.37	0.70	−0.36	−0.08
Family rules	0.08	−	0.09	0.00	0.20	0.15
Involvement in activities	0.19	0.10	*0.30*	0.40	−0.30	−0.10
Parental influence	0.68	0.12	0.28	*0.80*	−0.37	−0.16
Child opposi-tionalism	−0.47	−0.04	−0.28	−0.38	*0.23*	0.25
Rule dis-agreement	−0.23	0.05	−0.04	−0.16	0.16	*0.17*

[a]Fathers are below the diagonal and mothers are above. Correlations between the mother and father variables are printed in italics on the diagonal. Since Family Rules and Standards refers to families in general, no mother-father correlation is presented for this variable. $N = 100$ for all correlations. $r(0.05) = 0.20$. $r(0.01) = 0.26$. $r(0.001) = 0.32$.

ble to the equation. Thus, it "represents the pure quadratic variable" (Cohen and Cohen, 1983, p. 226). The same logic holds for all subsequent nonlinear terms.

An nth-order term yields a curve which has $n - 1$ bends. Given that our menarcheal status variable has four levels, only the linear, quadratic, and cubic terms were entered. Therefore, only two bends will be encountered, if any. The results of the multiple regression analyses for the effects of menarcheal status on all of the child-rearing and outcome variables are summarized in Table II. Although menarcheal status has been treated as a continuous variable in these regression analyses, it is easier to interpret the curvilinear findings when one is able to examine the means of the dependent variables at each level of menarcheal status. Table III is included for this purpose.

Rearing Variables

The three terms that represent the mother's rating of daughter menarcheal status accounted for 12% of the variance ($R = 0.34$) in the child's report of mother acceptance. Also, 4% of the variance ($R = 0.21$) in child's report of father acceptance is accounted for by the three terms that represent the father's rating of daughter menarcheal status. For mothers, the linear and cubic terms were significant. Given that the partial correlation for the linear term was negative, the trend is one of descending cubic curvilinearity (see Table III for menarcheal level means). For fathers, the linear term was marginally significant ($p < 0.10$, decending).

The three terms that represent the mother's and father's rating of daughter menarcheal status accounted for 4% ($R = 0.21$) and 6% ($R = 24$), respectively, of the variance in the daughters' rating of family rules and standards. As mentioned, the same set of items was used for this variable in the analyses for mother and fathers. Thus, the means in Table III represent the effects of mother's and father's ratings of menarcheal status for the same child ratings of family rules and standards. For both sets of analyses, a significant quadratic trend was found. The regression coefficients were negative, indicating that the best fitting curve has one bend, which is concave downward (see Table III).

OUTCOMES

Parental ratings of daughters' menarcheal status accounted for 16% ($R = .40$) and 2% ($R = 0.15$), respectively, of the variance in the mothers'

Table II. Summary of Regression Analyses of Effects of Menarcheal Status on Child-Rearing and Outcome Variables[a]

Variable	Step	Menarcheal status	Mothers			Fathers		
			Par $-r$[e]	R	R^2 – change	Par $-r$[e]	R	R^2 – change
Acceptance	1	M	-0.26	0.26	0.07[d]	-0.18	0.18	0.03[b]
(child report)	2	M²	0.07	0.27	0.00	0.10	0.20	0.01
	3	M³	-0.22	0.34	0.05[c]	-0.05	0.21	0.00
Family rules	1	M	-0.07	0.07	0.00	-0.04	0.04	0.00
and standards	2	M²	-0.20	0.21	0.04[c]	-0.23	0.24	0.05[c]
(child report)	3	M³	0.04	0.21	0.00	0.00	0.24	0.00
Family activities	1	M	-0.24	0.24	0.06[d]	-0.06	0.06	0.00
(parent report)	2	M²	-0.11	0.26	0.01	-0.12	0.14	0.02
	3	M³	-0.31	0.40	0.09[d]	-0.05	0.15	0.00
Parental	1	M	-0.28	0.28	0.08[d]	-0.29	0.29	0.08[d]
influence	2	M²	0.04	0.29	0.00	0.13	0.31	0.01
(child report)	3	M³	-0.27	0.39	0.07[d]	-0.15	0.34	0.02
Oppositionalism	1	M	0.04	0.04	0.00	0.00	0.00	0.00
(parent report)	2	M²	-0.11	0.12	0.01	-0.03	0.03	0.00
	3	M³	0.09	0.15	0.01	0.04	0.05	0.00
Disagreements	1	M	-0.15	0.15	0.02	-0.04	0.04	0.00
over rules	2	M²	-0.04	0.16	0.00	-0.05	0.07	0.00
(parent report)	3	M³	0.19	0.24	0.03[b]	-0.08	0.10	0.00

[a] $N = 100$.
[b] $p < 0.10$.
[c] $p < 0.05$.
[d] $p < 0.01$.
[e] Partial correlation.

Table III. Linearity of Relations Between Parental Ratings of Daughters' Menarcheal Status and Child-Rearing and Outcome Variables

	Parental rating of months since onset of menarche				
	0^a	6^b	12^c	$>12^d$	Trend[e]
Acceptance					
Mother	76.00	64.55	72.19	65.50	−L, −C
Father	59.75	54.76	55.28	55.57	−L(m)
Family rules and standards					
Mother	40.32	42.96	40.96	37.50	−Q
Father	40.18	42.63	41.30	36.28	−Q
Family activities					
Mother	30.35	28.01	30.73	26.64	−L, −C
Father	29.76	29.98	30.04	28.02	
Parental influence					
Mother	23.42	18.44	22.13	18.29	−L, −C
Father	21.87	18.08	19.42	18.28	−L
Oppositionalism					
Mother	6.20	6.82	6.35	6.20	
Father	6.43	6.62	6.42	6.43	
Disagreements over rules					
Mother	2.60	3.45	1.53	1.90	+C(m)
Father	2.56	2.31	2.74	1.71	

[a] n(mothers) = 62, n(fathers) = 61.
[b] n(mothers) = 11, n(fathers) = 13.
[c] n(mothers) = 17, n(fathers) = 19.
[d] n(mothers) = 10, n(fathers) = 7.
[e] L = linear trend, Q = quadratic trend (1 bend), C = cubic trend (2 bends), (m) = marginally significant; the directions of all trends are noted. Because different items were used for mother and father acceptance, the scale means for this variable are not comparable across parents. Such comparisons are possible for all other variables where mother and father means are present.

and fathers' ratings of the daughters' involvement in family activities. The mothers' linear menarcheal status term was significant and negatively predictive. Also, the cubic trend for the mothers' ratings was significant, indicating that the overall trend was one of descending curvilinearity. No significant findings emerged for the fathers' ratings.

Parental reports of their daughters' menarcheal status accounted for 15% ($R = 0.39$) and 12% ($R = 0.34$), respectively, of the variance in the children's ratings of their mothers' and fathers' influence in their life. The mothers' linear and cubic trends were significant. As Table III shows, the trend is one of descending cubic curvilinearity. The fathers' linear trend was significant and descending.

Given that acceptance and parental influence were highly intercorrelated for both dyads and that the results for each were quite similar, additional analyses were conducted to determine if any of the variance either variable shared with menarcheal status was unique to that variable. Regressions were run with one variable partialed from the second prior to adding the menarcheal status power polynomial terms to the equation. Menarcheal status was predictive in only one of the four analyses. For the father-daughter dyad the linear menarcheal term was predictive of parental influence after father acceptance was added to the equation. For the other three dyads, it appears that results for parental influence and acceptance are not independent.

Parental ratings of daughter menarcheal status accounted for 2% (R = 0.15) and 0% (R = 0.05), respectively, of the variance in the mothers' and fathers' ratings of children's oppositionalism. No significant trends were found.

Parental ratings of menarcheal status accounted for 6% (R = 0.24) and 1% (R = 0.10), respectively, of the variance in mothers' and fathers' ratings of disagreements over rules. The mothers' cubic term was marginally significant and positively predictive.

In summary, the effects of the mothers' menarcheal status rating were significant for the following child-rearing and outcome variables: mother acceptance (cubic and descending linearity), family rules and standards (quadratic and concave downward), family activities (cubic and descending linearity), and parental influence (cubic and descending linearity). A marginally significant effect of the mothers' rating of menarcheal status was found for disagreements over rules (cubic). The effects of the fathers' menarcheal status rating were significant for the following variables: family rules and standards (quadratic and concave downward) and parental influence (descending linearity). A marginally significant effect for the fathers' rating of menarcheal status was found for father acceptance (descending linearity).

DISCUSSION

One obvious feature of the multiple regression analyses reported above is that so little of the variance in the dependent measures can be attributed to menarcheal status. The percentage of variance accounted for ranges from 0% for oppositionalism (father-daughter) to 16% for involvement in family activities (mother-daughter). Nonetheless, the consistency of the curvilinear relations that emerged for the mother-daughter dyad commands our attention. Families where the daughter experienced menarche more than a year ago (early maturers) aside, the (then) quadratic trends look very much like those found by Steinberg and Hill (1978). That is, there are perturbations in parent-child relations (and, in the present case, in the outcome variables) 6 months after menarche; but by 12 months after menarche, the mean values look much like those of the premenarcheal group. Both the rather low percentage of variance accounted for and the curvilinearity of the relations are consonant with adaptational interpretations, rather than with persistent long-term effect interpretations.

Yet when the mother-daughter dyads where menarche occurred more than 12 months age (early maturers) are considered, the means for many of the variables for this group are commensurate with those of the 6-months-ago group. The timing of menarche may explain these cubic trends. When menarche occurs around the modal time, changes in parent-child relations of the sort tapped here may best be thought of as temporary perturbations. But when menarche occurs early—as, presumably, did the onset of the pubertal cycle—the effects persist: less participation in family activities, less parental influence, and less acceptance.

Another explanation for the double-bend, or sawtooth, effects may involve menarche and regular menstrual periods. Perturbations in family relations may occur just after menarche (the first bend) and again after the onset of regular menstrual periods (the second bend), which does not occur until well after menarche (Tanner, 1962). One or both of these explanations may be correct. Longitudinal study will be required to address the issues involved.

Only two significant results for fathers were found—a linear effect for parental influence as perceived by the daughter (the more biologically mature the daughter, the less parental influence was reported) and a quadratic effect for family rules and standards. A nearly significant effect of menarcheal status on acceptance was found for fathers (descending linearity). The means in Table III indicate that fathers of postmenarcheal daughters are viewed as less accepting. The effects for fathers cohere and resemble those involving mothers to the extent that, from a traditional standpoint, they suggest changes in parent-child relations with increasing maturation.

One obvious but incorrect assumption in accounting for fewer effects involving fathers would argue that fathers are not aware of daughters' menstrual status, an interpretation belied in the present instance by the high correlation between fathers' and mothers' judgments of the time since menarche ($r = 0.91$). Alternatively, fathers may be less reliable reporters of the outcome variables. Inspection of the correlations along the diagonal in Table I shows that children tend to see their parents similarly on parental acceptance and parental influence, but the parents probably disagree with each other on the parent-reported child outcome variables (i.e., involvement in family activities, oppositionalism, and disagreements over rules). Finally, menarche may simply impact less on fathers than on mothers (although some of our data on nonverbal behavior suggests that this is not the case).

The cubic trend for acceptance and the absence of such a trend for oppositionalism warrant comment. We labeled our scale acceptance instead of love-hostility (Schaefer's label) because no overtly hostile items were represented in this variable. What we have in low scores is the absence of warmth (or rejection) more than the presence of hostility. If acceptance did reflect parental hostility, then we might expect similar effects for child oppositionalism. We have neither here; nor have we evidence for the stronger forms of the psychoanalytic persuasion that adolescents are in "defiant rebellion against any and every authority" (Freud, 1966, p. 138) and that rebelliousness is fired by biological maturation (at least insofar as it is indexed by menarche). The frequencies for the items in the oppositionalism variable indicate that families rarely report the presence of frequent overt oppositionalism at any level of menarcheal status. Given the marginally significant result for disagreements over rules, however, there may be changes in the frequency of disagreements with increasing maturation.

Mothers are perceived by immediately postmenarcheal daughters as less accepting than are mothers of premenarcheal daughters, and the family is seen as being more controlling. In the first few months after menarche, there is less equalitarian treatment of the daughter and not more—at least as the daughter perceives it. Daughters also more frequently report being less influenced by their parents and seeking less guidance from them a few months after menarche than before. The findings are strengthened by the additional maternal report of less child participation in family activities in the immediately postmenarcheal group than in the premenarcheal group. If not outright storm, there certainly does appear to be a period of stress and strain in mother-daughter relations shortly after menarche. And if our speculation is correct, such stress and strain may persist in families of early maturing girls.

ACKNOWLEDGMENTS

The authors are grateful to Albert D. Farrell for his statistical advice and to Dale A. Blyth and Laurence D. Steinberg for their comments on an earlier draft.

REFERENCES

Alexander, J. F. (1973). Defensive and supportive communication in family systems. *J. Marr. Fam.* 35: 613-617.
Baumrind, D. (1968). Authoritarian vs. authoritative control. *Adolescence* 3: 255-272.
Block, J. H. (1978). Another look at sex differentiation in the socialization behaviors of mothers and fathers. In Sherman, J., and Denmark, F. (eds.), *Psychology of women: Future Directions of Research,* Psychological Dimensions, New York.
Blos, P. (1962). *On Adolescence: A Psychoanalytic Interpretation,* Free Press, New York.
Blos, P. (1979). *The Adolescent Passage,* International Universities Press, New York.

Blyth, D. A., Thiel, K., and Garbarino, J. (1978). Parent telephone interview from transition to adolescence study. Unpublished manuscript, Boys Town Center for the Study of Youth Development, Boys Town, Neb.

Brooks-Gunn, J., and Ruble, D. N. (1983). The experience of menarche from a developmental perspective. In J. Brooks-Gunn, J., and Petersen, A. C. (eds.), *Girls at Puberty: Biological and Psychosocial Perspectives,* Plenum, New York, pp. 155-178.

Cohen, J., and Cohen, P. (1983). *Applied Multiple Regression/Correlation Analysis for the Behavioral Sciences,* Erlbaum, Hillsdale, N.J.

Deutsch, H. (1944). *Psychology of Women,* Grune & Stratton, New York.

Devereux, E. C. (1970). The role of peer group experience in moral development. In Hill, J. P. (ed.), *Minnesota Symposia on Child Psychology,* (Vol. 4), University of Minnesota Press, Minneapolis, pp. 94-140.

Duncan, O. D. (1977). A socioeconomic index for all occupations. In Reiss, A. J., Jr. (ed.), *Occupations and Social Status,* Arno Press, New York, pp. 109-138.

Erikson, E. (1968). *Identity: Youth and Crisis,* Norton, New York.

Faust, M. S. (1960). Developmental maturity as a determinant of prestige of adolescent girls. *Child Dev.* 31: 173-184.

Freud, A. (1958). Adolescence. *Psychoanal. Stud. Child* 13: 231-258.

Freud, A. (1966). *The Ego and the Mechanisms of Defense,* International Universities Press, New York.

Garbarino, J. (1978). Family and neighborhood interview. Unpublished manuscript, Boys Town Center for the Study of Youth Development.

Greif, E., and Ulman, K. H. (1982). The psychological impact of menarche on early adolescent females: A review of the literature. *Child Dev.* 53: 1413-1430.

Hall, G. S. (1904). *Adolescence: Its Psychology and Its Relations to Physiology, Anthropology, Sociology, Sex, Crime, Religion, and Education,* Prentice-Hall, Englewood Cliffs, N.J.

Hetherington, E. M., Stouwie, R., and Ridberg, E. H. (1971). Patterns of family interaction and child-rearing attitudes related to three dimensions of juvenile delinquency. *J. Abnorm. Psychol.* 77: 160-176.

Hill, J. P. (1980). The family. In Johnson, M. (ed.), *Toward Adolescence: The Middle School Years. The Seventh-Ninth Yearbook of the National Society for the Study of Education,* University of Chicago Press, Chicago, pp. 32-55.

Hill, J. P., and Lynch, M. E. (1983). The intensification of gender-related role expectations during early adolescence. In Brooks-Gunn, J., and Petersen, A. C. (eds.), *Girls at Puberty: Biological and Psychosocial Perspectives,* Plenum, New York, pp. 201-228.

Kandel, D., and Lesser, G. S. (1972). *Youth in Two Worlds,* Jossey-Bass, San Francisco.

Kohn, M. L. (1977). *Class and Conformity,* 2nd ed., University of Chicago press, Chicago.

Newson, J., and Newson, E. (1968). *Four Years Old in an Urban Community,* Pelican, Harmondworth, Eng.

Petersen, A. C., and Taylor, B. (1980). The biological approach to adolescence: Biological change and psychological adaptation. In Adelson, J. (ed.), *Handbook of Adolescent Psychology,* Wiley, New York, pp. 117-155.

Schaefer, E. S. (1955). A circumplex model for maternal behavior. *J. Abnorm. Soc. Psychol.* 59: 226-235.

Schaefer, E. S., and Bayley, N. (1963). Maternal behavior, child behavior, and their intercorrelations from infancy through adolescence. *Monogr. Soc. Res. Child Dev.* 28 (Ser. No. 28).

Spence, J. T., and Helmreich, R. L. (1978). *Masculinity and Femininity: Their Psychological Dimensions, Correlates, and Antecedents,* University of Texas Press, Austin.

Steinberg, L. D. (1981). Transformations in family relations at puberty. *Dev. Psychol.* 17: 833-840.

Steinberg, L. D., and Hill, J. P. (1978). Patterns of family interaction as a function of age, the onset of puberty, and formal thinking. *Dev. Psychol.* 14: 683-684.

Tanner, J. (1962). *Growth at Adolescence,* 2nd ed., Charles C Thomas, Springfield, Ill.

Developmental Psychology
1987, Vol. 23, No. 3, 451–460

Impact of Puberty on Family Relations: Effects of Pubertal Status and Pubertal Timing

Laurence Steinberg
University of Wisconsin–Madison

This investigation examines the impact of pubertal status and pubertal timing, independent of each other and of chronological age, on the family relationships of adolescent boys and girls. The sample is composed of 204 families with a firstborn child between the ages of 10 and 15. Measures included adolescent and parental reports of closeness, conflict, and autonomy as well as assessments of each adolescent's pubertal status and pubertal timing (early, on time, or late maturing). Findings indicate that (a) pubertal maturation is associated with increased emotional distance between youngsters and their parents; (b) pubertal maturation (among girls) and early pubertal maturation (among boys) increase conflict between adolescents and their mothers, but not necessarily fathers; and (c) pubertal maturation and, especially, late maturation may be accompanied by increased behavioral autonomy for the adolescent.

Interest in the differential impact of early versus late maturation on parent–child relationships in adolescence dates back to the early days of the Berkeley Guidance and Oakland Growth Studies (see Clausen, 1975, and Livson & Peskin, 1980, for reviews). This interest has been rekindled with new fervor in recent years, as investigators have increasingly turned their attention to biological influences on social relations during early adolescence (e.g., Brooks-Gunn, Petersen, & Eichorn, 1985). During the last decade, researchers interested in the impact of pubertal status, independent of its timing, also have studied the impact of puberty on the family (e.g., Hill, Holmbeck, Marlow, Green, & Lynch, 1985a, 1985b; Steinberg, 1981), stressing that some of the effects of biological maturation involve adaptation to the changing competencies, concerns, and characteristics of the maturing youngster regardless of his or her age at the time of pubertal onset.

Considered together, the findings from studies of puberty and adolescent family relationships point to several general conclusions. First and most important, pubertal maturation appears to have an impact on the family system independent of changes that may be attributable to the adolescent's chronological age. With respect to *pubertal status*, studies suggest that pubertal maturation is associated with increased distance, dissatisfaction, or conflict in the parent–child relationship (Cantara, 1983; Hill et al., 1985a, 1985b, Papini & Sebby, 1985; Steinberg,

1977, 1981; Steinberg & Hill, 1978). This phenomenon appears to be most salient in relationships between adolescents and mothers and most apparent during the midpoint of the pubertal cycle (although the distance and dissatisfaction may continue beyond this stage, especially in families of girls; e.g., Hill et al., 1985b). There are, however, inconsistencies in this literature. For example, whereas Steinberg (1981) and Hill et al. (1985a, 1985b) report few effects of puberty on adolescent–father relationships, Papini and Sebby (1985) find that this dyad undergoes changes as negative and substantial as those experienced by mothers and adolescents.

Studies of *pubertal timing* and family relationships are more equivocal than studies of pubertal status and indicate that the impact of pubertal timing on family relationships may differ for adolescent boys and girls. Some studies, especially those of boys, suggest that early maturers enjoy more permissive family relationships and indicate that late maturers are likely to express higher "needs" for autonomy and greater dissatisfaction about what they perceive to be excessive parental control (e.g., Clausen, 1975; for a cross-cultural exception, however, see Young & Ferguson, 1981). Other studies, especially those of girls, indicate that early maturation may be accompanied by increased parental restrictiveness and vigilance and greater conflict between parents and the adolescent (e.g., Hill et al., 1985b; Petersen, 1985; Savin-Williams & Small, 1986). Many studies, however, report no or few systematic differences between the family relationships of early and late maturers (Savin-Williams & Small, 1986; Stone & Barker, 1939); and at least one study of family interaction suggests that interaction patterns are more strained in families of on-time youngsters than in homes of early or late maturers (Hauser et al., 1985).

One reason for discrepancies in the literature on pubertal timing and adolescent family relationships may be the variety of outcome measures used in these studies: Although some researchers have used standardized measures of adolescent personality traits (see Clausen, 1975), others have used self-report

---

The work described here was conducted during the author's tenure as a Faculty Scholar under the William T. Grant Foundation's Program in the Mental Health of Children and was supported by a grant from the Graduate School of the University of Wisconsin.

I am grateful to the administrators, teachers, and students of the Madison Unified School District and to Susan B. Silverberg, who directed our able staff of data collectors.

Correspondence concerning this article should be addressed to Laurence Steinberg, Child and Family Studies, 1430 Linden Drive, University of Wisconsin, Madison, Wisconsin 53706.

measures of various aspects of family relationships (e.g., Savin-Williams & Small, 1986), and still others have observed parent–adolescent interaction directly (e.g., Hauser et al., 1985). A second reason for inconsistency may be related to the source of information on family relationships. In some studies adolescents' reports are used (e.g., Blyth, Bulcroft, & Simmons, 1981; Simmons, Blyth, & McKinney, 1983); in others, both parents and adolescents provide information (e.g., Hill et al., 1985a, 1985b; Savin-Williams & Small, 1986); in still others, assessments are derived from independent raters (e.g., Hauser et al., 1985). To the extent that puberty affects individuals' perceptions of changes in the family more than it affects actual interactions between individuals, studies employing different sources may lead to different conclusions.

Measurement and source variability across investigations are not problems unique to the study of puberty and family relationships, of course. A third reason, however, for inconsistencies in this literature is particular to research on puberty and it creates an interesting methodological consideration in its own light: Studies of pubertal status and pubertal timing inherently confound one with the other and each with chronological age. To the extent that chronological age, pubertal status, and pubertal timing have different effects on family relationships, the fact that they usually are confounded may create problems in interpretation.

Disentangling the effects of pubertal status, pubertal timing, and chronological age in studies of the relation between biological development and adolescent social relationships presents an intriguing, if challenging, conundrum. Cross-sectional comparisons of adolescents in different pubertal timing groups (e.g., early maturers versus on-time maturers) inherently confound pubertal timing with pubertal status or with age, because early maturers are by definition either younger or more physically mature than their peers. Thus, effects that are attributed to early or late maturation may actually be due to chronological age alone (if the sample contains youngsters who range in age), pubertal status alone (if the sample is homogeneous with respect to age), or the interaction of the two (in which case, the effect is truly a pubertal-timing effect). Although this was noted by Peskin (1967), the implications seldom have been heeded. For example, Savin-Williams and Small (1986) examined an array of putative pubertal timing effects among 10- to 17-year-olds, but because they did not control for adolescent age, their attribution of group differences to differences in pubertal timing is suspect. Similarly, although Hauser et al. (1985) suggest that family interaction is more strained among on-time youngsters than among early or late maturers, group differences may be due to differences in adolescents' pubertal status (rather than pubertal timing) at the time of assessment. Cross-sectional studies of pubertal status (e.g., Hill et al., 1985a, 1985b; Papini & Sebby, 1985; Steinberg & Hill, 1978) are also problematic, because they confound pubertal status with pubertal timing (if the age range is restricted) or with chronological age (if the age range is wide).

This study was conducted for both substantive and methodological reasons. Substantively, it examines whether and in what ways puberty may distance adolescents from their parents. Methodologically, it is designed to examine whether the distanc-

ing effects of puberty, if apparent, are related to pubertal timing or pubertal status or, alternatively, to chronological age. It is hypothesized that pubertal maturation, independent of chronological age, is associated (either linearly or curvilinearly) with diminished parent–child closeness, increased parent–child conflict, and increased adolescent autonomy. Given the equivocal nature of previous research on pubertal timing and family relationships, it is not clear whether or how early or late maturation may moderate these relationships.

Method

Sample

The sample for this study is composed of 204 families with a firstborn child between the ages of 10 and 15. Participating families were selected via a two-step process, beginning with a representative sample of 865 adolescents attending Grades 5, 6, 8, and 9 in the Madison (Wisconsin) school district, who were surveyed in their classrooms, and ending with a subsample of 204 families with firstborn adolescents, who were surveyed in their homes. Participation rates in each phase of the data collection were adequate: 94% of all youngsters attending school on the day of the survey participated in the research and 70% of the families contacted by our research staff agreed to participate in the study (we contacted all families whose adolescent was firstborn). As a group, the participating families did not differ from the eligible nonparticipants on any of the demographic variables assessed (i.e., socioeconomic status, household composition, maternal employment status). Subsequent comparisons between the demographic characteristics of the study sample and that of the district's student population as a whole, on the basis of information provided by the district, indicate that the school sample and the family subsample are representative of the district population.

The sample of 204 families is evenly divided by target adolescent sex, predominantly White (88%), socioeconomically heterogeneous (39% blue collar, 37% white collar, 24% professional, as determined by parental occupation), from a variety of family structures (64% biologically intact, 21% single parent, 15% stepfamily), and with a variety of maternal work patterns (58% employed full-time, 31% employed part-time, 11% not working). At the time of data collection, the youngsters ranged in age from 10 to 15 years ($M = 12.71$, $SD = 1.62$, for boys; $M = 12.34$, $SD = 1.58$, for girls).

Data on family relations and pubertal maturation were collected during home visits conducted between April and June 1985. Adolescents, mothers, and fathers all completed the questionnaire battery independently. Of interest in this analysis are measures of adolescents' *pubertal maturation* and measures of *autonomy, conflict,* and *closeness* in the family.

Measures of Pubertal Maturation

Pubertal status. Adolescents' pubertal status was assessed surreptitiously during the home visit by two trained observers using a 5-point rating scale. Adolescents are assigned to one of five pubertal maturation categories (prepubertal, early pubertal, apex pubertal, postapex, and late pubertal) on the basis of visible signs of secondary sex characteristics, including facial shape and hair, body proportion, and chest and hip development. This measure has been used in previous studies linking pubertal maturation with changes in family interaction patterns (Steinberg, 1981) and in studies of the relation between adolescents' pubertal maturation and their friendship networks (Garbarino, Burston, Raber, Russell, & Crouter, 1978). In this study, the interrater reliability of the measure was .81, comparable to that reported in previous studies in which the measure was used (e.g., Steinberg, 1981). Disagreements between raters were resolved through discussion.

Pubertal timing. Adolescents' pubertal status scores also were used to assign youngsters to one of three pubertal timing groups according to a procedure identical to that used by Savin-Williams and Small (1986). Individuals within one standard deviation of their age (assessed in terms of school grade) norm for pubertal status in this sample were classified as *on-time maturers* (74 boys, 80 girls). Individuals more than one standard deviation above the norm were classified as *early maturers* (11 boys, 8 girls). Individuals more than one standard deviation below the norm were classified as *late maturers* (13 boys, 18 girls). This is a relatively conservative categorization procedure designed to ensure that "early" and "late" maturers are sufficiently advanced or behind their peers.

Measures of Autonomy

Adolescent emotional autonomy. This measure is based on Blos's (1979) perspective on individuation (see Steinberg and Silverberg, 1986, for details). The measure is composed of 20 Likert-scale items concerning four components of emotional autonomy: two cognitive components (the extent to which the adolescent perceives his or her parents as people and the extent to which he or she "deidealizes" them) and two affective components (an absence of feelings of dependency on parents and feelings of individuation). Scores on the measure increase linearly as a function of chronological age during the early adolescent period, consistent with the notion that adolescents become more emotionally autonomous with age, and providing some construct validation for the measure (Steinberg & Silverberg, 1986). The internal consistency of the measure, as determined by Cronbach's alpha, is .75.

Patterns of family decision making. Each family member completed a checklist concerning 17 areas of decision making on issues relevant to children in the age range studied (e.g., curfew, spending money, leisure activities, completing school assignments). For each item, individuals indicated whether the parents dictated how the adolescent should behave, asked the youngster's opinion but retained the final say on the matter, or left the decision entirely up to the youngster. Following Dornbusch et al. (1985), scores for authoritarianism (parents dictate), authoritativeness (parents ask opinion but maintain ultimate control), and permissiveness (child decides) were calculated for each individual by summing the number of items in each of the three categories and converting the total to a proportion of the total number of issues. The internal consistency of the measure, as determined by Cronbach's alpha, is .78 for adolescents, .77 for fathers, and .78 for mothers. Adolescents' scores derived from a similar measure have been shown to be significantly related to youngsters' involvement in deviant activities and with youngsters' susceptibility to peer pressure, with adolescent deviance and susceptibility positively correlated with parental permissiveness (Dornbusch et al., 1985; Steinberg, 1987).

Adolescents' reports of parental control and restrictiveness. Adolescents' characterizations of their parents' control and restrictiveness derived from these two subscales of the shortened form of the Child Report of Parent Behavior Inventory (CRPBI; Schludermann & Schludermann, 1970). The CRPBI is a Likert-scale format report of parental disciplinary practices that yields measures of perceived closeness (warmth-hostility), psychological control (control-autonomy), and restrictiveness (restrictiveness-permissiveness) for mothers and fathers separately. A substantial literature on parent-child relationships documents the usefulness of these dimensions in the study of family relationships (see Maccoby & Martin, 1983, for a recent review). As reported by Schwartz, Barton-Henry, and Pruzinsky, (1985), the revised version of the CRPBI has a reliability of .84.

Parents' reports of parental control. Measures of parental control

were also derived from mothers' and fathers' responses to the shortened form of the Parent Attitude Research Instrument (PARI; Schludermann & Schludermann, 1977). This measure is a report of parental disciplinary practices that yields an index of parental control comparable to that derived from the CRPBI. Slightly different forms of the PARI are administered to mothers and fathers. As reported by Schludermann & Schludermann (1977) the measure has a reliability of .82.

Measures of Conflict

The measures of adolescent-parent conflict were derived from adolescents' and parents' independent responses to a series of questions about the intensity of discussions that may have occurred across 17 different areas of day-to-day decision making (e.g., curfew, clothing, homework) within a particular dyad during the past 2 weeks. Adolescents completed the questions twice: once with regard to their mother and once with regard to their father. The specific items were chosen in view of previous studies indicating that conflict between teenagers and parents is likely to revolve around mundane issues of day-to-day living (Montemayor, 1986). For each of the 17 items the respondent is asked whether a discussion took place during the previous 2 weeks, and, if so, to rate the intensity of the discussion on a 5-point scale from *very calm* (1) to *very angry* (5). The instrument is modeled after the "Issues Checklist" first developed by Prinz, Foster, Kent, and O'Leary (1979; subsequently revised by Robin and Foster, 1984), who report that conflict scores derived from the measure significantly discriminate between families with and families without clinical problems. The internal consistency of the measure for adolescents with regard to mothers is .76; for adolescents with regard to fathers, .80; for mothers with regard to adolescents, .75; and for fathers with regard to adolescents, .80. In this analysis, two conflict scores were generated from the measure: *frequency of conflict* (the number of items discussed for which the respondent reported any anger at all in the discussion—i.e., scores of 2 or more on the scale) and *intensity of conflict* (the average level of intensity across all items for which a discussion took place).

Measures of Closeness

Frequency of calm communication. The checklist used to derive the measures of conflict was also used to derive a measure of calm communication between adolescent and parent. Calm communication was operationalized as the number of items discussed during the past 2 weeks for which the respondent reported no anger at all (i.e., a score of 1).

Parent-adolescent cohesion. Cohesion in each of the parent-child dyads was assessed via the cohesion subscale of the Family Adaptability and Cohesion Evaluation Scales (FACES)II inventory. The FACES inventory is a widely used measure of family relationships during adolescence in both clinical and nonclinical studies (see Olson, Sprenkle, & Russell, 1979, for details). In this study, the inventory is completed by all family members independently with reference to specific family dyads (e.g., the adolescent completes the inventory with reference to his or her mother and then again with reference to his or her father). Recent studies link positive scores on the FACES cohesion scale to positive scores on a measure of parent-adolescent communication and to positive scores on a measure of family satisfaction (Barnes & Olson, 1985). The internal consistency of the measure, as reported by its developers, is .87.

Plan of Analysis

In view of the need to disentangle the effects of pubertal status, chronological age, and pubertal timing, multiple regression analyses were used so that effects could be examined with and without controlling for possible confounding factors. In regressions examining the impact of

Table 1
Intercorrelations Within Sets of Dependent Variables: Conflict

Variable	1	2	3	4
1. P-Intensity		.448***	.361***	.238***
2. P-Frequency	.485***		.173**	.353***
3. C-Intensity	.064	.157*		.611***
4. C-Frequency	.147*	.264***	.510***	

Note. P = Parent's report, C = Child's report. Correlations for mother–child pairs are above the diagonal; correlations for father–child pairs are below the diagonal. *N*s range from 125 to 186.
* *p* < .05. ** *p* < .01. *** *p* < .001.

pubertal status this variable was entered into the regression equation and the regression coefficient was tested for significance. On the second step of the analysis chronological age (in months) was entered into the equation and the coefficient for pubertal status was reexamined.[1] The significance of the overall equation containing both pubertal status and age was also tested. Additional analyses were conducted to determine whether a significant curvilinear effect for pubertal status existed; in these analyses, the quadratic term for pubertal status was tested only after the linear term was in the equation.

In order to examine the effect of pubertal timing, this variable was effect coded and the two resultant vectors (one representing the contrast between early maturers and on-time youngsters, and one representing the contrast between late maturers and on-time youngsters) were entered into the equation on the first step. The regression coefficients were then examined. On the second step of the analysis, either chronological age or pubertal status was entered and the regression coefficients for the pubertal timing vectors were reexamined.

Results

Relations Among Dependent Variables

Patterns of correlations within the three sets of dependent variables are presented in Tables 1, 2, and 3. In general, the pattern of relations suggests that (a) when one individual's perceptions are examined, variables designed to measure similar constructs (e.g., closeness assessed via the measure of calm communication and closeness assessed via the FACES cohesion subscale) are significantly correlated in the expected direction; (b) adolescents' and parents' perceptions are generally positively correlated, particularly in the domains of conflict and closeness; and (c) adolescents' and fathers' perceptions are on the whole less strongly correlated with each other than are adolescents' and mothers' perceptions.

Impact of Puberty on Family Relations of Adolescent Boys

Adolescents' reports of closeness. In general, the findings support the hypothesis that pubertal maturation is associated with increased distance between sons and their parents. Sons who are more physically mature report less cohesion with their mother than do less mature boys, $b = .288$, $t(1, 89) = -2.836$, $p < .01$. Although this effect is diminished when age is entered into the equation along with pubertal status, the combined effect of pubertal status and age on cohesion with mother is sig-

nificant, $R = .30$, $F(2, 88) = 4.362$, $p < .05$, and neither predictor alone is significant when both are included in the equation simultaneously—suggesting that age and pubertal maturation have a similar and combined negative effect on boys' cohesion with their mothers.[2] Similarly, physically mature sons report less frequent calm communication with their fathers and see their fathers as less accepting than do less mature boys, $b = -.253$, $t(1, 69) = 2.169$, $p < .05$; and $b = -2.55$, $t(1, 72) = -2.238$, $p < .05$, respectively. Again, the patterns of relations suggest that pubertal maturation and age exert a similar and combined negative effect on closeness between sons and fathers. Adolescents' perceptions of maternal acceptance appear to vary curvilinearly with pubertal status, $b = 1.089$, $t(2, 83) = 1.878$, $p = .06$, with perceived acceptance lower among apex pubertal boys than among their more or less mature counterparts, an effect not diminished by controlling for age. Sons' reports of calm communication with their mother, or cohesion with their father, do not vary as a function of pubertal status.

In contrast to these effects of pubertal status, adolescent boys' perceptions of closeness with their mother or father do not vary as a function of pubertal timing.

Adolescents' reports of conflict. In contrast to cohesion, conflict between sons and parents is predicted by pubertal timing rather than pubertal status. Adolescent boys' pubertal status is unrelated to their reports of conflict with their mother or with their father. However, early maturing youngsters report more intense (although not more frequent) conflict with both mother and father than do on-time boys, $b = .357$, $t(2, 82) = 2.219$, $p < .05$; and $b = .550$, $t(2, 64) = 3.161$, $p < .01$, respectively; and late maturers report less intense conflict with their father, $b = -.425$, $t(2, 64) = -2.439$, $p < .05$. These relations are not changed when age or pubertal status is taken into account.

Adolescents' reports of autonomy. The findings concerning autonomy indicate that pubertal maturation is, as hypothesized, related to increased autonomy between sons and parents. Physically mature boys describe their parents as being more permissive, $b = .210$, $t(1, 91) = 1.97$, $p < .05$, and they feel more emotionally autonomous from them, $b = .222$, $t(1, 89) = 2.143$, $p < .05$; in both cases, the effects of pubertal status covary with chronological age. Although physically mature boys also describe their parents' decision making as less authoritarian, $b = -.274$, $t(1, 91) = -2.714$, $p < .001$, this relation is an artifact of chronological age. Sons' descriptions of their parents' degree of psychological control or restrictiveness, as assessed via the CRPBI, do not vary with pubertal status, however.

In contrast to the effects of pubertal status, only one pubertal timing effect reached significance: Late maturing boys describe their family's decision making as less authoritarian, $b = -.402$,

---

[1] The effect of adding age to the equation was only examined in cases in which pubertal status had been a significant predictor. If, after age was entered into the equation, both age and pubertal status were nonsignificant but the overall equation was significant, this was taken as evidence that age and pubertal maturation exerted similar and overlapping effects on the outcome in question.

[2] This pattern, suggesting that the effects of age and pubertal status covary, is observed across several dependent variables. For the sake of brevity, the pattern is elaborated here but not in subsequent examples.

Table 2
Intercorrelations Within Sets of Dependent Variables: Closeness

Variable	1	2	3	4	5
1. P-Cohesion		.330**	.418**	.169*	.415**
2. P-Communication	.038		.192*	.223**	.275**
3. C-Cohesion	.435**	−.068		.349**	.735**
4. C-Communication	.046	.033	.404**		.373**
5. C-Acceptance	.411**	−.083	.805**	.399**	

Note. P = Parent's report, C = Child's report. Correlations for mother–child pairs are above the diagonal; correlations for father–child pairs are below the diagonal. *N*s range from 125 to 186.
* *p* < .01. ** *p* < .001.

$t(2, 90) = -2.644$, $p < .01$, a relation that is neither an artifact of youngsters' age nor pubertal status.

Mothers' reports of closeness. Boys' pubertal status is not related to mothers' reports of closeness with their son. However, pubertal timing does exert an impact on mothers' reports of cohesion with sons; mothers report relatively less cohesion with late maturers and relatively more cohesion with early maturers, $b = .595$, $t(2, 43) = -2.929$, $p < .005$; and $b = .393$, $t(2, 43) = 1.937$, $p = .06$, respectively. These effects are not diminished when age or pubertal status is taken into account. Sons' pubertal timing and mothers' reports of calm communication are unrelated.

Mothers' reports of conflict. Neither pubertal status nor pubertal timing is related to mothers' reports of conflict with their sons.

Mothers' reports of autonomy. Mothers' reports of autonomy in the parent–child relationship appear to vary curvilinearly with sons' pubertal status: Mothers of midpubertal boys tend to characterize their families as more permissive than do other mothers, $b = -1.085$, $t(2, 87) = -1.900$, $p = .06$; and mothers of midpubertal boys describe themselves as less authoritarian on the PARI than do other mothers, $b = 1.179$, $t(2, 82) = 2.031$, $p < .05$. These relations are not artifacts of age.

Mothers of early maturing boys describe their families as more authoritarian, $b = .372$, $t(2, 87) = 2.41$, $p < .05$, a relation that is not due to age or pubertal status alone. Mothers' scores on the PARI are not related to their sons' pubertal timing.

Fathers' reports of closeness. Fathers' reports of closeness with sons are unrelated to their son's pubertal status or timing.

Fathers' reports of conflict. There appears to be a curvilinear relation between fathers' reports of conflict and their sons' pubertal status. Fathers of apex pubertal boys tend to report more intense and more frequent conflict with their sons than do fathers of less or more mature youngsters, $b = -.973$, $t(2, 94) = -1.762$, $p = .08$; and $b = -.967$, $t(2, 94) = -1.758$, $p = .08$, respectively. These trends are not diminished when age is taken into account.

Pubertal timing also is related to fathers' reports of conflict with their sons, but, contrary to sons' reports, more intense conflict is reported by fathers of late maturers, $b = .352$, $t(2, 64) = 1.935$, $p = .06$. This is not an artifact of age or of pubertal status. Frequency of conflict is not affected by pubertal timing.

Fathers' reports of autonomy. Fathers' self-characterizations derived from the PARI do not vary as a function of sons' puber-

tal status or pubertal timing. However, fathers tend to describe family decision making as less authoritative in households with physically mature boys, $b = -.210$, $t(1, 67) = -1.758$, $p = .08$, and describe decision making in these households as more permissive, $b = .339$, $t(1, 67) = 2.949$, $p < .01$; these effects are not diminished by controlling for age. Fathers' reports of decision-making styles do not differ across the pubertal timing groups.

The effects of pubertal status and timing on boys' family relationships are summarized in Table 4.

Impact of Puberty on Family Relations of Adolescent Girls

Adolescents' reports of closeness. Girls' reports of closeness with their parents show a similar pattern to that found among boys: Pubertal maturation, along with chronological age, is associated with diminished closeness between girls and their parents. Specifically, physically mature girls report less cohesion with their mothers than do other girls, $b = -.409$, $t(1, 101) = -4.508$, $p < .001$, report less calm communication with their mother, $b = -.343$, $t(1, 95) = -3.556$, $p < .001$, and see their mother as less accepting, $b = -.285$, $t(1, 91) = -2.835$, $p < .01$; in all three cases both age and pubertal maturation exert a similar and combined effect. A similar pattern is found in the father–daughter dyad: Physically mature girls report less cohesion with their fathers than do their less mature counterparts, $b = -.370$, $t(1, 79) = -3.544$, $p < .001$, report less calm communication with their father, $b = -281$, $t(1, 76) = -2.549$, $p < .01$, and describe their fathers as less accepting, $b = -.186$, $t(1, 69) = -2.788$, $p < .01$; again, the effects of pubertal status and age covary.

As is the case among boys, there are no significant effects of pubertal timing on daughters' reports of closeness with mother or with father.

Adolescents' reports of conflict. Physically mature girls report more intense, but not more frequent, conflict with their mothers than do other girls, $b = .253$, $t(1, 92) = 2.505$, $p < .01$, an effect that covaries with age. Late maturing girls tend to report less frequent conflict with their mothers, $b = -2.97$, $t(2, 94) = -1.870$, $p = .06$. However, although this is not an artifact of age, it is an artifact of pubertal status (the b becomes nonsignificant when pubertal status is in the equation) and suggests that the lower incidence of conflict among late maturing girls and their mothers may be due entirely to the girls' physical immaturity.

Table 3
Intercorrelations Within Sets of Dependent Variables: Autonomy

Variable	1	2	3	4	5	6	7	8	9	10
1. P-Authoritarian		-.528***	-.531***	.221**	.198**	-.089	-.144*	.029	.201**	.052
2. P-Authoritative	-.578***		-.439***	.022	.018	.080	-.099	.112	-.092	.113
3. P-Permissive	-.456***	-.464***		-.255***	-.229***	.010	.254***	-.142	-.120	.056
4. P-Control (PARI)	.265***	-.049	-.220***		.015	.063	-.080	-.068	.031	.187**
5. C-Authoritarian	.209**	.012	-.240**	.056		-.575***	-.601***	.179**	.230	-.079
6. C-Authoritative	-.213**	.093	.130	-.029	-.575***		-.309***	-.064	.012	-.032
7. C-Permissive	-.040	-.111	.160*	-.038	-.601***	-.309***		-.147*	-.274***	.123*
8. C-Control (CRPBI)	.092	.001	-.102	-.048	.115	-.043	-.092		-.156*	.311***
9. C-Restrictive (CRPBI)	-.138*	.046	.099	.007	.011	.025	-.037	-.111		-.061
10. C-Emotional autonomy	.089	-.102	.016	-.026	-.079	-.032	.123*	.299***	-.086	

Note. P = Parent's report, C = Child's report. PARI = Parent Attitude Research Instrument. CRPBI = Child Report of Parent Behavior Inventory. Correlations for mother–child pairs are above the diagonal; correlations for father–child pairs are below the diagonal. Ns range from 125 to 186.
* $p < .05.$ ** $p < .01.$ *** $p < .001.$

Neither pubertal status nor pubertal timing is related to daughters' reports of conflict with their fathers.

Adolescents' reports of autonomy. As is the case among boys, the relation between pubertal maturation and adolescents' reports of autonomy is most clear in the domain of emotional autonomy. Once again, the effect is consistent with the distancing hypothesis: Girls' reported emotional autonomy increases as a function of physical maturation, $b = .380$, $t(1, 92) = 3.948$, $p < .001$, an effect that covaries with age. Although physically mature girls are also less likely to describe their parents' decision making as authoritarian, $b = -.236$, $t(1, 100) = -2.430$, $p < .05$, and more likely to describe their parents' style as permissive, $b = .202$, $t(1, 100) = 2.066$, $p < .05$, these effects appear to be entirely due to age. Daughters' descriptions of the degree to which their fathers are psychologically controlling or restrictive, according to scores derived from the CRPBI, do not vary with pubertal status, but physically mature girls tend to be more likely to describe their mothers as psychologically controlling, $b = .191$, $t(1, 97) = 1.924$, $p = .06$, an effect that covaries with that of age.

Pubertal timing and adolescent autonomy are not clearly related. There is a tendency for late-maturing girls to describe their parents' decision making as less authoritarian, $b = -.279$, $t(2, 99) = -1.798$, $p = .08$. And, although late maturers also tend to describe their mothers as less psychologically controlling, $b = -.283$, $t(2, 96) = -1.805$, $p = .07$, this relation is due solely to the late maturers' lower pubertal status (see preceding paragraph).

Mothers' reports of closeness. Mothers report less cohesion with physically mature daughters than with less mature girls, $b = -2.05$, $t(1, 102) = -2.115$, $p < .05$, but this appears to be an artifact of chronological age, because the coefficient for pubertal status is greatly diminished, $b = .096$, whereas that for age is significant when the two predictors are considered simultaneously, $b = -.359$, $t(1, 101) = -2.049$, $p < .05$. Maternal reports of calm communication with daughters are also negatively related to pubertal status, $b = -.207$, $t(1, 100) = -2.119$, $p < .05$, but in this instance the effects of age and pubertal status appear to be overlapping. Mothers' reports of closeness with daughters are not affected by pubertal timing.

Mothers' reports of conflict. Mothers' reports of intensity of conflict with their daughters tend to be positively related to pubertal status, $b = .174$, $t(1, 100) = 1.768$, $p = .08$. Mothers' reports of frequency of conflict are unrelated to pubertal status, however.

As was the case for daughters' reports, mothers of late maturing girls report less frequent conflict with their daughters than do other mothers, $b = -.315$, $t(2, 99) = -2.065$, $p < .05$, but in this case the relation does not appear to be due either to age or pubertal status. Intensity of conflict, in contrast, is not related to pubertal timing.

Mothers' reports of autonomy. Mothers' reports concerning autonomy in the parent–child relationship are unrelated to their daughters' pubertal timing and not strongly related to pubertal status. Mothers of physically mature girls report less authoritarianism than do other mothers, $b = -.262$, $t(1, 98) = -2.692$, $p < .01$, a relation that covaries with age. Maternal reports of permissiveness, although appearing to vary positively

Table 4
Summary of Effects of Puberty on Family Relations of Boys

Outcome	Effect of pubertal status	Effect of pubertal timing
	Sons' reports	
Cohesion with mother	Negative***	ns
Calm communication with mother	ns	ns
Maternal acceptance	U-shaped*	ns
Cohesion with father	ns	ns
Calm communication with father	Negative**	ns
Paternal acceptance	Negative**	ns
Frequency of conflict with mother	ns	ns
Intensity of conflict with mother	ns	EM > on-time**
Frequency of conflict with father	ns	ns
Intensity of conflict with father	ns	EM > on-time > LM**
Authoritarian decisions	Age artifact	LM < on-time***
Authoritative decisions	ns	ns
Permissive decisions	Positive**	ns
Maternal control	ns	ns
Maternal restrictiveness	ns	ns
Paternal control	ns	ns
Paternal restrictiveness	ns	ns
Emotional autonomy	Positive**	ns
	Mothers' reports	
Cohesion	ns	EM > on-time > LM***
Calm communication	ns	ns
Intensity of conflict	ns	ns
Frequency of conflict	ns	ns
Authoritarian decisions	ns	EM > on-time**
Authoritative decisions	ns	ns
Permissive decisions	Inverted U-shaped*	ns
Maternal control	U-shaped**	ns
	Fathers' reports	
Cohesion	ns	ns
Calm communication	ns	ns
Frequency of conflict	Inverted U-shaped*	ns
Intensity of conflict	Inverted U-shaped*	LM > on-time*
Authoritarian decisions	ns	ns
Authoritative decisions	Negative*	ns
Permissive decisions	Positive***	ns
Paternal control	ns	ns

Note. EM = Early maturing; LM = Late maturing.
* $p < .10$. ** $p < .05$. *** $p < .01$.

with pubertal maturation, $b = .238$, $t(1, 98) = 2.425$, $p < .05$, are actually an artifact of chronological age.

Fathers' reports of closeness. Fathers report less cohesion with physically mature daughters than with less mature girls, $b = -.229$, $t(1, 78) = -2.076$, $p < .05$, an effect that covaries with age. Fathers' reports of calm communication do not vary as a function of daughters' pubertal status, however.

Fathers' reports of closeness with daughters are not affected by pubertal timing.

Fathers' reports of conflict. Fathers' reports of conflict with their daughters are unrelated to pubertal status or pubertal timing.

Fathers' reports of autonomy. Fathers' reports concerning autonomy in the parent–child relationship are unrelated to their daughters' pubertal status or timing. Although it appears that fathers of physically mature girls characterize family decision making as more authoritarian and fathers of early maturing girls as less authoritarian than do fathers of other girls, $b = -.213$, $t(1, 71) = -1.526$, $p = .07$, and $b = .335$, $t(2, 78) = 1.844$, $p = .07$, respectively, these relations actually are artifacts of chronological age. Because fathers' reports of authoritarianism decrease with age, they also appear to be lower among physically mature girls and higher among early maturers (the latter of whom are younger than their peers).

The effects of pubertal status and timing on girls' family relationships are summarized in Table 5.

Discussion

In this report the distancing impact of puberty on family relationships was examined through a series of analyses that permitted the disentangling of the effects of pubertal status, pubertal timing, and chronological age. The findings are generally consistent with the hypothesis that pubertal maturation increases emotional distance between youngsters and their parents. The effect of pubertal maturation appears to be independent of and additional to the similar distancing effect of chronological age.

The findings also suggest that researchers should be careful to distinguish among the effects of pubertal status, pubertal timing, and chronological age in studies of family relationships at puberty. In light of these findings and the results of previous studies, it would appear that the effects of pubertal status on family relationships are more consistent and more impressive than are those of pubertal timing. Pubertal timing, which has been shown to affect adolescents' peer relations (see Livson & Peskin, 1980), may be significant chiefly in contexts in which differences between early and late maturers are especially salient, such as the peer group. In the family, in contrast, individuals may be less aware of the adolescents' relative level of physical maturity and more sensitive to absolute changes in the youngster's appearance.

Although there are instances in which no significant pubertal status effect is observed, the number of significant or near significant relations between pubertal status and family relationships far exceeds that expected by chance, and virtually never is the direction of the relation contrary to the distancing hypothesis. Perhaps more important, the distancing effect of pu-

Table 5
Summary of Effects of Puberty on Family Relations of Girls

Outcome	Effect of pubertal status	Effect of pubertal timing
Daughters' reports		
Cohesion with mother	Negative****	ns
Calm communication with mother	Negative****	ns
Maternal acceptance	Negative***	ns
Cohesion with father	Negative****	ns
Calm communication with father	Negative***	ns
Paternal acceptance	Negative***	ns
Frequency of conflict with mother	ns	Maturation artifact
Intensity of conflict with mother	Positive***	ns
Frequency of conflict with father	ns	ns
Intensity of conflict with father	ns	ns
Authoritarian decisions	Age artifact	LM < on-time*
Authoritative decisions	ns	ns
Permissive decisions	Age artifact	ns
Maternal control	Positive*	Maturation artifact
Maternal restrictiveness	ns	ns
Paternal control	ns	ns
Paternal restrictiveness	ns	ns
Emotional autonomy	Positive****	ns
Mothers' reports		
Cohesion	Age artifact	ns
Calm communication	Negative**	ns
Intensity of conflict	Positive*	ns
Frequency of conflict	ns	LM < on-time**
Authoritarian decisions	Negative***	ns
Authoritative decisions	ns	ns
Permissive decisions	Age artifact	ns
Maternal control	ns	ns
Fathers' reports		
Cohesion	Negative**	ns
Calm communication	ns	ns
Intensity of conflict	ns	ns
Frequency of conflict	ns	ns
Authoritarian decisions	Age artifact	Age artifact
Authoritative decisions	ns	ns
Permissive decisions	ns	ns
Paternal control	ns	ns

Note. LM = Late maturing.
* $p < .10$. ** $p < .05$. *** $p < .01$. **** $p < .001$.

bertal maturation is seen across a range of variables, in the reports of adolescents as well as parents, in families of sons as well as daughters, and in relations with mothers as well as fathers.

Among adolescent boys and girls alike, reports of closeness with their parents decrease and reports of emotional autonomy from their parents increase with physical maturity. (For reasons that are not clarified by this study, in families of girls but not boys, adolescents' reports of diminished closeness are corroborated by parents.) Among boys diminished closeness is accompanied by decreases in perceived paternal acceptance; among girls physical maturity is accompanied by more negative descriptions of their mother on the CRPBI.

The impact of puberty on conflict in the family varies across different relational dyads. Puberty is related to increased conflict between adolescents and their mothers, although the pattern differs between adolescent sons and daughters. Among sons it is early maturation that is predictive of adolescent–mother conflict; among daughters conflict increases with physical maturity independent of the timing of puberty. This sex difference may inhere in the generally earlier maturation of girls relative to that of boys. One plausible hypothesis is that mother–adolescent conflict is more likely to result when puberty begins before a particular chronological age (e.g., before leaving elementary school). If this were the case, even among "on-time" girls, puberty would occur sufficiently early to provoke mother–child conflict. The relation between puberty and adolescent–father conflict, in contrast, is not apparent at all among families of daughters and neither consistent nor impressive in magnitude among families of sons.

This study as well as previous investigations (Hill et al., 1985a, 1985b; Steinberg, 1981) suggest that conflict in the family at puberty is more likely to surface between adolescents and their mothers than between adolescents and their fathers. At least four explanations seem reasonable. First, if adolescents perceive status differences between fathers and mothers, they may find it easier to act out their naturally developing ascendance and autonomy at the expense of the lower-status parent (see also Weisfeld & Berger, 1983). Second, according to object relations theory (e.g., Chodorow, 1978), both male and female adolescents may have a stronger need to individuate from their mother than from their father. To the extent that pubertal maturation may drive the individuation process (Freud, 1958), and to the extent that bickering and arguing may reflect attempts at individuation (Blos, 1979), the outward manifestations of the adolescent's attempt to establish emotional autonomy may be more apparent in the mother–child than in the father–child relationship. Third, most conflicts in the adolescent's family revolve around relatively mundane issues of daily living, and mothers are more active in matters of discipline in these arenas than are fathers (Montemayor, 1986). Finally, differences in the overall emotional quality of the relationships adolescents have with mothers versus fathers may account for differences in the display of conflict, whatever its causes may be. Conflict with fathers may be rare because adolescent–father relationships are so emotionally flat overall (Youniss & Smollar, 1985). Indeed, it is worth noting that there are very few significant relations of any sort between puberty and fathers' reports of their relationships with their children.

The findings concerning pubertal maturation and behavioral autonomy in the family also form an interpretable pattern. Where effects are seen, they tend to be reflected in individuals' descriptions of family decision making and not in adolescents' or parents' characterizations derived from the CRPBI or the PARI. The findings suggest that physical maturation may be accompanied by increased behavioral autonomy for the adolescent. Among boys, pubertal development may bring increases in parental permissiveness; among girls, maturation may be associated with declines in parental authoritarianism. Parental leniency may increase at puberty for both boys and girls, but, because parents generally rear girls more restrictively than boys, there are likely to be sex differences in the ways in which increases in leniency at puberty are manifested. In both cases, however, the shift toward greater autonomy at puberty appears to depend on the *timing* of the biological changes: Increases in autonomy at puberty are more likely for late maturers. Indeed, some early maturers may find themselves in the undesirable position of perceiving themselves not only as relatively more emotionally autonomous from their parents (and perhaps more "grown-up") but also as having parents who are not, in their view, sufficiently lenient. This notion is consistent with results reported by Savin-Williams and Small (1986).

In view of findings reported by several other teams of investigators using different measures, all of whom find that physical maturation is associated with higher levels of either actual or perceived independence from parents—especially among girls (e.g., Blyth et al., 1981; Hill et al., 1985a, 1985b; Magnusson, Stattin, & Allen, 1985; Simmons et al., 1983)—it seems reasonable to conclude that biological maturation accelerates the process through which youngsters become autonomous from their parents. This is especially interesting in light of observations that puberty distances offspring from their parents among virtually all nonhuman primates (Caine, 1986; Steinberg, 1986; Weisfeld & Berger, 1983). The distancing effect of puberty, however, may place early maturing youngsters growing up in contemporary society—especially girls, for whom early maturation is particularly early—at risk for excessive immersion in peer activities and early involvement in deviant behavior (Magnusson et al., 1985). In light of research indicating that emotional autonomy from parents is associated with increased susceptibility to antisocial peer pressure (Steinberg & Silverberg, 1986), further studies are needed in order to examine the process through which pubertal maturation may weaken family ties and stimulate youngsters' involvement in peer-related problem behavior.

References

Barnes, H., & Olson, D. (1985). Parent–adolescent communication and the circumplex model. *Child Development, 56,* 438–447.

Blos, P. (1979). *The adolescent passage.* New York: International Universities Press.

Blyth, D., Bulcroft, R., & Simmons, R. (1981, August). *The impact of puberty on adolescents: A longitudinal study.* Paper presented at the 89th meeting of the American Psychological Association, Los Angeles.

Brooks-Gunn, J., Petersen, A., & Eichorn, D. (Eds.) (1985). Time of maturation and psychosocial functioning in adolescence. [Special Issue]. *Journal of Youth and Adolescence, 14*(3–4).

Caine, N. (1986). Behavior during puberty and adolescence. In G. Mitchell & J. Erwin (Eds.), *Comparative primate biology: Vol. 2A.*

Behavior, conservation, and ecology (pp. 327–361). New York: Alan R. Liss.

Cantara, A. (1983). *Pubertal status and assertiveness in family interaction in early adolescent girls.* Unpublished master's thesis, Virginia Commonwealth University, Richmond.

Chodorow, N. (1978). *The reproduction of mothering: Psychoanalysis and the sociology of gender.* Berkeley: University of California Press.

Clausen, J. (1975). The social meaning of differential physical and sexual maturation. In S. Dragastin & G. Elder, Jr. (Eds.), *Adolescence in the life cycle* (pp. 25–47). New York: Wiley.

Dornbusch, S., Carlsmith, J., Bushwall, S., Ritter, P., Leiderman, H., Hastorf, A., & Gross, R. (1985). Single parents, extended households, and the control of adolescents. *Child Development, 56,* 326–341.

Freud, A. (1958). Adolescence. *Psychoanalytic Study of the Child, 13,* 255–278.

Garbarino, J., Burston, N., Raber, S., Russell, R., & Crouter, A. (1978). The social maps of children approaching adolescence: Studying the ecology of youth development. *Journal of Youth and Adolescence, 7,* 417–428.

Hauser, S., Liebman, W., Houlihan, J., Powers, S., Jacobson, A., Noam, G., Weiss, B., and Follansbee, D. (1985). Family contexts of pubertal timing. *Journal of Youth and Adolescence, 14,* 317–338.

Hill, J., Holmbeck, G., Marlow, L., Green, T., & Lynch, M. (1985a). Pubertal status and parent–child relations in families of seventh-grade boys. *Journal of Early Adolescence, 5,* 31–44.

Hill, J., Holmbeck, G., Marlow, L., Green, T., & Lynch, M. (1985b). Menarcheal status and parent–child relations in families of seventh-grade girls. *Journal of Youth and Adolescence, 14,* 301–316.

Livson, N., & Peskin, H. (1980). Perspectives on adolescence from longitudinal research. In J. Adelson (Ed.), *Handbook of adolescent psychology.* New York: Wiley.

Maccoby, E., & Martin, J. (1983). Socialization in the context of the family: Parent–child interaction. In P. H. Mussen (Series Ed.) & E. M. Hetherington (Vol. Ed.), *Handbook of child psychology: Vol. 4. Socialization, personality, and social development* (4th ed., pp. 103–196). New York: Wiley.

Magnusson, D., Stattin, H., & Allen, V. (1985). Biological maturation and social development: A longitudinal study of some adjustment processes from midadolescence to adulthood. *Journal of Youth and Adolescence, 14,* 267–284.

Montemayor, R. (1986). Family variation in parent–adolescent storm and stress. *Journal of Adolescent Research, 1,* 15–31.

Olson, D., Sprenkle, D., & Russell, C. (1979). Circumplex model of marital and family systems: 1. Cohesion and adaptability dimensions, family types, and clinical applications. *Family Process, 18,* 3–28.

Papini, D., & Sebby, R. (1985, April). *Multivariate assessment of adolescent physical maturation as a source of change in family relations.* Paper presented at the biennial meetings of the Society for Research in Child Development, Toronto, Ontario, Canada.

Peskin, H. (1967). Pubertal onset and ego functioning: A psychoanalytic approach. *Journal of Abnormal Psychology, 72,* 1–15.

Petersen, A. (1985). Pubertal development as a cause of disturbance: Myths, realities, and unanswered questions. *Genetic Psychology Monographs, 111,* 207–231.

Prinz, R., Foster, S., Kent, R., & O'Leary, K. (1979). Multivariate assessment of conflict in distressed and nondistressed mother–adolescent dyads. *Journal of Applied Behavioral Analysis, 12,* 691–700.

Robin, A., & Foster, S. (1984). Problem-solving communication training: A behavioral–family systems approach to parent–adolescent conflict. In P. Karoly & J. Steffen (Eds.), *Adolescent behavior disorders: Foundations and contemporary concerns* (Vol. 3, pp. 195–240). Lexington, MA: Lexington Books.

Savin-Williams, R., & Small, S. (1986). The timing of puberty and its relationship to adolescent and parent perceptions of family interactions. *Developmental Psychology, 22,* 322–347.

Schludermann, E., & Schludermann, S. (1970). Replicability of factors in children's report of parent behavior (CRPBI). *Journal of Psychology, 76,* 239–249.

Schludermann, E., & Schludermann, S. (1977). Methodological properties of the Parental Attitude Research Instrument. *Journal of Psychology, 96,* 15–23.

Schwartz, J., Barton-Henry, M., & Pruzinsky, T. (1985). Assessing child-rearing behaviors: A comparison of ratings made by mother, father, child, and sibling on the CRPBI. *Child Development, 56,* 462–479.

Simmons, R., Blyth, D., & McKinney, K. (1983). The social and psychological effects of puberty on white females. In J. Brooks-Gunn & A. Petersen (Eds.), *Girls at puberty* (pp. 229–272). New York: Plenum.

Steinberg, L. (1977). *A longitudinal study of physical growth, intellectual growth, and family interaction in early adolescence.* Unpublished doctoral dissertation, Cornell University, Ithaca, NY.

Steinberg, L. (1981). Transformations in family relations at puberty. *Developmental Psychology, 17,* 833–840.

Steinberg, L. (1986, November). *An evolutionary perspective on parent-adolescent conflict.* Paper presented at a symposium entitled "In Search of Man," Temple University School of Medicine, Philadelphia.

Steinberg, L. (1987). Single parents, stepparents, and the susceptibility of adolescents to antisocial peer pressure. *Child Development, 58,* 269–275.

Steinberg, L., & Hill, J. (1978). Patterns of family interaction as a function of age, the onset of puberty, and formal thinking. *Developmental Psychology, 14,* 683–684.

Steinberg, L., & Silverberg, S. (1986). The vicissitudes of autonomy in early adolescence. *Child Development, 57,* 841–851.

Stone, C., & Barker, R. (1939). The attitudes and interests of premenarcheal and postmenarcheal girls. *Journal of Genetic Psychology, 54,* 27–71.

Weisfeld, G., & Berger, J. (1983). Some features of human adolescence viewed in evolutionary perspective. *Human Development, 26,* 121–133.

Young, H., & Ferguson, L. (1981). *Puberty to manhood in Italy and America.* New York: Academic Press.

Youniss, J., & Smollar, J. (1985). *Adolescents' relations with mothers, fathers, and friends.* Chicago: University of Chicago Press.

Received July 10, 1986
Revision received December 5, 1986
Accepted December 9, 1986 ∎

Dialectics, Developmental Contextualism, and the Further Enhancement of Theory About Puberty and Psychosocial Development

Richard M. Lerner
Michigan State University

Contemporary theory in the study of human development in general and of adolescence in particular emphasizes reciprocal and changing relations between the developing person and his or her changing context. This article analyzes the Adams et al. dialectical model of the role of a key component of adolescent development—puberty—in such person-context relations. To interpret the model's meaning and critique its usefulness, the present article considers the place of this formulation within the recent history of theory development in the human developmental sciences. It is argued that dialectics is flawed as a means to understand variation in puberty-context relations because it involves an inherently teleological notion of change; as such, dialectics cannot be used successfully to model the multidirectionality and plasticity of adolescent development. A developmental contextual alternative formulation is presented.

The changes that occur during puberty are the most visible developments of adolescence. Arguably, they also represent the features of adolescence about which the most has been written in the scientific literature. Such topics as normative and atypical hormonal changes; secular trends in menarche; the influence of pubertal transitions on family relations, on achievement, and on psychosocial adjustment; pubertal rites; menstrual beliefs; sexuality; adolescent pregnancy and childbearing; and the role of pubertally based changes and/or "drives" in ego and cognitive development are among those concerning scholars from disciplines such as medicine, biology, psychology, sociology, anthropology, history, and human development. Across this literature, puberty has been linked to developments at levels of analysis ranging from the biological, through the psychological, social, and cultural, to the historical.

Preparation of this article was supported in part by National Institute of Child Health and Human Development grant HD23229. I thank Lisa J. Crockett for comments on a previous draft of this article.

Journal of Early Adolescence, Vol. 12 No. 4, November 1992 366-388
© 1992 Sage Publications, Inc.

Yet despite the prominence of conceptualizations about, and studies of, the role of puberty within and across these levels of organization, it is fair to argue—as do Adams, Day, Dyk, Frede, and Rogers (1992 [this issue])—that theories of the explanatory role or functional significance of puberty have not been articulated with the degree of precision or scope commensurate with the role attributed to puberty in the adolescent development literature. Indeed, as explained by Petersen and Taylor (1980), theories of the role of pubertal change in adolescent biopsychosocial development may be classified into two broad categories. "Direct effects" models stress that puberty has an unmediated influence on psychological functioning and social behavior. As epitomized by the psychoanalytic theories of A. Freud (1969) and Kestenberg (1967), these direct effect theories contend that biological change directly drives other changes of the person or that the biological processes (e.g., hereditary ones) that purportedly determine puberty are the same ones that shape personality and social functioning. The constitutional (somatic) theory of Sheldon (1940, 1942) is a case in point of this latter view.

"Mediated effects" models emphasize that the influence of pubertal change on the psychological and social behavior and development of the person occurs through an "interaction" with the environment—the context—within which the adolescent is embedded (e.g., Brooks-Gunn, 1987; Lerner & Lerner, 1989; Magnusson, 1988; Petersen & Taylor, 1980; Stattin & Magnusson, 1990). Although scholars following this general conception differ in regard to the meaning they attach to the term "interaction" and conceptualize, or model, the mediation of the context in different ways, all agree that the role of puberty in psychosocial functioning will be different under distinct contextual conditions.

Because the quantity *and quality* of the research literature on adolescent development has burgeoned over the course of the past 2 decades, the need to adopt some sort of mediated effects model has become increasingly apparent (Petersen, 1988). In turn, contemporary scholarship finds little evidence for, or utility of, a direct effects conceptualization of the role of puberty in psychosocial functioning (e.g., see Adams, Montemayor, & Gullotta, 1989; Brooks-Gunn, 1987; Brooks-Gunn & Petersen, 1983; Lerner & Foch, 1987; Magnusson, 1988).

A representative instance of this view was provided by Stattin and Magnusson (1990):

> There are few reasons to believe that pubertal timing, except in some few obvious ways, has a unidirectional influence on behavior. There are even fewer reasons to assume that its influence generally should be interpreted in a causal way. As Brooks-Gunn and Petersen (1984) have pointed out, the mere fact that there exists a relationship between pubertal growth and social behavior does

not imply a cause-effect relationship. What we witness might rather be the co-occurrence of different developmental factors. If so, the biological determinism model, which infers that observed changes in feelings, motivations, social relations, and so on are [causally] related to changes in the physical-bodily domain, has limited applicability. (p. 5)

Indeed, consistent with Stattin and Magnusson's view, there has been a compelling set of data generated indicating that puberty influences the adolescent's psychosocial behavior and development either in and/or through the context (e.g., the family, the peer group, or the school) within which the youth is embedded. However, due in part to the fact that the different scholars who have generated these data have done so through the use of different types of mediated effects models, there is considerably more information needed about the precise "parameters" of person and context that are involved in determining the conditions under which a particular instance of pubertal change interacts with the context to affect a specific instance of psychosocial functioning.

Thus, as Adams et al. maintain, there is a need for a more comprehensive theory of the interactive relation between pubertal change and the changes at the other levels of organization with which such change has been linked. In addition, Adams et al. are correct in asserting that a conceptualization that is associated with a research program is needed to help specify the conditions of puberty-context interaction that are linked to particular features of adolescent development.

The Adams et al. article was written to address these needs. The authors present an interesting and provocative outline of what they term a dialectical perspective regarding development. Their hope in making this presentation is threefold. First, they are interested in offering a framework for understanding extant data about the interactive role of puberty and psychosocial behavior and development. Second, they hope their perspective will be useful in generating new data about puberty-context interactions. Finally, they hope their article will lead colleagues into a series of theoretical discussions about the sort of person-context interactive model they presented. In this way, they believe, still more refined theoretical formulations may be generated.

The goals of Adams et al. are laudatory. In presenting their view of what constitutes a dialectical formulation about adolescent development in general and about puberty-context interactions in particular, they have provided the field with a stimulating basis for further thought, commentary, and theoretical advancement. As noted, such discussion and progress is the third goal of their article, and it is in this spirit of collegial exchange that the present article was prepared.

The purpose of the present commentary is also threefold. First, this article places the Adams et al. formulation within the context of a brief review of the recent history of theory development in the human developmental sciences so as to understand the formulation's meaning. This discussion leads to the second goal of this article, that is, a critique of the usefulness of their model. Finally, and to bring this article full circle to the third goal of Adams et al., the commentary offers an alternative to the Adams et al. formulation, one based not on a dialectical model but on a developmental contextual one.

The need for this last component of the present article arises because, as it will be argued, the Adams et al. formulation is flawed in its reliance on dialectics to understand the variation involved in puberty-context relations. As will be explained further, dialectics involves an inherently teleological notion of change (Dixon, Lerner, & Hultsch, 1991; Lerner & Kauffman, 1985), and such a conceptualization cannot be used successfully to model the multidirectionality and plasticity of development about which the model presented by Adams et al. is in large part concerned.

The limitations of the change processes involved in dialectics can be transcended through use of a developmental contextual formulation; thus it is important to present a brief overview of this model of human development. To reach this point, however, it is useful to turn to a discussion of the role of philosophies of science—of metamodels, or of worldviews—in the understanding of theories of human development.

PHILOSOPHY AND THEORY IN HUMAN DEVELOPMENT

"Theory" in human development has evolved quite dramatically over the past 20 years. At least two, interrelated changes have occurred. First, and due primarily to the contributions of Hayne W. Reese and Willis F. Overton (e.g., Overton & Reese, 1973; Reese & Overton, 1970), developmentalists have been reminded of the embeddedness of their theoretical, and derivative methodological, endeavors in superordinate philosophies of science. Second, and facilitated in large part by the work of Klaus F. Riegel (1975, 1976a, 1976b, 1978), developmentalists explored the potential of several different such philosophies for use in integrating existing data and for generating new data, especially insofar as information was sought about the plasticity and multidirectionality of relations between developing people and the changing contexts of life.

In regard to the first instance of change, Reese and Overton (1970) explained that two worldviews, or metamodels—termed organicism and mechanism—had been associated with the major theoretical formulations extant within the study of human development through the time of their writing. For example, organicism is associated with cognitive developmental theory, as represented for instance in the writings of Piaget (e.g., 1950, 1970). In turn, mechanism is associated with behavior analytic theory, as represented, for example, by the work of Bijou and Baer (1961).

Metamodels act to prescribe certain views (for instance, "development involves qualitative change," as in organismic stage theory; e.g., see Lerner, 1986) and to proscribe others (for instance, "development in a later stage cannot be reduced completely to phenomena involved in a prior stage," as also held in organismic stage theory; e.g., again see Lerner, 1986). Through these prescriptions and proscriptions, worldviews are associated with "families" of theories (Reese & Overton, 1970), such as the set of mechanistically oriented social learning theories generated from the 1940s through the early 1970s (e.g., Bandura, 1965; Bandura & Walters, 1959; Davis, 1944; Dollard & Miller, 1950; Gewirtz & Stingle, 1968; Homans, 1961; McCandless, 1970; Sears, 1957).

The renewed recognition of the role of worldviews in influencing the shape of theory was associated with the second change that occurred in developmental theory: Other worldviews were explored for their usefulness in, on one hand, the elaboration of new theoretical formulations and, on the other, in the integration of existing data on and the generation of new data about development (Baltes, 1979). Motivated by the works of Reese and Overton (1970; Overton & Reese, 1973), there was considerable intellectual excitement in the 1970s and early 1980s about the scientific potential of models derived from these "alternative" metamodels (Lerner, Hultsch, & Dixon, 1983), and, as well, there were numerous instances of these "new" models. The Sameroff (1975) "transactional" conception, the Looft (1973) "relational" notion, and the Lerner (1978, 1979) model of "dynamic interactionism" were all examples of such formulations. The instance provided by the work of Klaus Riegel, however, was particularly influential, and it is through a discussion of his contributions that the nature of the Adams et al. model can best be understood.

The Contributions of Klaus F. Riegel

It is within the milieu of the 1970s and early 1980s that the Adams et al. dialectical model fits, especially because it is derivative of arguably the most important example of these "new" models, that is, the dialectical view of human development formulated by Klaus F. Riegel (1975, 1976a, 1976b). In many ways, Riegel was both the intellectual leader of and catalyst for the exploration in the 1970s of the use of alternative models for the study of human development. This was the case, first, because he was a prolific and passionate writer—his book, *Psychology Mon Amour: A Countertext* (Riegel, 1978), being an excellent case in point—and, second, because he was editor of the journal *Human Development*, the prime outlet for theoretical scholarship in the field of human development.

Of the many important contributions of Riegel's scholarship, two are particularly pertinent to the present discussion. First, his dialectical model emphasized that the primary goal of a developmental analysis was the study of change, not stasis. Second, his model stressed that any level of organization —from inner-biological, through individual-psychological and physical-environmental, to the sociocultural—influences and is influenced by all other levels. Thus Riegel (1975, 1976a, 1976b) "developmentalized" and "contextualized" the study of the person by embedding the individual within an integrated and changing matrix of influences derived from multiple levels of organization.

However, the Riegel model, both a product and a producer of the 1970s' intellectual *Zeitgeist* in human development, was but an instance—albeit perhaps the prime one—of the growing interest during this period in the interactive role of the changing physical and social context for human behavior and development. Riegel's ideas, as well as those of Sameroff (1975), Looft (1973), Lerner (1978, 1979), and others (e.g., Baltes, 1979; Bronfenbrenner, 1977, 1979; Elder, 1974, 1975), were similar in their emphasis on change and context—and, to this extent, may be interpreted as being part of a common "family" of theories. However, as scholarship about this family advanced, it became increasingly clear that important distinctions existed among family members (e.g., compare Lerner, 1978, with Lerner, Skinner, & Sorell, 1980, with Lerner et al., 1983, and with Lerner & Kauffman, 1985). At least two, interrelated issues were raised in regard to Riegel's ideas.

First, Riegel (1976a) saw his dialectical views as both a model and a metamodel; that is, dialectics was, for Riegel (1975, 1976a, 1976b), both a worldview *and* a theory of developmental change derived from that worldview. Indeed, Riegel (1976b) was at pains to argue that dialectics constituted a metamodel of development distinct from organicism, arguing for instance that the (dialectical) model of cognitive development that he derived from his (dialectical) metamodel led to a formulation quite different from the one of Piaget (1950, 1970); for example, whereas Piaget proposed that after the development of formal operations no new cognitive structures emerged, Riegel argued that the dialectic resulted in a fifth, open-ended stage of cognitive development.

Thus, in merging his model with his metamodel, Riegel did not attend to the similarity between, or the association of, his emphases on change and context with the worldview of "contextualism." This latter metamodel not only stresses the very features of the human condition emphasized by Riegel—change and context—but, as well, was attracting considerable attention in the literature at the very time of Riegel's own writings (e.g., see Lerner et al., 1983, for a review). Nevertheless, the present writer can find no reference by Riegel to Pepper (1942), much less a discussion by Riegel of the embeddedness of his ideas in the contextual worldview described by Pepper (1942).

Second, Riegel's (1975, 1976a, 1976b) ideas, while similar to those of other theorists in the "family" in regard to the common stress on context and change, were distinct from many of these other formulations in respect to the *format* of change specified in his dialectical model. Indeed, in relying on the dialectic as a model for change, Riegel, it will be seen, was self-defeating. As will be argued, the nature of dialectical change is, in fact, entirely compatible with the view of change found in organicism. Thus, although Riegel (1976b) may have been correct in stressing that postformal operational thought is possible (e.g., see Alexander & Langer, 1990), his reliance on the dialectic to go beyond Piaget (1950, 1970) was ill conceived.

However, before explaining the essence of the shortcomings of the dialectical approach to understanding change and context, it is useful to note here the problems raised for the Adams et al. model because of their subscription to a Riegel-like dialectical conception.

The Dialectical Model of Adams et al.

In their reliance on dialectics, Adams et al. return to a model more of the 1970s than of the contemporary scene and, in so doing, fail to appreciate the reasons why the dialectical model of Riegel (1975, 1976a, 1976b) has not remained a conception of prime focus among developmental scholars. First, dialectics, as presented by Riegel, is but one instance of a superordinate philosophical concern with change and context, and, second, dialectics is a flawed conception in that it rests on a limited view of change—one quite difficult to use to integrate the wealth of empirical data existing on the multidirectionality and plasticity of human development (e.g., see Baltes, 1987; Brim & Kagan, 1980; Lerner, 1984, 1992), especially insofar as the role of puberty in psychosocial development is concerned (e.g., Brooks-Gunn & Petersen, 1983; Stattin & Magnusson, 1990).

Interestingly, however, the details of the Adams et al. formulation are not as dialectical as the authors propose. Certainly, there is little discussion of teleology, or goal directiveness, in their proposal, which, as explained below, are defining features of a dialectical view of change. In fact, the structure of the Adams et al. model (see their Figure 1) involves, quite centrally, plasticity and multidirectionality of developmental change: Not only are three distinct trajectories of change outlined, but insofar as the pathways for "progression" and "regression" are concerned, there is some degree of interpenetration of the processes associated with these points.

The nature of the contemporary literature about the role of pubertal change in psychosocial behavior and development is certainly more consistent with the presence of plasticity and multidirectionality than with uniformity and unidirectionality (e.g., Brooks-Gunn & Petersen, 1983; Stattin & Magnusson, 1990). Thus the figure used to depict the Adams et al. model is, by happenstance or intention, more closely aligned with this literature—and, as it happens, with the contextual metamodel, which emphasizes plasticity and multidirectionality—than with the dialectical worldview it was designed to illustrate.

Unfortunately, however, Adams et al. are not sufficiently operational and precise about the processes of change involved in a person's movement along the succession of pathway points depicted in their Figure 1. For instance, they state that "when discordant perceptions between self-assessment and social evaluations are dissonant . . . a tension occurs that stimulates the youth to resolve or diminish the stress through movement toward a reconciliation of differences" (p. 353). Not only does this description about the basis of change sound inconsistent with what was Riegel's (1976b) rejection of the balance of homeostasis theories but, in turn, the Adams et al. use of such concepts as the "stimulative value of tension reduction" is evocative of the drive-reduction mode of reinforcement in the McCandless (1970) mechanistic, social learning theory of adolescent behavior. Other examples may be given of the lack of sufficient clarity about the nature of the change processes associated with the terms used in the Adams et al. model; for instance, how are terms such as "compromise," "freedom," and "responsibility" operationalized, and how—through what exact change processes—do they constitute "the primary psychological conditions associated with growth"?

Because of the absence of requisite specificity about change processes, any correspondence between the Adams et al. model and contextualism is only descriptive. Indeed, without specification of the system or mechanisms involved in these change processes, it is fair to say that mechanistic, social learning conceptions could be used to model the plasticity and multidirectionality depicted in Adams et al.'s Figure 1.

In sum, then, there is a double-edged problem with the Adams et al. dialectical model. On one hand, their reliance on dialectics leads them to subscribe to a flawed conception of developmental change—one incompatible with the character of the puberty literature *and* with the actual structural details of the model they forward, a model which, at least descriptively, is more closely related to the ideas of plasticity and multidirectionality associated with contextualism. On the other hand, however, in failing to provide sufficient operationalization of key terms and specification of the exact processes of change involved with these terms, Adams et al. have provided a model that may be as readily linked with mechanistic conceptions of change as with either contextual or organismic ones.

However, as noted at the outset of the present article, Adams et al. prepared their article in order to "expand the dialogue" about the role of puberty in psychosocial behavior and development and to provoke colleagues to present critiques and alternative conceptual frameworks as part of this dialogue. Accordingly, to address the goals of Adams et al., the next section of this article presents the details of the shortcomings of the dialectical view of developmental change and, in so doing, explains why theorists, such as Adams et al., should not rely on such a perspective if there is an interest in modeling the variability of the developmental trajectories associated with puberty. This presentation will involve quite centrally a discussion of contrasts between contextualism and dialectics and, finally, will lead to the brief presentation of an "alternate," developmental contextual model of the role of puberty in behavior and development in adolescence.

ORGANISMIC VERSUS CONTEXTUAL VIEWS OF CHANGE

The focus of the second change that occurred in developmental theory over the past 2 decades—that is, the concern with philosophies of science other than organicism and mechanism—was not on dialectics but on the contextual worldview (Lerner, 1986; Lerner et al., 1983; Pepper, 1942). Indeed, it is arguably the case that the interest that occurred in regard to contextualism (e.g., see Bandura, 1978, 1986; Jenkins, 1974; Mischel, 1977; Rosnow & Georgoudi, 1986; Sarbin, 1977) resulted in the recession of the mechanistic and (to a much lesser extent) the organismic metamodels to the "back burner" of intellectual concern and empirical activity among developmentalists (Lerner, 1990). In their place, activity associated with the contextual worldview moved to the "cutting edge" of the scientific study of human development. As implied in the previous critique of the Riegel ideas, a key basis for the emergence of concern with contextualism was the view of human developmental change it involves. It is important, then, to focus on this view and to explain how it differs from the conception of change found in organicism and, as well, dialectics.

As explained by Pepper (1942), Overton and Reese (1981), and Lerner (1986; Lerner & Kauffman, 1985), organicism and contextualism are closely related. Both worldviews are nonreductionistic, involve the consideration of variables or events at multiple, qualitatively distinct levels of organization, and are change oriented. However, it is in this last similarity—change—that the two metamodels diverge as well. The process of change is seen quite differently in the two perspectives.

Within organicism, change is teleological (Lerner, 1986; Nagel, 1957). The final cause producing the goal-directedness of such change means that despite the "strands" (Pepper, 1942) of change that may exist over the course of life, development will eventually channel into a single direction; that is, despite individual differences in change, which may exist at some earlier time in life, development will have a common (i.e., interindividually invariant) end point—be it the attainment of formal operational thought, the emergence of the ego crisis of integrity versus despair, or the development of postconventional moral reasoning. People may differ only in how fast or in how far they develop toward this universal end point. In other words, because of the telos of change, development follows a predetermined path. Change, when seen from the perspective of the entire span of life, is thus unidirectional, and, accordingly, interindividual differences are not emphasized in such a conception of life span change.

By what process does the telos of development, that is, the final cause of change, pull the antecedent events of life toward this common, final point? From Plato to Piaget, the answer has been the dialectic (Pepper, 1942; Piaget, 1970; Riegel, 1975, 1976a, 1976b). As explained by Dixon, Lerner, and Hultsch (1991), the dialectic describes a teleological process of change: Thesis and antithesis (e.g., the "strands" of change, as in the Pepper, 1942, account) lead to synthesis. In other words, in the dialectic, as in the predetermined formulation of the direction of developmental change found in organicism, there is a universal, necessary, and single direction to change. It is through dialectical change that the telos of development is, therefore, revealed.

In their essence, then, a predetermined organismic view of change is isomorphic with a dialectical one: Both conceptions stress that a common developmental trajectory (Wohlwill, 1973), that change of a single pattern, characterizes human life. Plasticity of change (Lerner, 1984; Willis, 1990), multidirectionality of life-span development (Baltes, 1987), and increases across age in interindividual differences in intraindividual change (Schaie, 1979) cannot be dealt with adequately from a predetermined organismic, or dialectic, view of change (Dixon et al., 1991). Given the substantial empirical documentation that developmental change evidences such characteristics of diversity (e.g., Baltes, 1987; Brim & Kagan, 1980; Elder, 1974; Featherman, 1983; Gollin, 1981; Hetherington, Lerner, & Perlmutter, 1988; Lerner, 1984, 1986; Riley, 1979; Sorensen, Weinert, & Sherrod, 1986), it is not surprising that many human developmentalists have turned from organismic/dialectic models and directed their interest to a worldview that may seem to hold more promise for leading to formulations that can integrate data about the plasticity and multidirectionality of, and individual differences in, developmental changes across the life span. These interests, then, were the key bases for the burgeoning of attention to contextualism over the past 20 years (Lerner et al., 1983).

Within contextualism, change is dispersive (Pepper, 1942). The metaphor for this worldview is the historical event—the totality of phenomena, from all levels of organization, as they exist at a given instance in time (Pepper, 1942). Although all phenomena within an instant of history are interconnected (and here the parallel with the holism of organicism is apparent), the dispersiveness of contextualism arises because the multilevel structure of one historical event bears no *necessary* connection to the structure of a prior or succeeding event. Thus, although change is continuous within contextualism —that is, time, history, continues incessantly—there is no necessary intertime integration to the change.

Thus, if contextualism were to be adopted as the metamodel for developmental theory, it would be able to deal with plasticity, multidirectionality, and individual differences—but only in the most radical of ways. The extreme dispersiveness of the contextual worldview would mean that plasticity was infinite, that any direction of developmental change was possible, and that there were no necessary commonalities of human development. Clearly, these possibilities are counterfactual and, just as clearly, contextualism in its "pure" state—that is, as Pepper (1942) described it—cannot serve as a useful metamodel for the study of human development (Lerner & Kauffman, 1985).

Simply, plasticity is *relative,* not absolute; the levels of organization that combine to structure a historical event both *constrain* as well as permit particular instances of change and, as such, they promote or preclude certain patterns or directions of change. Finally, these same biological through social contextual variables act to make people *different from all others* in some respects, *different from some others* in some respects, and *similar to all others* in some respects (Lerner, 1988; Lerner & Tubman, 1989).

Accordingly, if contextualism were to serve as a metamodel for developmental theory alternative to predetermined organicism/dialectics, it could not do so in its "pure" form. For this reason, a conceptual framework which has attracted increasing interest among human developmentalists in general, and scholars of adolescence, in particular, is a modification of an extreme contextual worldview. This revised viewpoint is termed *developmental contextualism* (Lerner, 1986; Lerner & Kauffman, 1985).

FEATURES OF DEVELOPMENTAL CONTEXTUALISM

Developmental contextualism rests on two key ideas. First, there are variables from multiple, *qualitatively distinct* levels of analysis, or levels of organization, involved in human life and development (e.g., biology, psychology, society, and history). Of course, this conception is one with which scientists adhering to virtually *any* theoretical viewpoint would agree. However, some scientists would pursue inquiries aimed at the investigation of variables from one level of organization, in isolation from other levels (i.e., they would adopt a "main effects" approach to science); in turn, others would adopt a reductionistic orientation, seeking to study, or at least interpret, variables from multiple levels in terms of one level—a level conceived of by these scientists as the core, constituent, or elemental level. Developmental contextualists would reject both of these approaches and, instead, would adopt a nonreductionistic, interlevel-synthetic orientation to the multiple levels involved in human life. This perspective would be followed because of the second key idea within developmental contextualism.

Variables from the several levels of organization comprising human life exist in reciprocal relation: The structure and function of variables from any one level influence, and are influenced by, the structure and function of variables from the other levels. This reciprocal influence among levels, this "fusion" (Tobach & Greenberg, 1984) of interlevel relations, is termed *dynamic interactionism* within developmental contextualism (Lerner, 1978, 1979). As a consequence of the ubiquitous existence of these dynamic interactions, the potential for change is a continuous property of the multiple, interrelated levels of organization comprising human life. In other words, because levels of organization exist in an integrated, or fused, system, *relations* between levels of organization and *not* an isolated level per se become the key focus of developmental analysis and *changing relations among levels constitutes the basic process of human developmental change.*

When applied to the level of the individual, developmental contextualism stresses that neither variables belonging to levels of analysis lying within the person (e.g., biological or psychological ones) nor variables belonging to levels lying outside the person (i.e., involving either interpersonal, such as peer group relations or extrapersonal—institutional or physical ecological—relations) are the primary basis—or cause—of the individual's functioning or development. Rather, the structure (or "form"; Pepper, 1942) of the system—the pattern of relations—at a given point in time (at a specific moment in history; Pepper, 1942) is the "event" causing the person's functioning; and changes in the form of these relations are the cause of developmental change. Simply, not only do "A" and "B" simultaneously influence one another, but any change in A or B is a function of the organization of variables within which they are embedded.

Optimism About the Potential for Change

Given this "configural," or formal (Pepper, 1942), but nonetheless change-oriented, view of causality, developmental contextualism is an optimistic view of the character of human development (Brim & Kagan, 1980). The system of person-context relations comprising human development means that at any point in the life span there is some probability that means exist for altering significantly an individual's structural and/or functional characteristics. Because these characteristics are conceptualized in relational terms, such alteration may be possible through interventions aimed at any of the multiple levels of organization within which the person is embedded. Of course, complete alteration of the person or, more precisely, of the person-context system is not possible: The structure and function of a level influences other levels both through affording some changes and through delimiting or constraining others (Lerner, 1984, 1992).

Humans have two coupled change-related characteristics: a capacity for change and powerful stabilizing processes protecting existing arrangements and capabilities. Actual change (as contrasted to the potential for change) results from the interaction of these two coupled characteristics. In other words, plasticity—systematic change in structure and/or function—is not absolute but only relative. Nevertheless, the relational character of human life and/or human change means that development is seen as more open to influence and change when considered from a developmental contextual perspective than from one associated with other organismically or mechanistically derived theoretical perspectives (Brim & Kagan, 1980).

The Nature-Nurture Issue

Finally, a key theoretical feature of developmental contextualism is that it represents a quite distinct position within the controversy that has been the core conceptual issue in developmental psychology (Lerner, 1976, 1986) and, arguably, within psychology as a whole (Anastasi, 1958): the nature-nurture issue. Within developmental contextualism, variables from levels of organization associated with a person's biological or organismic character-istics (e.g., genes, tissues, or organ systems) are held to dynamically interact with variables from contextual levels of organization (i.e., involving intra-personal and extrapersonal variables), within which the biological or organ-ismic characteristics are embedded.

Because of the presence of dynamic interactions, biological variables *both* influence and, reciprocally, are influenced by contextual ones. Accordingly, stances about nature-nurture relations, which stress either the core determi-nation of human functioning and development by either context (e.g., cultural deterministic views) or biology (e.g., genetic or biological reductionistic, or deterministic, views), are explicitly rejected by a developmental contextual perspective (Lerner, 1992). In developmental contextualism, biological and contextual factors provide facilitating and constraining conditions that "set the stage" and through different patterns of interaction may produce many different "plays" with a diversity of "plots." In other words, changes in the causal field of fused, interlevel relationships provide the basis of human developmental change; and interindividual differences in the content and timing of these relationships creates distinct developmental trajectories (i.e., multidirectionality in development across life).

The Application of Developmental Contextualism to the Study of the Role of Puberty in Psychosocial Behavior and Development

As discussed in several recent essays (e.g., Lerner, 1987; Lerner & Lerner, 1989; Lerner, Lerner, & Tubman, 1989; see also Stattin & Magnusson, 1990), ideas associated with developmental contextualism may be used, for both descriptive and explanatory purposes, to study the role of puberty in psy-chosocial development. For example, within the laboratory of Lerner and Lerner (1989; Lerner et al., 1989), the fused, interlevel associations depicted within developmental contextualism have been represented by a model such as that displayed in Figure 1. This model represents the fusions within the adolescent between biological (e.g., pubertal) characteristics and other phys-ical, psychological, and behavioral attributes; in turn, fusions with the familial (e.g., parental), social network, community, societal, and cultural contexts are illustrated as well; finally, changes over time (history) in all these bidirectional, or reciprocal, relationships are represented in the model.

The descriptive use of the model, in regard to integrating extant data on puberty-psychosocial relations, may be illustrated by reference to the litera-

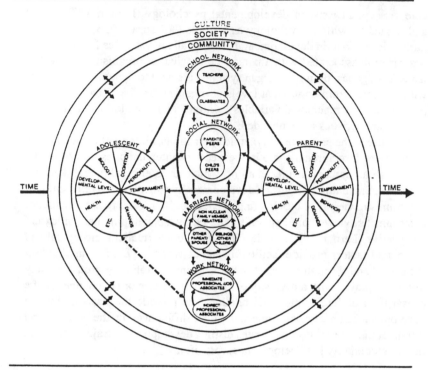

Figure 1: The Developmental Contextual Model of Development Used in the Research of Lerner and Lerner (e.g., Lerner & Lerner, 1989)

ture on menarche. This literature involves studies assessing the relationships, within the adolescent, of variation in timing of menarche (e.g., whether it occurs early, on time, or late) and other characteristics of individuality, for example, perceptions of self (Tobin-Richards, Boxer, & Petersen, 1983), cognition (Hamburg, 1974; Newcombe & Dubas, 1987; Petersen, 1983), or the experience of menstrual discomfort (Brooks-Gunn & Ruble, 1983). In turn, other studies assess how the occurrence of menarche is associated with a girl's relations with significant other people in her context (e.g., Anderson, Hetherington, & Clingempeel, 1989; Simmons, Blyth, & McKinney, 1983; Stattin & Magnusson, 1990; Steinberg, 1981; Steinberg & Hill, 1978). Such studies provide data illustrative of "adolescent effects" on the significant others in their social settings and constitute one component of the bidirectional effects (an adolescent → social context one) discussed in the literature on mediated effects models of puberty-context relations (Lerner & Foch, 1987; Magnusson, 1988; Petersen & Taylor, 1980; Stattin & Magnusson, 1990).

In contrast, other studies of menarche are "social context → adolescent" ones. These studies assess how adjustment to the transition of menarche is influenced by contextual features, such as parental demands regarding behavior desired in their adolescent children (e.g., Anthony, 1969; Windle et al., 1986), continuities or discontinuities in school structure (e.g., Crockett, Petersen, Graber, Schulenberg, & Ebata, 1989; Simmons & Blyth, 1987), or cultural beliefs regarding menstruation (e.g., Brooks-Gunn & Ruble, 1980; Ruble & Brooks-Gunn, 1979).

Additional studies in the adolescent literature assess how bidirectional relations between menarche and the social context (e.g., in regard to adolescents and their parents or peers) are associated with differences in developmental "outcomes" (e.g., the incidence of "adjusted" versus "problem" behaviors); these linkages are studied in relation to adolescents' embeddedness in more molar levels of the context, such as particular types of school or of physical activity settings (e.g., Brooks-Gunn, Attie, Burrow, Rosso, & Warren, 1989), different social classes (Hamburg, 1974; Simmons, Brown, Bush, & Blyth, 1978), different cultural or national settings (e.g., Lerner, Iwawaki, Chihara, & Sorell, 1980; Mussen & Bouterline-Young, 1964; Silbereisen, Petersen, Albrecht, & Kracke, 1989; Stattin, Gustafson, & Magnusson, 1989), or distinct historical eras (Elder, 1974; Nesselroade & Baltes, 1974).

To illustrate one instance of such findings, Stattin and Magnusson (1990) reported that in their study of 500 Swedish girls, minimal differences in social behavior (both problematic and well adjusted) in adolescence "will appear due to variations in maturational timing among females who do not engage with peers across the age border, who do not have peers outside the school environment, or who do not have stable opposite-sex relations" (p. 352). However, when girls do associate with these "nonconventional peers" Stattin and Magnusson found a greater role of puberty in social behavior.

Thus, at a descriptive level, the model shown in Figure 1 helps integrate extant portions of the puberty literature and, as such, also acts as a guide to studies of reciprocal puberty-context relations that need to be conducted. In turn, the relationships displayed in Figure 1 have been used as a basis for the formulation of theoretical models seeking to explain the nature of the outcomes derived from particular combinations of puberty and context.

Several instances of such theoretical formulations have been presented in the literature (e.g., Brooks-Gunn, 1987; Lerner & Lerner, 1989; Magnusson,

1988; Petersen, 1987; Stattin et al., 1989; Stattin & Magnusson, 1990). Despite the variation that exists in these instances of developmental contextual models, all involve (a) selection of a subset of the relationships displayed in Figure 1 and (b) specification of the conditions under which particular combinations of person and context are associated with specific developmental outcomes.

For example, in the Lerner and Lerner (1989) "goodness of fit" model, characteristics of physical individuality are predicted to be associated with healthy developmental outcomes when the characteristics meet the demands (or desires or expectations) of significant members of the adolescent's social context, for instance, peers, parents, or teachers; in turn, poor developmental outcomes are predicted when there is a poorness of fit (a mismatch, or incongruence) between the physical attributes the adolescent brings to a given social setting and the social demands of that context.

Several studies (e.g., Lerner, Delaney, Hess, Jovanovic, & von Eye, 1990; for reviews, see Lerner, 1987; Lerner & Jovanovic, 1990) have found that this developmental contextual, goodness of fit model is useful for understanding the role of physical (e.g., pubertal) variation in psychosocial behavior and development and adolescence. Moreover, the corresponding support in the literature for other developmental contextual models (e.g., Brooks-Gunn, 1987; Stattin & Magnusson, 1990) underscores the utility of such a family of theoretical approaches for advancing significantly knowledge of this key feature of adolescence.

CONCLUSIONS

Theory development is an arduous task. The success of any one effort should not be judged without the perspective afforded by years, if not decades, of presentations and evaluations of pertinent data. Thus theory development is a risky endeavor for academicians to undertake as part of their career development.

For these reasons, the field of adolescence is indebted to Adams et al. for, first, formulating a theoretical model of the role of puberty in psychosocial behavior and development *and*, second, presenting their ideas in the hope of inducing colleagues to evaluate their model and/or present alternatives. If judged only by the several components included in the present commentary, Adams et al. have succeeded in eliciting from at least one colleague a number of distinct ideas about the role of their model in past and current assessments of pubertal influences on adolescent development.

However, the ultimate value of both the Adams et al. formulation and the present reaction to it will be further significant advances in theory and research on adolescent developments, improvements derived from collegial debate, and the presentation and evaluation of alternative models. As was the case with the Adams et al. model, it is toward this end that the present article is directed.

REFERENCES

Adams, G., Day, T., Dyk, P., Frede, E., & Rogers, D.R.B. (1992). On the dialectics of pubescence and psychosocial development. *Journal of Early Adolescence, 12*, 348-365.

Adams, G. R., Montemayor, R., & Gullotta, T. (Eds.). (1989). *Advances in adolescent development*, Vol. 1. Beverly Hills, CA: Sage.

Alexander, C. N., & Langer, E. J. (Eds.). (1990). *Higher stages of human development: Perspectives on adult growth*. New York: Oxford University Press.

Anastasi, A. (1958). Heredity, environment, and the question "how?" *Psychological Review, 65*, 197-208.

Anderson, E. R., Hetherington, E. M., & Clingempeel, W. G. (1989). Transformations in family relations at puberty: Effects of family context. *Journal of Early Adolescence, 9*, 310-334.

Anthony, J. (1969). The reaction of adults to adolescents and their behavior. In G. Caplan & S. Lebovici (Eds.), *Adolescence: Psychological perspectives* (pp. 54-78). New York: Basic Books.

Baltes, P. B. (1979, Summer). On the potential and limits of child development: Life-span developmental perspectives. *Newsletter of the Society for Research in Child Development*, pp. 1-4.

Baltes, P. B. (1987). Theoretical propositions of life-span developmental psychology: On the dynamics between growth and decline. *Developmental Psychology, 23*, 611-626.

Bandura, A. (1965). Influence of models' reinforcement contingencies on the acquisition of imitative responses. *Journal of Personality and Social Psychology, 1*, 589-595.

Bandura, A. (1978). The self system in reciprocal determinism. *American Psychologist, 33*, 344-358.

Bandura, A. (1986). *Social foundations of thought and action: A social cognitive theory*. Englewood Cliffs, NJ: Prentice-Hall.

Bandura, A., & Walters, R. H. (1959). *Adolescent aggression*. New York: Ronald Press.

Bijou, S. W., & Baer, D. M. (1961). *Child development: A systematic and empirical theory*, Vol. 1. New York: Appleton-Century-Crofts.

Brim, O. G., Jr., & Kagan, J. (1980). Constancy and change: A view of the issues. In O. G. Brim, Jr. & J. Kagan (Eds.), *Constancy and change in human development* (pp. 1-25). Cambridge, MA: Harvard University Press.

Bronfenbrenner, U. (1977). Toward an experimental ecology of human development. *American Psychologist, 32*, 513-531.

Bronfenbrenner, U. (1979). *The ecology of human development*. Cambridge, MA: Harvard University Press.

Brooks-Gunn, J. (1987). Pubertal processes and girls' psychological adaptation. In R. M. Lerner & T. T. Foch (Eds.), *Biological-psychosocial interactions in early adolescence* (pp. 123-153). Hillsdale, NJ: Lawrence Erlbaum.

Brooks-Gunn, J., Attie, I., Burrow, C., Rosso, J. T., & Warren, M. P. (1989). The impact of puberty on body and eating concerns in athletic and nonathletic contexts. *Journal of Early Adolescence, 9,* 269-290.

Brooks-Gunn, J., & Petersen, A. C. (Eds.). (1983). *Girls at puberty: Biological and psychosocial perspectives.* New York: Plenum.

Brooks-Gunn, J., & Petersen, A. C. (1984). Problems in studying and defining pubertal events. *Journal of Youth and Adolescence, 13,* 181-196.

Brooks-Gunn, J., & Ruble, D. N. (1980). Menarche: The interaction of physiology, cultural, and social factors. In A. J. Dan, E. A. Graham, & C. P. Beecher (Eds.), *The menstrual cycle: A synthesis of interdisciplinary research* (pp. 141-159). New York: Springer.

Brooks-Gunn, J., & Ruble, D. N. (1983). The experience of menarche from a developmental perspective. In J. Brooks-Gunn & A. C. Petersen (Eds.), *Girls at puberty: Biological and psychosocial perspectives* (pp. 155-177). New York: Plenum.

Crockett, L. J., Petersen, A. C., Graber, J. A., Schulenberg, J. E., & Ebata, A. (1989). School transitions and adjustment during early adolescence. *Journal of Early Adolescence, 9,* 181-210.

Davis, A. (1944). Socialization and the adolescent personality. In *Forty-third yearbook of the national society for the study of education* (Vol. 43, Part 1). Chicago: University of Chicago Press.

Dixon, R. A., Lerner, R. M., & Hultsch, D. F. (1991). Maneuvering among models of developmental psychology. In P. van Geert & L. P. Mos (Eds.), *Annals of theoretical psychology* (vol. 7, pp. 279-323). New York: Plenum.

Dollard, J., & Miller, N. E. (1950). *Personality and psychotherapy.* New York: McGraw-Hill.

Elder, G. H., Jr. (1974). *Children of the Great Depression.* Chicago: University of Chicago Press.

Elder, G. H., Jr. (1975). Age differentiation and the life courses. In A. Inkeles, J. Coleman, & N. Smelser (Eds.), *Annual review of sociology* (Vol. 1, pp. 165-190). Palo Alto, CA: Annual Reviews.

Featherman, D. L. (1983). Life-span perspectives in social science research. In P. B. Baltes & O. G. Brim, Jr. (Eds.), *Life span development and behavior* (Vol. 5, pp. 1-57). New York: Academic Press.

Freud, A. (1969). Adolescence as a developmental disturbance. In G. Caplan & S. Lebovici (Eds.), *Adolescence* (pp. 5-10). New York: Basic Books.

Gewirtz, J. L., & Stingle, K. G. (1968). Learning of generalized imitation as the basis for identification. *Psychological Review, 75,* 374-397.

Gollin, E. S. (1981). Development and plasticity. In E. S. Gollin (Ed.), *Developmental plasticity: Behavioral and biological aspects of variations in development* (pp. 231-331). New York: Academic Press.

Hamburg, B. (1974). Early adolescence: A specific and stressful stage of the life cycle. In G. Coelho, D. A. Hamburg, & J. E. Adams (Eds.), *Coping and adaptation* (pp. 101-125). New York: Basic Books.

Hetherington, E. M., Lerner, R. M., & Perlmutter, M. (Eds.). (1988). *Child development in life span perspective.* Hillsdale, NJ: Lawrence Erlbaum.

Homans, G. C. (1961). *Social behavior: Its elementary forms.* New York: Harcourt, Brace & World.

Jenkins, J. J. (1974). Remember that old theory of memory? Well, forget it. *American Psychologist, 29,* 785-795.

326

Kestenberg, J. (1967). Phases of adolescence with suggestions for a correlation of psychic and hormonal organization: Part 1. Antecedents of adolescent organizations in childhood. *Journal of the American Academy of Child Psychiatry, 6,* 426-463.

Lerner, R. M. (1976). *Concepts and theories of human development.* Reading, MA: Addison-Wesley.

Lerner, R. M. (1978). Nature, nurture and dynamic interactionism. *Human Development, 21,* 1-20.

Lerner, R. M. (1979). A dynamic interactional concept of individual and social relationship development. In R. Burgess & T. Huston (Eds.), *Social exchange in developing relationships* (pp. 271-305). New York: Academic Press.

Lerner, R. M. (1984). *On the nature of human plasticity.* New York: Cambridge University Press.

Lerner, R. M. (1986). *Concepts and theories of human development* (2nd ed.). New York: Random House.

Lerner, R. M. (1987). A life-span perspective for early adolescence. In R. M. Lerner & T. T. Foch (Eds.), *Biological-psychosocial interactions in early adolescence* (pp. 1-6). Hillsdale, NJ: Lawrence Erlbaum.

Lerner, R. M. (1988). Personality development: A life-span perspective. In E. M. Hetherington, R. M. Lerner, & M. Perlmutter (Eds.), *Child development in life-span perspective* (pp. 21-46). Hillsdale, NJ: Lawrence Erlbaum.

Lerner, R. M. (1990). Weaving development into the fabric of personality and social psychology —On the significance of Bandura's *Social Foundations of Thought and Action. Psychological Inquiry, 1,* 92-95.

Lerner, R. M. (1992). *Final solutions: Biology, prejudice, and genocide.* University Park: Pennsylvania State University Press.

Lerner, R. M., Delaney, M., Hess, L. E., Jovanovic, J., & von Eye, A. (1990). Early adolescent physical attractiveness and academic competence. *Journal of Early Adolescence, 10,* 4-20.

Lerner, R. M., & Foch, T. T. (Eds.). (1987). *Biological-psychosocial interactions in early adolescence.* Hillsdale, NJ: Lawrence Erlbaum.

Lerner, R. M., Hultsch, D. F., & Dixon, R. A. (1983). Contextualism and the character of developmental psychology in the 1970s. *Annals of the New York Academy of Sciences, 412,* 101-128.

Lerner, R. M., Iwawaki, S., Chihara, T., & Sorell, G. T. (1980). Self-concept, self-esteem, and body attitudes among Japanese male and female adolescents. *Child Development, 51,* 847-855.

Lerner, R. M., & Jovanovic, J. (1990). The role of body image in psychosocial development across the life span: A developmental contextual perspective. In T. F. Cash & T. Pruzinsky (Eds.), *Body images: Development, deviance, and change* (pp. 110-127). New York: Guilford.

Lerner, R. M., & Kauffman, M. B. (1985). The concept of development in contextualism. *Developmental Review, 5,* 309-333.

Lerner, R. M., & Lerner, J. V. (1989). Organismic and social contextual bases of development: The sample case of adolescence. In W. Damon (Ed.), *Child development today and tomorrow* (pp. 69-85). San Francisco: Jossey-Bass.

Lerner, R. M., Lerner, J. V., & Tubman, J. (1989). Organismic and contextual bases of development in adolescence: A developmental contextual model. In G. R. Adams, T. Gullotta, & R. Montemayor (Eds.), *Advances in adolescent development* (Vol. 1, pp. 11-37). Newbury Park, CA: Sage.

Lerner, R. M., Skinner, E. A., & Sorell, G. T. (1980). Methodological implications of contextual/ dialectic theories of development. *Human Development, 23*, 225-235.

Lerner, R. M., & Tubman, J. (1989). Conceptual issues in studying continuity and discontinuity in personality development across life. *Journal of Personality, 57*, 343-373.

Looft, W. R. (1973). Socialization and personality throughout the life span: An examination of contemporary psychological approaches. In P. B. Baltes & K. W. Schaie (Eds.), *Life-span developmental psychology: Personality and socialization* (pp. 25-52). New York: Academic Press.

Magnusson, D. (1988). Individual development from an interactional perspective. In D. Magnusson (Ed.), *Paths through life* (Vol. 1, pp. 3-31). Hillsdale, NJ: Lawrence Erlbaum.

McCandless, B. R. (1970). *Adolescents*. Hinsdale, IL: Dryden.

Mischel, W. (1977). On the future of personality measurement. *American Psychologist, 32*, 246-254.

Mussen, P. H., & Bouterline-Young, H. (1964). Relationships between rate of physical maturing and personality among boys of Italian decent. *Vita Humana, 7*, 186-120.

Nagel, E. (1957). Determinism in development. In D. B. Harris (Ed.), *The concept of development* (pp. 15-24). Minneapolis: University of Minnesota Press.

Nesselroade, J. R., & Baltes, P. B. (1974). Adolescent personality development and historical change: 1970-1972. *Monographs of the Society for Research in Child Development*, No. 39.

Newcombe, N., & Dubas, J. S. (1987). Individual differences in cognitive ability: Are they related to timing of puberty? In R. M. Lerner & T. T. Foch (Eds.), *Biological-psychosocial interactions in early adolescence* (pp. 249-302). Hillsdale, NJ: Lawrence Erlbaum.

Overton, W. F., & Reese, H. W. (1973). Models of development: Methodological implications. In J. R. Nesselroade & H. W. Reese (Eds.), *Life-span developmental psychology: Methodological issues* (pp. 65-86). New York: Academic Press.

Overton, W. F., & Reese, H. W. (1981). Conceptual prerequisites for an understanding of stability-change and continuity-discontinuity. *International Journal of Behavioral Development, 4*, 99-123.

Pepper, S. C. (1942). *World hypotheses*. Berkeley: University of California Press.

Petersen, A. C. (1983). Pubertal change and cognition. In J. Brooks-Gunn & A. C. Petersen (Eds.), *Girls at puberty* (pp. 179-197). New York: Plenum.

Petersen, A. C. (1987). The nature of biological psychosocial interactions: The sample case of early adolescence. In R. M. Lerner & T. T. Foch (Eds.), *Biological-psychosocial interactions in early adolescence* (pp. 35-61). Hillsdale, NJ: Lawrence Erlbaum.

Petersen, A. C. (1988). Adolescent development. In M. R. Rosenzweig (Ed.), *Annual review of psychology* (Vol. 39, pp. 583-607). Palo Alto, CA: Annual Reviews, Inc.

Petersen, A. C., & Taylor, B. (1980). The biological approach to adolescence: Biological change and psychological adaptation. In J. Adelson (Ed.), *Handbook of adolescent psychology* (pp. 117-155). New York: Wiley.

Piaget, J. (1950). *The psychology of intelligence*. New York: Harcourt Brace.

Piaget, J. (1970). Piaget's theory. In P. H. Mussen (Ed.), *Carmichael's manual of child psychology* (Vol. 1, pp. 703-732). New York: Wiley.

Reese, H. W., & Overton, W. F. (1970). Models of development and theories of development. In L. R. Goulet & P. B. Baltes (Eds.), *Life-span developmental psychology: Research and theory* (pp. 115-145). New York: Academic Press.

Riegel, K. F. (1975). Toward a dialectical theory of development. *Human Development, 18*, 50-64.

Riegel, K. F. (1976a). The dialectics of human development. *American Psychologist, 31,* 689-700.

Riegel, K. F. (1976b). From traits and equilibrium toward developmental dialectics. In W. J. Arnold & J. K. Cole (Eds.), *Nebraska Symposium on Motivation, 1975* (pp. 349-408). Lincoln: University of Nebraska Press.

Riegel, K. F. (1978). *Psychology mon amour: A countertext.* Boston: Houghton Mifflin.

Riley, M. W. (Ed.). (1979). *Aging from birth to death.* Washington, DC: American Association for the Advancement of Science.

Rosnow, R., & Georgoudi, M. (Eds.). (1986). *Contextualism and understanding in behavioral research.* New York: Praeger.

Ruble, D. N., & Brooks-Gunn, J. (1979). Menstrual symptoms: A social cognition analysis. *Journal of Behavioral Medicine, 2,* 171-194.

Sameroff, A. (1975). Transactional models in early social relations. *Human Development, 18,* 65-79.

Sarbin, T. R. (1977). Contextualism: A world view for modern psychology. In J. K. Cole & A. W. Lundfield (Eds.), *Nebraska Symposium on Motivation, 1976* (pp. 1-41). Lincoln: University of Nebraska Press.

Schaie, K. W. (1979). The primary mental abilities in adulthood: An exploration in the development of psychometric intelligence. In P. B. Baltes & O. G. Brim, Jr. (Eds.), *Life-span development and behavior* (Vol. 2, pp. 67-115). New York: Academic Press.

Sears, R. R. (1957). Identification as a form of behavioral development. In D. B. Harris (Eds.), *The concept of development* (pp. 149-161). Minneapolis: University of Minnesota Press.

Sheldon, W. H. (1940). *The varieties of human physique.* New York: Harper.

Sheldon, W. H. (1942). *The varieties of temperament.* New York: Harper.

Silbereisen, R. K., Petersen, A. C., Albrecht, H. T., & Kracke, B. (1989). Maturational timing and the development of problem behavior: Longitudinal studies in adolescence. *Journal of Early Adolescence, 9,* 247-268.

Simmons, R. G., & Blyth, D. A. (1987). *Moving into adolescence: The impact of pubertal change and school context.* Hawthorne, NJ: Aldine.

Simmons, R. G., Blyth, D. A., & McKinney, K. L. (1983). The social and psychological effects of puberty on white females. In J. Brooks-Gunn & A. C. Petersen (Eds.), *Girls at puberty* (pp. 229-272). New York: Plenum.

Simmons, R. G., Brown, L., Bush, D. M., & Blyth, D. A. (1978). Self-esteem and achievement of black and white early adolescents. *Social Problems, 26,* 86-96.

Sorensen, B., Weinert, E., & Sherrod, L. R. (Eds.). (1986). *Human development and the life course: Multidisciplinary perspectives.* Hillsdale, NJ: Lawrence Erlbaum.

Stattin, H., Gustafson, S. B., & Magnusson, D. (1989). Peer influences on adolescent drinking: A social transition perspective. *Journal of Early Adolescence, 9,* 227-246.

Stattin, H., & Magnusson, D. (1990). *Pubertal maturation in female development.* Hillsdale, NJ: Lawrence Erlbaum.

Steinberg, L. D. (1981). Transformations in family relations at puberty. *Developmental Psychology, 17,* 833-840.

Steinberg, L. D., & Hill, J. P. (1978). Patterns of family interaction as a function of age, the onset of puberty, and formal thinking. *Developmental Psychology, 14,* 683-684.

Tobach, E., & Greenberg, G. (1984). The significance of T. C. Schneirla's contribution to the concept of integration. In G. Greenberg & E. Tobach (Eds.), *Behavioral evolution and integrative levels* (pp. 1-7). Hillsdale, NJ: Lawrence Erlbaum.

Tobin-Richards, M. H., Boxer, A. M., & Petersen, A. C. (1983). The psychological significance of pubertal change: Sex differences in perceptions of self during early adolescence. In J. Brooks-Gunn & A. C. Petersen (Eds.), *Girls at puberty* (pp. 127-154). New York: Plenum.

Willis, S. L. (1990). Cognitive training in later adulthood. *Developmental Psychology, 26,* 875-878.

Windle, M., Hooker, K., Lenerz, K., East, P. L., Lerner, J. V., & Lerner, R. M. (1986). Temperament, perceived competence, and depression in early- and late-adolescents. *Developmental Psychology, 22,* 384-392.

Wohlwill, J. F. (1973). *The study of behavioral development.* New York: Academic Press.

Requests for reprints should be addressed to Richard M. Lerner, Institute for Children, Youth, and Families, Unit 2 Paolucci Building, Michigan State University, East Lansing, MI 48824.

Journal of Adolescence 1989, **12**, 225–229

Brief Report

Objective and subjective attractiveness and early adolescent adjustment

JASNA JOVANOVIC, RICHARD M. LERNER*, AND
JACQUELINE V. LERNER

Using data from the Pennsylvania Early Adolescent Transitions Study
(PEATS), this study assessed how objective physical attractiveness (PA),
indexed by appraisals from others, and subjective PA, indexed by
self-appraisals, relate to each other and, in turn, to early adolescent
adjustment (indexed by self-esteem and anxiety). Findings indicated a low
relationship between objective and subjective PA. Only subjective PA was
associated with adjustment.

INTRODUCTION

Early adolescence is a period of important changes in the individual's
psychological, social, and physical characteristics. In regard to these latter
changes, a growing literature indicates that one attribute of physical
individuality—physical attractiveness (PA)—is linked to early adolescent
adjustment. For example, higher self-esteem (Lerner *et al.*, 1980), lower
anxiety (Lerner and Lerner, 1977), and lower depression (Noles, Cash and
Winstead, 1985) have been associated with higher PA.

PA may be indexed objectively (e.g. through other's appraisals of the
person) and subjectively (e.g. through the person's self-appraisal). However,
these two indexes may not be associated identically with adjustment. Indeed,
different links between objective and subjective PA and adjustment were
reported by Archer and Cash (1985) in a study of late adolescent through
adult psychiatric patients. However, to our knowledge these differential
relationships have not been examined longitudinally in a "normal" sample of
early adolescents. Yet, the early adolescent's changing physical, cognitive,
and emotional characteristics give such an assessment theoretical and
empirical value. Accordingly, using a portion of the data from the
Pennsylvania Early Adolescent Transitions Study (PEATS), we brought
some initial data to bear on the association, across the transition from
elementary to junior high school, between early adolescents' objective PA

* Reprint requests to Richard M. Lerner, College of Health and Human Develpment, The
Pennsylvania State University, University Park, PA 16802, U.S.A.

0140-1971/89/020225 + 05 $03.00/0

(indexed through teacher and college students' ratings), subjective PA (indexed through self-ratings) and adjustment (as represented by scores for self-esteem and anxiety).

METHOD

Subjects

The PEATS sample consists of 153 sixth graders (51·6 per cent male; 99 per cent white) from eight elementary schools within a north-western Pennsylvanian semirural, school district. A sample of these subjects ($N = 75$; 61 per cent male) was followed into the seventh grade of one junior high school within the same district. The sample was tested on six occasions, at periods separated by four months, from September, 1984 through May, 1986 (mean age of sample on Occasion 1 = 11·6 years, S.D. = 0·5 years). Since the measures of PA and adjustment of interest in the present study were only completely available at the end of Grade 6 and the beginning of Grade 7, these two points were focused on in the present study. Fuller details of the PEATS sample, design, and measures may be found in Lerner *et al.* (1988).

Measures

Subjective PA

Subjective PA ratings were derived from a subset of questions of the Harter (1983) Self-perception Profile (SPP), a psychometrically well-developed scale which assesses a subject's evaluation of his/her own physical appearance as well as scores assessing self-perceptions of scholastic competence, social acceptance, athletic competence, conduct adequacy, and self-worth. The SPP Physical Appearance domain, like the other domains, is measured by six items; each item is scored on a scale from "1" to "4," where "1" indicates the low end of an attribute (e.g. low perceived appearance) and a score of "4" reflects the high end of an attribute (e.g. high perceived appearance). Each domain score is the mean of the six items.

Objective PA

Teachers' ratings. To assess the subject's PA as judged by his/her teacher, one subscale of the Teacher's Behavior Rating Scale (TBRS) was used. The TBRS was developed by Harter (1983) to correspond to the SPP. Teachers rate subjects on the first five of the above-noted six SPP domains (i.e. all but self-worth). The TBRS contains three items for each domain. The physical appearance score was used; it, like all TBRS scores, is the mean of the three items. Within the PEATS (Lerner *et al.,* 1988), internal consistency reliabilities for all TBRS ratings exceed 0·90 at each measurement occasion.

College students' ratings. Another objective rating of the subjects' PA, one involving facial attractiveness, was derived from samples of college students through use of a method developed by Lerner and Lerner (1977). Standardly posed frontal view, midchest-to-head color slides of all subjects, at each time of measurement, are presented to large groups of college students enrolled in introductory human development or psychology courses. The students rated each slide for PA on a five-point scale, ranging from "1" = "very unattractive" to "5" = "very attractive." The mean of the ratings for each subject is used as the index of PA. For each time of testing a different sample of college students rated the slides. Lerner and Lerner (1977) found good interrater reliability and convergent validity data for PA indexed by this method.

Adjustment

Self-esteem. The early adolescent's general self-esteem was assessed using another, six item subscale of the Harter (1983) SPP, the self-worth domain. This scale indexes feelings of worth, or self-esteem, *independent* of any particular skill domain. The response format and scoring for this scale are the same as for all SPP domains.

Anxiety. To measure the early adolescent's trait anxiety the Reynolds and Richmond (1978) Revised Children's Manifest Anxiety Scale (RCMAS), a 37-item scale containing 28 anxiety and 9 "lie scale" items, was used. In the PEATS the RCMAS uses four response choices: "1" = "usually false;" "2" = "more false than true;" "3" = "more true than false;" and "4" = "usually true." The internal consistency reliability for this scale within the PEATS at the end of Grade 6 and the beginning of Grade 7 is 0·91 and 0·93, respectively.

Procedure

At each testing occasion all early adolescents were tested within a large school room (e.g. school cafeteria, library, or auditorium). After responding to the SPP and the RCMAS, photographs were taken of each subject. While the adolescents were tested the teachers responded to the TBRS.

RESULTS

Autocorrelations between the end of Grade 6 and the beginning of Grade 7 for the two objective PA measures (from college students and teachers), and from the subjective PA measure were 0·8, 0·4, and 0·7, respectively. However, the interrelations among the different PA measures were not high: The correlation between the two objective measures at the end of Grade 6 was $r(130) = 0·3$ ($P < 0·01$) and at the beginning of Grade 7 was $r(63) = 0·5$ ($P < 0·001$). Moreover, the relations within and across time between the two objective measures and the subjective measure are even lower: The correlation at the end of Grade 6 between the self-ratings and the college students' ratings was $r(140) = 0.15$, n.s., and the corresponding correlation involving teachers' ratings was $r(137) = 0.16$, n.s. The corresponding correlations at the beginning of Grade 7 were $r(60) = 0.17$ (n.s.) and $r(60) = 0.30$ (P <0.05), respectively. None of these findings (or in fact any discussed in this study) show sex differences.

PA and Adjustment

There is almost no significant relation between either objective measure of PA and the two indices of adjustment. At the end of Grade 6 the relations between self-worth and (a) the college students' ratings, or (b) the teachers' ratings, were $r(138) = 0.04$ (n.s.) and $r(135) = 0.14$ (n.s.), respectively. The corresponding relations involving anxiety were $r(108) = -0.08$ (n.s.) and $r(109) = -0.09$, respectively. At the beginning of Grade 7, the relations between self-worth and the two objective measures of PA were $r(62) = 0.13$ (n.s.) and $r(60) = 0.31$ (P <0.05), respectively; the corresponding relations involving anxiety were $r(53) = -0.07$ (n.s.) and $r(55) = -0.03$ (n.s.), respectively.

However, in regard to subjective PA, significant relations between PA and adjustment were found. At the end of Grade 6 the correlations between the subjective PA rating and self-worth was $r(145) = 0.71$ (P <0.001), and the corresponding correlation for anxiety was $r(114) = -0.46$ (P <0.001). At the beginning of Grade 7 the corresponding correlations were $r(60) = 0.78$ (P <0.001) and $r(52) = -0.49$ (P < 0.001), respectively. Thus, within and across time higher PA scores were associated with higher self-worth and lower anxiety; this constancy was maintained despite the across-time decrease in sample size and power.

DISCUSSION

This study's data point to the positive implications of self-perceptions of attractiveness for individual adjustment across the junior high school transition, associations which are consistent with stereotypes for beauty found in our culture (cf. Adams, 1977). In addition, while our results are of course bound by the particular measures and methods we employed, our findings of a lack of association between objective PA and adjustment, and of low relations between objective and subjective measures of PA, may have a substantive interpretation. It may be that the cognitive egocentrism purportedly characterizing early adolescents, and their emerging crisis of identity, or self-definition, conspire to foster a greater reliance on self-perceptions than on others' perceptions for their adjustment.

ACKNOWLEDGEMENTS

This research was supported in part by a grant from the William T. Grant Foundation to Richard M. Lerner and Jacqueline V. Lerner.

REFERENCES

Adams, G. R. (1977). Physical attractiveness: Toward a developmental social psychology of beauty. *Human Development, 20*, 217–230.

Archer, R. P. and Cash, T. F. (1985). Physical attractiveness and maladjustment among psychiatric inpatients. *Journal of Social and Clinical Psychology, 3*, 170–180.

Harter, S. (1983). *Supplementary description of the self-perception profile for children: Revision of the perceived competence scale for children.* Denver: University of Denver.

Lerner, R. M., Iwawaki, S., Chihara, T. and Sorell, G. T. (1980). Self-concept, self-esteem, and body attitudes among Japanese male and female adolescents. *Child Development, 51*, 874–855.

Lerner, R. M. and Lerner, J. V. (1977). Effects of age, sex and physical attractiveness on child-peer relations, academic performance, and elementary school adjustment. *Developmental Psychology, 13*, 585–590.

Lerner, R. M., Lerner, J. V., Jovanovic, J., Schwab, J., Talwar, R., Hess, L. E. and Kucher, J. S. (1988). *Physical attractiveness, body type, and psychosocial functioning among early adolescents.* Manuscript submitted for publication.

Noles, S. W., Cash, T. F. and Winstead, B. A. (1985). Body image, physical attractiveness, and depression. *Journal of Consulting and Clinical Psychology, 53*, 88–94.

Reynolds, C. R. and Richmond, B. O. (1973). What I Think and Feel: A revised measure of children's manifest anxiety. *Journal of Abnormal Child Psychology, 6*, 271–280.

Acknowledgments

Petersen, Anne C. "Presidential Address: Creating Adolescents: The Role of Context and Process in Developmental Trajectories." *Journal of Research on Adolescence* 3 (1993): 1–18. Reprinted with the permission of Lawrence Erlbaum Associates, Inc.

Muuss, Rolf E. "The Philosophical and Historical Roots of Theories of Adolescence." In *Theories of Adolescence* (New York: McGraw-Hill, 1996) (6th ed.): 1–17. Reprinted with the permission of the McGraw-Hill Companies.

Baltes, Paul B. "Theoretical Propositions of Life-Span Developmental Psychology: On the Dynamics Between Growth and Decline." *Developmental Psychology* 23 (1987): 611–26. Copyright 1987 by the American Psychological Association. Reprinted by permission.

Talwar, Rachna, and Jacqueline V. Lerner. "Theories of Adolescent Development." In *Encyclopedia of Adolescence*, Vol. II, edited by Richard M. Lerner, Anne C. Petersen, and Jeanne Brooks-Gunn (New York: Garland Publishing, 1991): 1141–47.

McAdoo, Harriette P. "Stress Absorbing Systems in Black Families." *Family Relations* 31 (1982): 479–88. Reprinted by permission. Copyright 1982 by the National Council on Family Relations, 3989 Central Ave NE, Suite 550, Minneapolis, MN 55421.

Elder, Glen H., Jr. "The Life Course as Developmental Theory." *Child Development* 69:1 (1998): 1-12. Reprinted with the permission of the Society for Research in Child Development.

Bandura, Albert. "The Stormy Decade: Fact or Fiction?" *Psychology in the Schools* 1 (1964): 224–31. Reprinted with the permission of John Wiley & Sons, Inc.

Rutter, Michael, Philip Graham, O.F.D. Chadwick, and W. Yule. "Adolescent Turmoil: Fact or Fiction?" *Journal of Child Psychology and Psychiatry and Allied Disciplines* 17 (1976): 35–56. Reprinted with the permission of Cambridge University Press.

Freud, Anna. "Adolescence as a Developmental Disturbance." In *Adolescence: Psychosocial Perspectives*, edited by Gerald Caplan and Serge Lebovici (New York: Basic Books, 1969): 5–10. Reprinted with the permission of HarperCollins Publishers.

Gilligan, Carol. "New Maps of Development: New Visions of Maturity." *American Journal of Orthopsychiatry* 52 (1982): 199–212. Copyright 1982 by the American Orthopsychiatric Association Inc. Reprinted by permission.

Magnusson, David. "Implications of an Interactional Paradigm for Research on Human Development." *International Journal of Behavioral Development* 8 (1985): 115–37. Reprinted with the permission of Taylor and Francis Ltd.

Bengston, Vern L., and Joseph A. Kuypers. "Generational Difference and the Developmental Stake." *Aging and Human Development* 2 (1971): 249–60. Reprinted with the permission of Greenwood Publishing Group Inc.

Lerner, Richard M. "Children and Adolescents as Producers of Their Own Development." *Developmental Review* 2 (1982): 342–70. Reprinted with the permission of Academic Press, Inc.

Lerner, Richard M. "Relative Plasticity, Integration, Temporality, and Diversity in Human Development: A Developmental Contextual Perspective about Theory, Process, and Method." *Developmental Psychology* 32 (1996): 781–86. Copyright 1996 by the American Psychological Association. Reprinted by permission.

Tanner, James M. "Menarche, Secular Trend in Age of." In *Encyclopedia of Adolescence,* Vol. II, edited by Richard M. Lerner, Anne C. Petersen, and Jeanne Brooks-Gunn (New York: Garland Publishing, 1991): 637–41. Reprinted with the permission of Garland Publishing Inc.

Susman, Elizabeth J., Gale Inoff-Germain, Editha D. Nottelmann, D. Lynn Loriaux, Gordon B. Cutler Jr., and George P. Chrousos. "Hormones, Emotional Dispositions, and Aggressive Attributes in Young Adolescents." *Child Development* 58 (1987): 1114–34. Reprinted with the permission of the Society for Research in Child Development.

Magnusson, David, Håkan Stattin, and Vernon L. Allen. "Biological Maturation and Social Development: A Longitudinal Study of Some Adjustment Processes from Mid-Adolescence to Adulthood." *Journal of Youth and Adolescence* 14 (1985): 267–83. Reprinted with the permission of Plenum Publishing Corp.

Brooks-Gunn, J., Anne C. Petersen, and Dorothy Eichorn. "The Study of Maturational Timing Effects in Adolescence." *Journal of Youth and Adolescence* 14 (1985): 149–61. Reprinted with the permission of Plenum Publishing Corp.

Brooks-Gunn, J., and Michelle P. Warren. "The Effects of Delayed Menarche in Different Contexts: Dance and Nondance Students." *Journal of Youth and Adolescence* 14 (1985): 285–300. Reprinted with the permission of Plenum Publishing Corp.

Hill, John P., Grayson N. Holmbeck, Lynn Marlow, Thomas M. Green, and Mary Ellen Lynch. "Menarcheal Status and Parent-Child Relations in Families of Seventh-Grade Girls." *Journal of Youth and Adolescence* 14 (1985): 301–16. Reprinted with the permission of Plenum Publishing Corp.

Steinberg, Laurence. "Impact of Puberty on Family Relations: Effects of Pubertal Status and Pubertal Timing." *Developmental Psychology* 23 (1987): 451–60. Copyright 1987 by the American Psychological Association. Reprinted by permission.

Lerner, Richard M. "Dialectics, Developmental Contextualism, and the Further
    Enhancement of Theory About Puberty and Psychosocial Development."
    Journal of Early Adolescence 12 (1992): 366–88. Reprinted with the
    permission of Sage Publications, Inc.
Jovanovic, Jasna, Richard M. Lerner, and Jacqueline V. Lerner. "Objective and
    Subjective Attractiveness and Early Adolescent Adjustment." *Journal of
    Adolescence* 12 (1989): 225–29. Reprinted with the permission of Academic
    Press Ltd.